A neoliberal revolution?

Manchester University Press

A neoliberal revolution?

Thatcherism and the reform of British pensions

Aled Davies, James Freeman,
and Hugh Pemberton

MANCHESTER UNIVERSITY PRESS

Copyright © Aled Davies, James Freeman, and Hugh Pemberton 2024

The right of Aled Davies, James Freeman, and Hugh Pemberton to be identified as the authors of this work has been asserted in accordance with the Copyright, Designs and Patents Act 1988.

Published by Manchester University Press
Oxford Road, Manchester, M13 9PL

www.manchesteruniversitypress.co.uk

British Library Cataloguing-in-Publication Data
A catalogue record for this book is available from the British Library

ISBN 978 1 5261 4652 6 hardback

First published 2024

The publisher has no responsibility for the persistence or accuracy of URLs for any external or third-party internet websites referred to in this book, and does not guarantee that any content on such websites is, or will remain, accurate or appropriate.

Typeset by Newgen Publishing UK

Contents

List of figures	*page* vi
List of tables	vii
Acknowledgements	viii
List of abbreviations	xi
Introduction	1

Part I: The neoliberal vision

1 Neoliberalism and Thatcherism	33
2 Neoliberalism and the UK state in the 1970s	75

Part II: The first term

3 The institutional inheritance	109
4 Pensions 'ratchet' and 'burden'	146

Part III: Planning a revolution, 1983–5

5 Personal pensions	187
6 The abolition of SERPS?	231

Part IV: Implementation and legacy

7 From revolution to evolution	269
8 Legacy	308
Conclusion	347
Bibliography	369
Index	393

Figures

2.1 Public expenditure as a percentage of GDP, 1952–79	*page* 87
3.1 Active occupational scheme members by sector, 1953–79	117
8.1 State pension as a percentage of average earnings at point of retirement for a worker on average earnings, 1950–2060	310
8.2 Frequency of the phrase 'pensions crisis' in published books in English, 1970–2019	313
8.3 Active occupational pension scheme membership, 1953–2012	315

Tables

2.1	Economic performance in the G7 economies, 1960–87	*page* 85
2.2	Structure of income tax in selected countries, c.1976	88
6.1	Government Actuary's prediction of the pensions 'support ratio' as at April 1984	237
7.1	Interim projections of public expenditure savings on a modified SERPS	287
7.2	Final projections of public expenditure savings on a modified SERPS	288

Acknowledgements

This book would not have been possible without the assistance, advice, and support of many individuals and organisations. Because primary archival materials lie at the heart of our study, we particularly thank the archives and special collections teams at the British Library, National Archives, Cabinet Office, Bodleian Libraries, and Royal Holloway. We are also grateful for the assistance of Jan Booth and Emma Wallis in the Treasury's Information & Records Division for access to then unreleased Private Office papers. We also owe a major debt of gratitude to the *Financial Times* and *Pensions World* for their commitment to excellent reporting of pensions policy and developments. We particularly thank the editor of *Pensions World* for allowing us to scan for research purposes historic issues of the magazine.

This research on which this book is based was funded by the UK Arts and Humanities Research Council (AH/L004739/1), to which we extend grateful thanks, as well as to the anonymous reviewers of our grant application. Over the course of the project we have, of course, also accumulated many intellectual debts to colleagues, reviewers, and conference audiences. We would especially like to thank organisers, commentators, and attendees at the following seminars and conferences: Modern British Studies, University of Birmingham in 2015; Political Science Association in 2016 and 2017; Economic History Society in 2016 and 2017; University College Dublin for its conference on 'The welfare state at the end of the long boom, 1965–1980' in 2016; Thatcher Network conference at the University of Durham, 2017; University of Oxford colloquium on 'Decentring conservatism' in 2017; Social Science History conference, Montreal, 2017; North Atlantic Conference on British Studies (Providence, RI, and Washington, DC); Institute and Faculty of Actuaries; and the Bristol Association of Actuaries.

We also thank anonymous journal article reviewers for the *Historical Journal*, *Journal of British Studies*, and *Twentieth Century British History*; their comments on submitted articles helped shaped our thinking at different stages of the project.

Acknowledgements

The wider project benefited from the expertise and advocacy of its advisory board (Nicholas Barr, Ed Cannon, Gordon Clark, Josephine Cumbo, Harry Cunliffe, and the late Frank Field) and partnership with the Institute of the Faculty of Actuaries, with which we organised a witness seminar and whose librarian, David Raymont, was immensely helpful in locating and giving us access to important material. We are grateful to our witnesses at that seminar (Sir Nicholas Montagu, Christopher Daykin, Sir Adam Ridley, Marshall Field), the chair of the panel, Greg McClymont, and all those who contributed to the subsequent plenary discussion. We also thank Lord (Nigel) Vinson and Lord (David) Willetts for contributing oral testimony in other settings.

A long list of scholars also helped us as the project unfolded. Notably, we extend thanks to Gordon Clark, Martin Farr, Matthew Francis, Ben Jackson, Kit Kowol, Peter Sloman, Florence Sutcliffe Braithwaite, Pat Thane, and Noel Whiteside. We owe a notable debt to Peter Blythe, whose doctoral work on historic occupational pensions data enriched considerably our analysis of reform legacies. Many other scholars were also helpful at various points either practically or intellectually, for which we are very grateful. The practical support and encouragement of the pension experts Norma Cohen, John Ralfe, and Mick McAteer is also gratefully acknowledged.

The research project out of which the book sprang was also fortunate in having a first-class doctoral student: (now Dr) Thomas Gould. His research on the changing actuarial profession, shifts in the dominant concepts of risk and uncertainty, and the evolving range of savings and investment products on offer by the 1980s complements this book's political story. It is also a hugely important contribution to knowledge on its own terms. Tom greatly assisted the wider project in numerous ways, but his work and detailed knowledge of the profession influenced our thinking considerably.

The project was based at the University of Bristol, and we are grateful for the support, encouragement, and intellectual input provided by Robert Bickers, Amy Edwards, Josie McLellan, the late Rodney Lowe, Martin Parr, Richard Sheldon, James Thompson, and Mark Wickham-Jones, among others. Roger Middleton, a principal investigator on the project in its first two years, was particularly missed after he took early retirement, with James Freeman stepping into the breach, but Roger's intellectual legacy continued to inform our work over the ensuing seven years. More generally, health problems, ill-health retirement, and major administrative tasks dogged the project, hence the nine years that have elapsed since it began, and we thank the university, our funders, and the publishers of this volume for their forbearance.

Aled Davies would like to thank his colleagues and students at Trinity Hall, Cambridge; Jesus College, Oxford; and St John's College, Oxford. He

x   *Acknowledgements*

is especially grateful to Ben Jackson and Patricia Clavin for all their support. Most importantly, he would like to thank Kate Davies for her love and encouragement throughout this project.

James Freeman thanks colleagues in the Arts Faculty Office – especially Michelle Coupland, Jayne Brown, Harriet Juniper, and Naomi Galliford – for their unfailing support, good humour, and understanding through some very turbulent times while parts of this book were being completed. He is grateful for the friendship of Amy Edwards, Leah Tether, Ben Pohl, and colleagues at Bristol. He thanks his family for their support and is especially grateful to David and Carol Freeman and Joan and Roger Hornsby for all their help and encouragement. His deepest thanks go to his partner, Hannah Charnock, for her love, friendship, and sound guidance. She has read large parts of the book from the perspective of a fellow historian, and many of the chapters have been immeasurably enhanced by her skill as an editor as well as her advice and insight.

Hugh Pemberton extends his heartfelt thanks to his partner, Susan Osborne, who put up with this project in one form or another for over 20 years and is, frankly, more than grateful to see the back of it.

Finally, any list of acknowledgements drawn up at the end of a very long project is bound to have inadvertently missed someone – probably more than one person, we suspect. If that is you, profound apologies, and belated but still sincere thanks from the three of us.

Abbreviations

ABCC	Association of British Chambers of Commerce
ABI	Association of British Insurers
ACA	Association of Consulting Actuaries
AVC	additional voluntary contribution [to an occupational pension]
BIBA	British Insurance Brokers' Association
BOPWG	Burden of Pensions Working Group
BSP	basic state pension
CBI	Confederation of British Industry
CPRS	Central Policy Review Staff
CPS	Centre for Policy Studies
DB	defined benefit [pension]
DC	defined contribution [pension]
DHSS	Department of Health and Social Security
DSS	Department of Social Security
EEF	Engineering Employers' Federation
FIMBRA	Financial Intermediaries, Managers and Brokers Regulatory Association
FSA	Financial Services Authority
FSAVC	free-standing additional voluntary contribution
GAD	Government Actuary's Department
GDP	gross domestic product
GMP	guaranteed minimum pension
IEA	Institute of Economic Affairs
IFoA	Institute and Faculty of Actuaries
IFS	Institute for Fiscal Studies
IMRO	Investment Management Regulatory Organization
IoD	Institute of Directors
IPPR	Institute for Public Policy Research
IPR	DHSS Public Inquiry into Provision for Retirement
IRA	individual retirement account [United States]
LAUTRO	Life Assurance and Unit Trust Regulatory Organization

LOA	Life Offices' Association
LPI	limited price indexation
MPS	Mont Pèlerin Society
NAO	National Audit Office
NAPF	National Association of Pension Funds
NHS	National Health Service
NI	National Insurance
OPB	Occupational Pensions Board
OPRA	Occupational Pensions Regulatory Authority [established 1995]
PAYG	pay-as-you-go [pension; abbreviated PAYGO in the USA]
PCFG	Personal Capital Formation Group [of the CPS]
PMQs	Prime Minister's Questions [in the House of Commons]
POP	portable occupational pension [as proposed by the CPRS in 1983]
PPP	portable personal pension/personal pension plan
PRA	personal retirement account [as proposed by Save & Prosper]
PSBR	public sector borrowing requirement
PU	No. 10 Policy Unit
QR	quinquennial review
RPB	Reserve Pension Board
RPI	retail prices index
S2P	Second State Pension [introduced 2002]
S&P	Save & Prosper
SERPS	State Earnings-Related Pension Scheme [introduced 1978]
SIB	Securities and Investments Board
SIPP	self-invested personal pension [introduced 1990]
SPA	state pension age
SPC	Society of Pensions Consultants
TUC	Trades Union Congress

Introduction

Between 1980 and 1983, relatively early in international terms, the United Kingdom government concluded that the country's unfunded state pensions were set to become a major fiscal problem when the postwar baby boom generation began to retire. Consequently, the government – led by Margaret Thatcher – began to pursue reforms expressly justified by the need to defuse this 'demographic time bomb' before it detonated in the early twenty-first century. Yet many within or advising Thatcher's government wanted much more ambitious reform than this. Informed by neoliberal ideas, they attempted to use state intervention to dismantle not just the country's then pay-as-you-go (PAYG) earnings-related state pension scheme (SERPS) but also collective occupational defined benefit (DB) pensions provided by many employers. Instead, they sought to compel every employee into an individualised defined contribution (DC) 'personal pension'. Thereby, individuals would be required to take responsibility for (and bear the risks of) providing their own old age income replacement. In the process, they were to be reconfigured into entrepreneurial investors with a clear personal investment in capitalism; individual freedom would be enhanced; the quantity and quality of investment capital available to British businesses would rise; and the concentration of ownership and power in large financial institutions would be dissipated.

This attempt at system replacement clearly represented the kind of 'neoliberal revolution' that Thatcher's governments are commonly seen to have been in the vanguard of. For all its ambition, however, key elements of this programme ran into the sands. It came much closer to enactment than is widely realised, but its advocates were forced to compromise and accept a neoliberal evolution instead: funded personal pensions would be introduced but without replacing occupational pensions, and SERPS would survive but with its benefits radically cut back over the long term to contain future public spending commitments. Nonetheless, although the revolutionary vision was unfulfilled, the resulting evolutionary policy package was still consistent with neoliberalism, with policy actors adapting their selection from the menu of neoliberal ideas available to them as they transited from one reform path to another.

This attempted policy revolution, its failure, and the subsequent salvaging of evolutionary reforms is important to the history of contemporary Britain and of international neoliberalism for three reasons. First, the compromises and recrafted neoliberal reforms left a malign legacy. Most notably, the United Kingdom ended up with the most complex and least adequate pension system of any advanced capitalist economy – and one that, ironically, still left it ill placed to deal with the inevitable coming challenge of an ageing society.

Second, the history of pension reform in this era reveals an important new way of thinking about the Thatcher governments. It encourages us to move beyond the concept of 'Thatcherism' (understood as a set of political and intellectual traditions to be 'implemented') and challenges interpretations that variously see Thatcher's governments as wholly pragmatic, largely unoriginal, centred on her own convictions, or riding wider societal currents rather than attempting actively to channel them, or, alternatively, as revolutionary in both intent and effect. Instead, it forces us to grapple with a more dynamic, less stable, yet deliberate project: one that moved rapidly between instincts for political continuity, caution, and financial prudence and a radical urge to break with the past, reset perceived distortions, and change individual behaviours. It was a project very often constructed 'in flight' by politicians, advisers, and civil servants as they negotiated the contradictions they found not just between Conservative and neoliberal influences but within the underlying neoliberal ideas themselves once these met the reality of practical policymaking and powerful existing interests.

Third, our findings demonstrate that detailed studies of neoliberalism can inject a similar complexity into histories of its political and policy manifestations as has been applied to its intellectual origins since the mid-2000s. The rich literature on neoliberalism has tended to fragment into intellectual histories of thought, political histories of influence, economic histories of capitalism, and sociological accounts of the rise of a neoliberal governmentality or selfhood. We show that a focus on policy history and newly released archival material can bring these approaches together and establish a more tangible – and more nuanced – understanding of neoliberal influence. The resulting analysis better explains how transnational ideas came to be influential within a highly nation-specific policy context and the tensions that arose as a result. Although we remain sceptical about the use of 'neoliberalism' as a synonym for all changes that took place in the 1980s and 1990s, our findings suggest that scholars have underestimated both the reach of neoliberal advocates within government and the level of their ambition in certain policy areas. Our study finds that there was a neoliberal diagnosis of what was wrong with the United Kingdom's pension system and a

Introduction 3

vision of what it should become. Because this was a vision, not a singular policy prescription, it could support multiple routes to implementation. We suggest that scholars of international neoliberalism can fruitfully draw upon theories of institutional change better to explain the routes considered by those sharing this neoliberal vision and understand how and why 'actually existing' neoliberal reforms took the shape they did.[1] Our application of this approach to the pension policy space suggests that the history of neoliberal ideas and networks in politics should be told not just through instances of straightforward adoption and implementation but through failed reform attempts, compromises with reality, and long-term impacts. If we have until recently been living through a supposedly neoliberal period, then it is a period that merits that label not so much because neoliberal ideas achieved a total supremacy in the 1980s but because – in the United Kingdom at least – we have been living with the consequences of policies salvaged from a failed revolution.

Britain's pension crisis and the history of policy failure

At the start of the twenty-first century, two decades on from the pension reforms of the Thatcher era, British politicians rather belatedly woke up to the fact that they had 'solved' one problem only to create another: the country's pension system, public and private, was now likely to prove utterly inadequate to deal with the significant challenge of a rapidly ageing society in need of retirement income. As that realisation dawned, the then Labour government appointed an independent commission of enquiry in 2002, the Pensions Commission, under the chairmanship of Adair Turner (former head of the Confederation of British Industry: CBI), to examine the adequacy of private pension saving in the United Kingdom and advise on appropriate changes to policy, including consideration of whether there was a need to 'move beyond the voluntary approach'. Its first report in 2004 was blunt: although longer lives for British citizens were to be welcomed, Britain faced a significant demographic challenge because of a reduction in birth rates, the ageing of the postwar baby boom generations, and rapidly rising longevity, which, in combination, could be expected to double the population aged 65 years and over by 2050. Yet, as the Pensions Commission noted, Britain's pension crisis was about more than demography, and about more than private saving. An ageing society was certainly a major policy problem but the challenge was made significantly greater by the failure of the country's pension system, broadly defined to include both state and private pensions, to provide a decent level of replacement income to British citizens in their old age.[2] System failure was evident on many fronts. The state pension, never munificent, had by design become progressively more meagre since the 1980s and was now 'amongst the least generous in the world'. Defined benefit occupational pension schemes run by employers, the success story of postwar pensions, had been exposed as a 'fool's paradise': the underlying trend in employer contributions had been in decline since the early 1980s, and levels of scheme funding were inadequate and falling.[3] To deal with the funding problem there was a growing trend for generous DB pension schemes (typically involving a promise to pay pension benefits based on 'final salary') to close to new members and for the employer to funnel employees into much less generous DC schemes (i.e. into schemes in which the contributions went into individualised accounts the final value of which was dependent both on the total value of contributions and, crucially, on long-term returns on investment, thus transferring investment and longevity risks from employers to individuals, who were often ill equipped to deal with them). At least such workers had some sort of pension. Although the government was then (and had been since the 1980s) encouraging workers without occupational pension provision to make their own private pension arrangements, 11.3 million of them in 2002/03 (40 per cent of the workforce) were not doing so, and thus, absent accrued occupational pension rights from earlier years, would be entirely dependent on their state pension entitlement. The result of all this, in combination with the government's assumption that, despite an ageing population, the increase in state spending on pensions over the next 50 years could be restricted to just 0.8 per cent of gross domestic product (GDP) (taking it from 6.1 to 6.9 per cent), was that 9 million people then in work could expect to receive an inadequate pension in retirement. That was clearly a major system failure in aggregate, with severe problems evident in all elements of the system.

Since the early 1990s the dominant paradigm for dealing with population ageing had been that of the World Bank – the so-called 'Washington consensus' that state involvement in pensions should be restricted to a mandatory but minimalist 'first pillar', with the slack taken up by a mandatory privately managed second pillar comprising occupational or personal pension savings plans, and a third pillar of voluntary pension savings for those wishing to have a higher retirement income.[4] Yet, in looking for solutions to Britain's particular problem at the start of the new century, the Pensions Commission concluded that there were significant barriers to raising the level of UK private pension savings given the low level of many people's financial understanding, high charges levied by private pension providers, and the behavioural barriers to savings posed by the 'bewildering complexity of the UK pension system, state and private combined'.[5] By 2004, therefore, we find a public acknowledgement that Britain's 'pension crisis' was a function not just of demography (seen by many not so much as a crisis but as a significant problem addressable via measures such as increased contributions, more subsidy from general taxation, and higher retirement ages) but of a pension system that – as our foremost historian of old age in Britain, Pat Thane, has noted and the Pensions Commission implicitly accepted – had become the most complicated and least effective in the world.[6]

How exactly this most unwelcome accolade had been gained was not explored by the Pensions Commission beyond its observation that something had changed in the 1980s. Nor has the cause really been explored subsequently. Indeed, our understanding of the detailed mechanics of policy change in Britain's postwar pension system in general remains surprisingly sketchy.[7] But how can we solve a problem effectively and enduringly without fully understanding its development? Most notably, the Thatcher governments ushered in changes with fundamental consequences, serving over time to shift the country to an individualised system of DC personal and occupational pensions; setting in train the implosion of the county's once successful DB occupational pension system; and radically degrading the value of state pension benefits in relation to average earnings. In short, it was the reforms of the 1980s that helped create the United Kingdom's twenty-first-century pension crisis.

The 'Thatcher project' in pensions had at its heart the intention of encouraging private initiative, raising the private ownership of capital, and increasing individual freedom by reducing the role of the state in pensions to the provision of a bare minimum of subsistence.[8] Indeed, the series of adjustments, small and large, made by the Thatcher governments to the country's system of providing an income in old age to its citizens represents a microcosmic example of neoliberal policy implementation in the UK context (a better example, in many ways, than that of privatisation – a policy approach that was mostly stumbled into in government).[9] These reforms to pensions served cumulatively over the succeeding decades radically to reshape Britain's pension landscape (not least by transferring to the individual risks hitherto borne by the state or by employers), marking a very significant step towards 'financialising' it in the sense that it became organised increasingly around the purchase of pension savings products by individuals within the market, but also helping (in conjunction with restrictions on the level of fund surpluses in the 1980s, that era's decline of manufacturing firms, and the privatisation of many large state-owned enterprises, each then key sponsors of workplace pensions) to weaken occupational provision.[10] It is the purpose of this book to explore and elucidate the causes and mechanics of the changes that were made, to place them within the context of the Thatcher governments' relationship to neoliberalism, and to consider their consequences over the medium to long term. We argue that these governments' reshaping of the system contributed significantly to the country's twenty-first-century pension crisis and, perhaps even more significantly, served also to constrain the array of available policy options for addressing that crisis.[11]

In telling this story, we position both planned and actual reforms to pensions within wider economic, political, and social transformations centred on the 1980s. There is marked agreement among historians that this period witnessed significant changes in politics, indicators (such as socio-economic inequality), policy frameworks, approaches to life cycle dependence, behaviours, and subjectivities, and the relationship between the UK economy and the rest of the world. Many of these changes are better located in what may be seen as the 'long' 1980s, and some historians make a case for even longer narratives in which the decade is but a focal point.[12] Yet there is broad agreement that the 1980s saw transformational change that (a) represented more than a continuation or amplification of the 1970s; and (b) began, matured, or in some cases completed, a reconfiguration of the United Kingdom's economy, politics and society into a pattern that explains much of its history since the 1990s. There, though, agreement ends. Historians and social scientists dispute which changes were real, rhetorical, realised, or unrealised, the terms used to describe before and after, the causes of change, the degree of contrast with earlier periods, and the extent to which changes can be connected or placed in an international context.

Much of this disagreement focuses on whether these changes should be attributed to 'Thatcherism' or described as 'neoliberal'.[13] As we discuss below and in Chapter One, these terms should not be used simplistically and are not coterminous. Many of the changes associated with the 1980s cannot be solely or even mainly attributed to Thatcher's governments or 'neoliberalism'. Recent work has revealed the roles that others played in pushing or enabling what are seen as Thatcherite reforms.[14] Not everyone who took on an entrepreneurial identity did so on neoliberal terms.[15] Left-wing activists and rights groups had their own criticisms of the welfare state.[16] Policies typically assigned to 'Thatcherism' and 'neoliberalism' also had a complex relationship with wider changes. Declining profits in the mid-1970s, the rise of multinational companies and communications technologies, increasing financialisation, and the (re)globalisation of trade sat alongside deindustrialisation and the growth of a service economy as processes that shaped the 1980s beyond the direct control of government.[17] Culturally, historians have also positioned Thatcher's governments as one expression of a rising tide of individualism, not its originator.[18] At a policy level, too, links have been emphasised between Thatcher's governments and their Conservative forebears.[19] 'Neoliberalism' is also often insufficient as an explanation. Britain's colonial links, credit liberalisation in the 1970s, and the Bank of England's role in facilitating the Euromarkets shaped or enabled many of

Introduction   7

the developments habitually described as neoliberal.[20] One might also point out that 1980s reforms relied on postwar changes: the United Kingdom's transformation into a country much less reliant on imported food than it had been, the floating of sterling on international currency markets after the collapse of the so-called 'Bretton Woods' system of fixed exchange rates, and its becoming a net exporter of energy all weakened the hold of sterling and the balance of trade on economic debate.[21] Indeed, even in the realm of ideas, our research confirms that neoliberal arguments do not wholly explain the policies pursued, and some of our findings support the sense that some postwar institutions and assumptions proved remarkably resilient.

It is possible, then, to over-credit the Thatcher governments and expand 'neoliberalism' to account for too many of the changes wrought in the 1980s. Yet risks also run in the other direction. Longer-run trends and processes certainly mattered, but governments could (and did) also elect to accelerate, harness, permit, or frustrate them. In certain policy areas – such as pensions – there is a risk that we underestimate the potential for political decisions taken by a small group of individuals to have outsize consequences, some of which still shape outcomes and behaviour long after those involved lost power. Likewise, some of the changes experienced in this period can helpfully be read as a further evolution of capitalism aimed at restoring profitability or as the reassertion of certain interests at the expense of others.[22] We would caution, though, that some of the reforms attempted actually set out to weaken interests normally seen as beneficiaries of 'Thatcherism' and push capitalism down quite a different path. As Ben Jackson argues, we need ideas (in this case neoliberal ideas) to understand the 'specific strategy to defend capitalism' in this period.[23] But we also need to understand the compromises and choices made by those pursuing this strategy if we are to understand some of the dynamics that characterise capitalism today.

The same balancing of risks applies when attempting to explain the Thatcher governments, describe the role of ideas in their policy decisions, and evaluate the extent of change. Although we often emphasise the incoherence of these governments' thinking, there is a danger in underplaying the degree to which ministers and advisers thought of and called for actions as part of a connected project. We certainly intend to substitute for a simplified model of neoliberal influence the reality of more circuitous, contested, and contingent routes to influence. Yet, in downplaying the role of neoliberal ideas, historians risk missing important stories about the advocacy of and resistance to these ideas and omit what was at stake in apparently small technical changes, pilot policies, or stakeholders' objections. We do not regard all neoliberal influence as attempting (or leading to) revolutionary change. Throughout the book we trace alternative strategies that attempted to outflank, problematise, replace, evolve, or degrade the status quo rather than directly replace it. Yet we also show that it is possible to underestimate the ambition and policy entrepreneurship of think tanks, advisers, ministers, and civil servants. Indeed, although we remain convinced that the study of 'actually existing' neoliberalism is vital, we caution that the reforms that eventually emerged can give the misleading impression of ideological moderation when in fact they were the result of forced compromises of revolutionary intent and bitter confrontations with reality.

For these reasons, we believe that 'neoliberalism' and the 'Thatcher project' can – when carefully defined – usefully describe *some* of the changes that were most transformative for Britain in the 1980s. Indeed, our research confirms that they are crucial to understanding pension reforms and the policy frameworks and politics that motivated them. By using newly released archival sources, we have been able to establish a clearer picture of how the Thatcher governments made policy in this relatively neglected area, and thereby show both the precise form and nature of neoliberal influence and the impact of these governments and ideas on the United Kingdom's subsequent development. In doing so, our intent is not to assert that they alone are sufficient as meta-narratives through which to understand international or British history at the end of the twentieth century. Instead, we hope that one result of bringing greater clarity to what government did and did not intend or accomplish is that we help future historians and social scientists to distinguish allied from unrelated agents of change and more precisely locate these governments in longer processes of transformation.

Because we do claim that there was significant change in this period, though, and that at least some of this was down to political actors and arguments about political economy, we need to state our general view on how it is best to think about what separated the United Kingdom before and after the Thatcher governments, not least because, if – as we claim – the pension reforms of the 1980s were intended to form part of a neoliberal revolution, we must first get a sense of what its architects thought they were revolting against. This requires us to engage with what is perhaps the most tedious debate in contemporary British history: whether there was or was not a 'postwar consensus' in the United Kingdom on the need for a mixed economy, welfare state, and Keynesian macroeconomic management; and whether, if there was, it collapsed in the mid-1970s. The scholarly underpinnings of the idea that a political consensus characterised the postwar decades lie in Paul Addison's famous analysis of the 'road to 1945'. He argued that fighting the Second World War required the government to mobilise 'the people' to support and prosecute the war effort by promising them that the state would deliver a better postwar world. It would do so by taking responsibility for ensuring economic growth and protecting British citizens 'from the cradle to the grave' via a newly constructed 'welfare state'.[24]

Victory in 1945 then demonstrated the capabilities of government action, thus raising expectations of what could be achieved in peacetime. Addison's analysis was very influential, but many scholars argued subsequently that the putative postwar political consensus was a 'myth' given clear differences of opinion between the two major political parties in each of the claimed vectors of consensus.[25] It is true that such differences can easily be found and that the gaps between interwar and post-1945 policies are smaller than once assumed. In both parties there were those who yearned for clearer distinctions, although economic and electoral realities sometimes suppressed disagreements on policy means (this was less true of ends).[26] Yet to repudiate the notion of 'consensus' – as opposed to the specific arguments made by its early advocates – makes it difficult to comprehend what happened in the 1980s. To understand the Thatcher governments and the political transformations of the 1970s and 1980s we must recognise the way in which the centre of gravity of British politics moved leftwards after 1945 with the election of a majority Labour government, even if that government continued a 'national' or 'liberal' policy in some areas and the Conservative party saw its role as *reconciling* this new reality with the continuation of liberty.[27] Perhaps most significantly, the parameters of political disagreement narrowed in the postwar years, as the Conservative party became the long-serving manager of a welfare system and national health service and eventually even conceded the need for the state to control wages and prices in peacetime. For its part, Labour accepted limits to physical economic controls and the constraints imposed by the need for currency stability, and over time its leadership arrived at less distinctive defence and European policies.

Although we do not wish to relitigate this debate, four points are relevant to our analysis. First, the focus on the existence (or not) of a consensus has stunted more complex understandings of political agreement that stress development and variation over time as well as the role of stakeholders in promoting or preventing agreement. As we show in Chapter Three, for most of the 1950s and 1960s Labour and the Conservatives disagreed on pensions, and there was thus no consensus. In the mid-1970s, however – years normally associated with policy divergence and the 'end of consensus' – a settlement was finally reached that commanded bipartisan support. Belatedly, therefore, a consensus was eventually built. Along the way, occupational pension funds and trades unions played important roles in preventing either party from establishing its respective preferred ideological reforms, and eventually exerted pressure for what was hoped would be a lasting agreement. Second, consensus mattered for political actors and had real effects in the policymaking process over several decades. The traditional narrative of consensus can fairly be criticised as too readily accepting of the Conservatives' self-narrated move to the centre after defeat in 1945. It is true that in the 1970s, just as cross-party agreement on pensions arrived, many associated with Thatcher explicitly conceived and rhetorically constructed their desired policy shift in terms of a repudiation of the prevailing political (in their view, 'socialist') consensus.[28] As we will see in Chapters Four and Five, however, these politicians' private recognition of consensus, and increasingly of stakeholders' investment in it, did initially constrain their appetite for reform in specific areas.

Third, we would maintain that – when carefully specified – the concept of an elite policy consensus across party lines is helpful in understanding the historical mechanics of policy change in the 1970s and 1980s, as the period in which the United Kingdom moved away from a framework that privileged Keynesian – or, perhaps better, 'post-Keynesian' – policy recommendations, initially to something called 'monetarism' and ultimately, by the 1990s, to a framework that we would now identify as aligned with some neoliberal precepts.[29] Although the comprehensiveness of this change and the influence of monetarism in particular can be overstated, there were significant efforts to rethink the management and structure of the British economy after the perceived failure of a modified Keynesian framework to deal with new economic problems arising in the 1970s.[30] In Chapter Two, we identify this perceived failure as creating a space for neoliberal influences, some of which proved important to pension reform. Finally, scepticism about the concept of consensus has dissuaded historians from exploring continuities outside the demand management plus welfare state formulation, such as the emergence of a corporatist developmental state and economic nationalism that David Edgerton has emphasised.[31] Ironically, the absence of a more nuanced framework for understanding the development of cross-party agreement has probably contributed to the use of the term 'social democratic' to characterise Britain's postwar political economy without recognition that this framework arguably owed more to liberalism for much of the period and became more generous, redistributive, and interventionist only in the 1970s.

Although we do not use the term 'consensus' with all its original meaning attached, then, we do ground our analysis in a periodisation that sees agreement between parties fall away. Unlike traditional accounts, we argue that consensus had not been reached about pensions until the mid-1970s. We maintain, though, that here, as in others areas of welfare provision and, indeed, in macroeconomic policy, consensus was not a 'mirage', and its dissolution after 1979 marked the start of a very different era and of a 'new politics' for Britain, for its welfare state in general, and for pensions in particular during the 'decade of revolution' that was the Thatcher premiership.[32] Crucially, then, we do believe that there is strong evidence for a policy consensus that was broken in the 1980s, and that this change can best be described as neoliberal.

Introduction

The landscape of pensions in 1979

What exactly was the nature of the pension consensus in late 1970s Britain? We explore this in more detail in Chapter Three, but, before we conduct our initial consideration of the nature of Britain's neoliberal revolution and the place of pensions within it, we need first to get a sense of what exactly the consensus was about. The need to do so is made more pressing precisely because pensions constituted an unusual area of welfare policy, in that for much of the postwar period there was no agreement at all between the major political parties on the ideal shape for the British system of pensions. There was, certainly, a consensus on pensions at the start of the period, inasmuch as both the Labour party (enthusiastically) and the Conservative party (reluctantly) had accepted the need to implement William Beveridge's proposals on National Insurance (NI), albeit with disagreement about the detail of implementation. In pensions, from 1948, that meant a 'universal' contributory state pension paid to women aged over 60 and men over the age of 65 (though, again, different parties held different views on the mechanics of its implementation, not least about the degree to which the new pension should be funded). We should remember, however, that Beveridge's vision of pensions was essentially a liberal one: the pension was intended to ensure only that basic needs were met and issues such as homelessness and hunger avoided among the old. As Beveridge had intended, the new universal National Insurance pension (universal in the sense that a flat-rate payment was to be paid to those making flat-rate workplace NI contributions and, in the case of male contributors, to their wives) was minimalist, being founded on the assumption that individuals had a responsibility to be thrifty and to save if they wanted something better.[33] Moreover, as implemented, the new state pension actually failed to deliver on its promise to meet the basic needs of its recipients (thus necessitating the continuation of means-tested state supplementation via National Assistance).[34] This was not just a pension consistent with politically 'liberal' minimalism, therefore; it was a profoundly ungenerous settlement. Its later characterisation by a former senior civil servant at the Department of Health and Social Security as 'fair shares in poverty' was at once a harsh but fair judgement.[35]

As the Second World War and the economic austerity that followed it, each with its emphasis on the fair sharing of hardship, began to fade in the 1950s the minimalism of UK state pensions began to look strikingly out of tune with the rising affluence of British workers in an era of historically unparalleled economic growth. Increasingly, workers wished to see this reflected in the pensions that they could expect to receive in retirement. Meeting that desire proved to be politically very divisive, however, with the major political parties advancing over the next two decades very different ideas about how best to translate rising earnings into better pensions for all. Little by way of legislation emerged (partly because of Treasury reluctance to see spending rise in the 1950s, and then in the 1960s and early 1970s because of frequent change in the political complexion of British government).

For many workers, however, the perceived inadequacy of the postwar settlement in pensions was being addressed not by government but by employers, who, in the very tight labour markets produced by rapid 'golden age' economic growth, saw the provision of occupational pensions to their employees as a useful tool for tying them to the firm. This was a complex and expensive endeavour, however, better suited to larger firms. Thus, in an economy dominated by small to medium-sized enterprises, most workers went without such benefits. This exclusion of the majority from occupational pensions created political pressure to improve their lot. For Labour, the answer lay in a state-administered 'national superannuation' fund, first advocated in 1957, that would pay pension benefits linked to earnings ('half-pay on retirement') and then 'dynamise'[36] those benefits in a way that linked them to future economic growth (something that occupational pensions could not hope to match and which would thus effectively put them out of business).[37] This profoundly statist solution, not surprisingly, was anathema to the then Conservative government. Instead, it explored the possibility of expanding occupational schemes to embrace the entire workforce, but found the insurance industry unenthusiastic about taking on a very large number of low-earning, expensive to service, and hence unprofitable new members. Consequently, Conservative governments first embraced a very limited 'pay-as-you-go' alternative to 'national superannuation' (implemented as the state 'graduated pension') in 1961; and then (with Labour having failed to get a watered-down version of national superannuation onto the statute book by the time it lost office in 1970) contemplated, in a 1971 White Paper, the idea of a 'modest' self-supporting and funded alternative for those without an occupational pension. This 'state reserve scheme' was to be run by an independent board of management. It was yet to come into force, however, when the government fell in the February 1974 general election.[38]

From the 1950s to the early 1970s, therefore, UK pension policy was far from consensual. That changed after Labour's return to power in March 1974. In September the new government published a White Paper, *Better Pensions*, that promised much-improved earnings-related benefits but, unlike the Labour party's earlier conceptions of 'national superannuation', assumed a productive partnership between state and market in which occupational schemes would be allowed to contract out of a new pay-as-you-go state earnings-related pension scheme on condition that they guaranteed

Introduction   13

benefits as least as good (and significantly better than those offered by the earlier Conservative 'state reserve scheme').[39] Crucially, the new state scheme was designed in a way that made it very similar to the most common model of occupational scheme (paying a pension of 1.25 per cent of salary for every year of service, or 50 per cent for someone retiring after 40 years of service), and the government undertook to provide for occupational schemes the inflation-proofing envisaged by the White Paper of the guaranteed minimum pension (GMP) that contracted-out schemes were required to provide. This, coupled with a widespread sense that the time had come to secure a lasting settlement, was the key that turned the lock, with the Conservative party effectively falling in behind the proposed scheme in 1975 and widespread support evident among professional actuaries, pension funds, employers, and trades unions. Consensus had finally arrived. It took the form of a two-pillar system, in which the first pillar was a minimalist basic state pension and the second a relatively generous earnings-related top-up provided either by funded private occupational schemes or via the new but unfunded pay-as-you-go 'State Earnings-Related Pension Scheme' (SERPS).

Thatcher's pension reforms and the neoliberal revolution

It is, of course, ironic that the rebuilding of consensus in British pensions came in 1975, a year that, in retrospect, saw the start of marked change in the Conservative party with the election of its new leader, Margaret Thatcher. Indeed, almost as soon as it had been constructed, the consensus began to unravel. New – or sometimes revitalised – thinking about both the economy and social policy (explored in detail in Part I of this volume) played the key role in that unravelling; and it was clearly bound in with what came to be called the 'neoliberal revolution'. Nevertheless, although it is easy to use the term 'neoliberalism' in the context of Thatcherism, it is in truth most 'slippery' term that is vulnerable to anachronism or oversimplification.[40] Most obviously, 'neoliberalism' does not entirely map onto the concept of 'the New Right', which initially informed much of the writing about (and thinking within) Thatcher's political project.[41] Nonetheless, scholarship increasingly has placed Thatcher's opposition and governments within (often at the heart of) the ideological development of neoliberalism.[42] We explore this in more detail in Part I, but it is important briefly to map out the basic contours of neoliberalism in order to show that the pension reforms of the 1980s are best understood as a product of neoliberal thought – albeit passed through a national context and Conservative party lens – and can be seen as a microcosm of British neoliberal policy in practice.

14   *A neoliberal revolution?*

What, then, do we mean by 'neoliberalism'? We certainly endorse David Harvey's observation that '[n]eoliberalism is in the first instance a theory of political economic practices that proposes that human well-being can best be advanced by liberating individual freedoms and skills with an institutional framework characterized by strong private property rights, free markets, and free trade'.[43] Yet, as Dieter Plehwe has observed, this is an approach that essentially reduces neoliberalism to neoclassical economics. Following Philip Mirowski and Plehwe, we take a more rounded view: one that emphasises neoliberalism's emergence as a 'neoliberal thought collective' with roots in the late 1930s and institutional expression in the formation of the Mont Pèlerin Society (MPS) in 1947, and that acknowledges a more complex interplay of ideas within that collective.[44] In particular, we conceptualise neoliberalism as a plural body of thought that goes considerably beyond neoclassical economics. It gained its coherence not through a single methodology or credo but through the intellectual exchanges that took place between members of a network that convened in the interwar period around the common belief that the world was witnessing a crisis of liberal civilisation. Most attributed this crisis both to the rise of collectivist ideologies and to the failures of intellectual liberalism to reconcile the social organisation of society with a competitive order. Several different groups of intellectuals, journalists, and others made distinctive contributions to this network and its diagnosis, but they also took forward the project of rebuilding liberalism and defending the competitive order on different lines, and the dominant emphasis within the thought collective changed as its constituent 'schools' gained and waned in influence over time.

In simplified terms, we identify three groups of contributors. Along with the work of Walter Lippmann, we see Friedrich Hayek as playing a crucial convening role, and his best-selling work *The Road to Serfdom* (1944) powerfully stated the concerns of the collective's members in the late 1930s and 1940s. Hayek's text – and to a lesser degree his later works on the legal framework necessary for the maintenance of liberty – came to influence many thinkers on the British Right (helped by the allied thinking of the London School of Economics academics Lionel Robbins and Arnold Plant).[45] We also acknowledge the importance of the Chicago school of economics, which had some roots in the reputation of the University of Chicago as a home to American critiques of the New Deal, but gained intellectual coherence only through a series of funded projects in the late 1940s and 1950s. Such projects and appointments created an institutional base and affiliation for a number of neoliberal thinkers, such as Ronald Coase, Richard Posner, George Stigler, Gary Becker, and Eugene Fama, as well as Milton Friedman.[46] Fundamental to Chicago school thinking, and of particular relevance to the United Kingdom's experience of Thatcherism, was

Introduction

its conceptualisation of neoliberalism not just as a body of ideas about the centrality of free markets to the freedom of the individual consumer but as a project that had to be *constructed* – a vision that meant that neoliberalism was 'first and foremost a theory of how to reengineer the state in order to guarantee the success of the market and its most important participants, modern corporations' and an acceptance of 'the (Leninist?) precept that they must organize politically to take over a strong government, and not simply predict it would "wither away" '.[47] Related to this – and, more unusually, in a British context – we see an important role for German ordoliberalism, a body of thought that emphasised the need to redesign society and its citizens' behaviours to support a competitive order and avoid the proletarianising effects of mass production and state welfare. Ordoliberal ideas were important in the British context in part because of the lively interest shown in them by Thatcher's mentor Keith Joseph (as noted by Werner Bonefeld), but also because of the influence that ordoliberalism had on neoliberal thought, especially in terms of its emphasis on the requirement for a strong state able to ensure that a competitive market economy is not taken over by rent seekers.[48]

The roots of neoliberalism and its vectors of influence on the British Right in the late 1970s and 1980s are explored in considerable detail in Part I. The association with the Right of British politics was not inevitable, and there are examples of Liberal and Labour thinkers attracted to some neoliberal ideas and instances when other elements of Conservative thinking limited the purchase of neoliberal ideas on policy.[49] Our key point at this stage, however, is to emphasise that the ambitions that lay at the heart of what *Marxism Today* dubbed the 'Thatcher project' were inextricably bound up with neoliberalism both as a plural body of ideas and as an ideological project – one that: placed individual liberty at the top of a hierarchy of human needs; saw liberty as primarily realisable through the exercise of individual choice in a market economy; and emphasised the need to restrict the role of the state (which was seen to be inherently less efficient than the market) in order to sustain a competitive economy; but also acknowledged the need for a proactive state determined both to enforce, create, and extend markets and to foster the entrepreneurial outlooks and dispersed ownership held to be most conducive to competition. Likewise, as we shall see, the Conservative vision for pensions in the 1980s was consistent with neoliberal visions of social policy: the state's responsibility for the welfare of individuals limited to providing a minimalist social 'safety net'; individuals expected to take responsibility for insuring themselves against personal risks; and the state expected to ensure freely operating and competitive markets in which those individuals would be free to choose and purchase the most appropriate form of such insurance.

16   *A neoliberal revolution?*

Ideas, interests, and institutions

Ideas therefore lay at the heart of the neoliberal project and were the well-spring of the economic and social change that those around Thatcher had in mind. Political scientists once tended to avoid accepting that ideas might be a driver of political change: in the jargon of that discipline, they were not an 'independent variable' that determined political outcomes. Rather, they had come to treat ideas as 'epiphenomenal' and thus unimportant.[50] It is now uncontroversial, however, to state that ideas matter in politics.[51] Yet, despite this acceptance, there has been much debate about how ideas should be defined, about how much, when, and why they matter, and about the ease with which their political impact can actually be measured.[52] Nonetheless, ideas along with interests and institutions have become, as Peter Hall put it, the 'primordial elements' within the analysis of political economy.[53] New ideas are seen as particularly important in driving the process of policy change.[54] This is especially the case when ideas are organised together into an ideology designed to achieve defined goals and 'championed by carriers or entrepreneurs, individuals or groups capable of persuading others to reconsider the ways they think and act'.[55] As Clifford Geertz puts it, 'Ideology … makes an autonomous politics possible by providing the authoritative concepts that render it meaningful, the suasive images by means of which it can sensibly be grasped.'[56] Thus, considering the rise of Thatcherism, and the ideas that underpinned it, Richard Heffernan argues that 'ideas are more significant in political life than they are often given credit for'; and he suggests that the 'Thatcher revolution' was an example of political change flowing directly from a new body of ideas coming to replace those which had hitherto shaped public policy in the United Kingdom.[57] Likewise, Peter Hall, writing nearly two decades earlier in a seminal article published in *Comparative Politics*, used the Kuhnian notion of scientific revolution to support his contention that 1979 ushered in an ideational 'paradigm shift' in UK economic policy-making, with Britain experiencing a fundamental change in the political and technocratic *gestalt* that saw the hierarchy of policy goals overturned and the dominant 'Keynesian' economic policy framework replaced.[58] Although Hall's analysis of the Thatcherite economic policy revolution was perhaps rather limited in his conceptualisation of that change (seeing it in terms of the replacement of a Keynesian policy paradigm by 'monetarism'), and might be said to have underestimated the complexity of the process and the time taken to change the framework of policy, his thesis has proved notably influential in analyses of the transition from a Keynesian to a 'neoliberal' economic policy framework in the United Kingdom.[59]

In this book, we make the case that what was broadly true of economic policy in the Thatcher era was if anything more definitively true of pension

Introduction   17

policy. We begin by placing the Thatcher governments' pension reforms in ideological context, providing an overview of the literature on 'Thatcherism', and then examining the ideological character of postwar 'neoliberalism'. We focus specifically on the ideas underpinning the 'Thatcher revolution' and explore the complex process by which a particular set of ideas from the broader ideational palette of neoliberalism came to be taken up by the architects of Thatcherism in the 1970s and then taken by them into government in 1979. Why, though, did much of the ensuing policy change prove inconsistent with the initial vision of a new neoliberal policy paradigm? We show that this 'implementation gap', as David Marsh and Rod Rhodes term it, was the product of a complex interplay of ideas, interests, and institutions in which institutional barriers to change and the opposition of interest groups was formidable.[60] Very significant change was wrought in the 1980s, certainly, but in the process of change compromises were forced that served to distort and reorientate the original vision. We seek to explain this process by drawing on the scholarly literature on 'historical institutionalism'.

Scholars in political science have long emphasised pensions as the epitome of institutional 'path dependence', because, as Hill notes, pension policy must give attention to needs and expectations 30 or more years ahead (actually, for even longer than that, as today's pensioners in their mid-90s may first have paid into the UK National Insurance system as long as 80 years ago).[61] In this sense, pensions are one of the most long-term of all areas of policymaking. Given the association between Thatcher's governments and the 'neoliberal revolution', it should not surprise us that pension policy, in the form of the Thatcher government's failure to abolish SERPs, formed a key example deployed by John Myles and Paul Pierson to support the idea that the long-term commitments embodied in state pension promises created significant barriers to those seeking to move from a pay-as-you-go to a funded pension system (as the Thatcher governments were attempting to do).[62] More generally, Myles and Pierson argue that pensions provide an example of a political process entirely different from the world of neoclassical economics in which decreasing marginal returns created negative feedback, leading to a single predictable equilibrium. Rather, as Pierson argues, politics was often characterised by 'increasing returns', or positive feedback effects, that served to embed the developmental path of a political institution and thus raise over time the cost of shifting to an alternative path (i.e. to an alternative institutional configuration).[63] As we explore in more detail in Chapter Three, as Myles and Pierson argue, this phenomenon of path dependence in political institutions explains why 'old welfare states' differed greatly from country to country, and why the 'new welfare states' emerging at the end of the twentieth century as a result of neoliberal-inspired retrenchment in the 1980s and 1990s turned out to exhibit a similar diversity, with reform in each country having to operate within the path-dependent constraints of the existing institutional order. As Giuliano Bonoli puts it, 'The institutional design of pension schemes is a powerful determinant of reform, in the sense that it limits the number and the range of possible options, and it points policymakers looking for political feasibility in some pre-determined directions.'[64] Politics, in this view, remained of fundamental importance, but it operated within path-dependent institutional constraints inasmuch as they made some solutions more politically attractive than others.

For a while the notion of path dependence proved a powerful influence on scholarly conceptualisation of institutional politics, but it did not take long for the concept to begin to be questioned. The principal critique was a very basic one: that path dependence was too static a theoretical construct, being inherently concerned with explaining institutional stability and not interested enough in the way that institutions change.[65] This criticism was given added weight by the accumulating evidence that pay-as-you-go pension programmes, central to so many accounts of institutional path dependence, *were* amenable to change. In 2006, for example, Maurizio Ferrara, Katherina Muller, and Karl Hinrichs each identified major changes to such programmes across Europe. Likewise, Bruno Palier's edited collection examining the politics of welfare reform in European systems variously identified as Bismarckian, Conservative-corporatist, Christian democratic, or 'continental' finds compelling evidence that pension systems were *not* frozen. Certainly, change was slow, and it was difficult, but it was clearly taking place.[66]

How did such critiques of path dependence conceptualise institutional dynamism? James Mahoney and Kathleen Thelen, in their 2010 book *Explaining Institutional Change*, emphasise the way in which apparently small changes over time could, incrementally and cumulatively, produce very significant change.[67] They identify four potential variables (pp. 10–14). First, *compliance*, in the sense that, when developments are inconsistent with existing institutional rules, the institutions themselves may be changed. Second, the *initial rules* of an institution may be implemented later, in different conditions and with different results. Third, institutions are embedded within *assumptions* (often implicit but amenable to change over time), Fourth, rules are not just designed but enforced, and may be enforced by *different actors*, thus opening up space for change.

Mahoney and Thelen also identify several different 'modes' of institutional change:

1) displacement, with existing rules being removed and replaced;
2) conversion, in which existing rules are enacted in different ways 'due to their strategic redeployment';

Introduction 19

3) drift, with inaction itself producing change over the long term as shifts in the environment lead existing rules to have different effects; and
4) layering, with new rules installed on top of or alongside existing rules.

They observe that 'drift and layering are more promising as strategies of change in political environments with strong veto players'.[68]

On the assumption that the United Kingdom, like the United States and many other liberal democracies, is just such a system, we therefore note Jacob Hacker's compelling analysis of the United States' 'divided welfare state' and his remark that

> actors who wish to change popular and embedded institutions in political environments that militate against authoritative reform may find it prudent not to attack such institutions directly. Instead, they may seek to shift those institutions' ground-level operation, prevent their adaptation to shifting external circumstances, or build new institutions on top of them.[69]

Thus, in his acute analysis of the hidden politics of social policy retrenchment in the United States over three decades, Hacker points not to 'path departure' per se but to a subtler process of change embodying the 'conversion' of old institutions to new ends; a process of 'drift' in which the state deliberately refrains from meeting new social needs through the welfare state, thus creating a vacuum in provision for the private sector to fill.[70] As a result, in this US example, we find 'layering', with system piled upon system. Bernard Ebbinghaus too argues that, although path dependence might indeed lock in a particular institutional configuration, and while path switching – though unlikely – might sometimes be possible, path departure was the most likely outcome when significant changes in the policy environment occurred, and that institutional layering could be an important means by which this change came about.[71]

In short, we believe that neoliberal visions of pensions were the wellspring of major policy change in all areas of Britain's pension system in the 1980s, but that the change wrought during the Thatcher years was the product not just of the initial neoliberal ideas but of their interplay with this complex amalgam of interests and historical institutional constraints. Ideas were not translated seamlessly into policy change. Thus, we explore what internal debates took place during the construction of new policies on pensions (both in opposition and in government), as well as considering how key actors interpreted concepts at the heart of the neoliberal project, such as 'freedom', 'choice', 'market', and the 'individual'. Likewise, we ask what compromises were forced, by whom, why, and how, in an implementation process involving the interaction of ideas with interests and institutions. What exactly were the policies that emerged from that process? How did changes within system elements system serve to alter the system as a whole? Finally, what was the long-term impact of the reforms? Plainly, in answering these questions, we assume that ideas matter; but we also recognise that their impact is not necessarily linear, in that interests and, particularly, institutions are both imbricated in the process by and extent to which these ideas change (or do not change) policy. We hypothesise that, in respect of institutional factors, path dependence was a barrier to change in pensions and that, consequently, political actors were forced away from 'big bang' change into more incremental approaches and 'layering' strategies. As will become clear, although our analysis covers the whole of the Thatcher era, our focus is particularly on the second Thatcher administration, for it is in the years 1983 to 1987, following the party's landslide victory in the 1983 general election and the definitive victory of Thatcherite 'dries' over Heathite 'wets' within the Cabinet, that the battle of ideas in pensions was mainly fought. We do, however, consider important policy developments both in the first Thatcher administration and in the remainder of the Thatcher era, as well as exploring their legacy over the short, medium, and long term.

Key terms and overview of the analysis

As we have highlighted, many of the terms we work with were coined by critics, and, more generally, many have gathered a considerable number of meanings over time. Before concluding this introduction with an overview of our analysis, then, we wish to condense the discussion above into a series of key terms that we hope cut through the miasma of competing understandings of both neoliberalism and Thatcherism.

Except in historiographical discussion, our use of the word *neoliberalism* refers to the ideas, values, and arguments of the 'neoliberal thought collective' – a network of connected thinkers whose work evolved over time (individually and in the dominance/emphasis of subnetworks or 'schools') but which cohered around those commonalities we identify in Chapter One and through significant interaction with each other.

We use the term *neoliberal project* to refer collectively both to the arguments this 'thought collective' made about how to reconfigure the state, economies, institutions, and individuals, and the work of an organised but looser network of individuals and institutions that attempted to turn these ideas into adopted policy. We occasionally make this specific to 'schools' within the thought collective, groupings within Britain, or individuals advocating change.

In discrete policy areas, we talk of *neoliberal visions* – a view both of an end state of what the economy, society and individual's behaviours should

Introduction 21

look like after reform and of the benefits of change. These visions allowed for flexibility, in that they could be achieved via several different policy routes at different paces following the strategies for institutional change we outline above. By drawing on different streams of neoliberal thought to greater or lesser extents, it was both possible for those associated with the neoliberal project to have different visions of a policy area and for them to refocus the vision when it was discovered to be contradictory or impractical to implement.

We use the term (*attempted*) *neoliberal revolution* to describe policy areas in which the concrete proposals equated to 'displacement' – a path-breaking system change intended to produce significantly different structures and behaviours from the status quo. As above, this was not the only policy-making strategy attempted. Later in the book we add *neoliberal evolution*, to describe the eventual layering route chosen. It is beyond the scope of this book to determine whether the overall impact of neoliberalism should be thought of as a 'neoliberal revolution', and so we use inverted commas when we use the term (infrequently) to refer to others' shorthand for the historical changes in 1980s Britain that are typically seen as a local expression of transnational neoliberalism.

The *Thatcher project* recognises that Margaret Thatcher – and, more importantly, many of her ministers and advisers – came to believe that parts of the British state, economy, and society needed to break with the 'consensus' status quo and that policies across government should be directed to that aim. They recognised potential electoral benefits from reform, but also that electoral strategies were needed to secure support. This political project did not always characterise all areas of government, was not always successful in its own terms, was not always driven at the same pace or even by Thatcher and her senior ministers, and could be dependent on wider trends.

Thatcherism refers to the motivations, objectives, ideas, values, arguments, and resulting actions that help us make sense of this project. In contrast to some who have used the term, we do not recognise a singular definition. Those strands of neoliberalism and neoliberal visions compatible with specific readings of a Conservative inheritance were an important part of its substance. We emphasise that the incoherence of these ideas demanded a dynamism and agility that meant Thatcherism's real-world expressions are better understood as the result of a *pathway* through its ideas, one constructed 'in flight' by many different political actors and stakeholders involved in responses both to the practical difficulties they came up against and the internal contradictions they discovered.

We use these terms to tell the story of an attempted neoliberal revolution in pensions in four parts. In Part I, Chapter One grounds our study within several existing approaches to Thatcherism and neoliberalism and draws attention to the problems that have arisen from the disconnections between these approaches. We examine the constituent 'schools' that developed within an international network of neoliberal thinkers and draw out their approaches to the welfare state and pension policy before characterising the relationship between Thatcherism and neoliberalism. Leading on from that, in Chapter Two we examine how neoliberal ideas on pensions entered the policy process, paying particular attention to the vectors of transmission and the key carriers of ideas into party policy, and into the policies of the Thatcher governments from May 1979.

In Part II we examine the pension system inherited by the incoming Conservative government in 1979 as well as exploring the first term of the Thatcher governments, from 1979 to 1983. We begin in Chapter Three by looking at institutional developments from 1945 to 1974 and describe the re-emergence of a pensions consensus in the mid- to late 1970s. Drawing on political science theories of historical institutionalism discussed above, a pattern of path dependence, incrementalism, and layering from 1948 to 1979 is mapped. The chapter ends by exploring emerging concerns about the compatibility of large occupational scheme funds with the Conservative party's vision of wider capital ownership. Chapter Four takes the story into 1979 to 1983. First, we show that the government came to see annual increases in the basic state pension (BSP) as a 'ratchet' working to expand state pension spending at the expense of working contributors. Constrained by earlier pledges but motivated to reduce public expenditure, it made technical changes within the existing system's architecture, linking annual increases in the BSP to price inflation alone rather than also to the rise in average earnings (a change that badly undermined the effectiveness of the United Kingdom's pension system over the long term). Second, we show that arguments about the 'burden of pensions' came to the fore in the first term. We examine how different actors used the research capabilities of the civil service to measure the share of society's resources pensions would eventually come to consume. We argue that this can be thought of as a process of neoliberal problem discovery, one that saw an issue defined, quantified, and then tied to policy agendas that exemplified a neoliberal vision of pensions.

In Part III we explore attempts to translate the neoliberal vision into policy after the Conservatives' landslide general election victory in 1983. Chapter Five looks at the attempt to substitute personal private pensions as the second tier of the UK pension system and, in the process, sweep away not just SERPS but the country's system of employer-provided occupational pensions. The emergence of this radical idea is explored, the investigations of the 'Fowler Inquiry' in respect of pensions are explored, the resistance from stakeholders encountered by the architects of change is delineated, and the outcome of policy development as embodied in the 1985 Green Paper

Introduction

on social security reform is described. Chapter Six then considers in detail the attempted abolition of SERPS, its justification, how policy was made, and the compromises forced on the government by key interests and institutional constraints as a policy for SERPS abolition was constructed in the lead-up to the 1985 Green Paper on social security.

Part IV then considers the policies actually implemented and explores the broader legacy of policy change in the 1980s. Chapter Seven explores the concentrated but decisive period between the Green Paper and legislation in 1986. Its focus is on the retreat from the revolutionary neoliberal vision of the Green Paper and the transition to a messy compromise, in which the original plan to substitute personal pensions for both SERPS and occupational pensions was abandoned. Instead, it outlines how the government was led into an evolutionary 'layering' strategy that saw personal pensions implemented as an addition to those existing elements of Britain's second pillar of pension provision, not as a replacement. In Chapter Eight we then turn our attention to the legacy of change. We describe the long-term consequences of the 1980s reforms, and the case is made that they played a key role in creating an emerging pensions crisis for the United Kingdom by the early years of the new century. In terms of state pensions, the role of these reforms in radically degrading the value of both the basic state pension and SERPS is analysed, and we explore the consequences in terms of pensioner poverty and increasing pressure on government to deal with the growing problem. The way in which cumulative change in the 1980s in the arena of occupational pensions served to create the conditions for their implosion is also explored. The growing complexity of the overall system is mapped and the consequences of that for decreased consumer understanding are considered. In personal pensions, the misselling scandal on the early 1990s, the growing need for government regulation, and emerging evidence of inadequacy are considered.

In our final chapter, we conclude that pension policy in the 1980s embodied a neoliberal vision at the heart of Thatcherism that *was* revolutionary, but that this ideology was forced to give way to political pragmatism in the face of interest-based resistance, institutional barriers to change, and the short- to medium-term costs of transition from the unfunded 'pay-as-you-go' SERPS to funded pensions attracting tax relief on contributions. In this sense, we argue, Thatcherite reformers in the field of pensions might perhaps be described as 'neoliberals mugged by reality'. The result, though much less radical than reformers had hoped, did nonetheless result in very significant change, implemented not via a revolutionary reconstruction of the system but via a series of incremental adjustments that were consistent with aspects of neoliberal thought that sought to shrink state involvement in social welfare but that emphasised individual freedom of choice in a competitive market for pension products rather than individual investment in the stock market. These changes had far-reaching effects. The system became much more complex and, when it came to private provision, consumers became increasingly confused; consumer confidence in pension saving declined; and individuals proved ill equipped to handle the complex financial decision making required to ensure adequate income replacement in old age. In addition, apparently small incremental adjustments to the system of state pensions and to occupational pensions in the 1980s, made mainly to deal with short-term financial pressures or as a result of the pragmatic withdrawal from grander ideological visions of change, had disastrous long-term consequences. These changes added up to a major reconfiguration of the system, and over time produced a marked shift away from generous collective provision to individualised and much lower and less secure pensions. Ultimately, however, the attempt to 'privatise' the pension problem, shift risk taking to the individual, and contain the long-term cost for government proved to be an illusion, because the state was eventually forced to confront the impending problem of mass pauperism that it had thereby created. As Britain faced the (much foreseen) twenty-first-century demographic crisis in pensions, its challenge was greater than most countries precisely because of the changes and added complexity introduced in the 1980s. Yet, because of the path-dependent institutional nature of pensions, those earlier reforms also served to limit options for addressing this crisis.

Notes

1 On 'actually existing neoliberalism': Jamie Peck, Neil Brenner, and Nik Theodore, 'Actually Existing Neoliberalism', in *The Sage Handbook of Neoliberalism*, ed. by Damien Cahill et al. (London: SAGE Publications, 2018), pp. 3–15.

2 Pensions Commission, *Pensions: Challenges and Choices: The First Report of the Pensions Commission* (London: TSO, 2004). Chapter 3 of that document lays out the failings of the then existing pensions system, broadly defined. The Commission, which included the trades unionist Jeannie Drake and the LSE academic John Hills in addition to Turner, had chosen to extend the terms of reference set for it by the government, which called on it to focus on state pensions – rightly judging that it was impossible to consider them without also examining private provision given the interrelationships between them.

3 Ibid., p. x. An average earner dependent entirely on the basic universal state pension and the top-up State Earnings-Related Pension could expect an income in old age of just 37 per cent of working-life earnings, compared with, for example, 70 per cent in the Netherlands or 71 per cent in France; it was less generous even than US Social Security, which had a replacement rate of 45 per cent.

Introduction

4 World Bank, *Averting the Old Age Crisis* (Oxford: Oxford University Press, 1994).

5 Pensions Commission, *First Report*, 'Executive Summary'; the quotation is at p. xiii.

6 Pat Thane, 'The "Scandal" of Women's Pensions in Britain', in *Britain's Pensions Crisis: History and Policy*, ed. by Hugh Pemberton, Pat Thane, and Noel Whiteside (Oxford: Oxford University Press, 2006), pp. 77–90. Some disputed the degree to which changing demography amounted to a crisis, as opposed to a policy problem; in the UK context, see, for example, Nicholas Barr, 'Pensions: Overview of the Issues', *Oxford Review of Economic Policy*, 22 (2006); Michael Hill, *Pensions* (Bristol: Policy Press, 2007), pp. 117–34; Phil Mullan, *The Imaginary Time Bomb: Why an Ageing Population Is Not a Social Problem* (London: I.B. Tauris, 2000). Nonetheless, the balance of opinion is that demographic change in combination with systemic problems in specific countries did (and does) pose a significant twenty-first-century challenge for the United Kingdom and other countries with developed pension systems; see, for example, Robin Blackburn, *Banking on Death or Investing in Life: The History and Future of Pensions* (London: Verso, 2002); Richard Disney, 'Crises in Public Pension Programmes in OECD: What Are the Reform Options?', *The Economic Journal*, 110 (2000); Paul Johnson, 'Fiscal Implications of Population Ageing', *Philosophical Transactions: Biological Sciences*, 352 (1997).

7 Significant books on the development of British pension policy since 1948 or on pension policymaking at particular points within that period are: Blackburn, *Banking on Death*; Giuliano Bonoli, *The Politics of Pension Reform: Institutions and Policy Change in Western Europe* (Cambridge: Cambridge University Press, 2000); Antoine Bozio, Rowena Crawford, and Gemma Tetlow, *The History of State Pensions in the UK: 1948–2010* (London: Institute for Fiscal Studies, 2010); Bryan Ellis, *Pensions in Britain, 1955–1975: A History in Five Acts* (London: HMSO, 1989); Steven Nesbitt, *British Pensions Policy Making in the 1980s: The Rise and Fall of a Policy Community* (Avebury: Ashgate, 1995); Tony Salter, Colin Redman, and Martin Hewitt, *100 Years of State Pension: Learning from the Past* (London: Faculty of Actuaries and Institute of Actuaries, 2008).

8 The term 'Thatcher project' was coined by early analysts working within a Marxian tradition; see, for example, Andrew Gamble, *The Free Economy and the Strong State: The Politics of Thatcherism* (Basingstoke: Macmillan, 1994). We use it here in the sense of a project informed by neoliberal ideas, among others, but also one that was seen by its proponents as demanding 'a sweeping transformation of institutions, attitudes and personnel', as Gamble puts it (p. 232).

9 On the specifics of the privatisation project, see David Parker, *The Official History of Privatisation*, vols. 1 and 2 (London: Routledge, 2009 and 2013).

10 Craig Berry, 'Austerity, Ageing and the Financialisation of Pensions Policy in the UK', *British Politics*, 11 (2016); Gordon L. Clark, 'The UK Occupational Pension System in Crisis', in *Britain's Pensions Crisis*, Pemberton, Thane, and Whiteside, pp. 145–68.

11 On the implications of the reshaped system for Britain's twenty-first-century pensions crisis, our analysis provides empirical support to Philip E. Davis, 'Is There a Pensions Crisis in the UK?', *Geneva Papers on Risk and Insurance Issues and Practice*, 29 (2004). See also Austin Vernon Mitchell and Prem Sikka, *Pensions Crisis: A Failure of Public Policy Making* (Basildon: Association for Accountancy & Business Affairs, 2006).

12 Jon Lawrence, *Me, Me, Me: The Search for Community in Post-War England* (Oxford: Oxford University Press, 2019); Amy Edwards, *Are We Rich Yet? The Rise of Mass Investment Culture in Contemporary Britain* (Oakland, CA: University of California Press, 2022); Florence Sutcliffe-Braithwaite, *Class, Politics, and the Decline of Deference in England, 1968–2000* (Oxford: Oxford University Press, 2018).

13 Stephen Brooke, 'Living in "New Times": Historicizing 1980s Britain', *History Compass*, 12 (2014); David Edgerton, 'What Came between Liberalism and Neoliberalism? Rethinking Keynesianism, the Welfare State, and Social Democracy', in *The Neoliberal Age? Britain since the 1970s*, ed. by Aled Davies, Ben Jackson, and Florence Sutcliffe-Braithwaite (London: UCL Press, 2021), pp. 30–51.

14 Amy Edwards, '"Financial Consumerism": Citizenship, Consumerism and Capital Ownership in the 1980s', *Contemporary British History*, 31 (2017); Neil Rollings, 'Organised Business and the Rise of Neoliberalism: The Confederation of British Industry, 1965–1990s', in *The Neoliberal Age?*, Davies, Jackson, and Sutcliffe-Braithwaite, pp. 279–98.

15 Sarah Mass, 'Where Was Entrepreneurship in Post-War Britain? Freedom, Family, and Choice in Modern British Shopping', in *The Neoliberal Age?*, Davies, Jackson, and Sutcliffe-Braithwaite, pp. 176–96.

16 Adam Lent, *British Social Movements since 1945: Sex, Colour, Peace, and Power* (Basingstoke: Palgrave, 2001); Daisy Payling, '"Socialist Republic of South Yorkshire": Grassroots Activism and Left-Wing Solidarity in 1980s Sheffield', *Twentieth Century British History*, 25 (2014).

17 David Edgerton, *The Rise and Fall of the British Nation: A Twentieth-Century History* (London: Penguin Books, 2018); Jim Tomlinson, 'De-Industrialization Not Decline: A New Meta-Narrative for Post-War British History', *Twentieth Century British History*, 27 (2016); Aled Davies, *The City of London and Social Democracy: The Political Economy of Finance in Britain, 1959–1979* (Oxford: Oxford University Press, 2017); Philip Cerny, 'The Dynamics of Financial Globalization: Technology, Market Structure, and Policy Response', *Policy Sciences*, 27 (1994); Edgerton, *The Rise and Fall of the British Nation*.

18 Emily Robinson and others, 'Telling Stories about Post-War Britain: Popular Individualism and the "Crisis" of the 1970s', *Twentieth Century British History*, 28 (2017).

19 Adrian Williamson, *Conservative Economic Policymaking and the Birth of Thatcherism, 1964–1979* (Basingstoke: Palgrave Macmillan, 2015).

20 Stuart Aveyard, Paul Corthorn, and Sean O'Connell, *The Politics of Consumer Credit in the UK, 1938–1992* (Oxford: Oxford University Press, 2018); James

Vernon, 'Heathrow and the Making of Neoliberal Britain', *Past & Present*, 252 (2021); Tehila Sasson, 'Afterword: British Neoliberalism and Its Subjects', in *The Neoliberal Age?*, Davies, Jackson, and Sutcliffe-Braithwaite, pp. 336–53.

21 Edgerton, 'What Came between Liberalism and Neoliberalism?'.

22 David Harvey, *A Brief History of Neoliberalism* (Oxford: Oxford University Press, 2005); Andrew Glyn, *Capitalism Unleashed: Finance, Globalization and Welfare* (Oxford: Oxford University Press, 2006).

23 Ben Jackson, 'Putting Neoliberalism in Its Place', *Modern Intellectual History*, 19 (2022).

24 Paul Addison, *The Road to 1945: British Politics and the Second World War* (London: Jonathan Cape, 1975). For the continuing influence of the 'consensus' idea, see David Dutton, *British Politics since 1945: The Rise, Fall and Rebirth of Consensus* (Oxford: Blackwell, 1997); Kevin Hickson, 'The Postwar Consensus Revisited', *Political Quarterly*, 75 (2004); Dean Blackburn, 'Reassessing Britain's "Post-war Consensus": The Politics of Reason 1945–1979)', *British Politics*, 13 (2017).

25 Ben Pimlott, Dennis Kavanagh, and P. Morris, 'Is the "Postwar Consensus" a Myth?', *Contemporary Record*, 2 (1989); Harriet Jones and Michael Kandiah, eds., *The Myth of Consensus: New Views on British History, 1945–1964* (Basingstoke: Macmillan, 1996).

26 Harriet Jones, 'The Cold War and the Santa Claus Syndrome', in *The Conservatives and British Society, 1880–1990*, ed. by Martin Francis and Ina Zweiniger-Bargielowska (Cardiff: University of Wales Press, 1996), pp. 240–54.

27 Edgerton, *The Rise and Fall of the British Nation*; James Freeman, 'Reconsidering "Set the People Free": Neoliberalism and Freedom Rhetoric in Churchill's Conservative Party', *Twentieth Century British History*, 29 (2018).

28 Richard Toye, 'From "Consensus" to "Common Ground": The Rhetoric of the Postwar Settlement and Its Collapse', *Journal of Contemporary History*, 48 (2013).

29 Michael J. Oliver and Hugh Pemberton, 'Learning and Change in 20th Century British Economic Policy', *Governance*, 17 (2004).

30 For the case that the change has been overstated: Jim Tomlinson, 'Tale of a Death Exaggerated: How Keynesian Policies Survived the 1970s', *Contemporary British History*, 21 (2007).

31 Edgerton, *The Rise and Fall of the British Nation*.

32 For discussion of the 'new politics' of British welfarism, see Rodney Lowe, 'The Second World War, Consensus, and the Foundation of the Welfare State', *Twentieth Century British History*, 1 (1990); Paul Pierson, ed., *The New Politics of the Welfare State* (Oxford: Oxford University Press, 2001). On early identifications of the Thatcher project as 'neoliberal', see, for example, John Grahl, 'Bump Starting Britain', *Marxism Today* (December 1984); Bob Jessop and others, 'Authoritarian Populism, Two Nations and Thatcherism', *New Left Review*, 147 (1984).

33 Jose Harris, *William Beveridge* (Oxford: Clarendon Press, 1997), pp. 414–15.

34 Hugh Pemberton, 'Politics and Pensions in Post-War Britain', in *Britain's Pensions Crisis*, Pemberton, Thane, and Whiteside, pp. 39–63, at pp. 46–47.

35 Ellis, *Pensions in Britain, 1955–1975*.

36 Labour Party, *National Superannuation: Labour's Policy for Security in Old Age* (London: Labour Party, 1957), pp. 25–29.

37 Oude Nijhuis, 'Rethinking the Beveridge Strait-Jacket: The Labour Party, the TUC and the Introduction of Superannuation', *Twentieth Century British History*, 20 (2009); Hugh Pemberton, 'The Failure of "Nationalization by Attraction": Britain's Cross-Class Alliance against Earnings-Related Pensions in the 1950s', *The Economic History Review*, 65 (2012); Stephen Thornton, *Richard Crossman and the Welfare State* (London: I.B. Tauris, 2009).

38 Department of Health and Social Security, *Strategy for Pensions: The Future Development of State and Occupational Provision*, Cmnd 4755 (London: HMSO, 1971).

39 Department of Health and Social Security, *Better Pensions – Fully Protected against Inflation: Proposals for a New Pensions Scheme*, Cmnd 5713 (London: HMSO, 1974).

40 The quotation is from Jamie Peck, *Constructions of Neoliberal Reason* (Oxford: Oxford University Press, 2010), p. 8.

41 For works approaching the Thatcher-era Conservative party in terms of the 'new Right', see, for example, Ian Gough, 'Thatcherism and the Welfare State', *Marxism Today* (July 1980); Nicholas Bosanquet, *After the New Right* (London: Heinemann, 1983); Arthur Seldon, ed., *The 'New Right' Enlightenment: The Spectre that Haunts the Left* (London: Economic and Literary Books, 1984).

42 Ben Jackson, 'The Think-Tank Archipelago: Thatcherism and Neo-Liberalism', in *Making Thatcher's Britain*, ed. by Ben Jackson and Robert Saunders (Cambridge: Cambridge University Press, 2012), pp. 43–61; Florence Sutcliffe-Braithwaite, 'Neo-Liberalism and Morality in the Making of Thatcherite Social Policy', *The Historical Journal*, 55 (2012).

43 Harvey, *A Brief History of Neoliberalism*, p. 2.

44 Philip Mirowski and Dieter Plehwe, eds., *The Road from Mont Pèlerin: The Making of the Neoliberal Thought Collective* (Cambridge, MA: Harvard University Press, 2009), p. 1. See also Ben Jackson, 'At the Origins of Neo-Liberalism: The Free Economy and the Strong State, 1930–1947', *The Historical Journal*, 53 (2010).

45 On a visit to the Conservative Research Department in 1975, Thatcher is reputed to have retrieved a copy of Hayek's *The Constitution of Liberty* from her handbag, banged it on the table, and stated firmly: 'This is what we believe.' (John Ranelagh, *Thatcher's People: An Insider's Account of the Politics, the Power and the Personalities* (London: Fontana, 1992), p. ix).

46 Robert Van Horn and Philip Mirowski, 'The Rise of the Chicago School of Economics and the Birth of Neoliberalism', in *The Road from Mont Pèlerin*, Mirowski and Plehwe, pp. 139–78.

47 Ibid., p. 161.

48 Werner Bonefeld, 'Freedom and the Strong State: On German Ordoliberalism', *New Political Economy*, 17 (2012); Michel Foucault, *The Birth of*

Biopolitics: Lectures at the Collège de France, 1978–79, ed. by Michel Senellart, trans. by Graham Burchell (Basingstoke: Palgrave Macmillan, 2008).

49 David Rooney, 'The Political Economy of Congestion: Road Pricing and the Neoliberal Project, 1952–2003', *Twentieth Century British History,* 25 (2014); Ben Jackson, 'Currents of Neo-Liberalism: British Political Ideologies and the New Right, c.1955–1979', *English Historical Review*, 131 (2016).

50 Sheri Berman, *The Social Democratic Moment* (Cambridge, MA: Harvard University Press, 1998), p. 16; Alan Finlayson, 'Political Science, Political Ideas and Rhetoric', *Economy and Society,* 33 (2004), p. 530; J. Goldstein and R. O. Keohane, 'Ideas and Foreign Policy: An Analytical Framework', in *Ideas and Foreign Policy: An Analytical Framework,* ed. by J. Goldstein and R. O. Keohane (Ithaca, NY: Cornell University Press, 1993), pp. 3–30, at p. 4.

51 Peter A. Hall, ed., *The Political Power of Economic Ideas* (Princeton, NJ: Princeton University Press, 1989).

52 Daniel Béland, 'Ideas and Social Policy: An Institutionalist Perspective', *Social Policy & Administration*, 39 (2005); Daniel Béland, Martin B. Carstensen, and Leonard Seabrooke, 'Ideas, Political Power and Public Policy', *Journal of European Public Policy,* 23 (2016); Berman, *The Social Democratic Moment*; Mark Blyth, *Great Transformations: Economic Ideas and Institutional Change in the Twentieth Century* (Cambridge: Cambridge University Press, 2002); Martin B. Carstensen and Vivien A. Schmidt, 'Power through, over and in Ideas: Conceptualizing Ideational Power in Discursive Institutionalism', *Journal of European Public Policy,* 23 (2016); Colin Hay, *Political Analysis* (Basingstoke: Palgrave, 2002); Matthias Matthijs, *Ideas and Economic Crises in Britain from Attlee to Blair (1945–2005)* (London: Routledge, 2010); Dietrich Rueschemeyer, 'Why and How Ideas Matter', in *The Oxford Handbook of Contextual Political Analysis*, ed. by Robert E. Goodin and Charles Tilly (Oxford: Oxford University Press, 2006), pp. 227–51.

53 Hall, *The Political Power of Economic Ideas*, p. 176.

54 Mark Blyth, 'Structures Do Not Come with an Instruction Sheet: Interests, Ideas, and Progress in Political Science', *Perspectives on Politics*, 1 (2003); Hay, *Political Analysis*.

55 Sheri Berman, 'Ideational Theorizing in the Social Sciences since "Policy Paradigms, Social Learning, and the State"', *Governance*, 26 (2013), pp. 225, 228.

56 Clifford Geertz, 'Ideology as a Cultural System', in *Ideology and Discontent*, ed. by David Apted (London: Free Press, 1964), pp. 47–76, at p. 63.

57 Richard Heffernan, *New Labour and Thatcherism: Political Change in Britain* (London: Palgrave Macmillan, 2001), p. 7.

58 Peter A. Hall, 'Policy Paradigms, Social Learning and the State: The Case of Economic Policy Making in Britain', *Comparative Politics*, 25 (1993).

59 On the need to take a longer-term and more evolutionary view of developments while accepting the basic utility of Hall's model, see Oliver and Pemberton, 'Learning and Change in 20th Century British Economic Policy'.

60 David Marsh and R. A. W. Rhodes, ed., *Implementing Thatcherite Policies: Audit of an Era* (Buckingham: Open University Press, 1992); David

Marsh and R. A. W. Rhodes, 'Implementing Thatcherism: Policy Change in the 1980s', *Parliamentary Affairs*, 45 (1992).

61 Hill, *Pensions*, p. 2.

62 John Myles and Paul Pierson, 'The Comparative Political Economy of Pension Reform', in *The New Politics of the Welfare State*, ed. by Paul Pierson (Oxford: Oxford University Press, 2001), pp. 305–33, at p. 306.

63 Paul Pierson, 'Increasing Returns, Path Dependence and the Study of Politics', *American Political Science Review*, 94 (2000). More generally, see, for example, James Mahoney, 'Path Dependence in Historical Sociology', *Theory and Society*, 29 (2000); Guy Peters, Jon Pierre, and Desmond King, 'The Politics of Path Dependency: Political Conflict in Historical Institutionalism', *Journal of Politics*, 67 (2005).

64 Bonoli, *The Politics of Pension Reform*, pp. 41–42.

65 Kathleen Thelen, 'Timing and Temporality in the Analysis of Institutional Evolution and Change', *Studies in American Political Development*, 14 (2000); Robert C. Lieberman, 'Ideas, Institutions, and Political Order: Explaining Political Change', *American Political Science Review*, 96 (2002); Peters, Pierre, and King, 'The Politics of Path Dependency'.

66 Maurizio Ferrera, 'Pension Reforms in Southern Europe: The Italian Experience', in *Britain's Pensions Crisis*, Pemberton, Thane, and Whiteside, pp. 208–22; Karl Hinrichs, 'New Century – New Paradigm: Pension Reforms in Germany', in *Ageing and Pension Reform around the World: Evidence from Eleven Countries*, ed. by Giuliano Bonoli and Toshimitsu Shinkawa (Cheltenham: Edward Elgar, 2005), pp. 47–73; Katherina Müller, 'Perspectives on Pensions in Eastern Europe', in *Britain's Pensions Crisis*, Pemberton, Thane, and Whiteside, pp. 223–40; Bruno Palier, ed., *A Long Goodbye to Bismarck? The Politics of Welfare Reform in Continental Europe* (Amsterdam: Amsterdam University Press, 2010).

67 James Mahoney and Kathleen Thelen, *Explaining Institutional Change: Ambiguity, Agency, and Power* (Cambridge: Cambridge University Press, 2010).

68 Ibid., pp. 10–14, 19.

69 Jacob S. Hacker, *The Divided Welfare State: The Battle over Public and Private Social Benefits in the United States* (Cambridge: Cambridge University Press, 2002). See also Jacob S. Hacker, 'Policy Drift: The Hidden Politics of US Welfare State Retrenchment', in *Beyond Continuity: Institutional Change in Advanced Political Economies*, ed. by Wolfgang Streeck and Kathleen Thelen (Oxford: Oxford University Press, 2005), pp. 40–82.

70 See also Streeck and Thelen, *Beyond Continuity*; Kathleen Thelen, 'How Institutions Evolve: Insights from Comparative Historical Analysis', in *Comparative Historical Analysis in the Social Sciences*, ed. by J. Mahoney and D. Rueschemeyer (Cambridge: Cambridge University Press, 2003), pp. 208–40.

71 Bernard Ebbinghaus, 'Can Path Dependence Explain Institutional Change? Two Approaches Applied to Welfare State Reform', Discussion Paper 05/2 (Cologne: Max-Planck-Institut für gesellschaftsforschung, 2005).

Part I

The neoliberal vision

1

Neoliberalism and Thatcherism

The reforms of the 1980s occurred in the context of longer-term social change, internationalisation, and economic and technological transformations, although such changes were not straightforwardly coterminous with a neoliberal project or Thatcher government. A central claim of this book, however, is that a significant attempt was made in the 1980s to reshape Britain's welfare state through reforms to pensions and that these can only credibly be understood with reference to neoliberalism and Thatcherism. Accordingly, this chapter sites our argument within existing approaches to Thatcherism and neoliberalism and draws attention to problems arising from the disconnections between them. We establish the foundations for our analysis by arguing that a distinctive set of neoliberal ideas and arguments took shape in the middle of the twentieth century. These gained their coherence through a network of thinkers interacting as a 'thought collective' with the common aim of reformulating liberalism. We highlight the constituent 'schools' that developed within this network and draw out their approaches to the welfare state and pension policy. The chapter concludes by evaluating the relationship between Thatcherism and neoliberalism. We argue this relationship can be best characterised as contingent, multi-layered, plural, embedded, dynamic, unstable, manifest, and (as we shall see) ironic. On this basis, we also claim that the most fruitful way to understand Thatcherism and neoliberalism is not to fully reconcile the differing perspectives outlined at the head of the chapter nor to leave these entirely disconnected but, instead, to write histories that foreground the interconnections and interdependences of the phenomena each describes.

Thatcherism

The policies of Margaret Thatcher's Conservative governments are popularly understood as expressing an ideological creed: 'Thatcherism'. Yet there has never been an agreed-upon definition of Thatcherism. In part, this is because contemporaries used the term to highlight and explain changes that were still unfolding. Close to events, they understandably tended to overemphasise particular aspects of Thatcher's leadership in opposition and in government and overstate their novelty and coherence. Subsequently, however, historians have perpetuated this initial debate through competing claims about the origins – political, material, and ideological – of the Thatcher project. Attempts to reconcile these perspectives into a singular definition of 'Thatcherism' applicable across all areas of government are unlikely to succeed or – at this stage – greatly add to understanding. This does not mean, however, that we should abandon any attempt to historicise the key motivations, objectives, arguments, and actions of the Thatcher governments. Indeed, our intention in this book is to set out how these operated within a particular policy space in the hope that this case study might be compared with further studies of 'Thatcherism in practice'. Yet we also want to move beyond identifying the different facets, influences, or strands within Thatcherism, or delineating its novelty. Our focus is the dynamics between them and the several routes through which political actors navigated Thatcherism's objectives and arguments to produce policy.

This more modest approach to comprehending the Thatcher governments and their motivations, policies, and achievements is a response to the findings of political scientists that her administrations were both less coherent, and less effective, than is often assumed. As early as 1988, for example, Andrew Gamble challenged the notion of Thatcherism as a monolithic project, asserting:

> The record of the Thatcher government, like that of all governments, has lacked symmetry, coherence and, often, purpose. What little coherence it has achieved has often been imposed by events and decisions outside its control. [...] The Government reacted pragmatically, its course shaped more by the pressure of events rather than its ideology or strategy.[1]

Subsequent assessments of the Thatcher governments have confirmed this view. In their evaluation of the implementation of Thatcherite policies, for example, Marsh and Rhodes concluded that the 'Thatcher effect' was far more limited than assumed, and that there was a substantial 'implementation gap' between aims and delivery. The structure of British government, interest group pressures, and economic context all served to constrain the scope of the Thatcher governments' actions. In some areas, no major policy changes were enacted – notably in defence, and law and order.[2] More recently, Stephen Farrall and Colin Hay have similarly shown that policymaking radicalism was not consistent over time.[3] The Thatcherism that emerges from these studies is less a blueprint and more an evolutionary, adaptive, and contingent strategy for government.

Yet we do not have to believe that Thatcherism was uniformly applied or that the Thatcher governments achieved their initial objectives to acknowledge that the post-1979 Conservative governments brought about far-reaching change. There are always limits on an administration's capacity to enact radical policy shifts, and so we must not lose sight of the substantial impacts of the three Thatcher governments. Most notable and far-reaching was the reformation of Britain's economy, and of the state's role in managing it, during the 1980s. The Thatcher governments' approach to economic management represented a significant break with the norms and practices prevalent since the Second World War. On entering government in 1979 the Conservatives' overriding objective was to reduce the high inflation that had dogged the economy in the 1970s. The chosen method, building on the Labour government's post-1976 commitment to monetary targets, was to adopt a nominally 'monetarist' strategy in which inflation would be cut by reducing the money supply.[4] The tight monetary policy and spending reductions required to overcome inflation in this way led to the deepest recession in Britain since the 1930s, with the rate of unemployment more than doubling between 1979 and 1983, to reach 12.2 per cent. With increased real interest rates, the effective exchange rate rose by 23 per cent between the first quarters of 1979 and 1981, forcing exporters to cut prices and reduce stock building (and, in the process, forcing many of them and their suppliers out of business).[5] This monetarist experiment – which caused profound concern in the still substantial 'Heathite' wing of the Conservative party – was a major departure from postwar 'Keynesian' norms, which had prioritised the maintenance of full employment as the key goal of macroeconomic policy.[6] The recession eventually gave way to a long boom after 1983, though unemployment remained at a high rate of 8 per cent in 1991.

In the longer term, the Thatcher governments undertook a thoroughgoing structural reform designed to shake the British economy from its supposed postwar underperformance. Thatcherites believed that the reasons for Britain's economic weakness in the 1970s lay in the corporatist consensus (that government should craft economic policy in consultation with major employers and trades unions) that had increasingly dominated the conduct of postwar economic policy. Future prosperity could be brought about only by a reduction in state intervention in the economy. In 1979, for example, exchange controls were abolished, eliminating government constraints on international capital flows.[7] Incomes and price controls were removed to liberalise labour, capital, and goods markets. State-owned enterprises and utilities were privatised.[8] Public sector housing was sold to tenants at heavily discounted rates under the 'right to buy' scheme to promote a 'property-owning democracy'.[9] Monopolies and restrictive practices were challenged in many areas of the public and private sector, with particular emphasis on undermining the power and influence of trades unions. The government was also committed to creating a more internationally 'competitive' taxation system in which taxes on personal income were cut substantially, especially for high earners, along with company taxation, capital gains, and stamp duty. The reduction in direct taxation was balanced by an increase in indirect tax, with value added tax (VAT) increased from 8 per cent to 17.5 per cent between 1979 and 1991. The overall effectiveness of this 'supply-side revolution' in improving Britain's economic performance has been subject to intense debate and disagreement – yet its far-reaching radicalism is beyond doubt.[10]

The priority that Thatcher's governments gave to economic reform after 1979 has shaped the way in which commentators and historians have interpreted Thatcherism. The earliest diagnoses of the Thatcherite phenomenon emerged from within a Marxist tradition of political analysis. From this vantage point, the crisis of the 1970s – in which profit rates were corroded by inflation and taxation, and the power of capitalists was challenged by industrial militancy and the threat of socialist policies – demanded state action to restore the supremacy of the capitalist order. To this end, it was argued, the Thatcher governments – on behalf of the capitalist class – constructed a new liberal-market accumulation regime by reducing worker rights, cutting taxation on corporate profits and high personal incomes, and liberating private enterprise.[11] For a group of radical Left thinkers associated with the journal *Marxism Today* at the turn of the 1980s, however, this simple material dynamic needed to be understood in a more nuanced political context. For Stuart Hall and Martin Jacques, the key issue was how and why this project gained popular support. Influenced by Antonio Gramsci, they understood Thatcherism as a hegemonic project of 'authoritarian populism' that enabled the Conservatives to build a coalition of voters and interest groups around a distinctive 'anti-collectivist' worldview, consisting of 'resonant traditional themes – nation, family, duty, authority, standards, self-reliance'. These drew on long-standing cultural tropes concerning law and order, social disorder, and race. Hall argued that working-class voters were attracted to these themes, and the broader anti-state message, as a result of their dissatisfaction with statist social democracy. This strategy enabled the Conservative party, working through the state, to construct a new capitalist accumulation strategy.[12]

Although the study of Thatcherism has its roots in the materialist explanatory framework of Marxism, subsequent assessments focused more upon the influence of ideas and ideology in determining its character. One key source of these ideas was supposedly Margaret Thatcher herself. Indeed, Thatcher was, according to herself and her supporters, a 'conviction politician'.[13] According to Eric Evans, her convictions were simply to oppose 'state interference with individual freedom; state initiatives that encourage an ethos of "dependency"; woolly consensuality; high levels of taxation; the propensity of both organised labour and entrenched professional interests to distort market forces; and a reluctance to be "pushed around" personally or as a nation state'.[14]

Peter Riddell alleges that this outlook was the expression of Thatcher's personal background, which had instilled in her 'an instinct, a series of moral values and an approach to leadership rather than an ideology'. Her politics expressed her Methodist upbringing and 'background of hard work and family responsibility, ambition and postponed satisfaction, duty and patriotism'.[15] Instead of a purely personal project, though, this way of understanding Thatcherism often led contemporaries and early analysts to see it as a British expression of a wider New Right combination of Conservative morality and market economics. Shirley Letwin puts forward perhaps the most convincing version of this thesis by stressing the importance of 'vigorous virtues'. If the essence of Thatcherite morality was its valorisation of the 'upright, self-sufficien[t], energetic, adventurous, independent minded' individual, then similar virtues could also be found motivating its political economy.[16] For both Letwin and Thatcher herself, these values amounted to a rejection of the so-called postwar political consensus in which the state took responsibility for collective well-being through economic and social interventions. Indeed, Thatcher sought to break explicitly with this consensus as a matter of principle. As she told a Conservative rally in Cardiff during the 1979 election campaign: 'The Old Testament prophets didn't go out into the highways saying, "Brothers, I want consensus." They said, "This is my faith and my vision! This is what I passionately believe!" And they preached it.'[17]

This rejection of the 'socialist' postwar consensus distanced Thatcher not only from Labour party socialism but also from the supposedly weak-willed collaborators in the governing elite of the postwar Tory party, who had accommodated themselves with a large state, a mixed economy, and a sectional trades union movement.[18] For these so-called Tory 'wets', Thatcher represented an anti-Conservative commitment to excessive individualism and extreme liberal economic doctrine that was not in keeping with the party's traditions of championing national community and sensible gradualism. Ian Gilmour, her most vocal Tory critic, alleged that she was not a true Conservative but simply a reconstructed nineteenth-century Manchester liberal.[19]

This claim that Thatcherism represented a break with the traditions of 'one nation' Conservatism has been debated extensively by historians.[20] Many identify a persistent liberal strand within Conservatism, and explain the party's policy as a product of tensions between this and its paternalism.[21]

Yet the differences between Thatcherism and Conservatism have been more successfully challenged by stressing different types of continuity. Jim Bulpitt, for instance, argues that the primary motivation of the Conservative party was 'statecraft' – 'the art of winning elections and achieving some necessary degree of governing competence in office'. By accommodating themselves with the postwar settlement, the Tories had been electorally successful; but, when faced with the inflation crisis of the 1970s, the party adapted and forged a new 'statecraft' by presenting itself as being more capable of bringing down inflation through strict monetary policy and cuts to government expenditure. This suggests that ideas and the content of policy are less important to Conservatism than the party's capacity to win power – and so, in this sense, Thatcher was a highly successful, typical Tory politician.[22]

Most students of Thatcherism have been less willing to downplay its ideological components, however, and have, rather, sought to place it within the longer intellectual history of Conservative ideas. Again, Thatcher and her supporters had their own vision of how their project fitted within the Conservative tradition, aligning their rhetoric with Winston Churchill's call to 'set the people free' in the late 1940s.[23] Yet, although some historians have endorsed the parallel and occasionally seen 'neoliberal' influences in late 1940s Conservatism, there is a considerable risk of teleology and anachronism in assuming that the similar rhetoric of two periods reflects the same beliefs or policy positions.[24] Instead, the most convincing connections between Thatcherism and earlier Conservatisms see the former as a product of long-standing arguments and trends in the party's subculture. As Ewen Green argued:

> [F]rom the very outset Conservative voices had been raised against the 'postwar settlement' and through the 1950s and 1960s elements of the Conservative party leadership, a substantial section of the backbenches and probably a majority of the middle and lower ranks of the party were predisposed to accept a liberal-market diagnosis of and prescription for their own and the nation's economic troubles.[25]

Green and others point out that some parts of the parliamentary party had shown antipathy towards the wartime Beveridge Report and that its grassroots had often been frustrated with apparently statist polices adopted in government during the 1950s and 1960s. Thatcher emerged from this ideological milieu and was able, in the context of amenable economic and social change, to pursue policies dedicated to individualism and personal freedom and especially appealing to the party's grassroots.

There are also links between Thatcher and the 'consensual' postwar Tory era, however.[26] Historians have explored the commonalities (and differences) with Enoch Powell's Conservatism or with members of the One Nation Group's emphasis on selective welfare. In policy terms, Peter

Thorneycroft's resignation from the Cabinet in 1958 is interpreted by Chris Cooper as a precursor to Thatcherite anti-inflation policies, and Adrian Williamson has demonstrated the extent to which many key Thatcherite approaches to economic policy – notably tax and trades union reform – were developed under Ted Heath's leadership of the party in the late 1960s.[27] Most significant, however, is the clear continuity in the Conservative commitment to building a 'property-owning democracy' through an expansion of home and share ownership. As Matthew Francis and others have shown, this was a vision shared by all elements of the party in the postwar decades.[28]

Thatcherism was not, therefore, one thing alone. As a political enterprise (what we refer to as the 'Thatcher project'), it was often radical in intent, but only partially implemented and at variable pace. As a set of motivations, ideas, arguments, and policies (what we refer to as 'Thatcherism'), it was novel in some respects, but many of its themes and policies also built on twentieth-century Conservatism. Faced with these contradictions, historians should not retreat from this complexity or discard the concept simply because it has been put to different uses. Instead, we must accept that the task is not a singular definition of Thatcherism or characterisation of the Thatcher project but an analysis of what specific policies and networks reveal about each of its several dimensions (personal/party, policy/ideology/statecraft, national/international) and the connections between these.

Neoliberalism

Much of the contemporary and initial historical dissection of Thatcherism was narrowly focused on domestic British politics. More recently, an alternative analysis has sought to look beyond the narrow confines of British politics and to place Thatcherism in a broader context. In particular, the focus turned to the relationship between Thatcherism and the phenomenon described as 'neoliberalism'. Neoliberalism is a highly contentious term, however, and its usage across a range of academic disciplines can often be vague or imprecise.[29] As with Thatcherism, it is notoriously difficult to define, with Jamie Peck noting that attempts to identify 'crisply unambiguous, essentialist definitions' of neoliberalism have 'become the bane of many a political lexicographer'.[30]

The primary reason for this difficulty is that there are two contrasting approaches to the definition of the term. The first defines neoliberalism according to the policies and practices of governments since the electoral victories of Margaret Thatcher and Ronald Reagan at the end of the 1970s. This approach attempts to distil the essence of neoliberalism from what actually happened, by way of policy changes and their supposed outcomes,

40   *The neoliberal vision*

over the past four decades. Within this, somewhat teleological, approach there are broadly two distinct interpretations. One is a Marxist analysis, which sees neoliberalism as the reassertion of 'class power' and, following the global economic crisis of the 1970s, the recreation by states of the conditions amenable to capital accumulation. In particular, it is argued that this was driven by 'the financial fraction of the ruling class', and that this resulted in the 'financialisation' of the accumulation process, in which, according to Greta Krippner, profits are increasingly extracted from financial sector activities.[31] For David Harvey, the most influential of the Marxist interpreters, neoliberalism is simply an ideological doctrine that gave direction and intellectual cover to the fundamental process of capitalist restructuring.[32]

An alternative to this straightforward, state-centric materialist analysis has been advanced by sociologists influenced by Michel Foucault's concept of 'governmentality'.[33] As part of his attempt to understand the exercise of power in liberal societies, Foucault identifies a form of 'neoliberal governmentality' in which individuals are required to take responsibility for their own self-government. From this perspective, neoliberalism is understood as a process of subjectification, in which the individual is reconstructed according to specific moral, ethical, and behavioural norms. According to Thomas Lemke, in his summary of Foucault's argument,

> [t]he key feature of the neo-liberal rationality is the congruence it endeavours to achieve between a responsible and moral individual and an economic-rational actor. It aspires to construct prudent subjects whose moral quality is based on the fact that they rationally assess the costs and benefits of a certain act as opposed to other alternative acts. As the choice of options for action is, or so the neo-liberal notion of rationality would have it, the expression of free will on the basis of a self-determined decision, the consequences of the action are borne by the subject alone, who is also solely responsible for them.[34]

This provides an important interpretive framework for understanding neoliberal society. Yet, although Foucault's lectures (which were never written up into a more substantive analysis) examined the influence of neoliberal ideas, his approach and that of his followers does not attempt to explain the causal factors that drove the supposed shift to neoliberal governmentality. Instead, it emphasises social relations, 'disciplinary institutions', and the production of knowledge. This has left an interpretive gap between Marxists and Foucauldians, with the former placing greater emphasis on explaining the causes of neoliberalism and its macroeconomic transformations and the latter offering a richer account of its consequences and impacts for individuals.[35]

The second method for defining neoliberalism has been to study the development of its key ideas, and the individuals and institutions who developed and propagated them. This intellectual history seeks to understand

Neoliberalism and Thatcherism

how neoliberal ideas formed and evolved over the course of the twentieth century, and to identify the core principles that underpinned them. The assumption in this literature is that ideas matter as much as material interests in politics and policymaking, and so are worthy of study.[36]

The question for historians concerned with *what actually happened* in politics and political economy in the final decades of the twentieth century is how to bridge the divide between neoliberal ideas and neoliberalism in practice and, in the process, unite these two modes of analysis. In this book, our approach is more concretely to show how neoliberal ideas impacted politics, partly because of economic transformations, and led to policy changes that aimed deliberately to promote subjectivities. The remainder of this chapter explains the intellectual development and distinctiveness of these neoliberal ideas.

Intellectual history of neoliberalism

A series of important studies have traced the origins and development of neoliberal ideas in the twentieth century.[37] Neoliberalism was much less monolithic than was sometimes supposed, consisting of multiple strands or 'schools', the dominance and emphasis of which shifted over time, as did the precise arguments of their major contributors. Yet this multiplicity existed within a transnational network that linked contributing intellectuals together, disseminated their work, and facilitated an exchange of ideas. It began to take shape in the 1930s, partly in response to the American journalist Walter Lippmann's *The Good Society* (1937) and the organising efforts of the French philosopher Louis Rougier. The Second World War disrupted early efforts to collaborate, but the Austrian economist Friedrich Hayek and German economist Wilhelm Röpke revived the network in a more permanent form in 1947 at the first meeting of the Mont Pèlerin Society near Vevey in Switzerland. Its annual meetings were by no means this network's only expression. Recent work suggests that the MPS is best seen in the context of a wider circle of business groups and funds, professional think tanks, bridgeheads in some university departments, and adjacent networks centred on international trade and economic organisations.[38] Yet the MPS was important because it initially brought together selected intellectuals from different disciplines to collaborate across national contexts and because it gradually enabled its academic members to connect with representatives from business, politics, and journalism and exert an influence at one remove from national party politics.

This network's intellectual coherence flowed from two sources. First, its members influenced each other's work, through the cross-pollination of ideas and mutual support but also through disputation within the network itself. The extent of this interaction over time has led scholars to think of neoliberalism as the product of a 'thought collective'.[39] Second, although they often disagreed on the preconditions and future shape of a liberal society, most of the network's members shared a double conviction that a rising tide of collectivism threatened 'liberal civilisation' and that it had revealed fatal inadequacies within liberalism itself. Most believed that these external and internal crises would need to be overcome if the capitalist social organisation necessary for free societies was to survive and prosper.

Especially in the MPS's early years, this shared conviction and reading of recent history encouraged participants to tolerate methodological differences in pursuit of a broad coalition and expansive project covering law, philosophy, and history as much as economics. Nevertheless, the agreement among early participants about who and what they opposed has created misleading impressions that neoliberals intended a return to a purified version of historic liberalism or that the distinction between nineteenth-century liberalism and neoliberalism lies in their respective attitudes to intervention.

In the late eighteenth century classical 'liberal' economists associated with the Scottish Enlightenment had argued that free exchange in markets – matched with the division of labour and capital accumulation – could best direct investment towards a nation's needs. Markets could deliver this result only under conditions of free trade, however, and in the absence of distorting tax or monopoly privileges. These arguments were regarded as calls for greater economic freedom, because the British state and interest groups within it had a history of circumscribing markets, granting monopolies, raising mercantilist tariffs to protect domestic production, restricting entry to trades, regulating lending and the formation of joint-stock companies, and discouraging the movement of people via the Poor Laws (although enforcement was varied).[40] By the middle of the nineteenth century, however, many statutory impediments to free trade had been repealed. The Manchester School and Anti Corn Law League had converted theory into a popular political campaign for free trade, securing the abolition of the Corn Laws and the removal of further duties in William Gladstone's 1853 and 1860 budgets.[41] When a Liberal party formed in 1859, there was still much to campaign for (many did not have an equal footing in the market or in democracy, and women would not until the next century), but it was possible to believe that liberal political economy was in the ascendance. For political liberalism there was also an obvious resonance between its leaders' involvement in the removal of economic privileges and ongoing campaigns for wider suffrage, religious disestablishment, education, and land reform.

Although Britain was the economic and intellectual centre for this liberalism, later neoliberals looked back on this history through an international

Neoliberalism and Thatcherism

43

lens. The United States had been founded on a fusion of Whig liberal and republican ideals, and the development of its domestic economy and culture could be understood as the flourishing of an enterprising liberal individualism played out in a society with less entrenched aristocratic privileges.[42] More importantly, a different form of liberalism was developing in the German-speaking world. *Rechtsstaat* liberalism aimed to establish the state as a constitutional entity limited by rule of law in place of a monarchical absolutism or unlimited popular sovereignty. Unlike British liberalism, freedom was made possible through the state.[43]

Even in the British context, this was not a story of a retreating or absent state. Proponents of free exchange did not necessarily entirely endorse a laissez faire approach. Adam Smith, for example, distinguished areas in which governments could intervene from those where it would be counterproductive. Free exchange, capital accumulation, and competition all required strong property rights and security of contract, and these in turn required the maintenance of law and defence. Taxes, in Smith's view, could legitimately be raised to fund these, but education and public works could also be justified as the means to functioning markets. British liberalism was also complicated by its relationship with utilitarianism.[44] In some ways, utilitarians bolstered liberalism's individualistic character, grounded opposition to privileges in the social philosophy of its utility principle, and constrained representative democracy to shield the individual from majorities. But the utilitarian liberalism of John Stuart Mill also created space for liberal interventionism by distinguishing private actions from those that impacted others, and a role for government in promoting the conditions of self-realisation. Mid-nineteenth-century liberal thinkers also identified cases for state intervention when markets failed. Liberal leaders acted to regulate markets to protect investors, safeguard employees, and curtail natural monopolies.[45] The introduction of death duties and land reform began to intervene in individual capital accumulation. At a local level, Liberals often led the public provision of water, gas, and electricity, and the party's members were motivated by causes, such as temperance, that opponents regarded as highly interventionist.[46]

From the 1860s liberalism was increasingly contested as it interacted with social reform movements, trades unionism, and the realities of technical and scientific change. One group of its advocates – associated with Herbert Spencer – emphasised an individualist reading of liberal economics and steeped this in a social philosophy that claimed individuals developed character through their independence and that civilisation progressed through the market's selective pressures. At the same time, T. H. Green, Leonard Hobhouse, and J. A. Hobson sought to reformulate liberalism's concept of freedom to emphasise the conditions needed to exercise it and began to reconcile liberty and the state by thinking of individuals both as discrete persons and as members of an organic community. Whereas Spencer's vision of liberalism remained popular in the United States, in Britain a political 'new liberalism' gradually became dominant from 1880.[47] This emphasised the creation of new freedoms through social reforms, measures to redistribute unearned wealth, and legislation to rebalance power in the market. As a political strategy it enabled collaboration with the emerging labour movement. The Britain of 1914 was one in which Liberal governments had introduced distinctions between earned and unearned income, graduated taxation, new labour laws, universal old age pensions, and a system of 'National Insurance'. The liberalisms of the past that neoliberals were responding to from the 1930s, then, had themselves already been reformulated.

The international progress of liberalism also looked more complicated. In Germany, unification was the triumph not of liberals but of militarist Prussia. The Bismarckian state embraced industrialisation and removed many impediments to enterprise. But from the late 1870s it abandoned free trade, sanctioned cartels, and sought to maintain unity around an authoritarian constitution by restricting political activity. Otto von Bismarck as chancellor also introduced health, disability, and accident insurance, and old age pensions. Germany's contributory 'welfare state' became a precedent for the reforms New Liberals favoured (although with a somewhat different nature and purpose). In the United States, the period between 1890 and 1916 saw the locus of American capitalism shift from owner-managed competitive enterprises to large corporations via mergers, distributed ownership, and administered markets.[48] Yet progressive politicians introduced anti-trust legislation and regulated railroads and food and drugs in the belief that larger-scale, cooperative capitalism was part of a natural evolution and that American liberalism's task was to manage this without the government usurping society.

There are limits to this characterisation. In Britain, the state remained relatively small in fiscal terms and its spending was focused on warfare. Political liberties, though much expanded in the nineteenth century, were still limited by gender, status, and property qualifications – although sufficient concessions had been made to ensure the demand for labour rights and social protections was relatively constrained. In Britain and other nations organised workers and socialist political parties did grow in influence in this period, and there was notable industrial unrest, but the pre-1914 liberal order was still relatively insulated from the demands of an increasingly mass democracy. For many, the gold standard was a cornerstone of the liberal international trading system (and was seen as a limit on government power), and the final quarter of the century saw many nations join Britain in adhering to it. Liberalism before 1914 certainly was not laissez faire in philosophy or political praxis, then, and it had been challenged and rethought. It was also distinct from what emerged after 1918, however.

The First World War brought about fundamental change both in Britain and for the international order. By its end David Lloyd George, who had been responsible for some of the Edwardian liberal reforms, had significantly extended the state's economic control. Britain's food supply was centrally organised and a significant proportion of its population subject to conscription or labour direction. Fighting the war had broken up the liberal international trading system, forced Britain and other countries off the gold standard, and massively raised government expenditure and indebtedness. Furthermore, although the 1917 Russian Revolution split the pan-European socialist movement, it also provided a genuine alternative – and threat – to liberal capitalism.

Following the war there was a concerted but ultimately failed international political effort to reconstruct pre-1914 economic liberalism and thereby return to the peace and prosperity of the *belle époque*. In Britain, the traumatic experience of postwar inflation, unemployment, and a national strike, combined with the further widening of the franchise, ensured the failure of this nostalgic project. As the gold standard fell apart in 1931, and tariff and trade barriers were erected in Britain and around the globe, liberalism faced an existential crisis, and in many nations it was discarded in favour of authoritarianism. Collectivist solutions to economic and social problems also gained greater salience.[49]

This international interwar crisis was both economic and political, and it pulled apart Britain's already fracturing political liberalism. Those attracted to new liberalism continued attempts to reconcile liberty and free markets with the democratic demands for economic and social security. Largely now achieved with or within other parties, this manifested in further social reforms (for example, Stanley Baldwin's Conservatives introduced 'liberal' measures of contributory National Insurance pensions and unemployment insurance), but it increasingly entailed the state taking on new responsibilities to provide the economic stability and security seen as necessary for the long-term survival of a liberal democracy. Among new liberalism's most significant figures was the economist John Maynard Keynes. A dogmatic adherent of laissez faire early in his career, Keynes reconsidered his understanding of economics during the interwar period in the face of self-evident market failure. His faith in the market's ability to self-regulate was abandoned and replaced with a belief in the essential duty of the state to maintain the conditions necessary to prevent mass unemployment.[50]

Following the Second World War, new liberalism, in coalition with socialist and social democratic ideas, emerged as the dominant governing paradigm in Britain, and to some extent in other Western nations. After an initial period of physical controls, rationing, and nationalisations, Keynesian demand management techniques and interest rate controls became the means of regulating economic growth to attain 'a high and stable rate of employment' without the direction of labour.[51] This was combined with the implementation of stronger labour market regulation, redistributive taxation, a significantly extended welfare system, and the growth of publicly provided goods and services, and was embedded in a new international monetary order in which international capital movements were controlled. Whether we emphasise its national orientation or its social democratic credentials, therefore, the postwar state extended collective security, provision, and ownership.[52]

In the minds of those who travelled to Paris for the Colloque Walter Lippmann in 1938 and those who gathered at Mont Pèlerin nine years later, these developments represented an 'epochal crisis'.[53] The first step in overcoming this crisis was to establish a liberal critique of collectivism. Although they were further elaborated, the four key arguments that formed this critique were already evident by the late 1930s. First, neoliberals asserted that economic, political, and intellectual freedoms were indivisible.[54] In part, this claim rested on their belief in historical connections between the development of liberty, property, and exchange, but the fuller claim of indivisibility rested on a refusal to separate life into strictly economic and political spheres.[55] In removing economic choices from individuals, collectivism was seen to diminish freedom in all aspects of their lives. Second, even if populations were willing to sacrifice their freedom in pursuit of efficiency or security, neoliberals doubted whether collectivist schemes could deliver their stated ends. Most doubted whether centralised planning could produce a more rational use of resources than free markets. Third, neoliberals made connections between centralised planning, protectionism, Keynesian demand management, and the Bismarckian corporatist state that suggested these were to some degree co-dependent. The adoption of each eventually necessitated the others, they argued, not least because one set of interventions led to another, as different interest groups began to compete for their own protective measures.[56] Fourth, neoliberals (most notably Hayek) gave these criticisms a spiralling historical logic, asserting that the eventual consequence was a slide into totalitarianism.[57] Still grounded in its nineteenth-century form, the liberal democratic state was said to be unable to manage conflicting interests. Amid the economic and social conflicts that arose from its failed interventions, neoliberals asserted, the state found that the only way to enforce planning and the required unifying purpose in peacetime was to resort to compulsion and autocratic leadership, and extend its reach into new areas of life. The result was arbitrary government by regulation in

Neoliberalism and Thatcherism

47

place of a legal framework and the subjugation of the inviolable individual that neoliberals saw at the core of liberalism.

This critique was not especially novel in its generalities, although some specific criticisms were. What set neoliberals apart was how they positioned the rise of collectivism and its slide into totalitarianism as the result of a crisis within liberalism as a body of ideas. Early neoliberals charged liberalism with having become a 'decadent' philosophy.[58] Once a challenge to established interests, it now defended the dominant interests of the status quo. Its thinkers had failed to recognise that the capitalist economy was dynamic and continually presented new economic phenomena. Finding that liberalism had little to say about contemporary social ills, younger generations of intellectuals instead flocked to collectivism or versions of liberalism that accommodated collectivist interventions. Although some neoliberals had sympathy with limited forms of the stabilising measures Keynes recommended, they saw new liberalism as unstable (for the reasons outlined above) and compromised by collectivist premises. Authentic liberal philosophy, neoliberals alleged, had withered in the hands of extreme individualists, who offered a crude version of the classical liberal authors' works embellished with an out-of-touch social Darwinism.

For neoliberals, though, the irrelevance of liberalism was but the symptom of its deeper intellectual crisis. Liberalism had failed to reconcile human society to the new mode of production that had been its animating principle: the division of labour and its power when operated through free exchange in ever-widening and competitive markets. According to neoliberals, eighteenth-century 'liberals' had discovered this new mode of production, and their early nineteenth-century heirs had done much to clear away impediments to its operation in trade and industry. Yet, because humanity's culture and societal organisation had been based on older modes of production, they lagged the economic changes wrought. Liberalism had failed to ease the resulting tensions, and – assuming its task complete – liberalism's thinkers were said to have abandoned its proper objective of creating a society harmonised with its mode of production.[59] In the neoliberal reading, both its leading thinkers and critics had wrongly assumed that nineteenth-century liberalism was liberalism fully developed.

In addition, from a neoliberal perspective, nineteenth-century liberalism had committed two serious errors. First, it had allowed laissez faire to degenerate from its original meaning as a reformist policy of freedom from restrictive measures into a defence of existing property interests.[60] Liberals had often refused to intervene to promote freedom, neoliberals claimed, because they perceived such interventions as extending the state into new arenas. Intervention would thereby diminish the realm of freedom and interfere with natural economic outcomes. In fact, from a neoliberal perspective, the state had always been involved in all aspects of property and work, and all freedom had been created and sustained by law.[61] Much of what nineteenth-century liberals assumed to be 'natural' was actually the result of questionable privilege. Rather than clearing this away to promote the division of labour and competitive markets, liberals had too often misapplied the principle of freedom from interference to justify the ossification of historic property relations.

According to neoliberals, nineteenth-century liberals' second error lay in their use of economic models. David Ricardo and other classical economists had, in Lippmann's words, necessarily simplified existing conditions to assume 'perfect and fair competition among equally intelligent, equally informed, equally placed and universally adaptable men'.[62] Under such conditions, outcomes would be 'natural' and socially just. As neoliberals pointed out, however, perfection was not the reality. Labour and capital were not perfectly mobile and ever-adaptable, competition was not free of restrictive practices, individuals did not have equal access to information or equal opportunity to develop their talents, and the time necessity of action could put one party at a considerable disadvantage. Neoliberals admitted that the classical economists acknowledged these 'distortions', but the liberal businessmen and politicians who read their work had passed over such caveats and assumed the models validated the actually existing circumstances as natural and just, especially when in some respects reforms had made competition freer than previously. The greater error, though, had been that liberals (and classical economists) failed to recognise the true value of their project: in defining the necessary assumptions for just outcomes, they had inadvertently identified the 'proper objectives of policy'. Liberalism's failure was that it had used classical economics to justify the world as it was rather than using it as 'a picture of the world as it needs to be remade'.[63]

The consequence of these errors was that liberalism seemed blind to the human costs of what its theorists referred to as 'frictions' and 'maladjustments'.[64] Personal suffering resulted from small margins of error in the price system's allocation of resources, for example, as individuals invested their careers in uneconomic industries. Likewise, because it had not recognised the development of new economic phenomena under this mode of production and too often refused to intercede, liberalism had allowed new concentrations of power in the form of monopolies, cartels, and restrictive practices to emerge out of measures such as corporation, patent, and labour laws. The result was social unrest and the rise of collectivist reactions against the market as groups sought to shield themselves from its dislocations or compete to entrench new privileges.

Liberals had also neglected social philosophy. For Frank Knight, the Chicago economist, the ultimate cause of the interwar 'crisis of civilisation' was the public's loss of faith in the 'fundamental equity of the values and terms of relationship established in the open market'.[65] More generally, neoliberals alleged that liberalism had neglected the consequences of the new economic organisation for human life, culture, and politics. Industrialisation, secularisation, population growth, and urbanisation had uprooted people from their organic communities and turned them into an atomistic but undifferentiated mass. This brought about social disintegration, the collapse of tradition, and the coalescing of society around large interest groups at the same time as a general rise in living standards (which raised expectations). Simultaneously, mass production and the division of labour had resulted in proletarianisation, leaving individuals isolated from their work, propertyless, and dependent on society. The ultimate risk lay in a mass version of politics based on interest groups, political populism, and rising voter expectations unmoored from economic realities. The state would collapse under the weight of competing expectations and – with the decay of the traditions and hierarchies that had restrained it – a popular will that crushed minorities in the name of majoritarian unity. Liberalism had not formulated robust, authentically liberal means to counteract these trends – which stemmed from its economic mechanism – and had instead abandoned the ground to collectivists and, worse still, left society hurtling towards the totalitarian governments that arose from such dislocations in the interwar years.

What, then, was the neoliberal way out of this double-sided crisis of collectivism and liberalism? They were certainly not pursuing a project of restoration.[66] Many measures they had cautioned against would need to be undone, but from a neoliberal perspective liberalism was an internally unstable ideology: its incompleteness and errors had led to the very conditions and expedients that would extinguish both its economic mechanism and its political and individual freedoms. Nor were neoliberals seeking a synthesis with collectivism or a compromise 'middle way', as advocated by the likes of Harold Macmillan.[67] Even those who strongly rejected the moral degeneration produced by industrial capitalism remained adamant that competitive markets were the only viable foundation for a liberal society. Instead, perhaps the most important point of unity among the groups that met in 1938 and 1947 was the conviction that their mission was to develop an alternative liberalism that eschewed collectivist premises but, by confronting the problems capitalism had created, was inherently more stable than nineteenth-century liberalism.[68] In Röpke's words: 'The non-collectivist world will only be able to deal with the dangers of collectivism

50   *The neoliberal vision*

successfully when it knows how to deal in *its own way* with the problems of the proletariat, large scale industrialism, monopolism, the multitudinous forms of exploitation and the mechanising effects of capitalist mass civilisation.'[69]

The novelty of this project did not lie in attitudes to intervention: liberalism had always permitted some forms of intervention. What drew neoliberals together was the desire to reformulate liberalism as a constructive programme of action – a different route to a new kind of liberal state and society. Its mission was to reorganise the state and society to work in harmony with the division of labour in free, competitive, and expanding markets.[70] This system – made possible by the coordinating power of prices – had shown itself most able to preserve space for individuals freely to pursue their interests. To preserve freedom, liberalism would no longer be about defining the market space the state should defend. Its first principle would be that 'the market must be preserved and perfected as the prime regulator of the division of labour' and that liberalism's 'uncompleted task is to show how law and public policy may best be adapted to this mode of production'.[71] In Foucault's insightful formulation, the aim was to create 'a state under supervision of the market, rather than a market supervised by the state'.[72]

Beyond this, early neoliberals could agree six broad areas of action. First, unlike nineteenth-century liberals, neoliberals did not believe markets were natural; they had to be created and maintained.[73] Repeated actions would be necessary as capitalism evolved, but a common thread would be removing privileges and countering concentrations of power.[74] Second, regulatory actions would be necessary – either to maintain the stability of markets and their conditions (such as prices) or to ease the rapid changes experienced with this new mode of production – but not when they frustrated or sought to avoid the market mechanism.[75] Third, neoliberals wanted to counter massification and proletarianisation, and the decaying culture and morality they felt they engendered.[76] For most, this involved actions to promote ownership and reduce dependence on the state. For some, though, it also tended towards a preference for the small scale – and action against large concentrations of wealth.[77] Fourth, neoliberals perceived the need for the state to overcome interest groups, confronting entrenched interests and concentrations of power, and ensure that it retained a monopoly of political power.[78] Fifth, neoliberals set out to root the case for market economies in persuasive social philosophies and epistemologies, rather than rely on utility arguments.[79] Sixth, over time they committed to the kinds of laws and governance mechanisms compatible with a liberal order.[80]

As we show in later chapters, the Thatcher governments' pension reforms should be understood as partly motivated by this project, albeit by a circuitous route, and in particular several of the different strands or 'schools' that developed within the neoliberal thought collective. Those schools emphasised different parts of the crisis of liberalism, and over time their (pre-existing) methodological differences led them to propose distinct sets of measures to make a revived (neo) liberalism a reality. How many schools there were within the collective is debatable, but for our purposes we outline three. In terms of dominance within the MPS, it is broadly accurate to say that the ordoliberal and Hayekian schools gradually gave way over time to a second iteration of the Chicago school, driven by Milton Friedman. As our analysis in later chapters shows, however, the ordoliberal tradition was influential for those orbiting Thatcher's Conservative party.

Ordoliberalism

Ordoliberalism originated in Germany during the interwar period, led by economists and legal thinkers: Walter Eucken, Franz Böhm, Alexander Rüstow, Wilhelm Röpke and Alfred Müller-Armack.[81] Their relationship to the 'neoliberal thought collective' is clear: Rüstow and Röpke attended the Lippmann Colloquium and the first Mont Pèlerin meeting; Eucken attended the latter. The term 'ordoliberal' was derived from the journal *Jahrbuch für die Ordnung von Wirtschaft und Gesellschaft* ('Yearbook for Social and Economic Order'), first published by Eucken and Böhm in 1948. Like other members of the neoliberal thought collective, ordoliberals believed the price system and competition were superior to the planned economy at allocating resources effectively. Similarly, ordoliberals believed that individual liberty could be sustained only in a competitive market economy.[82] They condemned nineteenth-century liberalism and laissez faire for its social and economic consequences, but also because it led to industrial concentration (cartels and monopolies that hindered competition, and harmed society through the waste and social ills that arose from wars between such interests) and the eventual capture of the state by dominant interests. Reformulated liberalism therefore needed a strong state to overcome these interests in favour of a free economy, in which individual actors would be free to compete and make their own decisions within a legal framework but would not be free to set the rules for themselves or constrain the freedom of others. The state therefore had to protect individual liberty from the threat of arbitrary state *and* private power.[83]

Ordoliberals conceived of their 'third way' as a reform project. The state's laws would not simply ratify the existing economic order; they would be an organising force creating a new economic order. Böhm made this clear through the concept of an 'economic constitution'.[84] Whereas a state's political arrangements might evolve naturally, its economic order had to flow from a deliberate decision to create this on specified principles, in this case a competitive order. All a state's laws and activities should seek to bring this competitive order into being, and those that did not would be reformed. Crucially, experts shielded from mass democracy would be needed to recommend these reforms and interventions as the only group free of the interests seeking to dominate.[85]

Beyond establishing this order, it would be necessary for the state to regulate the market. Regulations would be determined by their compatibility with the principles of the competitive order and apply to market conditions, not market mechanisms themselves.[86] Chief among these conditions was monetary stability.[87] Such regulation was to be undertaken within a wider restructuring, most clearly regarding economic concentration. Eucken, for example, argued that the postwar state should immediately move to destroy cartels and other concentrations of economic power so as to preserve competition in the market.[88] In some cases, however, a decision to break up cartels or monopolies could prove counterproductive: it might simply lead to the creation of new single-company monopolies or the creation of oligopolies. The solution here lay in regulation that attempted to ensure prices near to those achieved in perfect competition but, simultaneously, to reform the law to discourage economic concentration (for example, by outlawing loyalty schemes, preferential pricing, and loss leaders) and encourage foreign competitors. Thus, the ordoliberal state was intended not only to stand above interests but to carry out a far-reaching reform of laws and society, to create and sustain a competitive market order.

Ordoliberals rejected the separation of economic and social policy and saw both as examples of the repeated acts of state-led creation needed to sustain liberty and the competitive order. Social policy must promote competition by creating a population that was (a) equipped with the moral norms necessary for the market order to function effectively and (b) able to withstand the corrosive consequences of competition and division of labour that would otherwise undermine liberalism and the competitive order.[89] Röpke, Rüstow, and Müller-Armack connected this diagnosis with the competitive order through Vitalpolitik ('organic' or 'way of living' policy).[90] To combat dependence, they envisaged a mix of individual self-sufficiency alongside the market economy.[91] Ordoliberals also favoured small firms and giving workers a stake in the economy and in society.[92] Most of all, they promoted the ownership of property. In part, then, this was a social policy designed to enable the competitive order by reconciling it with the human need for social integration. But it can also be seen as the extension of the enterprise concept into social life, in two senses.[93] First, rather than an atomistic individual, the ordoliberal ideal was the individual integrated within a small enough group that they felt agency and meaning in the pursuit of a common purpose. Second, because independence was to be secured through property accumulation and investment over time, the individual could see their own life as an enterprise in securing this.

As we shall see, there are grounds to believe that ordoliberals' ideas and influence on the wider neoliberal thought collective shaped some of the aims of UK pension reform in the 1980s. Yet ordoliberalism's focus on the 'social market economy' was often conflated with the German postwar economic miracle. This failed to appreciate the difference between the ideologues who inspired it and the more social-democratic reality of postwar German political economy.[94] Whereas neoliberals in most advanced capitalist democracies were consigned to the political wilderness in the 1940s and 1950s, the ordoliberals exercised a degree of influence over the reconstruction of postwar West Germany.[95] Where commentators have recognised their ideological influence has been in Germany's commitment to a strong and independent central bank, which in turn was translated into a strict adherence to monetary orthodoxy.[96] On the whole, however, the focus of attention outside Germany has, until the late 2010s, been overwhelmingly on other strains of neoliberal thought.

Friedrich von Hayek

Hayek was perhaps the most important figure in the formation and development of the neoliberal project. He wrote extensively, and he was the first organiser of the 'neoliberal thought collective', securing funds to support the MPS and convening its initial meetings. It helped that, throughout his career, he spent time at each of the institutions associated with the schools within the collective.[97] Hayek was, therefore, a key link between neoliberals across Europe and North America, and he bridged some of the intellectual differences between participants.

Hayek's thought was wide-ranging and changed over time but it is possible to identify several contributions that shaped the 'neoliberal thought collective'. Foremost was his assertion that individual 'freedom' was the only moral value, and that other competing values, notably 'social justice', should be rejected.[98] In particular, Hayek challenged the new liberal reading of 'positive' freedom as a dangerous confusion between liberty and security, and stressed the need for individuals to make choices. For Hayek, responsibility and morality arose as a product of free choices: 'Only when we ourselves are responsible for our own interests and are free to sacrifice them, has our decision moral value … The members of a society who in all respects are *made* to do the good thing have no title to praise.' The freedom to decide between ends – especially when means were limited by material circumstances – was the precondition of morality. In contrast, collectivism offered 'relief from responsibility', and, in Hayek's view, it was therefore no coincidence that the virtues of an individualist society (independence, self-reliance, willingness to bear risk, etc.) were less evident under collectivism.[99] Through the concept of choice, then, Hayek made important connections with ordoliberal views of social crisis.

Hayek also emphasised that markets were the only means to secure individual liberty. The planned economy, he argued, necessarily removed individual freedom of choice over a much wider field than its advocates admitted. He based this claim on two lines of argument. First, he increasingly took up the insights of Walter Lippmann to claim that collectivist economic planning assumed a consensus about the common goods to which policy should be directed. The impossibility of a lasting consensus on such aims would lead planners to impose their will on the people. Individual freedom could not 'be reconciled with the supremacy of one single purpose to which the whole society must be entirely and permanently subordinated'. Second, Hayek saw the market as the only institution capable of managing the diversity of individual desires and subjective values. Although electorates increasingly sought shelter from the resulting 'impersonal forces' and mistakenly believed that markets were acting irrationally, the choice was between bending to impersonal forces they did not fully understand or submitting to the arbitrary choices of officials. Therefore, for Hayek, political liberty was contingent upon economic freedom. This did not amount to a rejection of the state, however. Like the ordoliberals, Hayek believed that the market had to be secured by a uniform application of laws enforced by a strong state.[100]

Ultimately, Hayek's views stemmed from his wider intellectual aim: to show the benefits of distributed knowledge and undirected systems. As a student of Ludwig von Mises, Hayek was closely involved in the 'economic calculation', or 'socialist calculation', debate that took place in the 1920s in which members of the Austrian school argued not that socialism was impossible (as sometimes claimed) but that socialised capital and planning together were incapable of rationally and efficiently distributing resources.[101] The Austrian school was said to have lost the debate in the 1930s, but after the war Hayek opened up a new line of attack: even if the calculation of a rational central allocation of resources was possible, he argued, the outcome would not be efficient because initial preferences were unknowable (existing only in the dispersed knowledge of individuals).[102] Markets, on the other hand, translated this dispersed information into prices that enabled coordination of activity and the rational allocation of resources to produce a spontaneous and efficient order. This order was in a sense 'democratic': the market drew upon the knowledge of all its participants and factored in their preferences. Hayek later extended this

Neoliberalism and Thatcherism 55

argument to see competition as a 'discovery procedure' in which 'entre-preneurs constantly search for unexploited opportunities that can also be taken advantage of by others'. In doing so, they discovered unknown 'facts' through price signals but also discovered new uses for materials and new demands. Outside the model of perfect competition (in which all relevant facts are known by market actors), competition was still superior to plan-ning, in Hayek's view, because it allowed a society's path of development to be determined by knowledge that was unknowable a priori. This in turn fed Hayek's criticism of 'social justice' as an attempt to maintain a group's current incomes against the outcome of this discovery process, in which the market signalled that a society's development now required its resources to flow to different opportunities.[103]

Chicago school

Hayek also played a role in the development of a 'Chicago school' through the connections he made promoting *The Road to Serfdom* in the United States. He persuaded Harold Luhnow, who oversaw the corporate-funded Volker Foundation, that the need was not simply an Americanisation of his warnings against collectivism but an extended examination of the policies necessary to bring about a competitive order. Luhnow agreed to fund this 'Free Market Study' project at the University of Chicago.[104] This location was not coincidental; during the interwar years Frank Knight, Henry Simons, and Jacob Viner had earned Chicago a reputation as the last American bastion of liberal economists.[105] Yet they had not thought of themselves as a coherent group. Indeed, as Rob Van Horn and Philip Mirowski have shown, it was not until Milton Friedman returned to Chicago's economics faculty in 1946 and George Stigler joined the Graduate Business School in 1958 that a more coher-ent 'Chicago' perspective formed, drawing in others such as Ronald Coase, Richard Posner, Gary Becker, and Eugene Fama.[106] The funding Hayek had secured was important both because it directly supported some members of this group (Friedman was a project member) and because it spawned succes-sor projects that took the research programme in new directions.

In its infancy, the Chicago school's intellectual position reflected that of the ordoliberals. Henry Simons' liberalism – centred on a fear of monopoly as the enemy of democracy – was aligned with the ordoliberal desire to maintain a strong state that could retain the liberal order.[107] Friedman's 1951 article published in the Norwegian business journal *Farmand*, entitled 'Neo-Liberalism and Its Prospects', replicated much of the ordoliberal per-spective. The project of neoliberalism, according to Friedman, should

> substitute for the nineteenth century goal of *laissez-faire* ... the goal of the com-petitive order. It would seek to use competition among producers to protect

consumers from exploitation, competition among employers to protect workers and owners of property, and competition among consumers to protect the enterprises themselves. The state would police the system, establish conditions favourable to competition and prevent monopoly, provide a stable monetary framework, and relieve acute misery and distress. The citizens would be protected against the state by the existence of a free private market; and against one another by the preservation of competition.[108]

The Chicago school gradually developed its own variation on the neoliberal theme, however: one that was much less circumspect about the virtues of market mechanisms. This both distinguished the postwar 'Chicago school' from Knight and Simons and came to dominate the MPS, while Friedman became the chief promulgator of neoliberal ideas in postwar North America.[109]

It is not possible to capture the nuanced ideas of all Chicago academics in generalisations, but it is fair to say that they developed and became known for a neoliberalism focused on economics and the extension of market principles and logics to understand most political and social phenomena. This was in part an epistemological change of approach from economics as the study of processes (production and exchange) to economics as the study of the choices actors made between ends in the presence of scarce means. For Friedman's part at least, this was related to a methodological difference. Friedman claimed that, although economic models oversimplified reality, they nevertheless represented objective knowledge if their falsifiable predictions were validated by empirical data.[110] A model's descriptive accuracy was irrelevant provided it held predictive power. This sat in contrast both with the Austrian approach, which derived its case for markets from logical deduction (which Friedman considered unfalsifiable), and the legal and historical arguments favoured by ordoliberals and Hayek.[111]

The result was three types of analysis. First, the Chicago school's members often re-evaluated economic phenomena. For example, the Free Market Study's empirical finding that the level of industrial concentration had been overstated led its successor, the Anti-Trust Project, to challenge apparently counterproductive parts of anti-trust legislation and argue that large corporations should no longer be seen as detrimental to a competitive order.[112] Likewise, the school's early work fused with that of Theodore Shultz, chair of the Chicago Economics Department, to develop a new theory of human capital. Together with Shultz, Gary Becker argued that many unusual economic phenomena could be explained by a focus on activities that influenced future income 'through the embedding of resources in people'.[113] Such investments in human capital ranged from education and on-the-job training through to parenting and investments that widened the information or job opportunities available to individuals. Governments should, in this view, widen access to capital so that people could invest in themselves and avoid underinvestment in human capital and consequent low productivity and falling returns. Second, the study of substitutable choices enabled Becker and others to apply market logics and rational self-interest (in the form of individual utility maximisation) to other policy areas, in particular crime and drugs policy.[114] The state's actions or suggested policies were usually assessed in terms of the extent to which they worked in alignment with the choices individuals would rationally make or how far they created new (adverse) rationalities. For Friedman in particular, an associated rhetorical strategy saw him often agree with his opponents on ends but show that their means were unnecessary or inefficient compared with a market.[115]

Third, a focus on choices, interests, and exchange rendered non-market phenomena susceptible to a similar style of economic analysis. George Stigler, for example, used this approach to argue that regulations did not normally achieve their goals and that regulators were subject to industry 'capture'. The related 'Virginia school' – led by James Buchanan – extended this approach to public institutions and democratic politics more generally. Like markets, democratic governance was an act of cooperation through exchange. Nonetheless, poorly designed institutions could, Buchanan claimed, inhibit that process and become open to rent seeking and corruption among politicians and bureaucrats.[116] Market-based solutions were to be preferred in part because they undermined the incentives that led administrators and experts to accumulate power.

The individual that emerged from the Chicago school's analysis, then, was one whose choices could be understood in economic terms, whose income was partly based on the entrepreneurial investments they made in their own capital, and who needed protection from the incentives public systems created for their employees. Ultimately, though, this was a governable subject: changes to rules or incentives could reliably shape future choices by individuals.

Neoliberals and the welfare state

It is clear, then, that ordoliberals, Hayek, and Chicago school economists emphasised different parts of the crisis of liberalism and collectivism. Their contexts and methodological assumptions also created different routes (and threats) to a competitive order. All, however, opposed features of postwar social insurance. Indeed, the welfare state became a focal point for neoliberal criticism once physical controls had mostly fallen into abeyance in the early 1950s in favour of economic 'management' using (neo-)Keynesian techniques.[117] Most neoliberals understood that it was not practical politics to eschew a minimum safety net of provision, but they attacked state

58   *The neoliberal vision*

provision above this minimum as a key example of the long-term limitations placed on freedom and of the unsustainable demands arising from mass democracy.

Although they had reservations, most neoliberals agreed that the provision of a minimum safety net was compatible with a liberal society and that a state system was probably the best way of achieving this quickly.[118] State welfare systems were not seen as an appropriate means of managing risk across the life cycle generally, however. Individuals should have a choice in how they planned to manage risk (in unemployment, sickness, and old age) above a minimum. Although ordoliberals gave it particular emphasis, Hayek and the Chicago school also agreed that welfare systems must avoid creating dependence. Crucially, contemporary welfare states were seen to have exceeded their remit by becoming redistributive; benefit should relate to contributions, and the welfare state should not use a principal of social justice to act as a counterweight to the distribution of incomes achieved via the market (not least because the sheer volumes of money collected and distributed gave the state enormous influence over disposable income and control of industry across the economy).

Within these principles, we can detect different emphases within these schools of thought and be more specific about their views on pensions. The ordoliberals were strong critics of the welfare state, stressing its failure to generate the ethical norms necessary to maintain a competitive order. In their view, it was the 'expedient' of a proletarian society that had undermined individuals' prudence but also detached them from the solidarity of small communities. The ordoliberal goal was, therefore, to replace both proletarian, centralised society and the welfare state. Beyond the latter's alleged redundancy, though, replacement was necessary, for several related reasons. First, compulsory state provision threatened to prolong proletarian status by degrading humankind to 'an obedient domesticated animal [kept] in the state's giant stables, into which we are being herded and more or less well fed'.[119] Second, mass welfare reduced responsibility and created an unsustainable burden.[120] Although welfare states might alleviate a 'few symptoms' of proletarianisation, ordoliberals believed their cost was 'gradual aggravation and eventual incurability'.[121] Third, this absence of self-reliance was said to undermine the competitive order. The social market economy would cease 'to flourish if the spiritual attitude on which it is based – that is the readiness to assume the responsibility for one's fate and to participate in honest and free competition – is undermined by seemingly social measures in neighbouring fields'.[122] Security, ordoliberals argued, was achieved through private property and investment, family and community, and the entrepreneurial norms of self-management and self-sufficiency. Progress should therefore be measured by 'widening the area of individual and voluntary group providence at the expense of compulsory public providence'.[123] In short, social policy should be 'market conforming' – facilitating the freedom and responsibility of individuals to allow them to escape dependence and play their role in maintaining the competitive order.[124]

Pensions had from the start been an ordoliberal example of state overreach. In 1942 Röpke partly positioned his 'third way' as an attempt to avoid the choice between laissez faire and 'an all-embracing public welfare system which aims at protecting each individual from the cradle to the grave against the vicissitudes of life as far as possible by means of retirement pensions'. Although many would look forward to 'everyone receiving an old age pension, given the insecurity and isolation already wrought by proletarization', the more far-sighted task was to 'pull up the evil by the roots and at last energetically oppose collectivization itself as the soil in which the idea of universal pensions thrives'. As soon as pension schemes were supplemented with taxation, 'the centre of life, welfare and community spirit is shifted from the natural and obvious mutual aid association of the family and other genuine communal units, to the state'.[125] More particularly, Röpke's later work critiqued 'pay-as-you-go' schemes both because they were redistributive and because they deprived capital markets of savings. Yet he was also concerned with the trend towards seeing pension funds as national resources.[126] Savings and insurance were 'provision against risks which belong to the area of economic rationality, the market, private law, and freedom'. National social security 'lock[ed] people in behind the bars of the national state'.[127] Given the strength of their opposition, then, it is not surprising that a significant example of the ordoliberals' limited influence on postwar West Germany is that they were unable to prevent the country's adoption of earnings-related pensions on a current expenditure basis in 1957.[128]

Although Hayek had acknowledged the necessity of a state-guaranteed minimum in *The Road to Serfdom*, critics pointed out that he had been vague about how this minimum could be provided without entering the spiral of interventions he described. His 1960 work *The Constitution of Liberty* sought to clarify both this and his views on welfare.[129] For Hayek, it was legitimate to (a) provide a needs-tested minimum and (b) coerce individuals to insure themselves against the unexpected and inevitable challenges of life. The latter avoided the wider coercion of the public into paying for their maintenance. Individuals should not be compelled into state-run national insurance schemes, however; they should be free to choose an insurance provider in a competitive market. Indeed, such a market was the means of discovering the best products for retirement savings and limiting the state's increasing control of income. Hayek was chiefly concerned, however, about two further elements of postwar social insurance and pensions provision.

First, many governments had abandoned the insurance-based principle in their use of general taxation and introduction of redistribution in the name of 'social justice'. This redistribution took several forms. Most schemes would begin paying members who had not yet had time to contribute fully. Nor were benefits determined by the value of contributions (lower earners received proportionately more, higher earners less). Moreover, inadequate contribution rates ensured that schemes would continue to be supplemented from general (redistributive) taxation. Hayek saw this as the quiet introduction of a 'household state', one that socialised income and granted it to those it felt were deserving. In place of social minimums, in which 'a majority of givers ... determine what should be given to the unfortunate few', the welfare state created 'a majority of takers who decide what they will take from a wealthy minority'.[130] To Hayek, there was no basis for this redistribution, which had been deliberately hidden behind the rhetoric of insurance.

Second, Hayek feared that state pension schemes had acquired a self-accelerating force. In part, this was because of their complexity: only the experts who ran them had a sufficient understanding, and they had a vested interest in a scheme's extension. Effective scrutiny of legislation was impossible in this context, but the schemes had also become a 'playball for vote-catching demagogues'. The rising expectations of each generation would increase a scheme's generosity, with voters confident that the bill would be paid by a future generation. Hayek was especially critical of advocacy for 'adequate pensions', and singled out Labour's plans for earnings-related pensions in the United Kingdom (discussed in Chapter Four) as allegedly embodying the unrealistic notion that retirees should continue living a similar standard of life to that when they were working without the majority making the necessary personal contributions. The result, Hayek predicted, would be a mounting 'burden' on younger generations that – if not addressed – would eventually lead to generational strife. He was very pessimistic about the likelihood of reform, however; future generations might inflate away the burden or simply breach the inter-generational contract, but it was unlikely that an electorate would ever vote for change. 'It would almost seem as if such a system, once introduced, would have to be continued in perpetuity or allowed to collapse entirely,' he concluded.[131]

As the most politically engaged member of the Chicago school, Milton Friedman was more confident about change but no less a public critic of the welfare state. In his influential book *Free to Choose*, Friedman echoed the ordoliberal concern that the welfare state created a culture of dependence, instilling

> in the one group a feeling of almost God-like power; in the other, a feeling of childlike dependence. The capacity of the beneficiaries for independence, for

Neoliberalism and Thatcherism

61

> making their own decisions, atrophies through disuse ... [T]he end result is to rot the moral fabric that holds a decent society together.[132]

Friedman also shared Hayek's concerns about redistribution, although, rather than simply a principled objection to social justice, he emphasised that, because redistribution occurred within schemes regardless of need, it led to perverse situations in which the young poor funded the aged rich. Similarly, Friedman shared the view that the state should not be the provider of pensions but articulated the argument in his typical style, focusing on the appropriateness of means rather than ends. So long as redistribution was not the aim and schemes were self-financing, there was no need for the state to be the sole provider. The economies of scale often alleged by proponents of state schemes could be put to a simple test: if such economies existed in a free market, a state-run option would outcompete and ultimately eliminate private providers. Individuals, Friedman believed, should have 'freedom to choose' but all things being equal, private provision should be preferred, as it reduced the size of the state. Like Hayek, Friedman was critical of the self-acceleration of state-run pension schemes caused by their reliance on experts who had a vested interest in the scheme's continuance and were not exposed to market incentives to drive efficiency. Where Friedman differed with Hayek, though, was over the question whether individuals should be compelled to enter such schemes at all. In so far as paternalists argued for compulsion to protect individuals from their short-sightedness, they were making a dangerously authoritarian argument that denied the 'freedom of individuals to make their own mistakes'. Liberals made the better argument that compulsion was about preventing the irresponsible becoming a cost to the community. Characteristically, though, Friedman regarded the latter not as an overriding logic but as a question of extent: compulsion would certainly be justified if 90 per cent of the population acted irresponsibly, but the irresponsible behaviour of 1 per cent could hardly justify restricting the freedom of the remaining 99 per cent.[133]

Neoliberals therefore shared a common hostility to the welfare state, social insurance, and state-run pension schemes. The emphasis of individual writers varied, however, according to the focus of their wider critique, optimism about the possibility of change, and approach to compulsion. Many of these individual arguments and tensions informed the debate about pension reform in the 1980s. Yet, stepping back, the logic of neoliberal authors' criticism and their alternatives also suggested three unstated claims. First, they strongly implied a reallocation of risk away from horizontal redistributions between members of the community embodied in pooled social insurance and towards individuals vertically distributing risk at different stages of their life cycle via individualised market investments.[134] Second, their arguments extended market approaches into other realms: individuals should see pensions as investments in their future security, and the difficulty of change should be understood through the lens of bureaucratic self-interest. Finally, their texts embodied the principle that social policy should reflect the needs of the competitive economy, whether in the form of investment in small business, improving the availability of capital, or job mobility.[135] As much as individual neoliberal arguments, it is these claims that we will see structuring Thatcher's pension reforms.

Conclusion

What, then, was the relationship of Thatcherism to these neoliberal ideas and to the Thatcher governments' attempted and actual reforms to pensions? One of our aims in this book is to move historical perspectives on the role of neoliberalism in Thatcherism beyond simple concepts that see one straightforwardly influencing or expressing the other. This chapter has established the foundations for that analysis in arguing for the distinctiveness of the neoliberal project, understanding it as a network that gained coherence through the interaction of its authors in a 'thought collective' and through their conviction that a new, more complete liberalism was needed. Its various schools took that project forward in different but related analyses. It is primarily the evidence of later chapters that shows how these ideas interacted with the Thatcher project and the objectives, ideas, values, arguments, and policy actions captured in the term 'Thatcherism'. At this stage, though, it is helpful to set out how we think about the wider relationship between these neoliberal ideas, the Thatcher project, and material and political contexts. Using eight headings, we can summarise our findings by stating that the relationship between Thatcherism and neoliberalism was contingent, multi-layered, plural, embedded, dynamic, unstable, manifest, and ironic.

We see the relationship as *contingent* because it was not inevitable that neoliberal ideas would become associated with the political Right or play an important role in late twentieth-century British politics. Certainly, the hostility that prominent neoliberals developed to social justice, redistribution, and the welfare state made the possibility of other configurations more remote. Yet these developments were themselves the result of historical trends within the neoliberal thought collective and of the forms that different welfare states took. More importantly, in the following chapters we stress (a) the opportunities that arose for greater ideological compatibility between neoliberalism and Conservatism; (b) the economic and political contexts that made neoliberal ideas attractive to the British Conservative party; and (c) the active agency of individuals within the policy process.

Neoliberalism and Thatcherism

We also see this as a *multi-layered* interaction. Following Ben Jackson, we highlight the different roles of neoliberal ideas. Sometimes they helped political actors perceive their actions within an overarching framework of arguments about the need actively to create freedom, insulate the state from interest groups, and escape the self-accelerating effects of democracy and expertise.[136] At other times neoliberal arguments provided them with a lens through which to extract meaning from (and understand) specific economic and political changes.[137] At a policy level, neoliberal principles or arguments could define problems and occasionally specify solutions. Our findings also suggest that this multi-layered character also applies to the agency of individuals in furthering this project. It was not only Thatcher and her closest ministers who brought neoliberal ideas into government or sustained their role in arguments: ministers, advisers and civil servants all played different roles; and their institutional opponents also had a significant impact on the types of policy these ideas came to justify.

We emphasise the *plurality* of neoliberal ideas and arguments available to combine with Conservative ideas or pragmatically to respond to context. At different times we shall see that those within and around Thatcher's governments believed that market competition could discover and provide new savings products. At the same time, though, we will see that concerns about concentrations of private capital and power made some of these political actors hostile to large institutions in the market. In part, their concern was over a capital infrastructure maladjusted to the needs of a dynamic competitive capitalism in the United Kingdom. Pension reforms, some believed, could become a means to promote small business and encourage risk-bearing entrepreneurial individualism. The individual would experience ownership – ideally, direct ownership as a company shareholder – so as not to be dependent on the state but also to create a population that intuitively understood the market as the source of its wealth, and so free mass democracy from the instability of its voters' cries for protection and rising expectations of the state. For reasons we explain in later chapters, though, choice making eventually displaced these arguments in the case for reform. Individuals would be free to choose from a wide range of products and providers in the market. Immediately, the question of whether to compel or merely incentivise individuals came into play. Similarly, the idea of a pension burden – and the inter-generational conflict that might result – came over time to drive a parallel set of reforms. Hostility to use of the welfare state as a redistributive programme and to the volume of income controlled by the state fuelled a serious attempt to rid the nation of a significant – and, alongside the NHS, arguably the most socially democratic – part of the British welfare state. Our point is not that all these arguments carried weight at the same time or in the minds of all political actors. Our claim is that, depending on which of these arguments they prioritised, it was possible to construct different neoliberal visions of pensions.

These neoliberal visions should not be seen as pure neoliberal thought when constructed by political actors, in our case chiefly Conservative politicians, their advisers, and think tanks. Neoliberal ideas and arguments were *embedded*, in two senses. First, some of the arguments had a grounding in Conservatism (albeit often as the result of quite different starting points). This allowed Conservatives to offer readings of neoliberalism that fitted their political tradition. Although it is important to recognise the specificity of these readings and the separate Conservative traditions that could produce similar arguments, we should not ignore the very real attempts to bring neoliberal thinkers directly into Conservative thinking. We wish to stress, for example, that those involved were exposed just as much to readings of ordoliberals as they were Chicago Friedmanites. For example, the Centre for Policy Studies think tank (which we go on to show was the primary instigator of personal pensions) published pamphlets on the German social market – and, indeed, a 'bibliography of freedom' – which listed both traditions.[138]

Florence Sutcliffe-Braithwaite has rightly emphasised a second sense of embeddedness, in that neoliberal ideas sat alongside Conservative ideas in the policymaking process and that the latter sometimes overruled the former.[139] We also find this, especially regarding paternalism and concepts of gradual rather than revolutionary change. We see this as one reason that the relationship between neoliberalism and the Thatcher project was a *dynamic* one, in that the arguments driving policy positions changed over time. As suggested in our introduction, though, this dynamic relationship was also affected by the political, economic, stakeholder, and system realities that neoliberal ideas faced when translated into specific proposals (especially within a path-dependent system). This confrontation with reality prevented some lines of argument developing further while encouraging others. But, on other occasions, political and institutional realities forced reformulation and an amended vision. Crucially, several different strategies for reform were pursued, and in this sense the realities of policymaking ensure there was no one way in which neoliberal policy was made. Yet we would also add that this dynamic relationship was driven by the internal inconsistencies found within neoliberal visions for pension policy or because other neoliberal ideas began to be reprioritised to overcome obstructions to reform. For these reasons, we see neoliberal ideas as a source of instability within the Thatcher project.

For all its contingency, pluralism, and dynamism, though, we miss something if we deny that the reforms undertaken were both attempted and partly achieved *manifestations* of neoliberalism. The story that unfolds is one in which a government set out to reform social policy to fit the needs of a market society, a reform in which risk was not to be managed across a society or between generations but across an individual's own lifetime via the market. These objectives and partly implemented realities speak directly to neoliberals' aims and the logic of their analysis of the welfare state. We would add, however, that this was in many ways an *ironic* manifestation – in the sense of a situational irony – in that neoliberal arguments aimed at one thing but their proponents found the reality of their reforms to be quite different. As our final chapters set out, for example, neoliberals' evolutionary reform in UK pensions actually created more of the system complexity they derided. The inducements thought necessary to incentivise and create the choice-making 'rational' individual merely replaced one source of redistribution with another, less efficient, solution, and the resulting pension landscape risked people entering old age much more dependent on the state and on future generations than they might have been. That was an outcome utterly at odds with the initial aims of neoliberal reformers.

Ultimately, this characterisation helps us resolve the questions that this chapter began with concerning differing analytical approaches to Thatcherism or neoliberalism. The way forward is not to reconcile these into a greater whole, give one priority, or leave them entirely disconnected as different perspectives on the same phenomena. Instead, we believe that the key lies in better describing their interconnections and interdependences, and the causes, impediments, and situational ironies that this produces. From this perspective, the Thatcher project looks very contingent and local, but at the same time the different responses that express this contingency relate back to a deeper and wider (national and international) history. Neoliberalism looks both plural and idea-centred, but in the hands of political and policy actors it could also appear surprisingly (if temporarily) integrated. It is vital we understand this, because the world the 1980s bequeathed us was the result of highly contingent and unstable pathways through ideas, policy visions, and welfare state systems with much longer histories.

Notes

1 Andrew Gamble, *The Free Economy and the Strong State: The Politics of Thatcherism* (Basingstoke: Macmillan, 1994), p. 222.
2 David Marsh and R. A. W. Rhodes, eds., *Implementing Thatcherite Policies: Audit of an Era* (Buckingham: Open University Press, 1992), pp. 4–10, 47–48.
3 Stephen Farrall and Colin Hay, eds., *The Legacy of Thatcherism: Assessing and Exploring Thatcherite Social and Economic Policies* (Oxford: Oxford University Press, 2014), p. 333.

4 On the monetarist experiment, see David Smith, *The Rise and Fall of Monetarism* (London: Penguin Books, 1987); Jim Tomlinson, 'Mrs Thatcher's Macroeconomic Adventurism, 1979–1981, and Its Political Consequences', *British Politics*, 2 (2007); Duncan Needham and Anthony Hotson, eds., *Expansionary Fiscal Contraction: The Thatcher Government's 1981 Budget in Perspective* (Cambridge: Cambridge University Press, 2014).

5 Roger Backhouse, 'The Macroeconomics of Margaret Thatcher', *Journal of the History of Economic Thought*, 24 (2002), pp. 323–25.

6 The claim that the Thatcher government brought the 'Keynesian' era to an end has been challenged: Jim Tomlinson, 'Tale of a Death Exaggerated: How Keynesian Policies Survived the 1970s', *Contemporary British History*, 21 (2007).

7 David Kynaston, 'The Long Life and Slow Death of Exchange Controls', *Journal of International Financial Markets*, 2 (2000).

8 David Parker, *The Official History of Privatisation*, vol. 1: *The Formative Years, 1970–1987* (London: Routledge, 2009).

9 Matthew Francis, '"A Crusade to Enfranchise the Many": Thatcherism and the "Property-Owning Democracy"', *Twentieth Century British History*, 23 (2012).

10 Nigel M. Healey, 'The Thatcher Supply-Side "Miracle": Myth or Reality?', *The American Economist*, 36 (1992); Richard Layard and Stephen Nickell, 'The Thatcher Miracle?', *The American Economic Review*, 79 (1989); Nick Crafts, 'Reversing Relative Economic Decline? The 1980s in Historical Perspective', *Oxford Review of Economic Policy*, 7 (1991); David Card, Richard Blundell, and Richard B. Freeman, *Seeking a Premier League Economy: The Economic Effects of British Economic Reforms, 1980–2000* (Chicago: University of Chicago Press, 2004).

11 Christopher Pierson, *Beyond the Welfare State? The New Political Economy of Welfare* (Cambridge: Polity, 2006), pp. 156–57; David Harvey, *A Brief History of Neoliberalism* (Oxford: Oxford University Press, 2005), pp. 1–13.

12 Stuart Hall and Martin Jacques, *The Politics of Thatcherism* (London: Lawrence & Wishart, 1983); Gamble, *The Free Economy and the Strong State*, pp. 23–25, 174–75, 79–85, 223.

13 As one of her biographers wrote, 'She stressed her unswerving convictions and dislike of consensus' (David Cannadine, 'Thatcher, Margaret Hilda', *Oxford Dictionary of National Biography* [www.oxforddnb.com]). He went on to add, however, that 'she could be more cautious and compromising than she admitted in public'.

14 Eric J. Evans, *Thatcher and Thatcherism* (London: Routledge, 2013), p. 3.

15 Peter Ridell, *The Thatcher Government* (Oxford: Blackwell, 1985), p. 7.

16 Shirley Robin Letwin, *The Anatomy of Thatcherism* (London: Fontana, 1992).

17 Margaret Thatcher Archive (hereafter MTA): Margaret Thatcher, 'Speech to Conservative Rally in Cardiff', 16 April 1979.

18 Thatcher and her mentor, Sir Keith Joseph, referred to this as the socialist 'ratchet effect' (MTA: Margaret Thatcher, 'Keith Joseph Memorial Lecture: Liberty and

Neoliberalism and Thatcherism

Limited Government', 11 January 1996 [www.margaretthatcher.org/document/108353]).

19 Ian Gilmour, *Dancing with Dogma: Britain under Thatcherism* (London: Simon & Schuster, 1992), p. 9.

20 Mark Garnett and Ian Gilmour, 'Thatcherism and the Conservative Tradition', in *The Conservatives and British Society, 1880–1990*, ed. by Martin Francis and Ina Zweiniger-Bargielowska (Cardiff: University of Wales Press, 1996), pp. 78–93; Andrew Denham and Mark Garnett, *Keith Joseph* (Chesham: Acumen, 2002), pp. 57–75; Peter Dorey, 'The Exhaustion of a Tradition: The Death of "One Nation" Toryism', *Contemporary Politics*, 2 (1996); Robert Walsha, 'The One Nation Group and One Nation Conservatism, 1950–2002', *Contemporary British History*, 17 (2003); Stephen Evans, 'The Not So Odd Couple: Margaret Thatcher and One Nation Conservatism', *Contemporary British History*, 23 (2009); David Seawright, *The British Conservative Party and One Nation Politics* (London: Continuum, 2010); Norman Barry, 'The "New Right"', in *The Political Thought of the Conservative Party since 1945*, ed. by Kevin Hickson (Basingstoke: Palgrave Macmillan, 2005), pp. 28–50; Andrew Roberts, *Eminent Churchillians* (London: Weidenfeld & Nicolson, 2010), pp. 252–53.

21 For an early example of this, see Robert F. Leach, 'Thatcherism, Liberalism and Tory Collectivism', *Politics*, 3 (1983). See also Keith Tribe, 'Liberalism and Neoliberalism in Britain, 1930–1980', in *The Road from Mont Pèlerin: The Making of a Neoliberal Thought Collective*, ed. by Philip Mirowski and Dieter Plehwe (Cambridge, MA: Harvard University Press, 2015), pp. 68–97; Florence Sutcliffe-Braithwaite, 'Neo-Liberalism and Morality in the Making of Thatcherite Social Policy', *The Historical Journal*, 55 (2012).

22 Jim Bulpitt, 'The Discipline of the New Democracy: Mrs Thatcher's Domestic Statecraft', *Political Studies*, 34 (1986). On the Conservative party as a machine for gaining power, see John Ramsden, *An Appetite for Power: A History of the Conservative Party since 1830* (London: HarperCollins, 1998).

23 David Willetts, 'The New Conservatism? 1945–1951', in *Recovering Power: The Conservatives in Opposition since 1867*, ed. by Stuart Ball and Anthony Seldon (Basingstoke: Palgrave Macmillan, 2005), pp. 169–91, at p. 190.

24 Harriet Jones, 'The Cold War and the Santa Claus Syndrome', in *The Conservatives and British Society*, Francis and Zweiniger-Bargielowska, pp. 240–54, at pp. 242–43; Seawright, *The British Conservative Party and One Nation Politics*, pp. 95–96. On the specificity of 1940s rhetoric: James Freeman, 'Reconsidering "Set the People Free": Neoliberalism and Freedom Rhetoric in Churchill's Conservative Party', *Twentieth Century British History*, 29 (2018).

25 E. H. H. Green, 'Thatcherism: An Historical Perspective', *Transactions of the Royal Historical Society*, 9 (1999), p. 39.

26 E. H. H. Green, *Thatcher* (London: Hodder Arnold, 2006), p. 40.

27 Chris Cooper, 'Little Local Difficulties Revisited: Peter Thorneycroft, the 1958 Treasury Resignations and the Origins of Thatcherism', *Contemporary British History*, 25 (2011); Dilwyn Porter, 'Government and the Economy', in *Britain*

The neoliberal vision

in the 1970s: The Troubled Economy, ed. by Richard Coopey and Nicholas Woodward (New York: St Martin's Press, 1996), pp. 34–54; Adrian Williamson, *Conservative Economic Policymaking and the Birth of Thatcherism, 1964–1979* (Basingstoke: Palgrave Macmillan, 2015).

28 Francis, ' "A Crusade to Enfranchise the Many" ', pp. 276–79; Evans, 'The Not So Odd Couple', pp. 108–9; Aled Davies, ' "Right to Buy": The Development of a Conservative Housing Policy, 1945–1980', *Contemporary British History*, 27 (2013).

29 William Davies, 'The Making of Neo-Liberalism', *Renewal*, 17 (2009), p. 88; Taylor C. Boas and Jordan Gans-Morse, 'Neoliberalism: From New Liberal Philosophy to Anti-Liberal Slogan', *Studies in Comparative International Development*, 44 (2009).

30 Jamie Peck, *Constructions of Neoliberal Reason* (Oxford: Oxford University Press, 2010), p. 83.

31 Greta R. Krippner, 'The Financialization of the American Economy', *Socio-Economic Review*, 3 (2005). See also Gerald A. Epstein, *Financialization and the World Economy* (Cheltenham: Edward Elgar, 2015); Costas Lapavitsas, *Profiting without Producing* (London: Verso Books, 2013).

32 Harvey, *A Brief History of Neoliberalism*, p. 2.

33 Michel Foucault, *The Birth of Biopolitics: Lectures at the Collège de France, 1978–79*, ed. by Michel Senellart, trans. by Graham Burchell (Basingstoke: Palgrave Macmillan, 2008); Nikolas Rose, *Governing the Soul: Shaping of the Private Self* (London: Free Association Books, 1999); Nikolas Rose and Peter Miller, 'Political Power beyond the State: Problematics of Government, 1992', *British Journal of Sociology*, 61 (2010); Nikolas Rose, Pat O'Malley, and Mariana Valverde, 'Governmentality', *Annual Review of Law and Social Science*, 2 (2006), pp. 90–91.

34 Thomas Lemke, ' "The Birth of Bio-Politics": Michel Foucault's Lecture at the Collège de France on Neo-Liberal Governmentality', *Economy and Society*, 30 (2001), p. 201.

35 Kean Birch, 'Neoliberalism: The Whys and Wherefores ... and Future Directions', *Sociology Compass*, 9 (2015), p. 575.

36 This in part reflects the 'ideational turn' in political science. See, for example, Peter A. Hall, ed., *The Political Power of Economic Ideas* (Princeton, NJ: Princeton University Press, 1989); J. Goldstein and R. O. Keohane, eds., *Ideas and Foreign Policy: An Analytical Framework* (Ithaca, NY: Cornell University Press, 1993); Mark Blyth, *Great Transformations: Economic Ideas and Institutional Change in the Twentieth Century* (Cambridge: Cambridge University Press, 2002).

37 Mirowski and Plehwe, *The Road from Mont Pèlerin*; Angus Burgin, *The Great Persuasion: Reinventing Free Markets since the Depression* (Cambridge, MA: Harvard University Press, 2012); Ben Jackson, 'At the Origins of Neo-Liberalism: The Free Economy and the Strong State, 1930–1947', *The Historical Journal*, 53 (2010); Daniel Stedman Jones, *Masters of the Universe: Hayek, Friedman, and the Birth of Neoliberal Politics* (Princeton, NJ: Princeton University Press, 2014).

Neoliberalism and Thatcherism   69

38 Quinn Slobodian, *Globalists: The End of Empire and the Birth of Neoliberalism* (Cambridge, MA: Harvard University Press, 2018). Neil Rollings, 'Organised Business and the Rise of Neoliberalism: The Confederation of British Industry, 1965–1990s', in *The Neoliberal Age? Britain since the 1970s*, ed. by Aled Davies, Ben Jackson, and Florence Sutcliffe-Braithwaite (London: UCL Press, 2021), pp. 279–98.

39 Mirowski and Plehwe, *The Road from Mont Pèlerin*.

40 For an overview: Ron Harris, 'Government and the Economy, 1688–1850', in *The Cambridge Economic History of Modern Britain*, ed. by Roderick Floud and Paul Johnson (Cambridge: Cambridge University Press, 2004), pp. 204–37.

41 For an account in global perspective: Marc-William Palen, *The 'Conspiracy' of Free Trade: The Anglo-American Struggle over Empire and Economic Globalisation, 1846–1896* (Cambridge: Cambridge University Press, 2016), ch. 1.

42 This was a thesis of Alexis de Tocqueville, *Democracy in America*, trans. by Harvey Mansfield and Delba Winthrop (Chicago: University of Chicago Press, 2012), ch. XVIII.

43 For an overview emphasising distinctions: Jens Meierhenrich, '*Rechtsstaat* versus the Rule of Law', in *The Cambridge Companion to the Rule of Law*, ed. by Jens Meierhenrich and Martin Loughlin (Cambridge: Cambridge University Press, 2021), pp. 39–67.

44 Rachel S. Turner, *Neo-Liberal Ideology: History, Concepts and Policies* (Edinburgh: Edinburgh University Press, 2011), ch. 2.

45 For example, the Joint Stock Act of 1844, Employers Liability Act 1880, and the 1847 Railways Act (which introduced price reductions on profitable lines and gave government the option to eventually purchase a line).

46 For an overview: Martin Pugh, *The Making of Modern British Politics 1867–1945* (Oxford: Blackwell, 2002), ch. 2.

47 The classic studies are Peter Clarke, *Lancashire and the New Liberalism* (Cambridge: Cambridge University Press, 1971); Michael Freeden, *The New Liberalism: An Ideology of Social Reform* (Oxford: Clarendon Press, 1978).

48 Martin J. Sklar, *The Corporate Reconstruction of American Capitalism, 1890–1916: The Market, the Law, and Politics* (Cambridge: Cambridge University Press, 1988).

49 In Britain, for example, an economic planning movement gained traction across all parties in the 1930s and the government intervened to consolidate industries, create chartered corporations and sector-based marketing boards, set import quotas, and dispense hundreds of millions of pounds in subsidies.

50 Robert Skidelsky, *John Maynard Keynes: The Economist as Saviour, 1920–1937* (London: Papermac, 1994). For a recent discussion of Keynes' relationship with 'New Liberalism', see Richard Toye, 'Keynes, Liberalism, and "the Emancipation of the Mind"', *The English Historical Review*, 130 (2015).

51 The shift had been heralded by a wartime White Paper: Minister of Reconstruction, *Employment Policy*, Cmd 6527 (London: HMSO, 1944).

52 Tony Judt, *Postwar: A History of Europe since 1945* (London: Vintage, 2010); John Gerard Ruggie, 'International Regimes, Transactions, and Change: Embedded

70 *The neoliberal vision*

Liberalism in the Postwar Economic Order', *International Organization*, 36 (1982).

53 Walter Lippmann, *The Good Society* (London: Allen & Unwin, 1937), p. 371. Lippmann's text is referenced below as an exemplar of early neoliberal views because its key arguments represented a starting point of agreement between key individuals involved in the thought collective: Burgin, *The Great Persuasion*, pp. 58–78.

54 Frank H. Knight and Hubert Bonner, 'The Meaning of Democracy: Its Politico-Economic Structure and Ideals', in *Freedom and Reform: Essays in Economics and Social Philosophy* (New York: Harper, 1947), pp. 184–204, at p. 203.

55 Frank H. Knight and Hubert Bonner, 'Ethics and Economic Reform', in ibid., pp. 45–128, at p. 52. As Hayek put it: 'Economic control is not merely control of a sector of human life which can be separated from the rest; it is the control of the means for all our ends.' F. A. von Hayek, *The Road to Serfdom* (London: Routledge & Kegan Paul, 1944), p. 95.

56 Lippmann, *The Good Society*, p. 112.

57 Hayek, *The Road to Serfdom*.

58 Lippmann, *The Good Society*, pp. 183–84; Wilhelm Röpke, *The Social Crisis of Our Time* (Chicago: University of Chicago Press, 1950), p. 9.

59 Lippmann, *The Good Society*, pp. 165–68, 174.

60 As we have seen, this was not a fair criticism to make of liberal praxis or of all liberal philosophy. We must remember, however, that (a) neoliberals were assessing liberalism not just from a British perspective but an international perspective; (b) their primary target here was Herbert Spencer; (c) they viewed many of the interventions that had been made as resulting from collectivist principles, not liberal ones; and (d) the case was being made to support significantly more action than social reform or regulatory measures.

61 Lippmann, *The Good Society*, p. 186.

62 Ibid., p. 199.

63 Ibid., p. 201.

64 Ibid., pp. 208–9.

65 Frank Knight, 'Lippmann's *The Good Society*', *Journal of Political Economy*, 46 (1938), p. 871.

66 The exception is Ludwig von Mises, who attended the MPS but was always isolated in his diagnosis that the problem was a failure properly to apply nineteenth-century liberalism.

67 Harold Macmillan, *The Middle Way: A Study of the Problem of Economic and Social Progress in a Free and Democratic Society* (London: Macmillan, 1938).

68 Walter Euken, 'Competition as the Basic Principle of the Economic Constitution [1942]', in *The Birth of Austerity: German Ordoliberalism and Contemporary Neoliberalism*, ed. by Thomas Biebricher and Frieder Vogelmann (London: Rowman & Littlefield, 2017), pp. 81–98.

69 Röpke, *The Social Crisis of Our Time*, p. 177, emphasis added.

70 Euken, 'Competition as the Basic Principle of the Economic Constitution'.

71 Lippmann, *The Good Society*, p. 174; Euken, 'Competition as the Basic Principle of the Economic Constitution'.

Neoliberalism and Thatcherism 71

72 Foucault, *The Birth of Biopolitics*, p. 116.
73 Röpke, *The Social Crisis of Our Time*, p. 227.
74 Lippmann, *The Good Society*, pp. 212–32. There was much less agreement on specifics but the field of action included reform to patent laws, anti-monopoly and restrictive practices laws, and changes to company law to limit the size of corporations, but also measures to promote the development of people, the mobility of capital, conservation, and perhaps even the euthanasia of unearned income.
75 Röpke, *The Social Crisis of Our Time*, pp. 160–2.
76 Lippmann, *The Good Society*, p. 214.
77 Röpke, *The Social Crisis of Our Time*, pp. 160–2.
78 Euken, 'Competition as the Basic Principle of the Economic Constitution'.
79 Burgin, *The Great Persuasion*, pp. 108–16.
80 The 'rule of law' featured in both the MPS's draft and agreed aims: Dieter Plehwe, 'Introduction', in *The Road from Mont Pèlerin*, Mirowski and Plehwe, pp. 1–42, at pp. 22–25.
81 Werner Bonefeld, 'Freedom and the Strong State: On German Ordoliberalism', *New Political Economy*, 17 (2012), p. 633.
82 Ralf Ptak, 'Neoliberalism in Germany: Revisiting the Ordoliberal Foundations of the Social Market Economy', in *The Road from Mont Pèlerin*, Mirowski and Plehwe, pp. 98–138, at pp. 101–2.
83 Turner, *Neo-Liberal Ideology*, pp. 81–83.
84 The relevant excerpts of his 1937 work are translated in English as: Franz Böhm, 'Economic Ordering as a Problem of the Economy and a Problem of the Economic Constitution', in *The Birth of Austerity*, Biebricher and Vogelmann, pp. 115–20.
85 Franz Böhm, Walter Euken, and Hans Grossmann-Doerth, 'The Ordo Manifesto of 1936', in *The Birth of Austerity*, Biebricher and Vogelmann, pp. 27–40.
86 Röpke, *The Social Crisis of Our Time*, pp. 159–63.
87 Turner, *Neo-Liberal Ideology*, pp. 81–83.
88 Euken, 'Competition as the Basic Principle of the Economic Constitution'.
89 These consequences were seen through the concepts of proletarianism and massification and the dependence, atomisation, and isolation from work and communities that resulted. See Alec Dinnin, 'Ortega y Gasset: The Fear of Mass Society', in *The Oxford Handbook of Ordoliberalism*, ed. by Thomas Biebricher, Werner Bonefeld, and Peter Nedergaard (Oxford: Oxford University Press, 2022), pp. 230–42.
90 Stefan Kolev and Nils Goldschmidt, 'Vitalpolitik ', in *The Oxford Handbook of Ordoliberalism*, Biebricher, Bonefeld, and Nedergaard, pp. 453–60.
91 Röpke, *The Social Crisis of Our Time*, pp. 199–223. For example, the survival of independent rural communities was celebrated in that they embodied households that both participated in markets and retained a way of life characterised by ownership, partial self-sufficiency, connection through collaborative work, and control over the mix of leisure and work.
92 They therefore preferred entrepreneurial small business and management practices that gave workers a sense of 'solidarity' and common purpose through

72 *The neoliberal vision*

actions such as control over processes, allotments, and community organisations. See Alexander Rüstow, 'Social Policy or Vitalpolitik (Organic) Policy [1951]', in *The Birth of Austerity*, Biebricher and Vogelmann, pp. 163–77.

93 Foucault, *The Birth of Biopolitics*, pp. 148–49.

94 Josef Hien, 'The Social Market Economy and Ordoliberalism: A Difficult Relationship', in *The Oxford Handbook of Ordoliberalism*, Biebricher, Bonefeld, and Nedergaard, pp. 333–46.

95 Jackson, 'At the Origins of Neo-Liberalism', p. 147.

96 This is seen to be an enduring legacy; see, for example, the argument that ordoliberalism shaped the construction of economic management within the Eurozone in Lars P. Feld, Ekkehard A. Köhler, and Daniel Nientiedt, 'Ordoliberalism, Pragmatism and the Eurozone Crisis: How the German Tradition Shaped Economic Policy in Europe', *European Review of International Studies*, 2 (2015).

97 As a student of Ludwig von Mises in Vienna, Hayek contributed to interwar debates involving the Austrian school of economics. While working at the London School of Economics, in the 1940s, he was the most public challenger of the emerging social democratic order through his best-selling work *The Road to Serfdom*. Published in 1944, the book's success deepened Hayek's ties in the United States, and he moved to the University of Chicago's Law School before joining the University of Freiburg, where his publications continued to engage with ordoliberals' focus on legal theory.

98 F. A. von Hayek, *The Constitution of Liberty* (Oxford: Routledge, 1960), pp. 11–35; Scott Gordon, 'The Political Economy of F. A. Hayek', *The Canadian Journal of Economics*, 14 (1981), p. 474.

99 Hayek, *The Road to Serfdom*, p. 217, emphasis in original.

100 Ben Jackson, 'Freedom, the Common Good, and the Rule of Law: Lippmann and Hayek on Economic Planning', *Journal of the History of Ideas*, 73 (2012); Hayek, *The Road to Serfdom*, p. 211; Philip Mirowski, 'Postface: Defining Neoliberalism', in *The Road from Mont Pèlerin*, Mirowski and Plehwe, pp. 417–56, at pp. 443–44; Chris Guest, 'Hayek on Government: Two Views or One?', *History of Economics Review*, 26 (1997), p. 52.

101 Andrew Gamble, *Hayek: The Iron Cage of Liberty* (Cambridge: Polity, 1996), pp. 50–74.

102 F. A. von Hayek, 'The Use of Knowledge in Society', *The American Economic Review*, 35 (1945).

103 F. A. von Hayek, 'Competition as a Discovery Procedure [1968]', *Quarterly Journal of Austrian Economics*, 5 (2002), pp. 17–18.

104 Robert Van Horn and Philip Mirowski, 'Neoliberalism and Chicago', in *The Elgar Companion to the Chicago School of Economics*, ed. by Ross Emmett (Cheltenham: Edward Elgar, 2010), pp. 196–206.

105 Burgin, *The Great Persuasion*, pp. 32–54. Knight had condemned both collectivism and laissez-faire liberalism, Simons had attacked Roosevelt's New Deal and Beveridge's welfare state, and both were involved in founding the MPS. See Knight, 'Lippmann's *The Good Society*'; Henry C. Simons, 'The Beveridge

Program: An Unsympathetic Interpretation', *Journal of Political Economy*, 53 (1945). Simons died before the Mont Pèlerin meeting took place.

106 Edward Nik-Khah and Robert Van Horn, 'The Ascendancy of Chicago Neoliberalism', in *Handbook of Neoliberalism*, ed. by Simon Springer, Kean Birch, and Julie MacLeavy (London: Routledge, 2016), pp. 27–38, at p. 29.

107 Jackson, 'At the Origins of Neo-Liberalism', p. 142.

108 Milton Friedman, 'Neo-Liberalism and Its Prospects', *Farmand* (17 February 1951).

109 Laurence H. Miller, 'On the "Chicago School of Economics"', *Journal of Political Economy*, 70 (1962); Philip Mirowski, 'Ordoliberalism within the Historical Trajectory of Neoliberalism', in *The Oxford Handbook of Ordoliberalism*, Biebricher, Bonefeld, and Nedergaard, pp. 57–75, at pp. 67–69.

110 Burgin, *The Great Persuasion*, pp. 160–62.

111 Van Horn and Mirowski, 'Neoliberalism and Chicago', pp. 197–99; Peck, *Constructions of Neoliberal Reason*, pp. 67–68.

112 Nik-Khah and Van Horn, 'The Ascendancy of Chicago Neoliberalism'.

113 Gary Becker, 'Investment in Human Capital: A Theoretical Analysis', *Journal of Political Economy*, 70 (1962), p. 9.

114 Foucault, *The Birth of Biopolitics*, pp. 248–60.

115 Burgin, *The Great Persuasion*, pp. 162–63.

116 Peter J. Boettke and Alain Marciano, 'The Past, Present and Future of Virginia Political Economy', *Public Choice*, 163 (2015); James D. Gwartney and Randall G. Holcombe, 'Politics as Exchange: The Classical Liberal Economics and Politics of James M. Buchanan', *Constitutional Political Economy*, 25 (2014).

117 See Hayek on 'The Decline of Socialism and the Rise of the Welfare State', in Hayek, *The Constitution of Liberty*, pp. 221–32.

118 See, for example, ibid., p. 249; Wilhelm Röpke, *A Humane Economy: The Social Framework of the Free Market* (Chicago: Henry Regnery Company, 1960), p. 175.

119 Röpke, *A Humane Economy*, pp. 154–55.

120 'The more the state takes care of us,' Röpke writes, 'the less shall we feel called upon to take care of ourselves and our family, with the result that the individuals' efforts declined just as they were demanding more of the state.' Röpke, *The Social Crisis of Our Time*, p. 164.

121 Röpke, *A Humane Economy*, pp. 164–65.

122 Ludwig Erhard, *Prosperity through Competition* (New York: Frederick A. Praeger, 1958), p. 185.

123 Röpke, *A Humane Economy*, p. 155.

124 Bonefeld, 'Freedom and the Strong State', p. 644.

125 Röpke, *The Social Crisis of Our Time*, pp. 164–65.

126 The tendency to identify pension funds as a resource for national renewal has been a persistent tendency in the United Kingdom – from Labour's 'national superannuation' proposal in 1957 to a developing cross-party assumption in 2023–4 that government should act to allow pension funds to take more risks

74 *The neoliberal vision*

and incentivise them to invest more in the United Kingdom, with a view both to long-term prospective fund returns and to the dynamisation of the domestic economy.

127 Röpke, *A Humane Economy*, p. 168.

128 Hien, 'The Social Market Economy and Ordoliberalism'. We should acknowledge, however, that, as with earnings-related pensions in the United Kingdom and elsewhere, this German welfare reform aimed to entrench inequality, not to eliminate it. The aim was 'social justice', in the sense of a just return on a worker's contributions, not 'social security', let alone 'social equality'. See Cornelius Torp, 'The Adenauer Government's Pensions Reform of 1957: A Question of Justice', *German History*, 34 (2016); Gordon L. Clark, 'The UK Pensions Crisis and Institutional Innovation: Beyond Corporatism and Neoliberalism', in *Challenges of Aging: Pensions, Retirement and Generational Justice*, ed. by Cornelius Torp (London: Palgrave Macmillan, 2015), pp. 105–32.

129 Hayek, *The Road to Serfdom*, pp. 124–25; *The Constitution of Liberty*, pp. 219–340.

130 Ibid., pp. 249, 251–53.

131 Ibid., pp. 253–64. The latter quotation is at p. 264.

132 Milton Friedman and Rose D. Friedman, *Free to Choose: A Personal Statement* (London: Secker & Warburg, 1980), p. 149.

133 Milton Friedman, *Capitalism and Freedom* (Chicago: University of Chicago Press, 1962), pp. 184–89.

134 Avner Offer, 'The Market Turn: From Social Democracy to Market Liberalism', *The Economic History Review*, 70 (2017).

135 Röpke, *A Humane Economy*, p. 180.

136 Ben Jackson, 'Intellectual Histories of Neoliberalism and Their Limits', in *The Neoliberal Age?*, Davies, Jackson, and Sutcliffe-Braithwaite, pp. 52–72.

137 Thomas Gould has shown how a wider layer of neoliberal concepts of uncertainty and risk interacted with material circumstances to make possible the alternative forms of individualised, dynamised old age provision that the Thatcher governments' reformers preferred: Thomas J. Gould, 'The Changing Practices of Managing Uncertainty and Risk in Post War British Political Economy: Investments, Insurance, Pensions and Professional Risk Managers c. 1945–1995' (PhD, University of Bristol, 2021).

138 Chris R. Tame, *A Bibliography of Freedom* (London: Centre for Policy Studies, 1980).

139 Sutcliffe-Braithwaite, 'Neo-Liberalism and Morality in the Making of Thatcherite Social Policy'.

2

Neoliberalism and the UK state in the 1970s

In the 1970s the neoliberal ideas discussed in the preceding chapter were transmitted from the neoliberal thought collective into British politics via a complex process widely acknowledged to have involved think tanks, journalists, and the building of personal links with political actors. That process was heavily conditioned by the context within which it occurred, however. This chapter therefore explores the political and economic environment of the 1970s that shaped the uptake of these ideas in Britain and their folding into a political project on the Conservative Right. The chapter begins by outlining the present state of knowledge about how a subset of neoliberal ideas gained political traction and reached policymakers. We highlight the growing compatibility between Conservative and neoliberal ideas and stress the range of individuals who acted as carriers or bridges between the two. The chapter then considers four environmental factors that served to make those ideas salient.

First, there is the impact of the economic crises of the 1970s and the way in which they called into question the prevailing economic policy model. The nature of the challenges is considered, with an initial focus on the problems for Keynesianism raised by simultaneous rising inflation and economic stagnation ('stagflation'). The poor economic growth experienced by the United Kingdom in this decade was far from unique among the advanced capitalist democracies. The particular UK experience is explored below, however, in terms of problems such as low productivity, low corporate profitability, relatively poor international competitiveness and the implications of that for the balance of payments and for the pound sterling, and levels of taxation. Second, we briefly elaborate the various attempts to address these multitudinous problems made by both Conservative and Labour governments during the decade. Third, we then explore key changes in British capitalism and in the composition of the UK labour force that served further to undermine existing assumptions about the operation of the economy. Finally, we widen the analysis to consider the 'crisis of consensus', examining the self-conscious break with the putative Keynesian and welfare state

76   *The neoliberal vision*

consensus to be found on both the Left and Right of British politics. Having
set out that environmental context, we proceed to consider how economic
crisis served to advance the neoliberal critique of the state in Britain. The
chapter concludes by connecting these developments with the Conservative
party's longer-term attitudes to the state and its pursuit of 'statecraft'.

The transfer of neoliberal ideas into British politics

As noted in Chapter One, by the 1970s an array of neoliberal ideas were
available to political actors seeking to push back against the prevailing economic orthodoxy and a state that was both much larger than it had been
before the Second World War and much more involved in life cycle provision and in the operation of the market. There are signs that these ideas
could have been of interest to some on the centre Left of British politics.
It was Conservatives, however, who proved most interested in some – but
not all – of that palette of neoliberal thought. The impact of neoliberalism
on the political project of the Conservative party in this decade is much
written about, but not necessarily well understood. In part, it was a matter of timing. Having lost office in 1974, the party began the customary
process of reflection and reorientation, using working groups to review its
policies. With the election of Margaret Thatcher as party leader in 1975,
some of the Conservatives already familiar with neoliberal ideas through
their existing contacts with right-wing think tanks, journalists, and advisers
found themselves leading the Conservative party's break with the policies it
had pursued in government. This created opportunities for proponents of
neoliberal ideas within the party's orbit. Reliant on its officers and MPs for
research, without the civil service advice it had received in government, and
identifying a need for fresh thinking, the party turned to external experts
to fill out its policy groups.[1] Consequently, the network of right-wing think
tanks (and their funders and supporters) along with those who were linked
to them, such as sympathetic academics, now had significant access to a
party seeking new ideas.[2]

Yet the Conservatives' interest in neoliberal ideas was also a matter of
compatibility. It was not inevitable that neoliberalism initially became intellectually aligned with the political Right in the United Kingdom, but three
factors made it more likely. First, the narratives presented in neoliberal
texts (or in popularisations of them) aligned with the Conservative party's
return to its familiar themes of a smaller state and the need to 'liberate' the
British people to arrest national decline. In previous periods of opposition,
in the late 1940s and 1960s, Conservative leaders had linked these themes
to national production and technocratic efficiency respectively.[3] The result

was that the aim of 'setting the people free' had not actually been wholly compatible with neoliberal positions on international trade and growth. In the 1970s, however, quite a different diagnosis underpinned this rhetoric. The party emphasised the unsustainability and damaging effects of government expenditure in the context of lacklustre tax revenues accompanying historically high peacetime rates of taxation, and the consequent rise in public borrowing that characterised the 1970s. This presented fewer contradictions with neoliberal theory.[4]

Second, some of the technical work associated with the neoliberal thought collective could lend a degree of intellectual credibility to the party's new approach. Specifically, the monetarist diagnosis, that public spending contributed to an expansion in the money supply and consequently to inflation, gained traction, but so too did the developing critique that high levels of taxation were serving to curb incentives to work (as demonstrated by the so-called 'Laffer curve') and thereby crimping economic growth.[5] These lines of argument could distinguish the opposition's approach from Labour and allow it to return to inflation as a political theme without fear of association with the Heath government's failed policies. At the same time, Conservatives were reading more widely within the work of the neoliberal thought collective. Whereas they had primarily encountered Hayek as a negative critique of planning, the more active policy suggestions of the Chicago school and 'social market' theorists appeared to meet the party's need for concrete steps towards its self-defined aims of creating a capital-owning society and bringing choice into the welfare state.[6]

Third, it is important to remember that Conservative leaders, MPs, and audiences were reading neoliberal ideas in the context of an emerging discourse known at the time as New Right thinking.[7] As Lawrence Black observes, the contributors to this amorphous New Right were 'a mix of activists, intellectuals, think tanks, neoliberals, authoritarians, libertarians, Eurosceptics, and marginal dead ends'.[8] Although to some extent they coalesced around a willingness to ignore tensions between economic liberalism and moral Conservatism, the New Right is better thought of as a style of Conservatism that emphasised the moral stakes of political economy and organised its arguments around the core motifs that Western capitalism still faced an existential threat from socialism and that a reaction to the ideas of the 1960s was necessary for its revival.[9]

This new style altered the relationship between neoliberalism and British Conservatism in several respects. Throughout the postwar years Conservative thinkers had separated neoliberals from their party's tradition, arguing that Hayek and his followers were making the same mistake as socialists when they attempted to reorganise society from first principles rather than accept its traditions and gradual evolution. A Conservative-run state eased this change by managing interest group conflict, striking ideological balance (such as by accepting the utility of a welfare state), and (increasingly) actively promoting growth. The New Right's meta-narratives disturbed this model in the 1970s, and in doing so offered new ways to locate neoliberalism within a Conservative worldview.[10] For example, within the frame of a cultural reaction it was possible to link the challenge neoliberals posed to mainstream economics and welfare theories with the wider reassertion of 'Conservative common sense' against an elite seen as dominated by Left-leaning experts.[11] Similarly, neoliberals' tough messages about the limits of the state and the role of individual responsibility could be seen as examples of the wider return to discipline required to combat the consequences of excessive permissiveness.[12] Furthermore, the argument that postwar attempts at tempering the perceived negative effects of capitalism had in practice ratcheted politics ever Leftwards provided a justification for ideas seeking to reform rather than just manage the status quo.[13] Combined with the claim that urgent action was needed to address decline, the result was an intellectual environment on the Right that was much less hostile to neoliberalism's basic premises.

Politically, the effect of the New Right was to shift the energy and focus of British Conservatism onto those issues that had the greatest potential for compatibility between Conservative aims and neoliberal ideas. As selective welfare, industrial relations, human capital, and burdensome government took on greater importance for Conservatives, the neoliberal thought collective's source material was rich enough in themes of individual responsibility, the use of authority to challenge the demands of interest groups, and the problems of over-government that its prescriptions often looked like modern policy options that accorded with the values Conservatives had long applied to these topics.[14] Crucially, many of the New Right's contributors began to articulate these issues and policy options in the language of 'vigorous virtues' and the logic of 'common sense'.[15] Dosed with populist framings, this 'authoritarian populism' appeared to offer a practical way of gaining majority support for some of the measures advocated by neoliberals, removing a major barrier that had hitherto restrained their influence.[16]

The New Right's emergence as a style of Conservatism rather than a clearly defined faction or univocal body of thought also encouraged a fusion of many different perspectives compatible with its meta-narratives and motifs. One consequence was that neoliberal ideas were interwoven with wider theories about the failures of Western governments. These included the idea that a growing state was taking an increasing share of income and in the process crowding out initiative in the (in the eyes of critics, more productive) private sector; that an enlarged state was increasingly overloaded and struggling to cope with its many functions; and that the growth of the state was intimately linked both to a systemic failure of modern democracy and to a systemic tendency for state bureaucracies to expand.[17] Partly because the communications experts advising the Conservative party at the time emphasised the importance of presenting these arguments as a cohesive worldview and partly because this totalising style was a favourite of some of the party's speakers (Keith Joseph, for example), neoliberal ideas were not simply injected into Conservative discourse but networked into it through their connection with related ideas to which Conservative political actors were attracted.[18]

The picture that emerges is thus an altered Conservatism that was more compatible with neoliberal ideas, even if the roots of that change spread much more widely than neoliberals' influence. This is only half the story, however. Although there was potential for tension between moral Conservatism and economic liberalism, neoliberal thought had itself arguably become more compatible with Conservatism – for instance, as Ben Jackson points out, via its implicit acceptance of the importance of family and of the male breadwinner model.[19] Hayek also was beginning to allow a larger role for tradition (and eventually religion) in neoliberal analysis.[20] In addition to the political timing, then, which meant that the party was open to new ideas, there was a growing conjunction between neoliberalism and Conservatism that made it much easier for policy ideas to cross from one network to another.

Nevertheless, although political timing and compatibility raised the likelihood of contact, they are insufficient explanations. Work by political scientists emphasises that policy change was the product of a complex mix of ideas, interests, and institutions (the triad of political economy's 'primordial elements', as Peter Hall puts it).[21] Many of the individual actors in the political process we mention below certainly represented vested interests. Peter Horden – who, as we shall see in Chapter Three, chaired the party's working group on wider ownership – was director of the F&C Smaller Companies Investment Trust. Nigel Vinson – who we meet serving on this working group but who later championed plans for personal pensions – was a successful businessman who had floated his plastic coatings company on the stock exchange. John Redwood – who, working in Thatcher's Policy Unit (PU), persuaded her to push on with these proposals – had been an investment adviser at Robert Fleming, the merchant bank, and then investment manager and director at N. M. Rothschild & Sons. As we explore in Chapters Four and Eight, institutions also played a powerful role, in the sense that political actors both anticipated their objections and found themselves having to react to their lobbying and opposition. Yet this does not mean we should reduce policy change to the interplay of interests and institutions. Historians and social scientists rightly understand ideas as

80 *The neoliberal vision*

helping shape perceived interests, not least by framing political visions of the world.[22] *Policy* timing is also important in determining whether such interests are able to advance their preferences and whether ideas are adopted. There is a general recognition that ideas that provide solutions to difficult policy problems are more easily taken up (and few decades in modern history have been as politically and economically difficult as the 1970s).[23] As we shall see, ideas played an important role in defining the problems that allowed one group of interests and politicians to challenge institutions, and vice versa. In themselves, however, abstract ideas do not directly influence politics; they need carriers (individual or institutional) who can inject them into political consciousness.[24]

In the British context, much of the analysis of such idea carriers has focused on the way in which neoliberal ideas entered politics via dedicated right-wing 'think-tanks'.[25] The first, and most prominent of these, was the Institute of Economic Affairs (IEA). This had been established in the late 1950s, but it moved to the centre stage both academically and in terms of policy influence in the 1970s (rather as the Heritage Foundation did in the United States), in the process moving from being the David to the Goliath of the New Right.[26] The IEA's close involvement with the Mont Pèlerin Society brought key neoliberal thinkers and their ideas to Britain.[27] Under the leadership of Ralph Harris and Arthur Seldon, each of whom was active within the MPS, and with widespread financial support from business donors, the IEA sought through its seminars and publications to influence elite political, media, and educational opinion to challenge the postwar settlement.[28] Perhaps its most significant achievement, however, was its early influence on a generation of young journalists and commentators with connections to government or with aspirations to political office (the most notable of the latter being Nigel Lawson, whose career had begun in the 1950s as a journalist on the *Financial Times*).[29] By 1980 Ralph Harris could justifiably claim, in the first issue of the IEA's new journal, *Economic Affairs*, that the Institute had made good progress in promoting an acceptance 'that the proper role of government ... is not to create the good life but to remove the obstacles in the way of millions trying to create it for themselves'.[30]

The IEA has been seen as a rather purist institution, committed more to the purity of free-market ideology than to pragmatic adjustment to the short-term expediencies of the 'politically possible'. That was certainly true of one of its founders, Arthur Seldon, who took a somewhat dim view of the right-wing think tanks that emerged in the 1970s.[31] Unlike the nominally non-partisan if plainly neoliberal IEA, these were both linked to the neoliberal thought collective and more closely aligned with the Conservative party than the IEA. The Centre for Policy Studies (CPS), for example, was established by Sir Keith Joseph, Alfred Sherman, and Thatcher herself in

Neoliberalism and the UK state in the 1970s

1974. It drew on neoliberal ideas and sought to package them into workable policy proposals as part of 'a radical free market programme'.[32] The CPS was explicitly intended by Joseph, who had himself expressed his conversion to 'true' Conservatism after the defeat of the Heath government, of which he had been a part, similarly to convert the Conservative party.[33] The CPS had a particularly Josephite moral and social agenda, certainly, but it also sought to bring neoliberal ideology into Conservative thinking.[34] Its director, Alfred Sherman, is said to have 'caught Mrs Thatcher's ear and wrote many of the speeches in the 1970s in which she and Joseph floated ideas of the radical right'.[35] The Adam Smith Institute was another think tank that, though less influential than the CPS, was nonetheless noteworthy in connecting the neoliberal thought collective with the Conservative party. Created by Madsen Pirie and Eamonn Butler in 1977, it too drew on neoliberal ideas in crafting policy ideas, which it then attempted to inject into Conservative thinking.[36]

These various think tanks on the Right wing of British politics are seen not just to have provided a conveyor belt by which neoliberal ideas were routed into the Conservative party in the 1970s but to have injected 'radical energy at moments when the government seemed to flag' after 1979.[37] They are commonly assumed, however, to have had most influence while the Conservatives were in opposition, during which time they are said to taken advantage of being outside the glare of publicity to absorb new ideas and process them into policy change.

Is there a danger of confusing correlation with causation, however? That, essentially, is the view of Adrian Williamson, who argues that the presence in policy of ideas promoted by think tanks is not a priori causal evidence.[38] There is a danger, certainly, that in focusing on (often somewhat triumphalist) accounts emphasising the key role played by think tanks in the transmission of neoliberal ideas in Britain we overlook the key role played by individuals. Embedded within international and national neoliberal networks and spanning the divide between academia and politics, they are seen as important in the process by which neoliberal ideas were absorbed into party policy and governing institutions (as they were in many other polities).[39] Neoliberal theorists such as Friedrich Hayek, James Buchanan, and Milton Friedman, have, of course, themselves been identified as crucial actors; but so too are specific individuals who played a key role as carriers of those ideas into and within British politics. As Stephanie Mudge puts it, neoliberalism did not just have an intellectual face; as ideas were turned into policies, it also came to have a political and a bureaucratic face.[40] Individuals were a key element in that process. As we have already observed, one way in which key individuals from the business world such as Ralph Harris, Arthur Seldon, Alfred Sherman, and Nigel Vinson played a part before, during, and after

82 *The neoliberal vision*

the 1970s was through the active role they played in establishing and running think tanks. But politicians too were important receivers and carriers of the neoliberal vision. As Ben Jackson notes, key politicians, such as Keith Joseph and Geoffrey Howe, 'imbibed the insight that in Britain too much power had been concentrated in the hands of democratic collective agencies, notably the state and the unions, at the expense of the individual'.[41] By imbibing the neoliberal critique, such individuals were well on the way to developing policies to address it.

One way in which many of these key actors could drink deeply of the neoliberal draught was by reading the work of financial journalists such as Peter Jay (writing in *The Times*) and Samuel Brittan (*Financial Times*) who were themselves influenced by the neoliberal critique, and who proved adept at translating it into language more easily understood by busy politicians and businesspeople who were not necessarily intellectually equipped to engage with neoliberal theory in its raw state.[42] It is easy to underestimate just how important they were in shaping not just the development of political ideas in Britain but the wider political discourse.

There was, of course, another set of individuals identified as 'carriers' of neoliberalism: political advisers. Despite Thatcher's initial scepticism about their utility, especially when employed outside No. 10, as the 1980s wore on the government made growing use of the 'rapidly increasing "private army" of special advisers'.[43] Intended to provide the political advice to which the civil service was seen as averse, special political advisers were a vital influence on Thatcher and her senior ministers. Through their use, '[p]ermanent officials who were deemed ideologically unsound, such as Sir Douglas Wass, the Permanent Secretary to the Treasury and a Keynesian, were to some extent bypassed as a primary source of advice'.[44] Most notably, economic advisers, formal or informal, played a key role in carrying economic ideas into politics: examples include Tim Congdon and Gordon Pepper, of Lombard Street Research on monetary policy; Patrick Minford, not least via his work at Liverpool University on the first rational expectations model of the UK economy; and, more formally, Alan Walters, as chief economic adviser to Thatcher from 1981 to 1983 and again from 1989 to 1990.[45] In the Treasury, Peter Cropper, a former head of the Conservative Research Department, George Cardona, Adam Ridley, and – later – Andrew Tyrie performed a similar service as special advisers in the Treasury by devising practical proposals for the implementation of neoliberal ideas. We should also note the key role played by John Redwood, the Rothschild director and investment manager whom Thatcher appointed to head the No. 10 Policy Unit between 1983 and 1985. As we shall see in later chapters, the PU ('a priesthood of true believers' in this era) played an exceptionally important role not just in injecting neoliberal ideas into policy discussions at the

Neoliberalism and the UK state in the 1970s　　83

heart of government but in acting as the motor of policy development across government.[46]

As well as widening the cast of carriers, recent research has also nuanced their roles in bringing neoliberal thinking into contact with British Conservatism. Rather than bringing unvarnished versions of neoliberal ideas into Conservative policymaking, the advisers and journalists involved had normally already parsed these through a Conservative lens that emphasised some but not all parts of the neoliberal thought collective's writings and thought. Many of the tensions often identified between moral Conservatism and economic liberalism were not end products of this transmission process but were, in fact, already present (and recognised) in the advice of those advocating neoliberal solutions. Rather than abstract ideas, neoliberal arguments and policies were also pitched very explicitly by carriers as solutions to the party's political problems and rhetorical needs.[47] We now also know that Thatcher and her allies read popularisations of neoliberal thought that deliberately set out to reconcile moral Conservatism with economic liberalism.[48]

The 'crisis' of the 1970s and the challenge to 'consensus'

Nevertheless, although it is possible to identify how neoliberal ideas may have gained a hold within the Conservative party, we still have to explain why. 'Say's law', that supply creates its own demand, is an insufficient explanation. Rather, we should analyse the process from the demand side, considering the policy environment and the way it created and shaped the demand for ideas among the early architects of 'Thatcherism'.

In British popular and political memory (and, until very recently, in scholarly memory) the 1970s are commonly seen as a 'dismal and benighted decade' in which the country's decline became all too obvious and 'the British economy was in serious trouble'.[49] Indeed, the term 'the 1970s' has become a shorthand for political and economic failure and the discrediting of what has been termed the 'social democratic consensus' that characterised British politics in the three decades after the Second World War. It should surprise nobody that a party forced out of office in 1974 by a combination of economic crisis and perceived government failure (not just the apparent inability to manage the economy effectively but also to control the trades unions) embraced a vision of the 1970s as a decade of political failure and national decline. In retrospect, it is possible to tell a more positive story of British politics in the 1970s than that which popular and political memory of the 1970s preserves. That was not how things were seen at the time, however. Rather, as the economist Patrick Minford puts it, 'the main feeling

84   *The neoliberal vision*

of those charged with running Britain's economy was one of hopelessness'.[50] Britain was perceived in these years to be in serious trouble economically and politically – being often dubbed 'the sick man of Europe', and not just by proto-Thatcherites such as Minford.[51] The crisis of confidence on both sides of British politics flowed in large part from economic challenges that were common to other advanced economies but with features that were seen to be distinctively British. Briefly, these can be encapsulated under four headings: high inflation, economic stagnation, high public borrowing, and poor international competitiveness (with implications for both the balance of payments and currency stability). One might also add very difficult industrial relations (encapsulated in popular and political memory by the 1978/79 'winter of discontent' but also a feature of the Heath years). Despite its obvious salience in the construction of a sense of governmental failure in the 1970s, however, we leave consideration of the latter to others and here focus on the specifically economic dimensions of the challenge.

Inflation

One result of a decades-long fiscal policy supportive of demand to keep unemployment at historically unprecedented low levels was that inflation was already edging up in the late 1960s.[52] In the 1970s, however, it took off, due to the quadrupling of oil prices by the Organization of the Petroleum Exporting Countries (OPEC) in 1973, a more general rise in commodity prices, and the fiscal policy reaction to rising unemployment in the wake of the oil price shock. A key issue for policymakers was that the United Kingdom's inflation experience was notably poor in comparison to most other G7 countries (see Table 2.1).

The rise in UK inflation was startling, reaching an annualised 26.9 per cent in late 1975. Not surprisingly, its rapid take-off was the source of much disquiet. The causes of the inflation surge were far from entirely understood. Nevertheless, one thing was clear to the New Right by the middle of the decade: as Geoffrey Howe put it, 'First, and above all, the nation need[ed] to be completely convinced of the Government's determination to control inflation.'[53] In 1975 Thatcher warned that 'rampant inflation, if unchecked, could destroy the whole fabric of our society' (not least by destroying the value of capital and thus reducing incentives to save).[54] Although opposition Conservative politicians remained attached to the idea that 'wage-push' factors were an important contributor to inflation, 'in spite of Friedman's emphatic denial', key political actors such as Howe proved receptive to the Friedmanite analysis that the expansion of the money supply was a cause of price inflation (an analysis that chimed with much earlier Powellite precepts about the evils of inflation and the role of monetary policy in controlling it).[55]

Neoliberalism and the UK state in the 1970s

Table 2.1 Economic performance in the G7 economies, 1960–87

	US	Japan	Germany	France	UK	Italy	Canada	Total	Total OECD
Growth rates of GDP (per cent per annum)									
1960–68	4.5	10.2	4.1	5.4	3.1	5.7	5.5	5.0	5.0
1968–73	3.2	8.7	4.9	5.5	3.3	4.5	5.4	4.4	4.5
1973–79	2.4	3.6	2.3	2.8	1.5	3.7	4.2	2.7	2.7
1979–87	2.6	3.8	1.4	1.7	1.8	2.2	2.9	2.6	2.5
Rates of inflation (consumer price indices)									
1960–68	2.0	5.7	2.7	3.6	3.6	4.0	2.4	2.7	2.9
1968–73	5.0	7.0	4.6	6.1	7.5	5.8	4.6	5.5	5.7
1973–79	8.5	10.0	4.7	10.7	15.6	16.1	9.2	9.4	9.9
1979–87	5.8	2.7	3.1	8.4	7.6	12.5	7.0	5.8	6.5
Unemployment (as a percentage of total labour force, average levels)									
1960–68	5.0	1.3	0.8	1.5	1.5	4.9	4.8	3.0	3.1
1968–73	4.6	1.2	0.8	..	2.4	5.7	5.4	3.2	3.4
1973–79	6.7	1.9	3.5	4.5	4.2	6.6	7.2	4.9	5.2
1979–87	7.6	2.5	6.9	8.9	10.1	9.5	9.7	7.1	7.8

Source: A. J. C. Britton, *Macroeconomic Policy in Britain, 1974–1987* (Cambridge: Cambridge University Press, 1994), p. 155.

Economic stagnation

Even as inflation rose in the 1970s, world economic growth stuttered as a result of the supply-side shock of rising commodity and oil prices (see the GDP figures in Table 2.1). In Britain, as in other advanced economies, the result was the first economic recession since the 1930s (lasting in the United Kingdom from mid 1973 to early 1974). Because of the very high political commitment to full employment in Britain, the prospect of unemployment going over a million in 1972 had already produced a decisive fiscal stimulus by the Heath government (giving rise to the so-called 'Barber boom', named after Anthony Barber, Heath's Chancellor of the Exchequer). Once recession set in, fiscal policy remained committed to restricting the growth in unemployment so far as was possible – and with considerable success, for the unemployment rate was kept below 6 per cent.[56] Nonetheless, even that represented a considerable political blow, given the exceptionally low levels of unemployment that had characterised the preceding quarter of a century.

Moreover, the conjunction of rising inflation and economic stagnation represented a major intellectual shock that called into question the (neo-)

86 *The neoliberal vision*

Keynesian framework, which since 1945 had underpinned economic policymaking by the Treasury under successive Labour and Conservative governments. It had assumed that macroeconomic policy could exploit a trade-off between inflation and economic growth embodied in and apparently endorsed by the 'Phillips' curve (first formulated in 1958, this appeared to provide empirical evidence of a long-term inverse relationship between inflation and unemployment). The stagflation phenomenon disproved that assumption, called into question the prevailing balance between state and market, and created a space for a revival of neoclassical economics.[57]

Moreover, Britain had a productivity problem. Productivity declined with the onset of recession because policy was strongly supportive of employment, and thus average output per worker fell, but, more generally, from the late 1960s a long-term downward trend in UK labour productivity growth had set in. This, of course, had consequences for international competitiveness. In conjunction with rates of earnings growth that were relatively high in comparison with international competitors (thus raising the cost of UK exports), this significantly weakened the balance of payments.

Public spending and international confidence in sterling

The policy response to the onset of stagflation under the Conservative government after 1972, and then under its Labour successor, was not just a marked fiscal loosening but action to try to contain wage-push inflationary pressures. This initially took the form of statutory incomes and price control (abjured by the Heath government in 1970 but re-embraced from 1972). When Labour took power in 1974 it initially sought to break with statutory controls by forging a 'social contract' with the trades unions under which they agreed voluntarily to moderate wage demands in return for additional state spending on welfare benefits, including what amounted to a deferred pay rise via the creation of a new state earnings-related pension and increases in the basic state pension. This rise in the 'social wage' was intended to provide compensation for nominal wages rising less quickly than prices.[58] In the event, this strategy (though it later moved from voluntarism to statutory control) played a major role in getting inflation under control by the end of Labour's term in office – rather to the surprise of the Treasury.[59] There was a cost, however, which was both financial and political. Most obviously, a higher social wage demanded more welfare spending even as spending on welfare benefits was rising anyway because of the so-called 'automatic stabilisers', such as the payment of unemployment benefit to those losing their jobs in the recession. Consequently, public spending rose markedly even as the recession eroded tax revenues as company profitability (and thus taxes raised on those profits) fell and real incomes (and thus, *ceteris paribus*, real income tax revenue) began to shrink.[60] As a proportion of GDP, public spending dropped somewhat at the end of the 1970s, but, as can clearly be seen in Figure 2.1, the trend in the mid-1970s was clearly upwards, as it had been since the mid-1950s. This, in short, was an era of profound expansion in the scope of the British state but without a concomitant rise in tax revenue to fund it.

The inevitable result was a worsening of what was then known as the 'public sector borrowing requirement' (PSBR). Consequently, a need to reduce the planned increase in government spending to contain the PSBR became increasingly pressing, and from 1976 the Labour government adopted a system of public spending 'cash limits' instead of volume-based expenditure planning to limit PSBR growth.[61] Likewise, the Conservative party moved decisively in favour of PSBR reduction, not least because it was seen as vital if the growth of the money supply was to be contained and inflation defeated.[62]

Nevertheless, even as borrowing rose to finance an expanding state in the 1970s, so taxes increased, in terms of both marginal rates of income tax and tax as a proportion of the overall economy. By the decade's end income tax rates were at levels that were high both historically and internationally (see Table 2.2). Moreover, both the number of people paying income tax and those paying it at the highest marginal rate were relatively high both historically and comparatively (not least because the rate of increase in tax thresholds lagged behind the rate of growth of earnings – the 'fiscal drag'

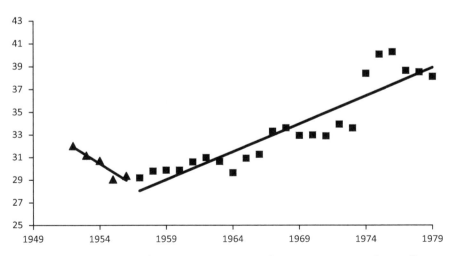

Figure 2.1 Public expenditure as a percentage of GDP, 1952–79 (with trendlines 1952–6 and 1957–79)
Source: National Statistics (based on historic data as at 8 March 2007).

88 *The neoliberal vision*

Table 2.2 Structure of income tax in selected countries, c.1976

	Threshold (£)	Initial rate (%)	Maximum rate (%)	Income for maximum rate (£)
UK	1,685	35	83	21,685
France	3,550	3.6	54	46,800
Germany	2,200	22	56	65,700
US	4,000	25	50 (55.5 incl. local taxes)	29,600

Source: Daunton, *Just Taxes*, p. 337.

effect). As Martin Daunton, the foremost historian of taxation in Britain, has noted, the consequence was an erosion of electoral support for the idea of redistributive taxation and concerns about its impact on economic growth and incentives.[63] In *The Right Approach to the Economy*, in 1975, for example, the Conservatives did not just prioritise the defeat of inflation ('the great destroyer – of jobs, living standards and a stable order'); they committed to reductions in income taxation and a smaller state as well as the encouragement of personal capital building.[64]

High inflation, economic stagnation, deteriorating international competitiveness, high taxation, and rising public borrowing to finance an expanding state were a toxic mix. An additional problem was the United Kingdom's degree of dependence on foreign lenders to finance its rising sovereign debt in the context of the collapse of the Bretton Woods system of fixed exchange rates in 1971, after the United States suddenly ended the dollar's convertibility into gold. Several years of confusion and volatility had ensued, with a series of 'prolonged and haphazard' adjustments to the international financial system.[65] Although the balance of payments surpluses accruing to OPEC countries after their 1973 oil price rise found their way back to London for investment, which tended to ease pressure on sterling, countervailing pressures in terms of the country's loss of competitiveness, worsening balance of payments, and a lessening of confidence among overseas investors meant that, as in the mid-1960s, the weakness of sterling became a pressing policy concern in the mid-1970s. This came to a head in 1976, when a severe run on the pound forced the government to negotiate an International Monetary Fund (IMF) loan of £3.9 billion (then the largest loan ever made by that institution).[66] This was a defining moment (presented by the media as a moment of national humiliation as the country went 'cap in hand' to beg the IMF for relief), which served to confirm the views of those in the New Right who saw a reduction in the scope of the state as essential to national survival. In pensions, as we shall see, this was to be a key force in shaping antipathy to the existing settlement and a desire radically to reform it on market lines.

The changing economy

In addition to these many economic challenges and their role in promoting a search for new solutions, the 1970s also saw profound shifts in the underlying nature of the British economy that, over the long term, were to prove significant for pension policy. For example, the male employment rate at the start of the 1970s was over 90 per cent, but there was a marked fall during the ensuing decade (a trend that would continue until the early 1990s), mainly because of the effect of recession on industrial jobs. Female employment, however, rose from around 55 to 60 per cent. The result was that, by the end of the 1970s, 41 per cent of the workforce was female, as compared with 36 per cent at the start. The decade thus saw the start of a long term 'feminisation' of the workforce, a change clearly linked to 'the more general rise in female emancipation and the change in attitudes around the 1960s'.[67] Likewise, manufacturing (which employed over 34 per cent of workers in 1970 but 29 per cent in 1979) was at the start of a long-term secular decline in importance that was common to all Organisation for Economic Co-operation and Development (OECD) economies, though one that was to accelerate markedly in the 1980s in the United Kingdom as the Thatcher governments became much less supportive of traditional heavy industries such as coal, steel, and shipbuilding.[68]

These were significant changes, with implications for political economy. For example, the structural shift in employment patterns clearly worked to the disadvantage of organised labour, historically strong in industrial employment. In 1978 Eric Hobsbawm presciently wrote of the 'forward march of labour' having been halted, and in retrospect we can clearly see that the late 1970s marked the high point of trades union membership, at a little over 50 per cent of all workers.[69] The changing labour market was also significant in terms of pension policy, however, because highly unionised male industrial workers were the most likely to benefit from funded occupational pensions, whereas women tended to have either an unfunded public sector pension (worth less because they also tended to earn less) or – more likely, as a result of high levels of female employment in the much less unionised private service sector – no pension provision at all over and above that provided by the state.

More generally, the 1970s saw demographic changes that even at the time were identified as having long-term implications. The twentieth-century decline in mortality rates continued, meaning that, on average, people were living longer (with all that implied for future pension costs), but

90 *The neoliberal vision*

two other changes were also evident. First, the rapid decline in the fertility rate that followed the end of the second wave of the postwar baby boom in the mid-1960s continued, dropping below the replacement rate in the 1970s and staying there, implying a marked shift over the long term in the ratio between those above retirement age and those of working age. Second, however, the products of that second, and much longer, wave of the baby boom began to enter the labour market from the early 1970s, a phenomenon that deferred the 'demographic time bomb' of old age income replacement for about three decades and thus created an acknowledged breathing space for public policy (albeit on what proved to be erroneous assumptions about continuing net emigration).[70] We should also note that, even as the economy began to move away from its domination by industrial production towards an increasing significance of business services, so the growing importance of the financial services sector was also in evidence by the time the Conservatives came into office in 1979.

The crisis of 'consensus'

The economic challenges of the 1970s described above (in conjunction with a common analysis in the leaderships of both the major parties that union power had become a destabilising force both politically and economically) served to call into question the Keynesian social democracy model of economic and social policymaking that had dominated UK government for nearly three decades. Once that would have been an uncontroversial statement, but, as discussed in our Introduction, although it was once widely accepted, the idea of a postwar 'consensus' is now controversial, with many contemporary historians emphasising the disagreement between the two major postwar political parties.[71] So comprehensive was the scholarly assault that it is now almost compulsory to place the term 'consensus' within inverted commas. Yet it is nonetheless possible to acknowledge significant disagreement between (and often within) the Conservative and Labour parties on the detail of both postwar economic and social policy while also recognising that, at the macro level, the notion of consensus continues to have some utility (and continues to have some scholarly purchase among social scientists).

Recognising this requires us to acknowledge that successive postwar governments of different political persuasions did largely embrace the idea of an active state intervening in the economy – partly via its ownership of key industries, partly by using Keynesian fiscal policy techniques to manage demand and maintain a high level of employment, and partly by using the welfare state to promote social security.[72] Indeed, given the post-1979

Thatcherite assault on Britain's prevailing Keynesian economic policy framework and, much less successfully, on its welfare state, an assault explicitly conceived as breaking with the prevailing political (in the view of Thatcher and others in the 'New Right', 'socialist') consensus of the mid-1970s, one could argue that we need to reinstate the consensus concept if we are to make sense of the changing contours of British politics since 1945.[73] In the context of the welfare state, although many ambitious Thatcherite plans for its shrinkage were to be disappointed, the financial and political environment became notably harsher from the mid-1970s.

This was even more evident once the Conservatives gained power in 1979 and brought a much more sceptical approach to welfare policy, even as the demands on the welfare state were increasing.[74] In that sense, the postwar consensus on welfare policy was not a 'mirage', and its dissolution at the end of 1970s marked the start of a very different era and of a 'new politics' for Britain's welfare state – particularly in the 'decade of change' that was the Thatcher premiership.[75] Consequently, scholars of Britain's welfare state have almost all identified the late 1970s as a defining stage in its history.[76] In Britain, as in other advanced capitalist democracies, the end of a quarter of a century of economic growth with the onset of recession in 1973 called into question the funding of expanded welfare provision for a very prosaic reason: it became harder to finance its scope in the context of rising demand for its services and benefits (for example, new medical techniques and rising numbers of out-of-work citizens entitled to unemployment benefits) even as lower or negative economic growth sapped government revenue-raising capability. The only real disagreement in the literature is about the precise timing of the transition.

The cuts in planned public spending increases required by the IMF in return for its loan in 1976 might be taken as the zenith of what Rodney Lowe called Britain's 'classic welfare state'.[77] That welfare settlement dated back to the 1945–51 Labour governments and their implementation of many of the proposals made by Beveridge in 1942 to slay the 'five giants on the road of reconstruction': want, disease, ignorance, squalor, and idleness.[78] During the ensuing three decades the 'welfare state' had expanded both in the scope of its coverage and the proportion of economic output that was devoted to it. Although the Conservatives had initially sought to cut back spending when they took office in 1951, once the party's 'reluctant collectivists' became dominant (most notably after Harold Macmillan became Prime Minister in 1957) they too came to see virtue in welfare spending (such as on education and on health) and of judicious intervention in the marketplace (for example, the institution of compensation for redundancy to promote labour mobility, or the embrace of a training levy rebate system to raise the quality and quantity of workplace training).[79] Their justification was not, as Labour's was, the promotion of greater equality; rather, it was grounded in economic efficiency (a healthier, better-educated, better-trained, and more secure workforce as a route to higher productivity).[80] To this extent, there was a degree of cross-party agreement on welfare policy means if not ends, and thus a form of 'consensus' in this era on the need for higher and more generous spending on welfare services and benefits and for targeted interventions in the market.[81]

Likewise, although there were plainly disagreements about economic policy between the two major parties in the postwar era, especially about the degree of state nationalisation of industry that was desirable, much of this disagreement was played out at the margin, most notably via the repeated nationalisation and denationalisation of the steel industry. Most of the nationalisation pushed through by Labour after 1945 remained intact. Similarly, despite inter-party disagreements about some of the detail of macroeconomic policy, in practice successive governments operated within a technocratic agreement that Keynesian-style management of aggregate demand could deliver full employment with relatively low inflation.[82] Once again, therefore, although there may have been disagreements about the ideological ends of policy, it is possible to identify a substantive amount of agreement between the major parties on policy means.[83]

In short, amidst much inter- and intra-party disagreement, from the mid-1950s to the mid-1970s it is possible to identify a degree of postwar cross-party agreement about the necessary balance between the state and the market. There may have been little agreement on policy objectives between the major parties, but the era of 'consensus' certainly saw a narrowing of the parameters of their disagreement and, indeed, a degree of agreement on the need for a welfare state, a measure of state ownership of industry, and active Keynesian-style management of the economy to maintain growth and full employment. The crises of the 1970s were the undoing of that consensus.

Although the United Kingdom was far from the only country encountering severe economic headwinds in the 1970s, as Table 2.1 shows, this tended not to be much acknowledged within British policymaking circles or political commentary at the time.[84] That was partly because the country's Keynesian policy framework was already giving some cause for concern before the onset of recession in 1973 and partly because Britain's problems were judged to be particularly awful. The apparently catastrophic failure of economic policy in so many dimensions had one obvious effect: it served to discredit both the existing Keynesian social democratic policy model and the Treasury as its administrator. As Peter Hall notes, that served to break open the policy process, creating a 'marketplace for ideas' in which both Left and Right competed to offer solutions.[85] Both sides of the Left/Right divide may have proceeded from a common analysis that the existing policy

Neoliberalism and the UK state in the 1970s

framework had failed, but their respective analyses of the causes of failure were markedly different. In the search for a remedy that would cure the ailing economy, each side came to embrace very different policy prescriptions. For the Left, the problem was one of profound market failure coupled with the timidity of the state in the face of powerful vested interests within British capitalism and its consequent unwillingness to control the market. The Left's proposed solution was a very significant increase in state ownership of economic resources and vastly greater state intervention in the remainder of the economy – the so-called 'Alternative Economic Strategy'.[86] (We should note, however, that in many ways this was not the programme of the Labour leadership in government from 1974 to 1979, during which time it pursued what Richard Coopey and Nicholas Woodward term a 'modified Keynesianism', by which it sought – with some success – to rescue the existing Keynesian social democratic model via pragmatic adjustment rather than replace it wholesale.)[87]

The crisis, neoliberals, and the state

Whereas the Left sought to address the economic crisis via an expansion of state ownership of industry and commerce and a much greater degree of state intervention in the market, the analysis of the 'New Right' after the Conservatives' loss of office in 1974 was that the cause of failure lay in the interventionist nature of an excessively large Keynesian social democratic state. The Heath government had entered office in 1970 promising to cut taxes, reduce market intervention by the state, and reform industrial relations (not least by ending state intervention in wage bargaining). To that end, it had initially tightened fiscal policy and adopted a more restrictive monetary policy, but then, in the face of rising unemployment, it had rapidly U-turned in 1972 back to the policy framework it had inherited.[88] For the architects of what came later to be termed 'Thatcherism', that U-turn betrayed a failure of nerve, a misdiagnosis of the problem, and a failure to recognise the underlying faults of postwar Keynesian social democracy as terminal. As Richard Vinen puts it, 'Heath's failure was a precondition for Thatcher's success' in the 1975 leadership election.[89]

As we saw in Chapter One, in the mid-1970s the so-called 'New Right' had a palette of neoliberal ideas on which to draw in developing an alternative policy prescription that could be the remedy for economic failure in the dimensions of policy failure outlined above. That remedy was to see the Conservative party re-embrace the market and the idea that the state should at once be smaller and both willing and able to enforce compliance with free-market requirements (for example, to bring the trades unions to

94   *The neoliberal vision*

heel).[90] The policy presumption in the United Kingdom, however, saw a notable emphasis placed on the unsustainability of an expanding state and on the damaging effects of state intervention in the market, high government spending, and public borrowing.

There were four key neoliberal elements to the critique of the prevailing Keynesian social democratic policy framework advanced by the New Right. First, most famous, and most influential, was the analysis of the 'monetarists'.[91] Monetarism, a product of the Chicago school, as discussed in Chapter One, gained purchase on the minds of policymakers in many countries as a product of the high inflation of the 1970s.[92] In the British context, there is often a tendency to see the 1979 general election as a contest between monetarism and Keynesianism.[93] This is a mistake, for it ignores both the degree to which Labour had adjusted the latter (despite much disagreement within the Cabinet) and exaggerates the extent to which the Conservative party (or, at least, the key players in its leadership) had reached agreement by 1979 on the need for monetarism.[94] Nonetheless, although (unreconstructed Heathite) members of the shadow Cabinet remained profoundly sceptical, the principal Conservative architects of policy change (Keith Joseph, Geoffrey Howe, Nigel Lawson, and Thatcher herself) used the party's period in opposition prior to 1979 to rethink economic policy and, in the process to repudiate attempting to control inflation via a highly interventionist prices and incomes policy. Instead, they embraced the idea that the expansion of the money supply, not least by debt-financed public spending, was the most important contributor to rising prices.[95] In this analysis, they were of course clearly influenced by Chicago school thinking, neatly summed up by Milton Friedman's famous proposition that 'inflation is always and everywhere a monetary phenomenon'.[96] Adrian Williamson is right, however, to remind us both that Friedman himself was not strictly a 'monetarist', on this definition, and that the architects of the new UK policy framework never embraced monetary control as the *only* weapon to be deployed in the battle against inflation. As Williamson puts it, 'The Conservatives enthusiastically embraced the new orthodoxy that control of the money supply was necessary, but not sufficient, to control inflation.'[97]

In short, the reinvention of Britain's macroeconomic policy framework from the late 1970s was about more than monetarism: 'Monetarism is not enough,' declared Keith Joseph in his Stockton Lecture of 1976.[98] The new, more broadly based, and recognisably 'neoliberal' policy stance also embraced alternative analyses of failure, most relevant to this study being critiques of an over-enlarged state.[99] One important example of the latter was the idea that the state was inherently less productive than the private sector and that a key explanation for the United Kingdom's relatively poor productivity was an enlarged state that 'crowded out' investment and output by private firms. As the principal exponents of this analysis in the United

Kingdom put it, Britain's economic problem was 'too few producers', and the solution to that problem was to shrink the state and liberate the economic potential of the market.[100]

Two other theories contributed to this analysis of state inefficiency and the deleterious effects of its expansion. The most publicly discussed in the mid- to late 1970s was a critique of the state that emphasised its increasing struggle to meet voters' rising expectations. Britain, in this analysis, was becoming harder, if not impossible, to govern effectively.[101] Different explanations for this were postulated, but from our perspective the most influential was the 'overload' thesis. This argued that the British state had taken on more than it could ever achieve in taking responsibility for promoting economic growth, maintaining full employment and relatively low inflation, raising productivity, and ensuring social security via the welfare state.[102] That it had done so, claimed Samuel Brittan in academic journal articles, in a book, and in columns in the *Financial Times* that proved influential on the New Right, was a product of 'the economic contradictions of democracy'.[103] Brittan argued not just that there were excessively high expectations of what government could achieve but that modern liberal democracy was inherently problematic. Political competition, Brittan asserted, encouraged parties to offer voters more public services and higher benefits. Over time, voter expectations tended to escalate, and the process was worsened by the pursuit of self-interest by the actions of rival collective groups, such as trades unions and employers.

A related explanation for the growth of government was provided by contemporary public choice theory. This proposed an 'economic theory of politics' rooted in Austrian economics and embracing an individualistic rational choice model of the state. By extension, it offered, a 'theory of government failure'.[104] In 1973 William Niskanen argued in an IEA pamphlet that government bureaucracy was not the servant of the people, but its master.[105] He outlined a theory of bureaucracy analogous to the theory of the firm: instead of maximising profits, bureaucrats aimed to maximise their budget. The individual self-interest of the bureaucrat thus provided the motive power for an inexorable expansion of the state irrespective of its social and economic utility. The affinities with neoliberalism of this analysis, both in terms of its critique of the state as antithetical to the maximisation of individual freedom and in terms of its rational choice theoretical underpinning, are clear.[106]

Conclusion

The reorientation of Conservative policy after 1975 can be seen as the start of a revolution in what Jim Bulpitt calls Conservative 'statecraft'.[107] Since the Second World War the Conservative party's electoral strategy had been to accommodate itself to voters' apparent preference for state intervention to ensure a high and stable level of employment in the economy and levels of state-provided welfare benefits and services considerably higher than those pertaining before 1939. Yet, as Ben Jackson and Robert Saunders have noted, although a preparedness to embrace the 'postwar consensus' had brought electoral dividends, by the mid-1970s 'the party had become trapped in a "statecraft game" that Conservatives no longer believed they could win, since the basis of governing competence had become the management of corporatist bargaining between government, employers, and trades unions'.[108] The profound economic crises of the 1970s served to discredit almost entirely that iteration of the postwar Keynesian social democratic settlement. The inflation explosion, economic stagnation, poor industrial relations, relatively poor productivity, and the seemingly remorseless tendency for the state to take an ever-growing share of national income all served to create in turn a perceived 'crisis of the state'. It is too glib to dismiss that crisis, as Colin Hay does, as a politically partisan media confection.[109] If there was one thing Britain's political class agreed on in the 1970s it was that the economic crisis was real, and that, one way or another, its resolution required at the very least very significant adjustments to the existing policy model.[110] On both the Right and Left of British politics the search for solutions to the crisis led to approaches that envisaged the complete replacement of the existing policy framework. Those alternatives were radically different, of course. Whereas the Left pursed its profoundly socialist alternative, on the Right of British Conservatism the search for new ways of governing competently (statecraft) led it to what we would now term a 'neoliberal' diagnosis of failure. The means by which a particular selection of available neoliberal ideas entered the thinking of Conservative policymakers was complex and dependent on the growing compatibility between neoliberalism and Conservatism, as well as on the actions of key idea carriers, both individual and institutional.

Notes

1 Adrian Williamson, *Conservative Economic Policymaking and the Birth of Thatcherism, 1964–1979* (Basingstoke: Palgrave Macmillan, 2015), pp. 50–51. Generally, however, Williamson sees neoliberals as somewhat less successful in influencing the party on economic policy than we do in our analysis of social policy.
2 On the importance of business support for those seeking to channel neoliberal ideas to the Conservatives, see Neil Rollings, 'Organised Business and the Rise of Neoliberalism: The Confederation of British Industry, 1965–1990s', in

The Neoliberal Age? Britain since the 1970s, ed. by Aled Davies, Ben Jackson, and Florence Sutcliffe-Braithwaite (London: UCL Press, 2021), pp. 279–98.

3 James Freeman, 'Reconsidering "Set the People Free": Neoliberalism and Freedom Rhetoric in Churchill's Conservative Party', *Twentieth Century British History*, 29 (2018).

4 Heather Whiteside, 'Neoliberalism as Austerity: The Theory, Practice, and Purpose of Fiscal Restraint since the 1970s', in *The Handbook of Neoliberalism* (London: Routledge, 2016), pp. 361–69, at p. 366.

5 On the impact of Friedman's monetarist diagnosis of inflation in the United Kingdom, see Williamson, *Conservative Economic Policymaking and the Birth of Thatcherism*, pp. 53–57. On the influence of the (subsequently discredited) Laffer curve, which purported to demonstrate that lower taxes would pay for themselves by stimulating growth, see Roger Middleton, 'The Laffer Curve', in *Famous Figures and Diagrams in Economics*, ed. by Mark Blaug and P. J. Lloyd (Cheltenham: Edward Elgar, 2010), pp. 412–19.

6 Aled Davies, James Freeman, and Hugh Pemberton, '"Everyman a Capitalist" or "Free to Choose"? Exploring the Tensions within Thatcherite Individualism', *The Historical Journal*, 61 (2017).

7 Ben Jackson, 'Currents of Neo-Liberalism: British Political Ideologies and the New Right, c.1955–1979', *The English Historical Review*, 131 (2016).

8 Lawrence Black, '1968 and All That(cher)', in *Inventing the Silent Majority in Western Europe and the United States: Conservatism in the 1960s and 1970s*, ed. by Anna Von der Goltz and Britta Waldschmidt-Nelson (Cambridge: Cambridge University Press, 2017), pp. 356–76, at p. 357.

9 Joan Isaac, 'The New Right and the Moral Society', *Parliamentary Affairs*, 43 (1990).

10 For wider arguments about the relationship between neoliberalism, the new right, and moral conservatism see Melinda Cooper, *Family Values: Between Neoliberalism and the New Social Conservatism* (New York: Zone Books, 2017); Jackson, 'Currents of Neo-Liberalism: British Political Ideologies and the New Right'.

11 For an international comparison: Roberto Romani, 'Varieties of Neoliberalism: On the Populism of Laissez-Faire in America, 1960–1985', *Global Intellectual History*, 6 (2021).

12 For work situating Thatcher's rhetoric as a response to permissiveness: Matthew Grimley, 'Thatcherism, Morality and Religion', in *Making Thatcher's Britain*, ed. by Ben Jackson and Robert Saunders (Cambridge: Cambridge University Press, 2012), pp. 78–94; Amy Whipple, 'Speaking for Whom? The 1971 Festival of Light and the Search for the "Silent Majority"', *Contemporary British History*, 24 (2010).

13 On the ratchet: Kevin Hickson, 'Lord Coleraine: The Neglected Prophet of the New Right', *Journal of Political Ideologies*, 14 (2009), p. 181.

14 Ben Jackson, 'Intellectual Histories of Neoliberalism and Their Limits', in *The Neoliberal Age?*, Davies, Jackson, and Sutcliffe-Braithwaite, pp. 52–72, at p. 63. For a similar process in an international context: Jacob Hamburger

and Daniel Steinmetz-Jenkins, 'Why Did Neoconservatives Join Forces with Neoliberals? Irving Kristol from Critic to Ally of Free-Market Economics', *Global Intellectual History*, 6 (2021).

15 Shirley Robin Letwin, *The Anatomy of Thatcherism* (London: Fontana, 1992), pp. 32–34; Jake Anthony Scott, '"There Is No Alternative"? The Role of Depoliticisation in the Emergence of Populism', *Politics*, 42 (2022).

16 Stuart Hall and others, *Policing the Crisis: Mugging, the State, and Law and Order* (London: Macmillan, 1977), chs. 8–9; Stuart Hall, 'The Great Moving Right Show', *Marxism Today* (January 1979).

17 Robert Bacon and Walter Eltis, *Britain's Economic Problem: Too Few Producers* (London: Macmillan, 1976); Anthony King, 'Overload: Problems of Governing in the 1970s', *Political Studies*, 23 (1975); Samuel Brittan, *The Economic Consequences of Democracy* (London: Temple Smith, 1977).

18 James Freeman, 'Neoliberalism and Conservatism in Britain', in *The Neoliberal Age?*, Davies, Jackson, and Sutcliffe-Braithwaite, pp. 254–75.

19 Ben Jackson, 'Free Markets and Feminism: The Neo-Liberal Defence of the Male Breadwinner Model in Britain, c.1980–1997', *Women's History Review*, 28 (2019).

20 Friedrich A. von Hayek and others, *Hayek on Hayek: An Autobiographical Dialogue* (London: Routledge, 1994), p. 72.

21 Peter A. Hall, 'The Movement from Keynesianism to Monetarism: Institutional Analysis and British Economic Policy in the 1970s', in *Structuring Politics: Historical Institutionalism in Comparative Analysis*, ed. by Sven Steinmo, Kathleen Thelen, and Frank Longstreth (Cambridge: Cambridge University Press, 1992), pp. 90–113; Peter A. Hall, 'The Role of Interests, Institutions and Ideas in the Comparative Political Economy of the Industrialized Nations', in *Comparative Politics: Rationality, Culture and Structure*, ed. by M. I. Lichbach and A. S. Zuckerman (Cambridge: Cambridge University Press, 1997), pp. 174–207. See also Colin Hay, 'Ideas, Interests and Institutions in the Comparative Political Economy of Great Transformations', *Review of International Political Economy*, 11 (2004).

22 Erik Bleich, 'Integrating Ideas into Policy-Making Analysis: Frames and Race Policies in Britain and France', *Comparative Political Studies*, 35 (2002), p. 1063; Colin Hay, *Political Analysis* (Basingstoke: Palgrave, 2002), p. 69.

23 Sheri Berman, 'Ideas, Norms, and Culture in Political Analysis', *Comparative Politics*, 33 (2001), pp. 234–35; Richard Heffernan, *New Labour and Thatcherism: Political Change in Britain* (London: Palgrave Macmillan, 2001), p. 9.

24 Sheri Berman, *The Social Democratic Moment* (Cambridge, MA: Harvard University Press, 1998), p. 25.

25 For example: Richard Cockett, *Thinking the Unthinkable: Think-Tanks and the Economic Counter-Revolution, 1931–1983* (London: Fontana, 1995); Daniel Stedman Jones, *Masters of the Universe: Hayek, Friedman, and the Birth of Neoliberal Politics* (Princeton, NJ: Princeton University Press, 2014), pp. 161–72.

26 Christopher Muller, 'The Institute of Economic Affairs: Undermining the Post-War Consensus', *Contemporary British History*, 10 (1996); David Harvey,

A Brief History of Neoliberalism (Oxford: Oxford University Press, 2005), p. 22; Nicholas Bosanquet, *After the New Right* (London: Heinemann, 1983), pp. 75–83.

27 'In effect, the IEA was the London branch of the MPS,' writes Williamson, in *Conservative Economic Policymaking and the Birth of Thatcherism*, p. 49.

28 Ben Jackson, 'The Think-Tank Archipelago: Thatcherism and Neo-Liberalism', in *Making Thatcher's Britain*, Jackson and Saunders, pp. 43–61, at pp. 44–45.

29 Keith Tribe, 'Liberalism and Neoliberalism in Britain, 1930–1980', in *The Road from Mont Pèlerin: The Making of a Neoliberal Thought Collective*, ed. by Philip Mirowski and Dieter Plehwe (Cambridge, MA: Harvard University Press, 2015), pp. 68–97, at p. 89.

30 Quoted in Peter Catterall, 'Twenty-Five Years of Promoting Free Markets: A History of Economic Affairs', *Economic Affairs*, 25 (2005), p. 48.

31 Simon James, 'The Idea Brokers: The Impact of Think Tanks on British Government', *Public Administration*, 71 (1993), p. 495.

32 Jackson, 'The Think-Tank Archipelago'; Cockett, *Thinking the Unthinkable*; Radhika Desai, 'Second-Hand Dealers in Ideas: Think-Tanks and Thatcherite Hegemony', *New Left Review*, 203 (1994); Brian Harrison, 'Mrs Thatcher and the Intellectuals', *Twentieth Century British History*, 5 (1994).

33 Andrew Denham and Mark Garnett, 'Influence without Responsibility: Think-Tanks in Britain', *Parliamentary Affairs*, 52 (1999), p. 48. On the significance of this conversion in the history of UK welfare policy, see Robert M. Page, *Clear Blue Water? The Conservative Party and the Welfare State since 1940* (Bristol: Policy Press, 2015), pp. 78–81.

34 Michael Harris, 'The Centre for Policy Studies: The Paradoxes of Power', *Contemporary British History*, 10 (1996).

35 James, 'The Idea Brokers', p. 495.

36 Madsen Pirie, *Think Tank: The Story of the Adam Smith Institute* (London: Biteback, 2012).

37 James, 'The Idea Brokers', p. 496.

38 Williamson, *Conservative Economic Policy Making and the Birth of Thatcherism*, pp. 44–49.

39 Stedman Jones, *Masters of the Universe*, pp. 173–79.

40 Stephanie Lee Mudge, 'What Is Neo-Liberalism?', *Socio-Economic Review*, 6 (2008).

41 Jackson, 'Currents of Neo-Liberalism: British Political Ideologies and the New Right', p. 842. Jackson sees such individuals as blind to concentrations of power in the private sector, though, as we shall see in later chapters, this was not in fact the case.

42 On Brittan, see Roger Middleton, 'Brittan on Britain: Decline, Declinism and the "Traumas of the 1970s"', in *Reassessing 1970s Britain*, ed. by Lawrence Black, Hugh Pemberton, and Pat Thane (Manchester: Manchester University Press, 2013), pp. 69–95; Roger Middleton, 'Brittan on Britain: "The Economic Contradictions of Democracy" Redux', *The Historical Journal*, 54 (2011). On Jay's more specific role in influencing Jim Callaghan, including his contribution to Callaghan's landmark speech to the Labour party conference in 1976,

see Kenneth O. Morgan, *Callaghan: A Life* (Oxford: Oxford University Press, 1998), pp. 507–8, 35–37. The importance of each in the neoliberal revolution in Britain, particularly their impact on key Conservative politicians, is emphasised by Jackson, 'Currents of Neo-Liberalism', pp. 843–49; and Stedman Jones, *Masters of the Universe*, p. 177.

43 Rodney Lowe and Hugh Pemberton, *The Official History of the British Civil Service: Reforming the Service*, vol. 2: *The Thatcher and Major Revolutions, 1982–97* (London: Routledge, 2020), pp. 168, 75–76.

44 Andrew Blick, *People Who Live in the Dark: The History of the Special Adviser in British Politics* (London: Politico's, 2004), pp. 185–222. The quotation is at p. 186.

45 Their contribution was not always positive; Alan Walters, for example, was to play a key role in Thatcher's downfall through his alienation of Nigel Lawson. See Andrew Blick and George Jones, *At Power's Elbow: Aides to the Prime Minister from Robert Walpole to David Cameron* (London: Biteback, 2013), p. 242.

46 The quotation is from Anthony Seldon, *John Major: A Political Life* (London: Weidenfeld & Nicholson, 1997), p. 141. The fundamental importance of the Policy Unit to the British neoliberal project in government is covered by Aled Davies, James Freeman, and Hugh Pemberton, 'Thatcher's Policy Unit and the "Neoliberal Vision"', *Journal of British Studies*, 62 (2023).

47 Freeman, 'Neoliberalism and Conservatism in Britain', pp. 261–66.

48 We need to pay attention to the role of American neoconservatives, who positioned neoliberal social policy as *part* of a twofold plan to save capitalism – one element being a reduction in democracy to address state 'overload', the other involving a critique of the state in moral terms and a championing of individual liberty: ibid., pp. 266–71. Also see Darren J. O'Byrne, 'The Rise of Populism, the Demise of the Neoliberal and Neoconservative Globalist Projects, and the War on Human Rights', *International Critical Thought*, 9 (2019).

49 Lawrence Black and Hugh Pemberton, 'Introduction. The Benighted Decade? Reassessing the 1970s', in *Reassessing 1970s Britain*, Black, Pemberton, and Thane, pp. 1–24; Richard Coopey and Nicholas Woodward, ed., *Britain in the 1970s: The Troubled Economy* (New York: St Martin's Press, 1996).

50 Patrick Minford, 'Inflation, Unemployment and the Pound', in *Margaret Thatcher's Revolution*, ed. by Subroto Roy (London: Continuum, 2005), pp. 50–66, at p. 50.

51 Kenneth O. Morgan, ed., *The Oxford History of Britain* (Oxford: Oxford University Press, 2001), p. 647. The political use of these worries can be seen in a Conservative party political broadcast for the 1979 general election: '[T]he fact is the world did have a bit of a cold. But it seems to be getting over the worst of it. In Britain that cold seems to have turned into double pneumonia' (*Party Political Broadcasts: The Greatest Hits*, VHS (London: Politico's, 1999).

52 In the 1950s and 1960s a rise in the unemployment rate above 1.4 per cent was judged to be sufficiently worrying to merit a loosening of fiscal policy.

53 Conservative Party Archive (hereafter CPA): CRD 4/7/61, speech by Sir Geoffrey Howe to the Insurance and Actuarial Society of Glasgow, 9 January

1975. In pensions, as Kenneth Clarke noted, a failure to get inflation down and restore returns on investment would, apart from anything else, mean that occupational schemes would be in 'real trouble' (CPA: CRD 4/7/61, Pensions Study Group, letter from Kenneth Clarke, 27 January 1975).

54 Quoted by Jim Tomlinson, 'Thatcher, Monetarism and the Politics of Inflation', in *Making Thatcher's Britain*, Jackson and Saunders, pp. 62–77, at p. 66.

55 On the enduring attachment to wage-push explanations, see Jackson, 'Currents of Neo-Liberalism', p. 839. On the linkage back to Enoch Powell, see E. H. H. Green, 'The Treasury Resignations of 1958: A Reconsideration', *Twentieth Century British History*, 11 (2000).

56 Britton, *Macroeconomic Policy in Britain, 1974–1987*, pp. 13–43.

57 Ibid., p. 94. See also Noel Thompson, 'Economic Ideas and the Development of Opinion', in *Britain in the 1970s: The Troubled Economy*, Coopey and Woodward, pp. 55–80, at p. 58.

58 Warren P. Fishbein, *Wage Restraint by Consensus* (London: Routledge & Kegan Paul, 1984); Peter Dorey, *Wage Politics in Britain: The Rise and Fall of Incomes Policies since 1945* (Brighton: Sussex Academic Press, 2002), pp. 105–72; Robert Taylor, *The TUC: From the General Strike to the New Unionism* (London: Palgrave, 2000), pp. 201–33.

59 Douglas Wass, *Decline to Fall: The Making of British Macro-Economic Policy and the 1976 IMF Crisis* (Oxford: Oxford University Press, 2008).

60 The decline in corporate profits, and the consequent decline in dividends paid to shareholders, was of course a significant concern to pension funds. As Thatcher noted, '[T]he great occupational pension and life insurance funds, together with the building societies', which she lauded as a form of 'people's capitalism' and 'a reserve army for freedom', were 'dependent on profits in the private sector where their funds are invested' (Margaret Thatcher Archive [hereafter MTA]: Margaret Thatcher, speech to the Zurich Economic Society 'The New Renaissance', 14 March 1977).

61 Edmund Dell, *A Hard Pounding: Politics and Economic Crisis in 1974–76* (Oxford: Oxford University Press, 1991), pp. 183–91; Leo Pliatzky, *Getting and Spending* (Oxford: Blackwell, 1982), pp. 122–75; Joel Barnett, *Inside the Treasury* (London: Andre Deutsch, 1982).

62 See, for example, section 2 of the Conservative party's 1979 general election manifesto and its emphasis on the centrality of PSBR reduction to the fight against inflation.

63 Martin Daunton, *Just Taxes: The Politics of Taxation in Britain, 1914–1979* (Cambridge: Cambridge University Press, 2002), pp. 336–37.

64 Geoffrey Howe and others, *The Right Approach to the Economy: Outline of an Economic Strategy for the Next Conservative Government* (London: Conservative Central Office, 1977). The defeat of inflation was number one of 'our five tasks' headlined in the Conservatives' 1979 general election manifesto. The creation of a property-owning democracy was also central to the equivalent (but unpublished) policy document 'The Right Approach to Social Policy': see CPA: CRD: 4/7/71. This began with a reference to the CPS' observation in *Why Britain Needs a Social Market Economy* that 'what the state owns,

nobody owns; and when nobody owns, nobody cares'. It set out its analysis that private property (and the family) were the principal defences against an over-mighty state, and its determination to focus more on wealth creation via private ownership and entrepreneurship than the redistribution of existing wealth.

65 Catherine Schenk, *The Decline of Sterling: Managing the Retreat of an International Currency, 1945–1992* (Cambridge: Cambridge University Press, 2010), pp. 316–56.

66 Kathleen Burk and Alec Cairncross, *'Goodbye Great Britain': The 1976 IMF Crisis* (New Haven, CT: Yale University Press, 1992); Kevin Hickson, *The IMF Crisis of 1976 and British Politics* (London: I.B. Tauris, 2005); Schenk, *The Decline of Sterling*, pp. 357–95; Richard Roberts, *When Britain Went Bust: The 1976 IMF Crisis* (London: OMFIF Press, 2016).

67 Craig Lindsay and Paul Doyle, 'Experimental Consistent Time Series of Historical Labour Force Survey Data', *Labour Market Trends*, 111 (2003); Craig Lindsay, 'A Century of Labour Market Change: An Overview of Labour Market Conditions in the Previous Century', *Labour Market Trends*, 111 (2003), p. 138.

68 Sally Hills, Ryland Thomas, and Nicholas Dimsdale, 'The Bank of England's Three Centuries Macroeconomic Dataset, Version 2.3', ed. by Bank of England (London, 2016), sheet A27.

69 Eric Hobsbawm, 'The Forward March of Labour Halted?', *Marxism Today*, September (1978).

70 For time series data, see National Statistics, *Pension Trends* (London: TSO, 2005), pp. 7–21. On the contemporary awareness of a three-decade breathing space, see *Pensions World*, 'Pension Costs in the Long Term', by E. Johnston (Government Actuary's Department), September 1982; and the Treasury analysis of the Government Actuary's 1982 Quinquennial Review of the National Insurance Fund for a Chancellor worried about the 'pensions time-bomb', at HM Treasury, Private Office papers: PO-CH-GH-0041 part A, G. W. Monger to Chancellor of the Exchequer, 'State Earnings-Related Pension Scheme', 1 July 1982.

71 Ben Pimlott, 'The Myth of Consensus', in *The Making of Britain*, ed. by Lesley M. Smith (Basingstoke: Macmillan, 1988), pp. 129–41; Ben Pimlott, Dennis Kavanagh, and P. Morris, 'Is the "Postwar Consensus" a Myth?', *Contemporary Record*, 2 (1989). On doubts about its utility as a framework for analysing the welfare state, see Noel Whiteside, 'Creating the Welfare State in Britain, 1945–1960', *Journal of Social Policy*, 25 (1996). For a good summary of the critical literature, see Duncan Fraser, 'The Postwar Consensus: A Debate Not Long Enough?', *Parliamentary Affairs*, 53 (2000).

72 See, for example, David Dutton, *British Politics since 1945: The Rise, Fall and Rebirth of Consensus* (Oxford: Blackwell, 1997); Kevin Hickson, 'The Postwar Consensus Revisited', *Political Quarterly*, 75 (2004); Hugh Pemberton, 'The United Kingdom', in *The State of Welfare: Comparative Studies of the Welfare State at the End of the Long Boom, 1965–1980*, ed. by Erik Eklund, Melanie Oppenheimer, and Joanne Scott (Oxford: Peter Lang, 2017), pp. 17–38.

Neoliberalism and the UK state in the 1970s   103

73 On the new Right's self-conscious break with 'consensus', see, for example, Keith Joseph's speech at the inauguration of the Centre for Policy Studies (co-written by another of its founders, Alfred Sherman), in which he accused postwar Conservative governments of failing 'to reverse the vast bulk of the accumulating detritus of Socialism', with the result that '[w]e are now more Socialist in many ways than any other developed country outside the Socialist bloc' (*Times,* 'Sir Keith Joseph says choice is to go down with socialism or prosper in a rational economy', 24 June 1974). Thatcher herself complained in her memoirs that postwar Conservative governments had 'failed to turn back the Socialist ratchet' and in a 1996 speech credited Keith Joseph with bringing both her and others to recognise that 'ratchet effect': see MTA: Margaret Thatcher, 'Keith Joseph Memorial Lecture ('Liberty and Limited Government') at SBC Warburg, London, 11 January 1996' [www.margaretthatcher.org/document/108353]. Joseph first publicly used the phrase in Keith Joseph, *Stranded on the Middle Ground? Reflections on Circumstances and Policies* (London: Centre for Policy Studies, 1976).

74 Paul Pierson, *Dismantling the Welfare State? Reagan, Thatcher and the Politics of Retrenchment* (Cambridge: Cambridge University Press, 1994).

75 Rodney Lowe, 'The Second World War, Consensus, and the Foundation of the Welfare State', *Twentieth Century British History*, 1 (1990); Paul Pierson, ed., *The New Politics of the Welfare State* (Oxford: Oxford University Press, 2001); Norman Johnson, *Reconstructing the Welfare State: A Decade of Change 1980–1990* (London: Harvester Wheatsheaf, 1990).

76 Rodney Lowe, *The Welfare State in Britain since 1945* (London: Palgrave Macmillan, 2005); Howard Glennerster, *British Social Policy, 1945 to the Present* (Oxford: Blackwell, 2007); Derek Fraser, *The Evolution of the British Welfare State* (Basingstoke: Macmillan, 2009).

77 Lowe, *The Welfare State in Britain since 1945*, p. 77.

78 William Beveridge, *Social Insurance and Allied Services*, Cmd 6404 (London: HMSO, 1942), para. 7, p. 6.

79 Paul Bridgen, 'Making a Mess of Modernisation: The State, Redundancy Pay and Economic Policy-Making in the Early 1960s', *Twentieth Century British History*, 11 (1999); Hugh Pemberton, *Policy Learning and British Governance in the 1960s* (London: Palgrave Macmillan, 2004).

80 Vic George and Paul Wilding, *Ideology and Social Welfare* (London: Routledge & Kegan Paul, 1984), pp. 44–68.

81 Hickson, 'The Postwar Consensus Revisited'.

82 Dutton, *British Politics since 1945*, pp. 57–58.

83 Hickson, 'The Postwar Consensus Revisited'.

84 Peter A. Gourevitch, *Politics in Hard Times* (Ithaca, NY: Cornell University Press, 1986); Niall Ferguson, and others, eds., *The Shock of the Global: The 1970s in Perspective* (Cambridge, MA: Harvard University Press, 2010); Britton, *Macroeconomic Policy in Britain, 1974–1987*, pp. 134–57.

85 Peter A. Hall, 'Policy Paradigms, Social Learning and the State: The Case of Economic Policy Making in Britain', *Comparative Politics*, 25 (1993).

86 The AES was first adopted as Labour party policy in 1973 and was central to Labour's increasingly interventionist official programme for the ensuing decade.

104 *The neoliberal vision*

Labour Party, *Labour's Programme 1973* (London: Labour Party, 1973); Mark Wickham-Jones, *Economic Strategy and the Labour Party: Politics and Policy-Making, 1970–83* (London: Macmillan, 1996).

87 Coopey and Woodward, *Britain in the 1970s*, p. 13.

88 Martin Holmes, *Political Pressure and Economic Policy: British Government 1970–1974* (London: Butterworths, 1982); Dennis Kavanagh, 'The Heath Government, 1970–74', in *Ruling Performance: British Governments from Attlee to Thatcher*, ed. by Peter Hennessy and Anthony Seldon (Oxford: Blackwell, 1987), pp. 216–40.

89 Richard Vinen, *Thatcher's Britain: The Politics and Social Upheaval of the 1980s* (London: Simon & Schuster, 2009), p. 41.

90 Andrew Gamble, *The Free Economy and the Strong State: The Politics of Thatcherism* (Basingstoke: Macmillan, 1994). On the centrality of the '1970s crisis' to the development of Thatcherism, see Colin Hay, 'Whatever Happened to Thatcherism?', *Political Studies Review*, 5 (2007), p. 190.

91 The monetarist critique also gained a certain amount of interest from some Treasury officials and, particularly, from officials in the Bank of England in the late 1970s, though in both cases it was received with more scepticism in that the setting of targets for money supply growth was from the start seen as but one element of a much broader anti-inflationary strategy in which rising inflation expectations inherited from earlier wage growth would be broken. See Lewis Allan, 'Thatcher's Economists: Ideas and Opposition in 1980s Britain' (D.Phil., Oxford University, 2008), pp. 87–88; Graham Hacche and Christopher Taylor, ed., *Inside the Bank of England: Memoirs of Christopher Dow, Chief Economist, 1973–84* (Basingstoke: Palgrave Macmillan, 2014).

92 Marion Fourcade-Gourinchas and Sarah L. Babb, 'The Rebirth of the Liberal Creed: Paths to Neoliberalism in Four Countries', *American Journal of Sociology*, 108 (2002).

93 For example, Hall, 'Policy Paradigms, Social Learning and the State'.

94 On Labour, see Dell, *A Hard Pounding: Politics and Economic Crisis in 1974–76*. Conservative divisions are well summed up by Britton, *Macroeconomic Policy in Britain, 1974–1987*, p. 44. For a critique of 1979 as the defining moment at which monetarism replaced Keynesianism, see Michael J. Oliver and Hugh Pemberton, 'Learning and Change in 20th Century British Economic Policy', *Governance*, 17 (2004).

95 Michael J. Oliver, *Whatever Happened to Monetarism?* (Aldershot: Ashgate, 1997), pp. 144–45.

96 Milton Friedman, *Counter-Revolution in Monetary Theory* (London: Institute of Economic Affairs, 1970), p. 24.

97 Williamson, *Conservative Economic Policy Making and the Birth of Thatcherism*, p. 119.

98 The speech was published by the CPS with a foreword by Thatcher: Keith Joseph, *Monetarism Is Not Enough* (Chichester: Centre for Policy Studies, 1976).

99 Oliver and Pemberton, 'Learning and Change in 20th Century British Economic Policy', pp. 430–31.

100 Bacon and Eltis, *Britain's Economic Problem*.

101 Anthony King, ed., *Why Is Britain Becoming Harder to Govern?* (London: BBC Books, 1976).

102 A useful contemporary discussion of the overload thesis, written by a member of the Conservative Research Department, is James Douglas, 'The Overloaded Crown', *British Journal of Political Science*, 6 (1976).

103 Samuel Brittan, 'The Economic Consequences of Democracy', *British Journal of Political Science*, 5 (1975); Brittan, *The Economic Consequences of Democracy*; Brittan, *The Role and Limits of Government: Essays in Political Economy* (London: Temple Smith, 1983). Brittan retrospectively explored his influence on the British New Right in the 1970s, while arguing trenchantly that he was 'never part of the Thatcher entourage': Samuel Brittan, 'A Time for Confession', in *Reassessing 1970s Britain*, Black, Pemberton, and Thane, pp. 61–68.

104 James M. Buchanan and Gordon Tullock, *The Calculus of Consent: Logical Foundations of Constitutional Democracy* (Ann Arbor, MI: University of Michigan Press, 1962); James M Buchanan, 'Politics without Romance: A Sketch of Positive Public Choice Theory and Its Normative Implications', in *The Theory of Public Choice,* ed. by James M. Buchanan and Robert D. Tollison (Ann Arbor, MI: University of Michigan Press, 1984), pp. 11–22, at p. 11. On the explicit links between Austrian economics and public choice theory, see Peter J. Boettke and Edward L. López, 'Austrian Economics and Public Choice', *The Review of Austrian Economics*, 15 (2002).

105 William A. Niskanen, *Bureaucracy: Servant or Master?* (London: Institute of Economic Affairs, 1973).

106 Patrick Dunleavy and Brendan O'Leary, *Theories of the State: The Politics of Liberal Democracy* (Basingstoke: Macmillan Education, 1987); Desmond King, *The New Right: Politics, Markets and Citizenship* (London: Macmillan, 1987).

107 Jim Bulpitt, 'The Discipline of the New Democracy: Mrs Thatcher's Domestic Statecraft', *Political Studies*, 34 (1986).

108 Ben Jackson and Robert Saunders, eds., *Making Thatcher's Britain* (Cambridge: Cambridge University Press, 2012), pp. 1–22, at p. 14.

109 Colin Hay, 'Narrating Crisis: The Discursive Construction of the Winter of Discontent', *Sociology*, 30 (1996); Colin Hay, 'The Winter of Discontent Thirty Years On', *Political Quarterly*, 80 (2009); Colin Hay, 'Chronicles of a Death Foretold: The Winter of Discontent and Construction of the Crisis of British Keynesianism', *Parliamentary Affairs*, 63 (2010). See also James Thomas, '"Bound in by History": The Winter of Discontent in British Politics, 1979–2004', *Media, Culture & Society*, 29 (2007).

110 See the similar diagnoses of the 'crisis of the state' revealed by the 'winter of discontent' that were provided retrospectively by the former Conservative Cabinet minister Kenneth Baker and Jim Callaghan's political adviser, David Lipsey, in Lawrence Black and Hugh Pemberton, 'The Winter of Discontent in British Politics', *Political Quarterly*, 80 (2009).

Part II

The first term

3

The institutional inheritance

In the previous chapter we explored the growing influence of neoliberalism on Conservative thinking as the 1970s unfolded. What, however, was the institutional inheritance for those who from 1979 sought to reform the United Kingdom's system of income replacement in old age? Similarly, what specific motivations, policy ideas, or known barriers to reform did the Thatcher governments inherit from their party's time thinking about savings, pensions, and capital ownership in opposition from 1974?

Past decisions and their consequences constrain many areas of government, but this is especially true of pensions. As Myles and Pierson note, anyone seeking to reform a pensions system must grapple with the system they have inherited, and so-called path dependence in the process of its development can make reform extremely difficult.[1] Decisions taken about pensions have among the longest time horizons in government. The consequences for individuals play out many decades later in uncertain demographic and economic contexts, and, given that understandings of fairness are implicit in many – if not all – of these decisions, current pension systems inevitably embody past moral norms. The result is that the object of reform is often not one system but a complex set of entitlements working in parallel, each of which may have implications for different cohorts that can become detached from an evolving society's priorities or sense of distributional fairness. If we are to understand fully reforms made to the British system in the 1980s, therefore, we must first understand the system that Conservative governments of that era inherited and the ways in which this inheritance created opportunities or obstacles for those who planned or resisted change.

The postwar history of pensions up to the election of the Conservatives in 1979 is, on one level, a tale of technical changes to entitlements and funding arrangements that could be told at one remove from party politics. Yet it is also the story of the rise, fall, and re-emergence of a political consensus on the best means to provide an income in retirement to British workers.[2] The end of the Second World War saw the construction of an initial political agreement on the need to implement a universal but minimalist pay-as-you-go (PAYG) state pension within the new system of National Insurance. That consensus then

110   *The first term*

dissolved into profound inter-party disagreement, however, as rapid economic growth and rising living standards for British workers during the 1950s made the inadequacy of the postwar settlement more obvious. By the tenth anniversary of the legislation setting up Britain's postwar 'welfare state' in 1946, its universal, flat-rate, minimalist 'National Insurance' pension looked increasingly like 'fair shares in poverty' and no longer met contributors' expectations. Rising discontent led to a battle between the two major political parties over very different solutions to the problem. This, in turn, produced successive institutional attempts (not always successful) to implement those alternative solutions under governments of different political complexions. Yet, as the political process consistently failed adequately to address workers' growing desire for earnings-related pensions, a vacuum emerged that was partially filled by larger employers, who increasingly offered their workers deferred pay in retirement as part of their contracts of employment. Eventually, in the mid-1970s a new consensus was constructed around the idea of a partnership between employers and the state when it came to providing earnings-related pensions for all workers. In the process, however, implemented policies each embodied a long-term commitment that would prove politically expensive to break (and financially expensive if losers were to be compensated). Consequently, change focused on new solutions, not on the repudiation of past promises and institutional configurations. The result was not just the evolution of the UK pension system towards better benefits but also the beginnings of rising complexity as the number of elements within the system rose.

This is, then, a different policy arc from the stereotype of a 'social democratic' consensus made in the 1940s falling apart in the 1970s; not only was its timeline different but it also shows how we can craft more complex accounts about the beliefs that motivated change alongside new narratives that foreground mounting complexity as a force in British politics.

The Beveridge consensus

There is no doubt that Labour's 1946 National Insurance Act, one of many reforms that flowed from the Beveridge Report, was an important and in some respects path-breaking change in British pensions. It introduced a new and nominally more generous flat-rate universal pension, paid to women retiring at the age of 60 and to men (and their wives) at 65. It was funded by, and entitlement was dependent upon, contributions from employees during their working life (but not the self-employed), a matching contribution from their employer, and a government top-up financed from general taxation. The new universal contributory pension, along with the many other postwar reforms of British welfare provision that flowed from the Beveridge Report, came into force on the 'appointed day' of 5 July 1948.

The institutional inheritance

It is often assumed that the Labour government's reforms represented a 'year zero' for Britain's new 'welfare state'. In fact, this was often not the case, with elements of the existing system frequently incorporated into the new.[3] That was certainly true in pensions. The inherited system embodied two elements: the contributory pension of 1925 (which provided a pension between state pension age [SPA] and 70 but did not cover all workers); and the system implemented by the Liberals in 1908 to provide non-contributory, means-tested (and very meagre) pensions for those over 70 who qualified.[4] The costs of the reforms that Beveridge wanted were substantial, and writing his report at a time when victory was far away and uncertain and while enormous amounts of treasure were being expended on fighting the war served to shape (and restrict) his recommendations.[5] First, he accepted that the pension paid would be below 'subsistence' for the first 20 years as contributions built up; means-tested top-up benefits for poorer pensioners therefore had to continue. Second, because of the cost of bringing in those not covered by the contributory 1925 scheme, Beveridge found himself unable to unite the 1908 and 1925 schemes under a single administrative umbrella. Those in receipt of the '1908' pension who had made no contributions to the '1925' contributory scheme would continue to receive it, Beveridge being forced to accept that the payment of a full pension as of right to these pensioners could not be afforded due to 'the vital need of conserving resources in the aftermath of war'. For these people, a residual non-contributory pension continued in the shape of access to means-tested state benefits.[6] We should also note that the 1948 pension was not implemented *de novo* in that the structure of the contributory and actuarially funded 1925 scheme was retained, as was its collection machinery.[7]

Nonetheless, the pension landscape was re-formed, with the 1908 and 1925 schemes eventually subsumed into a single universal contributory scheme that built on but ultimately replaced that introduced in 1925. Thus the 1946 legislative reform was not path-breaking in terms of the 1908 pension but, after a transition period, it was effectively path-eliminating in terms of the 1925 pension. That was a notable achievement: one of only two instances in the history of reforms to British pensions when a basic element of Britain's pension system was eliminated (the other being the 2013 unification of the flat-rate basic state pension and the earnings-related additional state pension into a new single flat-rate state pension).

That Beveridge achieved so much was due to two main factors. First, the Second World War paved the way for reform in that it contributed both to a perceived opportunity for solidaristic politics and, once victory had come, to a faith in the capabilities of the state to effect change.[8] Second, wartime inflation significantly eroded the real value of pre-war pensions, thus making it financially feasible to envisage their replacement by a nominally higher pension.[9] We should acknowledge, however, that the new pension was far from generous: when implemented by Labour several (inflationary) years after the Beveridge Report it was set at a slightly better rate than that proposed by Beveridge but, crucially, below the rate of means-tested National Assistance, with no commitment to move over time towards equivalence with that benefit, commonly seen as a poverty benchmark. Its flat-rate financing was also regressive.[10] Moreover, it was not actually universal, since entitlement to it was dependent on contributions.[11] As Pat Thane points out, although the new pension represented a significant achievement enjoyed by many people (not least married women, who, if they did not qualify by virtue of their own contributions, obtained an entitlement via their husband's contributions),

> [i]t was designed to relieve poverty rather than, like the pensions systems emerging in most other West European countries, to provide in old age an income related to income during working life, to stabilize income over the life cycle, preventing a catastrophic decline when paid work ceased.[12]

This was not exactly a 'socialist' vision of generous pensions for all.[13] In seeking merely to prevent destitution, the 'Beveridge pension' of 1948 was in fact entirely consistent with a liberal vision of social welfare (revealingly, the Liberal party was enthusiastic), with contributors expected to make private arrangements if they wanted something better. Nonetheless, it was the 'universal' nature of National Insurance that explained why Beveridge's plan had been warmly received by Labour intellectuals (with the significant exception of Beatrice Webb, precisely because of the acceptance of capitalism implicit in the plan) and endorsed strongly by many Labour constituency parties and trades unions. Its relatively limited ambition, commitment to building up a fund out of which pensions would be paid (a commitment significantly diluted by Labour once in office), and the fact that it was at once transformative and 'a masterly piece of consolidation' (as the Conservative MP Leo Amery put it) explained why many Conservatives could also support the Beveridge Report.[14] The new pension's lack of generosity was the reason why the consensus built around it in the mid-1940s was to prove so fleeting, however.

From consensus to political disagreement

Three features of the 1948 pension settlement proved particularly significant after the war: its inadequacy; its individualised character; and the establishment of the 'convenient fiction' that an individual's National Insurance contributions built up a fund out of which benefits (including their future pension) would be paid.[15] Certainly, it had been Beveridge's intention that contributions would fund future pensions – hence his proposed 20-year transition to full pension rights.[16] For Labour ministers, however, such a delay to allow contributions to build up was politically impracticable given the sacrifices

The institutional inheritance 113

made by those of working age during the 1930s Great Depression and the Second World War.[17] Labour's decision to pay full pensions immediately to those insured since 1925, with those who had joined after 1925 receiving a full pension after only ten years of contributions, made political sense (maximising short- to medium-term political benefits while pushing substantial costs beyond the electoral horizon) but it resulted in a definitively PAYG system with current pensions paid out of current contributions.[18] This was not made apparent to contributors, however, who often assumed the existence of a personal financial contract with the state in which an individual's contributions purchased rights to a fully funded future pension.[19]

This creation of an individualised pension 'contract' in 1948, myth though it was, proved to be a major constraint in an increasingly affluent postwar Britain. It was not just that such an implicit contract existed; its form was also a problem. A system of flat-rate contributions purchasing a flat-rate benefit, even though it reflected the spirit of wartime solidarity, tied the level of that contribution to what the lowest-paid worker could afford.[20] This 'Beveridge straitjacket' made it hard to improve the pension paid.[21] That suited a Treasury that was profoundly concerned by the move to PAYG, which foreshadowed substantial future public expenditure, but it was to prove both a major force for change and a major constraint on reform as the era of austerity receded and workers began to desire pensions that better reflected their rising earnings in the era of 'affluent Britain'.

The 'Beveridge straitjacket' was not just a problem for those seeking to raise the level of pensioner living standards; it also left the new system poorly placed to deal with postwar inflation, which served to erode further the already inadequate 1948 pension in real terms.[22] Several attempts to restore its value after 1951 failed consistently to raise it above the level of National Assistance – increasingly seen as a poverty benchmark. That was because rises were granted *ex post*, each being grudgingly conceded by a Treasury obsessed by the prospect of the 'growing army' of entitled pensioners (to be swollen by the 400,000 employees who would be retiring in 1958 on a full pension having paid only ten years' contributions), and concerned that any increase had to be financed out of current contributions that it wanted to use to bolster the finances of the National Insurance Fund.[23]

Demand for earnings-related pensions in the 1950s

This determined effort by the Treasury to avoid improvements to the level of the state pension occurred against a background of a booming economy in what later came to be called the 'golden age' of British capitalism.[24] Real wages were rising and, increasingly, workers wanted this to be reflected in

114   *The first term*

their pensions – not surprisingly, since, in the context of a minimalist flat-rate state pension, the better paid a worker was the greater would be the decline in their income on retirement. A substantial gap emerged between expectations and reality, and, in the tight labour markets of the 1950s, the result was that the demand by workers for pensions that better reflected their rising earnings was increasingly met by employers offering occupational pension schemes as an addition to the state pension.[25]

Hitherto, occupational pension schemes had been the preserve of a minority and provided by unregulated schemes. By 1956, however, the proportion of workers in such schemes had reached 33 per cent, most of this growth having occurred since the end of the war, and the figure was rising by 2.3 percentage points a year.[26] By 1966 the Institute of Actuaries estimated that the value of such funds had reached £7.35 billion – a startling figure given the immaturity of the schemes, and representing more than 12 per cent of households' financial wealth.[27] By 1967 there were around 65,000 occupational schemes, their total membership had reached around 12 million (about 53 per cent of the working population), and the net growth in the funds' value was running at £810 million a year.[28] Unbeknownst to analysts and commentators at the time, active scheme membership was now at its peak. Funds under management continued to grow rapidly, however, because of the relative youth of scheme members (which meant contributions vastly outweighed the value of pensions in payment) and returns on investment. By 1979 occupational pension scheme assets were worth £50 billion, about 3.7 times the 1967 figure when adjusted for inflation.[29] By 1981 occupational pension funds alone owned more than a quarter of the UK stock market with insurers, which also sold private pensions, holding another 20 per cent.[30]

Occupational pensions had thus moved from a 'niche' position in the late 1940s to a central role in Britain's system of pension provision. These funded schemes represented a major contractual commitment since, although each was owned by the sponsoring employer, they were provided by firms to their workers under contracts of employment.[31] Thus, because the 1948 settlement had resulted in a minimalist state pension locked in by the fiction of individualised National Insurance 'contracts', the conditions had been created for the development of a parallel and extensive system of private occupational pension provision itself embodying long-term individualised financial contracts. Consequently, even by the late 1950s, despite the final elimination of the 1925 scheme in 1958, Britain had developed two systems of mass pension provision to provide workers with an adequate pension, with each locked in by individualised contractual obligations.

Yet, even at the peak of occupational pension coverage in 1967, about half the workforce remained dependent on a flat-rate state pension that was not keeping pace with rising earnings. The desire to bring these excluded workers within the orbit of earnings-related pensions created significant political pressures for reform.[32] Consequently, in 1957 the opposition Labour party proposed a plan to extend the benefit of earnings-related pensions to all workers via an all-embracing state system of 'national superannuation'.[33] Championed by the MP Richard Crossman and designed by the London School of Economics and Political Science (LSE) academics Richard Titmuss, Peter Townsend, and Brian Abel-Smith, this envisaged a contributory scheme 'as advanced as any under discussion in the social democratic parties of Europe'. It would see the state build up an enormous superannuation fund with extensive investments in British industry and commerce out of which pensions would be paid (equivalent to 'half-pay on retirement' and 'dynamised' to allow pensioners to share in future economic growth).[34] This could be expected to put the existing occupational pensions sector out of business, because it could not hope to compete with the 'dynamisation' promise.[35] The plan had obvious electoral potential for Labour, and it encouraged the Conservative government to bring forward its own proposals in 1958.

In theory, further growth of occupational pensions could have satisfied the desire for universal earnings-related pensions. This was certainly the favoured solution of the then Conservative Minister for Pensions, John Boyd-Carpenter, and it fitted the ideological predilection for private sector solutions among many Conservatives and officials.[36] Yet, rather to the surprise of ministers, the private sector proved unenthusiastic. As the life assurance industry told the government, it had no desire to extend occupational pensions to all workers because it would be unprofitable to deal with the very large number of small firms in the British economy. This forced the government to examine an extension of the existing state pension. The questions were: how extensive should such a change be and how feasible was reform of the existing 1948 pension? Within government, there was high-level support for recasting the 1948 pension on an earnings-related basis from Iain Macleod and Harold Macmillan, then respectively Minister of Labour and Prime Minister. They faced several problems. First, as we have noted, the 1948 settlement had created the erroneous impression among workers that their National Insurance contributions purchased freedom from want in old age. This made replacing the inadequate flat-rate pension with an earnings-related pension that would pay benefits at least as good and in most cases better all but impossible – since to do so would require the government either to admit to nearly 23 million contributors that past contributions had not funded a decent pension for their old age (which would have been politically disastrous) or to crystallise the value of the accrued 'liability' implied by such a contract and compensate contributors by relating past contributions to future earnings-related benefits (a ruinously costly option with big implications for public finances). Consequently, the many options explored by Boyd-Carpenter all either explicitly or implicitly assumed the continuation of the flat-rate 1948 pension, with earnings-related pensions installed on top of it; and, likewise, Labour accepted a continuation of the flat-rate scheme. Related to this was the fact that the Treasury was more interested in bailing the 1948 state pension out of its unfunded financial crisis than in embarking on a potentially very costly long-term improvement to state pensions.

Policymakers inside and outside government also found their options constrained by powerful opposition from occupational pension funds (which were not afraid to use their now considerable financial resources to campaign in their own interests), insurers, institutes of actuaries, and trades unions eager to defend their members' occupational pension benefits.[37] Consequently, the Conservative government was forced to accept the proposal that occupational schemes be allowed to 'contract out' of any state earnings-related scheme in return for regulation by government to ensure their adequacy.[38] Likewise, occupational schemes would be allowed to 'contract out' of Labour's proposed system of National Superannuation. The continuation of occupational pensions therefore came to be accepted by both major parties even as they sought to build their state-run alternatives – even though contracting out tended to weaken the finances of any proposed new state scheme, because occupational scheme members tended on average to be better paid.[39]

Both the major parties had thus concluded that a state-run solution to bring earnings relation to those workers outside the occupational pension system *had* to be implemented as a new element in the system. In addition, the Conservative government's reform served to create a financial incentive for the expansion of occupational pensions, in that employers were required to contribute to the state graduated pension scheme if they did not start their own occupational scheme.[40] It is therefore no surprise, as Hugh Heclo noted, to find that formerly hostile pensions interests (most notably the Life Offices' Association [LOA] and the National Association of Pension Funds [NAPF]) offered their approval for Boyd-Carpenter's rather limited 'graduated pension' (implemented in 1961, having been passed into law in 1958), albeit somewhat cautiously, and that occupational pension coverage continued its expansion in the ensuing half-decade, as shown in Figure 3.1.[41]

The construction of Britain's first state earnings-related pension was therefore 'path-dependent', as Pierson describes it, being highly constrained by positive feedback effects within the existing system.[42] Such effects, the product of what Pierson dubs 'increasing returns', were generated in the state system by the rising number of contributors to the (basic) state pension, by growing user familiarity, and by institutional inertia (with officials in the Ministry of Pensions notably committed to defending the 1948

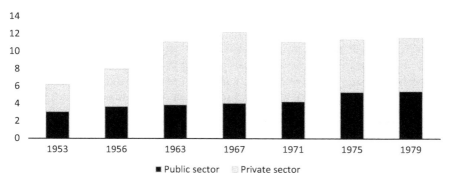

Figure 3.1 Active occupational scheme members by sector, 1953–79 (millions)
Source: Government Actuary, *Occupational Pension Schemes* survey, various years 1958–81.

settlement). In the occupational pension system, positive feedback arose from the rising number of workers covered, by the attachment of both employers and unions in terms of industrial relations (the latter were easily recruited by the pension industry as defenders of the status quo against Labour's National Superannuation plan), and by the growing financial heft of the occupational pension funds (which ran a well-funded marketing campaign against Labour while also running a sophisticated lobbying operation targeting employers and government alike).[43] The individualised nature of the 1948 pension 'contract' was plainly important too, however, in that it meant that the financial costs of folding that pension into an enhanced earnings-related system offering improved benefits were judged to be a non-starter. The result was a 'graduated state pension' that was limited in scope, with contributions used by the Treasury to bail out the National Insurance Fund over the short term, and installed on top of the existing state scheme. Rather than 'reform', therefore, a further element was added to the pensions system – one that embodied its own individualised implicit financial contract, and therefore created a path dependence of its own.

The Conservatives' new graduated pension was hardly generous, offering benefits that fell far short of those enjoyed by members of an occupational pension scheme. Leslie Hannah, not unfairly, notes that the pension industry saw it 'as political gimmick, not a pension scheme', although it supported it because it felt it was more attractive for it than Labour's alternative.[44] Its limitations meant that demand for decent earnings relation for all in pensions did not go away. The two major parties remained profoundly divided on the best means of meeting that demand, however. Thus, with Britain entering a period of alternating party government, the next decade and a half was to be characterised by competing solutions, policy paralysis, and a further expansion of occupational schemes.

118   *The first term*

Crossman Mark II

In 1964 Labour gained power after 13 years in opposition on a manifesto that noted that occupational pensions were not without problems, most notably the 'early leaver problem', whereby a worker's rights were lost on a change of employment. It promised to provide 'full transferability' of pension rights to those changing jobs. This had not been achieved by the time the party lost power in 1970, however. Its proposals for reform of the state pension system fared no better. Having noted that one in four state pensioners was in receipt of top-up National Assistance benefits, Labour promised in its 1964 manifesto to raise the level of the basic state pension, establish that as a guaranteed minimum income, index it to the rise in average earnings, and graft onto it a new and generous earnings-related scheme covering those workers outside an existing occupational pension scheme.[45] Little of this was delivered. The minimum income guarantee was 'abandoned as impractical and unaffordable' and the promised indexation to average earnings failed to materialise.[46] The level of the basic state pension did rise, but the determination of the Minister of Social Security, Peggy Herbison, to finance the increase without recourse to the graduated scheme (which she hoped to abolish) meant that, as Crossman noted in his diary, the Beveridge straitjacket continued to constrain room for manoeuvre and 'the net result [was] the worst of all worlds as we can't raise the flat-rate contribution any higher without imposing an intolerable burden on the lowest-paid worker'.[47]

Earnings-related 'national superannuation', which had languished with the appointment of Crossman as Minister of Housing and Local Government in 1964, returned to the fore in the wake of Labour's victory in the 1966 general election and Crossman's appointment in 1968 as Secretary of State for Health and Social Services. A year later, during which time he went considerably further than Boyd-Carpenter had done in consulting pension interest groups, Crossman published his proposals as a White Paper, *National Superannuation and Social Insurance*.[48] The new variant of his plan was, inevitably, claimed by Crossman to represent 'the most fundamental changes in social security' since the creation of the Beveridgean welfare state (a regular claim made by postwar ministers). It certainly would have marked a major expansion in the scope of state-earnings related pension provision when compared with Boyd-Carpenter's scheme of 1961. In some significant respects, however, it was much less revolutionary than claimed, in that it was recognisably derived from the earlier Crossman plan. Most obviously, it again embodied an element of redistribution between higher and lower earners, was relatively generous (providing 60 per cent of final earnings for workers up to the national average wage, though only 25 per cent above that level up to the limit of three times that average wage),

The Mark II Crossman plan also, like the 1959 revised version of his Mark I plan, envisaged occupational pension schemes being allowed to contract out of a state earnings-related pension. Crossman had learned the hard way that trades unions would not countenance any attack on the occupational pension benefits of their members. Moreover, the experience of his Mark I plan had taught Crossman that the pension funds and insurers were formidable lobbyists whose interests had necessarily to be considered. In short, Crossman had come definitively to recognise the path dependence produced by the development of an extensive system of occupational pensions. Accepting the need to allow private and occupational pension schemes to contract out of his proposed system of national superannuation made it more acceptable to the pension industry (though it continued to worry that the benefits proposed by Crossman would again be hard to match).[49] The industry had also shifted its ground since the late 1950s, however. As Hannah writes:

> The majority of the members of the renamed National Association of Pension Funds still stuck to the view ... that the state should confine itself to flat-rate pensions, leaving earnings-related provision to voluntary provision. However, broader political considerations led to support for Crossman's scheme from some former opponents of state provision. In the Legal & General, for example, the dominant firm in the insured pension market, the actuary Stewart Lyon was quietly arguing for a new approach. Much as the occupational pension movement had achieved in its breathing space, men such as Lyon could not but be aware of the strong political demand for more generous pensions and the superior achievements in other countries which had taken the state earnings-related route.[50]

The international comparisons were stark. Hannah notes that, at the time, the average German married man could expect to retire on a pension amounting to 60 per cent of his net final earnings. (Note that pensions were still invariably conceived by policymakers and experts mainly in terms of income for men in retirement, with women being considered overwhelmingly in terms of a widow's benefit derived from their relationship to the main household income earner.) Even in the United States, not normally thought of as a bastion of state provision, such a worker could expect a level of 56 per cent. In Britain, a worker dependent on state pension coverage could expect an income in retirement from the state of only 35 per cent of their final earnings.[51]

Crossman's preparedness to work with rather than against the occupational pension sector meant that his proposed scheme met relatively little opposition, the industry concentrating mainly on the terms under which schemes would be allowed to contract out. In some respects, however, the Crossman Mark II plan had some important differences when compared with Mark I. Most notably, it had been shorn of its Mark I desire to use the national superannuation fund to build up state equity stakes in British industry and commerce; it was now to be a PAYG scheme, albeit one that would initially be in surplus.[52] Other non-negligible changes included a better deal for women and replacing the existing flat-rate pension.[53]

This was, therefore, a proposal that envisaged a radical restructuring of the state pension system that would potentially be very costly (not just for the state but also for occupational schemes, which would be expected to offer a pension in complete substitution of the combined state pensions). To reduce the cost to the state, the government proposed that the changes be phased in over 20 years – though even then the National Insurance fund would be in surplus only for 15 years, and thus the system would remain 'pay-as-you-go'. The proposals, set out in a White Paper, were debated in the House of Commons in March 1969, and attacked by the Conservative opposition as undermining the insurance concept via redistribution within the earnings-related benefit formula. Much sound and fury signified little, however, for just over a year later the Conservatives, somewhat to their surprise, won the 1970 general election, and consequently Labour's pensions bill fell, having not yet completed its passage through Parliament.

The Conservatives' reserve scheme

With the election of the Conservatives in 1970, the way was cleared for them to implement an alternative solution. This did not emerge immediately, for, despite a thorough review of policies instigated by Heath after becoming party leader in 1965, the new government lacked detailed counterproposals to Crossman's legislation. Although it was clear that the new government intended to pursue a more selective approach to welfare benefits generally, its only significant manifesto promises on pensions were to extend the basic state pension to the small number of over-80s who were still not covered (because they had retired before 1948), review its level more regularly better to protect pensioners against inflation, and make sure that workers took their occupational pension rights with them when they changed job.[54] The latter problem was becoming an increasingly pressing concern. Employers had originally embraced occupational pension provision as a means of tying workers to their employment, and, consequently, rights were lost when a worker changed jobs or became unemployed. This loss of pension rights looked increasingly problematic as the labour market loosened in the

The institutional inheritance

less benign economic conditions of the 1970s, unemployment rose, and a shift away from the idea of a 'job for life' began to set in. That problem was addressed in 1973, when that year's Social Security Act required that, from 1975, schemes 'preserve' a member's pension rights if they switched employer (that Act also established the new Occupational Pensions Board [OPB], tasked with reviewing and certifying occupational schemes). This did not entirely solve the 'early leaver problem', however, since rising inflation rapidly eroded the real value of any preserved benefit. As we shall see, dealing with this issue was to be a major driver of policy change in the 1980s.

The 1970 Conservative manifesto had, however, made clear that party's continuing disdain for Labour's national superannuation plans. It saw these as imperilling the future of occupational schemes and, by extension, threatening a major source of private investment capital in the economy. It also worried that the substantial future public spending commitments generated would prevent the Conservatives' desired reduction of taxation.[55] Yet the only real hint of its alternative in that manifesto was a vague reference to the desirability of earnings-related pensions and an observation that this could and should be achieved through the expansion and improvement of occupational schemes, with a fallback state 'reserve scheme' for 'some people'. In 1971 this vague commitment on earnings relation was fleshed out by Keith Joseph, Secretary of State for Social Services, in a White Paper entitled *Strategy for Pensions.*[56] It proposed a very different approach from the one that had underpinned Labour's 1969 legislation, asserting that the government would put the state scheme 'on a sound financial basis' by moving it to a 'basically flat-rate' footing but funded by earnings-related contributions (the graduated pension would be discontinued but benefits accrued to date would be preserved, thus effectively putting it into 'cold storage' in order to avoid breaking the implicit financial contract it embodied). Earnings-related pensions would mainly be provided by funded occupational pension schemes, with a backstop reserve scheme 'of modest dimensions' run on the lines of an occupational scheme with a board of management independent of government (the Reserve Pension Board: RPB) with 'wide powers of investment'. Although the RPB would be allowed to invest in property and equities, it was to be prevented from building up a stake in any one company of more than 5 to 10 per cent (one should note here not just memories of the first version of the Crossman plan but Labour's policy proposals in 1973 promising 'radical new measures designed to provide workers, and the community as a whole, with a direct and increasing stake in the capital growth of companies', and its commitment in this so-called 'alternative economic strategy' substantially to extend government control of the economy).[57]

The Conservatives' proposed Reserve Pension Scheme would be financed by employer and employee contributions (as ever, the self-employed would not be covered). These contributions were to be set at a very low level, however (at 2.5 and 1.5 per cent of earnings respectively, up to a ceiling of one and a half times average earnings, with an Exchequer supplement of 18 per cent of the total contribution). Contributions would be collected via the PAYE system, at a cost to the Reserve Pension Scheme, and then channelled into it. Because contributions revenue from the scheme could be expected to exceed pensions paid for many years, the Reserve Pension Fund was forecast (on an assumed yield of 4 per cent per annum) to build up assets that would be worth about £5 billion by the end of the century – about a quarter of the value of all occupational pension funds when the scheme was proposed.[58] Ironically, therefore, this scheme (again inevitably claimed by the Secretary of State to be 'the most radical reform of pension arrangements since Beveridge')[59] would look somewhat like Crossman's Mark I proposal for funded national superannuation, but covering far fewer workers, with a much smaller fund and, crucially, one to be kept well away from state control.[60]

Benefits in the new Reserve Pension Scheme were to be earned according to a complex formula (based not just on the level of contributions paid but on the age at which they were paid and on gender), and it would take four decades to build up to full maturity. No benefits at all would be earned when sickness, unemployment, industrial injury, disability, or maternity meant that contributions were not paid. A man entering the new scheme at the age of 21 (the minimum age of entry) and paying contributions continuously could be expected eventually to earn a pension at the age of 65, all things being equal, equivalent to 41 per cent of earnings (paid in addition to the BSP) and a women of the same age would receive a pension at 60 equivalent to 26 per cent of her earnings (the lower figure justified by women's lower state pension age and longer average lifespan). The small print of the White Paper revealed that these figures assumed level earnings across a working life; if an individual's earnings rose with age, the pension paid as a proportion of final earnings would be lower. There would also be no inflation protection, although the fund would be allowed to pay bonuses if investment returns were sufficient to do so.

Thus, the Reserve Pension Scheme would offer benefits notably lower than those provided by the average occupational scheme. Moreover, as Tony Salter, Colin Redman, and Martin Hewitt point out, this was a solution for the long term; it would do relatively little to aid the half of the workforce without existing occupational pension benefits (the nearer they were to retirement, the less benefit they would derive from the new scheme). Nor would it do much to improve the treatment of women, not least because only 28 per cent of them were then in occupational schemes, compared to 62 per cent of men, and thus they would be much more reliant than men on

The institutional inheritance 123

the new scheme. This low level of occupational scheme coverage of women was becoming ever more obvious, partly because women were increasingly entering and staying in the labour force and partly because of the much greater political awareness of the disadvantages faced by women within the workplace that flowed from the campaigning of the Women's Liberation Movement from 1970.[61] Nonetheless, the government's approach was confirmed by the passing of the 1973 Social Security Act. As with Labour's aborted legislation in 1969, however, this legislation also fell victim to a general election, for it had not yet come into force by the time the government lost power in chaotic circumstances in February 1974.

By the time of this first general election of 1974, political agreement on the optimal means by which the benefits of a decent earnings-related pension in retirement might be extended to all workers looked no closer than it had been for nearly two decades. That the Conservatives had embarked on a different approach from Crossman had not been welcomed by the pension industry. Indeed, Hannah notes that the Life Offices' Association (LOA) and other pension interests were seriously concerned, for it thwarted their desire for a cross-party agreement, which they thought would bring certainty and stability. The political architects of change had ignored this professional scepticism. As Hannah observes, new Conservative architects proved to be equally sceptical:

> Thatcher and Joseph were contemptuous of the moderate, diplomatic liberalism of the actuaries and other professionals at the Life Offices' Association, finding more congenial the individual insurance brokers and company chairman who wanted to take a harder line in promoting the private sector of occupational pensions and blocking the expansion of the state scheme. Pension professionals, by contrast, were concerned that a state funded reserve scheme, with benefits not guaranteed but depending on investment performance and only maturing in forty years – the kind of scheme which met the ideological predilections of Conservative radicals – could not satisfy political urges for quicker and more secure earnings-related pensions.[62]

Between 1957 and 1974, therefore, the need to provide British workers with earnings-related pensions to supplement the minimum level of retirement income represented by the Beveridgean BSP had been accepted by the two main parties. So too had the need for bi-annual upratings of the state pension to adjust for inflation and earnings-related contributions to finance it. Within that basic agreement, however, and despite the evolution of their respective ideas over time, each party had taken a radically different approach when it came to how earnings-related pensions should be provided. In short, for nearly two decades consensus had been, and in early 1974 still appeared to be, most notable by its absence, and, except for Boyd-Carpenter's residual graduated pension of 1961, little of substance had been achieved other than the expansion of occupational pensions.

124 *The first term*

That latter change was never going to fill the vacuum completely, however, for, as insurance companies had made all too clear in the late 1950s, they had no interest in running occupational pensions for smaller firms that were unprofitable to service.

A consensus re-emerges

After nearly two decades of party political disagreement and relative policy paralysis, the political landscape then changed rapidly. Each party shifted its ground significantly as both they and what we would now call 'external stakeholders' crafted an agreement on the need cooperatively to build a second pillar of British pensions, which would be the joint responsibility of employers and the state operating in a public–private partnership. This was a remarkable change, the more so because it was forged against a very difficult economic backdrop, as the world economy stuttered in the face of severe headwinds including the breakdown of the Bretton Woods fixed exchange rate regime and the quadrupling of oil prices by OPEC in 1973 and with the economy, like other advanced industrial countries', entering recession (Britain's first since the 1930s).[63]

What were the roots of the new settlement that emerged in the mid- to late 1970s, and how was the new consensus forged around it? Several factors worked to bring the major political parties to an agreement on pensions. First, the willingness to reconfigure policy proposals and to compromise on long-held objectives flowed precisely from the lack of agreement that had characterised the preceding two decades, particularly the years 1968 to 1974. That both major parties had in relatively quick succession failed to implement their very different schemes at once discredited those earlier, contrasting, approaches and created public pressure for change. That the Labour White Paper of 1969 had emphasised the pressing need for change, and that the Conservative White Paper in 1971 had observed that '[t]he present state of uncertainly about the development of State and occupational pensions has lasted too long and must be brought to an end', served only to underline the parties' respective failures to deliver.[64]

Second, there was the fact that the incoming Labour government in March 1974 won only a minority of the votes cast in the 28 February election and only a plurality of seats. Lacking a majority in the House of Commons from then until the 10 October 1974 election, and then again once its small majority of three MPs in that election was rapidly eliminated, it was in a very weak position. This was unusual in modern British politics (the last time it had occurred had been in 1929 and it would not be seen again until 2010–15), and it meant that for much of its time in government

The institutional inheritance 125

Labour was on a knife's edge in House of Commons votes. That, in turn, created a strong incentive to compromise and secure the support of MPs across the House.

Third, Labour had 'won' the February 1974 election against a background of rapidly rising inflation (exacerbated by OPEC's quadrupling of oil prices in late 1973 and early 1974 but also, it was widely thought, the product of 'wage-push' pressures generated by strong and increasingly restive trades unions), economic stagnation, crippling industrial unrest, and with British firms operating for only three days a week as a result of government-ordered power supply restrictions to conserve oil and coal supplies. That Labour found itself in a position to form a new government was in large part a consequence of its claimed ability to work with the trades unions in addressing the economic and political crisis (rather than against them, as Heath had). Indeed, even as the election unfolded (and a Left-influenced radical manifesto was published by Labour – advocating a 'fundamental and irreversible shift in the balance of power and wealth in favour of working people and their families' and an 'alternative economic strategy' involving a significant extension of state intervention in the public sector), the Labour leadership was crafting with the Trades Union Congress (TUC) a set of less ambitious economic and social policies dubbed the 'social contract'.[65] This traded union restraint on wage demands and industrial action for the repeal of the Conservatives' 1971 Industrial Relations Act (the cause of much industrial unrest under Heath), the end of the previous government's statutory incomes policy, and a package of measures that would increase the 'social wage' by improving welfare benefits and services. Reflecting strong support within organised labour for the occupational pensions enjoyed by many unionised workers, these measures included a recognition of 'an integrated relationship between State and occupational pensions schemes', one that would radically improve the terms on offer in the Conservatives' state Reserve Pension Scheme by offering parity with the terms available through occupational schemes.[66]

Within weeks of Labour taking power the new Secretary of State for Health and Social Security, Barbara Castle, had raised both supplementary and National Insurance benefits by 14 per cent, in line with the rate of inflation since they had last been uprated the previous year. The basic state pension was increased by 29 per cent, however, taking it from £7.75 to £10 per week, equivalent to 24 per cent of then average earnings (Castle boasted that this was 'the greatest single uprating since the National Insurance Scheme was introduced 25 years ago', again demonstrating the powerful hold over the political imagination exercised by the reforms of 1948).[67] At the same time the government promised that the basic state pension would henceforth be reviewed annually and raised by the greater of the preceding year's rise in either prices or average earnings. This 'double lock' represented a very significant change. Over time, it had the potential not just to ensure that the state pension kept pace with rising average earnings but to raise its level in relation to that average (because years in which price inflation was used as the measure would lead to pension increases greater than those of average earnings).

Castle set out her strategy on pensions to the House of Commons on 10 April 1974 (on the same day as the proposal to raise benefits went through all its stages in a single sitting). She identified two aims: the abolition of poverty and a reduction in the amount of means testing within the benefit system (which had expanded significantly under the previous government as it sought to target benefits on the most needy).[68] Those were worthy aims (though, ironically, the decision to implement an equal rise in both National Insurance and supplementary benefits meant there would be no immediate diminution in means testing). It was the promise to index the level of the state pension to average earnings that represented the most significant long-term improvement for pensioners, however. For nearly two decades, since Crossman's espousal of 'dynamisation' within the state pension system, a battle had been fought to link state pensions to earnings and thus allow pensioners to benefit from the country's long-term economic growth. Castle's announcement met that need in respect of the basic state pension.

Castle's changes to the present and future level of the BSP, important as they were, still left open the question of what should happen in terms of a top-up to the BSP for those who were not in an occupational pension scheme. Most notably, what should be done about the Conservatives' Reserve Pension Scheme, which, though established in statute before Labour took office, had not yet begun operation? If allowed to go ahead, it would see about £300 million a year flowing into its fund and then onwards into market investments. In 1973 Castle had promised to repeal the Act that had established the reserve scheme and 'bring back the Crossman scheme'.[69] As the newly appointed Secretary of State for Social Services, however, Castle privately considered allowing the Reserve Pension Scheme to go ahead, albeit in improved form, but she was advised by both Brian O'Malley, her Minister of State for Social Security, and Edmund Dell, then Postmaster General, that its benefits would not flow soon enough to deliver political benefit either to pensioners or, by extension, to the government. She therefore decided only to let go forward the Conservatives' proposals for the earnings relation of state pension contributions and for those leaving occupational schemes to have their pensions 'preserved'. Beyond that, she hoped to make much more significant changes, but ones that would allow the continued development of good occupational pension schemes.[70] In formulating her proposals for those changes, Castle told the Commons in July

The institutional inheritance

that she had four ambitions: to ensure that the state pension was paid at a level that would not require supplementation; to give full equality to women (Castle having put this issue high on the agenda both through her '20 best years rule' and the concept of 'home responsibility protection', which would reduce qualifying years of service to compensate for periods of caring for children or parents); to provide adequately for widows who were dependent on their husband's pension; and to safeguard pensions against the ravages of inflation (then running at nearly 18 per cent a year, and on a rising trend that would see it reach nearly 27 per cent just over a year later).[71]

In September, shortly before Labour fought and won the second general election of 1974, Castle published her proposals.[72] Her *Better Pensions* White Paper promised to bring an end to 'the massive dependence on means-tested supplementary benefits'; to base earnings-related pensions on the best 20 years of income and then protect them against inflation; to build up to the full level of earnings-related benefit within 20 years (rather than 44, as was the case under the Joseph scheme); to embody within the scheme redistribution from the higher- to the lower-paid (who would receive a pension set at 100 per cent of earnings, as opposed to 44 per cent for a man earning £80 a week); and to end the treatment of women within the state system as 'second-class citizens', partly via the '20 best years' of earnings provision and partly by establishing their right to 100 per cent of their husband's pension entitlement. An appendix to the White Paper set out the Government Actuary estimate that the cost of the scheme by 2008/09, 20 years after its proposed introduction, would be between £5.5 and £5.8 billion, as compared with the projected £4 billion cost of the Reserve Pension Scheme. That would require contribution rates to rise by about two percentage points to 2008/09 to balance the higher expenditure. This looked affordable. Nevertheless, a harbinger of future public spending pressures lay in the Government Actuary's final observations about the expected strong upward momentum in benefits falling due in the ten years after the initial 20-year horizon used in the costing.

The reform proposals put forward by Castle and O'Malley were thus very different from Crossman's initial conception of national superannuation nearly two decades earlier. They assumed a productive cooperation between the state and the market rather than the effective destruction of the latter and thus accepted the reality of path dependence in the development of the system to date. A consultative document, *Partnership with Occupational Pension Schemes*, set out the desire for a cooperative relationship with good occupational pension schemes. Such schemes would be allowed to contract out of the proposed State Earnings-Related Pension Scheme, with their members paying a reduced National Insurance contribution in consequence, but in order to qualify they would have to provide pensions based on final

128   *The first term*

salary, or on average salary revalued in line with the change in average earnings, at a rate of at least 1.25 per cent of salary for every year of service, subject to the provision of a 'guaranteed minimum pension' (GMP) at least as good as the SERPS equivalent.[73] It was no accident that this was to be the required rate of accrual for schemes contracting out of SERPS. As the Institute and Faculty of Actuaries noted, it represented a 'very neat fit' with the most common 'one-eightieth of final salary per year of service' rate of accrual in occupational schemes (7.5 million workers were members of such schemes, and, generally, final salary schemes now represented 60 per cent of all occupational schemes).[74] In addition, a potential obstacle to gaining support from the occupational pension funds had also been removed with the government's promise to provide the required inflation proofing during the build-up of the new GMP, which they would be required to provide if they contracted out of SERPS.[75]

Many in the pension industry supported Castle's proposals. They were welcomed because, as one actuary observed, 'a firm and sensible basis for the future development of pension provision in this country on a partnership approach could at last be in the making'.[76] In September the *Financial Times* reported that the Conservatives' initial charge that occupational pension funds would be damaged by Labour's proposed scheme was at odds with the lack of opposition from the Life Offices' Association and Society of Pensions Consultants, and the positive welcome for the proposals that had come from the Companies' Pensions Association and from insurers such as Legal and General.[77] This is not to say there were no concerns at all. In November a meeting of the Institute and Faculty of Actuaries (IFoA) saw a significant minority of prominent speakers voicing their worries about the ability of pension funds to deliver the required inflation proofing of preserved benefits. Nonetheless, the *Financial Times* correspondent who attended that meeting (himself a professional actuary) reported that 'most actuaries supported the Government's proposals as a basis from which to build a firm and lasting structure for the future development of universal pension provision' and, crucially, that with some modification 'there was a real chance that … the proposals could be enacted without the threat of being overthrown at the next change of Government'.[78] In fact, a later IFoA analysis concluded that the well-run occupational scheme had 'little to fear and perhaps a lot to gain by being contracted out of SERPS'.[79]

In the House of Commons, Castle had already explicitly stated her hope that she would be able to 'forge an agreement on pensions policy which can stick' and which would 'end the chopping and changing and the uncertainties'.[80] In political terms, the omens looked good.[81] Indeed, although the Conservative shadow spokesman on social services, Geoffrey Howe, had indicated over the summer that the party would resuscitate the

The institutional inheritance 129

Reserve Pension Scheme if re-elected, the immediate Conservative response to the policies put forward in *Better Pensions* was surprisingly positive.[82] Thereafter, the opposition concentrated on amendments to make it easier for occupational schemes to coexist with the proposed State Earnings-Related Pension Scheme.[83] Consequently, by the time Castle tabled the legislation to create SERPS there were hopes that this might be 'third time lucky' for pension reform; by early 1975 the *Guardian* was reporting that the failures of the antithetical Crossman and Keith Joseph schemes seemed to have been transcended. There was now, it observed, 'a consensus among academics, commentators, and many pension industry leaders that Mrs Castle ha[d] adopted the better road'.[84] This did not mean that political opposition had disappeared at the rhetorical level; for example, Norman Fowler, the Conservative spokesman on pensions, noted in his response to Castle's introduction of the second reading of the Social Security Pensions Bill (just over a month after Thatcher became leader of the party), that the opposition remained concerned that SERPS would not be a funded scheme but would be 'pay as you go', thereby 'imposing a new and heavy burden on our children and grandchildren'.[85] Privately, however, a Conservative party policy group on pensions under the chairmanship of Kenneth Clarke had already revealed mounting concerns that the party's funded Reserve Pension Scheme was justifiably open to the damaging political criticism that it was second-rate.[86] The group also fretted about the Reserve Fund's potential growth, with fears that it might reach a size equal to the sum of all the other occupational schemes combined – seen by the group as a most unwelcome concentration of economic power in the hands of an institution potentially open to political manipulation.[87] That analysis implied the need for a robust occupational pensions system, but also for some rethinking on the state's role in earnings-related pension provision. One option considered by this group was to return to the idea of compelling employers to provide occupational pensions, but, as one member noted,

> employers [had] now been marched to the top of the hill twice in recent years only to be marched down again. The next Conservative government might well be marching them up for the fourth time. It must be expected that, on that occasion, employers will show much less readiness … and considerable consumer resistance, if not derision, is likely to be encountered.[88]

These sorts of concerns had led the opposition to consult the pension industry and employers. This revealed disquiet about the ability of occupational schemes to protect preserved pensions against inflation, but an acceptance that Labour's proposals represented a serious plan that, if implemented with some modification, could bring stability to the system while also allowing occupational schemes to thrive.[89] The party's policy group had therefore concluded that it would be better to work with the Labour proposals rather

130   *The first term*

than against them. Consequently, in his response to the Castle bill a month later Norman Fowler made it plain that the industry advice he had received was 'overwhelmingly … in favour of proceeding on the basis of the proposals contained in the Bill'.[90] Subsequently the opposition pushed merely for relatively minor adjustments to Labour's proposals (which were granted by the government): a greater reduction in National Insurance contribution for contracted-out occupational scheme members and a cap of 5 per cent on such schemes' annual revaluation of the GMP.[91] Fundamentally, therefore, Conservative opposition to the new scheme as it made its way through Parliament amounted to little more than a desire better to protect pension funds from the consequences of inflation-protecting preserved pensions. Indeed, the only fundamental point of difference over pensions that arose under this government was in 1976, over a separate government proposal to give trades unions statutory rights to 50 per cent representation on pension fund trustee boards.[92]

SERPS came into operation in April 1978, and Britain thus acquired a fully developed two-pillar system of pensions spanning the state–market divide, one with three basic elements: a flat-rate basic state pension, plus earnings-related top-up benefits provided either via SERPS or by an occupational pension of equivalent or greater generosity. The problem of 'two nations in retirement' that Crossman had originally highlighted in 1957 remained to an extent, but the incorporation of a high degree of redistribution within SERPS, and its more generous treatment of women (long the most disadvantaged among the old), held out the promise of substantial amelioration as SERPS matured. The greatest triumph, however, was the achieving of apparent concord over this settlement. Both major political parties, the pension industry, employers, and trades unions had all fallen in behind Labour's reform.[93] All looked forward to a lengthy period of stability and an end to the uncertainty that had dogged pensions, the most long-term of all areas of life, for so many years.

Outflanking consensus

Even as SERPS became law, however, some Conservatives came to see features of the new consensus as stifling the 'capital-owning democracy' they hoped to create. Indeed, by 1979 those advising Geoffrey Howe, then shadow Chancellor, were in search of policies that might allow a future Thatcher government to curtail the dominance of the occupational pension funds that underpinned the partnership between public and private savings. This surprising shift in perspective was the result of a feedback effect, as the growth

The institutional inheritance 131

of occupational funds outlined above started to interact with changes in Conservative party thinking about how best to spread capital ownership and address Britain's sluggish growth. In the late 1950s and 1960s a younger generation of Conservatives linked to the Bow Group associated wider capital ownership with investment literacy, savings schemes, unit trusts, or profit sharing via employee shares. By the early 1970s, though, Iain Macleod had developed a parallel strand within this theme that called for the elimination of distortions, namely the unequal treatment of 'earned' and 'unearned' income.[94] Although Heath's government backed away from Macleod's ideas, it took steps along the older policy path by introducing the legal scaffolding necessary for employee share ownership schemes, only for its own income controls to thwart their rollout. Back in opposition and under a new leader, David Howell convened a Wider Ownership Group that brought experts from the Wider Share Ownership Council together with party figures (notably Peter Cropper, from the Conservative Research Department [CRD], and later an adviser to Geoffrey Howe and Nigel Lawson) and individuals with links to the neoliberal thought collective (notably Nigel Vinson of the Centre for Policy Studies).[95] The group ensured that the opposition's interim policy statement *The Right Approach* (1976) included profit sharing, and it outlined a specific scheme in a 1977 Green Paper before falling into abeyance.

With that line of policy development, the party needed a more holistic view of capital ownership to make it an organising theme. After the Labour government had announced an almost identical profit-sharing scheme it also needed new proposals. When the Wider Ownership Group reconvened in December 1977 under a new chair – Peter Horden, an MP and Stock Exchange member – it refocused on two market distortions. The first was the favourable tax treatment given to some fixed-income assets (via capital gains tax relief on gilts), the products associated with them (pensions and life assurance), and mortgage interest payments. Shares in British industry offered a poor return in comparison given the impact of inflation on profits, caps on dividends, and a 15 per cent surcharge on investment income. Stamp duty and dealing costs were seen as further disincentivising active investment strategies that backed winners. Although the group thought the overall level of saving in the economy was appropriate, then, the volume channelled into fixed-income and housing assets was seen as too high and that into industrial capital as too low.[96] In a high-tax economy in which the top rate plus surcharge could reach 98 per cent (for a small number), Britons' savings were flowing towards safe assets with tax reliefs and away from 'risk capital and industrial investment'.[97]

A second layer of tax distortions was held responsible by the Wider Ownership Group for the excessive growth of intermediaries. As Tim

132   *The first term*

Boswell – a future MP who had headed the CRD's economic section until 1974 – reported of the group's meeting on 12 January 1978:

> At this meeting there developed a general feeling that personal savings were now channelled excessively through the hands of fiscal intermediaries like pension funds, who benefitted from a variety of tax concessions; while the individual wishing to operate his own portfolio or to invest directly in his own or another small business received little or no encouragement.[98]

As well as the reliefs for contributors, the group had in mind that pension funds' income and capital gains were free of tax and that life assurance companies paid a special rate. The problem was not only that these institutions dominated the inflows of private savings; their entrenched advantages and growth meant they were starting to dominate capital markets. The *Financial Times*, the group noted, projected that institutional funds would hold between 70 and 85 per cent by value of UK quoted companies by 2000 – a dominance tantamount to 'collectivisation in the investment market'.[99]

The size of these funds was seen as unsatisfactory for several reasons. First, it was felt that a lack of direct contact between investors and businesses prevented people experiencing capitalism. This had been a theme in the IEA's literature and for Conservatives such as Russell Lewis and Howell.[100] Second, institutions were thought to underinvest in British industry because they preferred fixed-return assets to meet liabilities and – given their size and risk appetite – were unlikely to be interested in investing in smaller businesses or new ventures. The dominance of institutional money, it was argued, thus inhibited dynamic investor-entrepreneurialism. We now know that Howe – who oversaw the group's work – was also aware of an American version of this critique, which argued that institutions managing large portfolios were less likely to be engaged shareholders and that schemes' fiduciary duties to their members made them more likely to sell than turn struggling businesses around.[101] Finally, both Horden's group and business leaders who Howe met in late 1977 were concerned that the funds' size had reached a point at which a case could be made for government control: 'The danger was that the Wilson Committee could build on this position by directing large agglomerations of institutional money into enterprises of doubtful profitability.'[102] Institutional funds were thus now seen as failing to support capitalism, linked to Britain's sluggish growth, and at risk of enabling state control of industry through the back door.

What was to be done? The simplest solution floated was to abolish all tax advantages in a return to 'fiscal equity'. Horden's group knew that the combined dismay of savers and a 'powerful lobby' of financial institutions made this politically untenable.[103] Instead, they discussed counterbalances that could limit the growth of occupational pension funds. A Conservative government could de-fund public sector schemes, introduce a flexible retirement age with access to lump sums, and explore the 'possibility of allowing individual employees to contract out and buy their own (approved) pension'.[104] Importantly, members noted that the latter could cause 'a mass exodus by young employees with damaging effects on the viability of funded schemes'.[105] Even this strategy was fraught with political risk, though. Like Crossman and Joseph before them, Boswell noted in a briefing paper: 'We would also have to face a powerful pension fund lobby and the cry that pensions were being tampered with would be very powerful. Moreover, this is one area where at last bipartisan policies have been established.'[106] More fundamentally, he argued, lower taxes and the abolition of privileges would not suffice to make wider share ownership a major plank of policy: '[A] political savings programme requires some positive discrimination in favour of new savings.'[107]

Boswell's strategy was therefore to 'confine ourselves to discreet and indirect measures'. A Conservative government would discourage the extension of funded pension schemes in the public sector, enlist 'inflation as our ally in encouraging private sector firms not to go for fully-funded schemes', and possibly tackle 'particularly blatant tax anomalies vis-à-vis the private citizen'.[108] The way to check the funds' dominance without political pain was to introduce new specific reliefs intended to balance the distortions created by existing concessions. Interestingly, he thought these could not only extend employee share schemes but eventually also cover new products: 'We could no doubt go on to devise e.g. "self-administered personal thrift/pension plans" and "venture capital plans".'[109] The group accordingly reported to Howe that its recommendation was to 'outflank the financial institutions, public sector and other vested interests' using new reliefs.[110]

Why, then, were pension innovations absent from the Conservatives' 1979 manifesto? In part it was an act of caution, but it was also because the group prioritised other measures as the means of redressing the dominance of institutional funds, namely individual investment allowances to encourage direct ownership of investments. In one scheme the first £1,000 of investment interest would be untaxed, and in another both a tax incentive and top-up would apply if investments were held for a certain period. Neither Howe nor Nigel Lawson – respectively the future Chancellor of the Exchequer and the Financial Secretary to the Treasury – were persuaded, and their reasons for scepticism foreshadowed the objections that the proposal for personal pensions would later run up against in the mid-1980s. Both allowances came with high administrative burdens and sacrificed tax revenue for uncertain benefits. Both were vulnerable to switching – selling existing assets to take advantage of the new tax shelter – and large volumes of small investments were thought unlikely to be economical for established providers to offer. Together, Howe and Lawson vetoed any mention of such schemes in the draft manifesto, and from the autumn of 1978 Horden's group was marginalised as Howe took control.

Howe's own position was complicated. He was hostile to further erosions of the tax base.[111] Yet he shared concerns about the 'facelessness' of institutions, explaining to one correspondent that 'I cannot dispel the fear that sooner or later a Socialist government will seek to take over the voting power lying (often dormant) in the hands of these giants'.[112] He was also troubled by a trend for larger organisations to buy out small capital holders. Recognising this would be difficult to reverse, however, he preferred initiatives that acknowledged the need for intermediaries but encouraged new solutions 'which could yet emerge from inventive entrepreneurial minds'.

Greater realism aside, Howe was nevertheless alive to the politics of wider ownership. As an election loomed, he had Cropper call a group of parliamentarians together in recognition that 'the Party need[ed] to move on' from Howell's profit-sharing proposals and instead 'produce something new and interesting for the next manifesto'.[113] The election came too soon for new policies, but the meeting notes and papers Howe commissioned from Cropper and Boswell reveal what Howe and those advising him intended just before they entered government.

This new group's first meeting, held on 1 December 1978, confirmed the basic political judgements made by Horden's Wider Ownership Group a year earlier.[114] The aim was not to increase savings but to spread ownership of equities. In pursuing this aim, though, 'it was agreed that it would be difficult to remove existing tax reliefs, e.g. on house purchase and institutional investment (via pension funds and insurance companies) in order to tip the balance more fairly in favour of direct personal investment in equities'. In summing up, Howe ruled that out, affirming that 'we cannot realistically be concerned with the curtailment of existing benefits or incentives'.[115] Instead, the scope for action lay in new counterbalancing encouragements, even if there was a limit to the revenue that could be 'sacrificed in pursuit of these objectives'. In devising these, Howe argued, Conservatives need not be hostile to new schemes that involved intermediaries, despite 'fear of Mr Benn' (i.e. socialist nationalisation as proposed by the principal tribune of the Labour Left, Tony Benn), but they 'much prefer direct private investment'. The trouble was that, although there was much agreement on principles, there was much less on means. Those sceptical about new incentives repeatedly returned to the abolition of pension funds' 'massive tax advantages' but baulked at the political cost.[116] The predictable result was a manifesto that made few specific pledges.

Yet one of the last papers commissioned for the group captured the beliefs and compromises those around the shadow Chancellor had arrived

The institutional inheritance 135

at by 1979. At its first meeting, the group asked Tim Boswell to 'bring the subject together' in a new 'Green Paper'. Boswell circulated his first draft of 'Encouraging Savings' in January 1979, which bullishly described the party's primary objective as linking 'personal savers with the demand for funds for industrial expansion'. This was desirable both to fuel investment and for the 'important moral and psychological benefit' of citizens having a stake in industry. A second objective was 'personal independence'. The party was not setting out 'to create (or recreate) a nation of rentiers', Boswell explained, but it did 'want as many people as possible to have a thousand pounds or two of "free" capital – in addition to house ownership and pension rights'. With this capital they could live comfortable, prudent lives: it might allow them to change jobs, become self-employed, retire in security, or go on holiday. But it might also allow them to experience risk: they could 'enjoy having a little income from an investment in Britain – or even an occasional experiment on the Stock Exchange'. Even at this stage, then, the future of savings was seen as an area of potential choice making. Indeed, the introduction of such choice was understood as a social project:

> [W]e see the need to encourage savings at least as much as a social, as an economic, imperative. The remaining 'rich' or well-off can already make use of advisers and decide for themselves whether to put a part of their portfolio into equities. Those less well favoured probably never look further than the Trustee Bank, the Building Society or the home service insurer. We would like to expand their range of choice.[117]

Boswell again identified the dominance of institutional money as an issue but considered abolishing tax distortions too disruptive, and – with a view to circulating the paper more widely – gave reassurances that Conservatives 'picked no quarrel' with the institutions. His party's 'sole reservation [was] that a number of savings media … have enjoyed such tax advantages that other means of saving, notably direct investment in equities, have been penalised'. Conservatives would offer people new choices to redress the balance.

These choices would not be the same for everyone, though. The employee, Boswell argued, could experience capital ownership through company profit-sharing schemes. The self-employed would no longer have to choose between decapitalising their business or retiring without an annuity. The 'middling investor' would be helped to retain direct ownership of shares by ensuring they did not normally pay a gains or investment income surcharge. Cuts to the top rate of income tax would free up capital for them to invest in companies directly and transaction and administrative costs would be lowered by waiving stamp duty on some transactions and investigating new ways for shares to be bought and sold. But doubts about the practicality of

136 *The first term*

escaping intermediaries meant that the 'small investor' (those with under £5,000 of free capital) was a more complicated case:

> We believe that he [*sic*] deserves encouragement in his own right, and we are also aware that one day the investment may grow bigger ... However we doubt whether, in all but exceptional cases (e.g. where the investor is perhaps unwisely prepared to stick to only two or three holdings) there is much future in encouraging direct investment. A financial intermediary (unit or investment trust) is almost certainly necessary. In many cases, the initial investment may be uneconomically small, even for the organised financial institution ...[118]

By the time they returned to office in 1979, then, senior Conservatives had concluded that institutional funds whose growth had been part of the solution to funding earnings-related pensions were now at the centre of a new problem. At the very same time, though, they recognised that the power of occupational funds and the new consensus created around them meant that only a flanking operation was possible and that, for all the moral benefits of direct ownership, intermediation was the only prudent reality for many.

Conclusion

The story that unfolds over the next four chapters is partly one of how the Conservative party in government – propelled by increasingly proactive proponents of neoliberalism – gradually forgot and then (painfully) rediscovered these constraints on its ability to reshape Britain's pensions system and rebalance ownership of capital away from institutions. Before turning our attention to that process, though, we should step back and draw out the common threads that explain the complex institutional configuration and political inheritances bequeathed to would-be reformers. The first is that the bipartisan assumption of the 1940s that implementing the Beveridgean National Insurance pension had solved the problem of British pensions proved short-lived. Within a decade profound disillusion with that settlement emerged and drew forth competing solutions for nearly two decades until the reconstruction of a cross-party consensus in the mid-1970s. The second is that, although many of those competing solutions never made it beyond the drawing board, the significant changes that were implemented did not re-form the existing system; they added to it. The result was that by the end of the 1970s Britain had not one but four means by which its workers could be paid a pension: the basic state pension, SERPS, the Graduated State Pension (albeit this latter was effectively in 'cold storage', with its benefit entitlements preserved for future payment), and occupational pensions.

To an extent, this accretion of system elements had been the product of vacuum filling as the inadequacy of the postwar settlement became clear. The growing gap between the 'fair shares in poverty' Beveridgean pension

The institutional inheritance 137

and the desire of British workers to see the fruits of postwar affluence reflected in their post-retirement income created a space for private initiative. It was filled by employers eager to hold onto workers in the tight labour markets of Britain's postwar full-employment economic 'golden age'. Consequently, occupational pensions moved rapidly from a niche position – provided by insurance companies for the better-off self-employed and, via so-called 'top-hat' schemes, for high-earners – to encompass virtually half the workforce by the mid-1960s via company-provided 'occupational' pension schemes. Once installed, however, it became hard either to abolish or reduce the benefits of occupational pensions, in large part because they were essentially deferred pay and were bargained for by trades unions as such. Although formal ownership of the pension fund lay with the employer, an occupational pension was to all intents and purposes a form of property acquired by a worker as part of a financial contract with their firm. As the number of workers in such schemes grew, so a strong positive feedback effect can be seen in that any abolition or degradation of such pensions would affect an increasing number of workers and pensioners within them. Moreover, the rapid rise in the value of funds under management, and their growing importance as investors in stocks, property, and government securities, had created its own feedback effect, with the occupational pension schemes and the insurers who managed many of them controlling a growing fraction of British capitalism and, consequently, having an increasing amount of money and power to defend their interests. As Crossman found in the late 1950s, and had to accept thereafter, in combination these effects created a very strong attachment to occupational pension schemes among members (many of them workers whose unions held power within the Labour party as well as within the labour market) and a strong corporate lobby with the willingness and money actively to pursue its interests. In the longer run, though, pension funds' expansion created a tension between them and their erstwhile political allies in the Conservative party as its wider ownership interest turned towards rebalancing the tax system to remove distortions favouring institutional investment. In short, once occupational pensions had become a mass phenomenon supported by powerful corporate and financial interests, the political (let alone the financial) cost to any government of abolishing or otherwise interfering with them in a way that reduced the benefits to their members would be high. At the same time, the arguments for counterbalancing their power crossed the political divide even as those seeking reform found themselves forced to take the interests of occupational pension funds into account.

Another positive feedback was important in the gradual accretion of elements within the British pension system: the implicit National Insurance 'contract'. Lowe may have been right to identify the concept of funded National Insurance as a political fiction but, for all that, it was a powerful fiction.[119] From the start National Insurance was presented as an individualised insurance arrangement, even though Labour's implementation of the new 'welfare state' in practice destroyed the 'insurance' link between an individual's contributions and benefit entitlement, not least in respect of the new state pension, by, essentially, moving it to a pay-as-you-go rather than a funded basis. The crucial point, however, is that this was not made clear to contributors. Subsequently, the assumption of an individualised National Insurance 'contract' created a barrier to policymakers seeking to reform the basic state pension. As noted above, the presence of that contract was why, when the Macmillan government sought to reform the state pension system to provide (a modicum of) earnings-related benefits, it found itself having to implement its new 'graduated pension' as an addition to the BSP, not as a replacement for it – the poorest workers being simply incapable of paying higher contributions. Likewise, the Castle reforms of the late 1970s had to assume the BSP's continuation. Although National Insurance contributions were moved to an earnings-related basis, SERPS provided an earnings-related pension in addition to the flat-rate basic pension. Why? Because, although earnings-related contributions would raise significant revenue, moving the very large number of existing pensioners to a fully earnings-related pension (i.e. paying benefits at least as good as and often better than the basic pension) would be fantastically expensive. Even as it was, SERPS envisaged higher contributions in the future that would probably be insufficient to cover spending promises implicit within that scheme. Abolishing the flat-rate BSP would only increase those costs further. Providing SERPS thus required the continuance of the BSP if the cost of reform was to be kept within reasonable bounds.

Thus, the incoming Conservative government in 1979 inherited a highly path-dependent and already quite complex system in which each element might be said to have been subject to the sort of 'lock-in' effects described by Pierson, which arose from institutional 'increasing returns', or positive feedback loops. Governments from the 1950s to the 1970s had found that the path dependences arising from these effects boxed them in when it came to reform, forcing them into incremental changes that added elements to the system rather than fundamentally reforming the system they had inherited. Once a consensus for change was formed, prior experiences of failure and the powerful interests created pressure against yet further change to any existing system element. The Conservatives in opposition from 1975 to 1979 were increasingly unhappy with some of the results of this settlement but were constrained to outflanking manoeuvres. From 1979 the Thatcher governments, now emboldened to bring wider ownership arguments directly into the pensions space, sought to break out of that policy box. In doing so, they attempted a profoundly path-breaking revolution, but – as we shall see – it was an ambition that eventually foundered on the rocks of path-dependent realities.

Notes

1 On path dependence, see W. Brian Arthur, 'Competing Technologies, Increasing Returns, and Lock-in by Historical Events', *The Economic Journal*, 99 (1989); Paul Pierson, 'When Effect Becomes Cause: Policy Feedback and Political Change', *World Politics*, 45 (1993); Paul Pierson, 'Increasing Returns, Path Dependence and the Study of Politics', *American Political Science Review*, 94 (2000); Kenneth J. Arrow, 'Increasing Returns: Historiographical Issues and Path Dependence', *European Journal of the History of Economic Thought*, 7 (2000); Paul David, 'Path Dependence: A Foundational Concept for Historical Social Science', *Cliometrica*, 1 (2007). On path dependence in pensions, see John Myles and Paul Pierson, 'The Comparative Political Economy of Pension Reform', in *The New Politics of the Welfare State*, ed. by Paul Pierson (Oxford: Oxford University Press, 2001), pp. 305–33.

2 On the ebb and flow of consensus on UK pension policy, see Hugh Pemberton, 'Politics and Pensions in Post-War Britain', in *Britain's Pensions Crisis: History and Policy*, ed. by Hugh Pemberton, Pat Thane, and Noel Whiteside (Oxford: Oxford University Press, 2006), pp. 39–63. For an excellent resumé of key attempts to reform the Beveridgean pension from the 1950s to the mid-1970s, see Bryan Ellis, *Pensions in Britain, 1955–1975: A History in Five Acts* (London: HMSO, 1989).

3 See Jose Harris, 'Enterprise and Welfare States: A Comparative Perspective', *Transactions of the Royal Historical Society*, 40 (1990), p. 183; Bernard Harris, *The Origins of the British Welfare State, 1800–1945* (London: Palgrave Macmillan, 2004), p. 300.

4 Harris, *Origins of the British Welfare State*, pp. 215–16.

5 John Macnicol, *The Politics of Retirement in Britain, 1878–1948* (Cambridge: Cambridge University Press, 1998), pp. 347–84.

6 Harris, *Origins of the British Welfare State*, pp. 398–404; William Beveridge, *Social Insurance and Allied Services*, Cmd 6404 (London: HMSO, 1942), paras. 240–41.

7 Ellis, *Pensions in Britain*, pp. 1–2; Howard Glennerster and Martin Evans, 'Beveridge and His Assumptive Worlds: The Incompatibilities of a Flawed Design', in *Beveridge and Social Security*, ed. by John Hills, John Ditch, and Howard Glennerster (Oxford: Oxford University Press, 1994), pp. 56–72, at p. 60.

8 Paul Addison, *The Road to 1945: British Politics and the Second World War* (London: Jonathan Cape, 1975). As Beveridge's biographer notes, it was a stroke of luck that his inquiry came in the wake of the August 1941 Atlantic Charter, in which Churchill and Roosevelt outlined a vision of 'a better future for the world' based on commitments including 'improved labour standards, economic advancement, and social security' (Jose Harris, *William Beveridge* (Oxford: Clarendon Press, 1997), pp. 369, 416–17).

9 Pemberton, 'Politics and Pensions in Post-War Britain', p. 43.

10 Harris, *William Beveridge*, p. 451.

140 *The first term*

11 John Macnicol, 'Beveridge and Old Age', in *Beveridge and Social Security*, Hills, Ditch, and Glennerster, pp. 73–96.

12 Pat Thane, *Old Age in English History* (Oxford: Oxford University Press, 2000), pp. 367–68.

13 It was hardly likely to be given that the Beveridge report, which formed the foundation of Labour's new welfare state, was written by a lifelong Liberal, as noted by Pat Thane, 'Labour and Welfare', in *Labour's First Century*, ed. by Duncan Tanner, Pat Thane, and Nick Tiratsoo (Cambridge: Cambridge University Press, 2000), pp. 80–118, at pp. 99–101.

14 Harris, *William Beveridge*, pp. 420–23.

15 Rodney Lowe, *The Welfare State in Britain since 1945* (London: Palgrave Macmillan, 2005), p. 159.

16 Paul Bridgen, 'A Straitjacket with Wriggle Room: The Beveridge Report, the Treasury and the Exchequer's Pension Liability, 1942–1959', *Twentieth Century British History*, 17 (2006).

17 Macnicol, *Politics of Retirement*; Nicholas Timmins, *The Five Giants: A Biography of the Welfare State* (London: HarperCollins, 2001).

18 David Gladstone, ed., *British Social Welfare* (London: UCL Press, 1995), p. 83.

19 Rodney Lowe, 'A Prophet Dishonoured in His Own Country? The Rejection of Beveridge in Britain, 1945–1970', in *Beveridge and Social Security*, Hills, Ditch, and Glennerster, pp. 118–33, at p. 123.

20 Addison, *The Road to 1945*; Harris, *William Beveridge*, pp. 406–7.

21 Helen Fawcett, 'The Beveridge Strait-Jacket: Policy Formulation and the Problem of Poverty in Old Age', *Contemporary British History*, 10 (1996).

22 Derek Fraser, *The Evolution of the British Welfare State* (Basingstoke: Macmillan, 2009), pp. 230–31.

23 Ellis, *Pensions in Britain*; Michael Hill, *The Welfare State in Britain: A Political History since 1945* (Aldershot: Edward Elgar, 1993), p. 57; Timmins, *Five Giants*, p. 193; Hugh Heclo, *Modern Social Politics in Britain and Sweden* (New Haven, CT: Yale University Press, 1974), p. 259.

24 Jim Tomlinson, 'The Decline of Empire and the Economic "Decline" of Britain', *Twentieth Century British History*, 14 (2003), p. 102.

25 Leslie Hannah, *Inventing Retirement: The Development of Occupational Pensions in Britain* (Cambridge: Cambridge University Press, 1986).

26 Government Actuary, *Occupational Pension Schemes: A Survey by the Government Actuary* (London: HMSO, 1958).

27 Institute of Actuaries, 'Extent of Private Pension Provision: Report of Working Party: Annual Pension Statistics – 1965', *Transactions of the Faculty of Actuaries*, 30:227 (1966–68), pp. 390–92. Two years earlier they had been valued at £5.8 billion, according to Laurie Dennett, *Mind over Data: An Actuarial History* (Cambridge: Granta Editions, 2004), p. 82.

28 Government Actuary, *Occupational Pensions Schemes: Third Survey by the Government Actuary* (London: HMSO, 1968).

29 Government Actuary, *Occupational Pension Schemes 1979: Sixth Survey by the Government Actuary* (London: HMSO, 1981), p. 2. The real-terms growth figure is from measuringworth.com.

The institutional inheritance   141

30 Office for National Statistics, 'Ownership of UK Quoted Shares: 2018', tab. 12 [www.ons.gov.uk/economy/investmentspensionsandtrusts/datasets/ownershipofukshares, accessed 9 February 2022].

31 Laurie Dennett, *A Sense of Security: 150 Years of the Prudential* (Cambridge: Granta Editions, 1998), p. 344; Hannah, *Inventing Retirement*, p. 44. Placing pensions in contracts of employment meant that, to all intents and purposes, and barring the bankruptcy of the fund, they amounted to 'deferred pay' that an employee could reasonably expect to receive after retirement.

32 Hannah, *Inventing Retirement*, p. 55; Noel Whiteside, 'Occupational Pensions and the Search for Security', in *Britain's Pensions Crisis: History and Policy*, Pemberton, Thane, and Whiteside, pp. 125–39.

33 Labour Party, *National Superannuation: Labour's Policy for Security in Old Age* (London: Labour Party, 1957).

34 Stephen Thornton, *Richard Crossman and the Welfare State* (London: I.B. Tauris, 2009), pp. 59–65; Fawcett, 'The Beveridge Strait-Jacket', p. 25. Labour envisaged a fund worth at least as much as those of all Britain's life assurance companies put together. As the Chief Actuary of the Prudential privately told Crossman, Labour would 'own the country in ten years at that rate!' (Hugh Pemberton, 'The Failure of "Nationalization by Attraction": Britain's Cross-Class Alliance against Earnings-Related Pensions in the 1950s', *The Economic History Review*, 65 (2012), p. 1434).

35 Pemberton, 'The Failure of "Nationalization by Attraction"'.

36 Paul Bridgen, 'Policy Paradigms, the "Beveridge Model" and UK Pensions Policy in the Early Post-War Period', paper given to the inaugural ESPANet conference, Copenhagen, Denmark, 14 November 2003; Noel Whiteside, 'Historical Perspectives and the Politics of Pensions Reform', in *Pensions Security in the 21st Century*, ed. by Gordon L. Clark and Noel Whiteside (Oxford: Oxford University Press, 2003), pp. 21–43.

37 Oude Nijhuis, 'Rethinking the Beveridge Strait-Jacket: The Labour Party, the TUC and the Introduction of Superannuation', *Twentieth Century British History*, 20 (2009); Pemberton, 'The Failure of "Nationalization by Attraction"'.

38 Contracting out involved an abatement of the national insurance contribution in return for an abatement of the state pension benefit. The lower benefit exceeded the reduction in contributions, however, thus 'creating the economic breathing space that would make private schemes profitable' (Heclo, *Modern Social Politics*, p. 276).

39 Labour Party, *National Superannuation*; Ministry of Pensions and National Insurance, *Provision for Old Age: The Future Development of the National Insurance Scheme*, Cmnd 538 (London: HMSO, 1958). In the event that only a minority of employers contracted their schemes out, however, because it was only in their interests to do so when their employees were earning near the national average wage (which represented the upper bound for contributions to the scheme), see Hannah, *Inventing Retirement*, p. 58.

40 Pemberton, 'Politics and Pensions in Post-War Britain'; Hannah, *Inventing Retirement*, pp. 58–59. Hannah notes that coverage of occupational pensions rose rapidly in the wake of the Boyd-Carpenter scheme.

41 Heclo, *Modern Social Politics*, pp. 272–23.
42 Paul Pierson, *Increasing Returns, Path Dependence and the Study of Politics* (Florence: European University Institute, Robert Schumann Centre, 1997).
43 Pemberton, 'The Failure of "Nationalization by Attraction" '.
44 Hannah, *Inventing Retirement*, p. 58.
45 Labour Party, *Let's Go with Labour for the New Britain* [1964 general election manifesto] (London: Labour Party, 1964).
46 Tony Salter, Colin Redman, and Martin Hewitt, *100 Years of State Pension: Learning from the Past* (London: Faculty of Actuaries and Institute of Actuaries, 2008), p. 59. Labour did make changes to the benefits system that served to help poor pensioners in other ways, however. The new Supplementary Benefit, which replaced National Assistance in 1966, increased the minimum standard of living guaranteed by the state (paradoxically making the basic pension look even more inadequate, with the number of claimants rising from 1.45 to 2 million). Around 800,000 pensioners also benefited from the more generous housing rate rebate scheme introduced in the same year. Data from Department of Health and Social Security, *National Superannuation and Social Insurance: Proposals for Earnings-Related Social Security*, Cmnd 3883 (London: HMSO, 1969).
47 Quoted in Thane, *Old Age in English History*, p. 377. On Herbison's vigorous opposition to the state graduated pension, see Ellis, *Pensions in Britain*, p. 21.
48 Cmnd 3883. On the consultation process, see Heclo, *Modern Social Politics*, p. 275.
49 Heclo, *Modern Social Politics*, p. 278.
50 Hannah, *Inventing Retirement*, p. 59.
51 Ibid.
52 Heclo, *Modern Social Politics*, p. 274; Cmnd 3883.
53 A married woman would now qualify for a pension based on the higher of her and her husband's earnings, and divorced women would qualify for a pension based on their ex-husband's earnings.
54 Conservative Central Office, *A Better Tomorrow* [1970 general election manifesto] (London: Conservative Central Office, 1970).
55 Howard Glennerster, *British Social Policy, 1945 to the Present* (Oxford: Blackwell, 2007), p. 112.
56 Department of Health and Social Security, *Strategy for Pensions: The Future Development of State and Occupational Provision*, Cmnd 4755 (London: HMSO, 1971).
57 Salter, and others, *100 Years of State Pension*, p. 70; Labour Party, *Labour's Programme 1973* (London: Labour Party, 1973), p. 11; Mark Wickham-Jones, *Economic Strategy and the Labour Party: Politics and Policy-Making, 1970–83* (London: Macmillan, 1996).
58 Cmnd 4755, para. 82. An estimate by the Government Actuary, however, suggested that the Reserve Fund would be worth £7 billion by the century's end, assuming it had a steady 7 million members; see Ellis, *Pensions in Britain*, p. 40.
59 Paul Dean (junior minister at DHSS), HC Debs, 28 November 1972, vol. 847, col. 363.
60 This conclusion at first sight is contrary to Hill, *The Welfare State in Britain*, p. 94. His view was that the reserve scheme was 'the only attempt ever made in

The institutional inheritance 143

Britain to institute a "funded" state pensions scheme', but the point being made here is simply that, although it certainly represented the only case of legislation being passed to set up such a scheme, the idea had already informed official Labour party policy in the 1950s and early 1960s.

61 Salter and others, *100 Years of State Pension*, pp. 70–71.

62 Hannah, *Inventing Retirement*, p. 60.

63 J. C. R. Dow, *Major Recessions: Britain and the World, 1920–1995* (Oxford: Oxford University Press, 2000), p. 273.

64 Cmnd 4755, para. 6.

65 Labour Party, *Let Us Work Together: Labour's Way out of the Crisis* [February 1974 general election manifesto] (London: Labour Party, 1974); James E. Cronin, *New Labour's Pasts: The Labour Party and Its Discontents* (Harlow: Longman, 2004), pp. 152–202; Wickham-Jones, *Economic Strategy and the Labour Party*; Chris Rogers, 'From Social Contract to "Social Contrick": The Depoliticisation of Economic Policy-Making under Harold Wilson, 1974–75', *British Journal of Politics and International Relations*, 11 (2009).

66 *Financial Times*, 'Labour's Views and Basic Aims', by Eric Short, 28 January 1974.

67 Salter, and others, *100 Years of State Pension*, pp. 100–1.

68 Castle's speech introducing the second reading of the National Insurance Bill at HC Debs, 10 April 1974, vol. 872, cols. 463–4; Ellis, *Pensions in Britain*, p. 46; Lowe, *The Welfare State in Britain since 1945*, pp. 256–58.

69 Salter, and others, *100 Years of State Pension*, p. 74.

70 *Financial Times*, 'Mrs Castle to Scrap Tory Pension Plan', by Stewart Fleming and Eric Short, 9 May 1979; Ellis, *Pensions in Britain, 1955–1975*, pp. 46–47; Barbara Castle, *The Castle Diaries, 1974–76* (London: Weidenfeld & Nicolson, 1980), pp. 65–76.

71 HC Debs, 1 July 1974, vol. 876, cols. 111–12.

72 Department of Health and Social Security, *Better Pensions – Fully Protected against Inflation: Proposals for a New Pensions Scheme*, Cmnd 5713 (London: HMSO, 1974).

73 Ibid., para. 58

74 Institute and Faculty of Actuaries, 'State and Occupational Pension Provision (Abstract of Sessional Meeting on 25 November 1974)', *Journal of the Institute of Actuaries*, 102 (1975); Salter, and others, *100 Years of State Pension*, p. 83. Those without the benefit of final salary benefits tended to be lower-paid manual workers in schemes providing a flat rate of pension entitlement per year of service.

75 The funds would therefore be responsible only for inflation-proofing the GMP once it was in payment. The GMP would be broadly equivalent to SERPS rights earned by those not contracted out.

76 Institute and Faculty of Actuaries, 'State and Occupational Pension Provision' (Abstract of Sessional Meeting on 25 November 1974)', Mr D. E. Fellows, at p. 20.

77 *Financial Times*, 'Labour Pension Plan Has Inflation Shield: Favourable Response from Insurance Industry', by Anthony Harris, 12 September 1974.

78 *Financial Times*, 'Actuaries Split on Pension Plans', by Eric Short, 26 November 1974.

79 W. B. McBride, 'The Interaction between State and Occupational Pension Schemes in the United Kingdom', *Transactions of the Faculty of Actuaries*, 35 (1975–77), p. 254.

80 HC Debs, 1 November 1974, vol. 880, col. 551.

81 There was, for example, a common acceptance that, as Lord Aberdare put it, the chopping and changing was 'becoming ridiculous' and that the need to provide the pension industry with long-term stability was 'paramount' (HL Debs, 24 June 1975, vol. 361, cols. 1324–74, second reading of the Social Security Pensions Bill, at cols. 1335–336).

82 *Financial Times*, 'Tories Will Revive Former Pension Scheme', by Stewart Fleming, 22 August 1974.

83 Ellis, *Pensions in Britain*, p. 53.

84 *Guardian*, 'Pensions: Third Time Lucky?', 28 February 1974.

85 HC Debs, 18 March 1975, vol. 888, cols. 1486–583, second reading of the Social Security Bill, at col. 1505.

86 Conservative Party Archive (hereafter CPA): CRD 4/7/73. Social Services Policy Groups (Post-1974) Second Pension Policy Group. Memorandum of Second Policy Group Meeting: Philosophy of the Scheme and the State Reserve Pension, 19 June 1974.

87 Not an unreasonable fear given the Left's still developing alternative economic strategy. For example, in April 1975 Tony Benn made public his intention to compel occupational pension funds to provide funding for the National Enterprise Board, nationalised industries, and investment projects approved under planning agreements – a proposal immediately dismissed by the Prime Minister (*Financial Times*, 'Wilson Disowns Pension Funds Plan', 29 April 1975), though Benn continued to advance the idea in his capacity as Industry Minister.

88 CPA: CRD 4/7/73, Social Services Policy Groups (Post-1974), Second Pension Policy Group. Alan Bradley, 'The Philosophy of the 1973 Act', 17 June 1974.

89 CPA: CRD 4/7/61, Pensions Study Group. CEB/JW, 'Conservative Strategy on Labour's Pensions Plan', 27 February 1975.

90 HC Debs, 18 March 1975, vol. 888, cols. 1486–583, second reading of the Social Security Bill, at col. 1505.

91 Salter and others, *100 Years of State Pension*, p. 89.

92 The proposal (linked to a broader movement towards worker participation in company boards) came in a White Paper: Department of Health and Social Security, *Occupational Pension Schemes: Role of Members in the Running of Schemes*, Cmnd 6514 (London: HMSO, 1976). It was vociferously opposed by both the employers' organisations and the NAPF, both of which disliked the idea of statutory compulsion, although they were open in principle to promoting more voluntary employee involvement. The Conservatives welcomed greater employee involvement but made clear their intention to 'fight Labour's plan to give this right exclusively to trade unions' (see Conservative Central Office, *The Right Approach: A Statement of Conservative Aims* (London: Conservative Central Office, 1976), p. 71).

93 Hannah, *Inventing Retirement*, p. 62.

The institutional inheritance 145

94 Clare Munro, 'The Fiscal Politics of Savings and Share Ownership in Britain, 1970–1980', *The Historical Journal*, 55 (2012).
95 For membership: Howe Papers (hereafter 'HP'): Dep 134, Peter Cropper, 'Wider Ownership Group', 16 November 1977. Kieran Heinemann includes a wider account of this reasoning that incorporates this earlier stage in the group's thinking from the perspective of the Wider Share Ownership Council's papers: *Playing the Market: Retail Investment and Speculation in Twentieth-Century Britain* (New York: Oxford University Press, 2021), ch. 4.
96 HP: Dep 134, minutes of the Wider Ownership Group, 6 December 1977.
97 HP: Dep 134, Tim Boswell, 'Tax Shelters for Savings', 10 January 1978. This memorandum was commissioned at the 6 December meeting.
98 HP: Dep 134, Tim Boswell, 'Wider Ownership Committee: Fair Tax Incentives for Savings', 25 January 1978.
99 *Financial Times*, 17 December 1977.
100 Heinemann, *Playing the Market*, ch. 4.
101 HP: Dep 134 contains a copy of Peter Drucker, 'American Business's New Owners', *Wall Street Journal*, 27 May 1976.
102 HP: Dep 134, Wider Ownership Committee Meeting, 6 December 1977. The Wilson Committee had been set up by the Labour government in October 1976 with the task of reviewing the functioning of UK financial institutions under the chairmanship of the former prime minister, Harold Wilson, but it was still deliberating as it prepared its report, which was not published until 1980.
103 HP: Dep 134, Tim Boswell, 'Tax Shelters for Savings', 10 January 1978.
104 HP: Dep 134, minutes of the Wider Ownership Group, 12 January 1978.
105 Ibid.
106 HP: Dep 134, Tim Boswell, 'Wider Ownership Committee: Fair Tax Incentives for Savings', 25 January 1978.
107 Ibid.
108 Ibid.
109 HP: Dep 134, Tim Boswell, 'Tax Shelters for Savings', 10 January 1978.
110 HP: Dep 134, First Draft of Second Report from Wider Share Ownership, 16 March 1978.
111 *Daily Telegraph*, 'Family Money-Go-Ground', by Geoffrey Howe, 23 September 1978.
112 HP: Dep 134, Howe to Brian Cole, 6 February 1979 (in defence of employee share ownership versus Cole's worries about dilution).
113 HP: Dep 134, Peter Cropper, 'Saving, Profit Sharing and Wider Ownership', 4 October 1978.
114 HP: Dep 134, minutes of the Wider Ownership Group, 1 December 1978.
115 Ibid.
116 HP: Dep 134, Peter Cropper, 'A Note on the Fundamental Merits of Equities', 5 December 1978.
117 HP: Dep 134, Tim Boswell, 'Encouraging Savings', 24 January 1979.
118 Ibid.
119 Lowe, *The Welfare State in Britain since 1945*, p. 159.

4

Pensions 'ratchet' and 'burden'

Margaret Thatcher's first four years in Downing Street started and ended with assurances that she had no intention of dismantling the pensions settlement that her government inherited. Beyond warning against trades union control of savings, the 1979 Conservative manifesto contained no signs of dissent from the model of public–private partnership embodied in SERPS. The incoming government pledged to honour its predecessor's promises – to phase out rules that discouraged pensioners from working, and to encourage saving by reducing the investment income surcharge – but it did not seek a mandate for radical reform. As we shall see, Thatcher's campaign for a second term in 1983 aimed to strike a similarly reassuring tone, and her government's record after its first four years in office did not include fundamental changes to pensions infrastructure. From a policy implementation perspective, then, the attempted pensions revolution at the centre of this book's concerns could appear to be the unexpected product of Thatcher's second term of 1983–7.

Yet this would be too narrow a view of 'Thatcherism in practice'. Legislative quietness in the first term hid important changes and connections with the second term. The forces pushing and pulling Thatcher's governments between ideological radicalism and the constraints of electoral politics were established between 1979 and 1983. Thatcher and her ministers proved willing to take political risks with retirement policies in pursuit of the spending cuts prescribed by monetarist theory to reduce inflation. The Cabinet's decision in 1980 to break the link between pensions and earnings revealed a willingness to pursue reform within the existing system to achieve this end, even if it made pensioners worse off in the long run. Yet more immediate radical reform was recognised as politically dangerous, especially if it implied the breaking of pledges. Rather than a government lacking the radical zeal of its successors, then, it was one frustrated by the feeling it had boxed itself in. This chapter therefore highlights the role that existing pledges played in determining how and to what extent neoliberal policy reforms could be realised (in this case, a reduction in the 'horizontal' redistribution of resources between working and retired generations).

These competing appetites for reform and political caution were not evenly distributed across the government. At the Treasury, Geoffrey Howe headed a team of ministers, special advisers, and officials who countenanced actions well beyond those that the Cabinet was willing to follow. At the Department for Health and Social Security (DHSS), Patrick Jenkin and his successor from 1981, Norman Fowler, often resisted the Treasury's proposals by highlighting political risks. The internal dynamics of Thatcher's Cabinet were more complex than a battle of 'dries' and 'wets', in that disagreements were often over political strategy, not simply ideology. In this context, debates about pension policy in Thatcher's first term evidence our wider claim that political actors' abilities to use, neutralise, or overcome arguments about electoral strategy shaped how a neoliberal vision of pensions was translated into policy.

Most importantly, between 1979 and 1983 politicians, special political advisers, civil servants, and the press began better to define (and discover) the problems that the second term's legislation claimed to resolve. What had been seen as technical problems increasingly became questions of economic and political principle. The ethics of 'inflation proofing', the 'burden' of pensions, and the lack (or dangers) of individual choice in the market were applied to the pensions politics of the first term before they were used to justify fundamental changes in the second. Advocates and opponents of later reforms had often already rehearsed some of their arguments before the 1983 election results were known. Reformers began to define their objections to the existing system with greater clarity, hitching their agendas to statutory reports on the National Insurance and occupational pensions systems and to recent market trends. These and other stakeholders' definitions of the problems facing government shaped the solutions advocated after 1983, which often had both to speak to a neoliberal vision of pensions and ostensibly solve the practical problems that seemed to demand action. In some policy fields, then, the first Thatcher government is best thought of as practising 'problem discovery' through a neoliberal lens. Rather than a neutral process, we show that advocates of reform both sought to define the scope of the work conducted by civil servants for their own purposes and use the resulting evidence to make a case for change.

Rather than a strictly chronological tour, this chapter considers the pension 'problems' that interested the 1979–83 government. The first was how to protect pensioners from inflation without creating an ever-widening gap between the retired and working generations. In different forms, this problem was understood as one of redistribution, inter-generational fairness, and an instance of a 'ratchet' effect whereby small measures led to ever more extreme distributional effects over time. The government sought to redress this not via system change but by changes to how it administered the existing

148   *The first term*

apparatus. The second problem focused on the proportion of resources that
society would need to devote to pensions of all kinds in future and whether
and when this would become unsustainable. This 'burden' of pensions was
debated and defined through both public political speeches and technical
work by officials within government. By 1983, though, it provided enough
of an imperative that the government that returned to office in June that
year no longer felt limited to outflanking industry interests and pursuing
reform within the existing system but, instead, began seriously to attempt
revolutionary change.

Inflation and the pensions 'ratchet'

The Thatcher government of 1979–83 is often remembered for its monetarist economic strategy and its attendant cuts to public spending and tol-
eration of high unemployment in pursuit of lower inflation (discussed in
Chapter Two). Inflation was a double-edged sword for pensioners in this
strategy. On the one hand, they were said to be some of the key beneficiaries
of price stability since inflation eroded the value of fixed incomes. On the
other hand, pensioners were seen as a group that would need to make sacrifices to lower inflation. The best-known example of such a sacrifice was the
decision to break the link between pensions and average earnings growth
in 1980, but the same drive to reduce social security spending was also the
backdrop to debates over the annual uprating of pensions. By reducing the
public sector borrowing requirement, cuts to public spending were thought
to constrain money supply growth and thereby control inflation at the same
time as freeing up investment capital for private enterprise and lowering
interest rates. In practice, the links between the PSBR, the money supply,
and inflation were less clear than the government's focus on public spending
restraint implied, but it did reduce the share of resources that would have
been transferred between the working and retired populations. That reform
must be understood, however, in the context of senior figures' ambitions to
go further and their concern that administrative rules and the pressures of
democratic politics had created a 'ratchet' effect that led to social security
taking an ever greater share of resources. To understand these concerns and
the paths to reform taken, we must first look to the politics of the 1979
general election.

In the mid-1970s advocates of the State Earnings Related Pension Scheme
had claimed that one of its virtues as a pay-as-you-go scheme was its superior ability to protect pensioners from inflation compared with funded
occupational schemes. Some Conservatives had reservations about exposing
taxpayers to such an open-ended liability, but, as we saw in Chapter Three,

the party eventually came out in support of SERPS and instead focused on attacking Labour's supposed plans to direct pension funds as a step towards a planned economy. Importantly, though, some hesitation about inflation-proofing pensions remained. The party's interim policy statement *The Right Approach* (1976) accepted SERPS but equivocated on inflation protection. In contrast to the statutory guarantees that Labour had built into its legislation, the Conservatives merely promised to 'do our best to keep the purchasing power of pensions and other long-term benefits in line with prices'.[1]

By the 1979 election, however, Thatcher had been forced into a firmer pledge. The Social Security Act 1975 created an annual duty to uprate the basic state pension and some other long-term benefits for the following year in line with forecast rises in *either* prices or average earnings (whichever was greater).[2] This provision had a weakness: actual inflation and wage demands could outrun the forecast and create a shortfall that left pensioners worse off in real terms, as happened in 1978. In March 1979 the Labour Prime Minister, James Callaghan, and his Cabinet agreed both to uprate benefits for the coming year and voluntarily make good the shortfall caused by the previous underestimate. The Cabinet pointed out that automatic indexation was a 'dangerous principle', not least because it was not clear that clawing back a future overshoot would be possible politically.[3] But, with the decision made, Callaghan sought to use it to maximum advantage in the dying hours of his administration by announcing it during the no confidence debate that triggered the 1979 election. Declaring this the mark of a government whose motto was 'Need, not greed', Callaghan sat down.[4] Five hours later his government lost the vote, by a margin of one.

The following day the leaders returned for Prime Minister's Questions (PMQs). Thatcher now sought to defuse Callaghan's election ploy by promising to honour his pensions commitment.[5] This pledge was not enough, though, to prevent questions about her party's commitment to protecting pensioners from inflation. The Conservative manifesto reiterated Thatcher's promise to 'honour the increases', but its only mention of inflation proofing was a factual defence of the party's plans to raise VAT, asserting that pensioners would not be unduly affected because 'the levels of State pensions and other benefits take price rises into account'.[6] During the campaign, however, Thatcher was pressed into a clearer commitment: her government would 'maintain the value of retirement pensions in terms of what they will buy in the shops'.[7] By 1979, then, Callaghan's campaign politics had extracted a firmer Conservative pledge to shield pensioners from inflation, but one that studiously avoided any mention of average earnings or enabling pensioners to share in the rise in national income.

On taking office, doubt was quickly cast on what the new Prime Minister had promised for November's uprating. The Treasury argued that Thatcher

150   *The first term*

had committed to honour only the total figures Callaghan had announced, not the underlying calculation. Thus, if the regular annual uprating calculation already met or exceeded those totals (or could be topped up to meet them), there would be no need also to add a shortfall correction relating to 1978.[8] On revised projections, this distinction could potentially reduce the PSBR by £90 million in 1979/80 and £230 million in a full year, and so Treasury officials urged Geoffrey Howe, now Chancellor of the Exchequer, to resist making up the shortfall given the need to reduce public expenditure.[9] Howe duly made the case to Patrick Jenkin, Secretary of State at the DHSS, arguing that 'there was some ambiguity' about what had been promised. Jenkin insisted that there was none, and proposed increases that both made good the shortfall and uprated pensions based on the forecasts for 1979. The Chancellor relented but left their meeting having agreed some technical changes to reduce the cost by £10 million.[10] At Cabinet, though, Jenkin secured a total victory, receiving the easy assent of his colleagues and managing to reverse the Chancellor's creative accounting.[11]

This early decision on pensions revealed two dynamics that characterised the 1979–83 government. First, the Treasury sought social security savings to reduce public borrowing but found itself boxed in by promises Thatcher had made under political pressure. Second, the DHSS typically outmanoeuvred the Treasury by highlighting the political risks of breaking those promises. Indeed, the importance of the firmer pledges extracted in the 1979 election campaign stretched beyond the issue of the shortfall. When in 1980 the Chancellor looked around the Cabinet table for savings, Thatcher's pledge of inflation proofing was cited as the reason why any reductions in social security would have to fall on short-term benefit claimants, not pensioners. Had Thatcher not supplemented the manifesto's dry statement of fact, the indications are that the Chancellor would have demanded otherwise and countenanced disposing with full inflation protection entirely.[12]

Indexation and the basic state pension

Jenkin's trump card when negotiating with the Chancellor had been that remedying the shortfall was a small price to pay for the chance to break the link between pensions and earnings by moving to prices-only uprating. In his first weeks as Chief Secretary to the Treasury, John Biffen was briefed on the logic behind breaking this link. Doing so was seen as removing a 'ratchet' mechanism that threatened to increase spending on the welfare state. Prices-only uprating would protect pensioners against increases in what they 'actually spend [their] money on', whereas uprating based on the better of prices or earnings meant that 'over time the pensioner does better than either, and increasingly improves his real position against the rest of the community'. Such improvements were, we would add, often from an inadequate or low starting point (around 1.7 million pensioner households still relied on supplementary benefit in 1983), but the Treasury focused on relative improvements in the past decade.[13] Since 1974, it argued, pensions had increased by 20 per cent in real terms. On top of swelling numbers of beneficiaries, this increase explained why social security benefits now made up 25 per cent of public expenditure. Prices-only uprating would thus rebalance the generational burden: although there would be a time lag, prices-only uprating would protect pensioners' purchasing power from the Chancellor's switch to indirect taxation but without increasing the retired population's dependence upon working contributors.[14]

The principled decision was understood to have already been taken in opposition, and Treasury ministers favoured 'getting it over with as soon as possible' given that it would 'cause a storm'.[15] Officials also advised swift action and urged the Chancellor to secure Jenkin's agreement that November's uprating and all thereafter would be based on prices only.[16] On 17 May 1979 Howe and Jenkin agreed that the uprating formula should 'immediately' be amended to prices only.[17] Although legislation might not strictly be needed (if prices outran earnings anyway), the ministers agreed that there 'might be advantage [in] grasping this nettle now' and that, 'if earnings looked like being materially ahead of prices, then legislation should certainly be introduced'.[18]

Despite this agreement, Jenkin was keen to put off changing the law so that he could in the meantime pass a first social security bill without the controversy likely to accompany a move to prices-only indexation.[19] His memorandum putting the change to the Cabinet highlighted the political risks of the latter and suggested a mitigating measure that appeared to backtrack on his agreement with Howe:

> The change will be severely criticised, but we can point out that will be open to the Govt to give a larger increase than the price movement if economic circumstances permit ... Indeed, at this uprating if the earnings forecast exceeds the price forecast by only a small amount, I propose to use the higher forecast.[20]

This was not the Treasury view, and in Cabinet discussion Jenkin clarified that his preference was to legislate in the current session. The Cabinet resolved on early legislation once the decision was announced in the Budget, which Howe did on 12 June 1979.[21] Yet, even with this agreement, Jenkin still managed to get his way on timing by starting negotiations with the opposition on his less controversial bill.[22] Outmanoeuvred, the Chief Secretary now refused to let Jenkin publish this first bill before securing firm commitments both that a second bill breaking the pensions link with earnings would

152   *The first term*

follow and that the Treasury could announce the next uprating in April 1980 on this basis with or without legislation passed.[23]

As we show in Chapter Eight, the decision to delink the state pension from average earnings had very significant long-term consequences for the adequacy of Britain's pension provision. It is important to note, though, that at the time the move was seen as a starting point rather than end to reform.[24] Peter Kemp, head of the Treasury's Social Security Group, wrote to a fellow civil servant:

> I suspect that it is not the last word. We have independently proposed to Treasury Ministers, who have agreed with DHSS Ministers, that there should be a longer term look at the whole role of social security and, amongst other things, what sort of uprating arrangements must be appropriate. It may well be that prices only is not the right long term solution. Indeed at a meeting the other day, the Chancellor asked why it was necessary to have any statutory formula at all; might it not be possible to go back to the early 1970s and earlier when pensions were uprated as and when the Government of the day thought necessary and/or appropriate in the light of the resources available. Politically, however, I do not see how they could now fail to stop off, so to speak, at the prices only stage; if only so as to be able to say, in the context of indirect tax increases, that pensioners remain protected as to their standard of living.[25]

Indeed, in advance of her interview on *Weekend World* in January 1980, the Chancellor tried to persuade Thatcher to qualify her commitment to indexation. If asked whether the government would continue to fully inflation protect pensions, he advised that she take the line that '[t]he Government had done so in the past, and would endeavour to do so in the future, though this must depend on the success of the Government's policies and the strength of the economy'.[26] As we shall see, the Prime Minister did not take this advice.

Uprating the basic state pension

The statutory duty to uprate pensions created an annual conflict between the Treasury's desire to keep more radical options open, the DHSS's political realism, and promises made by the Prime Minister. Although the prices-only formula was set by 1980, uprating decisions remained contentious because they relied on forecasts. If inflation turned out higher than forecast, the government came under pressure to make good the shortfall in the next year's uprating (as in 1979). But, if inflation fell further than expected, the government came under pressure to allow pensioners to keep the real-terms increase. As with indexation, arguments about inter-generational fairness (like those we saw some members of the neoliberal thought collective make about the redistributive welfare state in Chapter One) were applied to this second version of the 'ratchet'. In the process, the tension between the government's emphasis on reducing public spending and the pledges it had made (and still wanted to make) became clearer. Yet these annual arguments about uprating also created a consensus across government that more significant changes were needed to escape the cycle of political pressure.

The Chancellor's priorities were clear when, in November 1980, he proposed to uprate pensions by three percentage points less than prices. Reducing the real value of pensions, Howe recognised, would be portrayed as 'attacking the poor' and 'breaking pledges', but the potential savings (£159 million in 1981/82 and £470 million in each of the two following years) were necessary to reduce government borrowing.[27] He told the cabinet that one percentage point of the difference could be justified as a technical correction for the previous year's over-estimate of inflation, and another one percentage point might be justified as cancelling out the effect of VAT rises on alcohol and tobacco on inflation-linked benefits. But the further one percentage point difference rested upon an ethical case that those receiving benefits (including pensions) should not be doing better than those paying the National Insurance bill.[28] For Howe, this was a question of intergenerational fairness:

> More generally the reduction could be defended as not being unfair, at a time when most sections of the community would be having to accept reduced living standards, against the background that the real value of retirement pensions had increased by 31 per cent since 1971 and that the elderly were also entitled to a range of other valuable benefits.

Having made that argument, though, the Chancellor and Prime Minister found themselves facing 'the most serious political reverse' they had yet suffered.[29] At the time, the press was briefed that the 'Wets' (Jim Prior and Ian Gilmour) had formed an alliance with the so-called 'geriatrics' (Lord Soames, Lord Hailsham, and Willie Whitelaw) to defeat the Treasury hawks.[30] In fact, it was Jenkin who pushed back against Howe's plans by arguing that both he and Thatcher had regularly repeated their commitments to price-protect pensions and by warning the Cabinet that he would find it difficult to pass the necessary legislation. Cabinet minutes record Jenkin reminding fellow ministers that the 'Prime Minister, in a television broadcast on 6 January, had confirmed that the Government was pledged to the indexation of old age pensions for the lifetime of this Parliament'.[31] This was the interview Howe had urged the Prime Minister to use to soften her commitment to inflation protection, and she was reported to have 'turned puce' when the interview transcript was read out.[32] Asked directly about a possible move away from indexing pensions, she had said: 'No ... I'm pledged on that ... No, I'm absolutely pledged on that ... I'm pledged on that, and a

154   *The first term*

pledge must last.'[33] Jim Prior allegedly broke the awkward silence by saying 'Well, that's it, isn't it?', expecting the debate to close. But the Treasury,
backed by Thatcher, continued making the argument in a further hour and
a half of heated debate. Eventually, however, the Cabinet concluded that the
package as currently presented was just too politically sensitive:

> In discussion it was the general view that the Govt could not go back on
> its firm pledge to continue with indexation of retirement pensions. To do so
> would mean that this Govt, and the Conservative Party, would be charged
> both now and for many years in the future with breaking its faith with old
> people. It would moreover risk provoking social unrest at a time of deep dis-
> quiet, particularly outside the South East region, over rising unemployment.[34]

Howe extracted a small concession on principle: an agreement that the one
percentage point abatement related to the over-provision resulting from
inflation falling more rapidly than expected would not be inconsistent with
the party's pledges, since these concerned price protection over the course
of the Parliament. Even so, it was concluded that there was 'no case for
controversial legislation to secure this reduction alone', and the Cabinet's
search for cuts therefore turned to areas not covered by pledges (such as
unemployment benefit and healthcare). But, although on this occasion the
Cabinet deemed it 'better to accept tax increases than cuts to social security', the Chancellor and Prime Minister had set down a marker during the
discussion by opposing indexation.[35]

When the Cabinet reconvened a week later, the Treasury had worked out
a compromise whereby only the one percentage point abatement related to
the previous year's over-protection would be applied. Yet, against opposition from backbench Conservative MPs, the government settled for legislating for a one-off clawback rather than a permanent power to do so in future.
The government regretted that decision when the prospect of clawing back
over-protection again erupted into a significant political dispute, in 1982.
Over the summer Thatcher had commissioned the Central Policy Review
Staff (CPRS) to identify options for long-term public spending reductions.[36]
In September the Cabinet held an extended meeting to consider the public
spending situation and the CPRS's report, which, alongside the privatisation of health and education, put forward de-indexing social security as an
option.[37] The report's authors were linked to the Treasury, whose officials
saw such de-indexation as a 'front runner' option despite its political difficulty.[38] In preparing for Cabinet, they advised the Chancellor that he should
aim to agree further studies of the options but also secure a 'moratorium
on new commitments (or the renewal of old ones)'.[39] He should frame the
debate around the need to make 'radical changes of direction, if we are
to avoid creating in the longer term an economy – and a society – which

is dominated by the demands of the public sector, with all the depressing effects which that entails for individuals and enterprises'.[40] Governments around the world had made 'untenable commitments to indexation', and in Britain they were 'hedged in at present by too many pledges and commitments'.[41] To avoid tax rises, significant spending cuts would be needed.

Even the restricted circulation annex to the Cabinet conclusions glossed what was said to have been a torrid meeting. Ministers rounded on the paper for putting forward controversial policies without detail and harangued the Treasury for focusing on spending rather than growth.[42] Cabinet difficulties aside, the Prime Minister had from the start been concerned that the paper would leak.[43] It duly did, and *The Economist* carried an exclusive that highlighted both the privatisation proposals on health and those to de-index pensions.[44] Seen as another example of Cabinet splits, this caused the Prime Minister considerable embarrassment, and she was forced to use her conference speech to limit the damage and distance herself from the CPRS. For all the furore, though, the Cabinet minutes record agreement not to make further spending commitments and to 'avoid repeating former pledges that would otherwise expire'.[45] Treasury officials also agreed with the DHSS to undertake more detailed work on de-indexation. They were under instructions from the Prime Minister not to proceed formally until sensitive by-elections were over, however, and the Cabinet had considered more immediate reductions via the Public Expenditure Survey.

Against this backdrop, the Cabinet considered the 1983 uprating in November 1982. The previous uprating had assumed that inflation would run to 9 per cent. In fact, it now looked likely that prices would have increased only by between 6.1 and 6.8 per cent. The Treasury's Chief Secretary felt there was a 'cogent case for recovering the resulting excess'.[46] If they failed to act, there would be a 'ratchet effect' because pensioners would not just be protected against inflation but would do better when earnings rose more quickly than prices. The Treasury had agreed with the DHSS that the 1983 uprating would be abated by an amount decided at the Spring Budget but 'by no more than 2½ per cent'.[47] The Cabinet endorsed this plan but expressed 'considerable concern' about its presentation. If the inflation forecast remained at 5 per cent, an abatement of 2.5 percentage points would leave the uprating looking very small compared to previous years and could easily be framed by opponents as a cut that would 'face the Government with serious problems in both Parliament and the country'. Spokespersons were therefore asked to switch the focus of discussion onto the promise to protect pensioners against inflation *over the life* of the Parliament and 'words like "recovery" or "clawback" were to be avoided'.[48]

Howe announced these changes in his Autumn Statement, leaving the detail for the spring. As anticipated, though, he and the Prime Minister came under attack as the opposition decried the 'claw-back'.[49] Under pressure on the specifics at PMQs in the House of Commons, Thatcher turned to the rhetoric of generational fairness: increases were paid for 'not by Government, but by the working population of our country, who have had their National Insurance contributions put up to pay for it'.[50] Notably, over the next week, her rhetoric began to use inflation to draw distinctions between those exercising independence and those dependent on others. At the Lord Mayor's dinner she bemoaned the borrowing that had stoked inflation, 'ruining many a saver's nest egg and reducing many a non-index-linked pensioner to penury'.[51] Back in the Commons, however, she defended her government's plans to abate the uprating by explaining that, as a pay-as-you-go scheme, higher NI contributions had to fund increases and that 'pensioners would be the first to understand the burden on the working population'.[52] The status of the pensioner in Thatcherite rhetoric, then, was increasingly one that reflected the distinctions neoliberals made between those who invested in old age provision and those dependent on inter-generational transfers mediated by the state.

As the political pressure subsided, ministers turned to the detail of the 'clawback' and how to avoid such annual set piece attacks in future. By December Norman Fowler (who had succeeded Jenkin as Secretary of State for Health and Social Security) was seeking to deliver his department's required savings by taking at least 1.7 percentage points off the cost of 1983 social security uprating.[53] Legislation would be required if the uprating was less than the RPI forecast, however. The government had four options. It could again pass another exceptional act related only to one year (option A) – the least politically contentious option, but leaving the issue to recur almost annually. Alternatively, it could alter the uprating mechanism to give itself a permanent power, either mandatory or discretionary, to abate increases (option B) or add to option B a confirmation that it would make up undershoots (option C). Or the government could eliminate the forecasting problem entirely by switching to historical uprating (option D).

Most ministers viewed option D as the only long-term solution.[54] The Chancellor and Fowler's predecessor, Jenkin, had agreed the change in principle.[55] Yet, whereas Fowler himself considered historic upratings the best long-term solution, he thought it 'very contentious, and difficult to defend in 1983', as pensioners were likely to lose out as prices would probably rise more rapidly in 1983 than they had in 1982.[56] Timing the shift would be tough: it would look like an attempt to save money, and the party had made much of Labour's attempt to do the same when switching from historic data to forecasts in 1976. Recognising these difficulties, the Ministerial Group recommended option C.

When Cabinet met in March, however, the Prime Minister made the case for switching to historical uprating, citing the 'ratchet': '[W]hen outturn fell short of forecast, it was politically difficult for the Government to recover excess provision.'[57] Given the sensitivities, Thatcher now proposed abandoning any plans for clawing back the excess caused by previous overestimates and, instead, legislating to change to the historical system. On this compromise, pensioners would be better off in November 1983 than they would have been with an abatement.

Even so, electoral vulnerabilities continued to worry Fowler as the 1983 election approached. Updated forecasts suggested that using historical inflation would produce a less generous uprating than had been thought when Cabinet agreed the switch. He proposed to announce at the start of the election campaign that the government would uprate pensions by between 4 and 4.5 per cent regardless of the final RPI inflation figure.[58] The Chancellor riposted: '[I]f the Government abandoned its position of principle at the very first time of operation of the new method it would appear to have no confidence in its own arguments; and there would be no logical justification for whatever alternative figure it might select.' This time Thatcher backed Howe, not Fowler. The lower uprating simply reflected success in lowering inflation, and the government should 'stand firm during the General Election campaign on its previously declared policies'.[59]

Yet, if the Treasury had won on that occasion, it had lost the fight to keep open the prospects of removing inflation indexation entirely. In the run-up to the election, the Treasury and DHSS presented alternative views to the Prime Minister. The Chancellor made the case that the party should not repeat its pledge to price-protect pensions and other benefits given the need to control public expenditure and the unfair burden being placed on younger generations.[60] Fowler maintained that 'we cannot do less than promise to maintain what we achieved in this Parliament', however, and noted that decisions made in the first term had already made the pensioner materially less well off.[61] The DHSS noted the long-term impacts of breaking the link between pensions and earnings: 'If we had uprated pensions only in line with prices since 1948, a married couple's pension now would be £22 a week not £52.55 a week.'[62] Unlike the Chancellor, Fowler asserted that most of the first term's social security expenditure increase had come not from real-terms increases but from more pensioners and unemployed claimants. Pensioner numbers at least would stabilise until the mid-1990s. 'The course we have already set,' Fowler argued, 'implies that pensioners and other beneficiaries will become worse off in relation to those in work, and that the share of national resources going to the elderly by way of social security benefits is unlikely to change very much until the mid-1990s at least.'[63]

Perhaps most importantly, though, Fowler emphasised the political risks of de-indexation, inviting inevitable questions for which 'there are no politically sustainable answers'.[64] For example, if she used the suggested defence that it was irresponsible to make such pledges, Thatcher would be asked why she had done so in 1979. Rather than bow to pressure later, it was important to make a pledge now if the government accepted these arguments. In part, Fowler argued, this was because Labour had mishandled its own pension proposals, making it easier to defend the government's record 'despite the fact that, for reasons we all recognise, we have not been able to match the real increases of previous Governments, and UK pensions remain low by comparison with most comparable industrial nations'.[65] The opposition should be denied any chance to regain the initiative, he concluded. By the end of April Thatcher had sided with Fowler.[66]

If one of the aims of the settlement in 1975 had been to improve and protect the value of old age pensions, Thatcher's government had thus already taken steps away from this before the 1983 election. The Treasury saw cuts to social security as necessary initially to control inflation and subsequently to reduce the impact of government borrowing on interest rates and the availability of capital for private investment. Given pledges already made, it achieved these aims by targeting 'ratchet' effects that allowed pensioners – unfairly, from its perspective – to gain real-terms increases at the expense of those working. The ultimate effect of breaking the link between basic state pension and earnings and moving to historical uprating was to reduce the level of redistribution between generations and begin the process of recrafting Britain's pensions arrangements such that, if individuals wanted to continue sharing in the real-terms growth of the economy in retirement, they would need to redistribute more of their own income across the life cycle using investments. These changes were made within the existing pension system's architecture, but this hid the extent to which more radical breaches with the 1975 consensus were already being contemplated. Indeed, the direction of travel that arguments about generational fairness and changes to indexation represented can only really be understood alongside wider understandings of 'the burden of pensions'.

The burden of pensions

As noted above, Howe and Thatcher often invoked inter-generational fairness when arguing in favour of reductions in current public spending. The 'burden' that pensions allegedly placed on Britain's society and economy was also projected over a much longer time horizon, however, especially in relation to occupational pensions and SERPS. The remainder of this chapter shows how first term arguments about this 'burden' developed into a justification for departing from the consensus reached in 1975. We show not only how arguments about the 'burden' came to the fore in political rhetoric but also how different actors used the research capabilities of the civil service and Government Actuary to measure the 'burden', attract ministerial attention, and tie the findings to policy agendas that exemplified a neoliberal vision of pensions.

Some Conservatives had long opposed state earnings-related pensions on the grounds that this would weigh too heavily on the taxpayer or private companies.[67] In the mid-1970s most debate about the cost of pensions revolved around the merits of funded schemes versus an unfunded pay-as-you-go system. In 1974 Howe had pledged that if the Conservatives regained power then a new 'state reserve scheme' would be funded rather than being 'pay as you go', with future taxpayers picking up the bill.[68] Accordingly when Barbara Castle proposed SERPS, some members of the Conservative party's Pensions Study Group initially argued that it should oppose the legislation on the grounds that it 'would be on a pay-as-you-go basis and, therefore, imposed increasing burdens on future contributors and taxpayers as the pensions commitment built up'.[69]

As discussed in Chapter One, members of the neoliberal thought collective criticised the state's provision of pensions above a minimum because more expansive schemes extended the welfare state and grew into unsustainable burdens that relied on redistribution and taxpayer subsidy. Arthur Seldon – a member of the Mont Pèlerin Society and editorial director of the Institute of Economic Affairs – had made these arguments in the British context. In *Pensions in a Free Society* (1957), he had argued that state pensions diminished responsibility and self-worth: '[W]hat self-respecting man wants his neighbour to pay his milkman?' he wrote.[70] By the early 1980s, however, those arguing for pension reform within neoliberal think tanks had begun to focus on the future burdens created by demographic change. Arguing against automatic indexation in *The Daily Telegraph*, Alfred Sherman – director of the Centre for Policy Studies – claimed that

> the vast increase in the proportion of pre-work and post-work generations in the total population and their per capita share of resources – longer schooling, more in higher education, higher pensions but no lengthening of working life commensurate with increased life expectancy – throws a doubly increased burden on the economy.

In Sherman's view these pressures formed a looming generational and social crisis: 'increased dependence on the State, in one form or another, attenuates the link between effort and reward, and fosters group-political conflict to re-divide a shrinking cake, while inflation takes the hindmost. Economic man is elbowed aside by political animal. The social fabric comes under increasing strain.'[71]

160   *The first term*

Howe's speech to the National Association of Pension Funds

Howe brought these arguments about demographics, productivity, and a looming social crisis together as the 'burden of pensions' in May 1981, when he warned the National Association of Pension Funds (NAPF) that the pensions system was becoming 'unsustainable'.[72] Demographic change, the Chancellor claimed, placed a limit on how far society could protect pensioners from 'economic forces beyond their control'. With the proportion of pensioners having risen from 13.5 per cent in 1951 to about 17.5 per cent in 1982 and 'set to rise a little further', governments needed to be 'sure that those who are of working age will not have to bear an unsustainable burden'. This was a matter of democratic consent as well as economics: public spending on pensions, Howe claimed, had risen over 60 per cent in real terms since 1971 and there was 'a real risk that the working population may come to question the justice of further increases in this burden'.

Howe claimed that Britain's underperforming economy and unrealistic expectations had worsened this demographic problem. The 1975 *Better Pensions* White Paper had envisaged a 'transfer of income ... from the economically active sector of the community to those who have retired' but claimed that the cost would 'be far outweighed by the improvement in living standards generally resulting from economic growth'. Such growth had not materialised. Worse still, he argued, commitments to indexation prevented society offsetting some of its burden. Breaking the BSP's link with earnings was thus one step towards sustainability, but other forms of indexation were storing up worrying burdens in the longer term. Howe emphasised that occupational pensions would start to add to the taxpayer burden, as the 1975 settlement promised to protect against inflation the 'guaranteed minimum pension' of contracted-out occupational scheme members up to the same level as those who remained contracted in. Over time this cost could become significant; Howe predicted that 'a third to a half, or even higher', of a worker's occupational pension could end up being inflation-proofed by the state. Howe insisted he was not questioning the 'partnership between the state and the pensions industry' but noted that, although SERPS would reduce disparities between the protection available to public and private sector employees (but not the self-employed), it did so at an 'enormous cost to the Exchequer'.[73] Ideally, economic growth would absorb this accelerating expenditure, but in Howe's view a return to the higher growth rates of the 1950s and 1960s could not be guaranteed. His concern was that the 1975 Act had 'locked [society] into providing benefits without having made the economic adjustments necessary to sustain them'.

Crucially, in his NAPF speech Howe extended the concept of the burden of pensions to the private sector:

> We must ask also if private employers are not offering too generous pensions, in the sense that the real resources needed to meet them are placing too heavy a burden on the companies concerned. Is two-thirds of a final salary after 40 years too ambitious a target, when looked at from the point of view of competing demands on my resources?

The pension contributions necessary to sustain the benefits promised could, Howe argued, depress corporate profitability and investment, which were in turn needed to ensure the revenue growth required by the state system. This would have damaging impacts on the British economy. Pension funds needed to be more innovative in finding opportunities in Britain, but the *availability* of finance was not what limited investment in British businesses. Instead, it was the 'low real rate of return' that made investment unattractive.[74] Improved profits would thus be needed to reinvigorate investment in British industry, and, from this perspective, taking a realistic view of pensions promises was important for the success of pension funds themselves, which, despite foreign investment, were still heavily invested in Britain. The Chancellor had drawn together several arguments, then, to prophesy a formidable future pensions 'burden'. Like Sherman, Howe connected this burden with a looming conflict between the generations. He warned that, if the working population was required 'to provide more for the retired population than they are prepared to tolerate', then, 'in the far-from-distant future, expenditure on pensions could well provoke serious tensions'.

Howe also began to connect the 'burden' with arguments about the massive growth of institutional funds needed to fund occupational pensions in the future. Such funds might struggle to find assets and opportunities to match their promises, but the main economic risk was that they reduced opportunities for individual investors.[75] Those individuals brought the direct ownership associated with the more active role for shareholders that Howe believed necessary to restore higher returns. Framed more positively for this audience, Howe argued that, if they were to meet their future obligations, pension funds had to become more active shareholders and press for moderate pay settlements or corporate restructures in pursuit of increased profits. The looming burden was thus not just a demographic time bomb or looming social crisis. The increasing volume of resources devoted to pensions risked starting an economic feedback loop in which changes to capital markets made it harder to obtain the growth needed to ease their burden. Howe stressed that he was not criticising the funds themselves but admitted that he was 'not persuaded that it is necessarily right to leave things as they are'.[76]

Howe's speech generated a good deal of press interest.[77] It was also shortly followed by academic projections that SERPS would cost much more than hitherto realised.[78] It is likely that Howe knew of Richard

162   *The first term*

Hemming and John Kay's work at the Institute for Fiscal Studies (IFS) on the costs of the present pension system and that he was aware of John Ermisch's demographic projections on which their appraisal of the future costs of SERPS was based.[79] We should not overstate their influence, however. Howe's speech was primarily a product of mounting political pressure for higher pensions: Sir Bernard Scott's report on public sector pensions had suggested that the solution to the inequities between public and private provision was to extend index linking to the latter, for example. Nor was it just academics who were concerned with the mounting expenditure being mooted: Treasury civil servants had started to think about how to project the share of resources consumed by pensioners in the long run, and some of the figures in Howe's speech come from their briefing notes.[80]

Quantifying the burden

The origins of Howe's speech were less important, though, than the political sanction it gave to civil servants and ministers over the next two years. Howe had highlighted the long-term cost of pensions before two statutory reviews of the existing system were due from the Government Actuary's Department (GAD). The first of these, a review of the National Insurance rebates given to employers and employees who contracted out of SERPS, would eventually result in a Cabinet compromise in early 1982 that did little to change the overall picture.[81] The second was the first quinquennial review (QR) of SERPS mandated by the 1975 Act, and it was this technical review of the scheme's liabilities that gave civil servants and politicians the opportunity to quantify the 'burden' that pensions might place on Britain's future society and economy. In the process, that 'burden' was defined more precisely, but it also became clear that its existence was sensitive to the economic assumptions used and depended on which parts of the pensions system were included.

This process of quantification began two months after Howe's NAPF speech, when Treasury officials prepared a briefing on pensions issues ahead of the GAD starting work on the QR. The briefing advised ministers that it seemed likely that 'the review will show a substantial increase in the contributions needed to finance [SERPS]'.[82] The timing of this increase was unclear, but joint contributions for Class I employers might rise from 17.95 per cent in 1981/82 to 26 per cent in 2028/29. The QR would simply state the cost of SERPS, however. The government would need to plan its response separately. From their perspective, Treasury officials suggested that the likely increases in contributions already revealed 'the dichotomy between the expectations raised by the new pension scheme and the likely

Pensions 'ratchet' and 'burden' 163

ability of the economy to sustain them'. The transfer of resources between working and retired populations had been clear when SERPS was introduced, they argued, but a gloomier economic outlook now raised fundamental questions about its economic implications, whether the working population could or would be 'willing to afford, pension provisions on this scale', and whether the government should consider ways to 'reduce the cost of future pension provisions'.[83] As in Howe's speech to the NAPF, Treasury officials also predicted that occupational funds would also face future difficulties with a lower rate of return and worried that this too could have (indirect) consequences for the public finances.[84]

Howe, Jenkin, and their respective teams met to discuss these issues in July 1981. Jenkin and the DHSS questioned the Treasury's alarming projections: '[W]hile it would be right to sound warnings against adding new burdens, it was not necessarily the case that existing provisions represented an unmanageable burden.'[85] Jenkin pointed out that Ermisch's research suggested that the bulk of the rise would take place only from 2010 onwards. Resources that far out were difficult to predict, and in any case the United Kingdom's ratio of pensions to earnings 'was low by international standards'. An eight percentage point increase in contributions over an extended period looked relatively benign compared with the seven point increase seen over the last six years alone. Even before detailed work had taken place, then, there was no consensus that pensions promises already made would become an intolerable 'burden'. Nevertheless, the departments agreed that if the QR showed increasing costs after 2000 then the government should signal that changes to SERPS might be needed without arousing unnecessary fear about its immediate intentions. In the meantime, a joint working group should begin preparatory work to support the government's response.

In the event, timelines slipped, and the Treasury's focus did not return to the 'burden' until February 1982, when George Monger, the undersecretary now leading the Treasury's Social Services Group, produced some preliminary estimates for the Chancellor.[86] These seemed to suggest that the 'burden' of SERPS might be less worrisome than thought. Monger's figures suggested that, if flat rate benefits rose as quickly as earnings, then the overall National Insurance contribution (17 per cent in 1981) would need to rise to 18 or 19 per cent by 2005 and to 23 to 25 per cent by 2025, when the bulk of the demographic and SERPS maturity effects kicked in. If benefits were to rise only in line with prices then contributions should remain the same in percentage terms, and perhaps even fall. The prospect of SERPS placing an unbearable future burden on the economy could thus be significantly mitigated provided the government was willing to link benefit values to prices only. Monger recognised that this might be politically difficult in the long term, as the gap between earnings and benefits widened, and so he

164   *The first term*

suggested an array of other changes that might be considered to achieve the same ends. The calculation period for SERPS benefits, for example, could be extended from the 20 best years of earnings to 30 or even 40 years, or the scheme could made less generous to widows. In either case, the 'burden' produced by SERPS increasingly looked like one that could be managed and/or reduced with rule changes.

Monger's memorandum sparked attempts to push for a much wider review of the 'burden' beyond SERPS. Monger was not keen on a 'general review of the kind which so often leads to considerable work which Ministers then ignore'. Other Treasury officials, however, thought that there was a case for looking at the combined long-term effects of both SERPS and occupational schemes maturing. Monger's predecessor, Peter Kemp, and his deputy pressed for the joint Treasury/DHSS working group on the QR to undertake 'more exhaustive calculations about the likely burden of pensions'. Kemp, who now headed the Treasury's policy coordination unit, cited the Chancellor's NAPF speech as proof of ministerial interest and claimed that it was a major matter of public importance to know the 'point in time at which the working population decide that enough is enough and rebel against giving up their current living standards in order to provide for better living standards than would otherwise be the case for the retired'. Under continued pressure, Monger resisted a general review but conceded that the joint working group should look at what data on occupational schemes was available.[87] Over the next month, though, it became clear that this kind of data could be produced, combined with the QR's data on SERPS, and then set alongside expected spending on supplementary benefits and forecasts for macroeconomic indicators (such as GDP) to measure a total 'burden'.[88] Somewhat against the wishes of its lead civil servant, then, the Burden of Pensions Working Group (BOPWG) was formed, with a remit to report its findings into the existing joint working group.[89]

The BOPWG's efforts soon revealed how complex and uncertain future gazing could be. The weight of the future pensions 'burden' greatly depended on the time horizon and macroeconomic assumptions used.[90] The civil servants directly involved were keen to match the latter as closely as possible to those underpinning the QR but found themselves pressured into modelling alternative scenarios. For example, Kemp persuaded Dianna Seammen, the Treasury economist on the group, to send the GAD a new set of economic scenarios. This would expand the scope of the exercise still further, but Kemp's arguments for doing so show the political impetus behind efforts to quantify the burden and the link between measuring a problem and policy change:

> As you know, many people (including the Chancellor in a speech last year to the National Association of Pension Funds) think that this may be the great unexploded time bomb for the future, and it must be right to have a shot at

trying to measure it; I did not entirely go along with the view that is expressed by some people that this is a subject which no one will dare tackle, and that therefore time is wasted – if the bomb is large enough and the ticking frightening enough, there could be just a chance that something might be done.

The danger was greater in some scenarios than others, but many of the assumptions used to model these alternatives turned out to be incompatible with each other when stretched over the long time frames involved. The resulting haggling between departments meant that the basic assumptions sent to GAD in June 1982 were still being revised in December, and the group's work slipped into 1983.

Meanwhile, conflicting signals about the reality or otherwise of the 'burden of pensions' were coming from other sources. In July 1982 Monger briefed the Chancellor that the quinquennial review of SERPS was ready for publication, that its analysis was broadly in line with those presented previously, and that GAD's 'figures do not demonstrate any clear-cut conclusion that the burden of pensions will become intolerable for the working population'.[91] GAD's review of SERPS, which included forecasts for the National Insurance Fund, showed no significant increase in NI rates until the next century. After that, the increase 'would not be great', and even in the worst-case scenario would not be much beyond the 4.5 per cent seen since 1978 and could be mitigated by linking benefits to prices only.[92] Of course, Monger conceded, 'the way that the employed population regard such an increase will depend on general economic circumstances. If economic growth is low, any significant increase would come to appear a burden.' For now, though, he advised that the Chancellor agree a common line with Fowler (who had replaced Jenkin at DHSS) that neither would comment on the QR's substance and instead await public consultation and the joint working group's report.[93]

But, just as Howe was acting on this advice, Monger received more concerning news. The Government Actuary, Colin Stewart, had decided to pre-empt work for the BOPWG with his own study of the combined burden of pensions. 'If the pensions scene has to be described in two words, those words would be alarm and discord,' Stewart wrote.[94] He predicted that contributions to state and occupational schemes would eventually represent 28.75 per cent of total wages and salaries compared with 20.25 per cent in 1985/86. Alternatively, if looked at from the point of view of benefits (so that a rate of return could be factored in), pensions expenditure would rise from 16.75 per cent of total wages and salaries in 1985/86 to 31.75 per cent over the coming 50 years. 'Does this represent a greater allocation of resources to the retired members of the population than will ultimately be feasible?' Stewart wondered. It was possible that future economic growth would render such increases palatable, but 'the thought has been growing

166   *The first term*

that, as a nation, we have set our sights too high in holding out the hope of providing pensions of two-thirds of final salary for all, fully inflation-proofed, and that the difficulties already being faced by funded schemes is an early manifestation of further difficulties to come'. Stewart's paper was shared internally prior to publication, and Treasury officials began to draw out his worrying conclusion that the scale of investments needed for occupational schemes might be impossible given the number of opportunities and the funds' traditional bias towards domestic investment.

Arguments for system change and the political reception of the BOPWG's findings

Attempts to quantify the 'burden of pensions' gradually took on greater significance as Treasury ministers and their advisers started to countenance alternatives to the 1975 settlement. One early advocate of reform was Peter Cropper, who had supported the Conservative opposition's work on wider ownership before following Howe into the Treasury as a special adviser. In June 1979 Cropper wrote to Howe relaying a discussion at the Centre for Policy Studies about pensions, where, he reported, Nigel Vinson and Alfred Sherman were convinced that disparities between the inflation protection available to public sector employees, occupational scheme members, and the self-employed could not be resolved within Britain's existing system. It was financially 'impossible', they thought, for employers to replicate the inflation protection of public schemes but it was politically impossible to remove it from the latter. Having reached this impasse, they concluded that the 1975 Act had 'already lost its validity' and should be replaced with a substantially increased and inflation-proofed basic state pension and an additional layer left entirely to 'personal decision' and provided via 'private institutions with no State inflation guarantee of any sort'. In this system, existing funds would be 'closed down and the capital disbursed'. The CPS believed, Cropper reported, that the government had to choose between making a 'new start' along these lines or 'brush the problem under the carpet for a few years on the grounds that another major upheaval in pensions is unthinkable'.[95]

In the short term the Chancellor chose the latter, but Cropper continued to express hostility towards institutional life and pension funds, drafting speeches for Howe that argued that their tax privileges had led to shares 'rushing like lemmings out of private hands' and in effect allowed Labour to pursue 'collectivist intentions by impeccable market methods'.[96] The British economy was said to be suffering from the funds' cautious investment approaches and unsustainable defined benefit ('final salary') schemes

Pensions 'ratchet' and 'burden' 167

that used inter-generational redistribution to hide their true cost. Cropper's solution – which he proposed in July 1981 – was to replace occupational schemes' final salary promises and cross-subsidisation with personal investment holdings.[97] At this stage, Treasury officials roundly criticised the plan as unlikely to achieve its aim of wider ownership. Tellingly, though, Nigel Lawson (Financial Secretary at the time) supported measures that would put a 'much-needed curb on the growth of occupational pensions', and Howe circulated Cropper's paper as a 'thought provoking insight' for his discussions with Jenkin.[98] As we will see, this attack on institutional ownership would be a key driver of the personal pensions proposals that were developed in the second term, which are discussed in detail in Chapter Five.

Cropper left government later in 1981 to lead the Conservative Research Department. Thatcher asked him to link up the CRD and Centre for Policy Studies and produce options that might be of interest for the 1983 manifesto. He now placed pension reforms in a wider programme that sought the 'Extension of Choice in the Market Economy' and recommended the party consider 'how market influences may be brought to bear more swiftly in education (vouchers), universities (student loans), health (private health insurance), and pensions (switch from funded collective schemes to individual provision)'.[99] By late 1982 Howe was himself open to the idea of reform. In his submission to the Prime Minister's stocktaking review of her first term, he included pension system reform among his future aims, listing 'the pensions system, including in particular transferability of pension rights, solvency of pension funds and reconciling both with the need to ensure that undue burdens are not placed on future generations'.[100] Indeed, in a reflection of how far things had developed since 1979, he urged the Prime Minister not to make commitments that would prevent him changing the life assurance and pension industry's tax reliefs: the government should 'retain freedom to act in both areas, but not in any way to proclaim our intentions'.[101]

This ministerial interest in system reform began to impact the BOPWG's analysis. In October 1982 Seammen met with the Financial Secretary, Nicholas Ridley, who made it clear that he saw the group's work as a stepping stone to pursue his own aims. Ridley, Seammen reported, wanted to 'make participation in occupational schemes truly voluntary' (by modifying or eliminating their favourable tax treatment) and 'ensure that individuals were able to get their hands on their savings rather than allowing them to remain in the anonymous ownership of the pension funds themselves'. He was said to regard these funds as generally incompetent investors, unwilling to take entrepreneurial risks, and felt that the resources necessary to finance occupational schemes would eventually place too great a strain on businesses.[102] Over the Christmas holidays Ridley outlined a reform package along these lines. Aiming to restrict compulsion to a minimum safety net, he proposed raising the basic state pension to the level of supplementary benefit and removing the tax-free status of occupational pension contributions to pay for this. Above that minimum, contributions to SERPS or occupational pensions would be voluntary, with the latter run as individualised defined contribution ('money purchase') schemes. This would give more 'freedom to people to deal with their own money' but also 'enable us to dismantle the pension funds over time'.[103]

The most radical element of Ridley's scheme did not actually come from him, though. Invited to comment on Ridley's plans, Monger told his Treasury team that he was 'tempted to use this opportunity to float some of our ideas'.[104] In particular, he suggested that the abolition of SERPS might align with Ridley's objective to reduce the state's involvement to providing a minimum and generate the savings needed to raise the basic state pension over time. He explained to Ridley that an additional reason to do so was that there was concern that SERPS would become a significant part of future state expenditure (albeit noting that this could sometimes be exaggerated). It would be throwing out the hard-won pensions consensus of the late 1970s, however, and would probably face considerable opposition. Monger was careful to state that he was not himself suggesting abolition but, rather, pointing out that this would be a way to achieve Ridley's objectives. Nevertheless, his advice usefully illustrates the role civil servants could play in policy change by linking ministers' ideological visions with options that might also be seen as necessary or desirable for other reasons.[105]

It was in this context, then, that the BOPWG finally produced projections for the combined future costs of SERPS and occupational schemes just months before the 1983 election. The next step was to compare these combined costs with the future economy's performance to measure the 'burden'. Although these calculations were intended to be undertaken by the BOPWG itself, the Treasury pre-empted its estimates, partly out of frustration with DHSS economists. Stephanie Holmans led this work within the Treasury's Public Services Economic Division. Holmans was initially sceptical about whether the data justified the 'burden' framing. The historical trend suggested that the combined resources devoted to state and occupational pensions as a percentage of GDP over the next 45 years would change less rapidly than it had since 1951. It was also difficult objectively to say at what point the share of national income could be deemed 'worrying'.[106] Nevertheless, Holmans was the main author of the paper her division tabled at the Treasury's Policy Co-ordinating Committee (PCC) in May 1983 alongside a wider review of policy developments. This gave ministers and senior officials their first detailed empirical view of the 'the future burden of pensions'.[107]

The paper's opening paragraph set out what was at stake in arresting terms:

> The relative income of pensioners will rise significantly in the future as the State Earnings Related Pension Scheme (SERPS) and occupational pension schemes mature. The numbers of pensioners will also increase, especially after the turn of the century. A higher proportion of national income will therefore be used by the retired population, with correspondingly less for other uses including investment, public services, and consumption by the working age population and their families.

Holmans reported that the BOPWG (whose preliminary figures she used) expected that the number of pensioners would remain around 9.5 million between 1985/86 and 2004/05, but would increase thereafter to reach 11.5 million by 2025/26 as a consequence of baby boomer retirement. The BOPWG had projected a high annual economic growth scenario of 2 per cent and a low growth scenario of 0.5 per cent.[108] The real rate of return was assumed to be 3.5 per cent in the high-growth case and 1 per cent in low growth. On these assumptions, Holmans' basic conclusion for the PCC was that pension payments would rise from 9.1 per cent of GDP in 1981/82 to 14 per cent in 2025/26 under a high-growth scenario. They would climb to 16.1 per cent, however, if growth was low. Crucially, only a small part of this increase was due to demography.[109] Instead, the combination of low growth and the generosity of the fully mature state and defined benefit occupational schemes would be the main drivers of pensions' greater command over resources.

There would be change in the distribution of society's resources, then. But would it be sustainable? Holmans argued it might be. In the previous 30 years total pension payments as a percentage of GDP had risen by 4.7 points. The rises predicted for the next 40 years were therefore broadly in line with that seen previously (at 4.4 or 5.9) and over a longer period. Nonetheless, the economic effects of such a rise would depend on how the additional expenditure was funded and how workers experienced this change. Working generations might react to increased contributions by seeking higher wages, which would mean that the transfer of resources to pensioners ultimately came at the expense of corporate capital investment and profitability. Greater contributions flowing into occupational funds could offset this somewhat, but there was a danger that the funds would not be able to find enough UK opportunities to invest in, leaving them to invest abroad or simply contract back in to SERPS – a scheme that did nothing for investment.

The social consequences of the 'pension burden' were similarly dependent on the economic climate, in Holmans' view. Barbara Castle's original *Better Pensions* White Paper had recognised that SERPS involved a transfer of resources between generations but argued that the working

170   *The first term*

population was less likely to resent higher contributions in an economy experiencing healthy growth. But in either of the BOPWG's forecast scenarios, Holmans argued, the real growth of pensioners' incomes was likely to outrun the growth in the working population's average earnings.[110] Pensioners' increasing claim over resources would on average depress the working population's real annual gains by 0.06 percentage points under high-growth conditions and 0.11 under the low-growth scenario. 'On the face of it,' Holmans assessed, 'these impacts are small enough to be manageable. But this is a matter of judgement.' It could instead be argued that, in low-growth conditions, the pressure on wages would be severe enough that a 'shift in income which absorbed some 15 or 20 per cent of the rate of growth of income of the working age population could be unmanageable'. This would be especially so if they became 'aware that pensioners were becoming relatively better off'.[111]

Whether or not the combined burden was 'unbearable', Holmans suggested that adjustments to SERPS were the way to lighten it. SERPS was 'in some respects plainly very generous', her paper read, and there seemed enough academic criticism of earnings-related pensions to justify a rethink. Earnings-related state-supported schemes were very common in OECD nations, however, she warned, and the 'political tide behind SERPS [was] formidable'.[112] Facing this barrier to reform, the paper suggested that the government might instead focus its efforts on increasing the total resources available for consumption in later years; this should happen automatically, to some extent, via funded schemes' investments, but there was a limit to how far companies investing indirectly in each other's stocks actually increased the physical investment necessary for productivity gains, and SERPS contributed nothing to this process. Finally, Holmans suggested that the working population might become more accepting of rising contributions if they believed they were saving for their own retirement. Notional funding of unfunded schemes was one option here, but it had led to some unrealistic expectations when it had been tried previously. Holmans' paper was – by design – longer on diagnosis than on solutions, but it nonetheless marked a key moment in the discovery of a problem large enough that it could justify the political risks of disturbing the consensus reached in the mid-1970s.

The CPRS and the abolition of SERPS

By the spring of 1983, then, not only had Howe's 'burden' of pensions been quantified but it had also morphed from a problem of demography and future expense into a more specific (if somewhat ethereal) problem of SERPS

Pensions 'ratchet' and 'burden'

and occupational schemes' *designs* and the implication of these for future economic growth and capital ownership. In the process, the BOPWG had created the evidence that some could now use to suggest that radical change was required. The clearest expressions of this were a pair of CPRS reports presented to Thatcher in April 1983. One report detailed specific proposals for personal pensions, discussed in Chapter Five, but the other was a wider scene-setting paper that reviewed Britain's pension system against the aims of affordability, the values and behaviours it encouraged, the inequities it gave rise to, and its economic impacts.[113]

On affordability, the CPRS's conclusions followed the less optimistic assessments discussed above. Using BOPWG data, the paper claimed that Britain's pension system could lead to an unsustainable transfer of resources between the working and retired populations. In a low-growth scenario, the CPRS claimed this could lead to social tension and inflationary pay demands from the working population. Although pensioners were currently seen as 'one of the most deserving sections of the community', this might not remain the case once the burden became clear. Even though these problems were distant, the CPRS argued, 'the Government needs to act now to avert future problems'.[114]

The CPRS paper was notable, though, because it went beyond these warnings and started to integrate the BOPWG's findings with other criticisms and frame the pension burden as one of several reasons to limit the role of the state. SERPS was 'not a cost-effective way' of reducing pensioners' reliance on means-tested supplementary benefits, it argued. The scheme would do little to alleviate pensioner poverty over the next 20 years as entitlements built up, but its 'universal' rather than 'selective' principles meant that it would eventually devote most of its resources to providing benefits well above the supplementary benefit level. SERPS's relationship with occupational schemes also meant that large amounts of taxpayer money would be spent on contracted-out schemes – either through state-backed inflation proofing of the guaranteed minimum pension or because contracted-out members with a GMP below their full SERPS entitlements could draw upon the state scheme. The CPRS was similarly critical of the affordability of occupational schemes that relied on the system's long-running inequities. Occupational schemes, it argued, were never likely to remedy inequities between members (chiefly disadvantaging early leavers), because excessively generous final salary accrual promises required this cross-subsidisation.

Beyond affordability, present arrangements also did little for the 'objectives of promoting individual liberty and self-reliance'. The architects of SERPS had been right to recognise the deficiencies of occupational pensions, the paper argued, but 'the extension of state involvement into earnings-related pensions [was] difficult to reconcile with an aim of encouraging individuals to be more self-reliant when providing for their retirement' and gave 'little weight to personal freedom of choice'. Compulsory earnings-related pensions were 'paternalist' because they forced everyone to save in essentially the same way, whether through occupational or state variants. Private markets, on the other hand, were 'potentially better placed to cater for a wide variety of retirement plans – including irregular retirement saving or the building up of personal assets (including housing) with a view to subsequent encashment.'[115]

Nor, in the CPRS's view, did the present system support a dynamic economy. The paper alleged that occupational schemes discouraged job mobility (via discrimination against early leavers) and did little to educate the population about the connection between the economy's performance and their own retirement. The latter led to a 'general ignorance of individuals of their pension rights and pension costs' that made reform difficult. Moreover, the tax privileges for pension funds 'distort[ed] financial markets by providing unequal treatment to different channels of saving'. Like Ridley, the CPRS claimed this resulted in clogged capital markets, whereas equal treatment of savings and new products would 'widen choice and stimulate competition between, and thus innovation by, the various intermediaries', which could assist groups underserved at present.

The CPRS suggested that the alternative was to 'tackle the deficiencies of (non-state) pension arrangements directly' and focus the state's role on 'preventing poverty in old age'. Individuals would bear 'more responsibility for pension provision above the poverty level'. To bring these new arrangements into being, it advised that ministers 'consider the case for complete abolition of the earnings-related scheme', albeit recognising the 'very large' political difficulties. Even if they rejected abolition, the paper argued that ministers should consider ways of 'reducing the earnings-related element' of SERPS. Either route to reform could be made politically palatable by improving present-day minimum levels of entitlement to 'buttress the state's role in preventing poverty in old age'. Similar reform would be needed in occupational schemes. The paper argued that cuts to final salary promises should enable occupational pension schemes to eliminate the inequities that hindered job mobility and left some very exposed to inflation, while in the long run further reforms should aim to encourage new ways of retirement saving.

The CPRS recognised that a powerful political consensus and vocal interest groups weighed against most of the ideas it thought ministers should consider. Yet the looming burden of pensions provided a counterargument in favour of action. 'A major part of the background for decision is the risk of an excessive burden of pensions in the longer term,' the paper argued. The 'temptation' to ignore this would be great, but 'should be resisted, if it is not to become harder to deal with'. Regardless of whether ministers could countenance radical reforms, the CPRS thought 'the risk of an excessive burden of pensions in the long term' justified ministers examining 'ways of limiting, if not reducing, both state and non-state pension entitlements in ways which are consistent with their objectives'.[116]

The 'burden of pensions' had therefore now become integrated within a wider case for reform. Alongside objections to the paternalism of existing arrangements and their inequities, the future affordability and burden of pensions were seen as both a weakness of the system and a reason to take forward policy options that aligned with the government's objectives of widening freedom, fostering self-reliance, and bringing about a dynamic economy despite the political difficulty of doing so. For the Prime Minister, though, the balance between political risk and radical reform did not yet favour the latter. Even though the paper was only intended to survey the issues, such controversial conclusions were badly timed just before a general election. The leak and fallout of the CPRS's earlier report on health and education privatisation had already made Thatcher wary of its provocative horizon scanning, and she was decidedly unimpressed. On the opening page, she wrote:

> This paper indicates that its authors have <u>no idea</u> how to tackle a problem of this kind. It recommends policies as far apart as A and Z. In politics you can only at most go from about A-D at a time. This review ... would be seen to be absolutely disastrous if it were to go any further. I <u>reject</u> it.[117]

The Prime Minister was clearly concerned about leaks and ordered all copies to be recalled. Shortly after the election she disbanded the CPRS. Yet its arguments for change and the connections it made between the burden of pensions and neoliberal visions of reform did not go away. Indeed, the next two chapters reveal how the Prime Minister and her Cabinet came to support plans that were just as radical as those she emphatically rejected in April 1983.

Conclusion

Heading to the polls in June 1983, voters had little sense of the pension reforms that would be enacted by the government they were about to re-elect. In the weeks beforehand, rumours had circulated that more radical proposals might make it into the 1983 Conservative manifesto, but when it was published *The Challenge of Our Times* merely recommitted the party to protecting pensioners against price rises and investigating how injustices experienced by those who changed jobs might be lessened.[118] Labour warned that a 'hidden manifesto' lay behind the government's

174   *The first term*

pledges but went no further than suggesting that ministers secretly planned
to sever the link between pensions and the cost of living.[119] Indeed, the
Prime Minister appeared to rule out major structural change. During the
campaign Thatcher wrote to Labour's spokesman on social services, John
Brynmor, and flatly denied that there were any plans to change SERPS, a
system that, she reminded him, had been 'brought to the Statute Book with
the full support of Conservative members'.[120] She neglected to mention that
just a month before calling the election her government's internal think
tank had suggested changes to SERPS and mooted its abolition.[121] As we
have seen, Thatcher angrily rejected that paper as politically naive, but this
chapter has shown that many within or working for her government were
already contemplating radical reform.

What do these developments tell us about the Thatcher government and
the neoliberal vision of pensions in the first term? In some respects, her government had already broken with the system agreed in 1975 while retaining
its architecture. As we will see in Chapter Eight, the decision to break the
link between earnings and the basic state pension and uprate on a historical
basis significantly reduced the value of the basic state pension over time. In
doing so, it undermined one of aims of the consensus reached in 1975 (the
improvement of benefits to eliminate pensioner poverty). The effect was to
reduce the redistribution between generations to which members of the neoliberal thought collective objected and take the first step towards a system
that required individuals to invest in assets if they wished to share in the
nation's economic growth during their retirement. Political actors similarly
understood their actions in ways that had much in common with the neoliberal project: changes to indexation were thought of as undoing a 'ratchet'
that extended the welfare state but were also seen as necessary to achieve
price stability and the smaller state they associated with economic growth.
This interrelation of neoliberal arguments in favour of change is an under-
appreciated aspect of the role of neoliberal ideas in government, but the first
Thatcher administration also suggests that historians must pay closer attention to incremental change *within* the broad parameters of the existing system to understand policy change and the implementation of neoliberalism.

What the history of 1979 to 1983 shows, however, is that this incremental change was not delivered wholly according to plan. In fact, it was often
driven by policy actors with a significantly more radical vision of change
who found themselves constrained by political realities. Prior pledges
played an important role in this: the risk of being seen to break promises
limited the possible areas of change, not least because this argument could
be made by those sceptical of change within Cabinet without having to
confront the proposals directly. Advocates of reform were – in this case,
at least – more interested in securing subsequent freedom for manoeuvre

by committing colleagues not to make or renew pledges than they were in securing an explicit mandate for change. Yet there was also a more general sense in which the perception of a policy consensus supported by powerful stakeholders gave ministers reason for caution. In nearly every paper on the 'burden of pensions', the political difficulties of change were highlighted and forced the focus onto less radical options. The concept of consensus was therefore very real within the policymaking process and should prompt us to pay greater attention to how this constraint was escaped in Thatcher's second term.

Finally, the developments of Thatcher's first term suggest that we need to think about the relationship between the Thatcher project and neoliberalism as including a process of definition and discovery rather than straightforward implementation of a pre-formed programme. The 'burden of pensions' – as we have seen – had links with the neoliberal thought collective's view of the irresponsible extension of the welfare state and of intergenerational cross-subsidies. Initially applied to justify cuts to immediate spending, the concept was redefined, first to incorporate the effects of demographic projections, but later to describe the overall resources a society used for old age income replacement. Political interest in this was then used to justify technical investigations and expand their scope when the opportunity arose. This technical work further defined the policy problem to measure it. The resulting discovery of the size of the pensions 'burden' then quickly fed back into political agendas, offering a reason to overcome the status quo and a problem for which actors could pose favoured solutions.

Three points are worth further emphasis. First, the process from discovery to solutions was characterised initially by greater precision – as civil servants had to tie down parameters – but also by more uncertainty. The existence of a 'burden' was readily acknowledged to be dependent on assumptions and the time horizon or range of provision included. Yet, as the findings made their way into political briefings, such nuances were mostly lost. Second, although Thatcher's sponsorship or veto could at times prove decisive, those driving this discovery process were often ministers, special advisers, and civil servants. As well as departmental viewpoints, the latter anticipated the perspective of their political leadership in suggesting ideas, showing why proposed plans would not achieve these ends, or highlighting the political and practical constraints. In that sense, a much wider cast of actors shaped the particular neoliberal vision for pensions that emerged. Third, a neoliberal vision of pensions was not straightforwardly adopted or implemented (partially or otherwise). Instead, it gradually built up through the definition of problems and the matching of solutions to these; where neoliberal visions of pensions and neoliberal political economy exercised most influence was in connecting threads together (by showing, for example, that the 'burden'

176   *The first term*

was not just an affordability problem but a threat to investment and future economic growth) and by selecting solutions that met wider aims (increasing individual choice and favouring life cycle investment over redistribution). Over the next two chapters we will see these solutions be argued for, and eventually partly overcome, the counterweight of interests and political risk that kept them in Whitehall in the first term, and out of election manifestos at its start and end.

Notes

1 Conservative Central Office (hereafter CCO), *The Right Approach: A Statement of Conservative Aims* (London: CCO, 1975), p. 57.
2 Social Security Act 1975, Part IV, Section 124.
3 The National Archives (hereafter TNA): CAB 128/65/12, Cabinet Conclusions, 15 Mar 1979. Clawing back the shortfall cost £80 million.
4 HC Debs, 28 March 1979, vol. 965, cols. 481–82. Replying to Thatcher's motion, he announced that the Chancellor of the Exchequer would factor 1978's shortfall into 1979's uprating, resulting in increases of between £2.50 per week for single pensioners and £4 for married couples.
5 HC Debs, 29 March 1979, vol. 965, col. 619.
6 CCO, *1979 Conservative Party General Election Manifesto* (London: CCO, 1979).
7 Margaret Thatcher Archive (hereafter MTA): Margaret Thatcher, Speech to Conservatives in Gravesend, 17 April 1979.
8 His Majesty's Treasury, Private Office records (hereafter HMT): PO-CH-GH-00169 Part A, E. P. Kemp to Mr Bailey/Chief Secretary, 'Social Security', 11 May 1979.
9 Within the Treasury's Social Services Group, its under-secretary, Peter Kemp, concluded that, although it was a political decision, Hansard showed that there was no discrete commitment to make good the shortfall and recommended Treasury ministers oppose any additional uprating. For the full debate, see HMT: PO-CH-GH-00169 Part A: E. P. Kemp to Bailey/Chief Secretary, 'Social Security', 11 May 1979; A. M. Bailey to Chief Secretary, 'Social Security', 11 May 1979; A. M. Whit to Miss Whalley/Mr Kemp/Chancellor, 'Social Security Uprating', 16 May 1979; E. P. Kemp to Chancellor, 'Meeting with Mr Patrick Jenkin – Thursday 17 May 4 30 PM Social Security Uprating', 16 May 1979.
10 HMT: PO-CH-GH-00169 Part A, 'Note of a Meeting Held by the Chancellor of the Exchequer at H. M. Treasury on Thursday 17 May 1979'. The saving would be achieved by accounting for the shortfall via an additional margin on the Treasury's new forecast rather than applying the new forecast to an already corrected pension rate.
11 TNA: CAB 129/206/9, 'Uprating of Social Security Benefits: Memorandum by the Secretary of State for Social Services', 21 May 1979; CAB 128/66, Cabinet

Conclusions, Restricted Annex Minutes, 24 May 1979; Howe announced the changes during his 12 June 1979 budget speech.

12 TNA: CAB 128/67, Cabinet Conclusions, Restricted Annex, 24 January 1980. The Chancellor had asked his adviser, Adam Ridley, to check if the manifesto promised price protection. Ridley replied that it was the PM's speeches that made the promise whereas the manifesto commitments were 'not absolutely affirmative': HMT: PO-CH-GH-0041 Part A, A. Ridley to Chancellor of the Exchequer, 'Election Pledges on Pension Uprating and Health Charges', 7 January 1980.

13 Figures from TNA: PREM 19/1004, 'Pensions Issues and Policies: A Paper by the CPRS', April 1983.

14 HMT: PO-CH-GH-00169 Part A, E. P. Kemp to Bailey/Chief Secretary, 'Social Security', 11 May 1979.

15 HMT: PO-CH-GH-00170 Part A, Nigel Lawson to Chief Secretary, 'Social Security Bill', 23 May 1979.

16 HMT: PO-CH-GH-00169 Part B, E. P. Kemp to Pole, 'Social Security – The "Ratchet"', 21 May 1979; HMT: PO-CH-GH-00169 Part A, E. P. Kemp to Chancellor of the Exchequer, 'Meeting with Mr Patrick Jenkin – Thursday 17 May 4 30 PM Social Security Uprating', 16 May 1979. A CPRS memo also suggested breaking the link was a key expenditure reduction: HMT: PO-CH-GH-0093 Part A: CPRS, 'The Economy of the United Kingdom – Problems, Constraints, Opportunities', 4 May 1979.

17 HMT: PO-CH-GH-00169 Part A, 'Note of a Meeting Held by the Chancellor of the Exchequer at H. M. Treasury on Thursday 17 May', 17 May 1979.

18 Ibid.

19 TNA: CAB 134, H (79)7, Home and Social Affairs Committee, 'Social Security Bill', 19 May 1979.

20 TNA: CAB 129/206/9, 'Uprating of Social Security Benefits: Memorandum by the Secretary of State for Social Services', 21 May 1979.

21 TNA: CAB 128/66, Cabinet Conclusions, Limited Circulation Annex, 24 May 1979; HC Debs, 12 June 1979, vol. 968, col. 252.

22 HMT: PO-CH-GH-00170 Part A, E. P. Kemp to Chief Secretary, 'Social Security Legislation', 15 June 1979.

23 Ibid., John Biffen to Patrick Jenkin, 'Social Security Legislation', 18 June 1979. The only significance to the break happening in 1980 was that, after forecasts to the contrary, it turned out that earnings had risen more than prices in 1979.

24 Adam Ridley urged the Chancellor to leave the door open to more radical reforms such as ditching uprating in favour of indexing increases to the NI funds available: HMT: PO-CH-GH-0093 Part A, Adam Ridley to Chancellor, 'Savings on Social Security', 29 October 1979.

25 HMT: PO-CH-GH-00169 Part B, E. P. Kemp to Mr Pole, 'Social Security – The "Ratchet"', 21 May 1979.

26 HMT: PO-CH-GH-0045, Chancellor of the Exchequer to Prime Minister, 'Line for the PM to take in Weekend World Interview 6 Jan', 4 January 1980.

178 *The first term*

27 TNA: CAB 128/69, Cabinet Conclusions, Item 7, 'Most Confidential Record', 14 November 1980.
28 Howe argued that earnings would probably fall behind prices over the next few years (ibid.).
29 As described in the *Guardian*, 'Maggie Loses Fight on Cuts', by Adam Raphael, 16 November 1980.
30 Ibid.
31 TNA: CAB 128/69, Cabinet Conclusions, Item 7, 'Most Confidential Record', 14 November 1980.
32 *Guardian*, 'Maggie Loses Fight on Cuts', 16 November 1980.
33 MTA: 'Interview TV Interview for London Weekend Television Weekend World', 6 January 1980.
34 TNA: CAB 128/69, Cabinet Conclusions, Item 7, 'Most Confidential Record', 14 November 1980.
35 As soon as the government had reduced inflation to lower rates there would be a case for introducing legislation to remove the obligation to automatic indexation. Until this was done, the government's hands were tied over a major area of expenditure and the benefits of North Sea oil would continue to be channelled into consumption rather than investment. TNA: CAB 128/69, Cabinet Conclusions, Item 7, 'Most Confidential Record', 14 November 1980.
36 The CPRS was a unit within the Cabinet Office created by Edward Heath in 1971 to 'think the unthinkable' in terms of modernising government and improving its efficiency. Consisting of a small team of civil servants and outsiders and reporting to the Cabinet rather than directly to the Prime Minister, it was abolished by Thatcher after the 1983 general election. Tessa Blackstone and William Plowden, *Inside the Think Tank: Advising the Cabinet, 1971–1983* (London: Heinemann, 1988).
37 TNA: CAB 129/215–6, 'Longer-Term Options', 6 September 1982.
38 Alan Bailey – the report's author – was a Treasury Deputy Secretary on loan to the CPRS. Howe had also met with the authors about their report prior to its circulation. HMT: PO-CH-GH-0158 Part B, 'The Longer Term – Briefing for Cabinet on 9 September', 8 September 1982.
39 Ibid., 'Briefing on the Longer Term – Briefing for Cabinet on 9 September', 1 September 1982.
40 Ibid.
41 Ibid. The Cabinet minutes suggest that Howe followed this speaking note: TNA: CAB 128/74/11, Cabinet Conclusions, 9 September 1982.
42 TNA: CAB 128/74/11, Cabinet Conclusions, 9 September 1982; *The Observer*, 'Sinking the Unthinkable at Brighton', by Adam Raphael and Simon Hoggart, 10 October 1982.
43 HMT: PO-CH-GH-0158 Part B, J. O. Kerr to Chief Secretary, 2 September 1982.
44 The story's illustration included a crossed-out picture of the 1975 Social Security Act – see *The Economist*, 'Thatcher's Think Tank Takes Aim at the Welfare State', 18 September 1982.
45 TNA: CAB 128/74, Cabinet Conclusions, 9 September 1982.

46 Ibid., Cabinet Conclusions, 2 November 1982.

47 This would save £260 million in 1983/4 and £725 million in 1984/5, yielding a £180 million saving once it was offset by improvements to other benefits. The 2.5 per cent figure was a peg designed to deal with fact that the latest figures would not be available. The government was content to let pensioners keep any greater difference if it turned out inflation had fallen slightly further. TNA: CAB/130, MISC 88(82)1, Norman Fowler Memorandum, 9 December 1982.

48 TNA: CAB 128/74, Cabinet Conclusions, 2 November 1982.

49 HC Debs, 8 November 1982, vol. 31, col. 316.

50 HC Debs, 9 November 1982, vol. 31, col. 423. She would subsequently reframe it as a payment in advance.

51 MTA: Thatcher, Speech to Lord Mayor's Banquet, 15 November 1982.

52 HC Debs, 16 November 1982, vol. 32, cols. 144–45.

53 TNA: CAB 130/1219, Minutes of Ministerial Group on Social Security Issues, 14 December 1982. Fowler favoured abatement at the 1983 uprating of 2 per cent, despite the latest figures suggesting that inflation had been previously overestimated by 2.7 percentage points. As Norman Tebbit pointed out, that would leave pensioners with a 0.7 points real-terms increase.

54 As early as 1979 Treasury officials had recommended the switch 'to keep the burden of social security payments in check'. HMT: PO-CH-GH-00169 Part A, A. M. Bailey to Chief Secretary, 'Social Security', 11 May 1979.

55 Ibid., 'Note of a Meeting Held by the Chancellor of the Exchequer at H. M. Treasury on Thursday 17 May 1979', 17 May 1979.

56 TNA: CAB 130/1244, MISC 88, Ministerial Group on Social Security, Minutes, 31 January 1983.

57 TNA: CAB 128/77, Cabinet Conclusions, 3 March 1983. The decision had in fact already been taken at a meeting between the Prime Minister and a small group of Ministers: TNA: PREM 19/1957, M. Scholar to D. Clark, 'Uprating of Pensions and Other Benefits', 21 February 1983.

58 TNA: PREM 19/1957, Fowler to Thatcher, 'Pension Uprating', 11 May 1983.

59 TNA: CAB 128/76, Cabinet Conclusions, 12 May 1983.

60 TNA: T 496/436, G. W. Monger to Chancellor, 'Pledge on Future Pension Upratings', 8 April 1983. TNA: PREM 19/1957, Geoffrey Howe to Prime Minister, 12 April 1983.

61 TNA: PREM 19/1957, Fowler to Thatcher, 'Pledge on Future Pension Upratings', 31 March 1983.

62 HMT: PO-CH-GH-0098 Part A, S. A. Godber to J. O. Kerr, 'Pledge on Future Pension Upratings', 30 March 1983. The savings from having broken the link with earnings were also becoming clearer: £500 million a year in 1983, but potentially £2 to 3 billion by the end of the 1980s.

63 TNA: PREM 19/1957, Fowler to Thatcher, 'Pledge on Future Pension Upratings', 20 April 1983.

64 Ibid., 31 March 1983. The draft of this letter sent to the Treasury included this more provocative question: 'Does this mean that under your stewardship the country can no longer afford what it could previously afford?'

The first term

65 Ibid., 20 April 1983.

66 HMT: PO-CH-GH-0098 Part A, M. Scholar to J. Kerr, 'Pledge on Future Pension Upratings', 21 April 1983.

67 Conservative Party Archive (hereafter CPA): 4/10/81, Political Contact Programme Discussion Paper no. 55, 'Pensions for People', April/May 1973.

68 *Financial Times*, 'Tories Will Revive Former Pension Scheme', by Stewart Fleming, 22 August 1974; *Financial Times*, 'Traps for the Pay-As-You-Go Pension', by Anthony Harris and Eric Short, 12 September 1974.

69 CPA: CRD 4/7/60–64, Pensions Study Group, Minutes, 17 December 1974. Although the party then backed SERPS, its preference for funded schemes was one reason it pushed for the maximum number of occupational pensions under the proposals (despite subsequent reservations about the fund's size).

70 Arthur Seldon, *Pensions in a Free Society* (London: Institute of Economic Affairs, 1957), p. 36. Note the gendered nature of his language and thinking.

71 *Daily Telegraph*, 'Index-Linking Doesn't Really Help the Pensioner', by Alfred Sherman, 11 January 1980. Again, note the tendency for reformers to use a gendered frame of analysis.

72 Geoffrey Howe, Speech to NAPF Conference, Birmingham, May 1981 [reprinted in: *Pensions World*, June 1981].

73 He estimated that inflation proofing contracted-out pensions would cost '£1.25 million for 1980–81, £4 million this year and perhaps £9 million next. The corresponding figures for the total cost of the additional component are £7.5 million, £20 million and £43 million.'

74 Howe claimed that between the late 1950s and the late 1970s manufacturing profitability was said to have declined by 12 points to just 5 per cent (or 3 per cent if North Sea oil businesses were excluded).

75 Howe made clear he had no plans to restrict funds to UK investments but also said that interest-linked gilts were an instrument of monetary policy, not a stable means of indirect taxpayer funding.

76 Ibid.

77 *Financial Times*, 'Pension Costs Becoming Intolerable, Howe Warns', by Christine Moir, 8 May 1981; *Daily Mail,* 'Howe Hints at End of Index-Linked Pensions', by Anthony Bevins, 8 May 1981; *Guardian*, 'If Old Age Holds Terrors for You Now, Wait Till It's Time to Collect Your Pension', by Hamish McRae, 10 May 1981.

78 Richard Hemming and John A. Kay, 'The Costs of the State Earnings Related Pension Scheme', *The Economic Journal*, 92 (1982).

79 TNA: T 496/81, S. K. Holmans 'Economic Work on Social Security in the Longer Term: Some Introductory Notes', December 1980.

80 TNA: T 521/51, 'Index Linked Pensions', 14 April 1981.

81 The combined rebates were reduced to 6.25 per cent. GAD recommended a reduction to 6 per cent whereas Patrick Jenkin (now at the Department of Industry) argued for no less than 6.5 per cent to keep faith with the occupational funds. TNA: CAB 134, H (82) 4th meeting of the Home and Social Affairs Committee, 23 February 1982.

82 TNA: T 521/48, 'Pensions – A Note by the Treasury', 1 July 1981.

83 Ibid.

84 They worried that a lower rate of return could make it harder for funds to provide the guaranteed minimum pension needed to opt out of SERPS. Contributions would have to rise, leading to pressure for a higher contracting out rebate, which would in turn deprive the NI fund of income and mean that those contracted in would also need to pay more.

85 TNA: T 521/48, 'Note of a Meeting Held in the Chancellor of the Exchequer's Room', 27 July 1981.

86 TNA: T 521/51: G. W. Monger to Chancellor of the Exchequer, 26 February 1982.

87 Ibid.: C. D. Butler to D. R. Norgrove, 25 March 1981; N. J. Monck to G. W. Monger, 6 April 1981; D. R. Norgrove to G. W. Monger, 17 March 1982; E. P. Kemp to G. W. Monger, 6 April 1981; D. R. Norgrove to G. W. Monger, 8 April 1981; F. Cassell to G. W. Monger, 8 April 1981.

88 TNA: ACT 1/2372, Meeting Held between Civil Servants at DHSS, 23 July 1982. At an early stage the prospect of factoring in pensioners' claims on social and health services was excluded: C. S. Smee to M. J. Spackman, 22 July 1982. The group did, however, want to factor in taxation and pensioners' income from interest/dividends or employment.

89 TNA: T 496/81, G. W. Monger to T. S. Heppell, 27 April 1982. The study was agreed between Monger and DHSS on 21 May 1982: HMT: ACT 1/2372, C. S. Smee to M. J. Spackman, 22 July 1982.

90 Although DHSS initially wanted to focus on the next 20 years only, the group settled on a longer time frame ending in 2025/6, to match the QR.

91 HMT: PO-CH-GH-0041 Part A, G. W. Monger to Chancellor of the Exchequer, 'State Earnings-Related Pension Scheme', 1 July 1982. If earnings and prices rose at the same rate, and with unemployment at 6 per cent, Class I contributions would rise from 15.4 per cent in 1985/6 to 16.7 per cent by 2005/6 but then jump to 21.9 per cent by 2025/6. Further increases of up to two percentage points were to be expected thereafter. If, as was more likely, earnings rose ahead of prices (i.e. in conditions of real economic growth) then these contribution increases would be depressed by around two points. Indeed, if the flat-rate benefit element of the scheme was also uprated below earnings over a long period, the increase in the standard contribution rate could be less steep still and might not need to increase at all.

92 Ibid., G. W. Monger to Chancellor of the Exchequer, 'Quinquennial Review', n.d.

93 TNA: T 521/51, G. W. Monger to Chancellor, 1 July 1982.

94 TNA: ACT 1/273, C. M. Stewart, 'Pensions Problems and Their Solutions', submitted to the Institute and Faculty of Actuaries for publication in its journal, 24 January 1983.

95 HMT: PO-CH-GH-0093, P. Cropper, 'The Future of Pensions', 19 June 1979.

96 HMT: PO-CH-GH-0045, P. Cropper, 'Draft Speech for Delivery to CPC', 20 April 1980.

97 Cropper's proposals are summarised in TNA: T 521/48, 'Wider Ownership and the Pension System', 21 July 1981.

98 TNA: T 521/48: D. Willetts to Chancellor of the Exchequer, 24 June 1981; Chancellor of the Exchequer to Patrick Jenkin, 24 July 1981.

99 HMT: PO-CH-GH-0022, 'Policy Group Work', 1982.

100 HMT: PO-CH-GH-0096, 'Forward Look', 23 December 1982.

101 Ibid., Howe to Thatcher, 23 December 1982.

102 Seammen promised Ridley that the BOPWG would consider some measure of the funds' dominance over investment markets, although other members refused to extend the scope of the study, and so Ridley would have to find these estimates elsewhere.

103 TNA: T 496/135, Nicholas Ridley, 'Holiday Thoughts on Pensions', January 1983.

104 Ibid., G. W. Monger to S. K. Holmans, 'Holiday Thoughts on Pensions', 12 January 1983.

105 In the event Ridley did not take up Monger's suggestion. Instead, just days before the 1983 election, he wrote to the Chancellor in support of portable personal pensions designed for a small number of 'highflyers who expected to be mobile': HMT: PO-CH-GH-0098, Nicholas Ridley to Howe, 'Pensions', 6 May 1983.

106 Holmans compared it to debates in which 60 per cent of GDP had been arbitrarily set as the threshold at which the public sector started to imperil democracy. See TNA: T 496/139, S. K. Holmans to G. W. Monger, 'The Burden of Pensions in the Longer Term', 24 March 1983; S. K. Holmans to G. W. Monger, 'The Burden of Pensions in the Longer Term', 21 March 1983.

107 TNA: T 496/140, Public Services Economic Division, 'The Future Burden of Pensions', 12 May 1983.

108 These were, of course, the assumptions that Monger had provided the GAD earlier in the process. Holmans pointed out that the high-growth scenario was actually a 'central estimate' given that growth had been much higher in the 1951–70 period.

109 The changing number of pensioners accounted for only 1.2 percentage points of the increase.

110 Under a higher-growth scenario, pensioners could expect to see their income grow by 2.8 per cent per year, while the working population could expect 1.9 per cent growth. In a low-growth scenario, though, the 1.6 per cent growth in pensioners' incomes would outpace a meagre 0.5 per cent growth in average earnings.

111 TNA: T 496/140, Public Services Economic Division, 'The Future Burden of Pensions', 12 May 1983.

112 Ibid.

113 TNA: PREM 19/1004, 'Pensions and Individual Choice: A Paper by the CPRS', April 1983; ibid., 'Pensions Issues and Policies: A Paper by the CPRS', April 1983.

114 Ibid., 'Pensions Issues and Policies: A Paper by the CPRS ', April 1983.

115 Ibid., emphasis in original.

116 Ibid.

117 Ibid., emphasis in original.

118 *Financial Times*, 'Opting Out of Pension Plans May Be in Tory Manifesto', by Peter Riddell, 3 May 1983.
119 *Guardian*, 'Healey and Steel Attack Tories' "Hidden" Plans', by Colin Brown and Paul Keel, 31 May 1983.
120 TNA: BN 13/278, Prime Minister to John Brynmor, 20 May 1983.
121 TNA: PREM 19/1004, 'Pensions Issues and Policies: A Paper by the CPRS', April 1983.

Part III

Planning a revolution, 1983–5

5

Personal pensions

In Part III, we turn to a very different era for British pensions in the wake of the Conservatives' clear victory in the 1983 general election. As we saw in the preceding chapter, in the first Thatcher administration the government had acted in ways that were incremental, technical, and – as we shall see in Chapter Eight – very significant in the long term to contain the future cost of the basic state pension. Some within the government had been open to more radical reform but the focus of their activity had been defining – and to some extent discovering – the policy problems they wished to solve. Along with the 'ratcheting' effects of indexation, there had been a growing awareness of the rising importance of pension funds as holders of UK securities and government bonds (as highlighted by the 1980 Wilson Report on the functioning of financial institutions).[1] The government also worried that institutional conservatism on the part of the pension funds led to inefficient capital allocation. As we saw in Chapter Three, some Conservatives had feared this concentration of capital ownership at least since the late 1970s. Nevertheless, whereas in opposition they had concluded that no direct action could be taken against these interests, the first term of government had seen Treasury ministers and advisers begin to consider policies designed to tackle the power of institutional funds. Moreover, even as pension schemes accumulated very large asset holdings (£9 billion by 1979 and growing by about half a billion pounds a year), there were developing concerns that these were insufficient to meet rising liabilities, and emerging fears about the funds' long-term viability and, more generally, about the inter-generational implications of unfunded future liabilities.[2] The danger was beginning to be appreciated that occupational pension schemes might become, as Geoffrey Howe warned in 1981, 'an unsustainable burden on younger people'.[3] Again, however, although those concerns were evident and some options for both incremental and major system reform had been put forward before the 1983 election, no legislative steps towards systematic reform had been taken during the government's first term.

188   *Planning a revolution, 1983–5*

As we shall see, the second term proved very different. Emboldened by a landslide victory in June 1983 – partly the consequence of victory in the Falklands War the previous year, which rescued the Conservatives from their formerly dire level of unpopularity, but more the product of Labour weakness and the popularity of the new Social Democratic Party – there was a marked change in the tone of government, and a marked expansion of its ambitions and willingness to legislate.[4] Whereas Thatcher had not felt confident enough in her first term to ignore moderate Cabinet ministers (the so-called 'wets'), with a parliamentary majority of 144 she 'was now strong enough to insist that her own supporters dominate the cabinet'.[5]

The government's second term is remembered for key events such as the defeat of the National Union of Mineworkers during the 1984–85 miners' strike, the acceleration and greater boldness of privatisation as it became 'a dominant economic policy with the privatisation of major national-ised industries notably British Telecom and British Gas', and the reforms implemented to financial markets via the 1986 'Big Bang' and the conse-quent reinvigoration of the City of London as a global financial centre.[6] But nowhere was this ambition more obvious than in pension policy. Although the Conservatives' election manifesto had given no hint of radi-cal change, within months Thatcher's second government was embracing pension reforms of breathtaking ambition – a programme that, had it been implemented, would have led to the effective destruction of the occupational pensions enjoyed by about half the workforce, and of the State Earnings-Related Pension Scheme that covered the remainder, with their replacement by a new system of individualised, compulsory, and much more risky 'per-sonal portable pensions' backed up by a minimalist basic state pension.

In the next two chapters we explore the mechanics of this embrace of radical, even revolutionary, change. In this chapter we explore the personal pensions idea – its origins, its embrace at the heart of policymaking, and its fundamental role in the pension reform proposals embodied within the gov-ernment's 1985 Green Paper on social security. In the next chapter we turn our attention to another aspect of that Green Paper's proposals: the aboli-tion of SERPS. As we shall see, taken together these two policies amounted to a revolutionary overturning of the partnership between state and employ-ers that had been forged in the mid- to late 1970s, the substitution of a new idea of individualised pension provision, and an assault on the pension provisions of British workers and the financial (and political) power of pen-sion funds and insurance companies that, together, then owned about a half of all shares listed on the London Stock Exchange. It is hard to conceive of a more ambitious programme. Then, in Chapter Seven, we explore the mechanics of a substantial U-turn, with a rapid reconfiguration by the gov-ernment of its reform programme.

The Centre for Policy Studies and 'personal portable pensions'

Tracing the origin of a new idea adopted by any modern government is often problematic, not least because ministers and their special advisers were and are often cagey about acknowledging the influence of others. Ministers particularly tend to want to 'own' policies in which they invest their personal political capital. In the case of the Thatcher governments, however, there has long been a wealth of scholarship noting the importance of politically sympathetic think tanks, and their role in devising policy ideas that they then 'sold' to ministers and their advisers.[7] This was certainly the case in pensions, and in this section we consider the influence of one of these think tanks – the Centre for Policy Studies – and explore the means by which its radical pension reform proposals were injected into the heart of the government machine. First, however, we consider the origin of the CPS's proposed reform programme, which was intended to solve a technical problem in the occupational pension system that the government had inherited. In Chapter Four we discussed two sets of pension policy problems that the government grappled with between 1979 and 1983, but there was a third problem: 'the early leaver problem'. This acted as a lightning rod for criticisms of Britain's pension system as one built on unsustainable cross-subsidies that were unjust, inhibited labour mobility, and hid the true costs of occupational pensions. This problem had not seen as much technical investigation within government between 1979 and 1983 because Jim Callaghan's 1976–79 Labour government had commissioned a study of it by the Occupational Pensions Board. It would become the vehicle in which the CPS managed to drive its radical proposals for reform onto the government's second term agenda. For this reason, we briefly explain the early leaver problem and its development up until 1983 before turning to the CPS's proposed solution.

The 'early leaver problem'

Across the developed world in the 1970s the significant increase in the rate of inflation wrought economic and political difficulties.[8] In Britain, both the 1970–74 Conservative government and the Wilson and Callaghan Labour governments between 1974 and 1979 struggled to control rising prices. Despite Labour managing to reduce annual inflation from its peak of nearly 27 per cent in 1975, Britain entered the last year of the decade with inflation still high, at 9.3 per cent. As described in Chapter Three, high inflation coupled with a stagnant economy were two key factors in the election of a Conservative government in 1979 with an agenda that sought to curb inflation through tight monetary policy and reductions in public spending, even at the cost of recession. Although inflation had the far-reaching general effect of helping to dismantle the postwar macroeconomic consensus, however, it also had a significant local impact on the politics of pensions in Britain, which in turn created the conditions for the Thatcher governments to embrace the idea of radical change.

Stagflation presented occupational pension schemes with a problem. Since the 1950s pension funds had weighted investments towards equities for high returns, but the economic shocks of the 1970s saw reduced corporate profits (and thus dividend income) and lower stock prices.[9] Above-inflation returns were crucial to the funds, because future pensions were tied to final salaries, which tended to rise due to career progression and because earnings tended to increase at least as rapidly as prices over the long term. The funds were helped, however, by the fact that their generosity to pensioners did not extend to those who left the firm. Benefits accrued before 1975 were simply forfeited, and so too were benefits accrued after this by leavers who did not meet the qualifying criteria set out in the 1973 Social Security Act (which required them to have worked for the sponsoring company for at least five years and be aged over 26). Those who met these criteria had their post-1973 benefits 'preserved' – to be received when the individual reached retirement age. But schemes were under no obligation to protect preserved benefits against inflation; indeed, there was a positive incentive not to do so, because, as things stood, early leavers were subsiding stayers. Without such protection, the real value of preserved benefits was progressively eroded and ex-employees risked finding their preserved benefits worth very little in real terms when they retired.[10] This 'early leaver problem', as it was described, was widely accepted to be deeply unfair.[11]

To resolve the issue, the Labour government in 1978 instructed the OPB to investigate (by no means an easy task given conflicting interests). From the outset the OPB assumed it was unrealistic to solve the problem via improved transfer rights (the terms on which one occupational pension could be moved to another) because of the thousands of different occupational schemes with differing rules, the fact that not all employers organised such schemes, and that many early leavers did not go into further employment. Instead, it focused on revaluation, recommending in its 1981 report that schemes be required to preserve the real value of all early leavers' preserved benefits against inflation up to 5 per cent per annum compounded over the period of deferment.[12]

Revaluation had been considered but rejected by the Conservatives in opposition in the mid-1970s and in the lead-up to the 1973 legislation, not least because, with rapid inflation and a stagnant economy, it was far from clear that firms could afford it.[13] Likewise, in 1981 the government baulked at statutory revaluation, despite its commitment to bringing inflation down to a much lower rate and private acceptance that the present

Personal pensions 191

situation was inequitable. Against the background of severe recession and an impending requirement for employers to pay statutory sick pay, ministers hesitated to impose additional costs on firms. Instead, as a holding operation, the government merely commended to employers the OPB's recommendations on inflation proofing.[14] They proved unreceptive, however, since, even with a cap, they saw the prospective costs as too high and unpredictable.[15]

The early leaver problem was not so easily brushed aside by ministers, and it resurfaced a year later when Norman Fowler received the OPB's follow-up report on scheme member security and fund solvency.[16] Fowler warned the Cabinet's Home and Social Affairs Committee that the government's response to this report would inevitably highlight its inaction on early leavers. This led him to secure agreement to a slightly tougher line, whereby he would explicitly threaten legislation if progress was not made by the funds voluntarily.[17] Fowler stuck to this strategy throughout 1982 and 1983, but in reality his threat was a hollow one: the truth was that the government considered the costs of the OPB's proposals too high, and were anyway busy conceptualising the existing system as a burden on future workers. This is not to say that they disagreed with the OPB's central findings: perhaps more than the OPB, ministers objected to a system that they thought inhibited labour mobility and reflected the funds' attachment to cross-subsidisation and perceived indifference to former active members. In some ways, then, this was a government that had a diagnosis of the early leaver problem (courtesy of a Labour-commissioned OPB report) but was casting around for a more politically palatable solution.

The CPS's proposal: 'personal and portable pensions'

In 1983 the somewhat arcane debate about how to solve the early leaver problem was significantly reshaped by the Centre for Policy Studies. Founded in 1974 by the senior Conservative MP Sir Keith Joseph (alongside the journalist Alfred Sherman and soon-to-be Conservative party leader Margaret Thatcher), the CPS's purpose was to challenge the so-called postwar 'consensus' in British economic and social policy (characterised by government macroeconomic interventionism and limits on the operation of free markets). In the extensive literature on the origins and development of 'Thatcherism' in Britain, the CPS is understood, alongside the more longstanding think tank the Institute of Economic Affairs, to have provided a conduit for neoliberal ideas into the Conservative party.[18] In its early form, the CPS was largely the intellectual and ideological project of Joseph and Sherman. After the 1979 general election, with the former now a Cabinet minister, it became more policy-focused and divided itself up into a series of

192 *Planning a revolution, 1983–5*

study groups. It is from one of these that the CPS's contribution to the 'early leaver' debate emerged.[19]

In April 1983 the chairman of the CPS's Personal Capital Formation Group (PCFG), Nigel Vinson, and fellow group member Philip Chappell proposed a solution to the difficulties facing early leavers. Vinson had been a founding member of the CPS, following a successful career as the owner of a plastics firm (during which time he had also been chairman of the Industrial Participation Association); Chappell was a director of the merchant bank Morgan Grenfell.[20] In a policy paper entitled *Personal and Portable Pensions for All*, they condemned 'the grave injustice inflicted on those who change jobs' – something that was not only unfair to individuals but also discouraged them from moving between employers, thus producing an 'ossification of employment patterns'.[21] Their proposed solution was for individuals 'to be given the chance to run their own personalised pensions as if they were self-employed, through segregated funds'.

In other words, Vinson and Chappell proposed that the collective provision of employer-run occupational schemes be superseded by pensions tied to the individual worker. Both employers and employees would contribute to these individualised funds, and when the employee changed jobs the fund would not be left behind but would move with them. Moreover, the responsibility for managing and investing this personal fund would no longer be delegated to employers and their appointed fund managers but to the individual employee. Thereby, the successful model of so-called 'Section 226' pensions for the self-employed would be extended to all employees.[22] Such schemes would be 'money purchase' rather than 'final salary' (or, in more contemporary language, 'defined contribution' rather than 'defined benefit') – meaning that the pensionable income received would not be related to salary and guaranteed but, instead, determined by the contributions made by the individual to their fund over the course of their working life, coupled with its investment performance. By any standards, this would be a major change, serving to shift both responsibility for pension provision and all associated risks to the individual.

Although Vinson and Chappell presented 'personal and portable pensions' as an effective solution to the practical problem facing early leavers, their proposals were not simply motivated by their plight. Their aim was radically to change the pattern of ownership in British society. In their conclusion to *Personal and Portable Pensions for All*, they made their intention to promote individual capital ownership clear: 'To argue for the present status quo is to argue for the perpetuation of a gross injustice on most future pensioners. We believe our proposals would rectify this, and at the same time bring all the benefits that come from having a wider capital owning society.' In other words, although their personal pensions proposal offered

Personal pensions 193

a solution to a practical problem of social policy, solving that problem also offered a way to pursue a more far-reaching ideological project.

Although the CPS's Personal Capital Formation Group consisted of a wide range of individuals from industry, finance, and the Conservative party in Parliament, its leading figures were undoubtedly Vinson and Chappell.[23] They formulated and promoted a distinctly ideological agenda. Vinson told Thatcher in June 1981 that the PCFG's aim was 'to widen and make more personal the ownership of wealth in all forms'.[24] It was, for example, the progenitor of the government's November 1981 announcement of the Enterprise Allowance Scheme (an initiative that gave a guaranteed income of £40 a week to unemployed people setting up their own business) and of Nigel Lawson's creation of 'Personal Equity Plans' in his 1986 budget.[25] Vinson and Chappell were not concerned simply to continue the postwar Conservative party's long-standing notional commitment to creating a 'property-owning democracy', however, but in fact sought to achieve a more radical overhaul of ownership in Britain. In this, their primary concern was to dismantle the institutionalisation of capital ownership that had taken place since the war.[26]

The changing ownership of capital in postwar Britain had involved a significant decline in the importance of individual share ownership. A key factor in this was the growth of occupational pensions. As described in Chapter Three, prior to the Second World War only 13 per cent of workers had been covered by occupational pensions, but by 1967 this had risen to over 50 per cent, and active membership remained around that level in the mid-1980s.[27] This caused the market value of pension funds to rise to £31 billion by 1978.[28] This growth was also reflected in the parallel expansion of the holding of insurance companies (many of which ran pension schemes for small and medium-sized companies), which held assets of £44.6 billion in 1978.[29] These substantial funds had displaced individuals as the primary owners of British capital: at the start of the Second World War individuals owned over 80 per cent of the ordinary shares listed on the London Stock Exchange, but by 1963 that had reduced to 54 per cent.[30] By 1978 pension funds alone held £15.5 billion worth of ordinary shares, as well as £6.5 billion in British government securities and £5.4 billion in property – figures that continued to rise for many decades as contributions exceeded pensions paid by the funds.[31] By 1981 individual stock ownership was down to 28 per cent of total investment. Pension funds and insurers owned nearly half the London stock market by the end of the 1980s.[32]

Throughout the first three postwar decades the Conservative party had supported the growth of occupational pensions.[33] On the question of capital ownership, however, the Tories had little to say about the effect of the pension fund revolution prior to the mid-1970s.[34] Then, following the election of Thatcher as Leader of the Opposition in 1975, and as the party's commitment to the creation of a 'property-owning democracy' found a new and more enthusiastic champion, pension and insurance funds came to be viewed by the Conservatives as good examples of widening share ownership. The 1976 Conservative policy document *The Right Approach*, for example, recognised that, through them, 'millions of workers [were] already major equity owners at one remove'.[35] A subsequent paper, *The Right Approach to the Economy*, made a direct link between the party's programme for 'wider ownership and personal capital building' and the 'chance ... to acquire a proper stake (albeit at one remove) in the ownership of the wealth of the community.'[36] Thatcher herself built upon this view of the benefits of pension and insurance funds in a speech to the Zurich Economic Society in 1977, celebrating them as 'a kind of people's capitalism'.[37]

This optimism was tempered by a growing fear among Conservatives, however, that the Labour party and the trades unions were perilously close to nationalising or taking worker control of the funds as part of an attempted state-directed revitalisation of British industry. The economic crisis of the 1970s had encouraged the Left wing of the Labour party to view pension funds as a much-needed source of state-directed industrial investment. Meanwhile, the unions began to assert their members' claim to the rightful ownership and control of their retirement savings.[38] Peter Drucker's somewhat ironic reference to 'pension fund socialism' in the United States in 1976 looked as though it might become a reality if the Labour Left prevailed.[39]

Joseph and Sherman were particularly conscious of this threat, and in the late 1970s attempted to mobilise the funds against a socialist political takeover, trying to persuade them to educate their members about the need to defend the free-market economy and protect themselves against state or trades union control of workers' pension funds.[40] Sherman, an ex-Communist, described fund members as 'our reserve army', and told Thatcher that

> [o]ur battle against the Bullock [committee of inquiry on industrial democracy] would gain enormously if we were able to mobilise even part of the millions of people who are indirect shareholders, in that through their life insurance and pension funds they own half or more of industrial equity. It is estimated that up to 75% of British families hold a stake in quoted shares other than by direct ownership. This means approximately twice as many families as the TUC members and theirs. They represent a majority of voters, wage and salary earners, and probably of trade unionists too.[41]

This enthusiasm for rousing life and pensions institutions in defence of the free economy was ultimately disappointed by their reluctance to be politicised, and Sherman and Joseph's proposals faded away after 1977.[42]

Personal pensions 195

Nonetheless, Sherman's desire to bring 'institutional ownership ... into the framework of our [the CPS's] politico-economic overview' returned with Vinson and Chappell's proposal for 'personal and portable pensions' in 1983.[43] Those intervening six years had seen a radical shift; whereas Sherman had attempted to work constructively with the pension funds in the 1970s, Vinson and Chappell now sought nothing less than their ultimate destruction by replacing collective occupational pension saving with individual funds.

We have shown in Chapter Three that there were some early signs of this change in approach in the late 1970s. Vinson had been a member of the party's Wider Ownership Group (led by Peter Horden and reporting to Howe). This group attributed the growing dominance of institutional funds to unjustified taxation privileges but concluded that the only politically possible route to wider and more direct ownership was to outflank them through new forms of saving rather than confront these powerful interests directly. In Chapter Four we showed that some members of this group continued to criticise the funds within government and that some Treasury ministers tried to link the emerging 'burden of pensions' problem with their aim to weaken institutional funds. Vinson and Chappell's proposals represented a much bolder statement of these ideological objectives, however, and gained an *apparent* practicability and neatness from being packaged as a specific policy option for both rectifying a 'gross injustice' and delivering a wider capital-owning society.[44] Most importantly, though, they secured the Prime Minister's interest.

Vinson wrote to Thatcher in June 1981 to outline the developing vision of the CPS's PCFG.[45] In this letter, which attempted to give the government's agenda some overall direction that might cohere with Thatcher's stated desire to achieve 'a psychological revolution' throughout the country, Vinson argued for the need to 'widen and make more personal the ownership of wealth in all forms'. Interestingly, Vinson's focus was not on the sale of public assets (the Housing Act of 1980 had given tenants of council houses the right to purchase their homes at a discount, and several privatisations of public companies had already taken place during Thatcher's first term). Instead, he emphasised the PCFG's concern about 'the increasing concentration of wealth in the hands of institutions'. Beyond the concern for the 'early leaver' in occupational pensions, it was thus the institutionalisation of ownership and wealth that ultimately motivated the CPS's proposal for 'personal and portable pensions' as the most effective means of widening the understanding of wealth creation and first-hand experience of capitalism.[46]

Vinson and Chappell's primary criticism of institutional ownership was that the role of institutions as intermediaries served to obscure individual ownership rights. They were disturbed by the fact that, although capital ownership had in theory been spread to the wider public via pension and insurance funds in the postwar decades, this had not given individuals any 'personal identification' with their assets, and so they took no interest in them.[47] Vinson told Thatcher in 1981 that the PCFG wanted 'to encourage individual involvement in, and understanding of, the wealth creation process', because 'only thus can individuals really feel part of our society'.[48] As he put it in 1984:

> [U]nless some pension changes are introduced now to restore a greater sense of personal ownership, simplicity, and genuine involvement in the underlying asset, the nation's wealth, increasingly dominated by retirement provision, will be regarded as nobody's money.[49]

The aim, for Vinson and Chappell, was 'to turn "nobody's money" into "somebody's money"'.[50] In a letter to Howe a few days after the 1983 general election landslide, Vinson argued that breaking up the pension funds would 'give a new opportunity for 24 million people to have a real sense of involvement in the industrial success of this country' and 'create a national sense of common purpose and genuinely participatory society'.[51] This was necessary, in Vinson and Chappell's view, because the institutional barrier between individuals and the capital they unwittingly owned threatened the long-term stability and security of the free-market economy.[52]

Institutional concentration of pension fund capital ownership was a problem for the CPS for other reasons too. In the first instance, there was the fear that pension funds could be 'a socialist Trojan horse'; as Vinson remarked to Sherman in 1983, 'when pensions are personalised, they are harder to nationalise!'[53] Yet Vinson and Chappell were also deeply disturbed by the funds' size and power. In 1986 they asserted that 'institutionalised capitalism, because of its concentration of power and diminishment of individual enterprise, is just as much a betrayal of the open society as socialism itself'.[54]

As we have seen, some of these arguments had briefly been made just before the Conservative party entered government and occasionally by Treasury ministers and advisers in the first term (but with little traction). Vinson and Chappell's reinvigoration of this agenda represents an important and overlooked component of the Thatcherite ideological mix, however. There has been a great deal of emphasis placed on the Thatcher governments' commitment to creating a 'property-owning democracy' through the sale of council houses and privatisation of industry. This is commonly understood as representing the fundamental Thatcherite commitment to 'roll back the frontiers of the state' and allow the market to flourish. Yet the CPS's personal pension proposals amounted to an attack on the *existing* market provision of pensions, and on the associated pattern of capital ownership. Unlike previous attempts to make these arguments in government,

Personal pensions 197

Vinson and Chappell brought together the negative critique of institutional ownership with a positive policy alternative designed to promote the independence and entrepreneurial behaviours needed to revitalise British capitalism and solve both a technical problem and the risks of socialisation/industrial unrest said to arise from a society too detached from the mechanism that generated its wealth.

These arguments exhibit a close affinity with the neoliberal view of the welfare state and more specific neoliberal visions of pensions discussed in Chapter One. In particular, Vinson and Chappell's ideas had a close correspondence with the postwar German 'ordoliberal' school. Ralf Ptak and Werner Bonefeld have shown how the ordoliberals were committed to preserving individual liberty through free and competitive markets – a situation that they believed could be maintained only by a strong state that prevented the emergence of monopolies and concentrations of private economic power.[55] Furthermore, ordoliberals sought to create what they termed a 'social market economy', in which the state not only enforced law, order, and anti-monopolistic competition but also attempted to reform society so that individual citizens were equipped with the moral and behavioural norms necessary for the market order to function effectively. Ordoliberal social policy was intended to 'de-proletarianise' society by imbuing individuals with responsibility, ownership, and the values of the market.[56]

As we shall see, the CPS's proposals would eventually evolve to reflect some of the ideas emphasised by other neoliberal schools, but, if we compare the CPS's initial arguments for personalising pensions with the core ideas of ordoliberals, we can see a clear conceptual affinity. The policy was decidedly anti-laissez faire, seeking to use the state to intervene in the economy to break up concentrations of private economic power that had arisen through distortions created by its previous well-meaning but misguided paternalism and sustained by interest groups. Furthermore, the CPS's plans sought to secure the future sustainability of the market economy by creating entrepreneurial capitalist individuals in control of their own private property. The CPS placed a distinctive emphasis on the potential for the individual to control their investments and hold these directly. Vinson explicitly framed this as creating the means for employees to manage their savings 'as if they were self-employed' and giving rise to the 'motivational' ownership that came from disaggregated and first-hand holdings. This mirrored the ordoliberals' attraction to policies that sought to replicate the self-sufficiency they believed led to individual fulfilment and the preservation of liberalism in the context of mass production. The conceptual affinity between ordoliberalism and the CPS proposals is underlined by the fact that the CPS's first publication, which was co-authored by Nigel Vinson, was entitled *Why Britain Needs a Social Market Economy*.[57] In their biography of the CPS's

198   *Planning a revolution, 1983–5*

leading figure, Sir Keith Joseph, Andrew Denham and Mark Garnett suggest that this original interest in West Germany was superseded by 'other priorities' after 1975; but the ideological motivations of the 'personal pensions' proposal suggest that ordoliberalism continued to be a significant element within Thatcherism even in government.[58]

Reception

The CPS's 'personal and portable pensions' proposal served to remake the debate over the 'early leaver problem'. The idea was immediately well received by newspapers sympathetic to the government, receiving a strong endorsement from *The Times*, for example, in an editorial at the end of April 1983 that commended personal and portable pensions for being a 'much neater and simpler, and also more radical, solution' to the early leaver problem, helping to improve labour mobility and giving individuals a direct stake in the economy – thus making them 'more conscious of the merits of private property as an institution and more hostile to the threat of government direction of savings flows than if he [the employee] belongs to a group scheme'. Other papers sympathetic to the government took a similar line.[59]

The radicalism of the CPS's proposals and the evident support they were receiving forced the various stakeholder groups engaged in the early leaver debate to respond, but it also attracted the interest of Thatcher, which in turn led Norman Fowler, the Secretary of State for Health and Social Security, to act. In May 1983 he announced a one-day conference to be held at the DHSS in September to explore the early leaver problem and discuss the desirability and feasibility of 'personal and portable pensions' – which, after years of stalemate over revaluation of preserved benefits, suddenly appeared to offer a new route to tackling the problem.[60]

When it was held, however, the DHSS conference revealed a strong antipathy to the Vinson and Chappell proposals from almost every significant stakeholder group, including the National Association of Pension Funds, the Life Offices Association (LOA), the Association of Consulting Actuaries (ACA), and the Confederation of British Industry (the criticisms are discussed in detail in the next section).[61] Fowler attempted to moderate the debate but was clearly himself initially sceptical of the CPS's ideas. In early May he had reassured the annual NAPF conference that the government was not committed to the personal pension proposal and would 'not be hustled into decisions on this'.[62] The NAPF left the DHSS conference with the strong impression that Fowler preferred the OPB's proposals for the compulsory revaluation of preserved occupational pensions, and *The Economist* reported that he would probably merely use

Personal pensions   199

the threat of pension personalisation as 'a useful stick to wield if the pensions men [*sic*] should turn awkward when it comes to negotiating his considerably more conventional proposals [for revaluation]'.[63] Within government Fowler pressed hard for the OPB recommendations to be implemented.[64] At this early stage, therefore, Fowler plainly favoured reform of occupational pensions, not revolution via the implementation of personal pensions.

No. 10, however, had been swayed by the CPS's proposals. In the summer of 1983 John Redwood, a merchant banker and director of pension fund accounts at N. M. Rothschild, had been hired by Thatcher to help drive 'an autumn offensive' on pension reform by her Policy Unit.[65] Thatcher's official biographer has noted that personal pensions was one of several key policies identified by Redwood when he took over the PU that he thought could contribute to 'restoring individual freedom, responsibility and choice'.[66] Consequently, in late October Fowler was tasked by the Prime Minister with undertaking an inquiry into the possibility of implementing the CPS proposals.[67] It is evident that he was not enthusiastic, and he fought hard to ensure that his favoured solution to the early leaver problem – enforcing the OPB proposal on inflation protection – was implemented before agreeing to the inquiry. To satisfy Thatcher, however, Fowler promised that this would not 'impede progress toward [the] longer term goal' of replacing final salary occupational pensions.[68] Nevertheless, Fowler was not persuaded by the radical anti-institutionalism of the CPS and the Policy Unit. Although he accepted the creation of the inquiry, he made it clear that the review had to 'be presented as part of the normal process of Government to minimise the danger that it could be misrepresented as an attack on existing pension provisions'.[69]

The strong support for the CPS's vision evident in the PU was significant. Anthony Seldon noted that, under Thatcher, the Unit was 'a priesthood of true believers'. Its influence was at its height under Redwood's leadership (1983–85), during which time its function was 'thinking the unthinkable but also providing support for the Prime Minister'.[70] The support of the PU for personal pensions was therefore significant. It is worth noting, however, that its enthusiastic embrace of the CPS proposals was not the only source of support for personalising pensions at the centre of government. The CPRS, set up by Heath to be a sort of internal government think tank, had before the election conducted a rapid review of pensions, producing a paper in April 1983 entitled 'Pensions and Individual Choice' that proposed the creation of 'portable occupational pensions' (POPs) – almost identical to the 'personal and portable pensions' proposed by the CPS. Like the CPS, the CPRS proposals were concerned with discrimination against the early leaver, limits on individual freedom, and the lack of 'awareness of interest' on the part of scheme members about the underlying capital investments that funded their pension.[71] The CPRS's idea had been greeted with a degree of scepticism in the Treasury (though not outright hostility, for some Treasury officials had expanded their public sector focus on 'the burden of pensions' to encompass concerns about the future sustainability of occupational pension schemes, the distorting macroeconomic effects of a quest for safety in old age savings, and the increasing burden they would place on the working population).[72] At the DHSS, official scepticism was unqualified; its Deputy Secretary in charge of social security complained to the CPRS that defined contribution (DC) personal pensions were self-evidently much inferior to defined benefit (DB) occupational pension schemes, not least because workers lacked the necessary skills and financial knowledge to invest their retirement savings successfully.[73] Ultimately, however, the CPRS's POP proposal was sunk by its association with the proposal in a parallel CPRS report to abolish SERPS (explored in the next chapter), which the Prime Minister rejected out of hand as politically disastrous in the lead-up to a likely election (being mindful of the leaking in September 1982 of a CPRS 'Review of Long-Term Options', two of which, the de-indexation of pensions and privatisation of the NHS, had set off a firestorm of criticism).[74] She instructed the CPRS to recall every copy of its two reports.

By late 1983, however, political conditions were very different. Shortly after the election Thatcher had moved quickly to abolish the CPRS, which she saw as both politically maladroit and compromised by being formally responsible to the Cabinet rather than to her personally. Her preference was really for a full-blown Prime Minister's Department to support her, but this idea had been torpedoed early in her premiership by the Cabinet Secretary, who had warned darkly about its raising profound constitutional questions – 'mandarinate' code for 'likely to cause an almighty political row'. Uncharacteristically, she chose to duck this fight, choosing instead to expand her Policy Unit in the wake of the 1983 general election. At the start of 1984, as had been intended when he was first appointed, Redwood became its leader, and the PU 'now became central to the projection of Mrs Thatcher's will throughout government'.[75] Redwood saw mass personal pensions as a central plank in a government policy programme aimed at 'restoring individual freedom, responsibility and choice', and he was keen on their potential to give every worker a stake in the economy, believing that their implementation had the potential to make 'every man [*sic*] a capitalist'.[76] In short, by the end of 1983 personal pensions had in the person of Redwood gained an enthusiastic and powerful advocate at the heart of government, one operating with the support of a Prime Minister who had been converted to the idea and who, with her landslide majority, was at the height of her political power.

Personal pensions 201

The Fowler Inquiry

Remit and members

An obvious consequence of No. 10's enthusiasm for personal pensions, and of the Prime Minister's desire to implement them, was that Norman Fowler necessarily had to be seen to pursue the idea if he was to keep his job. His strategy was to set up a public Inquiry into Provision for Retirement (IPR) at the end of November, tasking it with studying 'the future development, adequacy and costs of State, occupational and private provision for retirement in the United Kingdom, including the portability of pension rights'. Chaired by Fowler himself, it had 11 other members: from within government, Rhodes Boyson, the Minister of State for Social Security, and his under-secretary, Ray Whitney; a Department of Trade and Industry (DTI) under-secretary, Alex Fletcher; the Minister for Employment, Peter Morrison, and a junior Treasury minister, Barney Hayhoe; plus senior representatives from the pensions sector, Marshall Field (an eminent actuary and general manager of Phoenix Assurance), Stewart Lyon, president of the Institute and Faculty of Actuaries, and Alan Peacock (professor of economics at the private University of Buckingham, former member of the IEA, and chief economic adviser to the Department of Trade and Industry). The Government Actuary, Edward Johnston, was also a member. As Steven Nesbitt has noted, the choice of members was significant, there being no representation of 'the social security lobby' and no direct representation from either side of industry.[77]

In the same month Fowler set out in a consultative document his proposals for improving the lot of future early leavers by implementing the OPB proposal on retail price indexation of preserved pensions, capped at 5 per cent per annum, and perhaps abolishing the age qualification for preservation.[78] Then, on 16 December 1983, he created a subgroup of the IPR, which he tasked with looking into 'the question of personal portable pensions'. The subgroup consisted of Fowler himself, Hayhoe, Field, Peacock, and Mark Weinberg (founder and managing director of Hambro Life Assurance, perhaps the most thrusting of the country's life assurers), who Fowler had brought into the Inquiry after its creation.[79] In a letter to stakeholders from the Inquiry's secretary, Nicholas Montagu, written evidence was invited in response to the 'main advantages claimed for portable pensions', which included giving workers more control over and a greater sense of involvement in their pensions; creating a 'fairer balance' between leavers and stayers in occupational schemes; encouraging job mobility; and stimulating 'a more effective investment policy by the funds concerned'. The letter asked, particularly, for a consideration of the 'practical and financial effects of portable pensions'.[80] Well over 1,500 items of written evidence

202 *Planning a revolution, 1983–5*

were subsequently submitted to the subgroup, which also took oral evidence in four public sessions during January and February 1984.[81]

Announcing a public inquiry is a favoured trick of ministers seeking to kick a proposal into the long grass. How was Fowler able to do this given the pressure he was under from No. 10? First, as already noted, the Conservatives' 1983 election manifesto had been notably reticent on possible pension reforms, thus increasing the political risks associated with radical change. Second, although Redwood was an enthusiastic proponent of personal pensions, Fowler was able to play on his fears of a repeat of the furore caused by the leak of the CPRS's proposals for NHS privatisation in 1982, and to persuade him that transparency would be advisable. It would be better, argued Fowler, to consider personal pensions in the context of his developing ideas for a broader review of social security, which he had heralded in a speech to the Conservative Bow Group in the autumn.[82] Of course, the PU understood what Fowler was up to. A minute from it to Thatcher observed that '[t]he DHSS strategy is to split off the problem of the early leaver from the other major issues at stake, tackling it by enacting in 1984/85 the feeble [OPB] proposals. They hope the impetus for more far-reaching reform will then go away.' The minute went on:

> In response to the growing pressure, Norman is now highlighting his Review of Provision for Retirement. In 1st thoughts, this was described merely as 'launching the exercise of public education and debate' and 'preparing the ground for moving forward later in this Parliament'. (In fact, this debate was launched long ago, and is already under full steam.) Now he promises a full-blown 'review', albeit one 'undertaken as part of the normal business of government'. But because its scope is to include every conceivable question relating to retirement, the chances of it coming up with radical proposals to give employees the same portability rights as the self-employed are virtually nil. We shall be told that 'it is all too complicated', and that 'there would be no demand for it'.[83]

Nonetheless, ultimately the Prime Minister agreed to an inquiry – persuaded not by Fowler but by Redwood, who had concluded that transparency was probably the better approach on a policy that promised such far-reaching change. The PU would be closely involved in the Inquiry, however, and intended to steer Fowler to acceptable conclusions.[84]

Supporters

It is notable that Vinson and Chappell did not provide a firm model of personal pensions to the IPR. Rather, in its written evidence the CPS asserted that it would be happy to accept any variant so long as it provided all individuals with 'an absolute right of transferability of accumulated assets' and stipulated that compulsory membership of occupational pension schemes

Personal pensions 203

for new employees was forbidden.[85] Additionally, it argued that a wide range of institutions, such as building societies and banks, should be permitted to provide personal pensions, but that 'the individual should be free, if he [*sic*] wishes, to determine absolutely his investment policy for his own portfolio, including personal stock selection', and allowed to take a loan from their pension savings as self-employed workers were permitted to do. Individual direct investment was clearly the ideal outcome for Vinson and Chappell, but in their evidence they were notably more circumspect than hitherto about the prospects of many individuals taking on such an active role in investment:

> Although we accept that the vast majority of PPPs [personal pension plans] would be managed by financial institutions, including those to be managed by existing occupational schemes, an individual will identify more closely with his [*sic*] accruing PPP, and watch its changing value and underlying assets, than is possible as regards his undefined and complex share in an existing occupational scheme. Personal evidence, and the unit trust movement, supports the view that ownership at first-hand matters to people.[86]

This was a considerable step back from the CPS's initial 'every man a capitalist' vision and undoubtedly a pre-emptive response to widespread scepticism that individuals could rise to the challenge of manage their own pension investments. Evidence submitted by the LOA to the DHSS conference on early leavers in September had already noted the strong likelihood that individuals would simply delegate this to an insurance company.[87] In the Treasury, the Chancellor's adviser, Adam Ridley, had expressed similar scepticism, being persuaded only that personal pensions could enable a small minority of pension savers to manage their associated investments.[88]

Nevertheless, the CPS had strong support from the Institute of Directors (IoD).[89] In particular, its director general, Walter Goldsmith, both embraced the CPS's ideological motivations and acted as an enthusiastic cheerleader for the ideals of individual capital ownership. In written evidence to the Inquiry, Goldsmith argued that 'if we accept that there is a lack of understanding in modern Britain of the wealth creating processes which underpin our free enterprise economy then only by increasing involvement in the creation of wealth can we continue to secure the freedoms which society holds to be important'.[90] He told the IPR subgroup that people 'have not tended to have any capital and they have not actually learned during their lives the process of managing their own affairs'.[91] 'Personal pensions would enlighten them by dispelling 'the mists of actuarial wizardry' in occupational pensions, which obscured each individual's recognition of their accumulating personal wealth.[92]

If Goldsmith bolstered the CPS's ideological campaign, a more practical level of support was provided by the insurance company Save & Prosper

(S&P). Its written evidence to the Inquiry offered a blueprint for how personal pensions might work: the 'personal retirement account' (PRA).[93] This had parallels with the United States' 'investment retirement account' (IRA), but in practice was based on the United Kingdom's existing 'Section 226' model of DC pensions for the self-employed. S&P proposed that all individuals be given the freedom to open a PRA with institutions such as banks, building societies, life insurance companies, and unit trust management groups, and be able freely to transfer their pension savings between them.[94]

Critics

This triumvirate of enthusiastic advocates for personal pensions in the inquiry process was counteracted by an overwhelming number of opponents. The first and most major criticism made by detractors was that giving individuals the freedom to opt out of occupational pension schemes would endanger the solvency of employer-run pensions (already facing strain as a result of inflation indexation), because schemes were dependent on the contributions of new members to meet prospective deficits.[95] As Tom Hayes, chairman of the NAPF, told the Inquiry, if young workers opted out the schemes would 'eventually wither and die'.[96] This fear was widely shared. The CBI, for example, believed that an exodus of young employees from DB schemes would result in their ultimate destruction.[97] More broadly, the TUC was concerned that personal pensions would weaken incentives for employers to provide good occupational pensions at all.[98] Fears about the implications of personal pensions for existing pension schemes were supported by evidence from the LOA, which told the Inquiry that it had attempted but failed to find a way to allow individuals to opt out of DB schemes without destroying existing occupational pensions.[99]

These were not disinterested voices, of course, but opposition also came from insurance interests that could be expected to profit from personal pensions. Legal & General, for example, though supportive of personal pensions as supplementary arrangements for a small number of individuals, expressed strong opposition to any attempt to substitute them for final salary schemes. It too worried that employers might withdraw from offering occupational pensions.[100] Its scepticism reflected its interest in running pension schemes for smaller employers, certainly, but its opposition was nonetheless revealing and stands out as a counterweight to the enthusiasm of Save & Prosper. The position of the 'insurance industry' on personal pensions was very mixed.

At the DHSS one-day conference on early leavers in late 1983, Vinson had expressed his exasperation at opposition of this sort and described feeling 'as if [he] was arguing the case for agrarian reform with members of the

Personal pensions 205

French aristocracy in the 1780s'. He asserted in his evidence that he was not seeking to 'destroy' occupational pensions but was concerned simply with 'seeking ... greater freedom of choice'.[101] This was reiterated in evidence in which the CPS outlined an approach that would allow only new employees, and employees changing jobs, to take out a personal pension.[102] This was an attempt to counter opponents' claims that portable pensions would be a 'bogey which will break the market'.[103] There was a very clear inconsistency in the CPS position, however, as its new position ran entirely counter to its earlier principled desire to disseminate wealth and assert individual control over capital assets.[104] Again, therefore, we see the CPS forced to trim its sails in its evidence to the Inquiry. Similarly, Goldsmith wrote to Fowler claiming that the IoD expected that most employees would remain in their company's scheme and that there was 'no suggestion that the entire occupational pensions system will suddenly be dismantled'.[105]

Save & Prosper, despite its early enthusiastic support for personal pensions, also rejected the argument that individual pensions of the sort they were proposing would have a significant effect on the solvency of DB schemes, since it would only be job changers who would be interested in a personal pension.[106] Thus, the clear opposition expressed by key stakeholders and their dire warnings about the endangering of occupational schemes' viability had forced proponents of personal pensions to reduce their ambitions.

Concern about the continuing viability of occupational pensions in a personal pensions world was not the only worry expressed to the IPR. There was also a widespread assumption that the adoption of DC would provide individuals with poorer and less secure pensions than DB.[107] In general, DB final salary schemes run by employers were viewed as superior to individualised DC by those giving evidence to the Inquiry because they were seen as far better equipped to manage the risks inherent in pensions saving and investment.[108] The CPS rejected claims that DC was 'inherently unsatisfactory'. It argued that DB security was 'illusory for all those who change jobs, or are forced into redundancy'. It also rebutted the assertion that DC was more vulnerable to inflation risk, Vinson and Chappell arguing that DB merely cloaked that risk under the promise of certainty.[109] Criticism of personal pensions on the grounds that they required the individual to carry the burden of inflation risk, exhibited poor investment performance, and ran the risk of short-term market weakness at time of retirement, plus the possibility that individuals might not save enough to avoid becoming a burden on the state in old age, were all routinely countered by Vinson and Chappell with the assertion that such freedoms were already permitted for the self-employed and not a problem (although they did not present any supporting evidence).[110] More fundamental, however, was Vinson and Chappell's belief in the moral superiority of DC 'money purchase', with its principle that 'what you get out reflects what you put in' reflecting 'a fundamental economic truth'.[111]

The CPS's proposals for personal pensions were based, of course, on a rejection of the paternalism inherent in occupational provisions.[112] Yet opponents of personal pensions argued that many individuals were not adequately equipped to save and invest for retirement, and so needed to be compelled, guided, and protected so that they could make the correct decisions in their long-term interest. The argument in favour of paternalism remained a powerful one, being based on four observations: individuals tended to be myopic; most individuals had inadequate financial knowledge or expertise; there was the possibility of bad investment, resulting in low retirement incomes; and the danger that pension providers might 'missell' personal pensions.

As we have already seen, critics of PPPs doubted that young people would make pension provisions unless forced to do so. For example, in his evidence to the IPR, the trade unionist Ken Thomas highlighted the dangers of youthful myopia and the need for compulsion.[113] Even companies and professionals who stood to make money out of personal pensions, such as the British Insurance Brokers' Association, were worried.[114] As Jonquil Lowe (a financial researcher at the consumer magazine *Which?*) noted in her evidence, it was 'doubtful that the majority of people have the inclination, time or expertise to manage their own pension fund'. She highlighted a Sun Life survey finding that a high proportion of self-employed people were saving relatively small amounts: 5 per cent made no pension contributions at all; one-third saved less than 10 per cent of their income through a pension scheme; 40 per cent had 'no idea' how much they were contributing.[115] In short, personal pensions might lead to significant under-pensioning, and in some cases to no pension at all. Such concerns were not shared by Vinson and Chappell.[116] They believed that 'virtually all individuals would make adequate savings for their old age (as the self-employed currently do)'.[117] Likewise, Goldsmith, while accepting there was a risk that some would fail to save enough for retirement, expressed his faith that 'most people' who left their employer's scheme would have 'the knowledge, initiative and incentives to accept greater responsibility for their pension futures'.[118] For those with less faith in individual responsibility than the CPS and IoD, one option could be to require minimum contributions to personal pensions (Save & Prosper, for example, proposed a minimum contribution of 10 per cent of earnings, of which six percentage points would come from the employer).[119] The demands this would place on employers were strongly opposed by them. The CBI warned that its members, though supportive of personal pensions for early leavers, or as an additional pension for occupational scheme members,

Personal pensions and personal pensions 207

would not accept employees opting out of an occupational scheme into a personal pension to which employers would be compelled to make contributions.[120] The NAPF's Derek Bandey agreed that there would be 'horrific' administrative costs if employers were forced to administer 'tens of thousands' of individual pension schemes, rather than a collective company pension.[121] As Bandey put it: 'We must recognise I think that if there is freedom for the individual to opt out then there must equally be freedom for the employer not to provide.'[122]

For concerned pensions experts and practitioners there was also a broader worry about lack of education and financial knowledge. A TUC representative to the IPR was blunt: it was 'quite laughable to imagine that the vast majority of working people of this country – and I am not insulting them – want the opportunity to play the stockmarkets themselves'.[123] The ex-chairman of the NAPF, Maurice Oldfield, neatly summarised his concern in his written evidence to the subgroup: 'Not everyone who bought one of the 3Ps [personal portable pensions] would be very well versed in the 3Rs [reading, 'riting, and 'rithmetic]. Mistakes, errors of judgement, bad luck even dishonesty on party of the broker or carrier could lead to the pension cupboard being bare.'[124]

In oral evidence to the subgroup, the IoD rejected the disparagement of the individual's ability 'to handle his [sic] own financial affairs', which Goldsmith described as 'one of the worst aspects of the opposition to personal pension portfolios'.[125] Goldsmith saw no problem in expecting people to understand the consequences of investment decisions made by them. Later in his oral evidence he added that, 'if we are going to embark upon a route which involves any increase in risk, then with that risk must come the possibility of loss, and I do not regard it as a totally unsympathetic approach to say that people who take risks should get the results of that risk'.[126] The Society of Pensions Consultants' greatest concern was that 'given choice and lack of understanding many individuals could make decisions they might live to regret', and it therefore cautioned that individualisation of pensions would be 'inadvisable' for most people.[127] The CBI also pointed out that it was likely that someone – most probably the state, but perhaps employers also – would have to pay to support individuals in retirement whose market investments had gone sour.[128]

In his evidence on behalf of Save & Prosper, Cholmeley Messer was uncompromising: he did not think it possible to 'stop people making fools of themselves' through poor investment choices. In his view, the only protection against this would be 'good advice' (no doubt from companies such as Save & Prosper).[129] But many of those giving evidence were sceptical that such advice would always be good. The TUC, for example, was concerned that financially naive workers would be easy prey for unscrupulous sales agents – 'sharks', as Ken Thomas called them – who would line up to invest workers' money on their behalf.[130] This fear was shared by the NAPF's Maurice Oldfield, who saw in personal pensions merely 'the prospect of some rich pickings for the commission only salesmen'. Even Save & Prosper expressed worries that people could become 'victims of dishonest or incompetent salesmen'.[131] This concern was shared by the Consumers' Association.[132]

As we have seen, a supplementary argument made by the advocates of personal pensions was that handing responsibility to the individual would bring about the deinstitutionalisation of saving and investment, and that this in turn would lead to a more dynamic capital market, which would benefit the national economy. Walter Goldsmith in particular was highly critical of pension funds' investment practices, arguing that they tended 'to adopt the lowest common denominator of risk when deciding investment policy'.[133] His view was that if pensions were individualised it would be possible for those with a greater appetite for risk to invest their funds more adventurously.[134] The idea that individuals would increase the supply of risk capital to the British economy was met with scepticism, however. Oldfield, drawing on his experience of managing a US subsidiary, argued that individuals there with individual retirement accounts were hardly entrepreneurial in their investments, preferring 'nifty fifty' stocks and fixed interest securities (dryly remarking that 'IBM did not grow from an IRA').[135] Jonquil Lowe cited a report by the Association of Pensioner Trustees on the assets of small self-administered pensions, which showed that a meagre 5 per cent of funds was directly invested in shares and unit trusts (slightly lower than the 7 per cent equivalent figure for IRAs). Lowe argued that existing pension funds were in a far better position to undertake risky investments, as they were able to pool risks, and thus if the investment turned bad it would not wipe out an individual's savings.[136] The Society of Pension Consultants, meanwhile, believed that, if 'a host of presently dormant entrepreneurs' wishing to manage their own portfolios was in fact liberated by personal pensions, the likely outcome would be a speculative crisis in the property market rather than a boost to industrial and commercial investment.[137] The TUC agreed with those who wanted pension funds to be 'more imaginative in their investments', but rejected the notion that to achieve this it would be necessary 'to hand over a pension to an individual person, and that such an individual would in the process act like a Victorian saver and invest in canals and railway companies' (firms that had been the financial graveyard of many nineteenth-century investors).[138] The TUC preferred instead that workers be given the opportunity through involvement on boards of trustees and management committees to influence how occupational funds were invested.[139]

Vinson and Chappell rejected the claim that individuals would be 'hyper-cautious' in investment, thus actually reducing the supply of investment capital for British industry. This, they argued, was because 'the overwhelming proportion of individuals would entrust total management of their pension plan to one of the institutions designated', thus giving 'far greater flexibility to capital markets'.[140] So, once again, Vinson and Chappell's evidence to the Inquiry about the likely outcome of personal pensions ran counter to their original intention of breaking up the institutions in favour of individual control of pension assets. Forced by the weight of opposing evidence to the IPR to restrain their ambition, their stated vision had morphed from promoting individual choice of underlying investment to advocating a choice in a market for institutionally administered investment products. Indeed, most of those giving evidence to the Inquiry assumed that individuals would delegate investment to a financial institution.[141] The response by the CPS and IoD was that consumer choice should be enhanced via a wider range of financial institutions being allowed to provide personal pensions. That was also opposed by the insurance industry, however. Indeed, the very idea that greater choice would be advantageous was questioned. According to the NAPF's Derek Bandey, the ultimate outcome would in fact be a reduction in the capacity of individuals to gain control over the investment of their pension savings. Bandey wondered 'just what control an individual is going to have over the board of directors of the Prudential Assurance Company or some other large institution'.[142] The counter to this charge was that individuals could exercise a greater degree of choice over where their funds were held, and that this would encourage a more competitive and dynamic approach to investing in the institutions. The chair of the NAPF was nonetheless sceptical that individuals would realistically exercise freedom of choice when most insurance companies imposed 'substantial termination penalties' and refused to disclose relevant information to individuals.[143]

Thus, Fowler's IPR had elicited much opposition to personal pensions, and reinforced the message received at his one-day stakeholders' conference in September 1983. It is worth noting that, when the IPR turned to considering the evidence submitted to it and crafting recommendations, none of its external members was supportive of personal pensions as a replacement for occupational schemes, as originally proposed by the CPS.[144] Although the evidence submitted indicated support for the CPS from the IoD and some firms in the insurance industry, the overwhelming weight of 'informed opinion' was against it. The CPS had anticipated this opposition by recrafting its personal pension proposal as a voluntary alternative to occupational pension schemes, rather than a replacement, in the process sacrificing its aim of individualising the pensions of all workers and thereby giving them an active engagement with and role in British capitalism. It had also accepted

210 *Planning a revolution, 1983–5*

that most personal pensions would be administered on the saver's behalf by an institution rather than directly invested. Nevertheless, even that reconceptualisation of the personal pensions vision had been subject to withering criticism from across the board.

Policymaking

It might have been expected that the width and volume of opposition to personal pensions expressed to the Fowler Inquiry would have caused the government to step back from personal pensions. Instead, it continued not just to pursue the idea but to expand its scope. In this section we explore the mechanics of this in our consideration of policymaking between the government's further consultation in mid-1984 on the mechanics of implementing personal pensions and its publication of the Green Paper on social security reform in June 1985, in which a maximalist personal pensions agenda was made clear.

Proposals for consultation

Following its gathering of evidence, the IPR's subgroup on personal pensions considered the issue and reported in May 1984. It acknowledged that there was enthusiasm from individuals for more portability and pensions choice, but also expressed a range of concerns, the most important of which were the risks to the individual involved in DC pensions; the threat to the viability of existing occupational pensions if young workers opted out in large numbers, or if employers were compelled to contribute to their personal pensions; and the consumer protections that would be necessary if personal pensions were sold directly to individuals.[145]

The subgroup's report was then developed into a set of proposals for implementing personal pensions, which was put out for further consultation by Fowler in May 1984. Its main elements were as follows.

1) Personal pensions should be available as of right to all employees.
2) Special arrangements should operate for those already in an occupational pension scheme to avoid any threat to the scheme's finances.
3) Personal pensions should qualify for contracting out of SERPS.
4) The test for contracting out should be based on a level of contributions calculated to deliver an adequate pension on retirement.
5) No employer contribution to a personal pension should be required, apart from an amount related to the National Insurance contribution rebate for employers whose scheme was contracted out.[146]

In launching the consultation, Fowler emphasised that the essence of the proposals was freedom of choice and flexibility, and to some extent the

Personal pensions   211

improvement of job mobility. He was at pains to make clear, however, that occupational pension schemes would continue to play a vital role. Personal pensions would therefore be but an additional element within the broader system of income replacement in old age encompassing occupational pensions and SERPS.[147]

In navigating from the 8 May report of the Inquiry's personal pensions subgroup to Fowler's consultation document in July, much of the internal debate within government centred on SERPS, which we discuss in the next chapter. On personal pensions, the subgroup had from the start been unwilling to follow the CPS's original path of ideological anti-institutionalism and the explicit promotion of individual capitalism via personal pensions as a means of breaking down the power of pension funds. Instead, it committed both to the introduction of personal pensions and to ensuring the stability and continuation of DB occupational pension schemes.[148] John Redwood – who had attended its meetings, alongside civil servants from the Treasury, Inland Revenue, and DHSS – had thus failed in what a Treasury official described as his desire to use personal pensions to 'destroy all final salary schemes'.[149] Subgroup members had from the start been sceptical about this aim. Alan Peacock had counselled against 'getting ... into an argument about the virtues of capitalism and the "every man a capitalist" theme', and his caution had informed the group's approach, with Fowler being personally concerned to 'not destabilise pension scheme or state scheme finances'.[150]

Despite the inquiry subgroup's continued support for DB schemes, however, it had still felt that individuals should be given the right to opt out of them. As Seammen noted, this was undoubtedly due to the Prime Minister being 'keen on personal pensions'.[151] Ideology was therefore an important driver. We can see this in the fact that personal pensions were not even viewed by the subgroup as the primary means to solve the 'early leaver problem'. This was instead dealt with by agreeing that individuals leaving an employer should be given the option of a 'transfer value' to take to their next pension.[152] A separate consultative document published on this proposal was widely welcomed (although the subsequent attempt to agree on how to calculate transfer values remained complex and contentious).[153]

The fundamental problem that confronted the subgroup in formulating its proposals to allow employees to opt out of an occupational scheme into a personal pension was that most of the evidence received by it suggested that those schemes would probably close in consequence. As an actuary, Marshall Field was most sympathetic to the argument that such schemes would be endangered. He was persuaded that permitting individuals to opt out would be 'administratively very complex'. He also worried about its potential to 'expose the employer to a financial selection'. His preference was to allow personal pensions to supplement, not replace, final salary schemes.[154] We can see a slightly different concern expressed by Field's subgroup colleague Mark Weinberg. Perhaps reflecting the latter's position as managing director of Hambro Life, he took the view that, 'in principle, everyone should be able to opt out of [an] occupational scheme'. He did not believe, however, that employers should be obliged to contribute to the personal pension of anyone who did so, because of the complex administration this would impose on firms.[155] Without those employer contributions, though, the effective outcome would essentially be the same as that envisaged by Field: for the employee in an occupational pension, a personal pension would be available as an additional option, not as a replacement. That was an outcome very much at odds with the wishes of Redwood, who continued to advocate total freedom to opt for a personal pension and for compulsory employer contributions into it, with all that would imply for the future unsustainability of occupational schemes.[156]

In an attempt to resolve the dilemma of how to implement personal pensions without endangering occupational scheme finances, the subgroup proposed that, while employers running contracted-out occupational pension schemes would continue to pay the lower (contracted-out) National Insurance contribution, they would be required only to make a minimum contribution to an employee's personal pension related to the age and sex of the employee (with the percentages to be laid down by government).[157] Leaving aside the distributional effects, this would be administratively very complex, and Field feared that the costs would be 'intolerable'.[158] This was a problem for Fowler, who believed that any successful personal pension policy 'should not place an unacceptable administrative burden on employers, government departments, or providers'.[159] To control administration costs, the subgroup proposed the creation of a 'clearing house' for employee and employer personal pension contributions, paid for and managed by pension providers.[160] This fix had featured not at all in the Inquiry hearings, was mentioned merely in passing by the DHSS official attending a subgroup meeting in early March, and then emerged in Fowler's note for the subgroup at the month's end on a possible framework for personal pensions.[161] Ultimately, it proved to be the key sticking point, as neither Save & Prosper nor Legal & General (two enthusiastic supporters and potential providers of personal pensions) supported the idea.[162]

Beyond the fundamental problem of how to introduce personal pensions without damaging occupational schemes, the IPR's personal pensions subgroup was also forced to respond to criticism that individuals might receive inadequate retirement incomes from DC personal pensions. It agreed that it would be necessary to set down minimum requirements for contributions (although nothing would or could be done about the possibility of poor

Personal pensions 213

investment returns). The best mechanism to achieve this appeared to be to allow contracting out of SERPS only if the personal pension met a contribution adequacy test. But how was this to be done? Plainly, the existing contracting-out requirements for DB occupational schemes (which were based on salary-related benefits) could not be applied to DC money purchase schemes; an alternative test would therefore be necessary. But, since only the level of contribution could be defined, not the ultimate benefits, what should this test be? The proposed solution was to set a minimum contribution based on a percentage of earnings, or a minimum cash requirement.[163] That was all well and good, but it in turn raised two questions. First, employees came in three basic varieties: those in a contracted-out DB scheme; those in a contracted-in DB scheme; and those whose employer offered no scheme at all. Plainly, different tests would have to apply in each case. Second, it was all very well seeking to ensure adequacy through minimum contributions to a DC personal pension, but, beyond this, whether the pension eventually secured would be adequate was still highly dependent on how well those contributions were invested. In any case, one major feature of Britain's pension system that the CPRS had decried as paternalistic would be retained: individuals would not have the freedom to choose not to save.

The July 1984 consultation document also considered the issue of who would be permitted to provide personal pensions, and what, if any, limits there should be on their investment. The DTI was concerned that employees have 'as wide a choice of [personal pensions] as possible', and to this end favoured 'maximum flexibility', albeit with 'limits to be set in order to ensure protection'. The Treasury was opposed to allowing building societies to provide PPPs, however, on the grounds that they would not be able to underwrite investments.[164] By the time the consultation document was published this issue had not been resolved, and, more generally, there was no agreement on the mechanics of providing personal pensions. Rather than make proposals, therefore, the consultation document merely invited views on how best to encourage supplementary voluntary provision. Indeed, when the consultation document was published in July 1984, the *Financial Times*' Eric Short noted the document's focus on principles, and its vagueness on the practicalities of how the system would actually work.[165]

Responses to the consultation

When the consultation document was published the IPR's secretary wrote to the CPS to acknowledge 'the considerable debt of gratitude' owed to it by the Inquiry 'for getting the portable pensions debate on the ground'.[166] Although its radical agenda had been eroded by the Inquiry process, Vinson and Chappell told Sherman that they were 'heartened' by the consultation document, which they believed would 'begin the process of personalising the wealth in pension funds'.[167] Yet the broader response to this latest consultation was, again, very negative. Despite the efforts made to safeguard occupational schemes and employers, the key interest groups and representative bodies expressed their continuing opposition to contracted-out personal pensions. The most high-profile public criticism came in November 1984, from Britain's largest insurance company: the Prudential. In a pamphlet for public consumption and a series of advertisements, it highlighted the absence of compulsory employer contributions, the lack of pension for a surviving spouse, unpredictable pension levels, the fact that the government had 'gloss[ed] over' the issue of investor protection, the immense costs imposed on employers, and the probability they would spell the end for occupational schemes. 'Radical reshaping is not the right course to take,' warned the Prudential. 'It is counterproductive. And it will cost you.' Ultimately, the company argued that personal pensions were 'completely unnecessary'.[168]

The DHSS summary of the responses received noted that the consultation had revealed support for 'more access to voluntary provision riding on top of occupational schemes'. Both the NAPF and CBI, for example, again argued that personal pensions should be additional to rather than a replacement for occupational schemes or SERPS.[169] Opinion was mixed on the right not to join an occupational scheme; for the CPS this was 'the single most important proposal' but, not surprisingly, pension funds, employers, and unions remained opposed. More generally, there was much concern that personal pensions would result in an overall reduction in pension provision. The IFoA, for example, warned that a combination of low personal pension take-up and a withdrawal of employers from occupational provision would result in poorer pensions all round.[170]

The ACA, the NAPF, and the Engineering Employers' Federation were all sceptical that the government's market research had demonstrated much demand for personal pensions.[171] Both the CPS and IoD had sought during the IPR to find ways that might increase demand, and had pushed the DHSS to go further in its encouragement of personalisation than in had initially desired. Vinson and Chappell wanted greater inducements for employees, which they believed could be achieved by encouraging employers to contribute no less to personal pensions than they would to their own occupational schemes, and, in the long term, by totally abolishing SERPS. Legal & General also criticised the proposals for not giving individuals enough encouragement to opt for a personal pension. Although the company did not support compelling employers to provide the option of a personal pension, it did argue that to make personal pensions more attractive employees should be able to claim up-front tax relief on contributions (rather than claiming

Personal pensions 215

a refund).[172] (At the behest of the Treasury, the Inquiry had been forbidden from examining tax changes.) The pensions consulting firm MPA was also sceptical, arguing that occupational scheme members, unless put under pressure by sales staff, would not opt for a DC personal pension because they were fundamentally so much less attractive than DB schemes.[173]

Overall, therefore, despite their involvement in the IPR, stakeholders had not been mollified by the translation of the personal pension idea into a framework for its implementation. Their responses to the consultation demonstrated their continuing scepticism about personal pensions. There was some softening in attitudes as compared with the evidence given to the IPR, in terms of some recognition of the merits of greater choice, but the overwhelming majority of interested organisations remained opposed to the personal pensions concept, particularly in its contracted-out form, and to the idea that employers should themselves contribute to and administer employee contributions to them.[174]

From consultation to the Green Paper on reform of social security

Following the publication of the July 1884 consultation document and the receipt of feedback, personal pensions were enveloped within the broader enquiry into provision for old age, which had itself become part of the government's now much broader review of social security. As policy was developed within government as it worked towards its Green Paper on the reform of social security, the main point at issue in pensions reform proved to be the future of SERPS (as discussed in the next chapter). When it came to personal pensions, however, there was a marked shift in the DHSS's approach. By January 1985 Fowler was leading internal DHSS discussions, which led to agreement on a new two-tier system: the BSP for all, with top-up either by an occupational pension or a personal pension; SERPS would be abolished, though rights already accrued would be honoured.[175] This idea (which had not been put to the IPR as a firm proposal by the time of its final meeting on 17 January) was then put to and endorsed by a subcommittee of the Cabinet working on social security reform (MISC 111) in February.[176] As we shall see in succeeding chapters, the key debate about personal pensions came to focus on whether or not they should be made compulsory in order to avoid a future crisis of old aged poverty and consequent pressure for higher welfare benefits as a result of abolishing SERPS.[177]

In the event, therefore, the key difference between the schema for personal pensions set out in the Green Paper and that proposed in Fowler's earlier consultation document related to their potential to be a replacement for occupational pensions. In the light of the government's decision to

216   *Planning a revolution, 1983–5*

legislate for compulsory alternatives to SERPS with the opportunity for employees to opt out of an occupational scheme into a personal pension (see next chapter), a complex regime of age- and sex-related rebates that had been proposed to preserve the stability of occupational schemes was dropped and it was decided that a minimum level of contribution to a personal pension of 4 per cent of earnings would be required, of which at least half had to be contributed by the employer (although only for permanent, full-time employees with high enough incomes). The Green Paper also stated that personal pension schemes would be required to offer minimum benefit conditions – notably, widower and widow benefits. The decision to enforce employer contributions to personal pensions was clearly a reflection of the broader decision, once the government had decided to abolish SERPS, to make private pension provision compulsory for those not in an occupational scheme.

This decision to make contributions to a personal pension compulsory for all employees not already in an occupational pension scheme had been promoted within government by the PU, Redwood and Willetts recommending it to Thatcher in April 1985.[178] But many of the details were still to be determined. It also remained to be decided what range of institutions would be permitted to provide personal pensions. The question of regulation was also unanswered (readers were referred to the government's recent White Paper on investor protection).[179] Why was policy detail lacking on personal pensions? As we shall see in Chapter Six, the personal pensions question became entangled with the attempted abolition of SERPS, a highly controversial reform even within the government, and with the concomitant need to make personal pensions compulsory (again, highly controversial, since the Treasury objected to the likely cost of the associated tax relief). Consideration of much of the detailed policy on personal pensions was simply squeezed out as the government sought swiftly to move to the Green Paper.

Conclusion

The idea of personalising pensions had entered the policy arena in 1983, ostensibly to solve the technical problem of preserving the pension benefits of individuals who changed jobs, but in reality motivated by a radical neoliberal political-economic agenda that sought to create a society of individual investor capitalists. The idea caught the attention of the Prime Minister and her Downing Street Policy Unit, with Redwood the conduit through which the CPS's personal pension idea flowed into the heart of government, and Thatcher subsequently tasked Fowler with introducing the new personal portable pension. From the start the idea received a hostile reception from employers, trades unions, and the pension industry. It was argued that allowing individuals to opt out of occupational schemes would

Personal pensions 217

be disastrous: it would destroy existing employer pension provision; result in significantly poorer overall pensions (by replacing DB with DC); and would expose individuals to their own financial ineptitude and the greed of unscrupulous sales agents. As with Labour's attempt to dismantle occupational pensions in the 1950s, therefore, we again see clear positive feedback effects working to encourage key institutional players to voice their opposition to wholesale reform of the existing system. In the face of this scepticism, the CPS was forced to trim its sails; whereas its original intention had been to give every individual employee direct control over how they invested their personal pension, it had instead embraced a more general aim of simply widening the number of financial institutions that might provide personal pensions.

Norman Fowler, who from the start had been sceptical about the CPS's agenda, was therefore successful in using his Inquiry into Provision for Retirement to highlight the scale of opposition to installing personal pensions as a replacement for occupational pensions. But, having revealed the scale of opposition, Fowler was less successful in resisting the PU's CPS-inspired revolutionary agenda. This is not to say he had no successes. His most notable achievement was the decision to deal with the early leaver problem via the indexation of preserved occupational pensions – as recommended by the OPB – and, by extension, the decision to retain and defend the financial sustainability of occupational pension schemes. His big defeat, however, was the decision to substitute personal pensions for SERPS. Thus, with the publication of the Green Paper, Fowler appeared to have lost his battle to install personal pensions as merely an additional element within the broad architecture of British pensions and, in doing so, allow workers to top up their existing earnings-related pension provision (whether SERPS or an occupational pension).

Notes

1 Harold Wilson, *Report of the Committee to Review the Functioning of Financial Institutions*, Cmnd 7937 [the Wilson Report] (London: HMSO, 1980).
2 Ibid., para. 307, p. 92.
3 Geoffrey Howe, Speech to the 1981 NAPF Annual Conference, Birmingham, 7–10 May 1981, reproduced in *Pensions World*, June 1981.
4 Anthony F. Heath, Roger M. Jowell, and John K. Curtice, *How Britain Votes* (Oxford: Pergamon Press, 1985), pp. 219–39; Steven Nesbitt, *British Pensions Policy Making in the 1980s: The Rise and Fall of a Policy Community* (Avebury: Ashgate, 1995), pp. 57–58; John Charmley, *A History of Conservative Politics since 1830* (Basingstoke: Palgrave Macmillan, 2008). On pensions specifically, see Nesbitt, *British Pensions Policy Making in the 1980s*, pp. 57–58.
5 Richard Vinen, *Thatcher's Britain: The Politics and Social Upheaval of the 1980s* (London: Simon & Schuster, 2009), p. 178.

6 David Parker, *The Official History of Privatisation*, vol. 1: *The Formative Years, 1970–1987* (London: Routledge, 2009), p. 166; Richard Roberts and David Kynaston, *City State: A Contemporary History of the City of London and How Money Triumphed* (London: Profile, 2002), pp. 19–21.

7 For early examples, see Simon James, 'The Idea Brokers: The Impact of Think Tanks on British Government', *Public Administration*, 71 (1993); Radhika Desai, 'Second-Hand Dealers in Ideas: Think-Tanks and Thatcherite Hegemony', *New Left Review*, 203 (1994); Richard Cockett, *Thinking the Unthinkable: Think-Tanks and the Economic Counter-Revolution, 1931–1983* (London: Fontana, 1995); Andrew Denham and Mark Garnett, 'The Nature and Impact of Think Tanks in Contemporary Britain', *Contemporary British History*, 10 (1996). The best more recent discussion is Ben Jackson, 'The Think-Tank Archipelago: Thatcherism and Neo-Liberalism', in *Making Thatcher's Britain*, ed. by Ben Jackson and Robert Saunders (Cambridge: Cambridge University Press, 2012), pp. 43–61.

8 Thomas Borstelmann, *The 1970s: A New Global History from Civil Rights to Economic Inequality* (Princeton, NJ: Princeton University Press, 2012).

9 Leslie Hannah, *Inventing Retirement: The Development of Occupational Pensions in Britain* (Cambridge: Cambridge University Press, 1986), p. 79.

10 David Blake, *Pension Schemes and Pension Funds in the United Kingdom* (Oxford: Oxford University Press, 2003), p. 146.

11 On the contemporary debate, see, for example: *The Economist*, 'Pity the Pensioner', by Paul Barry, 1 September 1979; *The Times*, 'The Great British Pensions Scandal', 24 June 1981; *Financial Times*, 'A Pension Stranglehold, but Legislation Is Difficult', by Barry Riley, 25 July 1981; *The Times*, 'How Employees Lose Out When They Change Jobs', by Lorna Bourke, 23 April 1983.

12 Occupational Pensions Board, *Improved Protection for the Occupational Pension Rights and Expectations of Early Leavers*, Cmnd 8271 (London: House of Commons, 1981). A useful précis of the report, and of pension industry reaction to it, can be found in *Pensions World*, August 1981, pp. 442–49.

13 Conservative Party Archive (hereafter CPA): CRD 4/7/61, 'Pensions Study Group: Minutes of Meeting Held in Interview Room F at the House of Commons at 6.15 p.m.', 4 February 1975.

14 The National Archives (hereafter TNA): CAB 134, Home and Social Affairs Committee, H (81) 40, Memorandum by the Secretary of State for Social Services, 'Occupational Pension Rights of Those Who Leave Employment', 3 June 1981; and Home and Social Affairs Committee, H (81) 19, Minutes of 19th Meeting, 8 June 1981.

15 CPA: CRD 4/7/60–64, 'British Institute of Management: A National Policy for Pensions', 19 November 1974. Consequently, employer and union representatives remained unable to find an agreeable solution (*Financial Times*, 'A Pension Stranglehold, but Legislation Is Difficult', by Barry Riley, 25 July 1981).

16 Occupational Pensions Board, *Greater Security for the Rights and Expectations of Members of Occupational Pension Schemes*, Cmnd 8649 (London: House of Commons, 1982).

Personal pensions

17 In the Treasury, the brutal assessment was this: 'What the DHSS are proposing is pretty pathetic': TNA: T 521/59, D. Seammen to G. W. Monger, 'OPB Report: Early Leavers and Solvency', 17 August 1982.

18 On the history of the CPS, see Jackson, 'The Think-Tank Archipelago'; Cockett, *Thinking the Unthinkable.*

19 Margaret Thatcher Archive [hereafter MTA]: Hugh Thomas to Caroline Stephens, 'The Centre for Policy Studies 1979–80: Report for the Prime Minister, May 1980', 3 July 1980; Nigel Vinson Personal Papers [hereafter NVP]: Nigel Vinson to Geoffrey Howe, 'Background Note for Meeting with the Personal Capital Formation Group at 1000 Wednesday 23 June 1983', 15 June 1983.

20 Gerald Frost, *Making Things Happen: The Life and Original Thinking of Nigel Vinson* (London: Biteback Publishing, 2015), pp. 77–131, 83–213.

21 Nigel Vinson and Philip Chappell, *Personal and Portable Pensions for All* (London: Centre for Policy Studies, 1983).

22 Thomas J. Gould, 'The Changing Practices of Managing Uncertainty and Risk in Post War British Political Economy: Investments, Insurance, Pensions and Professional Risk Managers c. 1945–1995' (PhD, University of Bristol, 2021). Gould notes that the strategy can be seen as building on the financial service sector's growing interest in selling individualised investment products such as unit trusts to better-off people of working age who began to save more during the postwar 'golden age' of economic growth and growing affluence. 'Section 226' pensions were retirement annuity contracts first introduced by the Finance Act 1956 but subsequently regulated by Section 226 of the Income and Corporation Taxes Act 1970.

23 MTA: Hugh Thomas to Caroline Stephens, 'The Centre for Policy Studies 1979–80: Report for the Prime Minister, May 1980', 3 July 1980.

24 MTA: Hugh Thomas and Alfred Sherman, 'Centre for Policy Studies: Reports of Study Groups 1980–81', February 1981; and Vinson to Thatcher, 11 June 1981.

25 Amy Edwards, '"Financial Consumerism": Citizenship, Consumerism and Capital Ownership in the 1980s', *Contemporary British History*, 31 (2017).

26 The importance of defusing economic power in Vinson's personal political philosophy is emphasised by Frost, *Making Things Happen*, pp. 183–97.

27 Joan C. Brown and Stephen Small, *Occupational Benefits as Social Security* (London: Policy Studies Institute, 1985), pp. 138, 53.

28 Cmnd 7937, app. 3, tab. 3.50, p. 467. The growth was driven by a combination of tax incentives and a 'cult of equity' among fund managers: see Brian R. Cheffins, *Corporate Ownership and Control: Evolution of the UK System* (Oxford: Oxford University Press, 2010), pp. 344–81; Yally Avrahampour, '"Cult of Equity": Actuaries and the Transformation of Pension Fund Investing, 1948–1960', *Business History Review*, 89 (2015).

29 Cmnd 7937, app. 3, tab. 3.47, p. 460.

30 Stock Exchange, *The Stock Exchange Survey of Share Ownership* (London: Stock Exchange, 1983), tab. 2.1b.

31 Cmnd 7937, app. 3, tab. 3.52, p. 469.

32 Stock Exchange, *Survey of Share Ownership*, tab. 2.1b; Office for National Statistics, 'Ownership of UK Quoted Shares: 2018' [www.ons.gov.uk/economy/investmentspensionsandtrusts/bulletins/ownershipofukquotedshares/2018, accessed 28 January 2020].

33 From the mid-1950s to the early 1970s their attraction was all the greater given the Labour party's support for the creation of a national, state-run funded earnings-related pension scheme; see Hugh Pemberton, 'The Failure of "Nationalization by Attraction": Britain's Cross-Class Alliance against Earnings-Related Pensions in the 1950s', *The Economic History Review*, 65 (2012), pp. 1436, 1446.

34 Ibid., p. 1435. As Prime Minister, Edward Heath became concerned with the failure of institutional investors (such as pension funds) to support British industry, despite owning large swathes of it; see Aled Davies, *The City of London and Social Democracy: The Political Economy of Finance in Britain, 1959–1979* (Oxford: Oxford University Press, 2017), pp. 42–52.

35 CCO, *The Right Approach: A Statement of Conservative Aims*.

36 MTA: 'The Right Approach to the Economy: Outline of an Economic Strategy for the Next Conservative Government', October 1977.

37 MTA: Margaret Thatcher, Speech to the Zurich Economic Society: 'The New Renaissance', 14 March 1977.

38 Davies, *City of London and Social Democracy*, pp. 37–74; Aled Davies, 'Pension Funds and the Politics of Ownership in Britain, c.1970–86', *Twentieth Century British History*, 30 (2019); James Reveley and John Singleton, 'Labour, Industrial Revitalization, and the Financial Sector, 1970–79', *Twentieth Century British History*, 27 (2016); Mark Wickham-Jones, *Economic Strategy and the Labour Party: Politics and Policy-Making, 1970–83* (London: Macmillan, 1996), pp. 80–81.

39 Peter F. Drucker, *The Unseen Revolution: How Pension Fund Socialism Came to America* (London: Heinemann, 1976). See also Tony Cutler and Barbara Waine, 'Social Insecurity and the Retreat from Social Democracy: Occupational Welfare in the Long Boom and Financialization', *Review of International Political Economy*, 8 (2001); Gordon L. Clark, *Pension Fund Capitalism* (Oxford: Oxford University Press, 2000).

40 On the history of the CPS, see Jackson, 'The Think-Tank Archipelago'; Cockett, *Thinking the Unthinkable*.

41 Alfred Sherman Papers (hereafter ASP): Sherman to Thatcher, 'Insurance and Pension Funds – Our Reserve Army', 24 January 1976.

42 ASP: AC 967, Letter from T. J. Palmer (General Manager, *Legal & General*) to David Howell, 22 January 1976; P. E. Moody (Joint Secretary and Investment Manager, *The Prudential Assurance Company*) to Sherman, 22 June 1976; Sherman to David Howell, 29 January 1979.

43 MTA: Alfred Sherman, Memorandum: 'CPS's Long-Term Publishing Programme', 8 August 1978.

44 Vinson and Chappell, *Personal and Portable Pensions for All*, p. 5.

45 MTA: Vinson to Thatcher, 11 June 1981.

Personal pensions 221

46 In a later submission to the Fowler Inquiry, Vinson was clear that pensions offered a much better opportunity in these respects than extending home ownership. See TNA: T 530/128, 'Centre for Policy Studies: Personal and Portable Pensions, Evidence to the Retirement Provision Inquiry', 6 January 1984.

47 ASP: AC 969–972: Vinson to Sherman, 'Option of Self Employed Pensions for All', 29 March 1983.

48 MTA: Vinson to Thatcher, 11 June 1981.

49 TNA: BN 147/27, Vinson and Chappell to N. Montagu, 9 February 1984.

50 TNA: BN 147/10, Nigel Vinson, 'Draft Statement to Be Issued by Centre for Policy Studies If and When the Government Announces the Option of Personal and Portable Pensions for All', July 1984.

51 NVP: Vinson to Geoffrey, 'Background Note for Meeting with the Personal Capital Formation Group at 1000 Wednesday 23 June 1983', 15 June 1983.

52 In a later pamphlet, Nigel Vinson and Phillip Chappell argued that 'only if individuals participate directly in the creation of wealth can they understand the benefits which it brings to society at large': 'Owners All: A Proposal for Personal Investment Pools' (London: Centre for Policy Studies, 1985), emphasis in original.

53 NVP: Vinson to Howe, 'Background Note for Meeting with the Personal Capital Formation Group at 1000 Wednesday 23 June 1983', 15 June 1983; ASP: AC 969–972: Vinson to Sherman, 'Option of Self Employed Pensions for All', 29 March 1983.

54 Vinson and Chappell, 'Owners All'.

55 Ralf Ptak, 'Neoliberalism in Germany: Revisiting the Ordoliberal Foundations of the Social Market Economy', in *The Road from Mont Pèlerin: The Making of the Neoliberal Thought Collective*, ed. by Philip Mirowski and Dieter Plehwe (Cambridge, MA: Harvard University Press, 2015), pp. 98–138; Werner Bonefeld, 'Freedom and the Strong State: On German Ordoliberalism', *New Political Economy*, 17 (2012).

56 Bonefeld, 'Freedom and the Strong State', p. 641.

57 Centre for Policy Studies, *Why Britain Needs a Social Market Economy* (London: CPS, 1975).

58 Andrew Denham and Mark Garnett, *Keith Joseph* (Chesham: Acumen, 2002), pp. 240–41.

59 *The Times*, 'Have Pension, Will Travel', 28 April 1983. See also the editorial on personal pensions in *The Daily Telegraph*, 29 April 1983, which praised the way in which they would enhance individual identification with economic growth; and in the *Financial Times* ('Freedom in Pensions', 4 May 1983), which praised personal pensions as an alternative to occupational pensions' 'particularly attenuated form of ownership'.

60 *Financial Times*, 'Fowler Promises Conference on Pension Scheme Early Leavers', by Barry Riley, 9 May 1983.

61 ASP: AC 946: The Life Offices' Association/Associated Scottish Life Offices, 'Occupational Pension Schemes Early Leavers' (paper presented to Joint Working Group at the One-Day Conference on Early Leavers at the DHSS,

222 *Planning a revolution, 1983–5*

14 September 1983); 'Discussion Paper to be presented by the Association of Consulting Actuaries' (presented to Joint Working Group at the One-Day Conference on Early Leavers at the DHSS, 14 September 1983); The National Association of Pension Funds, 'Early Leavers – A Policy Statement (presented to Joint Working Group at the One-Day Conference on Early Leavers at the DHSS, 14 September 1983)'.

62 *Financial Times*, 'Fowler Promises Conference'. The chairman of the NAPF, and the organisation itself, were vehemently opposed to the personal pensions proposal, viewing the CPS as a right-wing counterpoint to the Left in seeing pension funds as 'undefended prey' in a search for new sources of investment in British industry (Tom Hayes, 'Early Leavers: A Contribution to the Debate', *Pensions World*, October 1983, p. 640).

63 National Association of Pension Funds Archive (hereafter NAPFA), London Metropolitan Archives: LMA/4494/A/03/012, Minutes of the Parliamentary Committee Meeting, 11 October 1983; *The Economist*, 'At Last, a Law to Clear the Mess', 17 September 1983.

64 TNA: T 530/128, C. A. H. Phillips (DHSS) to Margaret O'Mara (HM Treasury), 28 October 1983; Fowler to the Prime Minister, 'Early Leavers and the Pensions Inquiry', November 1983.

65 *Sunday Times*, 'Thatcher Demands Pension Shake-Up', by Lionel Barber, 14 August 1983.

66 Charles Moore, *Margaret Thatcher*, vol. 2: *Everything She Wants* (London: Allen Lane, 2015), p. 94.

67 TNA: BN 13/278, M. J. A. Partridge to S. A. Godber, 'The Pensions Inquiry', 26 October 1983.

68 TNA: T 530/128, Andrew Turnbull to G. W. Watson (HM Treasury), 'Early Leavers, Portable Pensions and a Pensions Enquiry', 16 November 1983.

69 TNA: BN 13/278, S. A. Godber to Andrew Turnbull, 26 October 1983. Differing emphases within government on pension reform were clear in a meeting between Fowler and Redwood at the start of November, with Redwood's enthusiasm for personal pensions resisted by Fowler, who asserted that any inquiry would not be 'a backdoor way of eroding the rights of existing pensioners' (T 530/129, 'Portable Pensions: Discussion with John Redwood', Note of a Meeting, 1 November 1983).

70 Anthony Seldon, *John Major: A Political Life* (London: Weidenfeld & Nicolson, 1997), p. 141. For Hennessy, the PU at this time was Thatcher's 'to the last paperclip' (Peter Hennessy, *Whitehall* (London: Secker & Warburg, 1989), p. 653).

71 TNA: PREM 19/1004, CPRS, 'Pensions and Individual Choice', April 1983.

72 TNA: T 496/139, G. W. Monger to Mrs Holmans, 'Burden of Pensions in the Longer Term', 23 March 1983. Worries about the future impact on workers of a growing number and value of funded occupational pension commitments were derived from a recognition that even funded pensions were dependent on the level of economic output at the time they were paid out, a point later made by the Government Actuary in a seminar of the Institute and Faculty of Actuaries (*Pensions World*, 'Actuaries' Seminar on Pensions', February 1984, pp. 68–69).

Personal pensions
223

73 TNA: T 496/436, M. J. A. Partridge to G. A. Hart (CPRS), 'CPRS Work on Pensions', 22 March 1983.

74 TNA: PREM 19/1004, CPRS, 'Pensions Issues and Policy', April 1983. See Chapter Four.

75 Moore, *Margaret Thatcher*, vol. 2, p. 75. The abolition of the CPRS and expansion of the PU in 1983 are discussed in David Willetts, 'The Role of the Prime Minister's Policy Unit', *Public Administration*, 65 (1987); and Aled Davies, James Freeman, and Hugh Pemberton, 'Thatcher's Policy Unit and the "Neoliberal Vision"', *Journal of British Studies*, 62 (2023). The latter also covers Thatcher's thwarted attempt to create a Prime Minister's Department.

76 Moore, *Margaret Thatcher*, vol. 2, p. 94; TNA: PREM 19/2523, Redwood to Thatcher, 'Early Leavers and Portable Pensions', 14 November 1983.

77 Nesbitt, *British Pensions Policy Making in the 1980s*, p. 71.

78 Department of Health and Social Security, 'Consultative Document on Improved Protection for the Occupational Pension Rights and Expectations of Early Leavers from Occupational Pension Schemes' (London: DHSS, 29 November 1984).

79 TNA: BN 13/278, DHSS Press Release: 'First Task for the Pension Inquiry', 16 December 1983. The Inquiry's secretary noted the significance of Weinberg's appointment and the influence on it that he came to wield (Hugh Pemberton, ed., 'The Fowler Inquiry into Provision for Retirement and the Pension Reforms of 1986. A Witness Seminar Held at the Institute and Faculty of Actuaries High Holborn, London, 6 December 2017' [Bristol: University of Bristol, 2017], p. 19). A transcript of the witness seminar can be found online: https://research-information.bris.ac.uk/en/publications/the-fowler-inquiry-into-provision-for-retirement-and-the-pension--2.

80 TNA: BN 13/278, N. Montagu, 'Consultation Letter on Portable Pensions', 16 December 1983. Examples of issues to be explored cited in the letter included what the implications for existing occupational schemes would be if employees were given the right to remove their pension entitlements and transfer them into a portable scheme, or if new employees were not obliged to join company schemes; the effect of individuals' incentives to save for retirement; and the likely impact on financial markets.

81 TNA: BN 147/26, IPR (PP) 13, N. Montagu, IPR Sub-Group on Portable Pensions, 'Written Evidence on Portable Pensions: Note by the Secretary', 20 February 1984.

82 TNA: PREM 19/2523, S. A. Godber to Andrew Turnbull, 26 October 1983.

83 TNA: PREM 19/2523, Ferdinand Mount to Prime Minister, 'Portable Pensions', 28 October 1983.

84 TNA: T 530/77, Copy of Prime Minister's Private Secretary to S. Godber (DHSS), 'Portable Pensions', 31 October 1983; BN 13/278, 'Portable Pensions: Discussion with John Redwood, Note of a Meeting', 1 November 1983; PREM 19/2523, Redwood to Thatcher, 'Early Leavers and Portable Pensions', 14 November 1983.

85 TNA: T 530/128, Centre for Policy Studies, 'Personal and Portable Pensions, Evidence to the Retirement Provision Inquiry', 6 January 1984.

86 Ibid.

87 ASP: AC 946. The Life Offices' Association/Associated Scottish Life Offices, 'Occupational Pension Schemes Early Leavers (paper presented to Joint Working Group at the One-Day Conference on Early Leavers at the DHSS)', 14 September 1983.

88 TNA: T 530/128, Ridley to Chancellor of the Exchequer, 'Portable Pensions and All That', 11 November 1983.

89 The IoD, an institution with a large but mostly dormant membership, was a perennial advocate for neoliberal ideas in the Thatcher era, 'widely seen as having the ear of the Thatcher governments', which saw it as considerably more sympathetic to their agenda than the CBI (Desai, 'Second-Hand Dealers in Ideas', p. 30).

90 TNA: BN 147/30, Goldsmith to Fowler, 31 January 1984.

91 TNA: BN 147/36, Goldsmith, oral evidence to DHSS Public Inquiry into Provision for Retirement (hereafter 'IPR'), 14 February 1984.

92 TNA: BN 147/30, Goldsmith to Fowler, 31 January 1984.

93 NVP: Save & Prosper, 'Freedom in Pensions: A Blueprint for a Unified Personal Retirement Account', 6 December 1983; *Financial Times*, 'Portable Pension Scheme Launched by Save & Prosper', by Eric Short, 12 October 1984.

94 TNA: T 530/128, Save & Prosper, 'Memorandum on Portable Pensions', 6 January 1984. The authors, Cholmeley Messer and Tony Doggart, were frank about S&P's 'active commercial interest in the pensions market' and the fact that it stood to benefit from the implementation of personal pensions.

95 Indexation would be costly (as much as 7 to 7.5 per cent of payroll, estimated the chairman of the NAPF, *Pensions World*, August 1981, p. 442). In addition, as the Chancellor had been advised at the time of the OPB recommendations, earnings inflation running more rapidly than the rise in asset values had served to raise occupational pension liabilities and made the funds dependent on a constant stream of new workers to make up the deficiency (TNA: T 521/48, P. J. Cropper to Chancellor of the Exchequer, 'The Occupational Pensions Board Report on Early Leavers', 15 June 1981).

96 TNA: BN 147/36, Tom Hayes (chairman, NAPF), oral evidence to IPR, 24 January 1984.

97 TNA: BN 147/36, Michael Pilch, oral evidence to IPR, 21 February 1984. The CBI also argued that banning compulsory enrolment in occupational schemes amounted to an attack on the freedom of employers and employees to agree together on how employees' pension provisions might be arranged.

98 TNA: BN 147/36, Ken Thomas, oral evidence to IPR, 29 February 1984. Thomas, representing the TUC, explained that it had learned from experience that '[e]mployers ... do not hand out money like drunken sailors; every penny has to be fought for'. He argued that, faced with channelling contributions into personal pensions at the same time as voluntarily running administratively complex occupational pensions, many employers would think again about providing the latter.

99 TNA: BN 147/36, Roy Brimblecombe, oral evidence to IPR, 14 February 1984.

100 TNA: BN 147/26, 'Inquiry into Provision for Retirement, Portable Pensions, Evidence Submitted by Legal & General Assurance Society Ltd.', January 1984.

101 NVP: Nigel Vinson, 'DHSS Conference on Pensions – The Option of Personal Pensions for All', 14 September 1983.

102 TNA: T 530/128, 'Centre for Policy Studies: Personal and Portable Pensions, Evidence to the Retirement Provision Inquiry', 6 January 1984.

103 TNA: BN 147/36, Philip Chappell, quoted in 'DHSS Public Inquiry into Provision for Retirement', 24 January 1984.

104 Chappell even told the committee that the CPS believed there was 'relatively little demand for personal pensions', and so the damage to occupational schemes would be 'insignificant, if at all.'

105 TNA: BN 147/30, Goldsmith to Fowler, 31 January 1984.

106 TNA: T 530/128, Save & Prosper, memorandum on portable pensions, 6 January 1984.

107 The chair of the NAPF, for example, contrasted the certainty provided to individuals by final salary schemes with the unpredictability of a retirement income determined by luck in volatile markets (TNA: BN 147/36, Tom Hayes, oral evidence to IPR, 24 January 1984). The LOA pointed out that existing occupational schemes had often begun as DC schemes, but that dissatisfaction with them had resulted in the widespread transition to DB (BN 147/36, Barry Sherlock, oral evidence, 14 February 1984). Similarly, the Policy Studies Institute pointed out that the Federated Superannuation Scheme for universities had abandoned DC because it left many seriously 'under-pensioned' (BN 147/26, evidence of Prof. Michael P. Fogarty, 4 January 1984).

108 See, for example, TNA: BN 147/36, Roy Colbran (IFoA), oral evidence to IPR, 29 February 1984.

109 TNA: T 530/128, 'Centre for Policy Studies: Personal and Portable Pensions, Evidence to the Retirement Provision Inquiry', 6 January 1984.

110 Ibid. In fact, it is doubtful that the average self-employed pension saver had survived unscathed from the inflationary wave of the 1970s and early 1980s, and, in any event, they were probably better placed to weather such risks than the average employee.

111 TNA: BN 147/36, Nigel Vinson, quoted in 'DHSS Public Inquiry into Provision for Retirement', 24 January 1984.

112 This is most clearly expressed in a later pamphlet written for the CPS by Chappell, in which he criticised as erroneous the faith in the paternalist 'good employer': Philip Chappell, *Pensions and Privilege: How to End the Scandal, Simplify Taxes and Widen Ownership* (London: Centre for Policy Studies, 1988), p. 43.

113 TNA: BN 147/36, Ken Thomas, oral evidence to IPR, 29 February 1984.

114 TNA: BN 147/26, Michael S. Morris (director general, BIBA) to N. Montagu, 'Inquiry into Provision for Retirement: Personal Portable Pensions', 20 January 1984.

115 TNA: BN 147/27, Jonquil Lowe to N. Montagu, 14 February 1984. She also drew attention to the fact that one-third of respondents had no life insurance,

226   *Planning a revolution, 1983–5*

which suggested that people were unlikely to 'show more foresight in taking up voluntary pensions than they do voluntary taking up insurance'.

116 Vinson told the IPR that he had no issue with '[w]ine, women and song while young enough to enjoy it' (NVP: opening address by Mr Nigel Vinson to the Secretary of State's Inquiry on Pensions, 23 January 1984).

117 TNA: T 530/128, CPS, 'Personal and Portable Pensions, Evidence to the Retirement Provision Inquiry', 6 January 1984.

118 TNA: BN 147/30, Goldsmith to Fowler, 31 January 1984.

119 NVP: Save & Prosper, 'Freedom in Pensions: A Blueprint for a Unified Personal Retirement Account', 6 December 1983; TNA: T 530/128, Save & Prosper, memorandum on Portable Pensions, 6 January 1984.

120 TNA: BN 147/36, Peter Lobban (CBI), oral evidence to IPR, 21 February 1984. (See also the claim by the LOA's Barry Sherlock in evidence given on 14 February that the complexities and costs for employers of having to deal with personal pensions would prove so overwhelming that it would encourage some to abandon their occupational schemes.) The CBI was supportive of portable voluntary additional contributions on a DC basis, however: TNA: BN 147/36, IPR(PP)8, IPR Sub-Group on Portable Pensions. 'Summary of Written Submissions from Bodies Giving Oral Evidence', note by the secretary, 9 February 1984.

121 TNA: BN 147/36, oral evidence to IPR, 24 January 1984.

122 Ibid.

123 TNA: BN 147/36, Ken Thomas, oral evidence to IPR, 29 February 1984.

124 TNA: BN 147/26, Oldfield to Montagu, 'Inquiry into Provision for Retirement: Portable Pensions', 24 January 1984.

125 Goldsmith argued that 'if people have an interest in their financial affairs they will learn to handle them well, just as they learn to fill intricate combinations of football coupons and other things people actually have an interest in doing' (TNA: BN 147/36, Walter Goldsmith, oral evidence to IPR, 14 February 1984). We should note, however, the implicit acceptance by Goldsmith that the subject of personal pensions for all was no longer on the agenda; rather, it would be personal pensions for those who opted for them.

126 TNA: BN 147/36, Walter Goldsmith, oral evidence to IPR, 14 February 1984.

127 TNA: BN 147/27, Society of Pension Consultants, 'Précis of Society Evidence to Portable Pension Sub-Group of Fowler Inquiry', 30 January 1984.

128 TNA: BN 147/36, Richard Neale (CBI), oral evidence to IPR, 21 February 1984.

129 TNA: BN 147/36, Cholmeley Messer, oral evidence to IPR, 24 January 1984.

130 TNA: BN 147/36, Ken Thomas, oral evidence to IPR, 29 February 1984.

131 TNA: BN 147/26, Oldfield to Montagu, 'Inquiry into Provision for Retirement: Portable Pensions', 24 January 1984; BN 147/26, IPR(PP)6, N. Montagu, 'Further Notes by Save and Prosper Group', 25 January 1984.

132 TNA: BN 147/27, IPR(PP)15, IPR Sub-Group on Portable Pensions, 'Further Submissions from Consumers' Association and Society of Pension Consultants', note by the secretary, 14 February 1984.

133 TNA: BN 147/30, Goldsmith to Fowler, 31 January 1984.

Personal pensions

134 TNA: BN 147/36, Walter Goldsmith, oral evidence to IPR, 14 February 1984.

135 TNA: BN 147/26, Oldfield to Montagu, 'Inquiry into Provision for Retirement: Portable Pensions', 24 January 1984.

136 TNA: BN 147/27, Jonquil Lowe (Money Group – *Which?*) to Montagu, 14 February 1984.

137 TNA: BN 147/27, Society of Pension Consultants, 'Précis of Society Evidence to Portable Pension Sub-Group of Fowler Inquiry', 30 January 1984.

138 TNA: BN 147/36, Ken Thomas, oral evidence to IPR, 29 February 1984.

139 Davies, 'Pension Funds and the Politics of Ownership in Britain', p. 92.

140 TNA: T 530/128, Centre for Policy Studies, 'Personal and Portable Pensions, Evidence to the Retirement Provision Inquiry', 6 January 1984.

141 The British Insurance Brokers' Association believed, for example (in line with Save & Prosper and Legal & General), that the most likely system of personal pensions would see 'each individual worker having a contractual relationship with one or more investment institutions operating a competitive market', which would in turn result in the concentration of investment decisions into fewer hands, and that the market would thus become dominated by a small group of insurance companies and investment institutions. See TNA: BN 147/26, Michael S. Morris (director general, BIBA) to N. Montagu, 'Inquiry into Provision for Retirement: Personal Portable Pensions', 20 January 1984.

142 TNA: BN 147/36, Derek Bandey, oral evidence to IPR, 24 January 1984.

143 TNA: BN 147/36, Colin Lever, oral evidence to IPR, 24 January 1984.

144 TNA: BN 147/27, IPR(PP)21, IPR Sub-Group on Portable Pensions, 'Portable Pensions: Issues and Options. Note by the Secretary (N. Montagu)', 1 March 1984.

145 TNA: BN 147/33, Report of the Sub-Group on Personal Pensions, 8 May 1984, sect. 3. Research commissioned from Gallup by the IPR had demonstrated considerable public enthusiasm for personal pensions, though mostly among those without an occupational pension – and, even then, there was a marked difference depending on whether the employer would be expected to contribute: with such a requirement, four out of five employees would be interested; without it, only a third. Of those in an occupational scheme, just one in five expressed an interest (TNA: BN 147/10, 'The Demand for Portable Pensions: Summary of Gallup Research Carried Out for the Inquiry into Provision for Retirement', June 1984).

146 Department for Health and Social Security, *Personal Pensions: A Consultative Document* (London: DHSS, 1984).

147 *Financial Times*, 'The Do-It-Yourself Pension a Step Nearer' and 'Personal Pensions Plan Unveiled', by Eric Short, 17 July 1984.

148 TNA: T 530/129, D. J. Seammen to Peter Middleton, 'Mr Fowler's Pension Inquiry', 2 March 1984. As Weinberg put it to the other subgroup members: "The challenge is to design a structure for [personal pensions] where they are appropriate, without undermining the healthy continuance of final salary schemes for the many employees for whom they are the best solution.' TNA: BN 147/27, Mark Weinberg, 'Proposal for Personal Portable Pensions', n.d.

149 TNA: T 530/129, G. W. Watson to Minister of State, 'Portable Pensions', 6 March 1984; BN 147/27, Mark Weinberg, 'Proposal for Personal Portable Pensions', n.d.

150 TNA: BN 147/28, IPR(PP)39, IPR Sub-Group on Portable Pensions, 'A Personal Portable Pensions Framework', note by the chairman, 30 March 1984; BN 147/27, Alan Peacock, 'Portable Pensions: Some Notes on the Possible Contents of a Report', n.d.

151 As noted in TNA: T 530/129, D. Seammen to Sir Peter Middleton, 'Mr Fowler's Pension Inquiry', 2 March 1984.

152 TNA: BN 147/10, 84/166, DHSS Press Release, 'Improve Transfer Rights for Early Leavers', 23 May 1984; BN 147/28, IPR(PP)41, IPR Sub-Group on Portable Pensions, 'Consultative Document on Transfer Values', note by the chairman, 16 April 1984; BN 147/31, IPR(PP) 5th minutes of IPR Sub-Group on Portable Pensions, 20 March 1984.

153 Department of Health and Social Security, *Consultative Document on Improved Transferability for Early Leavers from Occupational Pension Schemes* (London: DHSS, 1984). On its reception and on disagreement about how to calculate transfer values, see Eric Short's coverage in the *Financial Times*: 'Accountants Welcome Pension Proposals', 3 August 1984; 'Self-Employed Back Pension Proposals', 9 August 1984; 'Actuaries' Report Unlikely to Remove Grievances on Pension Transfer Value', 28 February 1985; 'Accountants' Body Attacks Pension Transfer Proposals', 3 October 1985.

154 TNA: BN 147/27, M. H. Field to N. Montagu, 'Enquiry into Provision for Retirement: Subgroup on Portable Pensions', 17 February 1984.

155 TNA: BN 147/27, Mark Weinberg, 'Proposal for Personal Portable Pensions', n.d.

156 TNA: T 530/129, G. W. Watson to Minister of State, 'Portable Pensions', 6 March 1984.

157 TNA: T 530/129, Fowler to Whitelaw, 'Consultation Document on Personal Pensions', 15 June 1984. Employees in contracted-in schemes and those without an occupational pension would receive an age- and sex-related contribution directly into their personal pension from DHSS (TNA: BN 147/33, Report of the Sub-Group on Personal Pensions, sect. 3, 8 May 1984). The variations in the contribution level would compensate employers for the increasing cost of occupational schemes to the employer if younger employees opted out – a technically highly complex solution, described by the Treasury's Diana Seammen as 'theoretically justifiable' but 'derisory' and 'outrageous'. Other than its unequal distributional effects (younger workers would receive lower employer contributions than older colleagues; women less than men), she warned of increased administrative costs and complexities for employers. As the CBI's Michael Pilch had told the Inquiry in oral evidence, although it would be possible for actuaries to design a scheme for contracting out according to age- and sex-related contributions, 'in practice nobody could make it work at acceptable levels of administrative complexity and cost' (TNA: BN 147/36, 'DHSS Public Inquiry into Provision for Retirement', 21 February 1984).

Personal pensions   229

158 TNA: BN 147/27, M. H. Field to N. Montagu, 'Enquiry into Provision for Retirement: Subgroup on Portable Pensions', 17 February 1984.

159 TNA: BN 147/28, IPR(PP)39, IPR Sub-Group on Portable Pensions, 'A Personal Portable Pensions Framework', note by the chairman, 30 March 1984.

160 TNA: BN 147/31, IPR(PP) 6th Minutes of IPR Sub-Group on Portable Pensions, 4 April 1984; BN 147/33, I. D. Alexander to Mr Ward, 'Functions of PPP Clearing House', 9 April 1984; Ibid., Report of the Sub-Group on Personal Pensions, paras. 4.11–14, 8 May 1984.

161 TNA: BN 147/41, IPR(PP) 5th Minutes, 20 March 1984; BN 147/28, IPR(PP)39, 'A Personal Portable Pensions Framework', note by the chairman, 30 March 1984; ibid., IPR(PP)38, Inquiry into Provision for Retirement, Sub-Group on Portable Pensions, 'Contracted-out Portable Pensions: Comments from Mr Stewart Lyon, Note by the Secretary', 21 March 1984.

162 TNA: BN 147/31, IPR(PP) 7th Minutes of IPR Sub-Group on Portable Pensions, 2 May 1984; BN 147/33, T. S. Heppell to Mr Phillips, 'Discussions on PPPs with Legal and General', 9 May 1984.

163 TNA: T 530/129, Fowler to Whitelaw, 'Consultation Document on Personal Pensions', 15 June 1984.

164 TNA: BN 147/33, R. B. Saunders to D. Seammen, 'Portable Pensions: Building Societies', 9 July 1984.

165 *Financial Times*, 'The Do-It-Yourself Pension a Step Nearer', by Eric Short, 17 July 1984.

166 TNA: BN 147/10, N. Montagu to Philip Chappell, 'Personal Pensions: A Consultative Document', 16 July 1984; Montagu to Vinson, 'Personal Pensions: A Consultative Document', 16 July 1984.

167 ASP: AC 1240–1244, AR/M/MISC9/5/3 Box 32, letter from Vinson and Chappell to Sherman. 17 July 1984.

168 TNA: BN 147/33, G. J. Otton to Mr Hickey, 'Personal Pensions: Prudential Advertising Campaign', 21 November 1984.

169 TNA: BN 13/299, I. D. Alexander to Mr Hickey, 'Personal Pensions: Responses to the Consultative Document', 20 December 1984.

170 *Financial Times*, 'Actuaries Warn Government of Pitfalls in Pension Proposals', by Eric Short, 9 November 1984.

171 TNA: BN 13/299, I. D. Alexander to Mr Hickey, 'Personal Pensions: Responses to the Consultative Document', 20 December 1984.

172 *Financial Times*, 'Attack on Pension Proposals', by George Graham, 8 December 1984.

173 *Financial Times*, 'Consultants Fear Lower Pension Levels', by Eric Short, August 1984.

174 TNA: BN 13/299, I. D. Alexander to Mr Hickey, 'Personal Pensions: Responses to the Consultative Document', 20 December 1984.

175 TNA: BN 13/300, JW11.1, 'Outcome of January Week' (n.d.); ibid., 'Social Security Reviews: January Week – Session 3 (3–4 January): Pensions', 3 January 1985.

176 TNA: CAB 130/1293, MISC 111 (85) 1, 'Report on the Review of Social Security: Memorandum by the Secretary of State for Social Services', 1

February 1985; discussed by the committee on 6 February. The decision to abolish SERPS was taken by MISC 111 on 13 February.

177 The pros and cons of compulsion were first set out for MISC 111 in TNA: CAB 130/1293, MISC 111 (85) 5, 'Occupational Pension Provision: Encouragement or Compulsion?', memorandum by the Secretary of State for Social Services, 12 February 1985.

178 TNA: PREM 19/1639, Redwood and Willetts to the Prime Minister, 'State Earnings-Related Pension Scheme', 26 April 1985.

179 TNA: BN 13/305, 'Green Paper: Social Security Review Volume 2', June 1985.

6

The abolition of SERPS?

As described in Chapter Four, in the first of Thatcher's three terms the government had acted to contain what it saw as the unsustainable future public spending burden of Labour's indexing of the basic state pension to the higher of the rise in average earnings and prices. As described in Chapter Five, in its second term the government developed its proposals for solving the 'early leaver problem' in collective defined benefit (DB) occupational pensions by effectively replacing them with individualised defined contribution (DC) personal pensions. As policy developed, the idea of personal pensions as a solution to the early leaver problem in occupational pensions was expanded to embrace abolition of the State Earnings-Related Pension Scheme. In this chapter, after first briefly reviewing attitudes to SERPS in the government's first term, we explore the roots of the abolition proposal, in the process tracing two principal motivations: the desire to contain unfunded state spending on pensioners, a fear deepened by a growing awareness that SERPS could be a fiscal 'demographic time bomb' timed to detonate in the early decades of the twenty-first century; and the hope that, through privatisation and individualisation, its former members would be imbued with the 'vigorous virtues' of thrift and entrepreneurialism. We then examine the means by which this proposal became government policy in the 1985 Green Paper on the reform of social security, even though it had been opposed by the great majority of those giving evidence to Norman Fowler's Inquiry into Provision for Retirement (IPR). In the next chapter we then consider why the attempt to dismantle SERPS failed and ultimately, as Paul Pierson puts it, the pension policy of the Thatcher government moved from outright privatisation to a process of 'implicit privatisation'.[1]

From consensus to concern

As noted in Chapter Four, Geoffrey Howe, then Chancellor of the Exchequer, gave a speech to the National Association of Pension Funds in May 1981 in which he raised what he acknowledged was the 'highly emotive subject' of the affordability of UK state pensions. In part, Howe's fear of future unaffordability was driven by a realistic appraisal of future demographic change driven by the combination of the end of the postwar baby boom and the ageing of its product, but the main target of his criticism was Barbara Castle's 1974 *Better Pensions* White Paper. There were two aspects to the critique: first, the White Paper's failure to consider the sustainability of SERPS beyond a 20-year financial horizon; second, the cost to the state of protecting against inflation the 'guaranteed minimum pension' that occupational pension schemes contracted out of SERPS were required to provide. There were also, warned Howe, 'real dangers in planning public expenditure on the basis of assumed growth which may never materialise'.[2] Yet, although Howe and other Treasury ministers were concerned in 1981 about the long-term burden of state (and, for that matter, private occupational) pensions on future workers in the context of an ageing society, for the moment the Treasury had other more pressing pressures to deal with as it grappled with the most serious recession since the 1930s.

The issue returned to the Treasury's agenda following the Government Actuary's appraisal of SERPS's long-term costings in February 1982 (as part of the Quinquennial Review of the National Insurance Fund).[3] This gave rise to a proposal (by the unit responsible for budget policy coordination in the Treasury's Information Division) for a wide-ranging review of SERPS. This suggestion was initially resisted by the Treasury's Social Services Group, whose under-secretary, George Monger, at this point believed SERPS's future cost was containable via 'piecemeal and comparatively unobtrusive changes in the scheme'.[4] Nevertheless, by April 1982 work within the Treasury to assess the long-term costs of SERPS was well under way, influenced by a critical IFS analysis.[5] Despite reassurance from the government that the future cost of state pensions had been kept in acceptable bounds by the move to prices-only indexation of the BSP, the Treasury worried about future reignition of the problem via pressure to restore the earnings link. More fundamentally, and in the context of rapidly rising expenditure on social security generally (not least on unemployment benefits), it began reviewing a range of options for cutting back SERPS.[6] Overall, however, thinking within government about pension reform by early 1983 remained speculative.

Yet, by early 1983, radical action on SERPS had risen up the Treasury agenda, with proponents of pension reform, both ministerial and official, working within Thatcher's dictum 'There is a limit to the burden the government can put on the working population' in their assessment on the future 'burden of pensions'.[7] This is not to say that the abolition of SERPS lacked opponents within government. There was a clear perception that the Secretary of State for Health and Social Security, Norman Fowler, was opposed to the idea. Within the Treasury, his DHSS was seen as institutionally 'passionately attached to the present State pension system'.[8] The Deputy Secretary in charge of its Social Security Operations Group, Michael Partridge, was certainly a powerful opponent. At the Treasury, however, George Monger had reconsidered his view on SERPS sustainability as a consequence of chairing the Treasury's Burden of Pensions review; he now believed that it was worth considering the possibility of abolishing SERPS, as the CPRS was proposing, even though it 'would be enormously controversial'.[9] Ironically, however, as we saw in Chapter Four, the most immediate opponent to a dissolution of the prevailing consensus on pensions proved to be the Prime Minister, who, just a few weeks away from calling a general election, moved swiftly to suppress the CPRS's reports.[10] Tellingly, however, her notes on the CPRS's 'Pensions Issues and Policy' memorandum clearly show that Thatcher's objection was not so much to the radical ideas put forward therein but to the CPRS's political naivety in laying them out so bluntly and at such a politically sensitive juncture.[11]

Reflecting Thatcher's caution, as noted in Chapter Five, the Conservatives' May 1983 general election manifesto was reticent on pension policy, although, overall, it reflected the very different climate of opinion after the Falklands War and the benefits flowing to a party facing a divided opposition, being much more ambitious and much more clearly 'Thatcherite' than that of 1979. The focus of election campaigning on pensions was the promise to address the problem of early leavers from occupational pension schemes, and an assertion that Labour proposed to nationalise occupational pension funds. The manifesto promised nothing on state pensions other than continuing to uprate the BSP in line with price inflation and abolish the earnings rule. During the campaign Thatcher reiterated that there were no plans to make changes to SERPS.[12]

After the Conservatives' resounding electoral victory on 9 June, Thatcher reshuffled her Cabinet. Lawson (who, if anything, was more sceptical about SERPS than Howe, privately asserting that the expenditure promises within SERPS were a 'doomsday machine') became Chancellor of the Exchequer; Fowler, however, continued as Secretary of State for Health and Social Services.[13] Two months later the Prime Minister made another crucial appointment when she brought in John Redwood to run the No. 10 Policy Unit. As noted in Chapter Five, in the wake of the CPS's 'personal portable pensions' solution to the early leaver problem in DB occupational pensions, Thatcher tasked Redwood with action on the reform of pensions. He was anxious to avoid the impression of a secret plan to privatise SERPS, however, and of triggering an immediate backlash.[14] This led him to support Fowler's proposal for a public Inquiry into Provision for Retirement.

As Fowler moved towards setting up the IPR, the DHSS set out for him a possible framework for a new approach to pensions.[15] It had three components. First, giving as many employees as possible the chance of a job-related pension, either by allowing contracted-out DC occupational pensions or by simplifying contracting-out arrangements for DB schemes (in either case, financially incentivising contracting out and requiring the preservation of pension rights after two years of service rather than five). Second, giving all employees the right to opt out of SERPS into a contracted-out DB scheme (subject to improvements in inflation-proofing preserved pensions for leavers) or into a contracted-out DC personal pension. Third, improving the long-term affordability of SERPS by basing it on an individual's lifetime average earnings, not their best 20 years; cutting back to 50 per cent the spousal right to inheritance of SERPS benefits; and requiring contracted-out occupational schemes, not the state, to inflation-proof guaranteed minimum pensions in payment up to 5 per cent per annum (a change estimated by DHSS to remove half of all long-term projected SERPS spending). This was to be the framework within which the DHSS would conduct the public review of pensions that Fowler was shortly to announce, with a view to publishing a White Paper. Crucially, we should note the DHSS's underlying assumption at this stage that SERPS would be modified, not abolished.

The Inquiry into Provision for Retirement

Stage 1 of the IPR

As noted in Chapter Five, chaired by Fowler, the IPR brought three outside experts into the policy process to join ministers: Stewart Lyon, president of the Institute of Actuaries; Marshall Field, chair of the Occupational Pensions Schemes joint working group; and Professor Alan Peacock, vice-chancellor of Britain's only private university. It met for the first time on 14 December 1983, and was told by Fowler that its first task was to look at portable personal pensions (PPPs) – to which end a subgroup on personal pensions was formed.[16] Although it was not to the forefront of the IPR's enquiries, however, it was inevitable that the future shape of SERPS (indeed, whether or not it had a future) would also be a consideration. As Fowler had told Thatcher, the Inquiry would

> need to reach a conclusion on whether [SERPS], together with its sum total of provisions as enacted in the 1975 Pensions Act, can continue building up pension rights and expectations on the existing basis, or whether we ought to consider now steps to reduce the cost next century.[17]

Within and without government, this was to become a key issue as the IPR unfolded.

The abolition of SERPS? 235

Attitudes in the Treasury towards the Fowler Review in general and to SERPS in particular were mixed. As the *Financial Times* noted, one immediate result of the IPR's creation was the forestalling of attempts by the Chancellor to trim DHSS spending on pensions.[18] Lawson was otherwise very defensive of the Treasury's prerogatives, however, persuading Thatcher that Fowler's Inquiry should not be allowed to make recommendations with consequences for tax and National Insurance. Consequently, from the start the relationship between Fowler and the Treasury was fraught. Lawson, believing that SERPS – as currently configured – was unaffordable over the long term, took care to emphasise to Fowler the 'large public expenditure issues at stake', sought greater representation on the IPR (to include a Treasury official as well as a minister), and made plain his wish that the Inquiry consider the US system of individual retirement accounts rather than simply be captured by the CPS's proposals. He also argued that the IPR should consider reducing the generosity of the terms under which contracting out from SERPS was allowed as well as operating any new system without additional incentives; and he sought to ensure any inflation protection of the BSP continued to be limited to the increase in prices alone.[19]

A key Treasury concern was whether the new personal pensions would be contracted out of SERPS. There would be two implications if they were not (as might well be the case, for, as the Institute and Faculty of Actuaries pointed out to the IPR, a drawback of the CPS's personal portable pension concept was that its DC nature would mean 'it would not be possible to define minimum benefits for contracting out' of a continuing SERPS).[20] First, the somewhat paradoxical effect of individuals substituting a contracted-in personal pension for their contracted-out occupational pension would be to increase future SERPS liabilities. Second, because of that first effect, it would also, paradoxically, serve to shift the overall pension system away from funding towards pay-as-you-go. Another expressed concern was a likely tendency for index-linked gilts to form a considerable fraction of personal pension portfolios, thus transferring inflation risk to the state.[21] Each of these prospective effects would be wildly at odds with the desire among ministers to contain unfunded future state pension liabilities – which Thatcher, in an interview with *The New York Times* in January 1984 on the United Kingdom's broader review of social security, bluntly termed a 'social security time bomb' set to go off in the new millennium.[22]

There were also emerging concerns among senior Treasury officials about the cost of tax relief if personal pension plans proved popular with SERPS members – proponents of PPPs seeing tax relief on contributions as a key selling aid.[23] The problem was discussed by the IPR's personal pensions subgroup in late March 1984, but with no conclusion other than the commissioning of a joint study of the problem by Treasury officials and DHSS advisers.[24] A key issue here was that the most obvious way of containing the cost of such relief was to restrict it to the basic rate of income tax, yet higher-rate taxpayers were the ones most likely to be interested in taking out a PPP.[25] There was, of course, a read-across to SERPS, for its abolition, or curtailment, could be expected to increase the take-up of PPPs, and thus significantly raise the cost of tax relief on contributions to them.

Although Lawson was mindful of the need to manage down both short- and long-term SERPS expenditure, one of his special advisers, Adam Ridley, wanted robust action. He thought SERPS 'economically perverse' and accused it of embodying 'a very questionable contract over the generations and over time between workers and pensioners, in a manner which is insensitive to demographic change'.[26] In this important minute, Ridley made a case for the abolition of both SERPS and occupational schemes. He argued that 'personal occupational pensions', as proposed by the CPRS in 1983, were a 'chimera' and would prove impossible to implement. Instead, Ridley argued for a simplified system in which the entire panoply of earnings-related pensions as a top-up to the BSP (both public, in the shape of SERPS, and private, in the shape of occupational pensions) would be swept away and replaced by three clearly defined activities by the individual: private insurance against loss of income, savings, and investment. In doing so, Ridley essentially embraced a maximalist version of the CPS's agenda for personal pensions – essentially, a return to Beveridge, with a minimal flat-rate BSP and voluntary top-up private provision purchased by those who wanted it.[27]

Monger was doubtful, telling the Chancellor that Ridley overestimated the financial acumen of ordinary people, underestimated the attachment of members to their occupational pension schemes, and erroneously assumed that the BSP was adequate to meet basic needs when in fact an important argument for SERPS was that it would take as many as possible out of the supplementary benefit net into which those solely dependent on the BSP fell. SERPS abolition, Monger pointed out, would require either substantial continuing demands for supplementary benefits or the more expensive option of raising the BSP to the level necessary to avoid individuals needing recourse to that system (which, as we saw in Chapter Four, he had discussed with Ridley's distant cousin, Nicholas Ridley, when the latter was Financial Secretary in early 1983).[28] Clearly, therefore, there was a significant divide within the Treasury, as well as between it and the DHSS, running through the IPR in addition to the DHSS's more general review of social security: Fowler's principal desire was a cost-neutral reorganisation of social security that would see funds better targeted on those in need (especially poor families with children); Treasury officials, ministers, and advisers wanted cuts to or even, in many cases, the outright abolition of SERPS.[29]

The abolition of SERPS? 237

Ministerial concerns about SERPS's future costs had been reinforced by updated demographic projections, with a recent Government Actuary's Department paper on population trends reducing its forecast of the likely ratio between National Insurance contributors and pensioners from 2.3 to 1.8 by 2015–26, as can be seen in Table 6.1.[30]

Yet, as the Government Actuary recognised, although this further decline in the support ratio produced a concomitant increase in the prospective cost burden of SERPS, that system had been purposely designed to bring about a real improvement in the livings standards of pensioners relative to average earnings; in other words, SERPS had always embodied a growing burden on existing workers as a means of securing a better replacement income for them in old age. Assuming a 2 per cent per annum increase in average earnings, the BSP and SERPS combined could be expected to rise from 27.2 to 41.6 per cent of average earnings by 2025/26; but, if – like the BSP – SERPS was linked only to prices, there would be no real-terms improvement at all. As the Treasury acknowledged, that was not 'likely to be attractive in any but pure public expenditure terms'.[31] Leaving aside the political ramifications, however, it could certainly be expected to generate significant pressures on the broader benefits system over time as relative pensioner poverty worsened (although, revealingly, this point was not made by the Treasury). Despite this clear rationale for SERPS, there was weighty support within government for abolishing it. In discussions within the IPR's personal pensions subgroup, for example, John Redwood did not just argue strongly that those taking out a personal pension should be required both to contract out of SERPS and forced to make personal provision sufficient to prevent them requiring state support in old age; he also made clear his expectation that SERPS would be abolished (and that he wanted ultimately also to destroy all final salary occupational schemes).[32]

Table 6.1 Government Actuary's prediction of the pensions 'support ratio' as at April 1984

Year	Contributors	Pensioners	Ratio
1984/85	21,760	9,260	2.3
1995/96	21,940	9,780	2.2
2005–15	22,240	9,960	2.2
2015/16	22,390	11,120	2.0
2025/26	21,930	12,340	1.8
Ultimate	22,130	12,600	1.8

Source: TNA: BN 147/10, 'Inquiry into Provision for Retirement. Population and Pension Costs: Note by the Government Actuary's Department', 9 April 1984.

238 *Planning a revolution, 1983–5*

At the heart of the IPR, of course (as with the more general review of social security that Fowler announced on 2 April 1984 and within which it was embedded), was the philosophical question of what the right relationship should be between the individual and the state. Advocates of SERPS abolition, such as Redwood and Ridley, assumed that, above a bare minimum of state support, individuals should provide for their own retirement pension, not for those of others. Fowler too later claimed to be antipathetic to SERPS, not just because he deprecated the future liabilities of its unfunded pay-as-you-go nature but because he felt that the state should not really be in the business of providing an earnings-related top-up to the basic state pension:

> The second pension could be provided by an expanded pensions industry. My view was that most people would prefer a pension that was theirs by right rather than being dependent on the decisions of government. 'A pension of your own' could have the same kind of appeal as 'a house of your own'. The role of Government should be to ensure that such pensions met sensible regulation so that the public interest was protected.[33]

This was not apparent in 1984, however, when Fowler's focus was on the restriction, not the abolition, of SERPS.

Evidence submitted to the IPR certainly demonstrated strong backing from stakeholders for SERPS to continue. Both the Life Offices Association and the CBI, for instance, envisaged a three-tier system, with the BSP forming the first tier, the second formed either by SERPS or occupational schemes, and a third tier of top-up individual provision.[34] For the CBI, it would simply be inappropriate to expect individuals to bear the investment risks of a DC personal pension in the second tier, let alone allow 'gambling for higher returns on speculative ventures'. As far as the CBI was concerned, the present partnership between state and occupational schemes was 'working well', and, barring exceptionally disappointing economic growth over the ensuing three or four decades, was sustainable.[35] Privately, however, as a GAD staff member told the IPR's secretary, the CBI indicated that it was prepared to countenance restricting the costs of SERPS by cutting back its inheritance benefits and its '20 best years' provision.[36]

The Treasury, for reasons that became clearer as time went on, was less doctrinaire than the Policy Unit on SERPS, and more in line with the CBI's fallback position of cuts to SERPS rather than outright abolition. It was keen for the IPR to keep open the option of a considerable reduction in the scope of SERPS, as long as a way could be found of ensuring that those workers outside its ambit, or affected by reductions in its benefits, would retire with a minimum level of pension sufficient to avoid reliance on supplementary benefits (albeit not necessarily at the level of the GMP, which occupational schemes were required to provide to their members as the price of being allowed to contract out of SERPS – an amount intended to be 'broadly equivalent' to that which would have been received if the member had remained within SERPS).[37]

Stage 2 of the IPR

Having digested over 1,700 written submissions and taken much oral evidence in early 1984, the IPR subgroup on personal pensions produced its report for the main Inquiry in early May.[38] As we noted in Chapter Five, this recommended that personal portable pensions be made available to all employees, with contributions related to sex and age, and that they should qualify for contracting out of SERPS. In conformity with the Chancellor's early strictures on the need for the Fowler Inquiry to avoid trespassing on the Treasury's prerogative to determine tax policy, no recommendations were made about the tax treatment of personal pensions other than a general hope that they would be treated in the same way as Section 226 pension schemes for the self-employed (which received tax relief on contributions).

The Treasury was not impressed by what it saw as the IPR's failure to get to grips with state pension spending. The Treasury official who had attended the subgroup's meetings was damning in his summary for Barney Hayhoe: the report was 'extremely disappointing' and 'on all the difficult points ... vague and inconclusive and none of the practical problems is faced or resolved'.[39] The Chancellor now determined that the IPR needed next to look at the state scheme and 'examine in detail options for cutting the cost of SERPS' – to which end Hayhoe was enjoined to pressure Fowler. The aim was to end SERPS's calculation of benefit based on the best 20 years of earnings and modify its 'very generous inheritance provisions' (plus raise women's state pension age to 65 early in the new millennium).[40]

Fowler's review of social security now moved up a gear, with May and June 1984 spent taking written and oral evidence in all four dimensions of the review, including the main pensions Inquiry, and the preparation and publication (on 23 May) of a Green Paper on pension portability on a change of job.[41] In July the consultative paper on personal pensions was published, which included the proposal to allow contracting out of SERPS on the basis of a qualifying test based on the level of contribution.[42] The increased activity took place in the context of the publication in June of the Government Actuary's latest projections on population and pension costs, and of new DHSS forecasts of pensioner incomes. As Fowler put it in the foreword to his background paper for the IPR, expenditure on pensions was 'set to rise significantly as pensioners increase in number and live longer'. He went on,

240   *Planning a revolution, 1983–5*

> In pensions policy twenty or thirty years is a relatively short time. Even now there are younger workers who will not reach pension age until 2025. We will not be thanked by them and future generations if we do not address now the problems which they may face.[43]

According to this document, by 2025/26 the total value of public and private pensions in payment combined would amount to 21 per cent of total wages and salaries, with SERPS representing just over a quarter of that and the BSP more than a third.

The most decisive way of containing those long-term Exchequer costs, of course, would be to abolish SERPS (as the CPS, which had set off the reconsideration of the pension system, had suggested and which it had reiterated in its oral evidence to the IPR). Yet the IPR received much official evidence that favoured retention. As the official in charge of social security at the Government Actuary's Department pointed out to the DHSS official advising the Inquiry, the benefits of abolishing SERPS in expenditure terms would mainly be in the long term (the immediate saving would be the end of the contracted-out rebate on occupational scheme contributions, because there would be no SERPS to contract out of). It would leave a lot of people without an adequate pension, however – and even more so if the removal of the contracted-out rebate caused employers to cut back on occupational schemes. There would be problems even if everyone was enrolled in a personal pension, because those on low incomes would have correspondingly low pensions, there being no redistribution possible between individuals as there was in SERPS.[44]

The IPR was also presented with strong external support for SERPS as it took oral evidence in June and July. The TUC, for example, set out its strong objection to any break with the consensus so laboriously constructed around a public–private partnership on earnings-related pensions.[45] Muriel Turner, its representative, told the Inquiry that the TUC rejected 'totally' the idea that pensioners constituted a burden on the rest of the population and 'the view which we hear sometimes that the present arrangements are too generous'. The TUC did not challenge outright the estimates of the Government Actuary but made clear that it felt that the underlying assumptions about the future growth of the economy were too pessimistic. The TUC was concerned about the effect of the government's earlier breaking of the BSP link to earnings and it remained committed to the long-term aim of a basic state pension of half the average wage for a married couple and a third for a single person.[46] Pressed by Hayhoe on whether the TUC opposed any modifications of SERPS at all, Turner shot back: 'It would depend on what they were.'[47] On the other side of industry, the CBI was also strongly supportive of SERPS and of the consensus that had been constructed around it for a state–employer 'partnership in pensions'. Its deputy director general, Kenneth Edwards, firmly told the IPR that employers 'would not wish to see changes which might put this partnership at risk'.[48] Others giving evidence, such as the National Pensioners' Convention, also thought the government was underestimating the likely rate of future economic growth and felt that a more optimistic assumption called into question the government's fears about future sustainability.[49]

This is not to say that support for SERPS was universal among those giving evidence to the IPR. Those concerned by present-day pensioner poverty or by the way in which SERPS would increase inequality between pensioners were susceptible to the idea of abolishing it. The Policy Studies Institute, for example, argued that, although SERPS would eventually work considerably to reduce old age poverty, the long delay to 1998 while its benefits built up was unacceptable (the Institute favoured moving immediately to a fully flat-rate scheme, but at a much higher rate than the then BSP).[50] Age Concern also indicated that it was prepared to see SERPS abolished if that was accompanied by an increase in the BSP from 24 to 33 per cent of national average earnings. Like many other stakeholders, though, Age Concern noted in its oral evidence that the pessimistic government predictions for future growth indicated a surprising lack of faith in the government's own policies. Moreover, assuming the continuation of SERPS, Age Concern actually wanted to extend its coverage by bringing the self-employed within its scope as well as somehow 'crediting in' the present generation of pensioners.[51]

In its hearings in the spring and early summer of 1984, the IPR had explored several options for cutting back SERPS's costs, the main one being to abolish or amend the '20 best years' calculation to produce lower pensions and thus restrict the cost burden on future workers. In its evidence to the IPR, however, the TUC disputed the Treasury's assumption that workers would reject higher National Insurance contributions, arguing they would be prepared to accept them if they were assured they were purchasing a better pension. It also strongly opposed abolishing or amending the '20 best years' rule, on the grounds that the income of manual workers tended to decline as they aged. Age Concern was also opposed to cutting the '20 best years' provision, because of the impact it would have on the level of pension received by workers (mainly women) with caring responsibilities, or with variable and/or declining incomes during their working lives.[52] Not surprisingly, both the Equal Opportunities Commission and the Women's National Commission were also strongly in favour of retaining the rule, because it helped women, who often suffered from interrupted careers and low earnings (often the product of part-time working).[53]

Another proposal for reducing benefits under SERPS was to cut back inheritance rights, and the TUC was asked by Marshall Field if social change and the growing participation of women in the workforce did not mean that 'we should abandon any benefit to the wife derived from her husband's contribution and look after women's benefits quite separately from their husbands'. In replying, Muriel Turner was (justifiably) sceptical: 'While we may get there by the end of the century, or perhaps a little earlier, I do not think we are there yet.'[54] In doing so, she was pointing out the obvious: women had long been the most disadvantaged within the UK pension system, and SERPS had been specifically designed by Barbara Castle to reduce this disadvantage over time via the redistribution embodied within it. It is no surprise, then, given the large number of female pensioners then living in poverty, that Age Concern was also opposed to cutting back widows' benefits.[55]

The key point, therefore, is that the great majority of those giving evidence to the IPR had indicated a clear wish to see SERPS continue, and, although some had indicated a preparedness to see its benefits reduced in the interest of long-term cost control, many others – including the peak organisations on both sides of industry – were concerned by the potential effects of some or all cuts under consideration.

On 20 July 1984 Fowler published his consultative document on the portability of pension rights for early leavers from occupational schemes.[56] At this point there was still nothing to suggest publicly that the government would seek to abolish SERPS as opposed to contain its prospective future costs. Notwithstanding a descant voice, heard in September when the Adam Smith Institute published its 'Omega Report', in which it charged SERPS with being effectively a 'pyramid scheme' and recommended that it be abolished and replaced by a system of individual retirement accounts, the high level of support for SERPS remained clear in the remaining IPR oral evidence sessions held during the summer of 1984.[57]

From reform to abolition

Yet, even as the IPR considered the latest evidence presented to it, there were fears among stakeholders that the government intended to do something radical on SERPS. The NAPF Council, for instance, feared this had been the clear thrust of questioning within the oral evidence sessions.[58] They were right to be worried. The government had been embarrassed by a report from the House of Commons' Select Committee on Health and Social Security in which it noted that social security spending in 1983/84 had been underestimated by as much as £930 million.[59] Behind the scenes, the PU was moving to place SERPS abolition at the top of the agenda. In a personal letter to Fowler in July, Redwood wrote of SERPS that it was 'the best example of fool's gold the Government has yet devised'. SERPS involved 'paying too little now for something which will prove to be too expensive in the future', and the government should not be worried about 'owning up to the lack of arithmetical common sense in the current financing system'. One possibility, Redwood noted, would be to abolish the '20 best years' rule, but 'the best option would be complete abolition; this could be coupled with a compulsory private sector pension'.[60]

In a steering brief written for Thatcher ahead of a ministerial seminar on social security benefits in late September, Redwood's colleague David Willetts put her Policy Unit's view to her in robust terms.[61] He recommended that the BSP remain untouched, the government having 'achieved a clear and politically defensible position' as a result of the removal of the average earnings link, which would mean that the 'burden on the economy will fall as the economy grows'. On SERPS, however, the brief was blunt in its advocacy of swift abolition:

> Pensioner poverty is less of a problem than it was and so SERPS is dealing with a problem which is much less serious than it was. Moreover, when SERPS matures early in the next century, it will pose a major threat to the public finances of this country. Its complicated calculations linking pensions to earnings is a classic example of the public sector trying to ape what the private sector should do and can do better. So SERPS has to go. Instead, people should be encouraged (or even compelled?) to save directly for their own retirement. This carries forward your policy of individual property ownership: SERPS undermines it.

The only effective argument made against abolition, suggested Willetts, was the need for a compensatory higher basic pension. But his brief dismissed that argument:

> [T]he reply to this is simple. We should hold out against changing the current arrangements for indexing the state pension, and if people wish to top it up, they should look to the private sector. The poorest pensioners who have not saved themselves may still need to look to Supplementary Benefit, but there is not harm in that.[62]

A week later Thatcher reached agreement with ministers and senior officials on the need to abolish SERPS, subject to meeting obligations already incurred and protecting them against price inflation (it was also agreed that state pension ages would need to rise at some point).[63] This agreement remained secret, however, and the IPR examined three options for SERPS when it met again in late January: cuts to benefits within SERPS; abolition, with replacement by an 'intrinsic' earnings-related basic pension along the lines of those in the United States and Switzerland; or abolition with private provision above the BSP, either via occupational or personal pensions.[64] By this point, however, DHSS internal documents prepared to support a week of internal discussions of pension strategy at the start of 1985 were clearly focused on abolishing SERPS.[65] The outcome of those meetings was DHSS agreement that the long-term cost of SERPS was unsustainable, SERPS was too complex for the public to understand, its existence discouraged DC schemes because contracting out was so complex, and it gave too much of a role for the state in old age income replacement. With SERPS gone, the country would move to a 'twin pillar' system of a flat-rate pay-as-you-go BSP with supplementation by either an occupational pension or personal pension (though without compulsion).[66]

Given the DHSS's former attachment to the mid-1970s consensus on SERPS, it is no surprise that there was resistance to this from some officials. They pointed out that a 'major obstacle' to the abolition of SERPS was the 'funding gap' represented by the future cost of up to ten years of SERPS entitlements per member at the point of abolition, which it was recognised would have to be honoured. Another problem would be that, with SERPS gone, previously contracted-out scheme members would 'feel they had a poor deal', since their contributions would rise even as future benefits effectively declined. The loss of contracting out might also represent a disincentive to employers to provide occupational schemes. Likewise, the loss of the contracting-out rebate would remove 'a major financial incentive' to take out a personal pension. Nonetheless, in line with the secret high-level decision already taken in October, DHSS officials and ministers agreed that SERPS should be abolished.[67]

From Inquiry to Green Paper

Given the secrecy of the ministerial decision to abolish SERPS, the IPR continued to examine modifications to reduce its cost at its final meeting on 17 January 1985. Reading between the lines of this meeting, however, it is evident that Fowler was steering its members to a set of options including abolition and a move to a two-tier system in which the BSP would be supplemented by either an occupational pension or a personal pension.[68] At the same time, Fowler steered the IPR to an acceptance that the choice between those options (secretly already made, in fact) 'was primarily a matter for government'. Overall, the tone of the minutes for this meeting was notably more negative about SERPS than those for previous meetings: 'Getting rid of SERPS had obvious attractions,' it was noted.[69]

Despite a major row with Lawson, who complained that Fowler was trespassing on his prerogatives over fiscal policy by making proposals relating to National Insurance, on 1 February Fowler delivered his proposals for social security reform to a newly constituted ministerial Cabinet subcommittee, MISC 111 (created by Thatcher as a forum within which to discuss social security reform without recourse to debate in the full Cabinet).[70] Abolition of SERPS was to the fore. As Fowler wrote to the Prime Minister:

> If the proposals are agreed, they would amount to the biggest change in social security since the 1940s. Ever since Beveridge, successive Governments have based their policy more and more on the assumption that it is the responsibility of the Government to provide an all embracing social security system. I believe it is essential we turn this tide. We must move away from this perception of social security to a twin pillar approach, where one pillar is the state system but the other is private provision and builds on individual responsibility and initiative. [...]
>
> On pensions, we shall move to a position where the Government's role is to provide a decent basic pension, leaving it to individual and employer initiative to augment that with an occupational or personal pension. We should thus be rejecting the general view since the late 1950s that the Government has a responsibility to provide earnings related as well as flat rate pensions. It would be an integral part of this approach to encourage as wide a coverage of occupational and personal pensions as possible, since we do not want people to rely on means-tested help in addition.[71]

This was a long way from Fowler's starting point in the reform process, a tribute to the persuasive power of the PU, and clear evidence of its ability to shape policy within government.

With Thatcher in the chair, MISC 111 met for the first time on 6 February to consider Fowler's proposals, which embodied a draft of the first volume of his promised Green Paper on social security.[72] It opened with a bleak first sentence that would find its way into the final published version: 'To be blunt the British Social Security system has lost its way.' Although achievements were acknowledged, the costs of the system were presented as unacceptable, for it had

> grown five times faster than prices; twice as fast as the economy as a whole; and is set to rise steeply for the next forty years. But, for all that, resources have not always been directed to the most in need and under present plans will not be so in the future. The piecemeal development of the system has resulted in a multitude of benefits with overlapping purposes and differing entitlement conditions. The complexity and benefit rules has meant that Social Security is difficult to administer and impossible for many of the public to understand. While the overlap between Social Security and income tax means that significant numbers of people are paying tax and receiving means tested benefits.
>
> The fact is that each new development in social security since the war has been made for the best of motives. Overall, however, the effects all too often has been to confuse and complicate. Worse still understanding of what the social security system should be seeking to achieve has been obscured. Our relative responsibilities as individuals and collectively through the state had been left ill-defined.[73]

Briefly, the overall proposals within the draft Green Paper were threefold: to abolish SERPS and shift to a two-tier pension system consisting of a flat-rate state BSP topped up via occupational or personal pension provision; to simplify the supplementary benefits system via an income support scheme with rates varying only by family size and client group, backed up by a scheme of discretionary social aid for emergencies or people with exceptional needs; and to reduce the scope of housing benefits, with benefits paid in full only to those on supplementary benefits.

The justifications for change emphasised to MISC 111 were that the existing system gave too much responsibility to the state and too little to the individual; was 'extremely complex'; had failed to adapt to changing patterns of social need, in that working families, not pensioners, were now the greatest area of social need; and, finally, embodied a 'poverty trap', in that the gap between income in and out of work at the lower end of the pay scale was too narrow and the withdrawal of benefits on employment embodied a high marginal tax rate. A justification underlying the whole document, however, was that the proposed new system would be cheaper. In pensions, for example, the prospective costs of state pensions were to the fore (£45 billion a year by 2033/34 on the assumption of prices-linked upratings, or £66.5 billion with earnings-related upratings). On the latter basis, abolishing SERPS was estimated to yield savings of £500 million in 1993/94, rising to £22 billion in 2033/34.[74]

When MISC 111 met on 6 February to discuss Fowler's extensive proposals for reform of social security there was, from the start, strong support for his 'twin-pillar' plan for pensions, and a recognition that the proposals represented the output from an impressively comprehensive and deep review of the issues. The prospect of an annual saving on the overall social security budget of up to £750 million within three years was seen as attractive. Yet there was also a clear recognition of the difficult politics of pushing through such a reform that would entail 'radical change to almost every aspect of social security', represent a major break with the postwar order, and create many 'losers' and few obvious 'winners'. Nonetheless, on pensions the privatisation approach was agreed.[75]

In a minute to the Prime Minister, Redwood and Willetts strongly praised the proposed abolition of SERPS. 'None of this is easy politics,' they acknowledged, but they went on: 'No one has ever said it would be.' To stiffen Thatcher's resolve, they urged her to

> remember the origins of this exercise. By far and away the largest program in government has been growing like Topsy. 'Protected' and 'demand led' programs have to be scrutinised and cut if we are to stop the momentum of public expenditure. Moreover, the benefit system is cumbersome, widely disliked by

The abolition of SERPS? 247

the public, and costly in manpower and administrative resources. Worse still, the system is a disincentive to work and discouragement to self-help.

And it's not just basic principles that are wrong. It's practical politics as well. Because the government has to try to rein in the rate of growth of the program, it has had regular rows, has come to be seen as petty and mean minded, constantly tampering with the problem at the margins.

The government, wrote Redwood and Willetts, now had to choose from two options:

It could decide that the whole thing is too difficult. It could herald the idea of controlling public spending, and try and accommodate more of the pressure groups for more welfare spending, giving up the notion that they can bring this budget under control. It would involve either tearing up, or being seen to tear up, the rhetoric and ambitions of many years. And it would not necessarily end the arguments. All the evidence is that the more you give to client groups, the more they demand, the stronger the lobby becomes, and the more money they have to advertise against you. Having marched Norman Fowler to the top of the hill, we would then be marching him down again.

The second option is to go the Norman Fowler way, with sensible improvements, as a result of MISC 111 deliberations, to get the best trade-off between money saved and political cost. The advantage of the Fowler way is that by introducing a new structure, issuing a Green Paper, and restating your ambitions and principles for the system, you have a chance to change the debate in your favour. Norman's draft Green Paper is an excellent 1st draft.[76]

Redwood and Willetts' recommendation to Thatcher was therefore that MISC 111 endorse the PU's favoured option two: abolition of SERPS in favour of personal pensions. This was 'crucial to any sensible public expenditure planning for the future' and 'not as difficult as some people make out', for, they promised, the 'baying hordes of the pension industry, advisers, intermediaries, investors and others' would be on her side if the reform was 'put to them in the right way', as it would represent a 'bonanza of business opportunities'. 'The leading institutions might even be persuaded to argue and advertise in favour of the government's case', they reassured the Prime Minister.[77]

Voluntarism or compulsion?

MISC 111, having decided in principle to abolish SERPS with effect from April 1987, now recognised the danger of simply creating a vacuum that would remain unfilled, with all that implied for the future in terms of inadequate top-up pension provision and a potential need for state supplementation. Should the government merely encourage and financially incentivise occupational and personal pensions to fill that vacuum; or should there be compulsion? This fundamental question divided ministers.

In his initial memorandum for MISC 111 on the form of a post-SERPS landscape, Fowler had offered two options: government encouragement of greater occupational pension provision coupled with personal pensions for those who wanted them; or compulsion. He indicated that he favoured a transitional period of incentives followed by a requirement that all employers provide an occupational pension to those of their workers who did not opt for a personal pension. Compulsion, he argued, would prevent a vacuum opening up in pension provision and, more positively, it 'offer[ed] the attractions of near universal coverage and an end to the "two nations" in retirement'.[78] Recognising the practical problems of introducing compulsion by the target date of April 1987, Fowler proposed an initial transitional period during which employers would be incentivised to set up a qualifying occupational scheme via a temporary rebate on National Insurance contributions that would give them 100 per cent compensation for the minimum employer's contribution. Thereafter, the rebate would be phased out and all employers would have to provide a scheme that at least matched the minimum qualification. Regulation of this would be with a 'very light hand' (part of routine DHSS and Inland Revenue checking), and sanctions on defaulters would simply lead to a National Insurance (NI) 'surcharge' rather than criminal action. Taking out a personal pension with at least a 5 per cent contribution would be a permitted alternative if the employer paid the minimum 2.5 per cent of earnings towards it.

Perhaps surprisingly, at the heart of the debate on compulsion was not the question of individual freedom but the issue of public expenditure and its level over the long term. This was because that debate was taking place against a background of Treasury attempts in the lead-up to the 1985 budget to drive down social security expenditure over the near term by an additional £2 billion (the target savings for 1988/89 being raised from £1 to 2 billion to £3 to 4 billion). Fowler thought this totally unrealistic, and in minutes and meetings with the Prime Minister he attempted to defend his position.[79] He pointed out he was attempting to make fundamental structural changes to pensions to deliver huge long-term social security savings. In his view, that was the greater prize. His problem was that the changes he was envisaging were difficult to reconcile with cost cutting over the near term. In pensions, the fundamental truth was that compulsion would be costly both for companies and the state, because, although it would reduce SERPS commitments, the new arrangement would be an impost on employers, and the Exchequer would have to give tax relief on the new contributions, whether made to an occupational or personal pension.

More generally, the politics of compulsion were difficult. For one thing, as a No. 10 brief for Thatcher noted, whichever option was adopted the fact was that people would be worse off under post-SERPS arrangements, and compelling people to pay more for less would be a hard sell politically.[80] Redwood emphasised to Thatcher, however, that the alternative was that taxes would rise 'rapidly and dramatically over the next 30 years to pay for the generous Serps scheme – by much more than the modest increase required to buy a proper funded pension scheme for everybody'. Redwood acknowledged that the choice was still a difficult one: encouragement would be cheaper and more politically attractive; but, nonetheless, he argued that compulsion remained the better option, because it would ultimately be cheaper (because it 'stops people coming back on benefit and removes the need for NI rebates and incentives').[81]

Of course, as Lawson noted, compulsion would be a rather surprising policy for a government committed to promoting the freedom of the individual. Yet, as ministers acknowledged at their next MISC 111 meeting, in the absence of compulsion 'there was a high risk that there would be gaps in provision with an eventual burden on the state and hence on those who were conscientious in making provision for themselves'. The outcome of this meeting was that Fowler's proposal was accepted, with implementation of compulsion as soon as possible, preferably in 1987.[82] Ultimately, therefore, the long-term prize of a radical reduction in state spending commitments (and of individual dependence on the state) if SERPS was abolished had proved more compelling to MISC 111 than the issue of individual freedom or the prospective short-term costs, both economic and political.

Following acceptance by MISC 111 that a post-SERPS world would need compulsory occupational pensions with an allowed opt-out into a personal pension, Fowler fleshed out his proposals in a memorandum in late March. This favoured immediate implementation in 1987, partly because it would mean the scheme was operational before the likely date of the next election, partly for the sake of neatness, and partly because he thought that many of those employees most in need of an additional pension would be likely to work for employers who would resist setting up a pension scheme until the last possible moment. Fowler recognised, however, that the response to a consultative Green Paper might be negative, in which case his transitional period would apply, but for no more than three years. Nevertheless, the prize of full coverage would be worth having, he assured Thatcher, since the result would be over 80 per cent of the workforce within an occupational scheme, compared with the present 50 per cent. To keep down the cost to employers, the minimum level of contribution would be set at just 4 to 5 per cent of earnings.[83]

Yet the near-term costs of SERPS abolition continued to bedevil Fowler's proposal. Despite the tense relationship between the DHSS and the Treasury

250   *Planning a revolution, 1983–5*

in the spring of 1985, he thought he had gained the agreement of both the Chancellor and his Chief Secretary (Peter Rees) to overcome any difficulties arising from the decisions of MISC 111 on compulsion.[84] He was mistaken. Within days Lawson (now more clearly focused on the issue after several months of distractions) bluntly made clear to Fowler that 'while the Treasury would examine the DHSS proposals in good faith … he foresaw great difficulties'.[85] With both Lawson and Rees out of the country for much of April, those difficulties initially remained below the surface of the government's internal negotiations over the draft of the social security Green Paper, which Fowler presented to the full Cabinet on 19 April. In the memorandum covering that draft, Fowler expanded on the case for reform, bringing its different strands together in a way that had not been done beforehand and emphasising that the proposed reform would return Britain to a Beveridgean vision of minimalist social security with private top-up provision rather than break with it. Fowler wrote that SERPS was 'one – but only one – example' of how the system had evolved in a way that meant the balance between the state and the individual had been distorted in a way that gave too much of a role to the state. 'This dominance by the state,' wrote Fowler, 'was never intended by Beveridge who believed that they were important roles for <u>both</u> the state and the individual.' Indeed, Fowler went so far as to say that SERPS's very existence explained why the spread of occupational pensions had been halted (an inaccurate claim, given that the rise had ended a decade before SERPS came into effect).[86]

Fowler's defence of SERPS abolition cut little ice with Lawson. Having woken up late to the possible implications of Fowler's proposals both for the PSBR and for economic growth, the Chancellor now moved against him.[87] In a minute to Thatcher, he conceded that the abolition of SERPS would ultimately generate very substantial savings in public spending, but – and it was a very big 'but' – he pointed out that the price would be very substantial over the short to medium term. 'The immediate consequences will be a sharp increase in the burden of pension contributions from both public and private sectors' (and the impact of the former was likely to be an annual cost to the state of around £1 billion a year and a rise in the PSBR of the order of £1.25 billion). Moreover, with the envisaged expansion of occupational and private provision would come the substantial hit to annual tax revenues, assuming a continuation of tax relief on pension contributions. Lawson's conclusion was blunt: '[W]e must think very carefully before insisting on compulsory private provision for pensions.'[88] Fowler was livid. On 24 April he and Lawson had a blazing row, and Fowler insisted the Cabinet defer its discussion of his proposal until the issue between them had been settled.[89]

Thatcher's private secretary for economic affairs, the civil servant Andrew Turnbull, noted on Lawson's missive before passing it to Thatcher that he thought there was 'something fishy about the figures. […] How come everyone is worse off?' This reaction seems strange in retrospect, for what Lawson was pointing to was an important aspect of the 'double payment' that Pierson later noted was inevitable in any move from a pay-as-you-go system to a funded one.[90] Such moves resulted in a 'double payment', because it was necessary to continue paying through taxation or NI contributions for acrued benefits based on the pay-as-you-go model *and* simultaneously require firms and employees to invest in the funded schemes of the future. If existing incentives were maintained, the expansion of private schemes and savings also sacrificed immediate tax revenues, and therefore tightened public finances just as the government was itself paying more as an employer.

The fact that the double payment problem was still unconfronted so late in the day is notable. Fowler's response, that in devising a scheme based on a 2.5 per cent contribution from employers he had restricted the additional burden on employers to around 1 to 2 per cent of total payroll costs, should also be noted, since it was considerably lower than it could (and without doubt should) have been.[91] As he emphasised to the Prime Minister, 'We recognised all along that the end of SERPS would mean higher National Insurance contributions, for both employers and employees who are now contracted out because of the ending of the contracted out rebate.' He continued:

> The costs of the new pension arrangements will come from the tax relief on employers' and employees' contributions. While I recognise Nigel's concern about extra tax relief, the agreed note by officials shows that the cost is likely to be £200 million in 1987/88 rather than the £1 billion that the earlier estimates suggested.
>
> All of us in MISC 111 recognised that the end of SERPS and its replacement by a compulsory scheme would mean higher employment costs for some people but, as the note by officials shows, the overall effect on private sector employers as a whole is nil. We felt in MISC 111 – as I still do so – that stopping SERPS while we still can, with a huge long-term saving that offers, justified the public sector and other costs. And in a minimum pension requirement for all there was no dissent from your summing up of our discussions on 13 February (MISC 111 (85) 2nd meeting) when you said that 'it would inevitably impose greater costs on the contributors and arouse controversy, but should not be postponed'.[92]

Fowler went on to counsel Thatcher that 'abolishing SERPS without putting anything in its place would leave us very vulnerable to the charge that we are simply engaged in an exercise to reduce pension rights'. He warned that it might also prove to be counter-productive:

> Since the loss of SERPS pension rights would not be balanced by significant growth in private provision, we should be pressed to do more through state

provision, both by our supporters and more generally. The end result would be significantly higher expenditure on the basic retirement pension or on supplementary pensions – most likely on both.

Moreover, he warned Thatcher that the window of opportunity for SERPS abolition was closing fast. Deferring the end of SERPS would both leave the government politically 'extremely exposed' and see the cost of future abolition rise as the liabilities within it continued to grow. The alternative – modification of SERPS – would 'give us the worst of both worlds'. The system would be no less complex, there would be little incentive for employers to expand their pension provision, and

> most important of all we should be missing the opportunity – probably the last opportunity – of giving everyone the chance of a private pension. We should have accepted for good the dominance of the state scheme – and we would have undermined one of the main thrusts of the whole review.[93]

The robust tone of Fowler's intervention makes clear the fundamental threat that Lawson's objections posed for his reform plans. Lawson was having none of it, however, as a minute sent by him to Thatcher on the same day made clear. It was certainly important to have regard to long-term advantage, argued Lawson. 'But it is also prudent to consider the effects of what we are doing in the present century.' Citing a recent Treasury analysis not available to MISC 111 which shows a rise in the PSBR in 1988/89 of £1 billion as a result of the extra tax relief (which would effectively destroy the government's medium-term financial strategy), he warned Thatcher that to embark on Fowler's proposed abolition of SERPS in April 1987 and its replacement by a compulsory occupational pension regime 'would be more than a banana skin: it would be evidence of an electoral death wish'. It would be much better, Lawson argued, 'to keep a quasi-SERPS but in drastically modified form … as the Inquiry into Provision for Retirement itself concluded'. This, Lawson thought, would cut the long-term cost of SERPS to just over a third.[94]

Thus, Fowler's strategy of leading the IPR to embrace SERPS abolition as but one of its three final options of reform had backfired. Although he had intended that this would give him the political cover he needed to abolish SERPS, it had opened up a chink in his armour that Lawson was ruthlessly exploiting (and not just in internal discussions; a plethora of news stories about how abolition would 'hit business' was neither coincidental nor without effect).[95]

Thatcher now wobbled. Having enthusiastically endorsed Fowler's plans for SERPS only weeks beforehand, she was now notably reluctant to reiterate MISC 111's decisions on the abolition of SERPS and on compulsion when Lawson met her with Fowler on 30 April. Rather, her strategy was to allow the issue to go forward to Cabinet, effectively passing the buck to ministers within it.[96] In a meeting with the main protagonists two days later she was cooler still: 'The tone for the passage on pensions' in the Green Paper 'would have to be somewhat "greener" than the rest.'[97] The direction of travel was clear: abolition of SERPS was in play. This despite a rearguard fightback by the Policy Unit, in which it warned her that it was now or never for SERPS abolition, and that the cost of ducking it would be this: 'We lose all the big fundamental arguments ... and just look mean minded.'[98]

Fowler's draft Green Paper on social security was finally considered by the full Cabinet on 2 May. Despite much discussion within MISC 111 and between relevant ministers, this was the first time the Cabinet had considered the plan to abolish SERPS and replace it with compulsory private provision (now excluding the self-employed, at Lawson's insistence). It did so within a new political context, for the SERPS abolition plan was by now a matter of public knowledge, having been leaked to *The Daily Telegraph*, presumably by the Treasury, and duly reported on 18 April. That produced a denunciation in the Commons by the opposition spokesman on pensions, Michael Meacher, who called it 'a callous dismantling of the welfare state designed to provide even bigger tax handouts to the rich'.[99]

As widely noticed in the media, consideration of the proposal by the Cabinet would be a decisive moment.[100] Yet such was the scope of the overall social security reform package that consideration of the draft social security Green Paper at the 2 May Cabinet meeting spilled over to the next week's meeting (which also considered a memorandum from Fowler on pensions, sent to ministers only on 7 May, in which he reiterated his reasons for seeking the abolition of SERPS while also suggesting that its abolition would make the proposed system of personal pensions much easier to operate).[101] In the interim, supporters of radical reform, such as Norman Tebbit, sought to strengthen Thatcher's will; but she was also receiving warnings, for example from the Cabinet Secretary, Robert Armstrong, that the abolition of SERPS was going to be 'highly contentious' politically.[102]

In short, just weeks before the publication of the Green Paper, future policy on SERPS was becoming less rather than more certain. How did the government find itself in this position when it had been looking at the issue of pensions for 18 months? That question was the starting point for a No. 10 steering brief written by Andrew Turnbull for Thatcher to use in the 9 May Cabinet discussion. In it he noted: 'With 3 days to go before the Cabinet is supposed to take decisions, the policy on SERPS is far from clear.'[103] His answer boiled down thus: the enormously controversial policy to abolish SERPS had been under review only since February; and the Chancellor had only recently woken up to its near-term consequences for public spending and, potentially, for lower economic growth as a consequence of higher payroll costs for employers.

Under pressure, Fowler now conceded some ground. In his 7 May pensions memorandum to the Cabinet, he conceded that the 'double payment' problem was a serious concern. He also conceded that there needed to be

254   *Planning a revolution, 1983–5*

more recognition of disappointed public expectations, particularly the inability of older workers in the time left to them before retirement to build up their own pension to match the benefits they would lose from SERPS abolition. To meet those two key concerns, Fowler floated the possibility of a three-year phasing in of SERPS abolition and its replacement by compulsory occupational or private provision, but only for men under 50 and women under 45 – with SERPs continuing for those above these ages, albeit with a new age-related National Insurance contribution. The transition would work as follows: earned SERPS rights up to 1987 would be preserved in real terms; and there would then be reduced rates of accrual for 1987/88 and 1988/89, balanced by a minimum private pension contribution by employers and employees of 1 per cent each in 1987/88, 1.5 per cent in 1988/89, and 2 per cent (so 4 per cent in total) in 1989/90. The effects on the PSBR, on payroll costs, and on the take-home pay of the transition would, claimed Fowler, be 'manageable' (though the extra cost of tax reliefs on private pension contributions was notably absent from his projected costings for the Cabinet – something that, surprisingly, seems not to have been attacked by Lawson).[104]

This compromise had been hammered out at yet another summit meeting on 6 May attended by Thatcher, all the key protagonists (Fowler and Tony Newton, his Minister for Social Security, Lawson, Rees, and Michael Parkinson – then Secretary of State for Trade and Industry), as well as Willie Whitelaw (Thatcher's Deputy Prime Minister), John Wakeham (the Chief Whip), and Redwood and Willetts from the PU.[105] Discussion in this meeting, which sought to reach a decision on whether to adopt a phased abolition of SERPS or merely to modify it, laid bare the profound tension between the short and long term in public expenditure control. There were also clear concerns expressed by Fowler that opting merely to cut back benefits within SERPS would prove politically more challenging than the Chancellor thought and serve to discourage the take-up of personal pensions. Ultimately Fowler prevailed, and his proposal to abolish SERPS was accepted by the Cabinet on 9 May, but based on his revised proposals for phased abolition rather than the earlier proposal for outright abolition in 1987.[106] The decision was made public that evening. The Green Paper, containing both the proposal to abolish SERPs as well as proposals on the wider reform of social security, was published on 3 June.[107]

Conclusion

Our examination of policy development relating to SERPS has revealed a complex story. Conservative concerns about the prospective long-term costs of the benefit promises within SERPS were relatively long-standing, and worries about the increasing dependence of individuals on the state even more so. The Conservative party's landslide victory in the 1983 general election and Thatcher's subsequent appointment of John Redwood to her Policy Unit were defining moments, however, at which the abolition of SERPS was put on the government's policy agenda. At the DHSS, Norman Fowler responded to No. 10's new agenda by setting up, with Redwood's approval, a public inquiry on the issue of provision for retirement, setting a framework for it which involved trimming back SERPS benefits and encouraging workers to opt out of it into either a personal pension or a company-provided occupational pension scheme. Evidence to the Fowler Inquiry revealed some support for SERPS abolition from organisations interested in the issue of present-day pensioner poverty (because they hoped that money now flowing to SERPS could be diverted to improving the BSP). Overwhelmingly, however, evidence from stakeholders, and particularly from the peak organisations on both sides of industry, strongly supported the continuation of SERPS (though some, most notably the CBI, were prepared to countenance judicious cuts to its long-term benefits to contain future costs).

Despite overwhelming support for the continuation of SERPS expressed by those giving evidence to the IPR, within government the PU successfully persuaded the Prime Minister that SERPS had to go if a twenty-first-century state pensions time bomb was to be defused. Having been privately persuaded to abolish SERPS, Thatcher, as was her wont on difficult issues, set up a Cabinet subcommittee of ministers to develop policy. The decision to abolish SERPS may subsequently have been taken at a high level, but the politics of abolition remained to be navigated. For one thing, there was the small matter of the IPR, which had not yet delivered its report. Fowler's strategy was to steer the IPR to the idea of abolition by framing its deliberations around three possible options:

1. abolition of SERPS and a move to a two-tier system, in which the BSP would form the first tier, and the second tier would consist of either a personal or an occupational pension;
2. abolition of SERPS and its replacement with an 'intrinsic' earnings-related basic pension along the lines of the US or Swiss systems; or
3. continuation of SERPS but with a series of cuts to its benefits to contain its costs.

At the same time, Fowler successfully moved the IPR towards his first option while also getting it to accept that it would be the government that would decide (without the Inquiry members knowing that in fact it had already done so).

Within government, however, the politics of abolition, which increasingly focused on the issue of whether employees should be compelled to take out a personal pension if no occupational pension was available to them,

256   *Planning a revolution, 1983–5*

remained fraught. The argument in favour of compulsion was that, without it, millions would retire without any pension provision above the basic state pension, with all that implied for future pensioner poverty, and for the increased public spending that would be needed to address it. The key problem was that compelling millions of workers to exit SERPS into either an occupational or personal pension would be enormously costly in terms of tax relief on their contributions, and costly for employers because of the additional contributions required from them. When he woke up to the scale of the tax relief problem, Nigel Lawson acted decisively to oppose outright abolition. Yet, given the momentum that had built up in favour of it within the government, and despite a brief wobble by the Prime Minister, he was unable to stop it. Instead, the result was a compromise: compulsion would not apply to the self-employed, abolition would be phased over three years, and it would not apply to older workers (men aged 50 or over, and women aged 45 or more), although over time, of course, those workers would fall out of the equation on retirement and ultimately SERPS would disappear from the British pensions landscape. In just two years, therefore, the government had moved from Thatcher's promise in the 1983 general election that reform of SERPS was not on the agenda to embracing its abolition, with compulsory private pensions to replace it (in the shape of either a personal pension plan or occupational pension scheme).

Notes

1 Paul Pierson, *Dismantling the Welfare State? Reagan, Thatcher and the Politics of Retrenchment* (Cambridge: Cambridge University Press, 1994), p. 71.

2 The full text of Howe's 7 May NAPF speech is reproduced in 'Pension Funds and the Economy', *Pensions World*, June 1981, pp. 315–70.

3 The National Archive (hereafter TNA): T 521/51, N. Monck to Mr Monger, 'State Earnings Related Pension Scheme', 6 April 1982.

4 TNA: T 521/51, C. D. Butler to D. R. Norgrove, 'State Earnings Related Pension Scheme', 25 March 1982; ibid., Norgrove to Monger, 8 April 1982: T 496/135, Monger to Financial Secretary, 'Financial Secretary's Holiday Thoughts', 14 January 1983.

5 TNA: T 496/81, G. W. Monger to E. P. Kemp, 'State Earnings Related Pension Scheme', 15 April 1982; F. Cassell to Monger, 'State Earnings Related Pension Scheme', 8 April 1982. The IFS article was Richard Hemming and John A. Kay, 'The Costs of the State Earnings Related Pension Scheme', *The Economic Journal*, 92 (1982).

6 Government Actuary's Department, *National Insurance Fund Long-Term Financial Estimates: Report by the Government Actuary on the First Quinquennial Review under Section 137 of the Social Security Act 1975*, HC 451 (London: HMSO, 1982); HM Treasury, Howe Papers (hereafter 'HMT'): PO-CH-GH-0041 Part A, Monger to Chancellor of the Exchequer, 'State

Earnings-Related Pension Scheme', 1 July 1982. A detailed internal Treasury appraisal of the many forces driving up social security spending can be found at TNA: T 496/81, Holmans to Cassell, 'Medium Term Conference: Social Security Transfers', 27 July 1982.

7 *Financial Times*, 'Thatcher Forced on Defensive over Pensions', by Margaret Van Hattem, 2 March 1983.

8 See for example, TNA: T 496/139, Government Actuary, 'Projection of Occupational Pension Schemes', 16 March 1983; TNA: T 496/139, Holmans to Seammen, 'Projections of Occupational Pension Schemes', 8 March 1983. The GAD noted that those discussing figures that might be used to justify the abolition of SERPS were keenly opposed by the DHSS's economists (TNA: T 496/139, Government Actuary to Minister of State (Civil Service), HM Treasury, 1 March 1983).

9 TNA: T 496/436, Monger to Seammen, 'CPRS Work on Pensions', 25 March 1983. There is a good overview by the Treasury's Public Service, Economic Division, of the various parallel working groups as at April 1983, and of the lessons drawn in January from a survey of the academic literature on the sustainability of SERPS and the BSP (TNA: T 496/137, F. P. D Bird to Norgrove, 'Pensions', 18 April 1983).

10 Charles Moore, *Margaret Thatcher*, vol. 2: *Everything She Wants* (London: Allen Lane, 2015), pp. 27–29. TNA: PREM 19/1004, handwritten note from John Sparrow (head of CPRS) to the Prime Minister, 'Pensions', 22 April 1983. The demise of the CPRS followed swiftly thereafter.

11 TNA: PREM 19/1004, 'Pensions Issues and Policy: A Paper by the CPRS', April 1983, p. 1.

12 TNA: BN 13/278, Thatcher to Brynmor John, MP, 20 May 1983; Margaret Thatcher Archive (hereafter MTA): Margaret Thatcher and Norman Fowler, 'General Election Press Conference (Health and Welfare)', 24 May 1983. Brynmor John would have been a social security minister had Labour been elected.

13 Nigel Lawson, *The View from No. 11: Memoirs of a Tory Radical* (London: Bantam Press, 1992), p. 588.

14 Redwood later noted that the earlier furore over the leak of the CPRS memorandum proposing to privatise the NHS was 'engraved on my mind' at this point. Private interview, cited by Nicholas Timmins, *The Five Giants: A Biography of the Welfare State* (London: HarperCollins, 2001), p. 395.

15 TNA: BN 13/308, T. S. Heppell to Mr Laurance, 'A New Pensions Approach', 18 October 1983.

16 TNA: BN 13/278, 'DHSS Press Release: First Task for the Pension Inquiry', 16 December 1983.

17 TNA: T 530/128, Fowler to Thatcher, 'Early Leavers and the Pensions Inquiry', 11 November 1983.

18 *Financial Times*, 'Fowler to Investigate Pensions Provision', by Kevin Brown, 24 November 1983.

19 TNA: T 530/128, Lawson to Fowler, 'Pensions Enquiry', 21 November 1983; TNA: T 530/128, M. O'Mara to PS/Minister of State, 'Mr Fowler's Pension

258 *Planning a revolution, 1983–5*

Enquiry', 19 December 1983. On the structural nature of the historically tense relationship between the Treasury and DHSS, and on the particular tensions of our period, see Norman Fowler, *Ministers Decide: A Personal Memoir of the Thatcher Years* (London: Chapmans, 1991), pp. 206–9; Lawson, *The View from No. 11*, pp. 587–89. Despite the disagreement caused by near-term SERPS reform costs, both ministers were antipathetic to the recommendation by the House of Commons' Select Committee on Social Services that the state pension age for men and women be equalised at 63 (because the cost of reducing the SPA for men would outweigh the saving from raising it for women).

20 TNA: BN 147/26, IPR(PP)7, IPR Sub-Group on Portable Pensions, 'Written Submissions from Bodies giving Oral Evidence, Note by the Secretary (N. Montagu)', 2 February 1984. Later that month the OPB warned the DHSS that allowing personal pension plans to contract out of SERPS would require significant controls over the type of investments that might be made within them, an entirely new system of regulatory supervision of institutions selling PPPs, and detailed control of benefits and commutation and retirement dates. Even then, it would not be possible to guarantee a minimum pension, and, by extension, it would not be possible to replicate the existing system whereby the state protected the GMP against inflation. It concluded: 'Any system of PPP arrangements would … be much more complicated and have much wider implications than many of the advocates of PPPs appear to believe.' One of those implications was that the only way the OPB could envisage making contracting out work would be to move the entire contracting-out system, including that for occupational pensions, to an age-related system of contracting out contribution abatements in order to avoid holders of PPPs selecting against the state scheme via their contracting-out decision (TNA: BN 147/27, R. W. Abbott (Occupational Pensions Board) to Sir Geoffrey Otton (DHSS), 'Inquiry into Provision for Retirement', 29 February 1984). If that were the only option, Fowler thought 'the price might be too high' (TNA: BN 147/27, IPR(PP)26, 'Inquiry into Provision for Retirement, Sub-Group on Portable Pensions, Portable Pensions: The Choices before Us, Note by the Chairman', 9 March 1984).

21 TNA: T 530/128, Seammen to Watson, IPR, 'Evidence from NAPF and Mr Vinson', 10 January 1984 (the CPS's assertion in its evidence to the IPR that most such pensions would be contracted in if SERPS continued is noted at TNA: BN 147/26, IPR(PP)3, IPR Sub-Group on Portable Pensions, 'Evidence from Centre for Policy Studies, the National Association of Pension Funds, and the Save and Prosper Group, Note by Secretary', 13 January 1984).

22 MTA: Margaret Thatcher, 'Interview for *New York Times*', 20 January 1984.

23 TNA: T 530/129, A. J. G Isaac to Cassell, 'Tax Treatment of Pensions', 20 March 1984; TNA: BN 147/28; J. B. Craddock [Legal and General] to Fowler, 'Portable Pensions', 16 April 1984. Treasury concerns about the prospective cost of such tax reliefs had been prompted by an Inland Revenue analysis (N. Munro to Minister of State, 'Inquiry into Provision for Retirement: Portable Pensions: Revenue Paper on "Options"', 14 March 1984).

24 TNA: BN 147/31, IPR(PP) 5th Minutes, IPR Sub-Group on Portable Pensions, 20 March 1984.

The abolition of SERPS? 259

25 TNA: BN 147/31, IPR(PP) 6th Minutes, IPR Sub-Group on Portable Pensions, 4 April 1984.

26 TNA: T 530/128, Ridley to Lawson, 'Portable Pensions and All That', 11 November 1983.

27 It is worth noting that a DHSS analysis of the Beveridge Report, conducted as a background briefing for its Review of Social Security at the start of 1984, acknowledged that the setting of benefit rates below subsistence in 1948 had marked a profound break with Beveridge's initial objectives – its immediate effect being to make an increasing number of old people dependent on means-tested supplementation. The briefing also noted that the benefits system had become so complex over time as to inhibit a clear assessment of whether the failure to implement the intentions of the Beveridge Report had been due to a rejection of its principles, the problem of practical constraints, or the fact that the report was 'no longer relevant to the needs of society today'. It concluded that '[t]he principle of an insurance benefit which is sufficient to meet basic needs without means testing for an unlimited period remains relevant if hard to achieve', though it also observed that it was 'much less clear that the means of providing this was practicable then or now' (TNA: BN 13/278, 'The Beveridge Report: Summary of Findings and Principles', undated but probably January 1984).

28 TNA: T 530/128, G. W. Watson to Chancellor of the Exchequer, 'Pension Inquiry and Portable Pensions', 14 November 1983.

29 Fowler, *Ministers Decide*, p. 209.

30 TNA: BN 147/32, Government Actuary's Department, 'Population Trends', January 1984.

31 TNA: T 530/129, D. Seammen, 'Inquiry into Provision for Retirement: Population and Pension Costs (Note by Government Actuary)', 27 January 1984. She also noted the common misconception that those who complained about 'the cost of SERPS' missed the point that this calculation also included the cost of the BSP.

32 TNA: T 530/129, G. W. Watson to Minister of State, 'Portable Pensions', 6 March 1984 (Watson was a regular attender at the subgroup's discussions, as was Redwood).

33 Fowler, *Ministers Decide*, p. 211.

34 TNA: BN 147/26, IPR(PP)7, IPR Sub-Group on Portable Pensions, 'Written Submissions from Bodies giving Oral Evidence, Note by the Secretary (N Montagu)', 2 February 1984.

35 TNA: BN 147/37, 'DHSS: Public Inquiry into Provision for Retirement', 19 July 1984 – oral evidence given by Kenneth Edwards, CBI Deputy Director-General. One should note the emphasis on 'current commitments', however, for the CBI was most concerned about the long-term costs of inflation-proofing occupational pension. In this session of oral evidence, the CBI noted that these were likely to be 'substantial', told the IPR that much would depend on the rate of real economic growth in the future, and expressed concerns at possibly 'dramatic' impacts on business costs and efficiency.

36 TNA: BN 147/10, Stewart to Montagu, 'NPR 401: CBI', 25 April 1984. Colin M. Stewart (head of the GAD's directorate for social security and pensions policy) had recently published in a personal capacity a long and thoughtful article

260 *Planning a revolution, 1983–5*

on the issues facing the pensions system, in which he had concluded that the country might have 'set our sights too high' (C. M. Stewart, 'Pension Problems and Their Solution', *Journal of the Institute of Actuaries*, 110 (1983), p. 310.) The wisdom of publishing this article was the subject of quite extensive debate within Whitehall but it was finally agreed that the journal was so obscure that it would remain below the radar of all but the most committed expert.

37 TNA: T 530/129, Seammen to Watson/Minister of State, 'Inquiry into Provision for Retirement – Sub Group', 9 March 1984.

38 TNA: BN 147/33, Montagu to Phillips, 'IPR: Report of the Sub-Group on Portable Pensions', 8 May 1984.

39 TNA: T 530/129, Watson to Minister of State, 'IPR(PP): Meeting on 2 May', 1 May 1984. Watson was commenting on a draft but there were no substantive changes made between that and the final version.

40 TNA: T 530/129, Seammen to Minister of State, 'Inquiry into Provision for Retirement', 9 May 1984. See also ibid., 'IPR: Meeting on 21 May', 18 May 1984 – in which Seammen again pressed the official case in a brief in advance of a meeting on 21 May.

41 Department of Health and Social Security, *Consultative Document on Improved Transferability for Early Leavers from Occupational Pension Schemes* (London: DHSS, 1984).

42 Department of Health and Social Security, *Personal Pensions: A Consultative Document* (London: HMSO, 1984). Reviewing Fowler's proposals, a *Financial Times* editorial on 17 July concluded that, '[m]ore than anything else, the proposals look like an attempt to dilute the scope' of SERPS, but it also questioned the wisdom of contracting out into a personal pension given that the employee would lose the employer's contribution (typically 12 per cent) and get only the rebated employer's NI contribution (4.15 per cent).

43 Department of Health and Social Security and Government Actuary's Department, *Population, Pension Costs and Pensioners' Incomes: A Background Paper for the Inquiry into Provision for Retirement* (London: HMSO, 1984).

44 TNA: BN 147/10, Stewart to T. S. Heppell, 'NPR 276, Centre for Policy Studies', 12 June 1984.

45 TNA: BN 147/37, IPR, evidence from the TUC, 12 July 1984.

46 Note the underlying 'male breadwinner' assumption within the TUC analysis.

47 TNA: BN 147/37, IPR, 12 July 1984. Peter Jacques (head of the TUC's Social Insurance Department) followed up: 'If you are talking about the crediting in of existing pensioners in the earnings-related scheme, I think that is a very worthwhile suggestion. If it would mean cutting back, that we would oppose very strongly.' John Ermisch of the Policy Studies Institute, who gave evidence in the same session, was also concerned to do something for those retiring before the full maturity of SERPS.

48 TNA: BN 147/ 37, IPR, 19 July 1984, evidence from the CBI.

49 Ibid., 19 July 1984, evidence from the National Pensioners' Convention.

50 Ibid., 12 July 1984, evidence of John Ermisch.

51 TNA: BN 147/10, Stewart to Montagu, 'NPR 476 Submission from Age Concern', 18 June 1984; BN 147/37, DHSS, Public Session into Provision for Retirement, 25 July 1984.

52 TNA: BN 147/10, Stewart to Montagu, 'NPR 476 Submission from Age Concern', 18 June 1984.

53 Ibid., 'NPR 429 Submission from Equal Opportunities Commission', 18 June 1984.

54 TNA: BN 147/37, IPR, evidence from the TUC, 12 July 1984.

55 TNA: BN 147/10, Stewart to Montagu, 'NPR 476 Submission from Age Concern', 18 June 1984.

56 DHSS, *Consultative Document on Improved Transferability for Early Leavers*.

57 Adam Smith Institute, *Omega Report: Social Security* (London: Adam Smith Institute, 1984).

58 National Association of Pension Funds Archive (hereafter NAPFA), London Metropolitan Archives: LMA/4494/A/01/013, Minutes of the Meeting of Council, 12 September 1984.

59 House of Commons, Fourth Report of the Social Services Committee, 1983–84, 'Public Expenditure on the Social Services', 11 July 1984.

60 TNA: PREM 19/2523, Redwood to Fowler, 17 July 1984.

61 Willetts had been private secretary to Nicholas Ridley when he was Financial Secretary to the Treasury and then served in that department's Monetary Policy Division. After serving in the PU from 1984 to 1986 he went on to become Director of Studies at the Centre for Policy Studies.

62 TNA: PREM 19/2349, Seminars on Health and Social Security Matters, brief for the Prime Minister on 'The Benefits Seminar' by David Willetts, 28 September 1984. 'SERPS has to go' was triple-underlined by Thatcher – indicating her clear agreement with the sentiment expressed – and much of the rest of the brief was underlined, which itself was evidence of her close interest with the topic. On the meaning of Thatcher's handwritten underlining and marginalia on official documents, see Christopher Collins, quoted in "Thatcher Files: 'Squiggly Line' Revealed Thoughts", *The Scotsman*, 22 March 2013; and Moore, *Margaret Thatcher*, vol. 2, p. xv.

63 TNA: PREM 19/2349, 'Seminars on Health and Social Security Matters, Social Security Reviews: Note of a Meeting held at 10 Downing Street at 14.30 Hours on Thursday 4 October 1984'. The ministers present were Thatcher, Fowler, Lawson, John MacGregor (as Chief Secretary to the Treasury), and Lord Young (as Secretary of State for Employment). The senior civil servants in the room were Sir Peter Middleton (Treasury Permanent Secretary) and his deputy, A. M. Bailey; Sir Geoffrey Otton (Second Permanent Secretary at the DHSS); and three more minor officials from these departments: Heppell, Gregson, and Bailey. Redwood and Willetts were also present. Turnbull acted as secretary.

64 TNA: BN 13/302, 'Note of a Meeting: IPR Conclusions', 17 January 1985.

65 TNA: BN 13/300, JW11.1, 'Outcome of January Week', undated but January 1985.

66 TNA: BN 13/300, 'Social Security Reviews: January Week – Session 3 (3–4 January): 'Pensions', 3 January 1985.

262   *Planning a revolution, 1983–5*

67 Ibid.

68 The other two options considered were (a) move to a lower rate of benefit accrual, abolish the '20 best years' provision, and make contracted-out occupational pension schemes responsible for inflation-proofing the GMP; and (b) end SERPS and replace it with an 'intrinsic' privately provided earnings-related basic pension required to provide minimum standards of benefit accrual, funding, and vesting (on the lines of the Swiss system, or the United States' ERISA model).

69 TNA: BN 13/302, 'Note of a Meeting: DHSS Public Inquiry into Provision for Retirement, Conclusions', 17 January 1985.

70 There is an entertaining description of a robust argument between the two men on 31 January in Fowler, *Ministers Decide*, p. 214. Ad hoc subcommittees of the Cabinet were favoured by Thatcher as a means of managing contentious policy issues, since they weakened the full Cabinet's scope of action when it was presented with policies already agreed by key ministers. The members of MISC 111 were: Thatcher, William Whitelaw, Leon Brittan, Lawson, Keith Joseph, Fowler, Tom King, Peter Rees, Lord Young, John Wakeham, John Gummer, Anthony Newton, and William Waldegrave. Minutes of its meetings were not widely circulated.

71 TNA: BN 13/302, Fowler to Thatcher, 'Social Security Review', 1 February 1985.

72 TNA: CAB 130/1293, MISC 111 (85) 1, memorandum by the Secretary of State for Social Services, 1 February 1985, with the draft Green Paper at MISC 111 (85) 2.

73 Ibid.

74 Ibid.

75 TNA: CAB 130/1293, MISC 111 (85) 1st Meeting, 6 February 1985.

76 TNA: PREM 19/1638, Redwood and Willetts to Thatcher, 'MISC 111', 8 February 1985.

77 Ibid.

78 TNA: CAB 130/1293, MISC 111 (85) 5, 'Occupational Pension Provision: Encouragement or Compulsion? Memorandum by the Secretary of State for Social Services', 12 February 1985. Fowler's reference to 'two nations in retirement' was a nod back to Crossman's criticism in the late 1950s of the gap in retirement income between those with and without an occupational pension in a world in which the soon to be abolished SERPS had not yet been implemented.

79 TNA: BN 13/302, Fowler to Thatcher, 'MISC 111: Public Expenditure Outlook', March 1985; PREM 19/1638, Andrew Turnbull to Steve Godber (DHSS), 'Social Security Reviews', 6 March 1985, summarising a meeting between Fowler and Thatcher.

80 TNA: PREM 19/1638, P. L. Gregson to the Prime Minister, 'Provision for Retirement (MISC 111 (85) 1: appendix 1) (MISC 111 (85) 5)', 12 February 1985.

81 TNA: PREM 19/1638, Redwood to Thatcher, 'Pensions', 12 February 1985.

The abolition of SERPS? 263

82 TNA: CAB 130/1293, Ministerial Group on Social Security, 'Limited Circulation Annex, MISC 111(85) 2nd Meeting Minutes', 13 February 1985. On the issue of freedom, see Lawson, *The View from No. 11*, p. 590.

83 TNA: BN 13/302, Fowler to Thatcher, 'MISC 111: Provision for Retirement', 29 March 1985. See also the succeeding document in this file (S. A. Godber to Mark Addison, 'MISC 111: Provision for Retirement', 29 March 1985) for the modelled effects on employer and employee NI contributions across the range of earnings.

84 TNA: BN 13/302, Fowler to Rees, 'MISC 111: Pensions', 2 April 1985; ibid., Godber to Heppell, 'Meeting with the Chancellor on 4 April', 4 April 1985.

85 TNA: BN 13/303, Note of a Meeting held in No. 11 Downing Street at 10.45 a.m. on Thursday 4 April 1985. In his memoirs, Lawson noted that he had been distracted from the issue in early 1985 first by the sterling crisis in January and then by preparations for the March budget, but he also complained that the DHSS had failed to undertake any serious analysis of either the short-term PSBR implications or the potential impact on growth of raising employers' costs, and that it had failed to clear the plans with the Treasury (Lawson, *The View from No. 11*, p. 589).

86 TNA: CAB 129/219/9, C (85) 9, 'Social Security Review, Memorandum by the Secretary of State for Social Services', 19 April 1985, para. 7, emphasis in original. There is a strong whiff here of an earlier intervention by Willetts, who had written to Ann Bowtell (the DHSS civil servant in charge of its Supplementary Benefits Division) to 'challenge the custodians of the sacred texts', by asserting that they 'seriously misinterpret Beveridge's views on the National Insurance Fund' by assuming that he had always envisaged that it would be pay-as-you-go. In this minute, Willetts set out his case for abolition of SERPS (that it would deal with its financial unsustainability, remove future pressure for even more 'extravagant future provision', and 'generate extra investment and lower consumption now, so as to provide a bigger income stream in future') and detailed the reasons why the alternative option of making it a funded scheme run by the state would be unacceptable (TNA: PREM 19/1964, Willetts to Bowtell, 16 April 1985).

87 Lawson, *The View from No. 11*, p. 589.

88 TNA: PREM 19/1639, Lawson to Thatcher, 'Social Security Reviews', 23 April 1985.

89 Fowler denounced Lawson for behaving unacceptably and even unconstitutionally (Fowler, *Ministers Decide*, pp. 219–20). Lawson, in his own description of the row (*The View from No. 11*, p. 589), remarked that he 'had never seen Norman so cross', noting that Fowler 'was furious at what he saw as a last-minute attempt to sabotage his plans, and claimed I had no right to act in that way'. Lawson disputed Fowler's claim that he was wrong to intervene at such a late juncture, citing the potential Exchequer impact.

90 John Myles and Paul Pierson, 'The Comparative Political Economy of Pension Reform', in *The New Politics of the Welfare State*, ed. by Paul Pierson (Oxford: Oxford University Press, 2001), pp. 305–33, at pp. 313–15.

91 TNA: BN 13/301, 'Social Security Review: Brief for Cabinet: Speaking Note on Employment Cost Implications of Occupational Pension Proposals', 25 April 1985.

92 TNA: PREM 19/1639, Fowler to Thatcher, 'Social Security Review', 26 April 1985.

93 Ibid.

94 TNA: PREM 19/1639, Lawson to Thatcher, 'Social Security Review', 29 April 1985; Lawson, *The View from No. 11*, pp. 590–91. Just over a week later the government's Chief Economic Adviser added to Lawson's fears (TNA: PREM 19/1639, 'Note by the Chief Economic Advisor: Economic Implications of Increasing Pension Fund Income', 3 May 1985). He concluded that compulsory occupational pensions (not just for employees but for the self-employed) would see aggregate contributions rise, with 'consequential adverse supply-side effects' – though he noted that a short-term hit to growth might well pay off in terms of higher growth over the long term because of an increase in available investment funds.

95 See, for example, *Financial Times*, 'State Pension Changes "Would Hit Business"', by Peter Riddell, 1 May 1985. Lawson's use of the IPR report's alternative options to oppose Fowler's embrace of compulsion is acknowledged by him at Lawson, *The View from No. 11*, p. 588.

96 TNA: PREM 19/1639, Turnbull to Godber, 'Social Security Reviews: Pensions', 30 April 1985.

97 Ibid., 1 May 1985.

98 TNA: PREM 19/1639, Redwood and Willetts, 'State Earnings-Related Pension Scheme', 26 April 1985. See also ibid., Redwood to the Prime Minister, 'SERPS and the Welfare Reviews', 3 May 1985, in which Redwood warned Thatcher: 'The only possible outcome of any substance from the reviews is a shift towards more individual responsibility. The only serious runner is through replacing SERPS with private savings. If this is lost, the welfare reviews will be written off as a loss of nerve, the sign that the government will not back rhetoric with action about family responsibility or long-term public spending pressures.'

99 *Daily Telegraph*, 'Private Sector Task', by Frances Williams, 18 April 1985; HC Debs, 22 April 1985, vol. 77, col. 623.

100 See, for example, *Financial Times,* 'Why 11m Pensions Are in the Balance', by Michael Prowse, and 'Pension Scheme Plans Attacked', by Peter Riddell, 2 May 1985. Redwood was infuriated by this, complaining to Thatcher that there was 'still powerful political support' for replacing SERPS 'but this alliance will not last for long if leaks and counter leaks continue and the pressure groups are allowed to build up' (TNA: PREM 19/1639, Redwood to Thatcher, 'SERPS and the Welfare Reviews', 3 May 1985).

101 CAB 129/219, C (85) 12, 'Social Security Review: Pensions: Memorandum by the Secretary of State for Social Services', 7 May 1985.

102 TNA: PREM 19/1639; Tebbit to Thatcher, 7 May; ibid., R. Armstrong, 'A085/1288, "Social Security Review Briefing on Cabinet Memoranda C (85) 9 and 12"', 8 May 1985.

103 Ibid., Turnbull to Thatcher, 'Social Security Reviews', 3 May 1985.

104 The tax relief figures were set out in detailed costings made available to MISC 111 by the DHSS; see CAB 129/219, C (85) 12, 'Social Security Review: Pensions: Memorandum by the Secretary of State for Social Services', 7 May 1985. In this memorandum, Fowler projected that the effect in the first year of the transition would be to increase the PSBR by £100 million, to increase employer payroll costs by 0.2 per cent, and reduce take-home pay net of pension contributions by the same percentage. At the end of the transition those figures would be £1.3 billion, 0.2 per cent, and 0.5 per cent respectively. On the expenditure consequences of preserving SERPS for older workers, Fowler noted that £1 billion of savings by the end of the century had been forgone, but assured Thatcher that, despite ensuring that 'nobody retiring this century will be affected', the government would 'still achieve almost all the savings originally envisaged when SERPS would have been at its most expensive in the next century' (PREM 19/1639, Fowler to Thatcher, 6 May 1985). The detailed costings are at TNA: PREM 19/1639, Godber to Turnbull, 'Social Security Review: Pensions', 6 May 1985. Lawson's apparent lack of attention to the cost of additional tax relief on private pension contributions may have been because the Treasury took its eye off the ball, assuming that the battle over SERPS had been won on 29 April, though it might also be because, in retrospect, we can see that, at just £300 million per annum by the end of the three-year transition period, the costing was optimistic.

105 A summary of the discussion is at TNA: PREM 19/1639, Turnbull to Godber, 'Social Security Reviews: Pensions', 6 May 1985.

106 TNA: CAB 128, C (85) 16th Cabinet Conclusions, 9 May 1985.

107 Department of Health and Social Security, *Reform of Social Security*, vol. 1: *Reform of Social Security*, Cmnd 9517 (London: HMSO, 1985).

Part IV

Implementation and legacy

7

From revolution to evolution

In early May 1985, as the government moved towards publishing its Green Paper on social security reform, Thatcher emphasised in an interview for BBC Radio 4's *The World This Weekend* that she wanted 'people to have the right to property' via a funded private pension (rather than depending on the pay-as-you-go state earnings-related pension). In doing so, she stressed her fundamental belief in spreading property and share ownership as part of the creation of a classless society (more correctly, perhaps, a middle-class society).[1] At the same time, of course, the government remained committed to substantial cuts in future public spending even as ministers sought in advance of the Green Paper to extol the levels of spending on the NHS, education and pensions achieved during six years of Conservative government (somewhat disingenuously, since they focused on nominal, not real, figures).[2] The publication of the social security Green Paper in June brought these strands together in the field of pensions, with its emphasis on private pension provision above a minimum state guarantee and on substantial savings in public spending via the abolition of the State Earnings-Related Pension Scheme, and its proposal for a complete (and compulsory) shift to a private system of funded occupational and personal pensions above the minimal Basic State Pension (BSP) that would see every worker given an individual stake in British capitalism.

Whereas Labour's *Better Pensions* White Paper in 1974 had talked in terms of a partnership between the state and employers in the provision of earnings-related pensions above the BSP, now the talk in the July 1985 Green Paper *Reform of Social Security* was of a partnership between the state and individual.[3] The Green Paper sought to portray that new partnership in reassuring terms, with its proposals on pensions cast as a return to the founding principles of Britain's welfare state espoused by William Beveridge in 1942. In fact, its proposals were nothing short of revolutionary; and, whatever the Green Paper might say, they were a long way from Beveridge. Ultimately, certainly, they envisaged a return to the status quo of 1948. in that the state would get out of the top-up pensions business and provide merely a minimal basic state pension – itself a revolutionary change that would affect over half the workforce. But there would be none of the top-up voluntarism of Beveridge. Occupational pension provision, hitherto voluntary, would become mandatory, with employers required to set up a company pension scheme to cover all their workers; and that scheme might be defined benefit (DB) or newly allowed, cheaper, and easier to run defined contribution (DC). Individual freedom too would be notably constrained. Employees would not be forced into membership of an occupational scheme, but nor would they be allowed to make their own decision about whether to make voluntary provision for an income in retirement. Individual freedom would be limited to allowing each worker to choose their mode of pension saving, not whether to save at all. If an individual chose to leave their employer's pension scheme, their only option would be to take out and contribute to a personal pension plan (to which the employer would be required to contribute). Taken together, the Green Paper's planned abolition of SERPS, major changes to occupational pensions, and inauguration of personal pension plans (already heralded in the DHSS's July 1984 consultation document) amounted not just to an institutional overhaul of British pensions on an epic scale but to a major recalibration of the relationship between the state and individual, and of the individual's relationship to the economy. The irony was that, as in so many aspects of the Thatcher economic revolution, the promotion of economic freedom in this vision would result from the actions of a powerful state unafraid to exercise its powers of compulsion.[4]

Yet, proposed pensions revolution never happened – or, rather, it happened in a very different way from that envisaged by its architects. SERPS was not abolished; it was retained, albeit with modifications that would effectively halve its benefits in the long term. The changes to occupational pensions proved much more limited than had been proposed, not least the fact that employers were neither required to set up a company pension scheme nor to make contributions to an employee's personal pension. Personal pensions, which the architects of change (Vinson and Chappell in the CPS, Redwood and Willetts in the No. 10 Policy Unit) had hoped would ultimately replace both SERPS and occupational defined benefit schemes, became just another element within the country's system of top-up pension provision alongside occupational pensions and SERPS. Overall, moreover, whereas the aim had been to simplify the pensions system, in fact it became considerably more complex, both in terms of its number of elements and the interactions between them. Ultimately, therefore, as Paul Pierson famously put it, in the wake of the Green Paper the government moved from outright privatisation of the second tier of British pensions to a process of 'implicit privatisation'.[5] That was a much less ambitious, much more nuanced, and much more long-term aim than had been set out in the Green Paper. SERPS remained open to all, and thus collective state pension provision continued for those who remained in it, and personal pensions did not dominate private provision for an income in retirement.

In the literature on this topic there is widespread agreement that the ambitions for reform in the Green Paper proved greater than the results actually achieved.[6] When we look for diagnoses of the reasons for the disappointment of government hopes, Pierson's explanation for the failed abolition of SERPS is dominant.[7] He noted that SERPS, unlike the US social security system or systems of earnings-related social security on the Continent, was immature in the mid-1980s, and thus in theory easier to abolish, since the 'double-payment problem' inherent in moving from pay-as-you-go to funded pensions had, in theory, not yet become an insuperable barrier.[8] Thus, Pierson argued, the government saw a window of opportunity – during which it could be abolished at relatively little cost – albeit one that was closing rapidly.[9] Even so, the government still found abolition impossible. Explaining why this was so led Pierson to explore the economics and economic history literature on the way in which increasing returns on an initial investment by a first mover in a market or by a new technology can cause that company/technology to acquire an entrenched market dominance.[10] As discussed in Chapter Three, the key point of Pierson's ('historical institutionalist') argument was that, over time, a policy or a political institution is the product of a series of decisions the cumulative effect of which is increasingly to entrench, or 'lock in', that system.[11] In 2001 Pierson and John Myles identified pensions as the 'locus classicus' of institutional path dependence – arguing powerfully that those seeking to reform such systems must necessarily take into account choices made in the past (because decisions on pensions are among the most long-term of all decisions taken by policymakers, and by individuals, and because they embody long-term contracts, either financial or political, that convey either property rights or quasi-property rights).[12] In explaining why it proved politically impossible to abolish SERPS, despite its relative immaturity, Pierson therefore cited not just the 'double payment' problem but the positive and increasing returns generated by growing familiarity with the system and the attachment to it evident in a range of external institutions that saw abolition to be against their own institutional best interests and/or those of their members or employees.

Pierson's analysis of the government's failed attempt to abolish SERPS focused on the resistance encountered from trades unions, employers, and pension funds. This analysis found strong support in the work of Giuliano Bonoli, who located the failure not just in the Treasury's antipathy to the required 'double payment' and in the resistance of the Labour party and 'traditionally left-wing groups' (such as the TUC and the anti-poverty lobby), but also in the unexpected and substantial criticism 'from interest groups traditionally sympathetic to the Conservative government such as

272 *Implementation and legacy*

the CBI and NAPF'.[13] In this chapter we explore this phenomenon in an analysis that examines a much wider range of primary sources, most of it unavailable to scholars hitherto. In doing so, we find considerable support for the idea that institutional resistance proved to be central to the undoing of the Green Paper's programme.

Our analysis concludes, however, that the most important contributor to the government's U-turn on pensions was an additional set of institutions to those identified by Pierson and Bonoli: life assurance and insurance companies, which the government had assumed would welcome its personal pension proposals as a bonanza of business opportunities. At the same time, as we explore why the proposed revolution failed, we also examine the dynamic within government as different departments, and different political actors, within it fought out a major battle that had at its heart an ideological struggle between proponents of radical reform and the more politically pragmatic, as well as a struggle between different strands of Conservatism and different neoliberal visions of pensions.

The chapter starts by setting out in more detail the new system proposed by the Green Paper. We then go on to explore the mechanics of the counter-revolution via an analysis of the resistance evident in public debate about the proposals and in formal responses to the consultation set in train by the Green Paper. Having made clear both the width and depth of opposition, including hostility from a pension industry on which the government was relying to run the new personal pensions and which the government had assumed would welcome its proposals with alacrity, we then examine how the government was forced in short order to execute a humiliating U-turn, and we explore the mechanics of that reversal. As we do so, we unpick the forces at work both in constraining and shaping the government's options for change as the scale of the opposition to its proposed revolution became clear, and as it navigated its way to a very different pension reform programme during both the preparation for and the passage through Parliament of the 1986 Social Security and Financial Services Acts. After a brief digression on the latter as it related to pensions, we end with a set of conclusions that highlight the chronic underestimation by the revolution's architects of the scale of the institutional barriers to the radical changes they were seeking to achieve.

The Green Paper and immediate reactions

The publication of the social security Green Paper, on 3 June 1985, represented a major achievement for Norman Fowler. Volume One began with a forthright assertion, penned by him, that 'the British social security system

From revolution to evolution

has lost its way'. A well-meaning system with achievements to its credit was characterised as too costly and bedevilled by confusion and complexity. The Green Paper sought, therefore, to create a more streamlined and, crucially, cost-effective system 'capable of meeting the demands into the next century'.[14] The product of two years' hard work, a consultation process of unusual extent, and hard-fought battles within Whitehall, its three volumes (running to more than 240 pages) swept across the whole of social security (pensions, supplementary benefits, housing benefit, family support, maternity, death and widowhood, as well as the management of this labyrinthine construction) and set out both an analysis of and a proposed set of reforms to each of its foundational elements. Among many recommendations, the Green Paper proposed, for example, to simplify housing benefits, to treat both unemployed families bringing up children and single parents more generously while continuing to provide universal child benefit, and to allow unemployed people to earn up to £15 a week without affecting their benefit entitlement. The Green Paper claimed to have found a way to tackle both the 'poverty trap' and 'unemployment trap' within the benefits system (whereby someone moving into works did not just lost their benefits but also faced an effective marginal tax rate of more than 100 per cent) by basing a new family credit for low-income working families on net rather than gross pay. These examples of generosity were offset by savings, however. The most notable immediate proposed savings were in housing benefit, with a proposal that all households receiving it pay 20 per cent of their domestic and water rates, and hints that mortgage payments made by those qualifying for benefits would no longer be subsidised. For all the impressive extent of the proposed reforms in these policy areas, however, the most radical area of the Green Paper's many proposals lay in pensions.

The fact that pensions loomed large in the equation was not a surprise, for the cost of state pensions was by far the largest element within the broader social security system, with far more recipients (12 million) and much more significant current expenditure (£16.3 billion) than its other elements. Nonetheless, the pension proposals set out in Volume Two of the Green Paper were arresting, and they had several dimensions. By far the most radical was the abolition of SERPS. The objections to it set out therein had two fundamental foundations: demographic change; and SERPS's unsustainable generosity. The demographic focus was the claimed reduction in the 'support ratio' (between workers contributing to the National Insurance system and pensioners drawing benefits from it) that would progressively emerge as baby-boom-era workers retired over the ensuing half-century.

It was the emerging cost of state pensions that loomed largest in the justification for abolishing SERPS, however. Credit was taken for the government's earlier removal of earnings indexation from the BSP, without which, the Green Paper claimed, its cost would have more than quadrupled by 2035 (from £15.3 to £66.5 billion in constant prices), as opposed to tripling to £43 million with price indexation alone.[15] But there were dark warnings about the future cost of SERPS, which was projected to rise from virtually nothing in 1984/85 (because few people had yet qualified for its benefits) to reach £23 billion by 2033, a figure that would represent 44 per cent of total state pensions spending.[16] The Green Paper also hinted that abolition could reinvigorate occupational pension schemes, because the complexity of contracting out of SERPS was the reason why such schemes had failed to continue their expansion (a claim both lacking evidence and tendentious given that the peak of occupational scheme membership had come in 1967, a decade before SERPS).[17] The fundamental driver of SERPS's abolition, however, was evident in the desire to reduce dependence on the state and the assertion that it was 'preferable for individuals to make provision themselves during their working lives to supplement the basic pension than for the responsibility to be left wholly to the state and to taxes to be levied on the next generation'.[18]

To address the problem of SERPS, the Green Paper identified three options: outright abolition; reduction in its scope, but without provision of any alternative; and, third, its replacement by what was termed 'a new partnership' between (minimal) state provision and that from occupational and personal pensions. Having identified those options, it proposed a modified version of option three: no change for those within 15 years of retirement (men over 50 and women over 45); but abolition of SERPS, phased over three years from 1987, for younger cohorts who would 'have sufficient time to build up their own pension savings', although benefits earned to date within SERPS would be honoured. Implicitly, it was recognised that losing future SERPS benefits would make this younger group worse off; hence there was also a proposal to enhance existing SERPS entitlements of men aged 40 to 49 and women aged 35 to 44 (with between one and seven and a half years of added rights, representing an addition to SERPS entitlements of between 10 and 75 per cent, on a sliding scale across the age range).[19]

Under the proposed new regime, therefore, the second tier of pension provision above the BSP would by the start of the new century consist of just occupational and personal pensions. 'Many employees and employers' would 'find the option of personal pensions attractive', it was asserted.[20] All employers would be required to set up an occupational pensions scheme (either individually or sectorally), and employers and employees alike would be required to contribute to it, with a minimum level of contribution set at an amount equivalent to 4 per cent of earnings (following a transitional period of three years, during which the contribution would rise from 2 per cent in the first year to 3 per cent in the second, then 4 per cent in the third year). Employers would be expected to provide at least a half of this, and to contribute that sum to the personal pension of an individual worker should she or he elect to take one out rather than stay in their employer's scheme.[21] All employees would have the right to make additional voluntary contributions (AVCs) within Inland Revenue limits.[22] Contributions would be eligible for tax relief. The new employer schemes would be allowed to be defined contribution (and the Green Paper assumed this would touch off a substantial structural shift as a result, as it expected many employers with DB schemes to shift to DC). With the end of SERPS for workers more than 15 years from state pension age would come an end to contracting out, and hence the Green Paper proposed a new single National Insurance contribution rate for these cohorts of about 16.5 per cent combined employee/ employer (as opposed to the existing 19.5 per cent rate for those contracted in, and 13.2 per cent for those contracted out – again, to be phased in over three years).[23] The disappearance of SERPS, and thus the disappearance of contracting out, would also, claimed the Green Paper, remove the complications inherent in introducing personal pensions alongside SERPS by allowing their holders to contract out of it. On a change of job, members of an occupational scheme would be allowed to transfer their accrued rights into a personal pension, which would then follow them from job to job. The government was 'anxious that as wide a range of institutions as possible' should be allowed to offer the new personal pensions.[24] Regulation of those institutions would be as set out in the January White Paper *Financial Services in the United Kingdom*.[25]

In short, the pension proposals of the Green Paper set out an extremely ambitious agenda that sought to overturn the state–employer 'partnership in pensions' consensus of the late 1970s and remove the state from the provision of retirement income above the profoundly ungenerous BSP. Certainly, wary of the costs involved, the government had again dodged the question of equalising the SPA (action on which would have to wait for another decade), but it did promise to abolish the 'earnings rule' whereby those receiving a state pension had it progressively withdrawn if they continued to have earnings.[26] Taken together with the earlier consultation paper on personal pensions and the government's developing agenda on financial services, however, the government's programme for pensions amounted to a revolution not just in the institutional structure of UK pensioning but in the funding of pensions and the ownership of capital.

What was certain, noted the Green Paper, was that all workers would 'be able to rely on the fact that their pension is their own property'. It went on:

> They will be free to decide whether to invest in a personal pension, which they can control more easily, or with their employer's occupational scheme. And they will be able to decide for themselves whether they wish to increase their

276   *Implementation and legacy*

additional pension provision beyond the minimum level. The effect will be to give greater freedom and greater choice to individuals and to concentrate the resources of the state where they are most appropriately applied – in providing a reasonable National Insurance pension as the basis on which people can build.[27]

This emphasis on freedom of choice within an institutional context, whether a pension via an occupational pension scheme or via a personal pension taken out with a financial services provider, was not the 'every man a capitalist' vision of the CPS in 1983; individual workers (male *and* female) were not going to be given direct control over their pension investment portfolio. Nonetheless, the recrafting of the institutional structure of pensions and the absence of the state in the proposed new regime represented a revolution in both the institutional provision and funding of pensions. Moreover, the advent of personal pensions and the hoped-for shift from DB to DC occupational pension schemes would see a much clearer line of sight from the individual to their pension investments.

Responses to the consultation

Publication of the Green Paper represented a major achievement for Fowler, not least because it marked a victory against Treasury attempts to slash the DHSS budget to a level he was deeply unhappy with. It had been achieved in the face of the Chancellor's profound antipathy to replacing SERPS with funded pensions due to the financial cost of associated tax relief on contributions – from the government's perspective, an example of Pierson's 'double payment' problem. Nonetheless, although the battle Fowler had fought within the government had been hard won, the battle to come would be even harder – and it would be lost.

As soon as the Green Paper appeared it was immediately clear that implementing its proposals was going to be far from easy. Press reporting was mostly negative. For example, an editorial in *The Economist* welcomed the planned overhaul of the welfare system, and the abolition of SERPS, but bemoaned the length of time SERPS would be 'a-dying', noted that raising National Insurance now to benefit future taxpayers (not to mention a bill of some £1.24 billion for businesses required to contribute to private pensions) represented a bold step, and expressed doubts that the government would ultimately accept the electoral implications of creating so many present-day losers.[28] The *Financial Times*, a paper that one might have expected to prove supportive, mustered just 'one-and-a-half' cheers for a Green Paper that its correspondent found strangely unambitious – with the single exception of its pension proposals, which he forecast would command little support.[29]

The front page of the *Daily Mail*, normally an ardent government cheerleader, heralded the Green Paper as 'the greatest peacetime gamble the Thatcher cabinet has taken with its own future'.[30] Its editorial on the same day welcomed the attempt to 'start the rescue of the welfare state system before it impoverishes all of us', simplify a system that made Byzantine government look like 'an open book', improve targeting on the very poor, and do away with SERPS gradually and with existing promises honoured; but it predicted trouble ahead, as it expected Labour and vested interests vigorously to resist change on pensions. That warning was echoed by *The Daily Telegraph*.[31]

A hint of what lay ahead came in a *Guardian* editorial, which attacked the broad sweep of Fowler's proposals on social security and was highly sceptical of the proposal to phase out SERPS, complaining that the decision to abandon it had been taken on the basis of dubious forecasts of its future cost, 'without an electoral mandate and against the initial stand of Mr Fowler, who declared (in November, 1983) that his aim was not to call into question the fundamental pensions structure "that was established in the 1970s, with all-party agreement, and to which I was a party"'.[32] *The New Statesman* was even more blunt: Fowler's claim to be a reformer in the tradition of William Beveridge was bunk; instead, his broad proposals indicated his acceptance of 'the social evil of mass poverty and despair', and his proposals on personal pensions were criticised for transferring risks to powerless individuals ill-equipped to manage them.[33]

Not surprisingly, the leader of the Labour opposition, Neil Kinnock, attacked the Green Paper's proposals as 'a crude and cruel way of making the poor poorer, the insecure less secure and the needy more needy', and he promised a joint campaign of opposition by Labour and the unions.[34] Much of the criticism was directed at its proposals to cut at least £1 billion from the then £40 billion social security budget; but it was also immediately clear that SERPS was going to be the most highly contentious issue. Even before the publication of the Green Paper Kinnock had denounced the proposed SERPS abolition and pledged that the next Labour government would restore the scheme (some commentators wryly noted the somewhat unsocialist commitment to a scheme that by its nature entrenched rather than eliminated inequality). The plan to switch workers to private pensions, claimed Kinnock, amounted to an attempt to 'teach people to fly by chucking them off the Empire State Building', and he warned of potentially devastating consequences.[35] The breach of faith with workers in SERPS, who had, after all, been promised no changes to the scheme by Thatcher in the previous year's general election, was widely highlighted, as were its electoral risks.[36] It was immediately plain that the Labour party would place a 'save SERPS' campaign high on its agenda. Publication of the Green Paper was

278 *Implementation and legacy*

duly dubbed a 'black day for Britain' by Labour's social services spokesman Michael Meacher.[37] At the end of the summer the Labour party conference endorsed his condemnation of the government's SERPS proposals and adopted as party policy a commitment to reintroduce the scheme if it was abolished.[38]

The Times' economics editor had warned, when rumours of the Cabinet's decision to abolish SERPS had become public, that killing off SERPS 'would not be much political fun'.[39] So it was to prove. This should have surprised nobody, for Fowler's Inquiry into Provision for Retirement had already served to reveal the depth and width of stakeholders' antipathy to SERPS abolition. Despite strong approval from certain insurers for privatising SERPS, overwhelmingly those giving evidence to the IPR had favoured the 'consensus' status quo over revolution, although, as we saw in the preceding chapter, some were prepared to see reductions in SERPS's generosity.[40] Recognising this scepticism, as well as his technical dependence on such stakeholders in implementing reform, Fowler accompanied his publication of the Green Paper with a letter to key stakeholders, such as the CBI, TUC, and NAPF, seeking their help in translating his proposals on pensions into workable policy.[41]

The reaction to Fowler's appeal for cooperation was not positive. That of the NAPF was not untypical: its Parliamentary Committee welcomed the invitation to meet DHSS officials for discussions; but its members were both overwhelmingly opposed to Fowler's proposals and sceptical about whether constructively to engage with the government.[42] As one delegate to an NAPF seminar on the Green Paper forcefully put it, the industry needed its proposals 'like a hole in the head' (not least because the abolition of SERPS and promotion of personal pension plans were likely to produce lower pensions for most employees).[43] In September the head of the NAPF's Parliamentary Committee bluntly described the Green Paper as a 'false prospectus', criticised its proposals as 'undesirable, unworkable and destroying pensions stability', and highlighted the particular impact they were likely to have on part-time workers (overwhelmingly women) and those with interrupted careers (women and the unemployed) who currently gained SERPS entitlements that private pensions would not grant.[44] In its subsequent formal submission to the DHSS on the Green Paper, the NAPF expressed its 'strong distaste' for many elements of the proposals and called for a more careful examination of retaining a modified SERPS. It also dismissed the government's claim to be simplifying the system as 'blatantly untrue', called for a clear acknowledgement that contributions would rise even as benefits fell, and 'bitterly deplore[d]' the obvious attempt to undermine occupational pensions by allowing employees to opt out of them into a personal pension.[45]

By early August a leaked CBI discussion document had revealed similar sentiments within the employers' organisation. As a result of the Green

From revolution to evolution 279

Paper's pension proposals, businesses would pay more yet the pensions received by their workers 'would be both inadequate and insecure' (partly because the proposed minimum contribution was too low but also because administration costs would be much higher if companies were forced to contribute to a multitude of personal pensions). Consequently, the CBI's leaders were 'implacably opposed' to the government's proposals.[46] Its formal response to the Green Paper rejected Fowler's proposals on pensions, instead recommending (as the CBI had done in its evidence to the IPR) a three-tier system with personal pensions installed on top of the BSP and the second tier of occupational pensions and a retained SERPS (albeit, to contain future costs, one modified by abolition of the '20 best years' provision relating earnings to benefits and less generous inheritance rights). The CBI complained bitterly about the additional costs to be imposed on employers (which it estimated would increase payroll spending by 4 per cent) even as benefits to employees fell as compared to SERPS. Not surprisingly, given that it was privately the intention of the No. 10 Policy Unit, the CBI also expressed concern that implementation of the Green Paper's proposals would destabilise occupational schemes by sucking workers out of them into personal pensions. Finally, it condemned the timetable envisaged for reform as 'totally unrealistic and dangerous'.[47] In September the CBI returned to the fray, warning that the contributions of a low-paid worker to a personal pension would be too low to generate much of a pension, not least because up to a third of the contribution would be consumed by administration costs. It also emphasised the 'double burden' that would be placed on employers, who would be expected to pay not just for today's state pensioners via taxation but also for those of the next century as well because of the wholesale shift to funded pensions.[48] The CBI's president was blunt: the proposal to abolish SERPS should be 'thrown on the bonfire'.[49]

The TUC, like the CBI, was adamantly opposed to the abolition of SERPS.[50] In late July it decried the government's failure to honour its promise to protect SERPS, launched what it promised would be vigorous campaign to save it, promised a full debate at its annual conference in September, and announced a national march and rally in London on 27 October.[51] In its formal response to the Green Paper, the TUC expressed itself 'astounded' at the proposal to phase out SERPS and warned of 'potentially disastrous consequences'. Far from simplifying the system, complained the TUC, the proposed reforms would lead to much greater complexity (and much higher administrative costs) even as they produced poorer pensions. Moving to personal pensions would, inevitably, remove any possibility of redistribution, which the TUC saw as one of the key merits of SERPS; and it felt that the projected costs of SERPS were alarmist, arguing that future economic growth would allow the costs of SERPS to be financed without the need for any drop in the living standards of pensioners.[52] In early September the TUC's annual conference debated Fowler's proposals. The tone was bitter. Ray Buckton, the chairman of the TUC's Social and Industrial Welfare Committee, dismissed the review of social security as 'a cynical charade'.[53] 'It's our welfare state,' said one delegate. 'We've paid for it and we're going to fight like hell to defend it.'[54]

The TUC conference unanimously backed a proposed resistance campaign, and the unity of purpose on both sides of industry was evident when it issued jointly with the Engineering Employers' Federation (EEF) and the Association of British Chambers of Commerce (ABCC) a statement of opposition to the government's proposals. The EEF called them both 'impracticable and highly damaging' and its director general called for a more determined search for consensus to avoid making pensions once again 'a political shuttlecock'. The ABCC described the proposals as presenting 'real difficulties to industry and commerce'.[55]

It was not just pension funds, larger companies, and trades unions that proved problematic for the government; so did the financial services industry – even though, plainly, some firms in the sector hoped to profit from the proposal that private pensions infill for SERPS, not least because it promised an extra £2 to 3 billion a year in contributions. Life assurance companies with large sales forces and experience in handling individual accounts were expected to do notably well; on the day the Green Paper was published shares of Legal & General, Prudential, and other big insurers rose sharply.[56] Yet, despite positive investor sentiment, in fact many life assurers and insurance companies were unenthusiastic about the government's pension proposals. Legal & General, for example, expressed its profound concerns about the envisaged speed of reform and its worries about the destruction of the consensus on which SERPS was based (not least because gearing up for reform would require substantial investment by the company, which would prove worthless if a future Labour government rolled those reforms back).[57] More fundamental a problem was the proposed compulsory substitution of personal pensions for SERPS. It was one thing for a financial services firm to sell personal pensions to the better paid with money to invest, quite another to have to take on a huge number of expensive to service, and thus inherently unprofitable, low wage-earners. The largest firm in the industry, Prudential Assurance, for example, warned the DHSS that, as a major 'industrial' (doorstep) seller of pensions, it was likely to be saddled with a large number of lower-paid employees – something it saw as a 'worrying prospect, commercially' because of how expensive such small-value individual contracts would be to administer.[58] Shortly thereafter the Association of British Insurers (ABI) emphasised 'overwhelming problems handling small, infrequent contributions from the low paid under the new system', criticised Fowler's apparent dismissal of the option of modifying SERPS rather than abolishing it, and stressed the way in which good employers would face a 'double burden' even as their employees bore the risks of poor investment returns and inflation.[59] These complaints were reiterated in the ABI's formal response to the Green Paper, which also criticised the proposed 4 per cent minimum contribution as inadequate to replace SERPS. Taken as a whole, argued the ABI, the proposed reforms would also work to undermine the financial structure of occupational schemes.[60]

Thus, as an internal DHSS analysis of responses to the Green Paper noted, there had been a 'strongly adverse' response to the Green Paper's pensions proposals from both sides of industry, occupational pension funds, other representative organisations, and, crucially, a financial services sector on which the government was relying to deliver personal pensions. The break from the consensus constructed in the mid-1970s on the state–industry partnership on pensions had been generally decried, and the re-emergence of political disagreement about pensions, additional costs, and the loss of members to personal pensions were expected to weaken occupational schemes. There was a strong desire to see SERPS retained, albeit with some willingness to accept modifications to contain future costs.[61] There was certainly a preparedness to see personal pensions in the system, but as an additional element within it, not as a replacement; and even then there was a widespread perception that personal pensions were going to require 'very strong consumer protection'.

U-turn

As noted in Chapter Six, in the lead-up to the social security Green Paper the Cabinet Secretary, Sir Robert Armstrong, had warned Thatcher that 'abolition of SERPS is certain to be highly contentious' (emphasising the likelihood that the income of future pensioners would fall as a result and noting that different cohorts of working age adults were to be treated differently, with workers within 15 years of SPA treated much more generously than younger workers).[62] Responses to the Green Paper submitted to the DHSS over the summer had thus amply confirmed Armstrong's prediction. By the time the deadline for responses to the consultation on the Green Paper's proposals passed on 16 September, the 'near deafening chorus' of voices calling on the government to reconsider its proposed abolition of SERPS was all too obvious. 'Few others seem to want to join the Fowler bandwagon' apart from 'the right-wing Monday Club, the Institute of Directors and a handful of financial institutions such as Save and Prosper', noted Michael Prowse in the *Financial Times*. Ominously for the government, even though the Monday Club had praised the government 'for taking a course that is essential in the national interest', the praise had been accompanied by a warning that it was 'likely to cause some harm to its electoral standing'. Prowse also noted evidence of an emerging split within the Conservative party, with many on its centre and Left (such as the Tory Reform Group) favouring modification of SERPS rather than abolition.[63] At the Conservative party conference in early October Ian Gilmour, the former Conservative Cabinet minister, warned that the proposed abolition of SERPS was widely seen as a misplaced piece of ideology favouring the private sector at all costs. 'Wet' political pragmatism and 'dry' ideological ambition within the party were in clear tension. Fowler sought to present the party as a defender of the welfare state, prepared to reform it to render it sustainable for the long term. Its enemies were those who opposed reform. Significantly, however, Fowler's speech made no mention of SERPS, an omission that did not go unnoticed.[64] It was, essentially, a holding operation while he sought to reconstruct his policy, but, even so, Fowler was forced to give the first hint that the commitment to abolish SERPS could be reconsidered.[65] It was not just Fowler who felt at bay; Thatcher's speech was notably touchy about pensions, with a complaint about pensioners being 'the object of a sustained and particularly cruel campaign of false propaganda'. Nonetheless, her speech ended with the resounding peroration that 'step by step we are rolling back the frontiers of socialism and returning power to the people. Yes, we have set our sights high. But these goals are within our reach. Let us ensure that we bring them within our grasp.'[66]

Given the breadth of opposition, the Conservative party's internal qualms about SERPS abolition, and the need to work towards the publication of a White Paper in November, it is not surprising that Fowler had called a council of war for 1 October at Hannibal House, the DHSS's brutalist office block above the Elephant and Castle shopping centre in Southwark. In preparation for that day conference, Fowler asked Nicholas Montagu, the civil servant who had acted as secretary to the IPR, to collate and analyse responses to the Green Paper. The list of major industry bodies opposed to SERPS abolition revealed by Montagu's analysis the next day was long.[67] He noted that a survey of 196 major employers had found only 12 per cent favourable to the Green Paper's overall proposals, and only 2 per cent wanted SERPS abolished. Several large insurers opposed SERPS's abolition. Other bodies expressing more general doubts about abolition included professional pensions experts such as the Association of Consulting Actuaries and the Institute and Faculty of Actuaries. Objections were also noted from, among others, the National Consumer Council, the Consumers' Association, and the Equal Opportunities Commission. Montagu noted that the Tory Reform Group too had expressed its view that any justified concerns about SERPS could surely be met by reform rather than abolition.[68]

This was a devastating litany of criticism from virtually all those responding to the consultation. It was echoed by the government's Social Security Advisory Committee, which had expressed its strong preference for retention of SERPS, noting that the proposals were 'cause for a great deal of

From revolution to evolution 283

anxiety'. The idea of a minimum 4 per cent contribution to personal pensions as a replacement for SERPS was questioned on the grounds that it would not provide an adequate pension protected against inflation, and nor was it seen as addressing the problem of people with broken work records. The Committee also rejected the claim made both in the Green Paper and by ministers in internal government discussion that the projections of future SERPS costs justified its abolition. The Committee concluded that 'SERPS should be maintained, modified as necessary in the light of understandable concern about future costs'.[69]

Not surprisingly, the chorus of censure (which had a counterpart internally in terms of Lawson's criticisms of the proposal to abolish SERPS, which we explored in the previous chapter) had its effect. Fowler later wrote of how 'dangerously isolated' he had been left by the overwhelmingly negative responses, his sense that political support within the government for his reform proposals was ebbing away, and his recognition that to persist with his plans would be 'an extremely doubtful venture'.[70] On the eve of the Hannibal House conference the Policy Unit's David Willetts met Fowler to discuss his fears, noting afterwards in a brief for Thatcher that Fowler was now 'trying to escape from the MISC 111 deal'.[71] At that conference, which Fowler chaired, a range of options for SERPS was reviewed within the rubric that the resulting structure 'must encourage more private provision', broadly defined.[72] In addition to options proposed by Fowler to MISC 111, other options on the conference agenda as 'mainstream' possibilities were: to reduce the rate of accrual of SERPS benefits for those earning more than £150 a week (as suggested by the actuary Stewart Lyon); increase women's qualification age to 65; and reduce progressively the maximum earnings on which SERPS entitlements were calculated (the roots of the latter two options, along with the idea of moving to a '30 best years' rule, being ascribed to a speech made by David Owen, the leader of the Social Democratic Party, in a speech to the NAPF on 16 May).[73]

At the heart of the Hannibal House deliberations was a proposed alternative strategy: personal pensions introduced as an optional substitute for occupational pensions and a reformed SERPS. Their form would be simpler than envisaged in the earlier DHSS consultative document (most notably without mandatory employer involvement), however, and there would be encouragement of occupational pensions via provisions such as the right to make additional voluntary contributions and the preservation of benefits after one year of membership rather than five.[74] Perhaps more significantly, considerable thought had already been given to how to handle this abrupt change of course – especially through proposed behind-the-scenes discussions with key stakeholders to build support; a strategy for getting other ministers on-side via an emphasis on immediate political advantages; the

284 *Implementation and legacy*

necessary horse-trading of support (most notably with Nigel Lawson over his Green Paper on personal taxation); a subtle redrafting of pension priorities (now focused on affordability, widening occupational pension coverage, and promoting personal choice in the market); and an emphasis on the Green Paper having put forward a range of options (albeit only to dismiss all but the abolition of SERPS; but that was to be glossed over).[75]

Events now moved quickly. In the wake of the DHSS conference, and as Fowler sought to produced revised proposals for MISC 111, there was a whirlwind of detailed internal DHSS option reviews, meetings with the Prime Minister and key ministers such as Lawson and Tebbit, and private conversations with external stakeholders (Roy Brimblecome, general manager of Eagle Star and chairman of the Life Insurance Council's Parliamentary Committee; the NAPF chairman, Colin Lever; the CBI president, James Cleminson; and John Hoskyns, from the IoD).[76] In his memorandum for MISC 111 at its meeting on 15 October, Fowler wrote:

> I am convinced that we should stand by our agreed pension objectives – to reduce the cost of SERPS, to see an expansion of occupational provision and to increase choice through the option of personal pensions. But I have now concluded that we should follow a different path towards these objectives.[77]

In his notes for the meeting, Fowler acknowledged that the negative response of the government's 'natural supporters' (i.e. of employers and, most crucially, of firms in the financial services sector) had forced his search for new solutions, but he also expressed his hope that the new package of pension proposals he had crafted 'could form the basis of a new consensus.'[78] He noted the very large number of responses to the green paper (over 6,000 in total), emphasised the very negative reaction to the abolition of SERPS (including opposition 'from bodies who would normally be firm supporters and on whom we will depend heavily on getting new arrangements in place'), and set out his alternative strategy – 'to modify SERPS in order to reduce its emerging costs' and to undertake a further round of consultations on that basis.[79] He also noted, justifiably, that, although the consultation process had been difficult, it had produced a shift in sentiment, with a large number of stakeholders having indicated that they were now prepared to accept modification of SERPS.[80]

Fowler detailed the new strategy in an annex to this MISC 111 memorandum. From April 1988, a year later than originally envisaged, he proposed that SERPS be modified to base its benefits on 5 per cent of revalued earnings between the lower and upper earnings limits. Further changes would help to reduce its long-term costs: occupational schemes would be made responsible for inflation-proofing contracted-out pensions up to 5 per cent a year (thus saving £50 million of public expenditure in 1988/89, rising to

£3 billion by 2033); SERPS pensions would be based on the best 30 years of earnings since 1978, not on the best 20 (saving £4 billion by 2033); and inheritance would be restricted to half a dead spouse's SERPS rights. To secure the implementation of personal pensions, Fowler also proposed (a) to make simpler contracting out an occupational pension scheme from SERPS, including allowing DC schemes to contract out when the contribution exceeded a defined level (which he hoped might stimulate sector-based schemes); (b) to preserve pension rights for everyone who had been in a scheme for two years, rather than the present five; (c) to give everyone the right to opt for a contracted-out personal pension that would directly receive a contribution from the DHSS (to keep employers out of the administrative equation), with the rebated contribution to be age-related to avoid giving younger workers too great an incentive to opt out of their occupational scheme; and (d) to extend the range of institutions allowed to sell personal pensions to include, for example, banks, building societies, and unit trusts in order to 'end the virtual monopoly of the insurance companies in pension provision'.[81] It is notable, moreover, that his pitch to MISC 111 subtly recast the notion of pensions privatisation: whereas the Green Paper had placed personal pensions at the core of that concept, now it had been extended to embrace widening occupational pensions coverage, with personal pensions as a choice within an enhanced 'private' menu of alternatives to SERPS.

In its briefing note for the Prime Minister ahead of the MISC 111 meeting that considered Fowler's revised proposals, the PU tended to gloss over objections to SERPS's abolition, noting merely that the proposed timetable was unrealistic, and it reminded Thatcher that the option of abolition (with or without compulsory personal pensions as an alternative) was still available. Willetts wrote enthusiastically of that option: 'Abolishing Serps furthers the objective of a property-owning democracy and in the long run delivers big cuts in tax on public expenditure. Anything else looks like a retreat.' Yet the tone of his final recommendation was resigned, assuming SERPS would continue, thus defusing opposition from vested interests, but recommending that the government set off a process of slow strangulation by 'draining SERPS of the maximum number of people'. There was a recognition, however, that this too would be politically unpopular, the loss of benefits to present-day workers outweighing the benefits to future taxpayers and simply 'making SERPS meaner with no greater vision'.[82] A more positive steer for Thatcher came from the Cabinet Office. As a senior civil servant in the Cabinet Secretariat noted, since 'the proposal to abolish SERPS has clearly elicited quite unexpectedly hostile response not just from the government's political opponents but from most quarters representing the interests that would be involved in operating the new regime', MISC 111 might 'see

286   *Implementation and legacy*

advantage in moving quickly away from the plans to abolish SERPS before the government are committed to it any more deeply'.[83]

MISC 111 duly executed its U-turn. As both Douglas Hurd and Leon Brittan noted in letters of apology for their absence from the meeting, the lack of support from the pension industry, on which the government had been relying to fill the vacuum that would be created by the abolition of SERPS, left it with little option.[84] Consequently, MISC 111 authorised Fowler to change direction and proceed with consultations on modifying SERPS on the lines he proposed (albeit requiring savings of at least £9.5 billion be delivered by 2033).[85] This about-face on abolishing SERPS represented a considerable blow personally to Fowler, who was clearly identified with the policy politically and publicly. It was also a profound blow to the Policy Unit, however, and particularly to John Redwood, given his role in driving policy on SERPS abolition. In a minute to Thatcher, Redwood talked of the vital need now 'to rescue something from the rubble of SERPS' even as he restated his continuing belief in its abolition. He also complained that Fowler had 'lost ground on SERPS' because he had conducted two rounds of consultation in which opponents of radical change had been given a voice. Echoing Willetts, Redwood talked now of draining SERPS of members by incentivising contracting out to personal pensions and setting 'fairly penal rates for those remaining' – a death by slow strangulation.[86] Willetts himself continued to remind Thatcher that abolition had 'never just been about savings' but had as its crucial objective the encouragement of 'private pensions', and, like Redwood, he emphasised that it would not be enough to cut back SERPS benefits; there would now need to be incentives for 'companies and individuals' to make private provision and exit SERPS.[87]

Nevertheless, public expenditure reductions continued to loom large, with pressure on Fowler from both No. 10 and the Treasury to deliver further savings from SERPS' modification in addition to those mandated by MISC 111. Consequently, he was forced to concede further cuts. On 25 October Willetts summarised the revised situation for Thatcher.[88] By this point Fowler was proposing that, in addition to basing the calculation of SERPS benefits on earnings over a working life rather than its best 20 years, the value would also be reduced over ten years from 2000/01 from 25 to 20 per cent of earnings for new retirees; this would apply to all earnings since the scheme's inception in 1978, despite the promise to preserve benefits to date made in the Green Paper (the total saving would be £8 billion by 2033).[89] Reducing inheritance of SERPS rights to half, as already mooted, would generate another £1.7 billion by that year. That left Fowler with some headroom, which he used to reduce the planned shift to companies of responsibility for inflation protection of the GMP from 5 to 3 per cent a year

From revolution to evolution 287

(producing a net saving of £0.6 billion rather than £0.9 billion by 2033).[90] The combined effect of these further concessions was that the total savings in 2033 could now be expected to be £10.3 billion rather than £9.5 billion (see Table 7.1).[91] This was the package that Fowler took to MISC 111 at the end of the month.[92]

Nevertheless, there remained the problem of how best to encourage members of SERPS to contract out of it into private provision. In discussions with the CBI, occupational pensions schemes, and the British Insurance Brokers' Association, it had been made clear to Fowler that simply degrading the benefits offered by SERPS would not in itself generate either an expansion of occupational schemes or a large-scale shift to personal pensions. He therefore confirmed his intention to allow DC schemes to contract out of SERPS and simplify the contracting-out process. AVCs by members would be a right, not a privilege (as heralded by the Green Paper). He also confirmed that schemes would be expected to preserve rights after two years of membership. Fowler also proposed that for five years from 1988 there should be an additional National Insurance rebate of 2 per cent to schemes that decided to contract out (Nigel Lawson had been persuaded to support this in return for yet more savings on SERPS). This rebate would also be available to those opting for a personal pension, which would be available as of right to all employees (something that was to create tensions with Lawson, who wanted, but did not succeed in getting public sector workers in unfunded pension schemes excluded).[93] This 'special incentive' would provide a significant encouragement to take out a personal pension, as it was equal to half the minimum 4 per cent annual contribution. In addition, employers would be enabled (but not required) to make contributions to the personal pensions of their workers, and, again as heralded by the Green Paper, banks, unit trusts, and building societies as well as insurers would be allowed to offer personal pension schemes approved by the Occupational Pensions Board.[94]

Table 7.1 Interim projections of public expenditure savings on a modified SERPS (£ billion)

	2013	2023	2033
Full cost of unmodified SERPS	9.6	15.7	23.1
Savings from complete abolition	2.5	7.4	16.7
Savings under proposals of 11 October 1985	2.9	5.9	9.5
Savings under proposals as at 30 October 1985	2.3	5.7	10.3

Source: TNA: PREM 19/1640, Willetts to Thatcher, 'Savings on SERPS', 30 October 1985.

288   *Implementation and legacy*

Legislation

The Social Security Act 1986

The speed with which proposals on SERPS had been reconstructed was impressive, and on 31 October MISC 111 authorised Fowler to move rapidly towards legislation, the first stage of which was a draft White Paper ratified by the full Cabinet on 28 November.[95] By this point, by dint of some fiddling with the figures, the DHSS had managed to inflate the projected future cost of SERPS, and thus increase the savings generated by its proposed modifications to it, as can be seen in Table 7.2.

Moving from the draft to the published White Paper proved relatively easy. Ironically, the major sticking point with the Treasury was Fowler's text disparaging SERPS as unaffordable; this was 'just a little too apocalyptic', its officials warned Montagu. They went on:

> It is all too easy for critics to argue that SERPS is affordable, even on its present structure, if you assume 'a reasonable rate of growth' in GDP. The point is that, though the SERPS could be borne with reasonable economic growth, it is highly irresponsible to <u>assume</u> that growth and mortgage it in advance.[96]

The White Paper was published, with just minor changes to its wording, on 16 December.[97]

As the White Paper had taken shape there had been an awareness that selling reductions in the generosity of SERPS would not be easy. As Willetts warned Thatcher, 'Pensioner losers are very tricky politically.'[98] He had been in favour of a strong line, but Fowler had warned Thatcher that she needed to 'understand the political difficulty' of the changes he was 'being pushed

Table 7.2 Final projections of public expenditure savings on a modified SERPS (£ billion)

	2013	2023	2033
Full cost of unmodified SERPS	10.4	17.2	25.8
Total savings	2.9	7.0	12.8
Of which:			
- Abolition of '20 best years' rule, pension 20% not 25%	1.8	4.9	10.0
- Restrict inheritance of SERPS rights to 50%	1.1	1.8	2.2
- Contracted-out schemes to inflation-proof GMPs up to 3% p.a.	–	0.3	0.6

Source: TNA: PREM 19/1640, Willetts to Thatcher, 'Savings on SERPS,' 30 October 1985.

From revolution to evolution 289

into making'.[99] Willetts' perspective, however, was that the issue was presentational rather than fundamental: the changes would be but part of a much wider reform of social security that would bring benefits for many existing pensioners, transitional arrangements would mean that nobody currently in receipt of supplementary benefit would be worse off, and reform of the housing 'rates' system would work to the advantage of the many pensioners who lived alone. The assumption was that downgrading SERPS benefits for future pensioners would not attract the ire of existing ones.

Somewhat surprisingly, Willetts was not far off the mark in his prediction of a muted reception for the White Paper.[100] As the *Guardian* noted, the reaction of the pension industry could not be described as euphoric, but there was a widespread acceptance among large companies and insurers that SERPS's future costs could be said to justify cuts to its benefits, and that it was far better to have a modified SERPS than to see it abolished. Much as *The Daily Telegraph* might complain about the government's timidity in not abolishing SERPS, there was a general recognition that the scale of opposition to the Green Paper's pension proposals had required compromise.[101] As a spokesman for the Norwich Union, a large insurer, put it: 'Given the *status quo* with regard to SERPS was never an option, we are relieved to see the solution that has been reached.'[102] Insurance companies were, not surprisingly, pleased that they would no longer be required to sell personal pensions to unprofitable low earners, but could concentrate on the better paid.[103] Simplification of contracting out, and universal access to AVCs for occupational pension scheme members was widely welcomed. There were nonetheless concerns expressed about the effect on women of abandoning the '20 best years' rule, and pension industry companies were worried about the low level of pension that those taking out a personal pension might well receive. The industry also recognised that attention would have to be paid to the regulation of selling.[104]

As Eric Short, the *Financial Times*' pensions correspondent, pointed out although the White Paper might not encompass the abolition of SERPS, its proposals still shattered the pensions consensus of the late 1970s and would, ultimately, 'alter the whole concept of pension provision in the UK'. People retiring in the next century who relied on the state for their pension would 'be in for a shock'.[105] In the coming months Short continued to complain in the *Financial Times* about a continuing failure to understand the way in which women were disadvantaged by the proposed reforms. Presciently, he also attacked the failure to recognise that interrupted employment might in the future become a much greater feature of life.[106] Short was something of a lone voice, however. In fact, the only aspect of the White Paper that attracted significant criticism was the additional 2 per cent National Insurance rebate for new occupational schemes and private pensions. This 'rum bit of bribery' had been instituted at the insistence of the Policy Unit in its quest to strangle SERPS.[107] The 'bribe', as it was instantly dubbed in the pensions industry, was widely assumed to be an attractive incentive to take out a personal pension, especially to young people, though it was criticised by many as unethical politicking. It is notable, however, that no concerns were expressed about the potential for employees to be tempted out of their existing occupational pension scheme by the additional rebate.

As the government moved forward from the White Paper to legislation, publishing the Social Security Bill on 17 January 1986, its pension proposals continued to attract remarkably little serious opposition.[108] The only exception was the additional National Insurance rebate, which continued to attract criticism as a 'political bribe', but also because the decision to offer a flat-rate rebate was thought likely to distort the market by encouraging those who opted out of SERPS to gain it to opt back in again once it ceased to be paid.[109] The rebate was a particular target of the opposition as the Bill made its way through Parliament. At its second reading, for example, complaints about 'the bribe', led by the Labour MPs Archy Kirkwood and Frank Field, began even before Fowler had finished introducing the debate.[110] Labour's official spokesman, Michael Meacher, focused on querying the government's claims about the unaffordability of SERPS, however, and thus on the need for cuts to its benefits. Labour, he said, 'unequivocally reject the revised proposals on SERPS which reduce its value by nearly half ... [M]ost people are perfectly willing to contribute generously to others as long as they know they in their turn will get the same advantage.'[111] Fowler dismissed this line of attack by emphasising that nobody retiring before the end of the century would be affected. Meacher returned to the issue of SERPS later in the debate, but, again, the attack was somewhat half-hearted, though successful in emphasising the hit that workers retiring in the new century, particularly women and others with less than full contribution records, would take to their pension entitlement, and in asserting that 'the Fowler proposals are deliberately designed to make the SERPS scheme so unattractive that it can no longer compete with private pension schemes'.[112] Unusually, more Conservatives spoke against the Bill than MPs from other parties: Francis Pym, for example, bemoaned the loss of consensus, and Brandon Rhys Williams accused the government of taking the country back to Speenhamland with its proposals on social security.[113] Nevertheless, the government comfortably won the vote on whether the Bill should proceed to its committee stage (by 278 votes to 201).[114]

Since the Social Security Bill was lengthy, it was expected to be in committee for three to four months. Even so, the government found itself forced to resort to all-night sittings and imposing a guillotine (the first time this had been invoked for a major piece of pensions legislation).[115] Nonetheless,

From revolution to evolution
291

despite the significant debate that had taken place on it over many months, on pensions the Bill emerged essentially unchanged except for many relatively minor technical amendments. Likewise, the report stage in the House of Commons on 19–20 May saw no substantive changes. Indeed, so confident was Fowler that he left the handling of the Bill to his junior ministers, John Major and Tony Newton. Subsequently the Bill passed to the House of Lords, which held its second reading on 2–3 June, in which, again, there was substantial opposition to the 2 per cent personal pensions 'bribe', as well as some disquiet at the government's reticence on required regulation. Those concerns did not produce any substantive changes, however. During the Lords' committee stage, peers were lobbied quite intensively by opponents of the Bill, most notably by 'The Social Security Consortium', a loosely organised federation of charities and trades unions, which emphasised the plight of women, disabled people, and those experiencing unemployment and, thus, interrupted contribution records. They objected strongly to the 2 per cent rebate, as 'a regressive additional tax on all the working population' as well as 'a distortion of the free market in pensions provision'. In debate, the 'bribe' was in fact amended, Lady Trumpington, speaking for the government, recognising the strength of concerns that it threatened occupational schemes and tabling an amendment to modify the proposal such as to exclude people who had been members of a scheme for a reasonable period of time (but 'reasonable' was not defined, and remained subject to a consultation even after the legislative process was completed). Other than that, however, and despite peers having tabled over 230 amendments, the government was able to secure the passage of the Bill through the Lords without substantive concessions.[116] The Social Security Act 1986 passed into Law on 25 July, although, unusually, it was not completely enacted until 1988 because its consumer protection clauses relating to PPPs were so closely related to other legislation.

Other legislation

As Nesbitt observed, the implementation of personal pension plans was bound up not just with the Social Security Act but with the subsequent 1986 Financial Services Act (a landmark piece of legislation, not least because of its fundamental importance in the story of 'Big Bang', the deregulation of the City of London) and, to a lesser extent, the Building Societies Act 1986 (which extended the scope of institutions allowed to sell and administer personal pensions to include the societies as well as banks and unit trusts). As Nesbitt also noted, however, policymaking on pensions regulation was often chaotic, playing second fiddle to more pressing issues around deregulation of the City, with much of the necessary legislation delayed until the Financial Services Act 1988.[117] Such was the interrelation between the Financial Services and Social Security Acts of 1986 that, in August 1987, a delay in the implementation of the former required the implementation of personal pensions to be postponed at short notice from 1 January 1988 (embarrassingly, the Chancellor had in the 1987 budget brought the implementation forward by three months to that date) to 1 July.[118]

The Financial Services Act 1986, an enormous piece of legislation comprising 777 clauses, 15 schedules and 289 pages, received royal assent on 7 November. Among other things, it changed the way pensions and other investment products were sold. Amounting effectively to a watered-down version of the 1984 Gower Report, it introduced what the 1985 White Paper on financial services called a new system of 'self-regulation within a statutory framework'.[119] The new Securities and Investments Board (SIB) sat at the apex of what the shadow Chief Secretary to the Treasury, Bryan Gould, termed 'the wobbly structure' of regulation inaugurated by the Act.[120] Beneath the SIB, operating with a framework of rules defined by it and under its oversight, were a range of 'self-regulatory organisations', including the Life Assurance and Unit Trust Regulatory Organization (LAUTRO), Financial Intermediaries, Managers and Brokers Regulatory Association (FIMBRA), and the Investment Management Regulatory Organization (IMRO).

On 23 November the SIB set out the 'conduct of business rules' that would govern the selling of personal pensions: they should be sold only if the seller was certain it would provide better benefits for the individual, though that would not prevent door-to-door salespeople persuading people to leave their occupational pension scheme and take out a personal pension, taking advantage of the National Insurance 'bribe' (a fact already much criticised by the Consumers' Association).[121] As the Financial Services Bill had taken shape, it was significant that a key player in the Fowler Inquiry, Mark Weinberg, the chairman of Allied Dunbar, a UK life assurer with a reputation for cut-throat competitiveness, had been appointed to the advisory board, tasked with drawing up the detail of personal pension regulation.[122] Nonetheless, gone now was the ability of financial service companies to make their own rules on selling, and to participate in informal regulation. Henceforward sales operatives must be either truly independent intermediaries authorised by a regulator itself overseen by the SIB and free to recommend any appropriate product or a 'tied' representative of an authorised financial services provider restricted to selling just its products. All sales representatives, whether independent or not, were required to follow 'know your customer' rules and to offer 'best advice' to the customer. It became a crime to invest other people's money or offer investment advice without being authorised by a regulator. Some degree of transparency on

From revolution to evolution 293

commissions was mandated and rules on personal pensions illustrations established. This was all welcome, but there was of course a good deal of elasticity in the concept of 'best advice', and much would depend on the assertiveness of the regulators. Moreover, the government had chosen not to regulate charges, relying instead on market competition to minimise them.

We should also note the Chancellor of the Exchequer's unexpected announcement in his March 1986 budget of legislation to limit surpluses in occupational pensions. Concern about the size of these surpluses had been building against a background of the Lawson boom and the considerable rise in stock prices that flowed from it. In early 1985, for example, analysis by the stockbrokers Phillips & Drew showed that, thanks mainly to a rising stock market, pension funds' total assets had increased by £20 billion in 1984, taking them to over £126 billion, and that they had a gross annual return on investment of around 20 per cent. As *The Economist* noted of this report, sponsoring companies eyed these surpluses with relish, not least because reducing them by cutting a firm's contributions would enhance its profits.[123] The government, for its part, was concerned at the forgone tax implied by large surpluses, since 'excess' contributions still attracted tax relief. By the end of 1985 *The Economist* was reporting that 'British pension funds now have up to £50 billion more than they need to finance their obligations'.[124] The funds themselves noted that the surpluses were notional balances, subject to dramatic change in the event of alterations in, for example, stock prices or changes in the calculation of liabilities due to demographic change or alterations in gilt yields.[125] They were under no illusion, however, recognising that they were seen by both the political Right and Left as 'fat cats' ripe for plunder.[126]

Pension funds were right to be concerned. Action to allow the funds to divest themselves of 'objectively calculated surpluses', and perhaps compel them to do so if surpluses were above a certain level, was seen as 'a strong runner' in Treasury discussions on possible items for the spring 1986 budget.[127] By early March Lawson was telling Thatcher that dealing with 'the growing problem of pension fund surpluses' would be an important plank of his budget. 'Heavily, and undesirably, over-funded' schemes were

> a clear abuse of the tax privileges enjoyed by the funds. Nor are they in the interests of pension fund members who are denied the higher benefits or lower contributions they might otherwise enjoy. At the same time the [Inland] Revenue is having to use its discretionary powers to turn down many of the increasing number of requests for refunds from companies which, in the 70s, had to top up funds which were then in deficit.[128]

Consequently, in his budget speech Lawson announced that pension funds would be required to eliminate surpluses that represented more than

5 per cent of the fund's liabilities. The means by which that should be done was not mandated, leaving it open to do so by increasing member benefits, reducing or suspending employer contributions, or the sponsoring company taking a refund (though this would be liable to tax at the rate of 40 per cent). For the Exchequer, the payoff would be juicy: Lawson predicted £20 million in 1986/87 and £120 million in 1987/88.[129] There was widespread expert criticism that the 5 per cent over-funding level was much too low, however, paying scant attention to volatile markets or to the impact of changing assumptions in the calculation of liabilities, and shifting the scales away from occupational pension scheme members and pensioners and towards the sponsoring company.[130]

Conclusion

The analysis in this chapter has provided strong support for Pierson's explanation of the failure to abolish SERPS, though with less emphasis on the 'double payment' problem and rather more on the positive feedback effect of institutional attachment to the system evident among employers, trades unions, pension funds, and professional actuaries. In that sense, our findings also echo those of Bonoli. Yet, probably because we are looking at archival sources that were not available to either of these scholars, ultimately we find that none of those key institutional actors, either individually or severally, were the main cause of the government's U-turn. Indeed, their opposition had been expected. Rather, the key institutional barrier to the Green Paper's revolutionary proposals proved to be the very life insurance companies that the government was counting on not just to support abolition (on the assumption that it would be in their financial interest) but to sell the new personal pensions to former SERPS members and to any member of an occupational scheme who wanted one. Although opposition to the government's proposals in its Green Paper on social security reform, particularly the proposal to abolish SERPS, was intense and politically very problematic, much of it had been expected. It was growing evidence that finance sector companies that the government would normally count on as reliable supporters were implacably opposed to compulsory personal pensions – not least because selling them to low earners, and continuing to administer them for years, would be inherently loss making – that shifted thinking at the top of the government. By October 1985 it was clear to ministers that the policy as conceived in the Green Paper was untenable. To avoid utter humiliation, the only way out was to preserve the appearance of radical reform via a shift to modifying SERPS to contain its prospective long-term costs while continuing with the implementation of voluntary personal pensions, in the

From revolution to evolution 295

hope that a less generous SERPS coupled with the incentive of the 2 per cent National Insurance rebate ('the bribe') would tempt many of its members out into their own personal pension.

Thus, the autumn of 1985 saw a screeching U-turn as the government backed away from the revolutionary ambition of the June Green Paper and embraced an evolutionary alternative. In the process, the focus on SERPS moved from abolition to long-term strangulation, personal pensions moved from a compulsory replacement of SERPS (and ultimately of occupational pensions) to a voluntary alternative, and in the process moved from a mass-market product embracing workers across the salary range to a product that might be expected to appeal mainly to the better paid without an occupational pension. That was a very different world from that initially envisaged by the neoliberal architects of pension reform in the CPS and in the No. 10 Policy Unit: gone was compulsory personal pensions for all and the planned removal of SERPS and throttling of DB occupational pension schemes; gone too was the hope that personal pensions could be the vehicle for a new breed of investor capitalist in the United Kingdom. This was the source of anguish to the architects of neoliberal reform. Nigel Vinson, for example, complained in 1988 that the continued existence of occupational pension funds had embedded 'the greatest shift of ownership from individuals to institutions since the opposite had happened at the time of the Dissolution of the Monasteries'. He continued to advocate the urgent reversal of that shift 'before it is too late'.[131] Likewise, Redwood confessed that the failure to dismantle occupational pension funds and SERPS had been a 'missed opportunity'.[132] Still seeking 'to rescue something from the rubble', he continued to push 'clearly demarked individual pension funds' as one of 'ten basic points of popular capitalism [that would] provide the antidote to those of Marxism'.[133]

Yet we should not see this as an overwhelming defeat for neoliberalism, for, although SERPS survived and a compulsory transfer into personal pensions was ditched, and although the architects of reform had, even before the Green Paper, had to accept the continuation of occupational pensions, the new personal pensions did represent a significant change. Although those who opted for a personal pension would not be investing directly in the market (as the CPS had originally advocated, but which had prudently been rejected in favour of mandating professional financial service companies to handle the actual investment), they would be making a choice in a market of different private sector personal pension providers. Choice was thus enhanced, and so was the freedom of the individual to make that choice. In that sense, what the U-turn involved was a shift in the degree of reform and, crucially, a navigation from one form of neoliberalism to another. The reform process had been informed by neoliberal thought (mediated by the Centre for Policy Studies) in terms of a concern to shrink the role of the state, marketise pension saving, individualise capital ownership, liberate the individual from control by the state or big business, and promote individual initiative and entrepreneurialism. The collision between such neoliberal precepts and the practical realities of governing and of navigating widespread stakeholder resistance, including from companies the government was relying on to sell personal pensions, was an evolutionary settlement informed by an overlapping but different set of neoliberal ideas (notably emphasising the idea of individual freedom to choose within the market).

Charting the new course was no small task. In many ways Fowler navigated the exceptionally difficult setback in a masterly way, as he did with his relationship with the Chancellor of the Exchequer as the latter brought pressure to bear in a quest to minimise the 'double payment' problem. Setting the new course on personal pensions came at a price, however. Although the government had acted to cut back SERPS to contain long-term public spending, it had patently failed in its ambition radically to simplify the system. It had also, via the botched abolition of SERPS, failed to get the state out of the top-up pensions business. Reducing benefits in SERPS would certainly cut long-term state spending, and thus see a smaller state; but it would not be enough to secure the other ideological long-term aim: the promotion of individual freedom for every worker and the stimulation of individual responsibility, thrift, and entrepreneurialism. Moreover, by electing to cut back the scope of SERPS, the government had created a potential long-term problem. In conjunction with the government's earlier changes to the indexation of the BSP, its proposed reform of SERPS would slash the long-term value of pensions for those who elected to continue to be wholly dependent on the state for retirement income.

The intention to abolish SERPS was about much more than public expenditure control; it was about the hoped-for privatisation of responsibility for ensuring a decent income in old age. The original plan had been entirely to abolish SERPS and compel people into private alternatives; now that had been replaced by a combination of carrot (the 2 per cent National Insurance rebate as an incentive to take out a personal pension during the first five years of the new system) and stick (mainly cuts to SERPS affecting those retiring after 1999). At the same time, however, the government reforms as implemented did restrict occupational schemes (the National Insurance rebate had been specifically designed to encourage occupational scheme members as well as members of SERPS to take out personal pensions); and the Chancellor had also legislated in the 1986 budget to encourage occupational pension funds to reduce their surpluses. This meant that the success of the government's long-term strategy now depended almost entirely on its policy for personal pensions (the success of which, we should remember, had been seen by the No. 10 Policy Unit as completely dependent on the abolition of SERPS and on compelling individual workers to make

From revolution to evolution 297

alternative arrangements). As an editorial in the *Financial Times* observed, the existing system and the political consensus around it had been shattered, but the worry was that 'Fowler has neutered the state earnings related scheme, by halving its planned benefits, without showing convincingly that personal pensions can cost-effectively fill the gap'.[134] If it failed, Fowler's warning, issued as the government navigated its U-turn, that the United Kingdom could end up with the 'worst of both worlds' in pensions risked coming to pass. In the next chapter we turn to this vexed issue, as well as other aspects of the legacy left by the pension reforms of the early to mid-1980s.

Notes

1 Quoted in *Financial Times*, 'Cabinet to Discuss Pension Options', by Peter Riddell, 7 May 1985.

2 *Daily Telegraph*, 'Ministers Bang the Drum on Spending', by Valerie Elliott, 13 July 1985. There was substantial popular support for more, not less, social expenditure, however, with a Gallup poll indicating 74 per cent thought the government was spending too little on education, 76 per cent too little on the NHS, and 70 per cent too little on pensions (*Sunday Telegraph*, 'Gallup Highlights Doubts', 7 July 1985).

3 Department of Health and Social Security, *Better Pensions – Fully Protected against Inflation: Proposals for a New Pensions Scheme*, Cmnd 5713 (London: HMSO, 1974); Department of Health and Social Security, *Reform of Social Security*, vol. 1: *Reform of Social Security*, Cmnd 9517 (London: HMSO, 1985), p. 1.

4 Andrew Gamble, *The Free Economy and the Strong State: The Politics of Thatcherism* (Basingstoke: Macmillan, 1994).

5 Paul Pierson, *Dismantling the Welfare State? Reagan, Thatcher and the Politics of Retrenchment* (Cambridge: Cambridge University Press, 1994), p. 71.

6 See, for example, Rodney Lowe, *The Welfare State in Britain since 1945* (London: Palgrave Macmillan, 2005), pp. 337–39; Tony Lynes, 'The British Case', in *Enterprise and the Welfare State*, ed. by Martin Rein and Eskil Wadensjö (Cheltenham: Edward Elgar, 1997), pp. 316–22; Steven Nesbitt, *British Pensions Policy Making in the 1980s: The Rise and Fall of a Policy Community* (Avebury: Ashgate, 1995), pp. 118–19.

7 For the influence of Pierson's analysis, see Robin Blackburn, *Banking on Death or Investing in Life: The History and Future of Pensions* (London: Verso, 2002), pp. 285–94; Giuliano Bonoli, *The Politics of Pension Reform: Institutions and Policy Change in Western Europe* (Cambridge: Cambridge University Press, 2000), pp. 65–85.

8 Pierson, *Dismantling the Welfare State?*, pp. 56, 58–64.

9 Ibid., pp. 71–72.

298 *Implementation and legacy*

10 Paul Pierson, *Increasing Returns, Path Dependence and the Study of Politics* (Florence: European University Institute, Robert Schumann Centre, 1997).

11 Of those decisions, the initial implementation decision was the most significant: either the institution/policy got implemented or not. Thereafter each decision had the potential further to embed or to disembed that initial decision – but, over time, increasing returns (i.e. positive feedback, such as familiarity with the system, sunk investment costs, and so on) tended to favour the former. For the most detailed statements and exploration of the theory, see Paul Pierson, 'Increasing Returns, Path Dependence and the Study of Politics', *American Political Science Review*, 94 (2000); Paul Pierson, 'Not Just What, but When: Timing and Sequence in Political Processes', *Studies in American Political Development*, 14 (2000.

12 John Myles and Paul Pierson, 'The Comparative Political Economy of Pension Reform', in *The New Politics of the Welfare State*, ed. by Paul Pierson (Oxford: Oxford University Press, 2001), pp. 305–33, at p. 306.

13 Bonoli, *The Politics of Pension Reform*, p. 71. A much less theoretically sophisticated earlier analysis by Steven Nesbitt also noted the strong opposition to the proposal to abolish SERPS emanating from a wide range of institutions with an interest in the existing pensions system; see Nesbitt, *British Pensions Policy Making in the 1980s*, pp. 67–87. The NAPF was the National Association of Pension Funds, the representative body for employer-run occupational pension schemes.

14 Cmnd 9517, paras. 1.1–4. Volume Two (Cmnd 9518) set out the programme for change. Volume Three (Cmnd 9519) comprised the review's background papers. Housing benefit had a volume to itself: Department of Health and Social Security, *Housing Benefit Review: Report of the Review Team*, Cmnd 9520 (London: HMSO, 1985).

15 Department of Health and Social Security, *Reform of Social Security*, vol. 2: *Reform of Social Security: Programme for Change*, Cmnd 9518 (London: HMSO, 1985), para. 1.29. The detailed estimates are in background paper no. 2 in Department of Health and Social Security, *Reform of Social Security*, vol. 3: *Reform of Social Security: Background Papers*, Cmnd 9519 (London: HMSO, 1985) paras. 2.33–34.

16 Cmnd 9518, para. 1.30. The detailed demographic projections and projected costings from the Government Actuary are at Cmnd 9519, annex B, tab. 11. On the costs of SERPS, readers were also referred to Department of Health and Social Security and Government Actuary's Department, *Population, Pension Costs and Pensioners' Incomes: A Background Paper for the Inquiry into Provision for Retirement* (London: HMSO, 1984).

17 Cmnd 9518, paras. 1.31–34.

18 Ibid., para. 1.32.

19 Ibid., paras. 1.35–41.

20 Ibid., para. 1.50.

21 Ibid., paras. 1.45–46. Casual workers, the very low paid, and workers under 18 would be exempt from these requirements. Occupational and personal pension schemes alike would have to treat men and women equally (para. 1.54)

From revolution to evolution 299

and comply with minimum benefit conditions – e.g. death-in-service benefits, and inheritance by the widow/ers of deceased pensioners of half the pension generated by the minimum contribution (para. 1.52). Retiring members should be allowed to choose between an indexed pension and an enhanced pension, although views on this were invited (para. 1.53).

22 Ibid., para. 1.61.

23 Over time, of course, those within 15 years of state pension age would retire, and thus after that time had elapsed the country would have just a single rate of National Insurance. Note that the new rate of 16.5 per cent, though lower than the existing rate of 19.45 per cent, represented a one percentage point increase after factoring in the joint employer/employee minimum contribution of 4 per cent (para. 1.63).

24 Cmnd 9518, paras. 1.50–51, 1.57.

25 Department of Trade and Industry, *Financial Services in the United Kingdom: A New Framework for Investor Protection*, Cmnd 9432 (London: HMSO, 1985). On the development of this separate agenda, see Paul Draper, 'The New Framework for Investor Protection: Cmnd 9432', *Quarterly Economic Commentary*, 10 (1985).

26 Those costs would be in terms of public spending (if equalisation was either downwards to 60 or 'split the difference' at 63) or political (if equalised upwards). Interestingly, despite the concern within government about the future cost of the state pension, and despite EC Directive 79/7 on the need for equal treatment between the sexes in the calculation of benefits, there was still no desire to discuss openly the possibility of a common SPA of 65 (for the somewhat tortured discussion of this issue, see Cmnd 9518., paras. 1.70–74). Perhaps conscious of its lack of radicalism on this question, the Green Paper devoted the next five paragraphs to floating the idea of a flexible retirement age, although not very persuasively, given the obvious worries about its potential to impose 'unacceptably high extra costs' (ibid., para. 1.80).

27 Ibid., para. 1.67.

28 *The Economist*, 'To Oliver, from Granny', 8 June 1985. See also 'A Handsome Package, but What Is Inside?', in the same issue.

29 *Financial Times*, 'One-and-a-Half Cheers for the Green Paper', by Michael Prowse, 4 June 1985.

30 *Daily Mail*, 'The Great Welfare State Gamble', by Gordon Greig and David Hughes, 4 June 1985.

31 *Daily Telegraph*, editorial, 'The Case for Change', 4 June 1985.

32 *Guardian*, editorial, 'Mr Fowler Muffs His Chance', 4 June 1985.

33 *New Statesman*, editorial, 'Making Peace with Social Evil', 7 June 1985.

34 *Financial Times*, 'Cruel and Crude, Insists Kinnock', by Peter Riddell, 4 June 1985. Two weeks later Kinnock denounced Fowler's appeal to the principles set out by Beveridge in 1942 as a 'confidence trick' in a House of Commons debate on the Green Paper (HC Debs, 18 June 1985, vol. 81, cols. 199–200).

35 *Guardian*, 'Cabinet Agrees Deal to Phase Out Serps', by Ian Aitken, 10 May 1985; *The Times*, 'Phased Abolition of Serps Endorsed', by Philip Webster,

300   *Implementation and legacy*

10 May 1985. It is worth noting that Kinnock avoided a commitment to repeal the broader social security reforms, with the promise restricted to SERPS.

36 See, for example, *The Observer*, 'Mrs T Commits Pensions Suicide', by Adam Raphael, 12 May 1985; and *Daily Mail*, 'Fowler's Howler over Pensions', by Frank Chapple, 16 May 1985 (Chapple was a former general secretary of the Electrical, Electronic, Telecommunications and Plumbing Union – an adventurous choice by the *Daily Mail*'s editor, David English, and evidence of his disquiet).

37 *New Statesman*, 'Wrecking the Welfare State', by Gordon Brown, 17 May 1985; *Guardian*, 'Fowler Faces Storm over Serps Abolition', by David Hencke and James Naughtie, 4 June 1985.

38 *Report of the Annual Conference and Special Conference of the Labour Party, 1985* (London: Labour Party, 1985), p. 350.

39 *The Times*, 'Saving Time and Money on State Pensions', by Sarah Hogg, 20 May 1985.

40 An analysis by the IPR secretariat identified the following organisations being prepared in their evidence to the Inquiry to support a degree of modification of SERPS: the CBI, NAPF, ABI, SPC, ACA, IFoA, Pensions Management Institute, British Institute of Management, National Consumers' Council, Consumers' Association, EEF, ABCC, Prudential Assurance, Legal & General, Building Societies Association, Building Employers and Civil Engineers. It also noted support from the IFS and from David Owen in his speech to the NAPF conference. See TNA: BN 13/308, 'Bodies Supporting Modified SERPS', undated but probably early 1985.

41 *Financial Times*, 'Fowler Appeals to Pension Industry, CBI and TUC', by Eric Short, 6 June 1985.

42 National Association of Pension Funds Archive (hereafter NAPFA), London Metropolitan Archives: LMA/4494/A/03/014, Minutes of the Parliamentary Committee Meeting, 11 June and 13 August 1985.

43 *Financial Times*, 'Pensions Fund Body Split on Serps Plans', by Eric Short, 31 July 1985. The delegate was Anthony Davey of British Shipbuilders, who claimed to be speaking for the majority of NAPF members.

44 *Financial Times*, 'Pension Funds Group Attacks Serps Proposals', by Eric Short, 19 September 1985.

45 Its evidence is summarised in a detailed review of submissions at TNA: BN 13/299, HH 1.2, N. Montagu, 'Bodies Supporting Modifications for the State Earnings-Related Pension Scheme (SERPS) in Their Responses to the Green Paper, Annex', 24 September 1985.

46 *Financial Times*, 'CBI Steps Up Attack on Pension Proposals', by Eric Short, 3 August 1985.

47 Again, its evidence is summarised in TNA: BN 13/299, HH 1.2, Annex, 24 September 1985.

48 *Financial Times*, 'Why Few Wish to Join the Fowler Bandwagon', by Michael Prowse, 20 September 1985.

49 *The Times*, 'Cabinet Rethinking Pledge to Abolish Serps', by Philip Webster, 9 October 1985.

From revolution to evolution   301

50 At the time the Green Paper was published, its general secretary, Norman Willis, was promising that the unions would not allow it (*Guardian*, 'Reactions over Fowler's "Mouse"', by Martin Wainright, 4 June 1985).

51 *Guardian*, 'TUC Launches Campaign against Serps Abolition / Government's Welfare State Review', by David Hencke, 22 July 1985; *The Times*, 'TUC Will Fight Cuts in Benefits', by Nicholas Timmins, 22 July 1985.

52 See evidence summarised in TNA: BN 13/299, HH 1.2, Annex, 24 September 1985.

53 *Times*, 'TUC at Blackpool', 4 September 1985.

54 *Guardian*, 'TUC at Blackpool (Welfare): Campaign against Fowler Reform', 4 September 1985.

55 *The Times*, 'Employers Criticize SERPS Plan', by Edward Townsend and David Felton, 23 September 1985

56 Two days later ITT, an American conglomerate, sought to capitalise on this by announcing the sale of 48.2 per cent of its wholly owned subsidiary Abbey Life, a British life company with a sales force of 2,600, at £504 million; this was the most valuable share offering to date apart from privatisations (*The Economist*, 'British Pension Funds: the Fowler Factor', 8 June 1985).

57 *Financial Times*, 'Pension Plans Attacked by Legal and General', by Eric Short, 5 September 1985.

58 TNA: BN 13/308, G. J. Otton to Mr Heppell, 'Green Paper: Views of the Pru', 10 September 1985.

59 *Financial Times*, 'Insurance Industry Gives Warning on Pension Plans', by Eric Short, 19 September 1985.

60 TNA: BN 13/299, N. Montagu, 'HH 1.2: Bodies Supporting Modifications for the State Earnings-Related Pension Scheme (SERPS) in Their Responses to the Green Paper', Annex, 24 September 1985. Like many others, the ABI dismissed the proposed implementation timetable as 'impossible'.

61 TNA: BN 13/299, Mr Caslake, 'HH 1: Outcome of Consultations, 25 September 1985'. The only major organisations found to have expressed enthusiasm were the IoD and Save & Prosper.

62 TNA: PREM 19/1639, Armstrong to the Prime Minister, 8 May 1985

63 *Financial Times*, 'Why Few Wish to join the Fowler Bandwagon'.

64 *Financial Times*, 'The Conservatives at Blackpool', by Peter Riddell, 9 October 1985.

65 *Times*, 'Cabinet Rethinking Pledge to Abolish Serps'.

66 Margaret Thatcher Archive (hereafter MTA): 106145, 'Speech to Conservative Party Conference', 11 October 1985.

67 It included the CBI, Engineering Employers Federation, Association of British Chambers of Commerce, Building Employers Confederation, Federation of Civil Engineering Contractors, NAPF, ABI, Pensions Management Institute, British Institute of Management, Prudential Assurance, and Legal & General – to name but a few.

68 TNA: BN 13/299, N. Montagu, 'HH 1.2: Bodies Supporting Modifications for the State Earnings-Related Pension Scheme (SERPS) in Their Responses to the Green Paper', 24 September 1985.

302 *Implementation and legacy*

69 TNA: BN 13/299, HH 1.5, 'Summary of Draft Social Security Advisory Committee Response to the Green Paper', 1 October 1985.

70 Norman Fowler, *Ministers Decide: A Personal Memoir of the Thatcher Years* (London: Chapmans, 1991), p. 222.

71 TNA: PREM 19/1640, Willetts to Thatcher, 'Meeting with Norman Fowler: Social Security Savings', 30 September 1985. Willetts emphasised Fowler's fear that the number of gainers from reform would be heavily outweighed by the number of losers. It is not clear, however, why this should have suddenly been an issue; it had been built in from the start.

72 TNA: BN 13/299, HH 4A, 'Notes on SERPS Options', n.d.

73 TNA: BN 13/299, HH 4, 'Pensions: Main Elements of an Alternative Strategy', n.d. (the text of Owen's speech – which envisaged a three-tier system with a reformed SERPS within its second tier – is reproduced in *Pensions World*, July 1985, pp. 487–90). The Hannibal House conference also considered a second package (see ibid., HH 12, 'Alternative Pensions Framework', n.d.): a 'radical approach', which would see SERPS completely restructured (e.g. by calculating its benefits based on either 20 or 25 per cent of total revalued earnings based on the 30 best years, including those below the lower earnings limit, but with a ceiling of average male earnings; or integrating it with the BSP to give a total state pension of 25 per cent of total earnings).

74 TNA: BN 13/299, HH 4, 'Pensions: Main Elements of an Alternative Strategy', n.d.

75 TNA: BN 13/299, HH 5, 'An Alternative Pensions Strategy: Handling Issues' (the original options are to be found at Cmnd 9518, para. 1.37); and HH 8, 'Consultations with Colleagues'.

76 TNA: BN 13/299, HH 10, 'Consultation with Pensions Interests', n.d.

77 TNA: CAB 130/1293, MISC 111 (85) 14, 'Review of Social Security: The Next Steps, Memorandum by the Secretary of State for Social Services', 11 October 1985.

78 TNA: BN 13/308, Draft Speaking Note for MISC 111, n.d.

79 TNA: PREM 19/1640, MISC 111(85)14, 'Review of Social Security: The Next Steps, Memorandum by the Secretary of State for Social Services', 11 October 1985.

80 In his memoir of his time as a minister, Fowler noted that many of the organisations indicating their preparedness to accept modifications to SERPS had previously been opposed to any substantial modification of the status quo (Fowler, *Ministers Decide*, p. 223).

81 The decision to relate the rebated contribution to age was part of a developing recognition by Fowler that, without it, employers might be encouraged to close their existing schemes (to which the rebate would not apply) and open a replacement scheme that would qualify, transferring all their employees into it (most clearly stated by Fowler in TNA: CAB 130/1293, Ministerial Group on Social Security, 'Limited Circulation Annex, MISC 111 (85) 9th Meeting Minutes', 31 October 1985). Surprisingly, however, Fowler did not acknowledge that employees might act on their own initiative and transfer out of their occupational schemes en masse into personal pensions.

From revolution to evolution

303

82 TNA: PREM 19/1640, Willetts to Thatcher, 'What Should We Do about SERPS?', 11 October 1985.

83 TNA: PREM 19/1640, J. B. Unwin to the Prime Minister, 'Report on the Review of Social Security (MISC 111 (85) 14)', 11 October 1985.

84 TNA: PREM 19/1640, Hurd to Thatcher, 14 October 1985; ibid., Brittan to Thatcher, 'Review of Social Security: The Next Steps', 14 October 1985.

85 TNA: CAB 130/1293, Minutes of MISC 111 (85) 8th meeting, 'Limited Circulation Annex', 15 October 1985.

86 TNA: PREM 19/1640, Redwood to Thatcher, 'MISC 111', 14 October 1985.

87 TNA: PREM 19/1640, Willetts to Thatcher, 'SERPS', 25 October 1985.

88 Ibid.

89 The reduction of the SERPS pension calculation to 20 per cent of earnings would be mirrored by an equivalent drop in the required GMP in occupational schemes.

90 Fowler was acutely aware of the need to keep companies on board given the strength of their opposition to the Green Paper's proposals on pensions. To an extent, they would be compensated for taking on this inflation protection responsibility by a rise in the National Insurance contracted-out rebate. The cost of this, however, would be less than it appeared at first, because that rebate was anyway expected to fall by up to 0.75 percentage points (as a consequence of the proposed reduction in the value of SERPS benefits, which would in turn reduce the value of the GMP, which the National Insurance rebate was intended to compensate for) after the next quinquennial review of National Insurance in 1988. See TNA: BN 13/309, Montagu to Laurance, 'Social Security Review: Cabinet Meeting', 28 November 1985.

91 TNA: CAB 130/1293, Minutes of MISC 111 (85) 8th Meeting, 'Limited Circulation Annex', 15 October 1985; PREM 19/1640, Willetts to Thatcher, 'SERPS', 25 October 1985; ibid., 'Savings on SERPS', 30 October 1985.

92 TNA: CAB 130/1293, MISC 111 (85) 15, 'Pensions: Memorandum by the Secretary of State for Social Services', 29 October 1985.

93 TNA: BN 13/309, Lawson to Fowler, 'Personal Pensions and the Public Services', 25 November 1985; PREM 19/1640, Lawson to Thatcher, 'Personal Pensions and Public Services', 27 November 1985. Thatcher annotated the latter, which proposed that the government exercise its right not to contribute to an employee's personal pension to discourage public servants from taking them out and therefore adding to the PSBR, thus: 'I don't like this. I don't like our employees getting less good treatment than they could expect from other employers.'

94 TNA: CAB 130/1293, MISC 111 (85) 15, 'Pensions: Memorandum by the Secretary of State for Social Services', 29 October 1985.

95 Ibid., Minutes of MISC 111 (85) 9th Meeting, 'Limited Circulation Annex', 31 October 1985; CAB 128, CC (85) 34th Conclusions of the Cabinet, 'Limited Circulation Annex', 28 November 1985. The White Paper was published the following month; see Department of Health and Social Security, *Reform of Social Security: Programme for Action*, Cmnd 9691 (London: HMSO, 1985), para. 1.17.

304   *Implementation and legacy*

96 TNA: BN 13/309, G. M. Noble to N. Montagu, 'Draft Social Security White Paper', 3 December 1985, emphasis in original.
97 Cmnd 9691.
98 TNA: PREM 19/1640, Willetts to Thatcher, 'Meeting with Norman Fowler', 12 November 1985.
99 Ibid., D. Norgrove to Thatcher, 'Meeting with Mr Fowler', 12 November 1985.
100 For a good summary of the reactions to the White Paper, see Sue Ward, 'White Paper Reactions' and 'The Political Stage', in *Pensions World*, February 1986.
101 *Daily Telegraph*, 'A Step Forward', 17 December 1985.
102 *The Observer*, 'The Future of Pensions', by Diana Slaughter, 22 December 1985.
103 *The Times,* 'Applause for Fowler from Pensions People', 17 December 1985.
104 *The Times*, 'Women Lose and Families to Gain in Benefit Shift', by Nicholas Timmins, 14 December; *Pensions World*, 'White Paper Reactions', February 1986.
105 *Financial Times*, 'Not More than Two Years, Please', by Eric Short, 21 December 1985. It is clear from the text of this article that the sub-editor misread 'two yawns' as 'two years'.
106 See, for example, *Financial Times*, 'Era of Greater Choice', by Eric Short', 1 February 1986.
107 *Observer*, 'The Future of Pensions'; TNA: PREM 19/1640, Willetts to Thatcher, 'SERPS', 25 October 1985. Willetts advised Thatcher that the government 'should be trying to increase the contracted-out rebate as far as politically sustainable to give companies and individuals a greater incentive to take out their own private pension'. To do this, he proposed two options. The first was to encourage lower earners (those predominantly contracted into SERPS) to contract out by offering a full £6 rebate to those earning below £130 a week. The second option was to offer 'a special rebate of, say, an extra 2 per cent for the next 5 years to new schemes that contract out of SERPS'. Willetts suggested that this could go specifically to new contracted-out arrangements, but 'could also go to individuals who opt for their own personal pensions instead of the company scheme'.
108 The report of the House of Commons' Select Committee on Social Security, for example, restricted itself to querying the ability of individuals to perform the complex calculations necessary to determine if they would be better off contracting out of SERPS, observing that it would be much better to introduce a parallel equalisation of state pension ages between men and women, and recommending that the government consider delaying the introduction of changes, notably in pensions, which it thought business would struggle to accommodate by the envisaged deadline. See HC 180 (1985–1986), First Report, 19 January 1986, pp. ix–xi. The recommended delay echoed its earlier conclusion regarding the Green Paper's proposals.
109 See, for example, *Financial Times*, 'Bill "Unlikely to Provide Stable Pensions Policy"', by Eric Short, 25 February 1986; ibid., 'Widespread Anger over Fowler's Pensions "Bribe"', by Eric Short, 15 March 1986; ibid., 'CBI Condemns Plan for Pension Switch Bonus', by Eric Short, 21 April 1986; and ibid.,

From revolution to evolution 305

'Uncertainty over Pension Reform', by Nick Bunker, 19 June 1986. Ministers took exception to the use of the word 'bribe' but, as Eric Short observed, 'when such august bodies as the Institute of Actuaries and the National Association of Pension Funds put out statements which also refer to bribes, then the strength of feeling on the subject can be gauged' (*Financial Times*, 'Widespread Anger over Fowler's Pensions "Bribe"'). See also ibid., editorial, 'The Muddle over Pensions', 2 July 1986.

110 HC Debs, 28 January 1986, vol. 90, cols. 819–87.
111 Ibid., col. 834.
112 Ibid., col. 836. In March the Equal Opportunities Commission issued a briefing paper emphasising the fact that women would have a lower SERPS accrual rate than men in a reformed SERPS in the absence of an equalisation of state pension age, and asked how this could possibly be consistent with Article 4.1 of EC Directive 79/7 on equal treatment in the calculation of benefits (Sue Ward, 'The Political Stage', in *Pensions World*, May 1986, pp. 330–31). The inequality was made even more obvious by the government's publication in April of a consultation document on its proposal to require equal retirement ages in occupational schemes (*Sex Discrimination and Retirement*, Department of Employment, 1986).
113 HC Debs, 28 January 1986, cols. 842, 852. Rhys Williams was appointed to the Committee tasked with detailed analysis of the Bill, having sat on most Pensions Bill Committees over the past two decades.
114 The only notable concession to the opposition in the Bill's second reading was the government's acceptance of a 'cooling-off period' for anyone taking out a personal pension, although implementation of this was to be via the Financial Services Bill (then itself under consideration by its Bill Committee). It is worth noting that Labour had made it known that, were it to win an election before the Bill came into effect in 1988, it would immediately repeal it (Sue Ward, 'The Political Stage', *Pensions World*, March 1986, p. 158).
115 Ibid., p. 155.
116 Sue Ward, 'The Political Stage', *Pensions World*, August 1986, pp. 565–70. Again, however, there were many technical amendments, the most significant of which was to allow the GMP element in a transfer out of a DB occupational pension to purchase 'protected rights' in a personal pension or DC occupational scheme.
117 Nesbitt, *British Pensions Policy Making in the 1980s*, p. 120. See also Ranald C. Michie, *The London Stock Exchange: A History* (Oxford: Oxford University Press, 2001), ch. 12; David Kynaston, *The City of London*, vol. 4: *A Club No More, 1945–2000* (London: Chatto & Windus, 2001), ch. 24.
118 *The Economist*, 'Pensions Postponed', 27 August 1987; *Pensions World*, 'Personal Pensions Postponed', September 1987. Within government, concerns about the interactions between the two acts in the event of a delay were summarised in HM Treasury Private Office papers (hereafter HMT): PO-CH NL 0368 Part A, P. S. Hall to Mrs Lomax/Economic Secretary, 'FS Act Delayed Implementation: Personal Pension Problems', 14 July 1987. The danger of misselling personal pensions in the absence of the regulation envisaged in the

306   *Implementation and legacy*

Financial Services Act, and the consequent need for delay, was emphasised in ibid., John Moore to Lord Young of Graffham, 'Implementation of the Financial Services Act: Impact on Personal Pensions', 30 July 1987.

119 Cmnd 9432, para. 5.1; L. C. B. Gower, *Review of Investor Protection*, Part 1, Cmnd 9125 (London: HMSO, 1984). Gower himself noted that he preferred to see regulation put on a statutory basis, being profoundly sceptical about self-regulation, and that his 1984 proposals had received a hostile reception. Overall, however, Gower was happy with the Act, which he saw as effectively introducing 'statutory regulation monitored by self-regulatory organisations recognised by, and under the surveillance of, a self-standing Commission' (the Securities and Investments Board). See L. C. B. Gower, '"Big Bang" and City Regulation', *The Modern Law Review*, 51 (1988), pp. 8–12. For the Gower Report, see Cmnd 9125.

120 Bryan Gould, writing in *Tribune* but quoted in *Pensions World*, December 1986, p. 892. For a useful summary of the Financial Services Act 1986 (and his observation that 'only time will tell whether the self-regulation approach adopted in the Act will provide a high level of investor protection' (p. 356), see David M. Barnard, 'The United Kingdom Financial Services Act, 1986: A New Regulatory Framework', *The International Lawyer*, 21 (1987).

121 *Financial Times*, 'Attack on Plan for Doorstep Pension Sales', by Clive Wolman, 2 August 1986. The CA believed that cold calling for personal pensions would be 'even more pernicious' than for unit trusts and life assurance (which would also be permitted).

122 Conservative Party Archive (CPA): PPB 256/2. DHSS Press Release, 86/159, 'Norman Fowler Announces Membership of Advisory Group on Personal Pensions', 15 May 1986. Allied Dunbar's reputation for forceful sales agents meant that it was disparaged as 'Allied Crowbar' by other, more reticent, life assurers.

123 *The Economist*, 'Too Much of a Good Thing', 23 February 1985.

124 *The Economist*, 'A Happy Retirement', 30 November 1985.

125 Henry L. James (director general, NAPF), *Pensions World*, 'Comment: A Tax on Jobs', March 1985; *Financial Times*, 'Hopes Dashed over Plan for Pension Fund Surpluses', by Eric Short, 5 June 1986; and ibid., 'The Muddle over Pensions'.

126 *Pensions World*, 'Speech by Henry L. James to the NAPF Conference, 16–19 May 1985', July 1985.

127 Within days officials were instructed to start work on researching the issue and drawing up proposals. See HMT: PO-CH NL 0045 Part B, M. C. Scholar to Peter Middleton, 'Follow-on to Chevening: Work Priorities', 13 January 1986; ibid., R. Lomax, 'Chevening: 11–12 January 1986', 14 January 1986; and HMT: PO-CH NL 0039 Part A, R. Lomax, 'Record of the First Budget Overview Meeting: 9.30 am on 20 January 1986'.

128 HMT: PO-CH NL 0041 Part A, Lawson to Thatcher, 'Budget Proposals', 5 March 1986.

129 HC Debs, 18 March 1986, vol. 94, cols. 176–77. In this budget Lawson also announced the introduction of 'personal equity plans' (into which individuals

would be allowed to invest up to £2,400 a year and receive all dividends and capital gains tax-free), with the explicit intention of encouraging individual share ownership to rebalance capital ownership away from institutional holdings.

130 See, for example, S. M. Riley (Clay & Partners), 'Surpluses: The Start of a Funding Revolution or a Passing Phase?', *Pensions World*, December 1986.

131 Nigel Vinson, Foreword to Philip Chappell, *Pensions and Privilege: How to End the Scandal, Simplify Taxes and Widen Ownership* (London: Centre for Policy Studies, 1988).

132 John Redwood, *Equity for Everyman: New Ways to Widen Ownership* (London: Centre for Policy Studies, 1986), p. 8.

133 TNA: PREM 19/1640, Redwood to Thatcher, 'MISC 111', 14 October 1985; John Redwood, *The Popular Capitalist Manifesto* (London: British Young Conservatives, 1989).

134 *Financial Times*, 'The Muddle over Pensions'.

8

Legacy

The neoliberal architects of UK pension reform in the 1980s – most notably the Centre for Policy Studies outside government and the No. 10 Policy Unit at its heart – had set out to revolutionise British pensions and, in the process, defuse the country's twenty-first-century 'pensions time bomb'. At the same time, they had sought to reconfigure British workers if not into investor capitalists (as originally intended) then into investors with an indirect stake in British capitalism via defined contribution (DC) personal pension plans purchased from companies in the financial services sector, backed up to an extent by DC occupational pensions. Their 'back to Beveridge' strategy had been to restrict state involvement in pension provision to the bare minimum and transfer to the individual responsibility for income replacement in old age above that. In the process, they had planned to wipe out not just the country's State Earnings-Related Pension Scheme but also company-provided defined benefit (DB) occupational pensions, which, in tandem, then formed the second tier of British pension provision. As demonstrated in the previous chapter, they were therefore profoundly disappointed by the settlement embodied in the 1986 Social Security and Financial Services Acts. An unexpectedly broad coalition of opposition to their pension reform proposals in the 1985 Green Paper on social security had forced them to abandon their revolutionary strategy and instead adopt an incremental approach, with personal pensions added to the second tier of British pensions and a less disadvantageous regime for DB occupational schemes than envisaged. This 'Thatcher evolution' in pensions still amounted to a major reform for which the Conservatives took credit in their 1987 general election manifesto, adding a new element within Britain's mixed-economy pension system, and individualising not just responsibility for pension provision but also the associated investment and longevity risks. Evolution represented a significant step back from reformers' initial neoliberal vision, however. They were not just disappointed by this; they also feared that Britain might in the process have in the process ended up with the 'worst of both worlds', because of the compromises forced upon them. In this chapter, we turn our focus to the legacy of reform in the Thatcher era and ask whether they were right.

Our analysis is divided into four parts. We start with the state pension system and the long-term implications of delinking the basic state pension from earnings and reducing the generosity of the State Earnings-Related Pension Scheme (SERPS). We then turn our focus to DB occupational pensions, teasing out the consequences of reform for their long-term sustainability in four main dimensions. First, the impact on pension fund liabilities of a tendency to improve benefits, including solving the 'early leaver problem'. Second, the impact of employers' increasing desire to access (both legally and illegally) growing 'surpluses' in their pension schemes. Third, the consequences for pension funds of the government increasing scheme regulation (not least to protect members from illegal behaviour by employers), restricting surpluses, and limiting tax subsidies. Fourth, we consider the implications of these several factors for long-term fund sustainability and for the willingness of employers to sustain their commitment to DB occupational pensions. In the next section we consider personal pensions, beginning by acknowledging significant early successes in terms of sales. We then, however, explore two misselling scandals and their effects. Then we examine the consequences of poor performance, largely driven by high charges, inadequate contributions, and poor investment returns. Finally, in our last section, we draw the focus out to explore the ways in which the reforms of the 1980s served to generate market failure across state, personal, and occupational pensions, consider the consequences of increasing regulation, and describe the results in terms of reduced pension entitlement at the aggregate level. We conclude that all this amounted to a significant political failure that meant Britain did indeed end up with the worst of both worlds in pensions, though not entirely for the reasons identified by the Thatcher-era reform project's disappointed architects.

State pensions

In Chapter Four we noted that Thatcher's first term as Prime Minister saw no major structural reform of the country's pension system. Nevertheless, although the change in the annual indexation of the basic state pension in 1980, linking to prices rather than the higher of prices or earnings, looked like a relatively minor piece of tinkering at the time, in fact it markedly reduced its effectiveness over the ensuing decades. Once the early 1980s recession was over and inflation started to decline, earnings once again began to rise more rapidly than prices. Consequently, the value of the BSP relative to average earnings fell steadily – as Geoffrey Howe had intended in 1980. If this was not bad enough, the reduction in pensioner incomes relative to earnings was then compounded by the reduced generosity of SERPS. As we saw in Chapter Seven, for those above the 'lower earnings limit', and thus with entitlements under SERPS, changes made in the 1986 Social Security Act ensured a significant reduction in benefits even before the planned withdrawal of SERPS for workers retiring from 2000 onwards. The elimination of the '20 best years' rule meant that the pension paid would be based on earnings across the whole of a working life (with years of lower pay, or time out of employment, bringing the pension down). SERPS pensioners also suffered from the gradual reduction in the rate at which they accrued benefits – from 25 per cent for those retiring in 1999/2000 to 20 per cent for younger workers retiring in 2009/10. Moreover, subsequent changes to SERPS made by the Conservative government in the 1995 Pensions Act further penalised those retiring after this.[1] Taken together, and even with the advent in 2002 of 'new Labour's' State Second Pension (S2P) as a more generous replacement for the by then increasingly attenuated SERPS, the impact on retirement incomes by the end of the century, and on prospective retirement incomes in the twenty-first century, was profound – as the Pensions Commission demonstrated in 2004 (see Figure 8.1).[2]

In 1974 the Labour government's *Better Pensions* White Paper had looked forward to a new era of considerably improved state pensions, envisaging 'a gradually increasing transfer of income and therefore of claims on resources from the economically active section of the community to those who have retired'.[3] Labour's subsequent indexation of the Basic State Pension (BSP) to average earnings and the introduction of SERPs

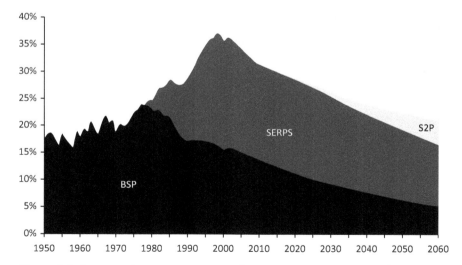

Figure 8.1 State pension as a percentage of average earnings at point of retirement for a worker on average earnings, 1950–2060
Source: Pensions Commission, *Pensions: Challenges and Choices: The First Report of the Pensions Commission* (London: TSO, 2004), p. 132 (Figure 4.3).

in 1978 had been intended to produce an overall state pension for a married contributor on average earnings equivalent to about 58 per cent of earnings by 1998.[4] In fact, as intended by the Conservatives, indexing the BSP to prices alone and then degrading top-up SERPS benefits contained the generosity and cost of state pensions. As clearly demonstrated in Figure 8.1, the effect was a startling reversal of the postwar trend – almost immediate in the case of the BSP, somewhat delayed when it came to SERPS. As demonstrated by Figure 8.1, by the end of the century the long-term reduction of the level of pension relative to prior earnings, and the impact on pensioners' lives, was profound. By the mid-2030s an average earner dependent wholly on state pensions could at best expect to retire on a pension equivalent to less than 25 per cent of those earnings (despite Labour's introduction in 2002 of the State Second Pension as a successor to SERPS). Thus, the Conservatives' state pension reforms of the 1980s succeeded in more than halving the pensions of late 1990s and early twenty-first century retirees with no private or occupational pension to supplement that received from the state.

This startling reduction in the long-term value of state pensions generated surprisingly few waves until the dawn of the new century. By the mid-1990s so inured had commentators become to the ungenerosity of present and future state pensions that two IFS economists could remark of the passage of the Pensions Bill through Parliament in 1995 that it was striking that 'barely a voice has been raised in protest at the further halving of state earnings-related pensions implicit in the Pensions Bill', despite the fact that the proposed cuts were retrospective, not just prospective.[5] That Act also (finally) equalised the state pension age for men and women, setting the new joint SPA at 65 – a long overdue response to demands for equal treatment in the labour market but one that served to further reduce the generosity of UK state pensions for women, because, of course, they would be paid a pension for fewer years, all things being equal, and so state spending on women's pensions would be reduced further. As Lady Hollis, the opposition spokesperson for social security, caustically remarked when responding for Labour to the second reading of that Bill, this was 'the Government's homoeopathic version of security; the more you dilute it the stronger it becomes'.[6]

In 1978 total state spending on pensions had amounted to around 4.3 per cent of GDP. By 1981/82 a rise in income support payments to pensioners had increased that figure to 5 per cent. In the 1974 *Better Pensions* White Paper the Government Actuary had calculated that the increasing generosity of SERPS would see the cost of state pensions rise by approximately 43 per cent by 2008/09.[7, 8] As the economy began to recover from the 1980–1 recession and inflation to decline, however, the fall in the value of the BSP relative to earnings ensured that the total cost of state pensions as a percentage of national income actually fell. Even with the build-up of SERPs benefits (crimped, of course, by the changes ushered in by the

312   *Implementation and legacy*

Social Security Act 1986 and Pensions Act 1995), state spending on pensions including means-tested top-up benefits was still under 5 per cent of GDP in the early 2000s. Only in 2008/09, with a significant increase in the BSP under new Labour coupled with more generous top-ups for the very poor, was the figure finally pushed to just over 5 per cent.[9]

The government headed by John Major basked in the glow of the Conservatives' success in having put a lid on UK state spending on pensions. In 1996, for example, Chancellor Ken Clarke told the House of Commons that during the 1980s 'across the rest of Europe, the modern state remorselessly took an ever-greater share of almost every nation's wealth'. He boasted that, in contrast, 'we have held the line'. Moreover, Clarke proudly promised a further drop in spending as a proportion of GDP.[10] This assumption that state spending on pensions must be contained if the 'pensions time bomb' was to be defused was now shared by other countries. As the postwar baby boomers aged, the prospect of the growing burden on a shrinking workforce of financing unfunded pay-as-you-go public pensions began to loom larger in the political imagination in ageing societies. At the same time, hopes faded of a return to the rates of economic growth experienced in the 30 years after the Second World War (what the French dubbed the *'trente glorieuses'*). In consequence, fears that had been at the forefront of Conservative policy concerns in the early 1980s began to be a concern internationally. This worry, shared by the incoming Labour government in 1997 despite previous governments' holding down of prospective state spending on pensions, meant that by the early 2000s talk of a worldwide 'pensions crisis' had become widespread; see Figure 8.2 for its prevalence in the anglophone world in the first decade of the new century.[11]

In its famous analysis of the problem in 1994, the World Bank was forthright about the unsustainability of publicly provided pay-as-you-go schemes, which it noted tended to have been set up in the postwar years, in conditions of high population growth and rapidly rising real incomes, which 'could not have been better' but which, unfortunately, no longer obtained. It therefore recommended a wholesale move to a 'three pillar' model of pensions: a public pillar, with the 'limited objective of alleviating old age poverty'; a mandatory second pillar, of privately managed actuarially funded pensions; and a voluntary third pillar, providing top-up private pension saving for those who wanted a higher income in retirement.[12] In Britain, however, the Conservative government of the mid-1990s assumed that the changes of the 1980s had addressed the issue of state pension unsustainability while the advent of personal pensions had already increased the level of funding, albeit with SERPS as a backstop. There was much self-congratulation in some quarters in the mid- to late 1990s, even in the early 2000s, about the

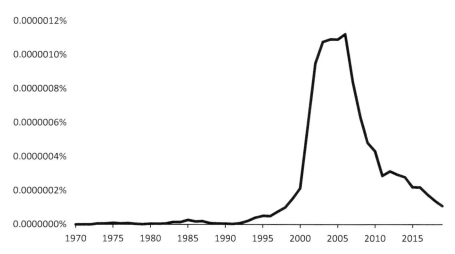

Figure 8.2 Frequency of the phrase 'pensions crisis' in published books in English, 1970–2019
Note: For comparison, the most frequent use of the term 'new Labour', in 1997 at 0.0000095%, was about nine times the frequency of 'pensions crisis' at its peak.
Source: Google Books Ngram Viewer, English corpus (https://books.google.com/ngrams), smoothing = 1.

United Kingdom's prescience, and relief that its consequence was that projections of the country's state spending on pensions stayed at levels equivalent to about 5 to 6 per cent of GDP as far as the eye could see. Typically, there was also considerable *schadenfreude* about the fact that European partners had not had such foresight.[13]

Within a few years, however, it became clear that this faith in Britain's 1980s pension settlement was misplaced. As we shall see, this was partly because of emerging problems in both occupational and personal pensions. Most obviously, however, it was a matter of simple arithmetic: keeping the overall cost of state pensions stable even as the population aged had required significant cuts in the level of those future pensions, with all that implied for a prospective rise in pensioner poverty. Labour somewhat overstated the problem in its 1997 general election manifesto when it said that, for the pensioner of the day, 'Conservative policies have created real poverty';[14] those with a decent level of entitlement to a defined benefit occupational pension tended to be far from poor. Nonetheless, for someone dependent on the increasingly nugatory BSP and SERPS, the problem was all too real, and would become even greater in the future as the cuts to the latter began increasingly to be felt. Hence the increasing focus on improved means-tested supplementary benefits. That was a problematic strategy, however, given its dependence on

314 *Implementation and legacy*

pensioners applying for supplementation, something they had always been reluctant to do because of the associated social stigma.[15]

In short, the Conservatives' reforms of the 1980s had not defused the twenty-first-century 'pensions time bomb'; they had merely privatised it – and with disastrous results. Far from eliminating pressure for higher state spending, the 1980s reforms had served to raise the pressure via the increasing inadequacy of retirement income for those without significant supplementation from personal or occupational pensions and, as we shall see, by long-run underinvestment in personal pensions.

When the Pensions Commission, set up by the Labour government of Tony Blair, reported in 2004 it noted that the impending retirement of the postwar baby boomers coupled with rising longevity was about to produce about 30 years of an increasing number of pensioners relative to the working population. It identified four options for dealing with this, between which society and individuals would have to choose.[16] The first was that pensioners would have to continue becoming poorer relative to the rest of society, an option that the Commission noted was 'unattractive' given that the value of state pension benefits for someone on average earnings throughout a full working life was expected to decline to just a fifth of those earnings by 2060.[17] The remaining options, not mutually exclusive, were that taxes and/or National Insurance contributions devoted to pensions would have to escalate, savings increase, or retirement ages rise. In its second report, a year later, the Commission recommended a combination of all three of these alternatives: the creation of a new low-cost national funded DC pension scheme (the later National Employment Savings Trust, created by the Pensions Act 2008) to expand top-up pension coverage, coupled with action to raise the incomes of the poorest pensioners by making state pensions and associated benefits more generous. This was to be financed by a mix of rising state pension ages and increased state spending (and of taxes to finance it). This 'new pensions settlement for the future', both a break with and consequence of the Thatcherite vision of pension reform, was that adopted and implemented by Labour.

Occupational pensions

As a recent study of British occupational pensions has noted, after peaking in 1967 in terms of active members a gradual decline was then accelerated by the reforms of the 1980s.[18] As can be seen in Figure 8.3, this decline was most obvious in private sector defined benefit schemes, the active membership of which declined precipitately (even as their funds under management grew as their active members aged). From the early 1990s, as Figure 8.3 also demonstrates, there was a parallel (if lesser) tendency for occupational

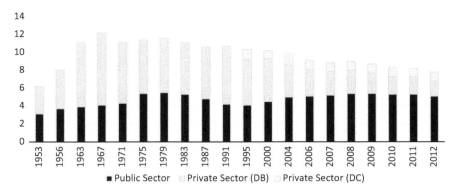

Figure 8.3 Active occupational pension scheme membership (millions), 1953–2012
Note: The decline of private sector schemes shown actually understates the transformation, since privatisation saw the official designation of very large public sector schemes transferred to private sector.
Source: Blythe, 'Why Did?', app. 4.1, p. 276 (1953–95), tab. 5.1, p. 190 (1995–2012).

scheme members to be in a defined contribution scheme. Defined benefit schemes in the public sector (many of which remained unfunded) were untouched by either of these transformations.

Although this transformation in the fortunes of private sector DB was a long-term process, the developments of the 1980s played a key role in the implosion. They did so via several effects: the rising future costs of improved benefits; growing regulation, and its raising of both administration costs and liabilities; 'asset stripping' of fund surpluses by sponsoring companies; changes in the taxation of DB pensions (not least to address surpluses that turned out to be temporary); a loss of faith in DB schemes by employers as the long-term costs of the promises embodied within them began to sink in; and the active promotion by government from 1986 of alternative 'money purchase' (DC) occupational scheme alternatives and of personal pensions. Whereas DB pensions had been the gold standard for occupational pension provision, and remained so in 1979, by the end of the 1980s they had been subjected to a decade of government scepticism as to their merits, coupled with changes that gradually undermined their long-term sustainability. Consequently, their future looked increasingly doubtful by the end of the century.

Improved benefits

At first sight it seems a paradox that an improvement in benefits that accompanied the growth of DB pensions continued even as government scepticism about them grew. Much of the improvement in occupational pension

316   *Implementation and legacy*

scheme benefits was driven by government, but not all. As Peter Blythe notes, DB had come to dominate occupational pension provision by 1983 (rising from 55 per cent of schemes in 1967 to over 90 per cent). This was the product of a voluntary shift that a 1992 CBI survey found to be largely a product of 'increasing concerns about the high levels of inflation experienced in the 1970s which made provision of a given level of replacement income on a money purchase basis difficult'.[19] It was, in effect, a product of a principled desire among good employers to provide high-quality pensions to their staff – even though labour markets were considerably softer than they had been in the heyday of occupational pension expansion in the full-employment decades of the 1950s and 1960s. At the same time, the momentum built up in those decades saw the benefits offered by DB schemes themselves improved. There was, for example, a long-term improvement in accrual rates: in 1967 40 per cent of scheme members accrued final salary benefits at the relatively ungenerous rate of 1/80th for each year of employment, but by 1983 that figure had fallen to 17 per cent, and by 1995 to just 5 per cent. In parallel, despite the government's negative attitude to occupational pensions in the 1980s, the proportion of DB scheme members accruing benefits at 1/60th a year or better had risen from 40 per cent to 73 per cent in 1983 and 94 per cent by 1995. As the rate at which members accrued benefits improved, so their normal retirement age also tended to fall overall. Increasingly, schemes also began guaranteeing that pensions in payment would rise to compensate pensioners for rising prices: in 1983 a mere 2 per cent of pensioners received such increases but by 1995 the level had risen to 52 per cent, even though for three-quarters of those members the link was capped at 5 per cent a year, thus managing the sponsor's risk but providing protection for the employee unless 1970s-style inflation should return. In practice, more members than this benefited, because the funds, seemingly awash with cash in the 1980s, often provided voluntary increases: Blythe finds that, by 1995, 93 per cent of members had received such an increase in the previous year.[20] Moreover, the proportion of schemes offering a pension to the surviving partner of a dead member rose from 89 per cent in 1979 to 97 per cent in 1991. At the same time, the definition of 'final salary' became more generous. The Thatcher era therefore saw not just a continuation but an acceleration of a trend towards voluntarily improved occupational pension scheme benefits, as the sector responded to the late 1970s 'partnership in pensions' agenda and professionalised and improved its offer to scheme members.[21]

Many changes in this era were the product of legislation and government regulation, however. Sometimes this could have negative consequences: for example, although the government's action to make membership of occupational pension schemes voluntary had been intended to open the way for members to substitute a personal pension instead, it had an unexpected side effect in that, in quest of a higher immediate net income, many simply opted out of their occupational pension, entering SERPS but in the process, of course, losing out on the better benefits of their company scheme.[22] Yet that negative experience was unusual. For instance, as we have seen in earlier chapters, government action in 1973 forced schemes to preserve the pension rights of those who changed jobs. Although this improved the position of early leavers somewhat, it was the Thatcher government's dissatisfaction with schemes' voluntary response to the desire for protection against inflation that led to its endorsement in principle of the 1981 recommendations of the Occupational Pensions Board on indexation of preserved pensions. This was resisted successfully by employers for a decade but from 1991 all schemes were required to revalue preserved pension benefits at a rate equal to or better than the government's newly constructed Limited Price Index (LPI) – with its 5 per cent per annum cap.[23] Likewise, the imperative to protect occupational scheme pensioners more broadly from the effect of inflation in the late 1970s and 1980s, though ducked at several points in the 1980s despite considerable pressure for action, did eventually lead to legislation in 1990, albeit without a commencement date being set (it was not until the Pensions Act 1995 that LPI indexation of DB occupational pensions in payment was required).[24] Statutory inflation protection of the guaranteed minimum pension (broadly equivalent to the benefits offered by SERPS) within an occupational pension had already been introduced in 1988, however, but capped at 3 per cent a year.

These improvements in the pension benefits of DB occupational pension schemes, whether voluntary or statutory, were significant, and were accompanied by a range of other voluntary improvements: in ill health retirement benefits, a lump sum on death in service, and improved pensions for the partners of members. The period between 1987 and 1991 was a particularly fecund one for such improvements. However welcome such enhancements were to members, though, they also acted to increase scheme liabilities. This added to the pressure on long-term sustainability created by rising longevity and the ageing of the postwar baby boomers. Blythe notes that it is difficult to put a figure on this because the very strong investment returns obtaining in the 1980s simultaneously bolstered fund 'surpluses' and allowed many employers to reduce contributions.[25] Nonetheless, the cost of improved benefits, voluntary or statutory, was to become a significant contributor to scheme deficits once investment returns began to decline from the early 1990s.

Fund holidays and asset stripping

In retrospect, we can see that the combination of the rapid growth in stock prices in the 1985–8 Lawson boom and the government's ultimate success in bringing inflation down in the 1980s (which left many occupational pension schemes

318   *Implementation and legacy*

holding long-term government bonds with improbably high yields) was a key contributor to what the Pensions Commission described as the 'fool's paradise' in British pensions.[26] The advent of large fund 'surpluses' touched off a debate about who exactly owned them: the employer sponsoring the scheme or the members benefiting from it? In law, however, ownership lay with the sponsoring firm, and companies started to cast an acquisitive eye over their pension fund. Consequently, a tendency for employers to take 'contribution holidays' set in during the mid-1980s, a trend reinforced by the Conservatives' statutory controls on the size of surpluses from 1986. In 1989, for example, 45 per cent of employers were not making contributions to their pension fund.[27] By 1991 research by the House of Commons Library, commissioned by the opposition, found that 80 per cent of the largest employers had either suspended or reduced the contributions to their pension fund. This led to accusations from the shadow minister for social security, among others, that companies were using contribution holidays to subsidise profits.[28] This was not an unjustified claim, although it was also true that companies often used the surpluses to fund expensive restructurings of their workforce in the 1980s and early 1990s by early-retiring many older workers.[29] In either case, however, the effect was to reduce fund 'surpluses' and leave funds badly exposed when economic headwinds began to blow against them.

Looking back in 2004, the Pensions Commission dryly observed of actions to reduce surpluses that '[i]n retrospect [they] were predicated on assumptions about the sustainability of long-term returns which were over optimistic'.[30] The problem, as one commentator noted at the time, was that the 'so-called surplus' was 'not a pot of gold but a purely theoretical construct'. A 'surplus' was the residual of a complex equation balancing the current investment value of the fund, likely future investment returns, and prospective benefit liabilities – a calculation that embodied a multitude of long-term assumptions, almost all of which were inevitably highly speculative.[31] Yet the prospect of gaining access to surpluses continued to be alluring after the Thatcher era, and not just to companies. For example, it lay behind the incoming Labour government's decision to change the rules on reclaiming Advance Corporation Tax (ACT) in Gordon Brown's first budget in 1997.[32] It also touched off a number of corporate takeovers in the late 1980s and early 1990s that were driven by the acquiring company's interest in the surplus in the target company's pension scheme.[33] Most of this was legal, albeit not in the interests of the scheme's members. The acquirer might, for example, intend to raise profitability by reducing pension contributions without breaching statutory lower limits on scheme funding or, more egregiously, use the fund to buy the company's own equity (the trust deeds of 24 per cent of fund trustees allowed this, even though there was

Legacy 319

plainly a potential conflict of interest that could work to the detriment of scheme members).[34] Some of it was simply illegal, the Maxwell scandal being the most shocking example.

Robert Maxwell, despite having been found by the Department of Trade in 1971 to be 'not in our opinion a person who can be relied on to exercise proper stewardship of a publicly quoted company', had by the early 1990s built a commercial empire spanning over 400 public and private companies mainly but not exclusively in the media. When the 'bouncing Czech', as *Private Eye* dubbed him, died in November 1991 (perhaps by suicide but probably from a heart attack before or after falling off his yacht in the Atlantic), the precarious edifice of his complex holdings collapsed.[35] It was almost immediately apparent that he had run down surpluses in the pension schemes of his companies via contribution holidays, directed 'his' pension funds to invest in other companies within the group, and simply appropriated share certificates owned by the funds and used them as collateral for company borrowing.[36] Evidence to the House of Commons' Select Committee on Social Security on the latter problem estimated that £420 million had gone missing from the funds, putting the pensions of up to 28,400 scheme members at risk.[37] Although Maxwell himself was ultimately responsible for the debacle, it raised profoundly troubling questions not just about the governance of pension schemes but about the probity of advice given by external professional advisers, the quality of audit by major accountants, and the robustness of pension scheme regulation in the United Kingdom.[38]

Given the number of pension fund members affected, the Maxwell scandal was of great political significance. A key problem arising from the saga, and from other instances of abuse of their pension schemes by employers in the late 1980s and early 1990s, was that it discredited occupational pensions and served to reduce the attachment of workers to them. Coming on top of the Thatcher government's attempt to woo occupational scheme members out into personal pensions, it often caused workers who might once have automatically enrolled in their company scheme to think twice about doing so. More specifically, the Maxwell scandal was widely seen utterly to have discredited the flawed system of pension fund regulation established under the 1986 Finance Act, and it precipitated a major rethink.

Re-regulation and taxation

In its report on the Maxwell scandal, the Select Committee on Social Security blamed regulators, City institutions, and professional advisers for failing to spot 'stealing on a massive scale'.[39] It recommended sweeping reform

320   *Implementation and legacy*

of the legal basis and regulation of occupational pensions, and the setting up of a House of Commons committee of inquiry intended to lead to a new Pensions Act.[40] The response of Peter Lilley, then Secretary of State for Social Security, to what he described as Maxwell's 'catalogue of crime' and the 'callous and despicable … pillaging of pension funds' to the detriment of their members was to set up in June 1992 an independent committee of inquiry under the chairmanship of the academic lawyer Sir Roy Goode.[41]

Goode reported in October 1993 (an impressive feat, given the complexity of the topic, the wide scope of his terms of reference, and the 82 questions posed by his committee in its initial consultation document a year earlier).[42] An array of 218 often interlinked reforms of occupational pensions was proposed. The most significant were these: a pensions compensation scheme to cover fraud, misappropriation, or theft, to be financed by a levy on all occupational schemes (a proposal already called for by the NAPF in November 1992); a new pensions regulator to replace the existing fragmented regulatory apparatus; strengthened roles for the pensions ombudsman and Occupational Pensions Advisory Service; a requirement that contribution holidays be allowed only when schemes met a minimum solvency standard of at least 90 per cent, with employers wishing to extract cash to be required to obtain permission from the pensions regulator; at least a third of trustees to be scheme members; and a modification to trust law to protect members' accrued rights when a scheme was amended, wound up, or subjected to benefit reduction or restriction (which employers would go on having the freedom to do). These changes were to be accompanied by a new Occupational Pension Schemes Act to codify the reforms.

The Goode Report is often seen as a landmark in the history of occupational pensions in Britain.[43] Although the country's system of DB occupational pensions was endorsed by Goode (the report noting their superiority over the DC alternative), its failures, particularly those in recent years, were laid bare. Interestingly, however, the report was not seen by the editor of the industry's trade magazine at the time as radical but as merely 'a fair start' in a process of reform.[44] This initial judgement was later endorsed by David Blake in his magisterial analysis of UK occupational pensions, noting that in retrospect it was astonishing that the report had been required at all given the basic common sense it embodied.[45] Goode's implication was clear: these were issues that could have been sorted out in the 1986 Financial Services Act, but were not; indeed, the Goode Report was effectively a rerun of the Gower Report a decade earlier.[46]

The Goode Report precipitated a major reform of the system, starting with the 1995 Pensions Act, which implemented many of its recommendations. Sue Ward, a member of Goode's committee, noted a watering down of its recommendations in the 1995 Act, however. For example, the new

Occupational Pensions Regulatory Authority (OPRA) was 'a much more limited body', and much more passive, than Goode had proposed – having no powers of enforcement. Ward also decried the continuing fragmentation of regulation. As Robin Blackburn observes, crucial aspects of regulatory enforcement were 'entrusted to other bodies or left without proper enforcement'.[47] *Pensions World*'s early conclusion that Goode would mark just the first step on a road to further reform was therefore prophetic. There were five full-blown Pension Acts in the ensuing 25 years (in 2004, 2007, 2008, 2011, and 2014) as well as three Pension Schemes Acts (2015, 2017, and 2021), plus the Welfare Reform and Pensions Act 1999 and sundry more minor pieces of legislation affecting occupational pensions. Nonetheless, the 1995 Act still represented a significant increase in the amount of regulation to which occupational pension schemes were subjected. That Act put right some of the failures of the 1986 Financial Services Act when it came to DB occupational pensions, but the greater security for members it provided came at a price: more complex administration coupled with more regulatory oversight and a higher reporting burden. This served further to increase pension fund costs, and thus put further pressure on the long-term sustainability of DB schemes. Blythe identifies 1995 as the turning point for occupational pensions in Britain, the moment at which a gradual decline began to accelerate markedly, and the rising cost of such schemes was an important driver of this process; but the roots of that acceleration clearly lay in the failures of the Financial Services Act 1986.[48]

The Goode Report marked a culmination of concerns about employers' abuse of pension funds for their own uses, but it was not just employers who had cast an acquisitive eye over the funds and their surpluses in the latter half of the 1980s; so too had the state. More generally, within government there remained an antipathy to large financial institutions as both too economically powerful and antithetical to individual freedom. In the summer of 1987, for example, Peter Cropper, former head of the Conservative Research Department and then a Treasury adviser, remarked to Lawson that the 'concern about the concentration of power in the hands of big institutions' was one that was generally shared by Treasury special political advisers and ministers alike.[49] The result was a much less accommodative – indeed, at times positively adversarial – attitude to occupational DB pensions and the sense in the Treasury that the pension funds at best received too great a tax subsidy and at worst acted as a vehicle for tax avoidance.

This latter assumption underpinned Lawson's action to reduce fund surpluses in the Finance Act 1986, which restricted surpluses to 5 per cent of the overall fund value, with any surplus required to be redistributed by reduced contributions, improved benefits, and/or taxable refunds to the employer. It also underlay Lawson's attempt to remove the benefit to members of a tax-free lump sum on retirement. His first essay on this had come in his 1985 budget but he had then rapidly withdrawn in the face of 'the most astonishing lobbying campaign of my entire career, devoted both to the preservation of the lump sum relief and to pension fund privileges in general'.[50] Lawson did, however, manage to limit to £150,000 the maximum value of the lump sum in his 1987 budget (in which he also introduced free-standing AVCs [FSAVCs] as well as completing the tax side of the 1986 pension reforms). At the same time, warning that 'the generous tax treatment of pensions can be justified only if it is not abused', Lawson acted to restrict the upper limit on benefit accruals to 1/30th of salary per annum as a prelude to measures to curb pension tax relief for highly paid employees.[51] Taken together, these changes in the occupational pensions tax and regulatory regime in 1987 significantly complicated both the schemes' tax situation and the administrative burden placed on them, as well as diluting their attraction for higher-paid members.[52]

Lawson's action on higher earners in 1985 marked the start of a long campaign by the Treasury and Inland Revenue against what was seen as occupational pensions' abuse of generous tax reliefs. In 1989, for example, Lawson acted to limit the amount of salary that could be invested in a tax-approved occupational pension scheme to £60,000 a year, or approximately four times the national average income of a male worker. The cap would apply only to new joiners, but because it was indexed to prices, not earnings, it would affect an increasing number of employees over time, and on that basis it was bitterly attacked by the NAPF, among others.[53] Although it is hard to feel much sympathy with the plight of high-paid executives experiencing a reduction in the generous tax benefits of their pension, Blythe perceptively notes that an unforeseen consequence was that it served gradually to alienate from their company schemes senior managers responsible for decisions affecting them. That in turn may have helped encourage companies to get prospective long-term cost under control, either by converting to DC or simply abandoning occupational pensions entirely.[54] More generally, the Finance Act 1989, which included measures to allow contracting out of SERPS into a DC occupational pension scheme, was seen by the industry as an outrage that had sent a shockwave through occupational pensioning and, by putting DB schemes under further pressure, considerably increased the likelihood of a shift away from DB to DC.[55]

What was really beginning to irritate the Treasury by the end of the 1980s, however, was pension funds' ability to reclaim Advance Corporation Tax on dividends received by them. This was seen as starting to erode the corporation tax base as the funds accumulated a rising proportion of UK equities.[56] It was this concern that lay behind the decision by Norman Lamont, then Chancellor, in 1993 to adjust down the benefit obtained from the funds'

Legacy   323

ability to reclaim ACT. Although views within the industry differed on the effects of this in terms of its implications for funds' investment strategies, there could be no doubt that the change decreased returns by reducing dividend income by 6.25 per cent. More seriously, Lamont had put the remainder of the ACT credit in play, and this set the stage for Gordon Brown's decision to abolish it entirely in 1997.[57] This was greeted in apocalyptic terms by the industry. The NAPF described it as 'the biggest attack on pension provision since the war' and *Pensions World* opined that it represented 'a near mortal blow' to occupational pensioning. The cost of the change for employers was estimated to be more than £50 billion over the next ten years. The NAPF chair, Peter Murray, wryly noted: 'Even Robert Maxwell only took £400m.'[58] An editorial in *Pensions World* noted that abolition of the ACT credit would push into deficit many of the 90 per cent of funds that then met the minimum funding requirement that had come into force in April 1996, following the Pensions Act 1995.[59]

Thus, the 1980s represented a turning point for occupational pension schemes, as the government turned against them philosophically, but also began to take practical measures to reduce their tax privileges. Most seriously, the changes of the Thatcher years became a template for change in the 1990s as governments of different political persuasions continued to increase regulation and push through changes to reduce the cost to government of the tax subsidy to occupational pension schemes. The effect was at once to reduce investment returns even as demographic change raised future liabilities, and a substantial increase in administrative complexity and cost. In combination, these changes too served increasingly to erode the financial sustainability of schemes. This had malign consequences, in that it further alienated companies from their pension scheme. It is to this problem that we now turn.

The decline of defined benefit pensions

After the economically easy years of the mid- to late 1980s, fund deficits started to become a defining feature of the DB occupational pensions landscape. This was an inevitable consequence of a range of factors, such as rising longevity, the less favourable tax regime just described, employers' contribution holidays, and the improved benefits because of the legislation discussed earlier in this chapter, as well as voluntary improvements to scheme benefits made by many companies when their funds were in surplus. The problem was exacerbated by a secular reduction in interest rates, first in the 'NICE' (non-inflationary, continuous expansion) decade and a half after the 1991/92 recession and, particularly, the United Kingdom's exit from the

European Exchange Rate Mechanism in September 1992, and then in the post-2008 financial crisis era of 'quantitative easing' in monetary policy. The advent of historically unparalleled low interest rates served further to increase pension scheme liabilities, because, to contain risks, guaranteed and increasingly costly future pension benefits had to be matched by scheme actuaries with investment-grade bonds whose yields were falling (reducing their return to the scheme) and prices rising (increasing their cost). At the same time, on the other side of the fund accounting equation, future pension obligations were discounted by a rate derived from those yields. This meant that fund liabilities ballooned even as the value of projected fund assets was negatively affected by the onset of lower investment returns across developed economies in a much more difficult economic climate than that of the 1980s. In consequence, the era of fund surpluses rapidly turned into one of deficits. That, of course, raised the potential future costs to employers of supporting their pension scheme – a problem made more pressing from 2000 by the Accounting Standards Board's requirement (via Financial Reporting Standard 17, or FRS 17: retirement benefits, which became fully effective from 2005) that companies henceforth reflect at fair value in their financial statements the assets and liabilities arising from their pension scheme's benefit obligations.[60]

At the same time, the traditional motivations for employers to provide DB schemes were weakening: in an increasingly 'flexible' labour market with higher unemployment than that experienced in the immediate postwar decades a company pension was no longer an important means of recruiting and retaining workers. Moreover, by the early 1990s paternalism was starting to look increasingly out of date in the new 'hire and fire' flexible labour market that flowed from the Conservative governments' market reforms after 1979. The result was that by 1992, as the CBI noted, 'most employers [had become] wary of the type of open-ended commitment which final salary schemes involve'. In consequence, 53 per cent of employers were by this point planning to contain the growth in their pension costs, and 15 per cent actively to reduce them. Almost a third of finance directors of FTSE 100 companies, all of which had a DB pension scheme, now thought that the burden had become too much to bear.[61] By the mid-1990s the capital value of many pension funds exceeded the quoted stock exchange value of the sponsoring company. As actuarial surpluses evaporated, DB pension schemes represented an increasingly onerous burden of support for their company sponsor. This dire situation was used by many to argue for a definitive shift from DB to DC – 'an idea whose time has come', as Nigel Vinson put it in 1996, and one that, as noted in the preceding chapter, had for a decade already been promoted by the government.[62]

Legacy 325

In consequence, in 2004 the Government Actuary's periodic report on occupational pensions noted a decline in DB pension coverage (three years earlier the Association of Consulting Actuaries had concluded that occupational pensions provision in smaller firms had fallen to a level not seen since the 1950s), and an increase in that for DC schemes.[63] Rising longevity, and its implications for future liabilities, were identified as significant contributory factors, but so too was the contribution to emerging scheme deficits of rising costs more generally against a background of more volatile investment returns. We should also note that the effect of making membership of occupational pension schemes voluntary was that barely half of new workers now chose to join their occupational scheme. Most notably, perhaps, employers were seeking to reduce their pension costs by a range of devices including increases to members' contributions, reductions in retirement benefits, and raising retirement ages. Increasingly, however, they were also choosing to close their DB pension scheme to new members as the means by which they might escape from the financial risks embodied in the defined benefit promise. Just over a third of DB schemes closed between 2000 and 2004, affecting 37 per cent of members overall; in the majority of cases a new DC scheme served more recently recruited staff.[64] The more ruthless, or desperate, companies simply closed down their DB scheme, ceasing to allow its active members to continue to accrue benefits (although this was still a relatively rare occurrence, it was becoming more common by 2004). Between 1995 and 2012 private sector membership of occupational schemes (whether DB or DC) fell by 3.5 million, a decline of 56 per cent.[65] Between the Government Actuary's tenth survey of occupational pension schemes, in 1995, and his eleventh report, in 2000, the number of active members in private sector DB schemes declined from 5.2 million to 4.6 million, of which half a million were in closed schemes – a closure rate of 16 per cent in five years. As the Pensions Commission noted in its first report, this was just the start of a closure wave, which accelerated after 2000. A survey by the ACA in 2003 found that 63 per cent of DB schemes had closed to new members, with a further 9 per cent closed to new accruals. The Pensions Commission estimated in 2004 that 60 per cent of active members of DB schemes were in closed schemes.[66]

Blythe notes that it was DB schemes with the highest accrual rates that tended to be targeted for closure, with the result that the overall average employer contribution to DB schemes as a proportion of salary fell.[67] It was in the growing number of DC schemes, however, that employer contributions declined most markedly, with companies using the transition to DC as an opportunity comprehensively to reduce their costs; in consequence, employer contributions per member of staff in a DC scheme were on average more than a third less than those made in DB schemes.[68] Members of DC schemes would therefore inevitably receive a much lower future pension than would have been the case if they had been in a DB scheme. In addition, of course, they were exposed to investment and longevity risks, which the employer bore in a DB scheme. Companies had thus acted to contain the rising costs of their DB pension schemes but in the process the defined benefit ideal had effectively evaporated in the private sector, leaving an increasing number of employees with an inadequate or non-existent occupational pension – a change that ran directly contrary to the Goode Report's endorsement of DB as superior to DC. In its second report, in 2005, the Pensions Commission concluded that the evident reduction in employers' willingness to provide pensions, in conjunction with the problems in personal pensions (which we consider in the next section), meant that voluntary pension provision by employers was by now 'in serious and probably irreversible decline'.[69]

Personal pensions

If government actions in the 1980s had touched off a process of decline in DB pensions, what of personal pensions, which the architects of reform in the 1980s had initially intended would come to replace not just SERPS but also occupational pensions?

Misselling to SERPS members

In late 1986, as the pension industry looked forward to what David Willetts had predicted would be a 'bonanza of business opportunities' in personal pensions, a delegate to a conference at the Institute for International Research commented:

> The Personal Pension had all the ingredients that any marketing man [*sic*] normally dreams about. It was a new opportunity – the first time people had been offered this choice. There was a free offer – the first part of the sell cost the client nothing. There was a bonus too. They normally had to make do with 1% or 2% – 5% was magnificent, 35% for five years was wonderful. And there was a closing date.[70]

For those tasked with selling the new personal pension plans, there was the added allure that two-thirds of employees had (erroneously) become convinced that they would offer them a better deal than a DB occupational pension – having been persuaded by the buzz created by the government and by financial services companies keen to sell them.[71] For the latter, the attraction was enhanced when the government decided not to take powers to

Legacy

restrict charges in the Financial Services Act 1986 (despite the very negative impact of high charges on long-term returns).[72]

Business proved to be brisk once sales of personal pensions began on 1 July 1988, a moment described by the Parliamentary Under-Secretary of State for Social Security, Michael Portillo, as marking 'both the completion and the beginning' of the government's 'pensions revolution'.[73] Within six months life assurance companies had sold more than a million personal pension plans (PPPs), with more than half the sales made to people contracting out of SERPS.[74] The personal pensions revolution was then extended when the Superannuation Funds Office cleared the way in October 1989 for the delivery of Lawson's promise in that year's budget to allow individuals the freedom to manage their own investment under a self-invested personal pension (SIPP) contract – first sold from 1990 – and the realisation of the CPS's vision of giving (at least some) individual pension savers full control over investment.[75] By the start of 1990 it was looking as if the launch of personal pensions had been 'an unqualified success', with more than three and a half million sold, mostly to those contracting out of SERPS, allowing talk of the government presenting a case at the next election that SERPS was no longer needed and could now be phased out.[76]

So successful had the sales effort been, in fact, that the government was now open to attack on the grounds that it had underestimated by a factor of ten the cost to the Exchequer of the associated National Insurance rebates and incentives.[77] That led to accusations that the National Insurance Fund had been 'plundered' to finance an ideological project. These allegations were dismissed by Gillian Shephard (Parliamentary Under-Secretary of State at the Department of Social Security [DSS]) in the House of Commons.[78] Nonetheless, when the National Audit Office (NAO) reported on the cost of the incentive (the 'bribe') in November 1990 it found that firms' success in selling over four million personal pensions to members of SERPS, eight times the DSS's original estimate, meant that the cost of associated rebates and incentives might now reach £9.3 billion, against savings in terms of lower SERPS pensions of just £3.4 billion, giving a net cost of almost £6 billion. Actuarial estimates suggested the cost would be much higher, however, because those contracting out tended to be younger than the NAO assumed, and because they were highly likely to contract back in once the incentive ended, thus radically reducing the future savings in public spending on SERPS.[79]

The high level of PPP sales to SERPS members also raised serious questions about adequacy. One obvious problem was that most of those opting out of SERPS were opting into an extremely minimalist 'appropriate personal pension' alternative. These were simply a vehicle for receiving the National Insurance rebate and incentive payment in a 'protected rights' contract (protected in the sense that it could not be cashed in but had to be used to purchase a pension, but not protected in the sense of guarantees about the level of benefit that would be received). That did not preclude additional contributions, but by late 1993 it was clear that some 60 per cent of personal pensions were not being used to do this.[80] These were thus nugatory savings vehicles, not a recipe for long-term savings towards adequate pensions.

Moreover, many of those tempted into contracting out of SERPS had done so against their own best interests. This was partly a matter of people not understanding the risks they were taking on and partly a consequence of outright misselling. In March 1990 a study by Pensions & Investment Research Consultants suggested that the risk of underperformance was being obscured by providers and that a large minority would end up with lower benefits than they could expect to receive if they stayed in SERPS.[81] Its author, Bryn Davies, noted that the practice of advisers assuming average returns in their marketing and sales processes obscured the inevitable reality of below-average performance by many providers. Even more seriously, Davies argued that providers of PPPs were recommending upper age limits for contracting out of between 45 and 54 for men and 35 and 50 for women, whereas ages of 40 and 30 respectively would have been more realistic. In the same month the Life Assurance and Unit Trust Regulatory Organization (LAUTRO) warned companies against misleading marketing and reminded them that selling a PPP without ensuring that it was fully suitable for the person buying it represented a breach of LAUTRO'S standards of conduct.[82]

Misselling of personal pensions to SERPS members was a particular problem when it came to women, many of whom earned too little to benefit from the incentives otherwise received by those contracting out of SERPS.[83] According to a DSS study in late 1993 (which also revealed that 18 per cent of personal pensions had been sold to customers with no earned income at all), 7 per cent of plans had been sold to individuals not earning enough to pay National Insurance, let alone tax. With such low or no earnings, personal pension saving was clearly inappropriate.[84]

Thus, although sales of personal pensions to members of SERPS had been an outstanding success in volume terms, unscrupulous marketing and dubious sales techniques meant it had been an abject failure when viewed from the perspective of many of those buying them. At least the problem was limited by the 5 April 1989 deadline for opting out of SERPS and receiving the incentive payment, and by the ease of opting back in (albeit without compensation for benefits forgone). The same could not be said of occupational pension scheme members.

Legacy

Misselling to occupational scheme members

Misselling to members of occupational schemes turned out to be a much bigger and more intractable problem, the consequences of what Anthony King and Ivor Crewe identified as a major blunder in the making of UK public policy.[85] Between 1988 and 1993 half a million members of such schemes transferred their assets to personal pension schemes. As many as 90 per cent of those who did so had been given inappropriate advice by high-pressure sales agents.[86]

By 1992, with over 4.5 million personal pensions having been sold, sentiment among providers and consumers alike was becoming much more sceptical. In part, this was because the government cut the National Insurance rebate from April 1992, meaning that between one and one and a half million purchasers of PPPs would be better off contracting back into SERPS. Consequently, the days of the 'something for nothing' marketing of 1988 began to recede into memory.[87] But it was also becoming clear that those who had been persuaded to transfer out of their occupational pension scheme into a PPP were increasingly complaining about poor advice.[88] The problem, first noted by LAUTRO in February 1992, led it to produce new rules in July that effectively banned sales agents from encouraging members of occupational schemes to switch to a personal pension; and it required firms to compensate those who had been improperly switched. One key problem was that around 50,000 such contracts had been terminated within two years of being taken out. This 'poor persistence' phenomenon, as it was known in the industry, was a good sign of misselling – the salesperson having pocketed the commission on the sale with little regard to the likelihood of the customer being able or willing to sustain future payments, let alone build up a fund capable of producing a decent pension.[89]

The blunt truth was that there were almost no circumstances in which selling an occupational pension scheme member a personal pension could be justified, as LAUTRO's guidance to sales agents made clear in 1992. At the end of 1993 that ineluctable fact led LAUTRO to order life companies to review almost half a million such sales with a view to compensation.[90] In short order, and because misselling of personal pensions was not just a problem with the sales forces of life assurance companies but was endemic across both independent financial advisers and tied agents, such as employees of building societies and high street banks, this led the SIB, along with LAUTRO, FIMBRA and IMRO, to form a panel of regulators and life industry representatives to set a uniform standard for determining when an individual had been misadvised and to define how compensation should be calculated.[91] Priority in the review and compensation process was to be given to older consumers who had been persuaded to leave DB schemes offering

330   *Implementation and legacy*

a fully inflation-indexed pension – an indicator of just how unscrupulous some firms and salespeople had been. As the *Financial Times* noted, the SIB's report on PPPs sold to occupational scheme members made 'grim reading', finding that no fewer than 91 per cent of transfers were problematic.[92] An investigation of pensions advice provided by bank and building society tied agents found 'lying by omission' to be endemic among advisers, with 'a widespread attempt to hide the light of the company scheme under a rather large bushel' of the personal pension.[93]

Although a deliberate intention to deceive (either on the part of the company or the salesperson) was a big factor in misselling, incompetent advice was also widespread. Much of the training provided to sales forces was entirely inadequate. As one adviser observed in 1994, they were under considerable pressure to achieve sales targets and knowledge was also poor; although she had not knowingly misled customers, she did not know enough about the products, and particularly about their disadvantages, to offer best advice. She had 'learnt to bluff my way through many situations where clients asked too many technical questions'. The four-week-long product training she had received 'was atrocious', in her view, focused almost entirely on sales techniques rather than on the products being sold, and assessed via 'a half-an-hour test that a monkey could have passed'. Nor were companies necessarily taking on high-quality sales staff. As another adviser observed, companies would 'take on just about anyone as long as they don't have a criminal record'. Moreover, the industry had a high rate of staff turnover, a shortage of experienced staff, and a notably high emphasis on commission earnings – all of which contributed further to misselling.[94] Management failure was thus fundamental to the misselling phenomenon. That this rather obvious fact was finally sinking in by early 1994 became clear when the Norwich Union, a large and respected life assurer, suspended its entire sales force (more than 800 agents) after LAUTRO identified a breakdown in management control, with a fine of £300,000 imposed on the firm by the regulator.[95]

High charges, poor outcomes

Misselling, widely forecast by expert critics of the Thatcher government's personal pension proposals between 1984 and 1986, was not the only issue. Customers were also poorly served by providers in other ways. High costs, driven by undisclosed generous commissions, high administrative charges, poor performance, and misleading benefit statements, were all highlighted by the Carsberg Report in mid-1993.[96] A highly critical report from the IPPR in May 1993 was also withering about marketing costs, commissions, and high administrative fees acting to consume much of the money being paid into personal pensions. Front-loaded charges and commissions, a particular feature of the business, were even more problematic when contributions were ended early, as many were, or the plan was cashed in.[97] Moreover, by mid-1993 it was also clear that unnecessary switching of investments was being widely recommended to customers by advisers in quest of further commission income. This was a mix of encouraging customers to switch providers (ruinously expensive for the customer, since upfront commissions and charges were estimated by Blake to consume between a quarter and a third of the switched sum) and switching between investment options within the personal pension.[98]

In addition to the effect of high charges on fund values, there was also the problem that inadequate contributions to PPPs, as was so often the case, would inevitably produce inadequate pensions.[99] Those on low earnings were, obviously, unable to pay much in. More generally, contribution levels were normally agreed with the adviser based on what the contributor was prepared to pay, without regard to the level of future pension needed. The result, as the editor of *Pensions World* observed in late 1993, was that the success of personal pensions was 'a dangerous mirage'. She rightly concluded that contribution levels were generally 'totally inadequate to fund a comfortable retirement'.[100]

Beyond this, of course, there was also the question of the prospective return on a plan holder's contribution, net of fees, charges, and commissions. Recent research has demonstrated the relatively poor performance of personal pension funds over the long term.[101] Typically, customers were steered into 'medium risk' balanced funds that produced relatively disappointing returns, but there were also huge variations in investment fund performance both between funds and relative to benchmarks. Blake, for example, estimated that the accumulated fund in the top quartile of UK Equity Growth funds would be 3.2 times larger than that in the bottom quartile for the same pattern of contributions over 40 years (different fund choices could produce an even worse result; investing in UK Smaller Companies, for example, would produce a more than fivefold difference).[102] Such variations were not easily understood by customers – indeed, were generally not apparent at all. Even plan holders who opted for an average fund did relatively poorly, but those choosing one of the many 'dog funds' on offer obtained exceptionally poor returns.

Regulatory failure

Plainly, misselling of personal pensions was a major scandal and poor outcomes a major problem. But this was not just a failure of those providing and selling personal pensions; it also amounted to a very serious indictment of

332 *Implementation and legacy*

the regulators. In the early years required standards for PPP sales and marketing were minimal. One head of sales at a firm with a poor track record in personal pension sales sought to wriggle out of criticism by observing that that they could hardly be blamed because '[i]n the past LAUTRO has told us we were well ahead of what was required'.[103] As Kit Jebens, then the chief executive of LAUTRO, said, 'When I joined, the brief I got from the then chief executive was that the industry consisted of good guys with a great deal of integrity – all we need to do is to produce a set of rules.'[104] That faith in the 'good chap' principle had been cruelly exposed as utterly misplaced.

Yet, when regulators and others observed that the government's enthusiasm for personal pensions had contributed to the problem, that was not entirely special pleading. As the Society of Pensions Consultants told the House of Commons' Treasury and Social Security Committees, the fundamental problem lay in the unsafe environment within which personal pensions were sold, one that owed much to the Thatcher governments' antipathy to collective provision and belief in individualisation both as a route to a more flexible labour market and a way of increasing individual freedom and experience of capital ownership.[105]

Given the high number of personal pensions sold, action to curb misselling was very much an exercise in shutting the stable door after the horse had bolted. Moreover, even though the door had been shut, it took a very long time to remedy the problem for those ensnared in the crisis (including those who had been missold FSAVCs, included in the review in 2000). As late as 2002 2 per cent of reviews had yet to lead to an offer of redress, and the Financial Services Authority (FSA) continued to identify new cases.[106] Along the way a succession of firms, many of them household names, had been fined for their tardiness in carrying out reviews. Once completed, over 1.1 million people had been identified as having been wrongly advised, and the cost of redress had risen to nearly £12 billion.[107] In 2001, however, it emerged that up to 25,000 people had received inadequate compensation due to miscalculations on the part of their pension provider.[108] Moreover, it also emerged that those compensated faced significantly reduced pensions because the vast majority could not be reinstated in their original occupational scheme; instead, they simply received a top-up from the insurer reflecting what they would have contributed to their DB scheme had they been in it. Such people were thus left without guarantees and were highly exposed in the event of disappointing investment returns. Nor was there any prospect of further compensation in this event, since they had been required to accept reimbursement as a full and final settlement.[109]

There also turned out to be many problems with the way in which many reviews had been conducted; in 2002, for example, the FSA fined Royal and Sun Alliance for failing to identify 13,500 victims of the misselling scandal.

In addition, the FSA estimated in the same year that between 0.3 million and 2.3 million purchasers of PPPs had simply been overlooked because they had not applied for review.[110] By then, however, there were severe limits on what could be done because many of the firms guilty of misselling had gone out of business. Overall, the debacle had put off those firms that were left from selling personal pensions, and, increasingly, many were directing older policy holders into SERPS for fear that poor returns would leave the firms liable to further accusations of misselling.[111]

Conclusion

The Conservative governments of the 1980s had set out not just to defuse the 'pensions time bomb' of unfunded future state pension commitments but also to reshape pension provision in the United Kingdom in ways that would encourage British workers to secure the income in retirement they desired via prudent saving, in the process converting them to the idea of individual investment in British capitalism. The aim was not simply to slash state pensions but to reconfigure the way in which retirement income was secured by individuals, and, in the process, to encourage higher pension saving that could potentially yield better future pensions while at the same time generating the funds needed to raise private investment in British industry. These hopes were not fulfilled, and the legacy of reform cannot be said to have been a good one.

Market failure

Ministers in the mid-1980s placed enormous faith in the capacity of the market to deliver personal pensions. That faith was misplaced. Companies marketing PPPs turned out to be efficient sellers of pension products but poor providers of pensions. By the first half of the 1990s it had become clear that the millions of SERPS members tempted into personal pensions had not been well served. This was even clearer in the case of those unfortunate enough to have been tempted out of occupational pensions (with generous defined benefits) into risky DC personal pensions. More conservative sections of the pension industry had in the lead-up to the 1986 legislation warned ministers about the potential for misselling; they were ignored. In the event, far too many companies and their sales agents proved to be more concerned with making the sale than with considering whether the product being sold was appropriate for the customer. Moreover, although ministers had disregarded widespread expert warnings about the likely inadequacy of personal pensions, their record did prove to be a poor one. Charges were high, investment performance was typically relatively poor, and contributions were too often agreed with the customer without regard for the retirement income that they would need. The market, in short, did not deliver decent personal pensions as ministers had expected.

As we have seen, market failure also became an increasing problem in the field of occupational pensions. Employers and the state, both dazzled by the large financial 'surpluses' that DB schemes were apparently piling up, sought to tap the funds: via contribution holidays and, sometimes, outright asset stripping on the part of employers; and via tweaks by successive governments to degrade the sector's tax advantages. Both sponsoring companies and the state were thus guilty of losing sight of the long-term nature of pensions, the inevitable future pressure of ageing baby boomers on the support ratio, future pressures of rising longevity, and the possibility that the short-term outperformance of underlying fund investments in the mid- to late 1980s would not be sustained. When companies substituted DC for DB, contributions were far too low to deliver a decent pension in retirement given the longevity and investment risk the member was taking on, not least because firms typically used the transfer to DC as the moment to cut their own contribution. The market for occupational pensions thus also failed. It did so overwhelmingly because of greed, short-termism, and myopia on the part of government and the companies running workplace pensions.

Regulatory failure

One reason for market failure was that controls over companies selling personal pensions and those overseeing occupational schemes were poorly designed by government. Initially, regulation was at once 'light touch' in nature but surprisingly complex, with regulatory responsibility divided between numerous bodies, both public and private. Thus, for example, the report by the SIB chairman, Andrew Large, on investment regulation, commissioned by Lamont in the wake of the Maxwell affair, though hardly the most objective analysis of the many failings in the regulatory apparatus set up by the Financial Services Act 1986, did highlight among other problems of self-regulation the sheer complexity of pensions regulation.[112] The Goode Report of 1993 also called for simplification.[113]

Calls for a simpler regulatory system were greeted with scepticism given that Fowler too had wanted this and the fact that the 1984 Gower Report's proposals for streamlining and improving investor protection had, as the editor of *Pensions World* observed, 'been transformed by legislation into the infamous, complex and immensely costly Financial Services Act' of 1986.[114] The sceptics had a point. Although the 1990s did see some consolidation of regulatory institutions, the market failure evident in both personal and occupational pensions produced a steady stream of new regulation designed both to secure and, in the occupational DB pensions arena, to improve benefits. These changes made pensions administration ever more complex, however, and thus ever more expensive. Personal pensions, thereby, became even less likely to generate the necessary retirement income for the plan holder. Well-intended measures to improve occupational pension benefits added costs even as a new era of lower investment returns made providing an occupational pension much more expensive for employers. In a looser and much more flexible labour market than in the heyday of DB, firms increasingly sought to move their staff into DC schemes – much riskier for the individual but much cheaper to run for the employer because of the lack of guarantee and the fact that they, typically, slashed their contribution. Sometimes, of course, the employer just got out of the occupational pensions business entirely. Ironically, therefore, greater regulation seeking to secure and even improve benefits served to degrade the quality of voluntary pension provision across the board. More than this, however, growing evidence of market failure coupled with the now extraordinary complexity of the British pensions landscape served to alienate workers and consumers. In his 2002 review for the Treasury, for example, Ron Sandler noted that consumers' loss of faith in long-term savings vehicles, including pensions, was acute and exacerbated by both their complexity and opacity.[115]

An early essay into pension policy by the new Labour government in 1998, the *Partnership in Pensions* Green Paper, noted that the improvement in pensioner incomes since 1979 had been driven by occupational pensions but that the 1986 reforms had served to degrade the acquisition of SERPS benefits for future pensioners. It noted too that personal pensions provided poor value if contributions were terminated (as was the case in a third of contracts) or irregular (an especial problem for women, as we have seen), and that high charges also reduced the value of the accumulated fund. Labour's Green Paper also acknowledged that personal pension contributions by low earners were inevitably too low to generate a worthwhile pension, with up to four million people earning between £9,000 and £20,000 a year paying only the compulsory minimum contribution. It also observed that trust in personal pensions had been badly dented by the misselling scandal, and that the Maxwell affair had eroded trust in the DB pensions system. Understanding of pensions was also low.[116]

Yet, in retrospect, Labour remained remarkably and somewhat naively positive about personal pensions. Having essentially accepted the Conservatives' recipe for improving pensions provision the new Labour government sought merely to tinker with the system (via the replacement of SERPS by a new State Second Pension, with better benefit accumulation, and 'stakeholder pensions', as a rebranded but also lower-cost alternative to

336 *Implementation and legacy*

PPPs). As the new century neared, therefore, Labour was not yet prepared to confront the manifest failings in personal pensions nor the growing evidence that employers were giving up on their voluntary provision of DB pensions and opting instead for lower-cost, and lower-benefit, DC pensions or exiting provision entirely. It was not until the Pensions Commission was established in December 2002, after a further four years of manifest failure, that a more sceptical approach to voluntarism became evident.

Political failure

Thus, the cumulative effect of reforms to pensions in the 1980s was to degrade prospective pensions in all elements of the system: SERPS benefits would be lower by design; occupational pension benefits would be lower because employers increasingly intended to withdraw from DB provision, at best closing their schemes to new entrants and substituting less generous and more risky DC arrangements; and personal pensions were now viewed with increasing scepticism by consumers as a result of misselling, the effects of high fees on investment performance, and growing evidence that on average the resulting pension would be low. Most workers were therefore facing a much more penurious old age than they would have wished for, or than they could reasonably have expected at the start of the 1980s.

Conservative ministers and their advisers in the mid-1980s had obviously not anticipated this outcome. The principal architects of reform had intended that good-quality personal pensions would, over time, effectively dominate pension provision in the United Kingdom, with SERPS at worst a rump scheme paying minimal benefits and at best abolished, and DB occupational schemes losing out in the market to superior personal pensions. Their dream of entirely individualising pension savings via personal pensions had died in hard bargaining within Whitehall in 1985–86 in the face of overwhelming opposition to revolutionary reform from virtually all external stakeholders – most devastatingly from firms providing financial services – as well as from the Treasury. The No. 10 Policy Unit had seen the failure of its attempt to abolish SERPS as a clear retreat from its neoliberal vision.

Norman Fowler had warned that the U-turn away from revolutionary to evolutionary neoliberal reform in 1985 carried with it the danger of compromises that might produce 'the worst of both worlds'.[117] His description turned out to be apposite, and was frequently used by later commentators, for, by adding personal pensions as another element within the country's pension system while simultaneously weakening its other elements, Britain ended up with a pension system that was at once the most Byzantine ('a maze of such complexity that users cannot make sensible decisions about their own lives') and among the least generous of any of the world's developed economies.[118]

Legacy   337

Was this the consequence of a failure by ministers to grasp the nettle of revolutionary reform, as the Policy Unit believed in 1986? Or, instead, was this outcome not virtually inevitable given the PU's surprisingly limited grasp of institutional and economic realities, including a misunderstanding of the profit motive in business, and its naive faith that individual pension saving in the market would get the state off the hook of future public pensions spending commitments even as British workers were reconfigured as well-informed investor capitalists?

Notes

1 Antoine Bozio, Rowena Crawford, and Gemma Tetlow, *The History of State Pensions in the UK: 1948–2010* (London: Institute for Fiscal Studies, 2010), pp. 35–36.
2 Note that the pension received would have been a lower percentage of average earnings than indicated in Figure 8.1, for its underlying assumptions that the individual would have been on average full-time earnings throughout their working life and possess a full contribution record would be a most untypical experience for any worker, and especially for a woman.
3 Department of Health and Social Security, *Better Pensions – Fully Protected against Inflation: Proposals for a New Pensions Scheme*, Cmnd 5713 (London: HMSO, 1974), pp. 2, 18.
4 At the lowest level of earnings, the proportion would rise to over 90 per cent; equally, at higher levels of earnings the proportion would fall. See ibid., pp. 3–4 (para. 8), 6; Bryan Ellis, *Pensions in Britain, 1955–1975: A History in Five Acts* (London: HMSO, 1989), p. 50.
5 *Financial Times*, 'The Strange Death of a Pension Scheme', by Richard Disney and Paul Johnson, 3 February 1995.
6 HL Debs, 24 January 1995, vol. 560, col. 980.
7 Cmnd 5713, appendix: 'Memorandum by the Government Actuary on the Finances of the Proposals', tab. 1, p. 27.
8 Bozio, Crawford, and Tetlow, *The History of State Pensions in the UK*, p. 64.
9 Pensions Commission, *Pensions: Challenges and Choices: The First Report the Pensions Commission* (London: TSO, 2004), p. 26.
10 HC Debs, 17 July 1996, vol. 281, col. 1159. Later that year the House of Commons Social Security Committee, chaired by the Labour MP Frank Field, argued that the United Kingdom's success in holding down public pension liabilities as compared with other members of the European Union was an argument not to participate in European monetary union, lest the country find itself called upon to finance the unfunded pensions of other, more profligate, member states (HC 23 (1996–97), Social Security Committee, First Report, 'Unfunded Pension Liabilities in the European Union', 1996–97, 23 October 1996, para. 3).
11 In the British context, on the eve of the Pensions Commission's second report the then Pensions Minister noted at the start of a keynote speech to the IPPR

that security in old age was, 'without doubt, one of the most important public policy challenges facing the country'. John Hutton, *Securing Our Future: The Pensions Challenge* (London: Institute for Public Policy Research, 2005), p. 1. On the nature and historical roots of the crisis in Britain, with comparisons to other European welfare states, see Hugh Pemberton, Pat Thane, and Noel Whiteside, ed., *Britain's Pensions Crisis: History and Policy* (Oxford: Oxford University Press, 2006).

12 World Bank, *Averting the Old Age Crisis* (Oxford: Oxford University Press, 1994), pp. 16, 105.

13 *The Times*, 'Europe's Pensions Time Bomb', by Tim Congdon, 1 March 1997; *Daily Telegraph*, 'Europe Facing Pension Crisis, Says Hague', by Andrew Sparrow, 21 May 1999. In 1996 *The Economist* ('Thinking the Unthinkable', 27 April, pp. 32–36) praised the United Kingdom as 'uniquely well placed' when compared with other countries' prospective public spending on pensions – despite acknowledging that one reason for this was that the BSP could end up being worth just 8 per cent of average earnings by 2030. Likewise, a month beforehand Peter Lilley, then Secretary of State for Social Security, had boasted that the country was 'uniquely placed' to deal with the 'fiscal time bomb' faced by countries in the rest of Europe with unreformed pay-as-you-go pension schemes (*Pensions World*, April 1996, pp. 61–62).

14 Labour Party, *New Labour: Because Britain Deserves Better* (London: Labour Party, 1997).

15 New Labour's favourite think tank, the IPPR, concluded that a means-tested 'minimum income guarantee' was a flawed strategy due to low take-up; the only solution was to address the problem at source by raising the BSP to a level that people could actually live on it. See Richard Brooks, Sue Regan, and Peter Robinson, *A New Contract for Retirement* (London: Institute for Public Policy Research, 2002), pp. 36–39, 108–10.

16 Pensions Commission, *A New Pensions Settlement for the Twenty-First Century: The Second Report of the Pensions Commission* (London: TSO, 2005). Although it had been asked by the government to review the United Kingdom's system of private pension provision, the Pensions Commission had wisely reinterpreted its terms of reference as extending to reviewing the state pension system, and the interactions between these different means of receiving an income in old age.

17 Pensions Commission, *First Report*, pp. ix–x, 132.

18 Peter Blythe, 'Why Did UK Private Sector Defined Benefit Occupational Pension Schemes Grow So Strongly in the Middle Years of the Twentieth Century, Then Decline So Rapidly at the End of the Century and the Beginning of the Twenty First?' (PhD, King's College London, 2021). Blythe's thesis is rich in data, some of which has been used to inform the analysis in this section.

19 Confederation of British Industry and Clay & Partners, *Occupational Pension Schemes: Securing the Future* (London: Confederation of British Industry, 1992). It is noteworthy that the CBI perspective here was concerned with the management of inflation risk from the employee's perspective, not from that of the employer.

20 Blythe, 'Why Did?', p. 152.

21 The occupational pensions sector's enthusiastic embrace of more professionalisation and the provision of better-defined benefits can be seen in the pages of *Pensions World* throughout the decade. Note that the improvement in benefits was not driven by competitive pressures within the labour market, given the much higher rates of unemployment that obtained after 1979, but by a continuing paternalistic desire to take care of employees.

22 *Financial Times*, 'SIB Orders Fresh Study of Opt-Out Sales', by Alison Smith, 28 April 1994.

23 Blythe, 'Why Did?', pp. 153–54.

24 Djuna Thurley, 'Occupational Pension Increases', Briefing Paper 5656 (London: House of Commons Library, 2021), pp. 15–16. Once retired, for pensions in payment the only legal requirement between 1978 and 1997 was to index the GMP (which represented a relatively small proportion of the overall DB pension entitlement, and much of the cost of indexation was borne by the government). A 1983 study found that only a third of pensioners were entitled to a guaranteed annual increase to an occupational pension in payment (and just 2 per cent to an increase linked to RPI or LPI); but by 1995 these figures were 81 and 52 per cent respectively. These improvements represented a significant and entirely voluntary improvement in benefits by employers, but, of course, they still left many excluded from such guarantees. See Blythe, 'Why Did?', pp. 146–52.

25 Blythe, 'Why Did?', pp. 155–62.

26 Pensions Commission, *First Report*, p. xi. Across the 1980s the FTSE All Share Index rose more than fivefold (a compound rate of 18 per cent a year), comfortably outpacing total inflation of 95 per cent (John Littlewood, *The Stock Market: 50 Years of Capitalism at Work* (London: Financial Times, 1998), p. 410). By 1989 the market value of UK securities held by pension funds had risen eightfold, reaching £165 billion, compared with £19 billion in 1979. By 1990 the funds owned 31.4 per cent of all the shares listed on the London Stock Exchange. See HC 61, House of Commons' Select Committee on Social Security, Second Report, *The Operation of Pension Funds* (London: House of Commons, 1992), p. ix.

27 *Financial Times*, 'Two Fifths of Employers Taking Pensions Holiday', by Eric Short, 25 November 1988; Henry L. James (director general, NAPF), 'Uncharted Waters', *Pensions World*, April 1990.

28 Sue Ward, 'Equality – No Holding Back!', *Pensions World*, May 1991, pp. 59–62.

29 Pensions Commission, *First Report*, pp. 34, 124.

30 Ibid., p. 124.

31 *Financial Times*, 'Who Gets What in Pensions', by Barry Riley, 23/24 May 1992.

32 A spirited attack on Brown can be found in Alex Brummer, *The Great Pensions Robbery* (London: Random House, 2010). Though journalistic and guilty of underestimating the scale of earlier 'asset stripping' of fund surpluses, it is both entertaining and powerful in how it puts the case that Brown's action inevitably weakened the long-term sustainability of occupational pension promises.

33 The 'bid fever' that characterised the five years from 'Big Bang' in 1987 is well described by Littlewood, *The Stock Market: 50 Years of Capitalism at Work*. Although he does not identify fund surpluses as a factor, the Bank of England did find that financial surpluses in the target company were a significant factor in 1980s takeovers (Bank of England, *Quarterly Bulletin*, Q1, 1989, pp. 85–87). The problem continued for many years. For example, the acquisition of British Home Stores and its pensions scheme by Philip Green in 2000 and subsequent disposal for just £1 in 2015 was described as ' "lawful" looting' by Ian Clark, 'The British Home Stores Pension Scheme: Privatised Looting?', *Industrial Relations Journal*, 50 (2019). As fund surpluses evaporated, however, the existence of a deficit in a company pension fund increasingly became a 'poison pill' discouraging potential buyers: Jayesh Kumar, 'Impact of Pension Plan Funding Status on M&A Activity', Technical Paper 2006-TR-05 (London: Watson Wyatt, 2006).

34 The collapse of Belling in 1992, for example, revealed the extent to which it had abused its trusteeship of the company pension fund to support the company's share price. See Cm 2342, Royston Goode, *Pension Law Reform: The Report of the Pension Law Review Committee* [the Goode Report] (London: HMSO, 1993), para. 4.10.11.

35 The best analyses of Maxwell are Tom Bower, *Maxwell: The Final Verdict* (London: HarperCollins, 1995); and John Preston, *Fall: The Mystery of Robert Maxwell* (London: Penguin Books, 2020).

36 The modus operandi were clear early on in the enquiries of the Select Committee on Social Security, which on 4 February 1992 was told by trustees of the Mirror Group Newspapers pension scheme (which had been left with a £38 million hole in its fund) that Maxwell had not just stopped contributions but also made fund investment decisions personally even though he was not authorised to conduct investment business (*Financial Times*, 'Unauthorised Decisions on Pensions by Maxwell', by Norma Cohen, 5 February 1992). The scale of the consequent alteration in pension fund investment was extraordinary; in seven years the fund had been transformed from one focused on UK blue chip stocks to one with none among its top 20 holdings (*Financial Times*, 'Questions over the Maxwell Pension Funds', by Norma Cohen, 22 January 1992). Within a month of Maxwell's death the DHSS had activated a clause in the 1990 Social Security Act, which had yet to come into force, to require pension scheme trustees to cap investment in the controlling company at 5 per cent of total assets (*Financial Times*, 'Government to Restrict Pension Fund Investment', by Ivo Dawnay, 6 December 1991).

37 HC 61, *The Operation of Pension Funds*, p. xxii. The number of pensioners potentially affected is from Bower, *Maxwell: The Final Verdict*, p. 50.

38 The Social Security Committee observed that 'Pontius Pilate would have blushed at the spectacle of so many witnesses washing their hands in public before the Committee of their responsibilities in this affair': HC 61, *The Operation of Pension Funds*, para. 173.

39 HC 61, *The Operation of Pension Funds*, p. vi.

40 Ibid.

Legacy 341

41 HC Debs, 8 June 1992, vol. 209, col. 19.

42 Cm 2342.

43 Gordon L. Clark, *Pension Fund Capitalism* (Oxford: Oxford University Press, 2000), p. 54.

44 Stephanie Hawthorne, 'The Road to Hell Is Paved ...', *Pensions World*, November 1993, pp. 15–20. In the same issue, see also Robin Ellison, 'A Goode Result', pp. 63–5.

45 David Blake, *Pension Schemes and Pension Funds in the United Kingdom* (Oxford: Clarendon Press, 2003), p. 356.

46 As Gower later observed, the 1986 legislation was 'a total disaster' and a missed opportunity (quoted in Terry Arthur, 'Pensions and Public Choice: The Road to Myners', *Economic Affairs*, 22 (2002), p. 43). The report itself is L. C. B. Gower, *Review of Investor Protection*, Part 1, Cmnd 9125 (London: HMSO, 1984).

47 Sue Ward, 'Regulation of Pensions in the UK', in *The Role of the State in Pension Provision: Employer, Regulator, Provider*, ed. by Gerard Hughes and Jim Stewart (Boston: Springer, 1999), pp. 63–73, at p. 66; Robin Blackburn, *Banking on Death or Investing in Life: The History and Future of Pensions* (London: Verso, 2002), p. 138.

48 Blythe, 'Why Did?', pp. 251–57.

49 HM Treasury Private Office papers (hereafter HMT): PO-CH NL 0147 Part A, P. J. Cropper to Lawson, 'Letter from Sir Keith Joseph', 3 July 1987. The tax advantages enjoyed by pensions funds were the subject of an attack by Philip Chappell in a 1988 CPS pamphlet, which described the funds as latter-day barons that had developed an 'immoderate greatness' undiluted by the changes of the past five years: Philip Chappell, *Pensions and Privilege: How to End the Scandal, Simplify Taxes and Widen Ownership* (London: Centre for Policy Studies, 1988).

50 Nigel Lawson, *The View from No. 11: Memoirs of a Tory Radical* (London: Bantam Press, 1992), p. 368.

51 HC Debs, 17 March 1987, vol. 112, col. 825. A parallel change to the new FSAVCs saw Lawson remove the ability to take a tax-free lump sum from them (it would have to come solely from the main pension) in combination with contribution limits and restrictions on the value of an overall pension, the complex assessment of which would fall to the company scheme, not the Inland Revenue. This rendered FSAVCs virtually unworkable, as well as ensuring that the take-up of what had been seen as an attractive prospect for employees would be predictably low: *Financial Times*, 'Taxman Scuppers Freedom of Choice', by Eric Short, 8 August 1987).

52 A detailed analysis of the various changes can be found in Alan Maxwell, 'The Finance Act, 1987', *Pensions World*, August 1987, pp. 596–600.

53 In its pamphlet 'Truth, Honour and Democracy: The Finance Bill 1989' (London: NAPF, 1989), the NAPF accused Lawson of going back on a 1985 promise to issue a Green Paper before undertaking any fundamental reform of pensions taxation: *Financial Times*, 'Pensions Tax Relief Limit Attacked', by Eric Short, 31 May 1989; see also a comment piece by Peter Stirrup, the

342   *Implementation and legacy*

incoming chair of the NAPF: 'Taking Up the Cudgels', *Pensions World*, June 1989.

54 Blythe, 'Why Did?', p. 175.

55 *Pensions World*'s July and August 1989 issues contain several articles about that year's budget's measures relating to pensions and the passage of the Finance Act. On the impact of the change to allow contracted-out DC schemes, see, especially, the perspective a year later in Adrian Mathias, 'The Money Purchase Takeover?', *Pensions World*, August 1990.

56 The problem is nicely encapsulated by *Financial Times*, 'Tighter Tax Lid for Pensions Honeypot', by Clive Wolman, 22 February 1988.

57 The figure for the dividend reduction (as a consequence of funds now being able to claim only 20 per cent rather than 25 per cent of ACT) is from a more detailed discussion in 'Budget Hammers Pension Funds', *Pensions World*, April 1993, p. 5 – which also notes that the reduction would serve to reduce and potentially eliminate fund surpluses.

58 'ACT: The Chancellor Has Stolen All the Credit', *Pensions World*, August 1997, p. 9. A year earlier the NAPF director general had decried the 1993 restriction of ACT credits as a stealth tax eroding the tax structure of occupational pensions (Ann Robinson, 'A Taxing Subject', *Pensions World*, October 1996, p. 3). In the wake of Brown's abolition of the credit she observed: 'With a few simple words, the Chancellor, Gordon Brown demolished a large part of one of the central planks of the tax regime which underpins the UK's huge voluntary pensions savings movement' (Ann Robinson, 'Caught in the ACT', *Pensions World*, August 1997, p. 3).

59 *Pensions World*, August 1997, p. 9.

60 Blythe, 'Why Did?', p. 224; Blake, *Pension Schemes and Pension Funds in the United Kingdom*, pp. 388–89. The implications of FRS 17 are discussed in more detail in Geoffrey Whittington, 'Accounting Standards for Pension Costs', in *The Oxford Handbook of Pensions and Retirement Income*, ed. by Gordon. L. Clark, Alicia H. Munnell, and J. Michael Orszag (Oxford: Oxford University Press, 2006), pp. 521–38.

61 Confederation of British Industry and Clay & Partners, *Occupational Pension Schemes: Securing the Future*; Blythe, 'Why Did?', pp. 140–41.

62 Nigel Vinson, 'Going for Broke', *Pensions World*, January 1996, pp. 25–28

63 Association of Consulting Actuaries, *Pensions in Smaller Firms Survey 2001: Occupational Pensions: The End of an Era?* (London: Association of Consulting Actuaries, 2001).

64 Government Actuary, *Occupational Pension Schemes 2004: Twelfth Survey by the Government Actuary* (London: Government Actuary's Department, 2005), pp. 44–48. On the implications of voluntary DB scheme membership, see David Blake, 'The UK Pension System: Key Issues', *Pensions: An International Journal*, 8 (2003), p. 334; Richard Disney and Gary Stears, 'Why Is There a Decline in Defined Benefit Pension Plan Membership in Britain?', Working Paper 96/04 (London: Institute for Fiscal Studies, 1996); Association of Consulting Actuaries, *Pensions in Smaller Firms Survey 2001: Occupational*

Pensions: The End of an Era?; and Blake, *Pension Schemes and Pension Funds in the United Kingdom*, pp. 367–68.

65 Blythe, 'Why Did?', p. 192. Blythe notes that the situation was worse than this headline figure implies due to ONS's 2000 recategorisation from private to public sector of organisation such as the Post Office, BBC, and passenger transport authorities (he estimates that at least 214,000 scheme members were so reclassified). The giant Universities' Superannuation Scheme, which had always been categorised as private in this schema, was also growing strongly in this period, thus offsetting the decline of 'pure' private sector occupational pension scheme membership.

66 Pensions Commission, *First Report*, p. 85.

67 Blythe, 'Why Did?', pp. 222–30.

68 The Pensions Commission (*First Report*, p. 88) reported in 2004 that employer DB contributions were broadly in the range 11 to 14 per cent of salary, whereas those to DC were around 7 to 11 per cent. Contributions from employees were also lower, meaning that the total contributions were in the ranges 16 to 20 per cent and 7 to 11 per cent respectively – with all that this implied for the level of DC members' future pensions.

69 Ibid., p. 85; Pensions Commission, *Second Report*, p. 2.

70 *Pensions World*, 'Personal Pensions Opportunities', January 1987, pp. 42–48.

71 *Financial Times*, 'Poll Shows Staff Prefer Private Pensions', by Eric Short, 16 April 1987. Just 20 per cent thought that a workplace pension would be better.

72 Blake, 'The UK Pension System: Key Issues', p. 335.

73 *Pensions World*, 'Pensions Revolution Underway?', August 1988. 'The beginning' because, as Portillo went on to explain, there was 'a long way to go yet' in a process by which the government hoped over time to 'break the habit of passive reliance, either on the state or on an employer'.

74 *Financial Times*, 'Life Groups Sell 1m Personal Pensions', by Eric Short, 11 February 1989. The business was worth £809 million in premium income, excluding National Insurance rebates.

75 *Financial Times*, 'Path Cleared for Pension Fund Freedom', by Eric Short, 12 October 1989.

76 *Financial Times*, 'You Get What You Pay For', by Eric Short, 20 January 1990. As Short had observed earlier, sales of PPPs to those wishing to contract out of SERPS could have been even higher but for the fact that so many workers didn't realise they were in it (*Financial Times*, 'Deadline on Pensions Nears', 25 March 1989).

77 'Already £1.5 billion has been frittered away on this ill-considered ideological venture, which will rise to more than £3 billion by 1993,' observed Michael Meacher; quoted in Sue Ward, 'Shuffling the Pack', *Pensions World*, January 1990.

78 HC Debs, 3 April 1990, cols. 1122–25.

79 National Audit Office, *The Elderly: Information Requirements for Supporting the Elderly and Implications of Personal Pensions for the National Insurance*

344   *Implementation and legacy*

Fund (London: HMSO, 1990), para. 14; *Financial Times*, 'Footing the Pensions Bill', by Eric Short, 15 December 1990.

80 *Financial Times*, 'Pensions Switch May Have Cost Taxpayers £1.3bn', by Norma Cohen, 28 February 1994.

81 Pensions & Investment Research Consultants, 'Approved Personal Pensions: Advice Given on Contracting Out', Pension Services Report 1 (London: PIRC, 1990). The report estimated that 30 per cent of men who chose a personal pension at age 30 would end up with lower benefits than if they had stayed in SERPS. It is usefully summarised in *Pensions World*, 'A Right Honourable Skirmish', by Sue Ward, April 1990, pp. 55–56.

82 *Financial Times*, 'Lautro Warns Life Companies', by Eric Short, 14 March 1990. The warning was contained in LAUTRO's Enforcement Bulletin no. 7.

83 *Financial Times*, 'Poor Advice on Pensions Feared for 1m Women', by Norma Cohen, 18 December 1993.

84 Ibid.

85 Anthony King and Ivor Crewe, *The Blunders of Our Governments* (London: Oneworld, 2013), pp. 65–78.

86 *Financial Times*, 'Regulating the Pensions Revolution', by Eric Short, 13 April 1987; Blake, 'The UK Pension System: Key Issues', p. 334.

87 *Financial Times*, 'Personal Pensions Fervour Cools Off', by Debbie Harrison, 15 February 1992.

88 *Financial Times*, 'Steep Rise in Complaints over Life Assurance Sales', by Norma Cohen, 18 February 1992.

89 *Financial Times*, 'Watchdog Seeks Pensions Review', 16 July 1992.

90 *Financial Times*, 'Insurance Companies Will Have to Review 5m Pensions', by Norma Cohen, 15 November 1993.

91 *Financial Times*, 'Pensions Probe after Fears over Bad Sales Advice', by Norma Cohen and Alison Smith, 3 December 1993.

92 *Financial Times*, 'Grim Litany of Pension Faults', by Alison Smith, 18 December 1993.

93 *Pensions World*, 'Streetwise', by Rachel Pope, March 1994, 19.

94 *Financial Times*, 'Short Lautro Test that "a Monkey Could Pass"', by Peter Marsh, 24 March 1994.

95 *Financial Times*, 'Norwich Union Suspends Pensions Direct Sales Force', by Alison Smith, 30 March 1994; and 'Norwich Union Fined £300,000', by Alison Smith, 30 April 1994.

96 Sir Bryan Carsberg, *Financial Services Act 1986: The Marketing and Sale of Investment-Linked Insurance Products: The Rules of the Securities and Investments Board and the Life Assurance and Unit Trust Regulatory Organisation, a Report to the Chancellor of the Exchequer by the Director General of Fair Trading* (London: Office of Fair Trading, 1993).

97 Based on firms' published information on the impact of expenses on yields, which he rightly thought underestimated the problem, they would on average consume up to 20 per cent of total contributions over a lifetime, and considerably more for a lower earner facing fixed charges: Bryn Davies, *Better Pensions for All* (London: Institute for Public Policy Research, 1993), pp. 27–29.

A slightly more optimistic estimate of 10 to 20 per cent, produced by the Institute of Actuaries, is cited by David Blake, 'Does It Matter What Type of Pension Scheme You Have?', *The Economic Journal*, 110 (2000), F57. Like Davies, however, Blake's own estimate was at the upper end of that band.

98 *Financial Times*, 'Pensions Alert over Spread of "Churning"', by Barbara Ellis, 8 May 1993; Blake, 'Does It Matter What Type of Pension Scheme You Have?', F58. The impact of switching from DB was even greater, at 61 to 68 percent.

99 Philip E. Davis, 'Is There a Pensions Crisis in the UK?', *Geneva Papers on Risk and Insurance Issues and Practice*, 29 (2004), p. 357.

100 Stephanie Hawthorne, 'The Pensions Time Bomb', *Pensions World*, November 1993, p. 3. See also Davies, *Better Pensions for All*.

101 Anastasia Petraki and Anna Zalewska, 'Jumping over a Low Hurdle: Personal Pension Fund Performance', *Review of Quantitative Finance and Accounting*, 48 (2017). Their conclusions are distinctly more negative than an earlier study: Alan Gregory and Ian Tonks, 'Performance of Personal Pension Schemes in the UK', Research Paper 06/11 (Exeter: University of Exeter, Xfi Centre for Finance and Investment, 2006). The latter had a narrower focus, however, being principally interested in the persistence of under- and overperformance between a narrower range of funds.

102 Blake, 'Does It Matter What Type of Pension Scheme You Have?', F71.

103 *Financial Times*, 'Short Lautro Test that "a Monkey Could Pass"'.

104 *Financial Times*, 'Slow Response by Regulators Is Exposed', by Alison Smith, 1 March 1994.

105 *Pensions World*, 'SIB and SPC Offer Transfer Solutions', May 1994, p. 7.

106 FSA Summary Annual Report, 2001/2, June 2002, p. 35 [https://webarchive.nationalarchives.gov.uk/ukgwa/20081231204446mp_/www.fsa.gov.uk/pubs/annual/ar01_02summary.pdf, accessed 20 January 2022]; and address by Howard Davies to the annual meeting of the FSA, 18 July 2002 [https://webarchive.nationalarchives.gov.uk/ukgwa/20081231082812/www.fsa.gov.uk/Pages/Library/Communication/Speeches/2002/SP102.shtml, accessed 20 January 2022].

107 FSA Annual Report, 2003/4, June 2004, p. 31 [https://webarchive.nationalarchives.gov.uk/ukgwa/20081231205428mp_/www.fsa.gov.uk/pubs/annual/ar03_04/ar03_04.pdf, accessed 20 January 2022].

108 *Financial Times*, 'More Cash for Many Who Were Mis-sold Pensions', 24 March 2001. The year beforehand the Treasury had won a Whitehall battle limiting compensation to widows facing big losses of income because of their late husband having contracted out of SERPS as a result of misselling; see *Financial Times*, 'Treasury Wins Whitehall Fight to Cut Pensions Scandal Costs', by Nicholas Timmins, 14 March 2000. This even though the Exchequer had received an unexpected bonus as a result of those who had been misled into opting out of SERPs being contracted back in and their contributions made up (*Financial Times*, 'Brown to Reap £3bn Pension "Windfall"', by Nicholas Timmins, 2 October 1999).

109 *Financial Times*, 'Victims of Mis-selling Face Another Blow', by Nic Cicutti, 17 August 2002.

346 *Implementation and legacy*

110 *Financial Times*, 'Fewer than Expected Take Up Pensions Review Offers', by Nic Cicutti, 31 August 2002.

111 *Financial Times*, 'Spectre of Mis-selling Prompts Rethink on SERPS', by Nic Cicutti, 14 March 2002.

112 *Financial Times*, 'Large Urges Clampdown on Investment Fraud', by Robert Peston, 26 May 1993. For the full report, see Andrew Large, *Financial Services Regulation: Making the Two Tier System Work* (London: Securities and Investment Board, 1993). On Large's unsuitability for the role given his obvious vested interest, and on the regime's many problems, see Jimmy M. Hinchliffe, 'The Financial Services Act: A Case Study in Regulatory Capture' (PhD, Sheffield Hallam University, 1999).

113 Cm 2342.

114 Hawthorne, 'The Road to Hell Is Paved ...', pp. 15–20.

115 Ron Sandler, *Sandler Review: Medium and Long-Term Retail Savings in the UK* (London: HM Treasury, 2002). Sandler estimated that the result was an aggregate shortfall of 20 per cent of annual savings, amounting to £27 billion. Optimistically, as the route to lower charges he recommended a 'lighter touch' regime for sales and advice on investment products, as well as greater competition between providers. More usefully, perhaps, he endorsed the government's planned simplification of the eight extant pension tax regimes.

116 Department of Social Security, *A New Contract for Welfare: Partnership in Pensions*, Cm 4179 (London: Department of Social Security, 1998), pp. 11, 19, 24, 26–27.

117 The National Archive: PREM 1640, Redwood to Thatcher, 'MISC 111', 14 October 1985; ibid., Fowler to Thatcher, 'Social Security Review', 26 April 1985.

118 Howard Glennerster, 'Why So Different? Why So Bad a Future?', in *Britain's Pensions Crisis: History and Policy*, ed. by Hugh Pemberton, Pat Thane, and Noel Whiteside (Oxford: Oxford University Press, 2006), pp. 64–73, at p. 66; Pensions Commission, *First Report*, pp. 58, 80.

Conclusion

Attempts to write histories of neoliberalism are now caught between the greater complexity introduced by new accounts of its intellectual development and the legacy of its more monolithic conceptualisations. The last 15 years have seen necessary challenges to the impression that neoliberal intellectuals subscribed to a single, unchanging body of thought and the view that all economic, social, political, and cultural transformations experienced since the late 1970s can be attributed to a common project. Scholars have rightly emphasised the evolving strands of thinking within a 'neoliberal thought collective' rather than a single body of thought, as well as the specificity of the national contexts and party traditions through which some of these ideas were refracted across the political spectrum.[1] They have also placed the arguments and political project of neoliberal intellectuals within the wider stories of twentieth-century history.[2] Others have reminded us that appearances can be deceiving; some of what we might habitually attribute to neoliberalism actually represents the revival of older ideas, the continuation of trends, or something else entirely.[3] Others still have begun to surface the capacity of neoliberal thought to justify policies that do not fit the stereotypical image of market fundamentalism as well as the wider cast of actors and institutions involved in its dissemination and enactment.[4]

Yet this more sophisticated history of neoliberalism sits somewhat in tension with the cruder, totalising claim made by its object of study – the 'neo', the 'liberal', and the 'ism' are each now hotly contested – and the rich body of scholarly work that still seeks to draw together the transnational influence of ideas, the economic transformations, and the emergence of new subjectivities or modes of government under its banner. The connections made between different national contexts and policy spaces have frequently been just as enlightening as hyper-specificities and have sometimes lifted analysis up from overly parochial interpretations. Moreover, the different understandings of and approaches to the study of neoliberalism have rendered visible the very phenomena that have then been rightly eroded to reveal something more contingent and precise. It is also as yet unclear whether ostensibly more neutral bundles of intellectual positions or phenomena ('liberal market', 'national-global', 'deindustrialisation') will prove any less reductionist in practice once they are applied beyond their advocates' carefully delimited arguments.

It is all too easy to dismiss the more expansive sense of 'neoliberalism' as an oversimplification, a thin veil for interests, or a redundant term of abuse.[5] Certainly, neoliberalism is susceptible to these usages and all the problems of a term used both in scholarship and in public debate. We agree that oversimplification and illusory coherence are unhelpful and that 'neoliberal' as a chronological period is, on its own, too totalising a view or explanation of contemporary history. Likewise, we suspect that the expansive meaning of the term has often allowed scholars of all fields (including ourselves) to make the analysis of many transformations feasible and to draw firmer conclusions about the late twentieth- and early twenty-first-century worlds than their complexity perhaps yet allows.

We would, however, argue two points. First, although it is important to point out these weaknesses, they are not necessarily the ones that have most inhibited historical understanding. Rather, in our view, the biggest limiting factors have been the persistent separateness of economic, intellectual, and governmentality literatures on neoliberalism and the relative lack of detailed consideration of specific case studies of governance and policymaking compared with national and international intellectual histories. Second, we do not feel that forgoing the term 'neoliberalism' is the *only* appropriate response to the discovery of a need for greater complexity in how we think about the origins or ideas of a group of connected intellectuals or how we explain change over the last four decades. Instead, the challenge is to introduce greater rigour, nuance, and complexity into the term's wider historical usage beyond intellectual histories. We need to make it signify not a completely implemented or stable ideology but a much more interesting process involving the interaction of ideas, visions, constraints, advocates, stakeholders, resisters, contradictions, and legacies. In short, we believe that neoliberalism is a worthwhile object of study – but one that needs the self-imposed limits of being more tightly defined than is sometimes the case, applied using a relatively high bar for inclusion, and elaborated not to encompass ever more phenomena at the exclusion of other histories but deepened to show more of its political reality.

This book has made that case for deepening rather than abandoning 'neoliberalism' through a detailed study of British pension reforms in the 1980s. The remainder of this conclusion serves not only to summarise its empirical findings but also to draw out the strategies that we have deployed in our analysis and that we believe can yield a productive approach to

Conclusion 349

complex neoliberalism. The first strategy is to position the analysis at the intersection of the different facets of neoliberalism. Second, we embrace the complexity of neoliberalism's multiple strands, its localisation, and the consequences of this plurality for policymaking. Third, we apply a similar level of detailed scrutiny to pathways of influence, networks of policy actors, and the policymaking process as it has been applied to neoliberalism's intellectual history (in doing so, combining the strengths of a historical multi-archival study with social science concepts to understand different routes to policy change). Fourth, we avoid positioning neoliberalism as causal in itself; instead, we follow Ben Jackson in stressing the range of functions that ideas can perform.[6] We add an emphasis on the power and influence that ideas gain both from their advocates' links to power and from their ability to help solve problems, make sense of situations, and be compatible with other beliefs. Finally, we emphasise the weight of existing policies, contingency, and the legacies of decisions taken.

In the following sections we relate each of these strategies to our empirical findings before turning to consider the implications of the latter for our understanding of political change (and British politics in the 1980s specifically), international neoliberalism, and the long shadow cast by the United Kingdom's neoliberal pension reforms of the 1980s.

Neoliberal aims

Our study has been consciously restricted to a political stage; it is not a fully integrated political, economic, and socio-cultural study of pensions. Instead, we have shown how a political history can nonetheless be positioned to emphasise the connections between intellectual, political, and economic contexts, and delineate the means by which political actors attempted to reconfigure how individuals perceived themselves and their relationship to the state and capitalism. Rather than attempt to reconcile different approaches to neoliberalism (or Thatcherism) into a single definition, we have stressed the connections and interdependences between ideas, the economy, and attempts to promote new subjectivities. The resulting analysis has confirmed that UK pension policy objectives in all three of Thatcher's terms can be said to have been 'neoliberal' in each of these senses.

Nevertheless, the specific ideas underpinning the party's development of a coherent pension policy represented a very particular selection from the rich palette of neoliberal ideas available; and the ideas that eventually informed enacted reforms represented a sub-selection from those ideas that were transmitted to policymakers by think tanks and others within the neoliberal thought collective. The desire to rein in the state, for example, loomed large in the equation in terms of reducing its spending on pensions as a proportion of the economy (both to avoid 'crowding out' private investment, seen by neoliberals as inherently more efficient, and contribute to the 'monetarist' reduction of inflation via control of the money supply). It was also assumed that cutting the role of the state in old age income replacement would liberate the individual from an oppressive state apparatus as well as increase the efficient allocation of capital. Expanding the economic freedom of the individual in the market, and by extension expanding political liberty, as argued by Hayek, was thus clearly a key part of the idea selection dynamic.[7] So too was the desire to reinvigorate the 'vigorous virtues' of British entrepreneurialism and promote the free operation of market forces – even if that required, as advocated by ordoliberals (and by Hayek), action by a strong state prepared actively to intervene to implement and enforce market freedom.[8]

Even more clearly, we have shown the strong affinity between the government's motivations and neoliberal approaches to the welfare state and to pensions in particular (in terms of opposition to distorting privileges, hostility to in-scheme redistribution, fear of the burden placed on future generations, and the desire for individuals to take responsibility for investing in their own old age provision over the life cycle rather than sharing risk across society or distributing resources between generations). These political theories and policy visions can be placed alongside the wider understandings of governance that informed ministers' views of pension policymaking, namely that their objective was to curtail the welfare state's in-built self-expansion, combat the self-interest of technocratic experts, and factor in the inadequacies of democracy (at all stages the government believed its reforms were not ones for which a mandate should be sought). What emerges is a government in which some ministers and influential advisers were aligned with multiple layers of neoliberal thought, not just with a pre-packaged proposal.

In selecting from the menu of ideas within a far from monolithic neoliberalism, the government's objectives in pension policy, as in other areas of its economic policy, were partly a product of the crisis of the 1970s and the struggle to deal with these using the existing policy framework. Also important, however, was the perception among both Thatcher and those around her that, by its 1972 'U-turn' from its earlier attempt to break with state intervention in private markets, the Heath government had failed to turn back the 'socialist ratchet'.[9] In combination, these factors have generally been seen to have created a 'crisis of consensus' in Britain via the discrediting of the postwar Keynesian 'social democratic' orthodoxy, which, in turn, stimulated a demand across the political spectrum for new ideas. On the Left, that demand had been filled by the 'alternative economic strategy' advanced by Labour's left wing. On the Right, we have confirmed that the

Conclusion   351

demand for new thinking was satisfied by the neoliberal thought collective. Its ideas were helped into the Conservative party by a 'New Right' version of political Conservatism that made both the British Right and neoliberalism more compatible. Specific and sustained exchange between the ideas of Conservatism and neoliberalism took place in a complex process involving think tanks, journalists, and the building of personal links with key political actors within what came to be termed the 'Thatcher project'.

Albeit more nuanced in its content, this is nonetheless a familiar narrative. It is also a problematic one when it comes to pensions, however. In this policy field, the late 1970s were in fact the high point of postwar political consensus. As outlined in Chapter Three, the Conservative opposition swung behind the Labour government in endorsing Barbara Castle and Brian O'Malley's creation of a 'partnership in pensions' between the state and employers – a partnership that gave earnings-related pensions to all workers from 1978, whether provided by the employer or by the state. A small number of Conservatives around Geoffrey Howe had doubts about the long-term impacts of this settlement on capital ownership almost as soon as the legislation was passed, but the fear that powerful interests would fight to preserve this consensus led them to dismiss any prospect of a direct confrontation. It was only after its election in May 1979 that the new Conservative government sought to think seriously about how to begin reversing what it now characterised as the 'socialist ratchet' of the postwar decades in pensions by dismantling a system perceived as successful by most political and business actors at the end of the 1970s.

Although the repudiation of the 'postwar consensus' by the Conservatives in the field of pensions had to await the party's coming to power in 1979, the mechanics of neoliberal idea transmission in the arena of pensions were much the same as those in other areas of economic and social policy. Right-wing think tanks that were part of the neoliberal thought collective (in our case, the Centre for Policy Studies) drew neoliberal ideas from the palette of thinking circulating within it and incubated them with a view to implementation in a UK context. They then pushed those ideas towards Conservative politicians on the Right of the party and to their political advisers (most notably, in our case, those in the Treasury and No. 10 Downing Street). In doing so, these neoliberal think tanks drew on the close relationship with policy actors that they had carefully cultivated. This process was already evident while the Conservative party was in opposition but it most obviously began to shape practical ideas for pension reform once the party entered government.

Certainly, policy ambitions in the first term were relatively limited, as described in Chapter Four. There was much thinking about pensions by the Conservative government and much identifying of problems; but there was little legislation. When there was change it was shaped by the party's developing neoliberal iteration of Conservatism, specifically the objective of a smaller state and, by extension, the promotion of individual freedom. The main change was the 1980 linking of increases in the basic state pension to annual retail price inflation, rather than the higher of the annual rise in prices or average earnings as hitherto. This reform, which took advantage of an unusual period in which earnings were rising more slowly than prices, was driven by a desire to reduce state spending (and thus the size of the public sector borrowing requirement) over the short to medium term. It was undertaken, however, with the intention of also delivering long-term policy ambitions to defuse the perceived 'pensions time bomb', in the form of unfunded future state pension liabilities in an ageing society. Thus, it would also over time play an important role in the delivery of a smaller welfare state with more scope for individual decision making in general and, specifically, more room for voluntary top-up saving and pension provision by individuals.

Viewing this process through the archives has revealed a more complicated picture of how neoliberal ideas and arguments influenced policy. In addition to think tanks and advisers, we have shown that civil servants were also participants in this process, either by anticipating their political masters' needs, reducing the field of options by highlighting problems, or providing the detail that made quite loosely sketched options more viable. As discussed in Chapter Four, some aspects of neoliberal policymaking in the first term can be seen as a discovery process in which problems were identified in broad political terms (albeit with strongly neoliberal-aligned assumptions) before officials carried out work to define and quantify the scope of a problem, which could then serve as an impetus to radical – and not necessarily related – reform. Crucially, the caveats and uncertainties officials assigned to their findings did not always persist into the political use of their work in justifying the need for change.

As explored in Chapters Five and Six, Thatcher's second term saw much more radical ambition. The idea that the state should intervene actively to reshape and vastly expand the market by individualising pensions (in terms not just of ownership but of investment and risk) firmly entered the policy arena in 1983. Although it was not the only group to promote the concept, the CPS was the first to achieve political traction with a proposal ostensibly designed to solve the technical problem of preserving the occupational pension benefits of individuals who changed jobs.[10] In reality, this was but a lever to open the pension policy door to a much more radical political-economic agenda – one that was plainly neoliberal, and understood as aiming to bring 'market influences' to bear in social policy.[11] It was a reform project enthusiastically embraced by key actors within the No. 10 Policy Unit with past

Conclusion
353

and future links to the CPS: John Redwood and David Willetts. By seeking to dismantle both the pay-as-you-go State Earnings-Related Pension System (SERPS) and the United Kingdom's 'defined benefit' (DB) occupational pensions system, they sought to substitute personal pensions as the second tier of UK pension provision, in the process disintermediating occupational pension funds covering around half the workforce as well as abolishing state earnings-related pensions for the other half. These architects of reform thereby hoped to achieve a number of objectives. Most notably, they sought to get the state off the hook of financing long-term unfunded SERPS benefits, thus rolling back the planned future growth of state involvement in providing earnings-related income in old age (in some senses, the most social democratic feature of Britain's welfare state alongside the NHS). In the process, they also intended to end 'welfare dependence' and curtail redistribution within and across generations, promoting as alternatives the vigorous virtues of individual thrift, risk bearing, and entrepreneurialism. Abolishing SERPS would encourage individual freedom of action and choice within a market context, with individuals saving for a personal pension via capital accumulation and, in the initial vision, investing directly in British capitalism (on the lines of a modern self-invested personal pension, or a US investment retirement account).

As we have seen, it was decided that this creation of a nation of investor-capitalists could not be left to voluntarism: the Hayekian assumption that order would arise spontaneously through the market was rejected; so too was the Chicago school assumption that self-interested and rational individuals acting within the market to maximise their personal utility would automatically take steps to provide for their old age. Instead, recognising individuals' tendency to avoid thinking about old age, and drawing on ordoliberal ideas about the duty of the state to act to shape society to conform to the market, and to deproletarianise society by creating citizens imbued with individualist values of 'entrepreneurialism', the state would act to compel current members of SERPS to take out a personal pension. Individuals would have the consumer's freedom to choose the form of their investment (in line with the Chicago school's emphasis) but they would not have the freedom to choose whether and when they saved, even above a minimum.

If that was not radical enough, reformers also sought to destroy employer-provided DB pensions, hitherto seen and supported by Conservatives (not least Thatcher) as a species of 'peoples' capitalism' but now seen by neoliberal policy actors in the CPS and the No. 10 Policy Unit as monopolistic concentrations of economic power antithetical to individual freedom (a major concern for ordoliberals) and also as institutions that were intrinsically averse to risk taking and thus to the market-oriented entrepreneurialism that they saw as key to reversing the country's economic 'decline'.[12] In short, in this vision of reform, most workers would eventually end up not just saving into their own

354   *A neoliberal revolution?*

personal pension but investing its capital themselves in stocks and bonds, in the process bearing all the associated investment and longevity risks.

At the same time, the architects of reform sought to move not just those in the new personal pensions but also those remaining in surviving DB occupational pension schemes to this 'defined contribution' (DC) model. Defined contribution occupational pensions had been comprehensively discredited in the postwar decades because of their poor record on delivering decent pensions. We have shown, however, that by the mid-1980s DC schemes had come to be seen by those in and orbiting the Conservative government as fundamental to its creation of a nation of individual investor capitalists. Action by the state to individualise pension investment and risk in this way, it was argued, would create a substantial pool of risk-oriented capital to be deployed in UK investment markets for the regeneration of UK capitalism, with investment decision making by individuals seen as inherently superior to that by institutional investment managers. In sum, in the Thatcher administration's second term reformers initially sought to use the state actively to reconstruct almost every British worker in a process of Foucauldian-style neoliberal governmentality that would make those individuals responsible for their own self-government.[13]

In the third term the policy ambition was smaller and, essentially, reactive in its tying up of loose ends left over from second term reform. Most significant was the adjustment of the tax system to reduce DB scheme surpluses, in the process reducing state spending on pension fund tax reliefs, and continuing encouragement of the DC model whether in occupational pension schemes or via personal pensions. This was, of course, also consonant with the neoliberal aim of reducing the role of the state in the economy (incidentally reducing the near-term public sector borrowing requirement and thus creating headroom for the government's tax-cutting agenda) as well as creating more scope for marketised individual decision making as well as more engagement by individuals with their wealth.

Translating the neoliberal vision into policy

Geoffrey Howe's breaking of the link between the basic state pension and average earnings growth in 1980 marked the beginning of the practical implementation of the government's neoliberal pensions reform project, but the 1985 Green Paper on social security represented the high point for those advocating neoliberal reform in pensions.[14] By this point, compromises had already been made with the original ambition to satisfy those in government who were sceptical about the reform project being driven by the No. 10 Policy Unit (most notably to assuage Nigel Lawson's concerns about the near-term costs of reform

Conclusion 355

if SERPS was instantly abolished and its members forced into personal pensions with tax relief awarded on their contributions). Nonetheless, the core of the programme remained in the Green Paper on social security, which was published in June 1985. The complete abolition of SERPS was merely postponed until the end of the century for older workers (men over 50 and women over 45), with plenty of incentive for them to opt out in the shorter term, and there would be a near-term three-year phased implementation of SERPS abolition for younger workers. The Green Paper's proposals on personal pensions also, although now accepting a role for financial service companies in investment, still meant that occupational pension funds could be expected to wither away over time as incoming staff were incentivised to take out a personal pension rather than join their company scheme. By any standards, this was therefore still a revolutionary package, and one that was clearly neoliberal in its ambition radically to cut back state involvement, promote voluntary provision by individuals, enhance individual freedom, tackle vested interests and powerful private sector institutions seen as acting against the best interests of individuals, and stimulate entrepreneurialism.

There was a U-turn between the Green Paper and legislation in 1986, however – as we saw in Chapter Seven. In consequence, a significant implementation gap opened up between the neoliberal vision of the Green Paper and the policies actually embodied in the 1986 Social Security and Financial Services Acts.[15] In this highly contingent process, neoliberal revolution became neoliberal evolution, with personal pensions implemented merely as an additional element within the United Kingdom's system of top-up pension provision rather than as the sole element, as had initially been envisaged. We also see a distinct shift in neoliberal policy aims: from creating a nation of individual capitalists, free to invest their pension savings directly in any company they saw fit, to promoting individual freedom of choice in the market for personal pension products provided by – typically very large – firms in the financial services sector. Even as they were forced to compromise further, therefore, the architects of reform sought to recraft their policy programme by selecting from a different set of neoliberal ideas, ones based mainly on individual freedom and choice in the market. Thus, the policies remained neoliberal even as significant compromises were made vis-à-vis the original agenda. Nonetheless, those driving reform both within and without government saw the failure to attain the original neoliberal vision as significant and regrettable.

What forced the architects of reform to recraft their proposals? One factor was their failure to recognise the significant constraints on reform posed by path dependences within the system as it had evolved over many decades. For example, a barrier to outright abolition of SERPS was Paul Pierson's 'double payment' problem in pay-as-you-go state pensions – a system delivering past spending promises paid out of current spending, which must necessarily continue even if there was a move to present-day funding of future pensions by workers, employers, and/or the state.[16] The bigger path-dependent constraint, however, turned out to be institutional attachments to the 'partnership in pensions' political and institutional settlement of the late 1970s, itself the product of what Pierson dubbed 'increasing returns' within the system.[17] These formative positive feedbacks and resulting path-dependent effects can be seen in many dimensions. First, the post-war growth of occupational pensions and the attachment to them evident among employers, pension schemes, their members, and their trades union representatives had already forced Barbara Castle to work with rather than against the pension funds in the mid-1970s, unlike her Labour forerunner Richard Crossman (thereby ensuring that her proposals were implemented, whereas his were not). Second, the attachment to SERPS among these stakeholders was itself a product of the two-decade-long political battle from the mid-1950s to provide earnings-related pensions for those not in an occupational scheme. Taken together, the result was an attachment to the 'partnership in pensions' compromise forged by Castle among all these actors as well as the pension industry more broadly and civil servants in the DHSS. Thus, path dependence in pensions had produced a gradual accumulation of 'locked-in' system elements, with the existence of each element also constraining options for reform.[18]

Our study therefore highlights the need for assessments of neoliberal policymaking to take account of policymaking failures and to acknowledge better the constraints on reform, the entrenchment of existing arrangements, and the significant stakeholder resistance that characterised the 1980s and shaped the eventual form that 'actually existing' neoliberalism took. Recognising these limitations places further emphasis not just on the localised national instances of neoliberal policy but also on the contingency that arose from the political skill of its advocates. The fact was that the architects of reform in the No. 10 Policy Unit failed fully to appreciate the attachment of these institutions to the existing order and, in consequence, underestimated the scale of their likely resistance. This is not to say that the attachment of employers, pension funds, their members, and trades unions to the 'partnership in pensions' consensus of the late 1970s and early 1980s was entirely unexpected; but it was certainly underestimated.

What was entirely unanticipated by No. 10, however, was that the financial services sector, which had been expected by ministers and their political advisers to jump at the 'bonanza of business opportunities' that they thought would flow from personal pensions, proved overwhelmingly resistant to key parts of the personal pensions reform agenda, as did the industry's pension professionals, most notably the actuarial profession. Remarkably, given that the Conservatives saw themselves as the party of business and of

Conclusion 357

free markets, we have identified a significant failure within the Policy Unit to understand the way in which the profit motive would shape financial services sector reactions to reform. Both Redwood and Willetts simply failed to grasp that providing personal pensions to the very large number of low-paid employees in the workforce would be an administratively expensive and inherently unprofitable business for private sector providers. Thus, even those insurance companies that were highly supportive of personal pensions in principle proved highly resistant to the idea that they should be compulsory. These were powerful institutions with deep reservoirs of money to spend on lobbying, extensive links across business, finance, and politics, and a history of practical moral and financial support for the Conservative party. Moreover, by 1985 the government was relying on these companies to deliver personal pensions. As Thatcher realised, to alienate them would be profoundly risky. Hence her realisation that to take the pension proposals in the 1985 social security Green Paper forward to legislation was untenable, and the subsequent search for a face-saving alternative.

From revolution to evolution

Exploring the political mechanics of this U-turn on personal pensions in 1985 in Chapter Seven has allowed us to understand the ways in which those driving revolutionary reform were ultimately forced to accept its impossibility. It has also, however, revealed the ways in which an evolutionary alternative to revolution was then constructed by those reformers via a different selection from the available menu of neoliberal ideas and the use of different strategies to achieve policy change. In this sense, we draw a wider lesson for studies of international neoliberalism: that, rather than the straightforward comparison of neoliberal ideas, policies, and implementation, we must also understand the pressures shaping the selection of ideas, modifications made, and chosen routes to reform.

The initial preference of Norman Fowler, as Minister for Health and Social Services, had been to reform rather than replace the existing second tier of the pension system. Early in the reform process the Inquiry set up by Fowler to examine the issue revealed significant opposition to a wholesale replacement of earnings-related SERPS and occupational pension provision by individualised DC personal pensions. This early phase of policy development forced proponents of radical reform in No. 10 into some early compromises – most notably around implementation phasing. Fowler's ability to resist the Policy Unit's agenda was limited, however, because at this stage it had the active support of the Prime Minister. Despite her prior enthusiasm for occupational pensions, she had then been persuaded by the PU's argument that, as well as implementing personal pensions, the government should use them to abolish SERPS and incentivise members of occupational pension schemes to take out a personal pension. At this stage, therefore, Thatcher was prepared to countenance the substitution of personal pensions for both SERPS and occupational pensions, and thus had embraced the idea of a neoliberal revolution in pensions.

Unfortunately for Thatcher, normally an uncommonly astute reader of political possibilities, she had allowed her enthusiasm for the 'every man a capitalist' programme to blind her to the likely political costs of such a radical reform.[19] In 1983 she had dismissed a similar agenda with these words: 'It recommends policies as far apart as A and Z. In politics you can only at most go from about A – D at a time.'[20] That she subsequently came to embrace an 'A to Z' approach was a tribute to the persuasive power of her advisers. She would have been better advised, however, to stick to her pragmatic instinct, for she had notably underestimated how the Treasury would react (possibly because under Howe it, rather than No. 10, had pushed reform). Under Lawson, the Treasury's opposition was muted at first, but, as it came better to appreciate what the Policy Unit was trying to do, the Treasury became alarmed by the prospective Exchequer cost.[21] Compulsorily transferring all SERPS members into personal pensions would very significantly increase the cost of present-day tax relief on their contributions – which the Treasury had hitherto assumed would in aggregate be relatively low in a voluntary system (and offset by very substantial future savings on SERPS benefits) – even as the government continued to pay out on past (pay-as-you-go) state pension promises. Faced with this 'double payment', the Treasury forced further important compromises: the exclusion of the self-employed; the phasing of SERPS reform over three years; and an effective 15-year delay in the time taken for it to disappear entirely, by excluding older workers from its immediate abolition.

As ministers and officials worked frantically to recraft the government's proposals in the face of overwhelming opposition, the way out they identified was to preserve the appearance of radical reform while reducing its scope and selecting much longer-term means to achieve their ends. Rather than abolish SERPS, the government chose instead to modify it to contain its long-term costs while continuing to implement voluntary personal pensions. Reformers hoped that financial incentives would tempt members of a less generous SERPS to leave and take out a personal pension. Thus, personal pensions now became a voluntary alternative to SERPS, not a replacement, and were expected to be a relatively niche product given the absence of compulsion. Moreover, occupational pensions' early leaver problem (the original motivation for CPS-inspired 'portable personal pensions') would now be addressed via limited price indexation of preserved occupational pensions – as

Conclusion 359

recommended by the Occupational Pension Board in 1981 – and thus, by extension, occupational pension schemes would be retained and (via government issuance of index-linked gilts from 1981 to be used by the schemes to manage future inflation) effectively defended.[22] Nor, in this new world, would personal pensions be disintermediated. Powerful private sector institutions seen as antithetical to individual freedom would not be replaced by a nation of individual investor-capitalists reconciled with capitalism through their direct ownership of shares. Instead, personal pensions products would be sold to individual consumers but be managed and invested by financial service sector firms. All this amounted to an incremental neoliberal adjustment to the existing system via the addition of personal pensions and measures to attenuate future SERPS liabilities; but such institutional evolution, with its 'system layering' approach, was a very different outcome from the 'system displacement' revolution originally envisaged by the neoliberal architects of pension reform in the CPS and the No. 10 Policy Unit.

The legacy

We would stress, then, that the study of international neoliberalism needs to account not simply for whether neoliberal reforms were implemented but how reforms interacted with and sat alongside the existing policy infrastructure. Beyond that, though, histories of neoliberalism must also evaluate not just the immediate policy impact of the ideas themselves but also the long-term consequences of the combination of ideas, the routes to reform taken, and the compromises reached. As we saw in Chapter Seven, tasked with implementing personal pensions, Norman Fowler had advised the Prime Minister that modifying rather than replacing SERPS would 'give us the worst of both worlds'. The complexity of the existing two-tier system would continue (and, implicitly, be worsened by the addition of personal pensions to the mix) and 'probably the last opportunity' to give everyone a personal pension would be lost.[23] The architects of neoliberal pension reform at the centre of government in No. 10 shared that analysis and were profoundly disappointed by the retreat from the objectives of the Green Paper. When Redwood and Willetts talked about the need 'to rescue something from the rubble of SERPS' they were clear that its abolition was the only way in which the government could expand 'the boundaries of individual responsibility' in a welfare state in which everything else was 'politically inviolate and well defended'.[24] Merely seeking to drain members out of SERPS over the long term was for them a clear defeat. If the dream of a wholesale neoliberal reconstruction of Britain's second tier of pensions was dead, though, what did that leave? Was Fowler right that the compromises forced by general resistance to the Policy Unit's revolutionary reform were in danger of leaving Britain with the worst of both worlds in pensions? More generally, what was the legacy of the more general array of neoliberal pensions reforms undertaken during the 1980s?

The first of those changes, linking the BSP to price inflation alone, proved to be disastrous in the long term. As was obvious at the time, the predictable result was that the BSP declined relative to average earnings. By the turn of the century it was clear to all, and central to the findings of the Pensions Commission in 2004, that the country by then had one of the least generous state pensions among advanced economies and that it faced a major problem of future poverty among the retired, a problem that would be exacerbated by the decline in SERPS benefits flowing from other Conservative reforms in the 1980s.[25] Moreover, the net result of the 1985 U-turn on personal pensions was not the simpler system originally envisaged but a more complicated system with a new element in the shape of personal pensions, along with an array of interlinkages between them, SERPS, and occupational pensions. This more complex system was a harder and more expensive system to run and to regulate as well as harder for consumers to navigate (again, as noted by the Pensions Commission). It was also, however, a system in which potential pension savers had declining levels of trust, partly because its complexity meant they found it hard to understand but also because the (widely predicted) personal pensions missellings scandals of the late 1980s and early 1990s, together with financial misconduct in relatively lightly regulated occupational schemes, were destructive of public confidence in pensions generally. When combined with the historic propensity for individuals to avoid thinking too much about old age, the result was ultimately reduced rather than increased demand for personal pensions, often inadequate contributions, and a tendency for those who did take one out to let it lapse in fairly short order. All this was coupled with high charges and poor investment returns generated by personal pension providers and was hugely destructive of their future value.

Moreover, although personal pensions were implemented alongside rather than as a replacement for SERPS and occupational pensions, their introduction had profoundly negative consequences for both. As a result of the 1985 U-turn, SERPS had been subjected by the government to changes that ensured a slow bleeding away of its benefits, which could be expected by 2050 to slash its value by half relative to earnings. That would serve to reinforce the problem of inadequate state pensions for those dependent on them. Yet, for the reasons just stated, personal pensions failed to fill the expanding vacuum of state provision. At the same time, DB occupational pensions were also severely weakened – by the government's legislation to make membership voluntary, the incentive to leave and take out a personal

Conclusion 361

pension, its encouragement of DC occupational schemes, raids on fund 'surpluses' executed both by employers and the state, and by rising administrative costs flowing from greater regulation in the wake of scandals relating to fraud and/or maladministration. In consequence, DB occupational pension schemes were left ill prepared for the onset of a much harsher operating environment – brought about by growing liabilities driven by more generous benefits, rising longevity and more realistic valuation methods, and greater difficulties in meeting those liabilities because of lower investment returns as profitability in the British economy, and in other advanced economies, declined and rates of return on government bonds also dropped in conditions of much lower inflation (the latter also, somewhat paradoxically, serving to increase the size of the fund liabilities, because bond yields, which moved downwards as inflation was vanquished, were used to discount their future value).[26] Consequently, DB occupational pensions embarked on a substantial contraction, slowly at first and then precipitately from the dawn of the new century. Increasingly, firms began to close their DB schemes to new entrants, and sometimes to existing members. Typically, they slashed the employer's contribution even as they substituted DC for DB, in the process transferring investment and longevity risks to the individual member, who now faced a much lower and more uncertain future pension. Alternatively, employers simply got out of pensions entirely, leaving their workers with no top-up occupational pension provision at all.

Thatcherism and political change

How do these findings recast what we know about the Thatcher project and political change in the 1980s more generally? We would stress the dynamism and instability of the Thatcher project. Instead of a stable set of ideas entirely or partially implemented, we should imagine the Thatcher governments' policymaking as a pathway through the variety of aims, ideas, motivations, and arguments available to it. Some of these had a firmly Conservative heritage, but others were drawn from neoliberal thought (albeit in the complex process of Conservative readings of these ideas). To us, the term 'Thatcherism' is best used to signify these ideational materials and the particular pathways through them taken by Thatcherites in different policy areas. In our case study, these pathways frequently experienced quite sudden course corrections, partly because those travelling them met with opposition from stakeholders but partly because they discovered contradictions and tensions (between, say, choice and responsibility) or that the policies embodied a particular combination of ideas that turned out to have insurmountable practical difficulties of implementation. We would further stress the contingency of this process: policy was formulated and reformulated at speed, and the personal political access and skill of those involved affected the outcome. Nor was this a political project driven by the singular figure of Thatcher. We have highlighted the role of Howe, Lawson, and Fowler but also the fundamental importance of political advisers; and we have also shown that, on occasion, reform was actually prevented by Thatcher's political caution.

The 'Thatcher project' that emerges from our case study is one concerned with the economic crises of the 1970s and the apparent inability of existing prescriptions to fight inflation. Interestingly, however, it was also a project orientated around the assumption of low growth and the consequences of predicted low returns on capital. Economic historians of Thatcherism initially stressed these attributes in thinking about the project as the reassertion of the interests of capital, but there is a case for revisiting the connections between these economic assumptions and the new subjectivities associated with Thatcherism. Subjectivities such as the individual as risk-taking investor were not simply political constructs or mere rhetorical cover for the reassertion of capitalist interests. Instead, the fostering of such subjectivities could be a key aim of policy decisions, and their widespread adoption was often understood as a long-term answer to Britain's economic difficulties.

We also need to appreciate that the Thatcher project was capable of multiple types of policy change and that the status quo played a significant role in shaping its record. Pension reforms, as we have shown, were a product of a complex interplay between ideas, institutions, and interests (Peter Hall's 'primordial elements' of political economy).[27] Reform was also a product of path dependences within the system. In combination, they forced policymakers into an incremental series of evolutionary reforms, which, among other things, saw a further, personal pensions layer added to the state–employer partnership in pensions implemented in 1978, rather than replacing the two existing elements within the United Kingdom's second tier of pension provision. Neoliberal revolution this was not, but the implemented evolutionary change still amounted to a big reform, if one achieved by layering as opposed to system displacement (on the lines suggested by Mahoney and Thelen and by Hacker and Ebbinghaus). It demonstrates how major change can be produced by evolution, as argued by Mahoney and Thelen.[28] This evolutionary process and the change it gave rise to ('actually existing neoliberalism') was, nevertheless, a reform project which still drew on neoliberal ideas, even if a rather different set from those that had initially informed the architects of policy change.

Although we would not advocate a British history of the 1980s that sees everything of importance between then and now as a product of Thatcherism, we do note that, in pension policy, the profound consequences of that decade's politics were not fully felt until long afterwards. Changes to pension arrangements had greater effects for many more people than

Conclusion   363

the 'Big Bang' in the City of London or privatisation, and represented a significant reconstruction away from a welfare state that had, just a few years beforehand, become much more redistributionist. Moreover, the new structures and incentives generated through this political process shaped the choices that individuals made about their lives. They may not have regarded them as overtly political, but the options available to people stemmed from a very self-consciously (and neoliberal) political project.

Neoliberalism and the long shadow of reform

With that bigger picture in mind, how does this case study of neoliberal policy change in pensions suggest we might think about neoliberalism differently? One obvious lesson is that we could profitably adopt a more complex model of ideational 'influence', given the importance of behind-the-scenes advisers as the vector by which neoliberal ideas were translated into pension policy on multiple occasions in the 1980s and through multiple routes, as well as fitted into an older Conservative tradition of property ownership. Moreover, it was not just the specific neoliberal vision of pensions or the welfare state that mattered in the process of translating ideas into implemented policies; it was also the broader context of interests, institutions, and the challenges of democratic governance – each of which shaped the way ideas were selected and injected into policy.

Second, neoliberal ideas had more complicated relationships with capitalist interests than often imagined. In our case, neoliberal argument led the Conservative party away from the interests of major institutional holders of capital assets. This was to prove a significant problem when the latter's pursuit of profits ultimately thwarted the neoliberal vision of a more fundamental reconfiguration of the welfare state. We should also note that an important feature of the neoliberal policy reforms that were nonetheless carried out is that they worsened the position of groups that were especially vulnerable to the precarious employment and the low and disrupted earnings that came to characterise the transition to a globalised and services-led model of less-regulated capitalism. Historians of neoliberalism can therefore productively understand neoliberal reform as choices between interests but only if they avoid simplistic equivalence between the interests of capital and neoliberal argument.

Third, we are better off thinking of 'neoliberal visions' rather than singular neoliberal ideas or policy options. Our case study suggests that the reason multiple routes to neoliberal reform were available was because political actors could utilise different neoliberal visions of the problems posed by the status quo and of what a neoliberal policy end state would look like. They could – and did – also switch between routes to achieving their goals, modulate the pace and scope of change, and subtly shift the vision or set of problems they were attempting to solve when opposition to reform became intractable. The reform programme altered in consequence but nonetheless remained neoliberal, though this does not mean that the architects of reform were necessarily happy with the policy outcomes or their long-term results. Thus, historians of 'actually existing neoliberalism' also need to confront and explain the weaknesses of its arguments, ideas, and implementation on its own terms.

Nevertheless, for all its partial implementation of a particularly radical vision of neoliberal reform, and the disappointments of those driving change, Britain did switch its old age provision from a system with multiple forms of redistribution and intergenerational mutuality towards one in which individuals were increasingly responsible for investing in their own old age income replacement across the life cycle through the choices they made in a market. With this in mind, we close by considering the long shadow that decisions taken in the 1980s on pensions have cast on a crucial element of the welfare state. As noted above, early in the personal pensions reform process Fowler had predicted that, if reform was badly handled, the country could end up with the 'worst of both worlds' in pensions. That indeed proved to be the case, as we outlined in Chapter Eight. In failing to revolutionise the system via the replacement of its second tier, the architects of reform had fallen back on evolutionary changes, which were added to the earlier delinking of the BSP from earnings growth, and to which were added further changes that increased regulation in response to emerging failures, and in the process weakened DB pension fund finances. In aggregate, these changes served at once vastly to complicate the system, to weaken all its elements, and to exacerbate rather than solve the impending problem of pensioner poverty linked to the retirement of the baby boomers and rising longevity. The result of this political, regulatory, and market failure was a system that was at once the most complicated and least generous in the world by the start of the new century, and a system whose elements all embodied profound path dependences, constraining reform options.

Ironically, moreover, the pensions time bomb had not been defused, as ministers had assumed it would be. Responsibility for solving the problem had merely been passed from the state to individuals, almost all of whom lacked the knowledge, expertise, or inclination to deal with it. In the longer term the (widely predicted) inability of individuals to manage the problem themselves by raising their level of savings, investing them effectively, and managing both investment and longevity risk became obvious. Given the clear and overwhelming advice to the government in the mid-1980s that this would inevitably happen, this should have surprised nobody. Considering the enormous complexity of the decisions that were being required of workers, who typically had relatively low pay (and thus little scope for adequate, or sometimes any, pension contributions), low levels of numeracy, and even lower levels of financial understanding, it was virtually inevitable that personal pensions would fail to deliver their promised benefits.

The result of all this was that in 2005 the Pensions Commission's second report concluded that, far from growing, as neoliberal reformers of the 1980s had intended, voluntary private pension saving (whether via personal pensions or occupational pension schemes) was 'in serious and probably irreversible decline'.[29] State pension provision was also becoming wholly inadequate as a result of the reduction in the BSP in relation to earnings and the attenuation of SERPS benefits and its eventual abolition. Taken together, this represented a major political failure. It was all very well to boast, as the Secretary of State for Social Security, Peter Lilley, had done in 1996, that the United Kingdom was 'almost uniquely placed' among advanced capitalist democracies in having moved away from pay-as-you-go state pensions to funded pensions, thereby 'solving' the future problem of pensions, subject to some additional relatively minor reforms further to stimulate personal pension saving.[30] (Lilley was not alone, for British politicians on both sides of the ideological divide in the 1990s complacently assumed that the problem of unfunded future state spending on pensions had effectively been solved by subjecting SERPS to slow strangulation and substituting DC in the shape of either personal or occupational pensions.) In fact, the consequences of the 1980s 'neoliberal evolution' in British pensions were profoundly negative and profoundly counterproductive.

Most obviously, perhaps, although the government persuaded itself that it had cunningly defused the pensions time bomb and reduced dependence on the state, in the long term its evolutionary neoliberal reforms in fact ultimately managed to create greater welfare dependence and greater state spending. Increasingly, poorer retired people (among whom women were disproportionately represented) were forced to fall back on state benefits to supplement their inadequate pensions (whether state, occupational, or personal). The result was an expanding pensions underclass and every prospect that it would continue to expand well into the twenty-first century. Ironically, therefore, the neoliberal attempt to promote individual responsibility and in the process pass the 'burden of pensions' from the state to the individual eventually served merely to return to the state responsibility for the (now much greater) problem of inadequate income in old age among those without a generous SERPS or good DB occupational pension, and, in the process, radically degrade the effectiveness of Britain's overall system of providing an income to those in retirement. Brave new dawn this was not; instead, the neoliberal evolution in British pensions had produced precisely the 'worst of both worlds' that Norman Fowler had warned Margaret Thatcher it might do, and that John Redwood and David Willetts in the No. 10 Policy Unit had come to fear it would as their hopes for a neoliberal revolution in British pensions crumbled.

Notes

1 Philip Mirowski and Dieter Plehwe, eds., *The Road from Mont Pèlerin: The Making of the Neoliberal Thought Collective* (Cambridge, MA: Harvard University Press, 2009); Ben Jackson, 'Currents of Neo-Liberalism: British Political Ideologies and the New Right, c.1955–1979', *The English Historical Review*, 131 (2016).

2 Quinn Slobodian, *Globalists: The End of Empire and the Birth of Neoliberalism* (Cambridge, MA: Harvard University Press, 2018).

3 Emily Robinson and others, 'Telling Stories about Post-War Britain: Popular Individualism and the "Crisis" of the 1970s', *Twentieth Century British History*, 28 (2017).

4 Peter Sloman, 'Welfare in a Neoliberal Age: The Politics of Redistributive Market Liberalism', in *Neoliberalism and Conservatism in Britain*, ed. by Aled Davies, Ben Jackson, and Florence Sutcliffe-Braithwaite (London: UCL Press, 2021), pp. 75–93.

5 For a sophisticated version of this argument, see David Edgerton, 'What Came between Liberalism and Neoliberalism? Rethinking Keynesianism, the Welfare State, and Social Democracy', in *The Neoliberal Age? Britain since the 1970s*, ed. by Aled Davies, Ben Jackson, and Florence Sutcliffe-Braithwaite (London: UCL Press, 2021), pp. 30–51.

6 Ben Jackson, 'Intellectual Histories of Neoliberalism and Their Limits', in *The Neoliberal Age?*, Davies, Jackson, and Sutcliffe-Braithwaite, pp. 52–72.

7 F. A. von Hayek, *The Road to Serfdom* (London: Routledge & Kegan Paul, 1944), p. 211. See also Philip Mirowski, 'Postface: Defining Neoliberalism', in *The Road from Mont Pèlerin*, Mirowski and Plehwe, pp. 417–56, at pp. 443–44.

8 Werner Bonefeld, 'Freedom and the Strong State: On German Ordoliberalism', *New Political Economy*, 17 (2012); Chris Guest, 'Hayek on Government: Two Views or One?', *History of Economics Review*, 26 (1997), p. 52.

9 Annotations on Margaret Thatcher Archive: Margaret Thatcher, 'Keith Joseph Memorial Lecture: Liberty and Limited Government', 11 January 1996.

10 Nigel Vinson and Philip Chappell, *Personal and Portable Pensions for All* (London: Centre for Policy Studies, 1983).

11 HM Treasury Private Office papers (hereafter HMT): PO-CH-GH-0022, 'Policy Group Work', 1982.

12 This is a finding at odds with a common assumption that UK neoliberal politics in the 1980s was accepting of concentrations of power in the private sector; see, for example, Jackson, 'Currents of Neo-Liberalism: British Political Ideologies and the New Right', p. 842.

13 Michel Foucault, *The Birth of Biopolitics: Lectures at the Collège de France, 1978–79*, ed. by Michel Senellart, trans. by Graham Burchell (Basingstoke: Palgrave Macmillan, 2008). See also Nikolas Rose, *Governing the Soul: Shaping of the Private Self* (London: Free Association Books, 1999); and Nikolas Rose, Pat O'Malley, and Mariana Valverde, 'Governmentality', *Annual Review of Law and Social Science*, 2 (2006).

14 Department of Health and Social Security, *Reform of Social Security*, vol. 2: *Reform of Social Security: Programme for Change*, Cmnd 9518 (London: HMSO, 1985).

15 We thus confirm the early and perceptive identification of an implementation gap between the Thatcher governments' aims and achievements in the work of David Marsh and R. A. W. Rhodes, 'Implementing Thatcherism: Policy Change in the 1980s', *Parliamentary Affairs*, 45 (1992). As Thatcherism was an evolutionary, adaptive, and contingent strategy for government, as argued by Marsh and Rhodes, so too was the neoliberal project as implemented by those governments.

16 John Myles and Paul Pierson, 'The Comparative Political Economy of Pension Reform', in *The New Politics of the Welfare State*, ed. by Paul Pierson (Oxford: Oxford University Press, 2001), pp. 305–33, at pp. 313–15.

17 Paul Pierson, *Increasing Returns, Path Dependence and the Study of Politics* (Florence: European University Institute, Robert Schumann Centre, 1997).

18 For a condensed summary of this phenomenon, see Hugh Pemberton, 'Politics and Pensions in Post-War Britain', in *Britain's Pensions Crisis: History and Policy*, ed. by Hugh Pemberton, Pat Thane, and Noel Whiteside (Oxford: Oxford University Press, 2006), pp. 39–63.

19 As we noted in Chapter Five, this was an overwhelmingly 'every *man*', male-oriented reform programme. It was also a decidedly middle-class vision. Thus, it did not bother itself with the problems of those with low earnings and interrupted contributions because of time out of the labour market, and it had no concern with redistribution within the system to address the problems that would arise from this in terms of inadequate retirement earnings.

20 The National Archive (hereafter TNA): PREM 19/1004, 'Pensions and Individual Choice: A Paper by the CPRS', April 1983.

21 Something that both Lawson and Howe had, in opposition, been clear was a limitation on wider ownership schemes.

22 On the introduction of index-linked gilts, see Michael J. Oliver and Janette Rutterford, '"The Capital Market Is Dead": The Difficult Birth of Index-Linked Gilts in the UK', *The Economic History Review*, 73 (2020).

23 TNA: PREM 19/1639, Fowler to Thatcher, 'Social Security Review', 26 April 1985.

24 TNA: PREM 19/1640, Redwood to Thatcher, 'MISC 111', 14 October 1985.

25 Pensions Commission, *Pensions: Challenges and Choices. The First Report of the Pensions Commission* (London: TSO, 2004).

26 Lower gilt yields created particular problems in the wake of the 2005 requirement (under FRS 17) that, in calculating their pension fund's financial position (which had from 1988 had to be stated in the company's balance sheet, thus vastly increasing its visibility), pension fund assets had to be marked to market and future liabilities discounted using the yield on investment-grade bonds (which meant that a lower yield served to increase the liability, all other things being equal).

27 Peter A. Hall, ed., *The Political Power of Economic Ideas* (Princeton, NJ: Princeton University Press, 1989), p. 176.

28 Jacob S. Hacker, *The Divided Welfare State: The Battle over Public and Private Social Benefits in the United States* (Cambridge: Cambridge University Press, 2002); Bernard Ebbinghaus, 'Can Path Dependence Explain Institutional Change? Two Approaches Applied to Welfare State Reform', Discussion Paper 05/2 (Cologne: Max-Planck-Institut für gesellschaftsforschung, 2005); James Mahoney and Kathleen Thelen, *Explaining Institutional Change: Ambiguity, Agency, and Power* (Cambridge: Cambridge University Press, 2010).

29 Pensions Commission, *A New Pensions Settlement for the Twenty-First Century. The Second Report of the Pensions Commission* (London: TSO, 2005), p. 2.

30 Sue Ward, 'Tables Turned', *Pensions World*, April 1996, pp. 61–62.

Bibliography

Archives

Alfred Sherman papers, Royal Holloway, University of London (ASP)
Conservative Party Archive, University of Oxford (CPA)
Geoffrey Howe papers, University of Oxford (HP)
HM Treasury, Private Office papers (Geoffrey Howe and Nigel Lawson), London (HMT)
Margaret Thatcher Archive, via the website of the Thatcher Foundation (MTA)
The National Archives, Kew, London (TNA)
     ACT   Government Actuary's Department
     BN   Department of Health and Social Security
     CAB   Cabinet Office, including minutes and memoranda of the Cabinet and Cabinet Committees
     PREM Prime Ministerial and No. 10 Downing Street files
     T   HM Treasury
National Association of Pension Funds Archive, London Metropolitan Archives, London (NAPFA)
Nigel Vinson papers, Institute of Economic Affairs, London (NVP)

Hansard

House of Commons debates (HC Debs)
House of Lords debates (HL Debs)

Newspapers and trade journals

Daily Mail
Daily Telegraph
Economist
Evening Standard
Financial Times
Guardian
New Statesman
Observer

370 *Bibliography*

Pensions World
Sunday Telegraph
Sunday Times
Times

Official publications

Command Papers

Note: the papers are ordered by date.

Cmd 6404: William Beveridge, *Social Insurance and Allied Services* (London: HMSO, 1942).

Cmd 6527: Minister of Reconstruction, *Employment Policy* (London: HMSO, 1944).

Cmnd 538: Ministry of Pensions and National Insurance, *Provision for Old Age: The Future Development of the National Insurance Scheme* (London: HMSO, 1958).

Cmnd 3883: Department of Health and Social Security, *National Superannuation and Social Insurance: Proposals for Earnings-Related Social Security* (London: HMSO, 1969).

Cmnd 4755: Department of Health and Social Security, *Strategy for Pensions: The Future Development of State and Occupational Provision* (London: HMSO, 1971).

Cmnd 5713: Department of Health and Social Security, *Better Pensions – Fully Protected against Inflation: Proposals for a New Pensions Scheme* (London: HMSO, 1974).

Cmnd 6514: Department of Health and Social Security, *Occupational Pension Schemes: Role of Members in the Running of Schemes* (London: HMSO, 1976).

Cmnd 7937: Harold Wilson, *Report of the Committee to Review the Functioning of Financial Institutions* [the Wilson Report] (London: HMSO, 1980).

Cmnd 8271: Occupational Pensions Board, *Improved Protection for the Occupational Pension Rights and Expectations of Early Leavers* (London: House of Commons, 1981).

Cmnd 8649: Occupational Pensions Board, *Greater Security for the Rights and Expectations of Members of Occupational Pension Schemes* (London: House of Commons, 1982).

Cmnd 9125: L. C. B. Gower, *Review of Investor Protection*, Part 1 [the Gower Report] (London: HMSO, 1984).

Cmnd 9432: Department of Trade and Industry, *Financial Services in the United Kingdom: A New Framework for Investor Protection* (London: HMSO, 1985).

Cmnd 9517: Department of Health and Social Security, *Reform of Social Security*, vol. 1: *Reform of Social Security* (London: HMSO, 1985).

Cmnd 9518: Department of Health and Social Security, *Reform of Social Security*, vol. 2: *Reform of Social Security: Programme for Change* (London: HMSO, 1985).

Cmnd 9519: Department of Health and Social Security, *Reform of Social Security*, vol. 3: *Reform of Social Security: Background Papers* (London: HMSO, 1985).

Cmnd 9520: Department of Health and Social Security, *Housing Benefit Review: Report of the Review Team* (London: HMSO, 1985).

Cmnd 9691: Department of Health and Social Security, *Reform of Social Security: Programme for Action* (London: HMSO, 1985).

Cm 2342: Royston Goode, *Pension Law Reform: The Report of the Pension Law Review Committee* [the Goode Report] (London: HMSO, 1993).

Cm 4179: Department of Social Security, *A New Contract for Welfare: Partnership in Pensions* (London: Department of Social Security, 1998).

Bibliography

Other official publications

Department of Health and Social Security, *Consultative Document on Improved Transferability for Early Leavers from Occupational Pension Schemes* (London: DHSS, 1984).

Department of Health and Social Security, *Personal Pensions: A Consultative Document* (London: HMSO, 1984).

Department of Health and Social Security and Government Actuary's Department, *Population, Pension Costs and Pensioners' Incomes: A Background Paper for the Inquiry into Provision for Retirement* (London: HMSO, 1984).

Financial Services Agency, Annual Reports.

Government Actuary, *Occupational Pension Schemes: A Survey by the Government Actuary* (London: HMSO, 1958).

———, *Occupational Pensions Schemes: Third Survey by the Government Actuary* (London: HMSO, 1968).

———, *Occupational Pension Schemes 1979: Sixth Survey by the Government Actuary* (London: HMSO, 1981).

———, *National Insurance Fund Long-Term Financial Estimates: Report by the Government Actuary on the First Quinquennial Review under Section 137 of the Social Security Act 1975*, HC 451 (London: HMSO, 1982).

———, *Occupational Pension Schemes 2004: Twelfth Survey by the Government Actuary* (London: Government Actuary's Department, 2005).

House of Commons' Select Committee on Social Security, *The Operation of Pension Funds*, HC 61 (London: House of Commons, 1992).

Andrew Large, *Financial Services Regulation: Making the Two Tier System Work* (London: Securities and Investment Board, 1993).

National Audit Office, *The Elderly: Information Requirements for Supporting the Elderly and Implications of Personal Pensions for the National Insurance Fund* (London: HMSO, 1990).

National Statistics, *Pension Trends* (London: TSO, 2005), and online supplements.

Pensions Commission, *Pensions: Challenges and Choices. The First Report of the Pensions Commission* (London: TSO, 2004).

———, *A New Pensions Settlement for the Twenty-First Century. The Second Report of the Pensions Commission* (London: TSO, 2005).

Ron Sandler, *Sandler Review: Medium and Long-Term Retail Savings in the UK* (London: HM Treasury, 2002).

Other primary sources

Adam Smith Institute, *Omega Report: Social Security* (London: Adam Smith Institute, 1984).

Association of Consulting Actuaries, *Pensions in Smaller Firms Survey 2001: Occupational Pensions: The End of an Era?* (London: Association of Consulting Actuaries, 2001).

Sir Bryan Carsberg, *Financial Services Act 1986: The Marketing and Sale of Investment-Linked Insurance Products: The Rules of the Securities and Investments Board and the Life Assurance and Unit Trust Regulatory Organisation, a Report to the Chancellor of the Exchequer by the Director General of Fair Trading* [the Carsberg Report] (London: Office of Fair Trading, 1993).

Bibliography

Centre for Policy Studies, with foreword by Sir Keith Joseph, *Why Britain Needs a Social Market Economy* (London: Centre for Policy Studies, 1975).

Philip Chappell, *Pensions and Privilege: How to End the Scandal, Simplify Taxes and Widen Ownership* (London: Centre for Policy Studies, 1988).

Confederation of British Industry and Clay & Partners, *Occupational Pension Schemes: Securing the Future* (London: Confederation of British Industry, 1992).

Conservative Central Office, *A Better Tomorrow* [1970 general election manifesto] (London: Conservative Central Office, 1970).

———, *The Right Approach: A Statement of Conservative Aims* (London: Conservative Central Office, 1976).

———, *1979 Conservative Party General Election Manifesto* (London: Conservative Central Office, 1979).

———, *The Challenge of Our Times* [1983 general election manifesto] (London: Conservative Central Office, 1983).

———, *The Next Moves Forward* [1987 general election manifesto] (London: Conservative Central Office, 1987).

Peter F. Drucker, *The Unseen Revolution: How Pension Fund Socialism Came to America* (London: Heinemann, 1976).

Ludwig Erhard, *Prosperity through Competition* (New York: Frederick A. Praeger, 1958).

Walter Euken, 'Competition as the Basic Principle of the Economic Constitution [1942]', in *The Birth of Austerity: German Ordoliberalism and Contemporary Neoliberalism*, ed. by Thomas Biebricher and Frieder Vogelmann (London: Rowman & Littlefield, 2017), pp. 81–98.

Milton Friedman, 'Neo-Liberalism and Its Prospects', *Farmand* (17 February 1951), 89–93.

———, *Capitalism and Freedom* (Chicago: University of Chicago Press, 1962).

———, *Counter-Revolution in Monetary Theory* (London: Institute of Economic Affairs, 1970).

Milton Friedman and Rose D. Friedman, *Free to Choose: A Personal Statement* (London: Secker & Warburg, 1980).

F. A. von Hayek, *The Road to Serfdom* (London: Routledge & Kegan Paul, 1944).

———, 'The Use of Knowledge in Society', *The American Economic Review*, 35:4 (1945), 519–30.

———, *The Constitution of Liberty* (Oxford: Routledge, 1960).

———, 'Competition as a Discovery Procedure [1968]', *Quarterly Journal of Austrian Economics*, 5:3 (2002), 9–23.

F. A. von Hayek, Stephen Kresge, Leif Wenar, Stephen Kresge, and Leif Wenar, *Hayek on Hayek: An Autobiographical Dialogue, Collected Works of F.A. Hayek* (London: Routledge, 1994).

Geoffrey Howe, Keith Joseph, James Prior, and David Howell, *The Right Approach to the Economy: Outline of an Economic Strategy for the Next Conservative Government* (London: Conservative Central Office, 1977).

John Hutton, *Securing Our Future: The Pensions Challenge* (London: Institute for Public Policy Research, 2005).

Keith Joseph, *Stranded on the Middle Ground? Reflections on Circumstances and Policies* (London: Centre for Policy Studies, 1976).

———, *Monetarism Is Not Enough* (Chichester: Centre for Policy Studies, 1976).

Institute and Faculty of Actuaries, 'State and Occupational Pension Provision (Abstract of Sessional Meeting on 25 November 1974)', *Journal of the Institute of Actuaries*, 102 (1975), 17–33.

Frank Knight, 'Lippmann's *The Good Society*', *Journal of Political Economy*, 46:6 (1938), 864–72.

Labour Party, *National Superannuation: Labour's Policy for Security in Old Age* (London: Labour Party, 1957).

———, *Let's Go with Labour for the New Britain* [1964 general election manifesto] (London: Labour Party, 1964).

———, *Labour's Programme 1973* (London: Labour Party, 1973).

———, *Let Us Work Together: Labour's Way Out of the Crisis* [February 1974 general election manifesto] (London: Labour Party, 1974).

———, *Report of the Annual Conference and Special Conference of the Labour Party, 1985* (London: Labour Party, 1985).

———, *New Labour: Because Britain Deserves Better* [1997 general election manifesto] (London: Labour Party, 1997).

Walter Lippmann, *The Good Society* (London: Allen & Unwin, 1937).

Harold Macmillan, *The Middle Way: A Study of the Problem of Economic and Social Progress in a Free and Democratic Society* (London: Macmillan, 1938).

Karl Marx and Friedrich Engels, *The Communist Manifesto* (London: Penguin Books, 2002).

National Association of Pension Funds, 'Truth, Honour and Democracy: The Finance Bill 1989' (London: NAPF, 1989).

William A. Niskanen, *Bureaucracy: Servant or Master?* (London: Institute of Economic Affairs, 1973).

Hugh Pemberton, ed., 'The Fowler Inquiry into Provision for Retirement and the Pension Reforms of 1986. A Witness Seminar Held at the Institute and Faculty of Actuaries High Holborn, London, 6 December 2017' (Bristol: University of Bristol, 2017). Transcript available online: https://research-information.bris.ac.uk/en/publications/the-fowler-inquiry-into-provision-for-retirement-and-the-pension–2.

Pensions & Investment Research Consultants, 'Approved Personal Pensions: Advice Given on Contracting Out', Pension Services Report 1 (London: PIRC, 1990).

Politico's, *Party Political Broadcasts: The Greatest Hits*, VHS (London: Politico's, 1999).

John Redwood, *Equity for Everyman: New Ways to Widen Ownership* (London: Centre for Policy Studies, 1986).

———, *The Popular Capitalist Manifesto* (London: British Young Conservatives, 1989).

Alexander Rüstow, 'Social Policy or Vitalpolitik (Organic) Policy [1951]', in *The Birth of Austerity: German Ordoliberalism and Contemporary Neoliberalism*, ed. by Thomas Biebricher and Frieder Vogelmann (London: Rowman & Littlefield, 2017), pp. 163–77.

Stock Exchange, *The Stock Exchange Survey of Share Ownership* (London: Stock Exchange, 1983).

Nigel Vinson and Philip Chappell, *Personal and Portable Pensions for All* (London: Centre for Policy Studies, 1983).

———, 'Owners All: A Proposal for Personal Investment Pools' (London: Centre for Policy Studies, 1985).

World Bank, *Averting the Old Age Crisis* (Oxford: Oxford University Press, 1994).

374   *Bibliography*

Autobiographies

Joel Barnett, *Inside the Treasury* (London: Andre Deutsch, 1982).

Barbara Castle, *The Castle Diaries, 1974–76* (London: Weidenfeld & Nicolson, 1980).

Edmund Dell, *A Hard Pounding: Politics and Economic Crisis in 1974–76* (Oxford: Oxford University Press, 1991).

Norman Fowler, *Ministers Decide: A Personal Memoir of the Thatcher Years* (London: Chapmans, 1991).

Nigel Lawson, *The View from No. 11: Memoirs of a Tory Radical* (London: Bantam Press, 1992).

Leo Pliatzky, *Getting and Spending* (Oxford: Blackwell, 1982).

Margaret Thatcher, *The Downing Street Years* (London: HarperCollins, 1993).

Secondary sources

Paul Addison, *The Road to 1945: British Politics and the Second World War* (London: Jonathan Cape, 1975).

Lewis Allan, 'Thatcher's Economists: Ideas and Opposition in 1980s Britain' (D.Phil., Oxford University, 2008).

Kenneth J. Arrow, 'Increasing Returns: Historiographical Issues and Path Dependence', *European Journal of the History of Economic Thought*, 7:2 (2000), 171–80.

Terry Arthur, 'Pensions and Public Choice: The Road to Myners', *Economic Affairs*, 22:3 (2002), 43–47.

W. Brian Arthur, 'Competing Technologies, Increasing Returns, and Lock-in by Historical Events', *The Economic Journal*, 99:394 (1989), 116–31.

———, *Increasing Returns and Path Dependence in the Economy* (Ann Arbor, MI: University of Michigan Press, 1994).

Stuart Aveyard, Paul Corthorn, and Sean O'Connell, *The Politics of Consumer Credit in the UK, 1938–1992* (Oxford: Oxford University Press, 2018).

Yally Avrahampour, '"Cult of Equity": Actuaries and the Transformation of Pension Fund Investing, 1948–1960', *Business History Review*, 89:2 (2015). 281–304.

Roger Backhouse, 'The Macroeconomics of Margaret Thatcher', *Journal of the History of Economic Thought*, 24:3 (2002), 313–34.

Robert Bacon and Walter Eltis, *Britain's Economic Problem: Too Few Producers* (London: Macmillan, 1976).

David M. Barnard, 'The United Kingdom Financial Services Act, 1986: A New Regulatory Framework', *The International Lawyer*, 21:2 (1987), 343–56.

Nicholas Barr, 'Pensions: Overview of the Issues', *Oxford Review of Economic Policy*, 22:1 (2006), 1–14.

Norman Barry, 'The "New Right"', in *The Political Thought of the Conservative Party since 1945*, ed. by Kevin Hickson (Basingstoke: Palgrave Macmillan, 2005), pp. 28–50.

Gary Becker, 'Investment in Human Capital: A Theoretical Analysis', *Journal of Political Economy*, 70:5 (1962), 9–49.

Daniel Béland, 'Ideas and Social Policy: An Institutionalist Perspective', *Social Policy & Administration*, 39:1 (2005), 1–18.

Daniel Béland, Martin B. Carstensen, and Leonard Seabrooke, 'Ideas, Political Power and Public Policy', *Journal of European Public Policy*, 23:3 (2016), 315–17.

Bibliography

Sheri Berman, *The Social Democratic Moment* (Cambridge, MA: Harvard University Press, 1998).

——, 'Ideas, Norms, and Culture in Political Analysis', *Comparative Politics*, 33:2 (2001), 231–50.

——, 'Ideational Theorizing in the Social Sciences since "Policy Paradigms, Social Learning, and the State"', *Governance*, 26:2 (2013), 217–37.

Craig Berry, 'Austerity, Ageing and the Financialisation of Pensions Policy in the UK', *British Politics*, 11:1 (2016), 2–25.

Kean Birch, 'Neoliberalism: The Whys and Wherefores … and Future Directions', *Sociology Compass*, 9:7 (2015), 571–84.

Lawrence Black, '1968 and All That(cher)', in *Inventing the Silent Majority in Western Europe and the United States: Conservatism in the 1960s and 1970s*, ed. by Anna Von der Goltz and Britta Waldschmidt-Nelson (Cambridge: Cambridge University Press, 2017), pp. 356–76.

Lawrence Black and Hugh Pemberton, 'The Winter of Discontent in British Politics', *Political Quarterly*, 80:4 (2009), 553–61.

——, 'Introduction. The Benighted Decade? Reassessing the 1970s', in *Reassessing 1970s Britain*, ed. by Lawrence Black, Hugh Pemberton, and Pat Thane (Manchester: Manchester University Press, 2013), pp. 1–24.

Dean Blackburn, 'Reassessing Britain's "Post-war Consensus": The Politics of Reason 1945-1979)', *British Politics*, 13:2 (2017), 195–214.

Robin Blackburn, *Banking on Death or Investing in Life: The History and Future of Pensions* (London: Verso, 2002).

David Blake, 'Does It Matter What Type of Pension Scheme You Have?', *The Economic Journal*, 110:461 (2000), F46–F81.

——, *Pension Schemes and Pension Funds in the United Kingdom* (Oxford: Oxford University Press, 2003).

——, 'The UK Pension System: Key Issues', *Pensions: An International Journal*, 8:4 (2003), 330–75.

Erik Bleich, 'Integrating Ideas into Policy-Making Analysis: Frames and Race Policies in Britain and France', *Comparative Political Studies*, 35:9 (2002), 1054–76.

Andrew Blick, *People Who Live in the Dark: The History of the Special Adviser in British Politics* (London: Politico's, 2004).

Andrew Blick and George Jones, *At Power's Elbow: Aides to the Prime Minister from Robert Walpole to David Cameron* (London: Biteback, 2013).

Mark Blyth, *Great Transformations: Economic Ideas and Institutional Change in the Twentieth Century* (Cambridge: Cambridge University Press, 2002).

——, 'Structures Do Not Come with an Instruction Sheet: Interests, Ideas, and Progress in Political Science', *Perspectives on Politics*, 1:4 (2003), 695–706.

Peter Blythe, 'Why Did UK Private Sector Defined Benefit Occupational Pension Schemes Grow So Strongly in the Middle Years of the Twentieth Century, Then Decline So Rapidly at the End of the Century and the Beginning of the Twenty First?' (PhD, King's College London, 2021).

Taylor C. Boas and Jordan Gans-Morse, 'Neoliberalism: From New Liberal Philosophy to Anti-Liberal Slogan', *Studies in Comparative International Development*, 44:2 (2009), 137–61.

Peter J. Boettke and Edward L. López, 'Austrian Economics and Public Choice', *The Review of Austrian Economics*, 15:2/3 (2002), 111–19.

Peter J. Boettke and Alain Marciano, 'The Past, Present and Future of Virginia Political Economy', *Public Choice*, 163:1 (2015), 53–65.

Bibliography

Franz Böhm, 'Economic Ordering as a Problem of the Economy and a Problem of the Economic Constitution', in *The Birth of Austerity: German Ordoliberalism and Contemporary Neoliberalism*, ed. by Thomas Biebricher and Frieder Vogelmann (London: Rowman & Littlefield, 2017), pp. 115–20.

Franz Böhm, Walter Euken, and Hans Grossmann-Doerth, 'The Ordo Manifesto of 1936', in *The Birth of Austerity: German Ordoliberalism and Contemporary Neoliberalism*, ed. by Thomas Biebricher and Frieder Vogelmann (London: Rowman & Littlefield, 2017), pp. 27–40.

Werner Bonefeld, 'Freedom and the Strong State: On German Ordoliberalism', *New Political Economy*, 17:5 (2012), 633–56.

Giuliano Bonoli, *The Politics of Pension Reform: Institutions and Policy Change in Western Europe* (Cambridge: Cambridge University Press, 2000).

Thomas Borstelmann, *The 1970s: A New Global History from Civil Rights to Economic Inequality* (Princeton, NJ: Princeton University Press, 2012).

Nicholas Bosanquet, *After the New Right* (London: Heinemann, 1983).

Tom Bower, *Maxwell: The Final Verdict* (London: HarperCollins, 1995).

Antoine Bozio, Rowena Crawford, and Gemma Tetlow, *The History of State Pensions in the UK: 1948–2010* (London: Institute for Fiscal Studies, 2010).

Paul Bridgen, 'Making a Mess of Modernisation: The State, Redundancy Pay and Economic Policy-Making in the Early 1960s', *Twentieth Century British History*, 11:3 (1999), 233–58.

——, 'Policy Paradigms, the "Beveridge Model" and UK Pensions Policy in the Early Post-War Period', paper given to the inaugural ESPANet conference, Copenhagen, Denmark (14 November 2003).

——, 'A Straitjacket with Wriggle Room: The Beveridge Report, the Treasury and the Exchequer's Pension Liability, 1942–1959', *Twentieth Century British History*, 17:1 (2006), 1–25.

Samuel Brittan, 'The Economic Consequences of Democracy', *British Journal of Political Science*, 5:2 (1975), 129–59.

——, *The Economic Consequences of Democracy* (London: Temple Smith, 1977).

——, *The Role and Limits of Government: Essays in Political Economy* (London: Temple Smith, 1983).

——, 'A Time for Confession', in *Reassessing 1970s Britain*, ed. by Lawrence Black, Hugh Pemberton, and Pat Thane (Manchester: Manchester University Press, 2013), pp. 61–68.

A. J. C. Britton, *Macroeconomic Policy in Britain, 1974–1987* (Cambridge: Cambridge University Press, 1994).

Stephen Brooke, 'Living in "New Times": Historicizing 1980s Britain', *History Compass*, 12:1 (2014), 20–32.

Richard Brooks, Sue Regan, and Peter Robinson, *A New Contract for Retirement* (London: Institute for Public Policy Research, 2002).

Joan C. Brown and Stephen Small, *Occupational Benefits as Social Security* (London: Policy Studies Institute, 1985).

Alex Brummer, *The Great Pensions Robbery* (London: Random House, 2010).

James M Buchanan, 'Politics without Romance: A Sketch of Positive Public Choice Theory and Its Normative Implications', in *The Theory of Public Choice*, ed. by James M. Buchanan and Robert D. Tollison (Ann Arbor, MI: University of Michigan Press, 1984), pp. 11–22.

Bibliography

James M. Buchanan and Gordon Tullock, *The Calculus of Consent: Logical Foundations of Constitutional Democracy* (Ann Arbor, MI: University of Michigan Press: 1962).

Jim Bulpitt, 'The Discipline of the New Democracy: Mrs Thatcher's Domestic Statecraft', *Political Studies*, 34:1 (1986), 19–39.

Angus Burgin, *The Great Persuasion: Reinventing Free Markets since the Depression* (Cambridge, MA: Harvard University Press, 2012).

Kathleen Burk and Alec Cairncross, *'Goodbye Great Britain': The 1976 IMF Crisis* (New Haven, CT: Yale University Press, 1992).

David Card, Richard Blundell, and Richard B. Freeman, *Seeking a Premier League Economy: The Economic Effects of British Economic Reforms, 1980–2000* (Chicago: University of Chicago Press, 2004).

Martin B. Carstensen and Vivien A. Schmidt, 'Power through, over and in Ideas: Conceptualizing Ideational Power in Discursive Institutionalism', *Journal of European Public Policy*, 23:3 (2016), 318–37.

Peter Catterall, 'Twenty-Five Years of Promoting Free Markets: A History of Economic Affairs', *Economic Affairs*, 25:4 (2005), 48–53.

Philip Cerny, 'The Dynamics of Financial Globalization: Technology, Market Structure, and Policy Response', *Policy Sciences*, 27:4 (1994), 319–42.

John Charmley, *A History of Conservative Politics since 1830* (Basingstoke: Palgrave Macmillan, 2008).

Brian R. Cheffins, *Corporate Ownership and Control: Evolution of the UK System* (Oxford: Oxford University Press, 2010).

Gordon L. Clark, *Pension Fund Capitalism* (Oxford: Oxford University Press, 2000).

———, 'The UK Occupational Pension System in Crisis', in *Britain's Pensions Crisis: History and Policy*, ed. by Hugh Pemberton, Pat Thane, and Noel Whiteside (Oxford: Oxford University Press, 2006), pp. 145–68.

Ian Clark, 'The British Home Stores Pension Scheme: Privatised Looting?', *Industrial Relations Journal*, 50:4 (2019), 331–47.

P. F. Clarke, *Lancashire and the New Liberalism* (Cambridge: Cambridge University Press, 1971).

Richard Cockett, *Thinking the Unthinkable: Think-Tanks and the Economic Counter-Revolution, 1931–1983* (London: Fontana, 1995).

Chris Cooper, 'Little Local Difficulties Revisited: Peter Thorneycroft, the 1958 Treasury Resignations and the Origins of Thatcherism', *Contemporary British History*, 25:2 (2011), 224–50.

Melinda Cooper, *Family Values: Between Neoliberalism and the New Social Conservatism* (New York: Zone Books, 2017).

Richard Coopey and Nicholas Woodward, eds., *Britain in the 1970s: The Troubled Economy* (New York: St Martin's Press, 1996).

Nick Crafts, 'Reversing Relative Economic Decline? The 1980s in Historical Perspective', *Oxford Review of Economic Policy*, 7:3 (1991), 81–98.

James E. Cronin, *New Labour's Pasts: The Labour Party and Its Discontents* (Harlow: Longman, 2004).

Tony Cutler and Barbara Waine, 'Social Insecurity and the Retreat from Social Democracy: Occupational Welfare in the Long Boom and Financialization', *Review of International Political Economy*, 8:1 (2001), 96–118.

Martin Daunton, *Just Taxes: The Politics of Taxation in Britain, 1914–1979* (Cambridge: Cambridge University Press, 2002).

Paul David, 'Path Dependence: A Foundational Concept for Historical Social Science', *Cliometrica*, 1:2 (2007), 91–114.

Aled Davies, '"Right to Buy": The Development of a Conservative Housing Policy, 1945–1980', *Contemporary British History*, 27:4 (2013), 421–44.

———, *The City of London and Social Democracy: The Political Economy of Finance in Britain, 1959–1979* (Oxford: Oxford University Press, 2017).

———, 'Pension Funds and the Politics of Ownership in Britain, c.1970–86', *Twentieth Century British History*, 30:1 (2019), 81–107.

Aled Davies, James Freeman, and Hugh Pemberton, '"Everyman a Capitalist" or "Free to Choose"? Exploring the Tensions within Thatcherite Individualism', *The Historical Journal*, 61:2 (2017), 477–501.

———, 'Thatcher's Policy Unit and the "Neoliberal Vision"', *Journal of British Studies*, 62:1 (2023), 77–103.

Bryn Davies, *Better Pensions for All* (London: Institute for Public Policy Research, 1993).

Philip E. Davis, 'Is There a Pensions Crisis in the UK?', *Geneva Papers on Risk and Insurance Issues and Practice*, 29:3 (2004), 343–70.

William Davies, 'The Making of Neo-Liberalism', *Renewal*, 17:4 (2009), 88–92.

Andrew Denham and Mark Garnett, 'The Nature and Impact of Think Tanks in Contemporary Britain', *Contemporary British History*, 10:1 (1996), 43–91.

———, 'Influence without Responsibility: Think-Tanks in Britain', *Parliamentary Affairs*, 52:1 (1999), 46–57.

———, *Keith Joseph* (Chesham: Acumen, 2002).

Laurie Dennett, *A Sense of Security: 150 Years of the Prudential* (Cambridge: Granta Editions, 1998).

———, *Mind over Data: An Actuarial History* (Cambridge: Granta Editions, 2004).

Radhika Desai, 'Second-Hand Dealers in Ideas: Think-Tanks and Thatcherite Hegemony', *New Left Review*, 203 (1994), 27–64.

Alec Dinnin, 'Ortega y Gasset: The Fear of Mass Society', in *The Oxford Handbook of Ordoliberalism*, ed. by Thomas Biebricher, Werner Bonefeld, and Peter Nedergaard (Oxford: Oxford University Press, 2022), pp. 230–42.

Richard Disney, 'Crises in Public Pension Programmes in OECD: What Are the Reform Options?', *The Economic Journal*, 110:461 (2000), F1–F23.

Richard Disney and Gary Stears, 'Why Is There a Decline in Defined Benefit Pension Plan Membership in Britain?', Working Paper 96/04 (London: Institute for Fiscal Studies, 1996).

Peter Dorey, 'The Exhaustion of a Tradition: The Death of "One Nation" Toryism', *Contemporary Politics*, 2:4 (1996), 47–66.

———, *Wage Politics in Britain: The Rise and Fall of Incomes Policies since 1945* (Brighton: Sussex Academic Press, 2002).

James Douglas, 'The Overloaded Crown', *British Journal of Political Science*, 6:4 (1976), 483–505.

J. C. R. Dow, *Major Recessions: Britain and the World, 1920–1995* (Oxford: Oxford University Press, 2000).

Paul Draper, 'The New Framework for Investor Protection: Cmnd 9432', *Quarterly Economic Commentary*, 10:3 (1985), 64–67.

Patrick Dunleavy and Brendan O'Leary, *Theories of the State: The Politics of Liberal Democracy* (Basingstoke: Macmillan Education, 1987).

David Dutton, *British Politics since 1945: The Rise, Fall and Rebirth of Consensus* (Oxford: Blackwell, 1997).

Bibliography

Bernard Ebbinghaus, 'Can Path Dependence Explain Institutional Change? Two Approaches Applied to Welfare State Reform', Discussion Paper 05/2 (Cologne: Max-Planck-Institut für gesellschaftsforschung, 2005).

David Edgerton, *The Rise and Fall of the British Nation: A Twentieth-Century History* (London: Penguin Books, 2018).

———, 'What Came between Liberalism and Neoliberalism? Rethinking Keynesianism, the Welfare State, and Social Democracy', in *The Neoliberal Age? Britain since the 1970s*, ed. by Aled Davies, Ben Jackson, and Florence Sutcliffe-Braithwaite (London: UCL Press, 2021), pp. 30–51.

Amy Edwards, '"Financial Consumerism": Citizenship, Consumerism and Capital Ownership in the 1980s', *Contemporary British History*, 31:2 (2017), 210–29.

———, *Are We Rich Yet? The Rise of Mass Investment Culture in Contemporary Britain* (Oakland, CA: University of California Press, 2022).

Bryan Ellis, *Pensions in Britain, 1955–1975: A History in Five Acts* (London: HMSO, 1989).

Gerald A. Epstein, *Financialization and the World Economy* (Cheltenham: Edward Elgar, 2015).

Eric J. Evans, *Thatcher and Thatcherism* (London: Routledge, 2013).

Stephen Evans, 'The Not So Odd Couple: Margaret Thatcher and One Nation Conservatism', *Contemporary British History*, 23:1 (2009), 101–21.

Stephen Farrall and Colin Hay, eds., *The Legacy of Thatcherism: Assessing and Exploring Thatcherite Social and Economic Policies* (Oxford: Oxford University Press, 2014).

Helen Fawcett, 'The Beveridge Strait-Jacket: Policy Formulation and the Problem of Poverty in Old Age', *Contemporary British History*, 10:1 (1996), 20–42.

Lars P. Feld, Ekkehard A. Köhler, and Daniel Nientiedt, 'Ordoliberalism, Pragmatism and the Eurozone Crisis: How the German Tradition Shaped Economic Policy in Europe', *European Review of International Studies*, 2:3 (2015), 48–61.

Niall Ferguson, Charles S. Maier, Erez Manella, and Daniel J. Sargent, eds., *The Shock of the Global: The 1970s in Perspective* (Cambridge, MA: Harvard University Press, 2010).

Maurizio Ferrera, 'Pension Reforms in Southern Europe: The Italian Experience', in *Britain's Pensions Crisis: History and Policy*, ed. by Hugh Pemberton, Pat Thane, and Noel Whiteside (Oxford: Oxford University Press, 2006), pp. 208–22.

Alan Finlayson, 'Political Science, Political Ideas and Rhetoric', *Economy and Society*, 33:4 (2004), 528–49.

Warren P. Fishbein, *Wage Restraint by Consensus* (London: Routledge & Kegan Paul, 1984).

Michel Foucault, *The Birth of Biopolitics: Lectures at the Collège de France, 1978–79*, ed. by Michel Senellart, trans. by Graham Burchell (Basingstoke: Palgrave Macmillan, 2008).

Marion Fourcade-Gourinchas and Sarah L. Babb, 'The Rebirth of the Liberal Creed: Paths to Neoliberalism in Four Countries', *American Journal of Sociology*, 108:3 (2002), 533–79.

Matthew Francis, '"A Crusade to Enfranchise the Many": Thatcherism and the "Property-Owning Democracy"', *Twentieth Century British History*, 23:2 (2012), 275–97.

Derek Fraser, *The Evolution of the British Welfare State* (Basingstoke: Macmillan, 2009).

Duncan Fraser, 'The Postwar Consensus: A Debate Not Long Enough?', *Parliamentary Affairs*, 53:2 (2000), 347–62.

Michael Freeden, *The New Liberalism: An Ideology of Social Reform* (Oxford: Clarendon Press, 1978).

James Freeman, 'Reconsidering "Set the People Free": Neoliberalism and Freedom Rhetoric in Churchill's Conservative Party', *Twentieth Century British History*, 29:4 (2018), 522–46.

———, 'Neoliberalism and Conservatism in Britain', in *The Neoliberal Age? Britain since the 1970s*, ed. by Aled Davies, Ben Jackson, and Florence Sutcliffe-Braithwaite (London: UCL Press, 2021), pp. 254–75.

Gerald Frost, *Making Things Happen: The Life and Original Thinking of Nigel Vinson* (London: Biteback Publishing, 2015).

Andrew Gamble, *The Free Economy and the Strong State: The Politics of Thatcherism* (Basingstoke: Macmillan, 1994).

———, *Hayek: The Iron Cage of Liberty* (Cambridge: Polity, 1996).

Mark Garnett and Ian Gilmour, 'Thatcherism and the Conservative Tradition', in *The Conservatives and British Society, 1880–1990*, ed. by Martin Francis and Ina Zweiniger-Bargielowska (Cardiff: University of Wales Press, 1996), pp. 78–93.

Clifford Geertz, 'Ideology as a Cultural System', in *Ideology and Discontent*, ed. by David Apted (London: Free Press, 1964), pp. 47–76.

Vic George and Paul Wilding, *Ideology and Social Welfare* (London: Routledge & Kegan Paul, 1984).

Ian Gilmour, *Dancing with Dogma: Britain under Thatcherism* (London: Simon & Schuster, 1992).

David Gladstone, ed., *British Social Welfare* (London: UCL Press, 1995).

Howard Glennerster, 'Why So Different? Why So Bad a Future?', in *Britain's Pensions Crisis: History and Policy*, ed. by Hugh Pemberton, Pat Thane, and Noel Whiteside (Oxford: Oxford University Press, 2006), pp. 64–73.

———, *British Social Policy, 1945 to the Present* (Oxford: Blackwell, 2007).

Howard Glennerster and Martin Evans, 'Beveridge and His Assumptive Worlds: The Incompatibilities of a Flawed Design', in *Beveridge and Social Security*, ed. by John Hills, John Ditch, and Howard Glennerster (Oxford: Oxford University Press, 1994), pp. 56–72.

Andrew Glyn, *Capitalism Unleashed: Finance, Globalization and Welfare* (Oxford: Oxford University Press, 2006).

J. Goldstein and R. O. Keohane, 'Ideas and Foreign Policy: An Analytical Framework', in *Ideas and Foreign Policy: An Analytical Framework*, ed. by J. Goldstein and R. O. Keohane (Ithaca, NY: Cornell University Press, 1993), pp. 3–30.

———, eds., *Ideas and Foreign Policy: An Analytical Framework* (Ithaca, NY: Cornell University Press, 1993).

Scott Gordon, 'The Political Economy of F. A. Hayek', *The Canadian Journal of Economics*, 14:3 (1981), 470–87.

Ian Gough, 'Thatcherism and the Welfare State', *Marxism Today* (July 1980), 7–12.

Thomas J. Gould, 'The Changing Practices of Managing Uncertainty and Risk in Post War British Political Economy: Investments, Insurance, Pensions and Professional Risk Managers c. 1945–1995' (PhD, University of Bristol, 2021).

Peter A. Gourevitch, *Politics in Hard Times* (Ithaca, NY: Cornell University Press, 1986).

L. C. B. Gower, '"Big Bang" and City Regulation', *The Modern Law Review*, 51:1 (1988), 1–22.

John Grahl, 'Bump Starting Britain', *Marxism Today* (December 1984), 7–12.

E. H. H. Green, 'Thatcherism: An Historical Perspective', *Transactions of the Royal Historical Society*, 9 (1999), 17–52.

———, 'The Treasury Resignations of 1958: A Reconsideration', *Twentieth Century British History*, 11:4 (2000), 409–30.

———, *Thatcher* (London: Hodder Arnold, 2006).

Alan Gregory and Ian Tonks, 'Performance of Personal Pension Schemes in the UK', Research Paper 06/11 (Exeter: University of Exeter, Xfi Centre for Finance and Investment, 2006).

Matthew Grimley, 'Thatcherism, Morality and Religion', in *Making Thatcher's Britain*, ed. by Ben Jackson and Robert Saunders (Cambridge: Cambridge University Press, 2012), pp. 78–94.

Chris Guest, 'Hayek on Government: Two Views or One?', *History of Economics Review*, 26:1 (1997), 51–67.

James D. Gwartney and Randall G. Holcombe, 'Politics as Exchange: The Classical Liberal Economics and Politics of James M. Buchanan', *Constitutional Political Economy*, 25:3 (2014), 265–79.

Graham Hacche and Christopher Taylor, eds., *Inside the Bank of England: Memoirs of Christopher Dow, Chief Economist, 1973–84* (Basingstoke: Palgrave Macmillan, 2014).

Jacob S. Hacker, *The Divided Welfare State: The Battle over Public and Private Social Benefits in the United States* (Cambridge: Cambridge University Press, 2002).

———, 'Policy Drift: The Hidden Politics of US Welfare State Retrenchment', in *Beyond Continuity: Institutional Change in Advanced Political Economies*, ed. by Wolfgang Streeck and Kathleen Thelen (Oxford: Oxford University Press, 2005), pp. 40–82.

Peter A. Hall, 'The Movement from Keynesianism to Monetarism: Institutional Analysis and British Economic Policy in the 1970s', in *Structuring Politics: Historical Institutionalism in Comparative Analysis*, ed. by Sven Steinmo, Kathleen Thelen, and Frank Longstreth (Cambridge: Cambridge University Press, 1992), pp. 90–113.

———, 'Policy Paradigms, Social Learning and the State: The Case of Economic Policy Making in Britain', *Comparative Politics*, 25:3 (1993), 275–96.

———, 'The Role of Interests, Institutions and Ideas in the Comparative Political Economy of the Industrialized Nations', in *Comparative Politics: Rationality, Culture and Structure*, ed. by M. I. Lichbach and A. S. Zuckerman (Cambridge: Cambridge University Press, 1997), pp. 174–207.

———, ed., *The Political Power of Economic Ideas* (Princeton, NJ: Princeton University Press, 1989).

Stuart Hall, 'The Great Moving Right Show', *Marxism Today* (January 1979), 14–20.

Stuart Hall, Chas Critcher, Tony Jefferson, John Clarke, and Brian Roberts, *Policing the Crisis: Mugging, the State, and Law and Order* (London: Macmillan, 1977).

Stuart Hall and Martin Jacques, *The Politics of Thatcherism* (London: Lawrence & Wishart, 1983).

Jacob Hamburger and Daniel Steinmetz-Jenkins, 'Why Did Neoconservatives Join Forces with Neoliberals? Irving Kristol from Critic to Ally of Free-Market Economics', *Global Intellectual History*, 6:2 (2021), 215–30.

Leslie Hannah, *Inventing Retirement: The Development of Occupational Pensions in Britain* (Cambridge: Cambridge University Press, 1986).

Bernard Harris, *The Origins of the British Welfare State, 1800–1945* (London: Palgrave Macmillan, 2004).

Jose Harris, 'Enterprise and Welfare States: A Comparative Perspective', *Transactions of the Royal Historical Society*, 40 (1990), 175–95.

———, *William Beveridge* (Oxford: Clarendon Press, 1997).

Michael Harris, 'The Centre for Policy Studies: The Paradoxes of Power', *Contemporary British History*, 10:2 (1996), 51–64.

Ron Harris, 'Government and the Economy, 1688–1850', in *The Cambridge Economic History of Modern Britain*, ed. by Roderick Floud and Paul Johnson (Cambridge: Cambridge University Press, 2004), pp. 204–37.

Brian Harrison, 'Mrs Thatcher and the Intellectuals', *Twentieth Century British History*, 5:2 (1994), 206–45.

David Harvey, *A Brief History of Neoliberalism* (Oxford: Oxford University Press, 2005).

Colin Hay, 'Narrating Crisis: The Discursive Construction of the Winter of Discontent', *Sociology*, 30:1 (1996), 253–77.

———, *Political Analysis* (Basingstoke: Palgrave, 2002).

———, 'Ideas, Interests and Institutions in the Comparative Political Economy of Great Transformations', *Review of International Political Economy*, 11:1 (2004), 204–26.

———, 'Whatever Happened to Thatcherism?', *Political Studies Review*, 5:2 (2007), 183–201.

———, 'The Winter of Discontent Thirty Years On', *Political Quarterly*, 80:4 (2009), 545–52.

———, 'Chronicles of a Death Foretold: The Winter of Discontent and Construction of the Crisis of British Keynesianism', *Parliamentary Affairs*, 63:3 (2010), 446–70.

Nigel M. Healey, 'The Thatcher Supply-Side "Miracle": Myth or Reality?', *The American Economist*, 36:1 (1992), 7–12.

Anthony F. Heath, Roger M. Jowell, and John K. Curtice, *How Britain Votes* (Oxford: Pergamon Press, 1985).

Hugh Heclo, *Modern Social Politics in Britain and Sweden* (New Haven, CT: Yale University Press, 1974).

Richard Heffernan, *New Labour and Thatcherism: Political Change in Britain* (London: Palgrave Macmillan, 2001).

Kieran Heinemann, *Playing the Market: Retail Investment and Speculation in Twentieth-Century Britain* (New York: Oxford University Press, 2021).

Richard Hemming and John A. Kay, 'The Costs of the State Earnings Related Pension Scheme', *The Economic Journal*, 92:366 (1982), 300–19.

Peter Hennessy, *Whitehall* (London: Secker & Warburg, 1989).

Kevin Hickson, 'The Postwar Consensus Revisited', *Political Quarterly*, 75:2 (2004), 142–54.

———, *The IMF Crisis of 1976 and British Politics* (London: I.B. Tauris, 2005).

———, 'Lord Coleraine: The Neglected Prophet of the New Right', *Journal of Political Ideologies*, 14:2 (2009), 173–87.

Josef Hien, 'The Social Market Economy and Ordoliberalism: A Difficult Relationship', in *The Oxford Handbook of Ordoliberalism*, ed. by Thomas Biebricher, Werner Bonefeld, and Peter Nedergaard (Oxford: Oxford University Press, 2022), pp. 333–46.

Michael Hill, *The Welfare State in Britain: A Political History since 1945* (Aldershot: Edward Elgar, 1993).

————, *Pensions* (Bristol: Policy Press, 2007).

Sally Hills, Ryland Thomas, and Nicholas Dimsdale, 'The Bank of England's Three Centuries Macroeconomic Dataset, Version 2.3', ed. by Bank of England (London: 2016).

Jimmy M. Hinchliffe, 'The Financial Services Act: A Case Study in Regulatory Capture' (PhD, Sheffield Hallam University, 1999).

Karl Hinrichs, 'New Century – New Paradigm: Pension Reforms in Germany', in *Ageing and Pension Reform around the World: Evidence from Eleven Countries*, ed. by Giuliano Bonoli and Toshimitsu Shinkawa (Cheltenham: Edward Elgar, 2005), pp. 47–73.

Eric Hobsbawm, 'The Forward March of Labour Halted?', *Marxism Today* (September 1978), 279–86.

Martin Holmes, *Political Pressure and Economic Policy: British Government 1970–1974* (London: Butterworths, 1982).

Joan Isaac, 'The New Right and the Moral Society', *Parliamentary Affairs*, 43:2 (1990), 209–26.

Ben Jackson, 'At the Origins of Neo-Liberalism: The Free Economy and the Strong State, 1930–1947', *The Historical Journal*, 53:1 (2010), 129–51.

————, 'Freedom, the Common Good, and the Rule of Law: Lippmann and Hayek on Economic Planning', *Journal of the History of Ideas*, 73:1 (2012), 47–68.

————, 'The Think-Tank Archipelago: Thatcherism and Neo-Liberalism', in *Making Thatcher's Britain*, ed. by Ben Jackson and Robert Saunders (Cambridge: Cambridge University Press, 2012), pp. 43–61.

————, 'Currents of Neo-Liberalism: British Political Ideologies and the New Right, c.1955–1979', *The English Historical Review*, 131:551 (2016), 823–50.

————, 'Free Markets and Feminism: The Neo-Liberal Defence of the Male Breadwinner Model in Britain, c.1980–1997', *Women's History Review*, 28:2 (2019), 297–316.

————, 'Intellectual Histories of Neoliberalism and Their Limits', in *The Neoliberal Age? Britain since the 1970s*, ed. by Aled Davies, Ben Jackson, and Florence Sutcliffe-Braithwaite (London: UCL Press, 2021), pp. 52–72.

————, 'Putting Neoliberalism in Its Place', *Modern Intellectual History*, 19:3 (2022), 982–95.

Ben Jackson and Robert Saunders, eds., *Making Thatcher's Britain* (Cambridge: Cambridge University Press, 2012).

Simon James, 'The Idea Brokers: The Impact of Think Tanks on British Government', *Public Administration*, 71:4 (1993), 491–506.

Bob Jessop, Kevin Bonnett, Simon Bromley, and Tom Ling, 'Authoritarian Populism, Two Nations and Thatcherism', *New Left Review*, 147 (1984), 32.

Norman Johnson, *Reconstructing the Welfare State: A Decade of Change 1980–1990* (London: Harvester Wheatsheaf, 1990).

Paul Johnson, 'Fiscal Implications of Population Ageing', *Philosophical Transactions: Biological Sciences*, 352:1363 (1997), 1895–903.

Harriet Jones, 'The Cold War and the Santa Claus Syndrome', in *The Conservatives and British Society, 1880–1990*, ed. by Martin Francis and Ina Zweiniger-Bargielowska (Cardiff: University of Wales Press, 1996), pp. 240–54.

Harriet Jones and Michael Kandiah, eds., *The Myth of Consensus: New Views on British History, 1945–1964* (Basingstoke: Macmillan, 1996).

Tony Judt, *Postwar: A History of Europe since 1945* (London: Vintage, 2010).

384   *Bibliography*

Michael Kandiah and Anthony Seldon, *Ideas and Think Tanks in Contemporary Britain*, 2 vols. (London: Routledge, 2013).

Dennis Kavanagh, 'The Heath Government, 1970–74', in *Ruling Performance: British Governments from Attlee to Thatcher*, ed. by Peter Hennessy and Anthony Seldon (Oxford: Blackwell, 1987), pp. 216–40.

Anthony King, 'Overload: Problems of Governing in the 1970s', *Political Studies*, 23:2/3 (1975), 284–96.

———, *Why Is Britain Becoming Harder to Govern?* (London: BBC Books, 1976).

Anthony King and Ivor Crewe, *The Blunders of Our Governments* (London: Oneworld, 2013).

Desmond King, *The New Right: Politics, Markets and Citizenship* (London: Macmillan, 1987).

Frank H. Knight and Hubert Bonner, 'Ethics and Economic Reform', in *Freedom and Reform: Essays in Economics and Social Philosophy* (New York: Harper, 1947), pp. 45–128.

———, 'The Meaning of Democracy: Its Politico-Economic Structure and Ideals', in *Freedom and Reform: Essays in Economics and Social Philosophy* (New York: Harper, 1947), pp. 184–204.

Stefan Kolev and Nils Goldschmidt, 'Vitalpolitik', in *The Oxford Handbook of Ordoliberalism*, ed. by Thomas Biebricher, Werner Bonefeld, and Peter Nedergaard (Oxford: Oxford University Press, 2022), pp. 453–60.

Greta R. Krippner, 'The Financialization of the American Economy', *Socio-Economic Review*, 3:2 (2005), 173–208.

Jayesh Kumar, 'Impact of Pension Plan Funding Status on M&A Activity', Technical Paper 2006-TR-05 (London: Watson Wyatt, 2006).

David Kynaston, 'The Long Life and Slow Death of Exchange Controls', *Journal of International Financial Markets*, 2:2 (2000), 37–42.

———, *The City of London*, vol. 4: *A Club No More, 1945–2000* (London: Chatto & Windus, 2001).

Costas Lapavitsas, *Profiting without Producing* (London: Verso Books, 2013).

Jon Lawrence, *Me, Me, Me?: The Search for Community in Post-War England* (Oxford: Oxford University Press, 2019).

Richard Layard and Stephen Nickell, 'The Thatcher Miracle?', *The American Economic Review*, 79:2 (1989), 215–19.

Robert F. Leach, 'Thatcherism, Liberalism and Tory Collectivism', *Politics*, 3:1 (1983), 9–14.

Thomas Lemke, '"The Birth of Bio-Politics": Michel Foucault's Lecture at the Collège de France on Neo-Liberal Governmentality', *Economy and Society*, 30:2 (2001), 190–207.

Adam Lent, *British Social Movements since 1945: Sex, Colour, Peace, and Power* (Basingstoke: Palgrave, 2001).

Shirley Robin Letwin, *The Anatomy of Thatcherism* (London: Fontana, 1992).

Robert C. Lieberman, 'Ideas, Institutions, and Political Order: Explaining Political Change', *American Political Science Review*, 96:4 (2002), 697–712.

Craig Lindsay, 'A Century of Labour Market Change: An Overview of Labour Market Conditions in the Previous Century', *Labour Market Trends*, 111:9 (2003), 133–44.

Craig Lindsay and Paul Doyle, 'Experimental Consistent Time Series of Historical Labour Force Survey Data', *Labour Market Trends*, 111:9 (2003), 467–75.

Bibliography

John Littlewood, *The Stock Market: 50 Years of Capitalism at Work* (London: Financial Times, 1998).

Rodney Lowe, 'The Second World War, Consensus, and the Foundation of the Welfare State', *Twentieth Century British History*, 1:2 (1990), 152–82.

———, 'A Prophet Dishonoured in His Own Country? The Rejection of Beveridge in Britain, 1945–1970', in *Beveridge and Social Security*, ed. by John Hills, John Ditch, and Howard Glennerster (Oxford: Oxford University Press, 1994), pp. 118–33.

———, *The Welfare State in Britain since 1945* (London: Palgrave Macmillan, 2005).

Rodney Lowe and Hugh Pemberton, *The Official History of the British Civil Service: Reforming the Service*, vol. 2: *The Thatcher and Major Revolutions, 1982–97* (London: Routledge, 2020).

Tony Lynes, 'The British Case', in *Enterprise and the Welfare State*, ed. by Martin Rein and Eskil Wadensjö (Cheltenham: Edward Elgar, 1997), pp. 309–51.

John Macnicol, 'Beveridge and Old Age', in *Beveridge and Social Security*, ed. by John Hills, John Ditch, and Howard Glennerster (Oxford: Clarendon Press, 1994), pp. 73–96.

———, *The Politics of Retirement in Britain, 1878–1948* (Cambridge: Cambridge University Press, 1998).

James Mahoney, 'Path Dependence in Historical Sociology', *Theory and Society*, 29:4 (2000), 507–48.

James Mahoney and Kathleen Thelen, *Explaining Institutional Change: Ambiguity, Agency, and Power* (Cambridge: Cambridge University Press, 2010).

David Marsh and R. A. W. Rhodes, 'Implementing Thatcherism: Policy Change in the 1980s', *Parliamentary Affairs*, 45:1 (1992), 33–50.

———, eds., *Implementing Thatcherite Policies: Audit of an Era* (Buckingham: Open University Press, 1992).

Sarah Mass, 'Where Was Entrepreneurship in Post-War Britain? Freedom, Family, and Choice in Modern British Shopping', in *The Neoliberal Age? Britain since the 1970s*, ed. by Aled Davies, Ben Jackson, and Florence Sutcliffe-Braithwaite (London: UCL Press, 2021), pp. 176–96.

Matthias Matthijs, *Ideas and Economic Crises in Britain from Attlee to Blair (1945–2005)* (London: Routledge, 2010).

W. B. McBride, 'The Interaction between State and Occupational Pension Schemes in the United Kingdom', *Transactions of the Faculty of Actuaries*, 35 (1975–77), 199–280.

Jens Meierhenrich, 'Rechtsstaat versus the Rule of Law' in *The Cambridge Companion to the Rule of Law*, ed. by Jens Meierhenrich and Martin Loughlin (Cambridge: Cambridge University Press, 2021), pp. 39–67

Ranald C. Michie, *The London Stock Exchange: A History* (Oxford: Oxford University Press, 2001).

Roger Middleton, 'The Laffer Curve', in *Famous Figures and Diagrams in Economics*, ed. by Mark Blaug and P. J. Lloyd (Cheltenham: Edward Elgar, 2010), pp. 412–19.

———, 'Brittan on Britain: "The Economic Contradictions of Democracy" Redux', *The Historical Journal*, 54:4 (2011), 1141–68.

———, 'Brittan on Britain: Decline, Declinism and the "Traumas of the 1970s"', in *Reassessing 1970s Britain*, ed. by Lawrence Black, Hugh Pemberton, and Pat Thane (Manchester: Manchester University Press, 2013), pp. 69–95.

Bibliography

Laurence H. Miller, 'On the "Chicago School of Economics"', *Journal of Political Economy*, 70:1 (1962), 64–69.

Patrick Minford, 'Inflation, Unemployment and the Pound', in *Margaret Thatcher's Revolution*, ed. by Subroto Roy (London: Continuum, 2005), pp. 50–66.

Philip Mirowski, 'Postface: Defining Neoliberalism', in *The Road from Mont Pèlerin: The Making of the Neoliberal Thought Collective*, ed. by Philip Mirowski and Dieter Plehwe (Cambridge, MA: Harvard University Press, 2009), pp. 417–56.

———, 'Ordoliberalism within the Historical Trajectory of Neoliberalism', in *The Oxford Handbook of Ordoliberalism*, ed. by Thomas Biebricher, Werner Bonefeld, and Peter Nedergaard (Oxford: Oxford University Press, 2022), pp. 57–75.

Philip Mirowski and Dieter Plehwe, eds., *The Road from Mont Pèlerin: The Making of the Neoliberal Thought Collective* (Cambridge, MA: Harvard University Press, 2009).

Austin Mitchell and Prem Sikka, *Pensions Crisis: A Failure of Public Policy Making* (Basildon: Association for Accountancy & Business Affairs, 2006).

Charles Moore, *Margaret Thatcher*, vol. 2: *Everything She Wants* (London: Allen Lane, 2015).

Kenneth O. Morgan, *Callaghan: A Life* (Oxford: Oxford University Press, 1998).

———, ed., *The Oxford History of Britain* (Oxford: Oxford University Press, 2001).

Stephanie Lee Mudge, 'What Is Neo-Liberalism?', *Socio-Economic Review*, 6:4 (2008), 703–31.

Phil Mullan, *The Imaginary Time Bomb: Why an Ageing Population Is Not a Social Problem* (London: I.B. Tauris, 2000).

Christopher Muller, 'The Institute of Economic Affairs: Undermining the Post-War Consensus', *Contemporary British History*, 10:1 (1996), 88–110.

Katherina Müller, 'Perspectives on Pensions in Eastern Europe', in *Britain's Pensions Crisis: History and Policy*, ed. by Hugh Pemberton, Pat Thane, and Noel Whiteside (Oxford: Oxford University Press, 2006), pp. 223–40.

Clare Munro, 'The Fiscal Politics of Savings and Share Ownership in Britain, 1970–1980', *The Historical Journal*, 55:3 (2012), 757–78.

John Myles and Paul Pierson, 'The Comparative Political Economy of Pension Reform', in *The New Politics of the Welfare State*, ed. by Paul Pierson (Oxford: Oxford University Press, 2001), pp. 305–33.

Duncan Needham and Anthony Hotson, eds., *Expansionary Fiscal Contraction: The Thatcher Government's 1981 Budget in Perspective* (Cambridge: Cambridge University Press, 2014).

Steven Nesbitt, *British Pensions Policy Making in the 1980s: The Rise and Fall of a Policy Community* (Avebury: Ashgate, 1995).

Oude Nijhuis, 'Rethinking the Beveridge Strait-Jacket: The Labour Party, the TUC and the Introduction of Superannuation', *Twentieth Century British History*, 20:3 (2009), 370–95.

Edward Nik-Khah and Robert Van Horn, 'The Ascendancy of Chicago Neoliberalism', in *Handbook of Neoliberalism*, ed. by Simon Springer, Kean Birch, and Julie MacLeavy (London: Routledge, 2016), pp. 27–38.

Darren J. O'Byrne, 'The Rise of Populism, the Demise of the Neoliberal and Neoconservative Globalist Projects, and the War on Human Rights', *International Critical Thought*, 9:2 (2019), 254–68.

Bibliography

Avner Offer, 'The Market Turn: From Social Democracy to Market Liberalism', *The Economic History Review*, 70:4 (2017), 1051–71.

Michael J. Oliver, *Whatever Happened to Monetarism?* (Aldershot: Ashgate, 1997).

Michael J. Oliver and Hugh Pemberton, 'Learning and Change in 20th Century British Economic Policy', *Governance*, 17:3 (2004), 415–41.

Michael J. Oliver and Janette Rutterford, '"The Capital Market Is Dead": The Difficult Birth of Index-Linked Gilts in the UK', *The Economic History Review*, 73:1 (2020), 258–80.

Robert M. Page, *Clear Blue Water? The Conservative Party and the Welfare State since 1940* (Bristol: Policy Press, 2015).

Marc-William Palen, *The 'Conspiracy' of Free Trade: The Anglo-American Struggle over Empire and Economic Globalisation, 1846–1896* (Cambridge: Cambridge University Press, 2016).

Bruno Palier, ed., *A Long Goodbye to Bismarck? The Politics of Welfare Reform in Continental Europe* (Amsterdam: Amsterdam University Press, 2010).

David Parker, *The Official History of Privatisation*, vol. 1: *The Formative Years, 1970–1987* (London: Routledge, 2009).

——, *The Official History of Privatisation*, vol. 2: *Popular Capitalism, 1987–97* (London: Routledge, 2013).

Daisy Payling, '"Socialist Republic of South Yorkshire": Grassroots Activism and Left-Wing Solidarity in 1980s Sheffield', *Twentieth Century British History*, 25:4 (2014), 602–27.

Jamie Peck, *Constructions of Neoliberal Reason* (Oxford: Oxford University Press, 2010).

Jamie Peck, Neil Brenner, and Nik Theodore, 'Actually Existing Neoliberalism', in *The Sage Handbook of Neoliberalism*, ed. by Damien Cahill, Melinda Cooper, Martijn Konings, and David Primrose (London: SAGE Publications, 2018), pp. 3–15.

Hugh Pemberton, *Policy Learning and British Governance in the 1960s* (London: Palgrave Macmillan, 2004).

——, 'Politics and Pensions in Post-War Britain', in *Britain's Pensions Crisis: History and Policy*, ed. by Hugh Pemberton, Pat Thane, and Noel Whiteside (Oxford: Oxford University Press, 2006), pp. 39–63.

——, 'The Failure of "Nationalization by Attraction": Britain's Cross-Class Alliance against Earnings-Related Pensions in the 1950s', *The Economic History Review*, 65:4 (2012), 1428–49.

——, 'The United Kingdom', in *The State of Welfare: Comparative Studies of the Welfare State at the End of the Long Boom, 1965–1980*, ed. by Erik Eklund, Melanie Oppenheimer, and Joanne Scott (Oxford: Peter Lang, 2017), pp. 17–38.

Hugh Pemberton, Pat Thane, and Noel Whiteside, eds., *Britain's Pensions Crisis: History and Policy* (Oxford: Oxford University Press, 2006).

Guy Peters, Jon Pierre, and Desmond King, 'The Politics of Path Dependency: Political Conflict in Historical Institutionalism', *Journal of Politics*, 67:4 (2005), 1275–300.

Anastasia Petraki and Anna Zalewska, 'Jumping over a Low Hurdle: Personal Pension Fund Performance', *Review of Quantitative Finance and Accounting*, 48:1 (2017), 153–90.

Christopher Pierson, *Beyond the Welfare State? The New Political Economy of Welfare* (Cambridge: Polity, 2006).

Paul Pierson, 'When Effect Becomes Cause: Policy Feedback and Political Change', *World Politics*, 45:4 (1993), 595–628.

———, *Dismantling the Welfare State? Reagan, Thatcher and the Politics of Retrenchment* (Cambridge: Cambridge University Press, 1994).

———, *Increasing Returns, Path Dependence and the Study of Politics* (Florence: European University Institute, Robert Schumann Centre, 1997).

———, 'Increasing Returns, Path Dependence and the Study of Politics', *American Political Science Review*, 94:2 (2000), 251–67.

———, 'Not Just What, but When: Timing and Sequence in Political Processes', *Studies in American Political Development*, 14:1 (2000), 79–92.

———, ed., *The New Politics of the Welfare State* (Oxford: Oxford University Press, 2001).

Ben Pimlott, 'The Myth of Consensus', in *The Making of Britain*, ed. by Lesley M. Smith (Basingstoke: Macmillan, 1988), pp. 129–41.

Ben Pimlott, Dennis Kavanagh, and P. Morris, 'Is the "Postwar Consensus" a Myth?', *Contemporary Record*, 2:6 (1989), 12–15.

Dilwyn Porter, 'Government and the Economy', in *Britain in the 1970s: The Troubled Economy*, ed. by Richard Coopey and Nicholas Woodward (New York: St Martin's Press, 1996), pp. 34–54.

John Preston, *Fall: The Mystery of Robert Maxwell* (London: Penguin Books, 2020).

Martin Pugh, *The Making of Modern British Politics 1867–1945* (Oxford: Blackwell, 2002).

Ralf Ptak, 'Neoliberalism in Germany: Revisiting the Ordoliberal Foundations of the Social Market Economy', in *The Road from Mont Pèlerin: The Making of the Neoliberal Thought Collective*, ed. by Philip Mirowski and Dieter Plehwe (Cambridge, MA: Harvard University Press, 2015), pp. 98–138.

John Ramsden, *An Appetite for Power: A History of the Conservative Party since 1830* (London: HarperCollins, 1998).

John Ranelagh, *Thatcher's People: An Insider's Account of the Politics, the Power and the Personalities* (London: Fontana, 1992).

James Reveley and John Singleton, 'Labour, Industrial Revitalization, and the Financial Sector, 1970–79', *Twentieth Century British History*, 27:4 (2016), 599–620.

Peter Riddell, *The Thatcher Government* (Oxford: Blackwell, 1985).

Andrew Roberts, *Eminent Churchillians* (London: Weidenfeld & Nicolson, 2010).

Richard Roberts, *When Britain Went Bust: The 1976 IMF Crisis* (London: OMFIF Press, 2016).

Richard Roberts and David Kynaston, *City State: A Contemporary History of the City of London and How Money Triumphed* (London: Profile, 2002).

Emily Robinson, Camilla Schofield, Florence Sutcliffe-Braithwaite, and Natalie Thomlinson, 'Telling Stories about Post-War Britain: Popular Individualism and the "Crisis" of the 1970s', *Twentieth Century British History*, 28:2 (2017), 268–304.

Chris Rogers, 'From Social Contract to "Social Contrick": The Depoliticisation of Economic Policy-Making under Harold Wilson, 1974–75', *British Journal of Politics and International Relations*, 11:4 (2009), 634–51.

Neil Rollings, 'Organised Business and the Rise of Neoliberalism: The Confederation of British Industry, 1965–1990s', in *The Neoliberal Age? Britain since the 1970s*, ed. by Aled Davies, Ben Jackson, and Florence Sutcliffe-Braithwaite (London: UCL Press, 2021), pp. 279–98.

Bibliography

Roberto Romani, 'Varieties of Neoliberalism: On the Populism of Laissez-Faire in America, 1960–1985', *Global Intellectual History*, 6:1 (2021), 931–55.

David Rooney, 'The Political Economy of Congestion: Road Pricing and the Neoliberal Project, 1952–2003', *Twentieth Century British History*, 25:4 (2014), 628–50.

Wilhelm Röpke, *The Social Crisis of Our Time* (Chicago: University of Chicago Press, 1950).

———, *A Humane Economy: The Social Framework of the Free Market* (Chicago: Henry Regnery Company, 1960).

Nikolas Rose, *Governing the Soul: Shaping of the Private Self* (London: Free Association Books, 1999).

Nikolas Rose and Peter Miller, 'Political Power beyond the State: Problematics of Government, 1992', *British Journal of Sociology*, 61: Suppl.1 (2010), 271–303.

Nikolas Rose, Pat O'Malley, and Mariana Valverde, 'Governmentality', *Annual Review of Law and Social Science*, 2 (2006), 83–104.

Dietrich Rueschemeyer, 'Why and How Ideas Matter', in *The Oxford Handbook of Contextual Political Analysis*, ed. by Robert E. Goodin and Charles Tilly (Oxford: Oxford University Press, 2006), pp. 227–51.

John Gerard Ruggie, 'International Regimes, Transactions, and Change: Embedded Liberalism in the Postwar Economic Order', *International Organization*, 36:2 (1982), 379–415.

Tony Salter, Colin Redman, and Martin Hewitt, *100 Years of State Pension: Learning from the Past* (London: Faculty of Actuaries and Institute of Actuaries, 2008).

Tehila Sasson, 'Afterword: British Neoliberalism and Its Subjects', in *The Neoliberal Age? Britain since the 1970s*, ed. by Aled Davies, Ben Jackson, and Florence Sutcliffe-Braithwaite (London: UCL Press, 2021), pp. 336–53.

Catherine Schenk, *The Decline of Sterling: Managing the Retreat of an International Currency, 1945–1992* (Cambridge: Cambridge University Press, 2010).

Jake Anthony Scott, '"There Is No Alternative"? The Role of Depoliticisation in the Emergence of Populism', *Politics*, 42:3 (2022), 325–39.

David Seawright, *The British Conservative Party and One Nation Politics* (London: Continuum, 2010).

Anthony Seldon, *John Major: A Political Life* (London: Weidenfeld & Nicholson, 1997).

Arthur Seldon, *Pensions in a Free Society* (London: Institute of Economic Affairs, 1957).

———, ed., *The 'New Right' Enlightenment: The Spectre that Haunts the Left* (London: Economic and Literary Books, 1984).

Henry C. Simons, 'The Beveridge Program: An Unsympathetic Interpretation', *Journal of Political Economy*, 53:3 (1945), 212–33.

Robert Skidelsky, *John Maynard Keynes: The Economist as Saviour, 1920–1937* (London: Papermac, 1994).

Martin J. Sklar, *The Corporate Reconstruction of American Capitalism, 1890–1916: The Market, the Law, and Politics* (Cambridge: Cambridge University Press, 1988).

Quinn Slobodian, *Globalists: The End of Empire and the Birth of Neoliberalism* (Cambridge, MA: Harvard University Press, 2018).

Peter Sloman, 'Welfare in a Neoliberal Age: The Politics of Redistributive Market Liberalism', in *Neoliberalism and Conservatism in Britain*, ed. by Aled Davies,

390   *Bibliography*

Ben Jackson, and Florence Sutcliffe-Braithwaite (London: UCL Press, 2021), pp. 75–93.

David Smith, *The Rise and Fall of Monetarism* (London: Penguin Books, 1987).

Daniel Stedman Jones, *Masters of the Universe: Hayek, Friedman, and the Birth of Neoliberal Politics* (Princeton, NJ: Princeton University Press, 2014).

C. M. Stewart, 'Pension Problems and Their Solution', *Journal of the Institute of Actuaries*, 110:2 (1983), 289–331.

Wolfgang Streeck and Kathleen Thelen, eds., *Beyond Continuity: Institutional Change in Advanced Political Economies* (Oxford: Oxford University Press, 2005).

Florence Sutcliffe-Braithwaite, 'Neo-Liberalism and Morality in the Making of Thatcherite Social Policy', *The Historical Journal*, 55:2 (2012), 497–520.

———, *Class, Politics, and the Decline of Deference in England, 1968–2000* (Oxford: Oxford University Press, 2018).

Chris R. Tame, *A Bibliography of Freedom* (London: Centre for Policy Studies, 1980).

Robert Taylor, *The TUC: From the General Strike to the New Unionism* (London: Palgrave, 2000).

Pat Thane, 'Labour and Welfare', in *Labour's First Century*, ed. by Duncan Tanner, Pat Thane, and Nick Tiratsoo (Cambridge: Cambridge University Press, 2000), pp. 80–118.

———, *Old Age in English History* (Oxford: Oxford University Press, 2000).

———, 'The "Scandal" of Women's Pensions in Britain', in *Britain's Pensions Crisis: History and Policy*, ed. by Hugh Pemberton, Pat Thane, and Noel Whiteside (Oxford: Oxford University Press, 2006), pp. 77–90.

Kathleen Thelen, 'Timing and Temporality in the Analysis of Institutional Evolution and Change', *Studies in American Political Development*, 14:1 (2000), 101–8.

———, 'How Institutions Evolve: Insights from Comparative Historical Analysis', in *Comparative Historical Analysis in the Social Sciences*, ed. by J. Mahoney and D. Rueschemeyer (Cambridge: Cambridge University Press, 2003), pp. 208–40.

James Thomas, '"Bound in by History": The Winter of Discontent in British Politics, 1979–2004', *Media, Culture & Society*, 29:2 (2007), 263–83.

Noel Thompson, 'Economic Ideas and the Development of Opinion', in *Britain in the 1970s: The Troubled Economy*, ed. by Richard Coopey and Nicholas Woodward (New York: St Martin's Press, 1996), pp. 55–80.

Stephen Thornton, *Richard Crossman and the Welfare State* (London: I.B. Tauris, 2009).

Djuna Thurley, 'Occupational Pension Increases', Briefing Paper 5656 (London: House of Commons Library, 2021).

Nicholas Timmins, *The Five Giants: A Biography of the Welfare State* (London: HarperCollins, 2001).

Alexis de Tocqueville, *Democracy in America*, trans. by Harvey Mansfield and Delba Winthrop (Chicago: University of Chicago Press, 2012).

Jim Tomlinson, 'The Decline of Empire and the Economic "Decline" of Britain', *Twentieth Century British History*, 14:3 (2003), 201–21.

———, 'Mrs Thatcher's Macroeconomic Adventurism, 1979–1981, and Its Political Consequences', *British Politics*, 2:1 (2007), 3–19.

———, 'Tale of a Death Exaggerated: How Keynesian Policies Survived the 1970s', *Contemporary British History*, 21:4 (2007), 429–48.

—, 'Thatcher, Monetarism and the Politics of Inflation', in *Making Thatcher's Britain*, ed. by Ben Jackson and Robert Saunders (Cambridge: Cambridge University Press, 2012), pp. 62–77.

—, 'De-Industrialization Not Decline: A New Meta-Narrative for Post-War British History', *Twentieth Century British History*, 27:1 (2016), 76–99.

Cornelius Torp, 'The Adenauer Government's Pensions Reform of 1957: A Question of Justice', *German History*, 34:2 (2016), 237–57.

Richard Toye, 'From "Consensus" to "Common Ground": The Rhetoric of the Postwar Settlement and Its Collapse', *Journal of Contemporary History*, 48:1 (2013), 3–23.

—, 'Keynes, Liberalism, and "the Emancipation of the Mind"', *The English Historical Review*, 130:546 (2015), 1162–91.

Keith Tribe, 'Liberalism and Neoliberalism in Britain, 1930–1980', in *The Road from Mont Pèlerin: The Making of a Neoliberal Thought Collective*, ed. by Philip Mirowski and Dieter Plehwe (Cambridge, MA: Harvard University Press, 2015), pp. 68–97.

Rachel S. Turner, *Neo-Liberal Ideology: History, Concepts and Policies* (Edinburgh: Edinburgh University Press, 2011).

Robert Van Horn and Philip Mirowski, 'The Rise of the Chicago School of Economics and the Birth of Neoliberalism', in *The Road from Mont Pèlerin: The Making of the Neoliberal Thought Collective*, ed. by Philip Mirowski and Dieter Plehwe (Cambridge, MA: Harvard University Press, 2009), pp. 139–78.

—, 'Neoliberalism and Chicago', in *The Elgar Companion to the Chicago School of Economics*, ed. by Ross Emmett (Cheltenham: Edward Elgar, 2010), pp. 196–206.

James Vernon, 'Heathrow and the Making of Neoliberal Britain', *Past & Present*, 252 (2021), 213–47.

Richard Vinen, *Thatcher's Britain: The Politics and Social Upheaval of the 1980s* (London: Simon & Schuster, 2009).

Robert Walsha, 'The One Nation Group and One Nation Conservatism, 1950–2002', *Contemporary British History*, 17:2 (2003), 69–120.

Sue Ward, 'Regulation of Pensions in the UK', in *The Role of the State in Pension Provision: Employer, Regulator, Provider*, ed. by Gerard Hughes and Jim Stewart (Boston: Springer, 1999), pp. 63–73.

Douglas Wass, *Decline to Fall: The Making of British Macro-Economic Policy and the 1976 IMF Crisis* (Oxford: Oxford University Press, 2008).

Amy Whipple, 'Speaking for Whom? The 1971 Festival of Light and the Search for the "Silent Majority"', *Contemporary British History*, 24:3 (2010), 319–39.

Heather Whiteside, 'Neoliberalism as Austerity: The Theory, Practice, and Purpose of Fiscal Restraint since the 1970s', in *The Handbook of Neoliberalism* (London: Routledge, 2016), pp. 361–69.

Noel Whiteside, 'Creating the Welfare State in Britain, 1945–1960', *Journal of Social Policy*, 25:01 (1996), 83–103.

—, 'Historical Perspectives and the Politics of Pensions Reform', in *Pensions Security in the 21st Century*, ed. by Gordon L. Clark and Noel Whiteside (Oxford: Oxford University Press, 2003), pp. 21–43.

—, 'Occupational Pensions and the Search for Security', in *Britain's Pensions Crisis: History and Policy*, ed. by Hugh Pemberton, Pat Thane, and Noel Whiteside (Oxford: Oxford University Press, 2006), pp. 125–39.

—, 'The UK Pensions Crisis and Institutional Innovation: Beyond Corporatism and Neoliberalism', in *Challenges of Aging: Pensions, Retirement and Generational Justice*, ed. by Cornelius Torp (London: Palgrave Macmillan, 2015), pp. 105–32.

Geoffrey Whittington, 'Accounting Standards for Pension Costs', in *The Oxford Handbook of Pensions and Retirement Income*, ed. by Gordon. L. Clark, Alicia H. Munnell, and J. Michael Orszag (Oxford: Oxford University Press, 2006), pp. 521–38.

Mark Wickham-Jones, *Economic Strategy and the Labour Party: Politics and Policy-Making, 1970–83* (London: Macmillan, 1996).

David Willetts, 'The Role of the Prime Minister's Policy Unit', *Public Administration*, 65:4 (1987), 443–54.

—, 'The New Conservatism? 1945–1951', in *Recovering Power: The Conservatives in Opposition since 1867*, ed. by Stuart Ball and Anthony Seldon (Basingstoke: Palgrave Macmillan, 2005), pp. 169–91.

Adrian Williamson, *Conservative Economic Policymaking and the Birth of Thatcherism, 1964–1979* (Basingstoke: Palgrave Macmillan, 2015).

Index

Abel-Smith, Brian 115
Accounting Standards Board 324
actuaries 13, 128, 283, 327
Adam Smith Institute 81, 242
Advance Corporation Tax (ACT)
    322, 323
Age Concern 241, 242
Allied Dunbar 292
Amery, Leo 112
Anti Corn Law League 42
Anti-Trust Project 56
Armstrong, Robert 253, 281
Association of British Chambers of
    Commerce (ABCC) 280
Association of British Insurers (ABI)
    280, 281
Association of Consulting Actuaries
    (ACA) 198, 214, 282, 325
Association of Pensioner
    Trustees 208
Austrian school 54, 56, 95
authoritarian populism 36, 78

Baldwin, Stanley 45
Bandey, Derek 207, 209
Bank of England 6
basic state pension 13, 22, 86, 113,
    116, 118, 120, 122, 123, 125,
    126, 130, 136, 138, 150, 152,
    166, 168, 187, 188, 231, 237,
    238, 240, 241, 243, 246, 256,
    269, 274, 275, 279
  delinking from earnings 148, 150–2,
    158, 160, 174, 232, 273, 309,
    352, 354, 364
  double lock 126

equalised retirement age 275, 311
individualised contract fiction
    112–13, 117
origins of 110–12
uprating of 22, 125, 149–50,
    152–8
value of 23, 309–14, 360
Becker, Gary 14, 55, 56, 57
Benn, Tony 134
Beveridge Report 38, 110, 112
Beveridge, William 11, 91, 112,
    245, 277
  pensions straightjacket 113, 118
  reforms to pensions 112
  vision of welfare state 136, 236,
    250, 269, 308
Biffen, John 150, 151
Bismarck, Otto von 44
Böhm, Franz 51
Bonefeld, Werner 15
Boswell, Tim 132, 133, 134, 135
Boyd-Carpenter, John 115, 116,
    118, 123
Boyson, Rhodes 201
Bretton Woods system 7, 88, 124
Brimblecome, Roy 284
British Gas 188
British Insurance Brokers' Association
    (BIBA) 206, 287
British Telecom 188
Brittan, Leon 286
Brittan, Samuel 82, 95, 98
Brown, Gordon 318, 323
Brynmor, John 174
Buchanan, James 57, 81, 105
Buckton, Ray 280

394   *Index*

burden of pensions 60, 148, 158–70,
  172, 175, 350
  Burden of Pensions Working Group
    (BOPWG) 164–5, 171, 233
  reported findings of 168–70
Butler, Eamonn 81

Callaghan, James 149, 150, 189
Cardona, George 82
Carsberg Report 1993 330
Castle, Barbara 159, 232, 242,
    351, 356
  1970s pensions reforms 125–30, 138
Central Policy Review Staff (CPRS)
    154, 155, 200, 202, 213,
    233, 236
  pensions reform proposals 170–3,
    199–200
Centre for Policy Studies (CPS) 64, 80,
    81, 131, 159, 166, 167, 191,
    197, 198, 199, 211, 213, 214,
    216, 217, 233, 235, 236, 240,
    270, 276, 295, 308, 327, 351,
    352, 353, 358, 359
  at Inquiry into Provision for
    Retirement 201–10
  origins of 191–2
  Personal Capital Formation Group
    (PCFG) 192, 193, 195, 196
  *Personal and Portable Pensions
    for All*
    origins and arguments of 189–98
    reception of 198–9
  *Why Britain Needs a Social Market
    Economy* 197
Chappell, Philip 192, 193, 195, 196,
    197, 198, 202, 203, 205, 206,
    209, 213, 214, 270
Chicago school 14, 49, 51, 57, 58, 60,
    64, 77, 94, 353
  on choice 57
  on epistemological approach 56
  on human capital 56
  on monopolies 56
  overview and key ideas 55–7
  on rational individual 57, 353
  on regulatory capture 57
Churchill, Winston 38
City of London 188, 291, 363
Clarke, Kenneth 129, 312

Cleminson, James 284
Coase, Ronald 14, 55
Colloque Walter Lippmann 46, 49, 51
Companies' Pensions Association 128
Confederation of British Industry (CBI)
    3, 198, 204, 206, 207, 214,
    238, 240, 255, 272, 278, 279,
    284, 287, 316, 324, 338
Congdon, Tim 82
'consensus' 37, 90–3
  challenges to 13, 35, 37, 38, 75,
    95, 350
  emergence in pensions 9, 12–13,
    109–10, 124–30, 275, 351
  histories of 8–10
  lack of in pensions to 1974 9,
    11–12, 109–10, 112–24
  role of stakeholders 9, 116, 117, 175
Conservative governments
  1951–64 12, 91, 115, 116, 138
  1970–74 12, 75, 77, 81, 84, 85,
    86, 93, 120, 123, 125, 131,
    189, 350
  1990–97 310, 312
Conservative party 9, 11, 13, 15, 21,
    22, 36, 37, 38, 39, 45, 62, 64,
    80, 90, 91, 112, 120, 128,
    154, 191, 193, 254, 272, 281,
    311, 357, 363
  beliefs and intellectual tradition 37,
    38, 77, 94
  nationalisation, fear of 121
  property-owning democracy 39,
    193, 196
  role of the state 76, 78, 93, 167
  wider capital ownership 22, 131,
    187, 193, 194, 269
  worries about dominance of
    institutional funds 132
  Bow Group 131, 202
  Conservative Research Department
    (CRD) 82, 131, 132, 167, 321
  grassroots members 38
  interest in neoliberal ideas 76–9, 83
  late 1970s plans to widen capital
    ownership 130–6
  Monday Club 281
  One Nation Group 38
  parliamentary party 154, 290
  Pensions Study Group 159

Index

publications
The Challenge of Our Times 173
The Right Approach 131,
149, 194
The Right Approach to the
Economy 88, 194
relationship to New Right 77–9
relationship to think tanks
80–1, 351
response to Better Pensions White
Paper 1974 129
Second Pension Policy Group 129
statecraft 38, 76, 95–6
support for occupational pensions
193, 353
Tory Reform Group 282
Wider Ownership Group 131,
134, 195
consultative documents
Improved Transferability for Early
Leavers from Occupational
Pension Schemes 1984 211
Partnership with Occupational
Pension Schemes 1974 127
Personal Pensions 1984 210–13, 239
Consumers' Association 208, 282, 292
contributory National Insurance
pensions 1925 111, 114
Cropper, Peter 82, 131, 134, 166–7, 321
Crossman, Richard 120, 121, 123, 129,
130, 133, 137, 356
Mark I pension proposals 115, 122,
126, 127
Mark II pension proposals 120
crowding out 78, 94, 350

Daily Mail 277
Daily Telegraph 159, 253, 277, 289
Davies, Bryn 328
Dell, Edmund 126
demography 160, 170
ageing population 2, 3, 90, 159,
232, 317, 352
population projections 3, 273
Department for Health and Social
Security (DHSS) 11, 147, 150,
152, 155, 157, 163, 164, 165,
168, 200, 202, 203, 211, 212,
214, 215, 228, 233, 234, 235,
236, 239, 240, 243, 244, 248,

249, 250, 255, 270, 276, 278,
280, 281, 282, 283, 284, 285,
288, 356
day conference 1983 198, 204
Social Security Operations
Group 233
Department of Trade and Industry
(DTI) 201, 213, 319
Drucker, Peter 194

Eagle Star 284
Economist 155, 198, 276, 293
economy, the
affluence 113
balance of trade 7, 88–9
capital allocation 1, 62, 354
credit liberalisation 6
employment patterns 89
Euromarkets 6
exchange controls 35
growth 85
inflation 35, 84, 94, 111, 113, 121,
125, 129, 189
international competitivenes 86
job mobility 62, 172
productivity 86, 94
public spending 86–7
rate of return 6, 161
stagflation 86, 190
taxation 87, 88
unemployment 35
Edwards, Kenneth 240
Engineering Employers' Federation
(EEF) 214, 280
Enterprise Allowance Scheme 193
Equal Opportunities Commission
241, 282
Ermisch, John 162, 163
Eucken, Walter 51, 52
European Exchange Rate
Mechanism 324

Falklands War 188
Fama, Eugene 14, 55
Field, Frank 290
Field, Marshall 201, 211, 212,
234, 241
Financial Intermediaries, Managers
and Brokers Regulatory
Association (FIMBRA) 292

Financial Services Authority (FSA) 332
financial services industry 12
  opposition to reforms 272,
    280–1, 356
Financial Times 80, 82, 95, 128, 132,
    213, 235, 276, 281, 289,
    297, 330
financialisation 6, 40
First World War 45
Fleming, Robert 79
Fletcher, Alex 201
Foucault, Michel 40, 50, 354
Fowler, Norman 129, 130, 147, 156,
    157, 158, 165, 191, 198, 199,
    212, 216, 217, 232, 233, 234,
    242, 247, 250, 252, 254, 255,
    272, 276, 277, 278, 279, 280,
    286, 290, 292, 296, 297, 301,
    334, 336, 357, 359, 362,
    364, 365
  on cost of abolishing SERPS 249–52
  on draft 1985 Green Paper
    and phased abolition of
    SERPS 252–4
  role in Cabinet U-turn on 1985
    Green Paper 281–7
  role in MISC 111 proposals to
    abolish SERPS 244–7
  role in passing Social Security Act
    1986 288–91
  on SERPS transitional
    arrangements 247–9
  speeches 202, 282
  views on role of the state in social
    security 250
  views on SERPS 238
  see also Inquiry into Provision
    for Retirement; Green
    Papers: *Reform of Social
    Security* 1985
'Free Market Study' project 55, 56
freedom 46, 47, 48, 51, 173, 296
  choice 15, 23, 46, 53, 54, 61, 95,
    270, 276, 295, 296, 353, 355
  economic 42, 54, 270, 350
  individual 1, 5, 15, 37, 53, 54, 95,
    270, 321, 352, 353, 355, 359
  markets 54
Friedman, Milton 14, 51, 55, 56, 57,
    81, 84, 94
  Free to Choose 60

on pensions 61
on welfare states 60–1

general elections and manifestos
  1964 118
  1966 118
  1970 120, 121
  1974 (February) 123, 124, 125
  1974 (October) 159
  1979 16, 37, 94, 133, 146, 148–9,
    150, 189, 233, 351
  1983 20, 22, 146, 147, 157–8, 167,
    173, 187, 188, 196, 200, 202,
    233, 255, 256
  1987 308
  1997 313
generational fairness 60, 147, 151, 152,
    153, 156, 158, 169, 350
  conflict over 159, 161, 171
Germany 43, 44, 51, 53, 59, 64, 198
Gilmour, Ian 37, 153, 282
Gladstone, William 42
Goldsmith, Walter 203, 205, 206,
    207, 208
Goode Report 1993 320–1, 326, 334
Gould, Bryan 292
Government Actuary 127, 159, 162,
    164, 165, 201, 232, 237, 238,
    239, 240, 311, 325
Gower Report 1984 292, 320, 334
Gramsci, Antonio 36
Green Papers
  *A New Contract for Welfare:
    Partnership in Pensions* 1998 335
  Reform of Social Security 1985 23,
    188, 231, 250, 269–72, 308,
    354–5, 357, 359
    Cabinet U-turn on 281–7
    personal pensions 216, 274, 275
    response to 276–81
    SERPS and occupational
    pensions 272–6
    transferability 275
Green, T. H. 43
Guardian 129, 277, 289

Hailsham, Lord 153
Hambro Life Assurance 201, 212
Harris, Ralph 80, 81
Hayek, Friedrich 14, 41, 46, 55, 56, 57,
    58, 61, 77, 79, 81, 350, 353

markets and competition 54–5
overview and key ideas 53–5
on pensions 60
school of thought 51
The Constitution of Liberty 59
The Road to Serfdom 14, 55, 59
on welfare states 59–60
Hayes, Tom 204
Hayhoe, Barney 201, 239, 240
Heath, Edward 39, 93, 120, 125, 199
Hemming, Richard 162
Herbison, Peggy 118
Heritage Foundation 80
HM Treasury 12, 82, 86, 92, 104,
113, 116, 117, 147, 149, 150,
151, 152, 153, 154, 155, 157,
158, 162, 163, 164, 166, 167,
168, 187, 195, 196, 200, 201,
203, 211, 213, 215, 216, 232,
233, 235, 236, 237, 238, 239,
241, 248, 250, 252, 253, 271,
276, 286, 288, 292, 293, 321,
322, 332, 335, 336, 345,
351, 358
Information Division 232
Public Services Economic
Division 168
Social Security Group 232
Social Services Group 163
Hobhouse, Leonard 43
Hobson, J. A. 43
Hollis, Lady 311
Holmans, Stephanie 168–70
Horden, Peter 79, 131, 132, 134, 195
Hoskyns, John 284
Howe, Geoffrey 82, 84, 94, 128, 130,
131, 132, 133, 134, 147, 150,
151, 152, 153, 154, 155, 157,
158, 159, 162, 163, 165, 166,
167, 170, 195, 196, 233, 309,
351, 354, 358, 362
speech to National Association of
Pension Funds 1981 160–2,
163, 164, 187, 231–2
Howell, David 131, 132
Hurd, Douglas 286

Industrial Participation
Association 192
Inland Revenue 211, 248, 275, 322

Inquiry into Provision for Retirement
(IPR) 22, 201–10, 231,
278, 279
consultation responses to 213–15
opposition to personal
pensions 204–10
origins 199, 233
proposals to abolish or modify
SERPS 244
proposals for consultation 210–13
remit and members 201–2
stakeholder views on future of/
modifications to SERPS
234–9, 242
support for personal pensions 202–4
Institute of Actuaries 114, 116,
128, 234
Institute of Directors (IoD) 203, 205,
206, 207, 209, 214, 281, 284
Institute of Economic Affairs (IEA) 80,
132, 159, 191, 201
Economic Affairs 80
Institute and Faculty of Actuaries (IFoA)
128, 201, 214, 235, 282
Institute for Fiscal Studies (IFS) 162,
232, 311
Institute for International Research 326
Institute for Public Policy Research
(IPPR) 330
institutional funds 271, 353
asset ownership 114, 132, 187, 193
criticism of 131–3, 166
investment strategies of 161,
187, 354
lobbying of 116, 117, 119, 133, 172,
217, 351, 357
size and power of 1, 114, 129, 132,
161, 167, 187, 193, 196,
321, 353
tax reliefs 131, 133, 166, 167, 172,
195, 321, 322, 354
International Monetary Fund
(IMF) 88, 91
Investment Management Regulatory
Organization (IMRO)
292, 329

Jay, Peter 82
Jenkin, Patrick 147, 150, 151, 153,
156, 163, 165, 167

Index

Johnston, Edward 201
Joseph, Keith 15, 79, 80, 81, 82, 94,
    121, 127, 129, 133, 191,
    194, 198

Kay, John 162
Kemp, Peter 152, 164
Keynes, John Maynard 45, 47
Keynesian demand management 10, 35,
    46, 57, 75, 90–3, 94
Kinnock, Neil 277
Kirkwood, Archy 290
Knight, Frank 49, 55, 56

Labour governments
    1945–51 9, 91, 92, 110, 111,
      112, 113
    1964–70 12, 118
    1974–9 12, 35, 75, 77, 86, 87, 94,
      124, 131, 189, 190, 191, 231,
      310, 351
    1997–2010 3, 4, 310, 312, 314,
      318, 335
Labour party 9, 11, 12, 15, 60, 90,
    112, 115, 116, 117, 118, 125,
    128, 137, 173, 194, 217, 271,
    277, 280, 290, 311, 313, 335
    alternative economic strategy 93,
      121, 125, 350
    constituency parties 112
    party conference 278
    social contract 86
Laffer curve 77
Lamont, Norman 322, 323, 334
Large, Andrew 334
Lawson, Nigel 80, 94, 131, 133, 134,
    167, 193, 233, 235, 236, 239,
    244, 249, 250, 251, 252, 253,
    254, 256, 276, 283, 284, 287,
    292, 293, 294, 296, 317, 321,
    322, 327, 354, 358
Legal & General 128, 204, 212,
    214, 280
legislation
    Building Societies Act 1986 291
    Finance Act 1986 319, 321
    Finance Act 1989 322
    Financial Services Act 1986 272,
      291–3, 308, 320, 321, 327,
      334, 355

    Housing Act 1980 195
    Industrial Relations Act 1971 125
    National Insurance Act 1946 110
    Pension Schemes Act 2015 321
    Pension Schemes Act 2017 321
    Pension Schemes Act 2021 321
    Pensions Act 1995 310, 311, 312,
      317, 320, 321, 323
    Pensions Act 2004 321
    Pensions Act 2007 321
    Pensions Act 2008 314, 321
    Pensions Act 2011 321
    Pensions Act 2014 321
    Social Security Act 1973 121,
      123, 190
    Social Security Act 1975 149
    Social Security Act 1986 23, 272,
      288–91, 308, 310, 312, 355
    Social Security and Pensions Act
      1975 129, 160, 166
    Welfare Reform and Pensions Act
      1999 321
Lewis, Russell 132
Liberal party 15, 42, 112
liberalism
    American variant 43, 44
    crisis of liberal civilisation 14. 46,
      49, 57
    Edwardian reforms 44
    eighteenth-century 42, 47
    free trade 42
    impact of First World War 45
    international trading system 44
    intervention 43
    interwar crisis of 45
    laissez-faire 43, 44, 47, 51
    Manchester school 37, 42
    markets 42
    'new liberalism' 44
    Rechtsstaat liberalism 43
    as response to mode of
      production 47
    Scottish Enlightenment 42
    splits within 43
    utilitarianism 43
Life Assurance and Unit Trust
    Regulatory Organization
    (LAUTRO) 292, 328, 329,
    330, 332
Life Insurance Council 284

Life Offices Association (LOA) 116, 123, 128, 198, 203, 204, 238
Lilley, Peter 320, 365
Limited Price Index 317
Lippmann, Walter 14, 41, 46, 48, 54
Lloyd George, David, 45
Lombard Street Research 82
London Stock Exchange 193, 305
Lowe, Jonquil 206, 208
Luhnow, Harold 55
Lyon, Stewart 119, 201, 234, 283

Macleod, Iain 115, 131
Macmillan, Harold 49, 91, 115
Major, John 291
Marxism Today 15, 36
massification 49, 50
Maxwell, Robert 319, 320, 323, 334, 335
Meacher, Michael 253, 278, 290
Messer, Cholmeley 207
Mill, John Stuart 43
Minford, Patrick 82, 83, 84
Ministry of Pensions 116, 141
Mises, Ludwig von 54
monetarism 10, 35, 84, 94, 148, 350
Monger, George 163, 164, 165, 168, 232, 233, 236
Mont Pèlerin Society (MPS) 14, 41, 42, 46, 49, 51, 53, 56, 80, 159
Montagu, Nicholas 201, 282, 288
Morgan Grenfell 192
Morrison, Peter 201
Müller-Armack, Alfred 51, 52
Murray, Peter 323

National Assistance 112, 113, 118
National Association of Pension Funds (NAPF) 116, 119, 160–2, 163, 164, 198, 204, 207, 208, 209, 214, 231, 242, 272, 278, 284, 320, 322, 323
National Audit Office (NAO) 327
National Consumer Council 282
National Employment Savings Trust 314
National Insurance (NI) 17, 109, 112, 114, 125, 126, 136, 137, 138, 147, 153, 237, 244

contributions 127, 130, 156, 162, 163, 165, 212, 248, 251, 275, 276
rebate 162, 287, 289, 290, 291, 292, 296, 327, 329
National Insurance Fund 113, 117, 120, 165, 232, 327
National Pensioners' Convention 241
'National Superannuation' 12, 60, 114–15, 116, 117, 118–20, 121, 122, 127
National Union of Mineworkers 188
neoclassical economics 14, 17
neoliberalism
    'actually existing' 8, 41, 175, 348, 356, 364
    constraints on 8, 19, 23, 174, 296, 336, 355, 356
    critique of collectivism 42, 46–7
    critique of liberalism 14, 42, 47–9
    definitions of 2, 7, 8, 13, 14, 20, 39, 347–9
    family and breadwinner model 79
    governmentality 2, 40, 347, 354
    histories of 2, 8, 41–57, 347, 348, 359
    long-term impacts of 3, 20, 359–61
    as neoliberal evolution 1, 21, 295, 357, 362, 365
    as neoliberal project 15, 20, 50
    as neoliberal revolution 1, 21
    origins of 51
    as palette of ideas 2, 17, 349, 350, 351, 357
    policy failures 3, 355, 356, 364
    as policy visions 3, 19, 20, 176, 197, 272, 349, 350, 355, 363
    as problem discovery 22, 147, 176, 352
    promotion
        by government advisers 82–3
        by journalists 82
        by think tanks 80–1
    as reformulated liberalism 49–51
    relation to interests 7, 19, 79–80, 356, 363
    relationship to conservatism 33, 76–9, 83, 351, 363
    as revival of capital 7, 40, 348, 363
    role of the state 51, 54

neoliberalism (*continued*)
  social security 57–8, 62, 152, 159, 197, 350
  sociological approaches to 2, 40
  as thought collective and network 14, 33, 41–2, 51, 53, 347, 349
New Right 13, 37, 77–9, 80, 88, 91, 93, 94, 95, 351
New Statesman 277
New York Times 235
Newton, Tony 254, 291
Niskanen, William 95
No. 10 Policy Unit (PU) 79, 82, 199, 200, 202, 216, 217, 233, 238, 242, 243, 245, 253, 254, 255, 270, 279, 283, 285, 286, 295, 296, 308, 336, 337, 352, 353, 354, 356, 357, 358, 359, 360, 365
  defeat of proposals to abolish SERPS 285–6
  National Insurance contribution rebate incentive 290
  proposals to abolish SERPS 242–3, 246–7
  proposals to drain SERPS of members 285–6
non-contributory pensions 1908 111
Norwich Union 289, 330

occupational pensions 12, 116, 119, 274, 279, 353, 359
  additional voluntary contributions 275, 283, 287
    free-standing 322, 332
  administrative costs of 321, 361
  asset stripping of 317–19, 321, 360
  compulsory or voluntary 168, 172, 249, 270, 325
  contracting out 234
  contribution holidays 317–19
  cross-subsidisation 171
  defined benefit (DB) schemes
    decline of 315, 323–65
    final salary 128, 172
    improved benefits 315–17
    rise of 316, 356
  defined contribution (DC) schemes 168, 275, 285, 308

substitution for defined benefit 4, 275, 325, 354
impacts of economic and demographic change on 160, 163, 190, 324, 361
impacts of personal pensions on 211, 212, 278, 279, 290, 360
inflation indexation 128, 160, 316, 358
lack of industry support for universality in 1950s 115
legacy of reforms to 364–5
membership numbers 113–16, 193
minimum contribution 275
surpluses 293–4, 318, 321, 354, 361
survivor benefits 316
sustainability of 4, 160, 200, 212, 217, 321, 323
taxation of 321–3
tax-free lump sum 322
transferability 120, 190, 203, 275
  preserved benefits 129, 130, 190, 201, 234, 287, 317
see also pensions systems: early leaver problem
Occupational Pensions Advisory Service 320
Occupational Pensions Board (OPB) 121, 189, 198, 199, 201, 202, 217, 287, 317
  report on early leaver problem 1981 190–1
Occupational Pensions Regulatory Authority (OPRA) 321
Oldfield, Maurice 207, 208
O'Malley, Brian 126, 127, 351
ordoliberalism 15, 51, 197
  affinity with CPS proposals 197
  democracy and role of the state 52
  entrepreneurship and enterprise 53
  interest groups 15, 51
  markets 51
  monopolies 52
  overview of and key ideas 51–3
  regulation 52
  social policy 52–3, 58, 197
  social security and pensions 59
  strong state 15

Index

Organisation for Economic
Co-operation and Development
(OECD) 89, 170
overloaded state 49, 78, 95, 350
Owen, David 283
ownership
capital 5, 171, 192, 196, 275,
296, 351
decline in share ownership 193
direct forms 134, 135, 276, 353,
354, 359
intermediated forms 134, 355, 359
property 52
stake in capitalism 1, 172, 196, 308

Parkinson, Michael 254
Partridge, Michael 233
Peacock, Alan 201, 211, 234
Pensions Commission 3, 4, 5, 310, 314,
318, 325, 326, 336, 360, 365
Pensions & Investment Research
Consultants (PIRC) 328
pensions systems
adequacy of provision 3, 314
complexity 2, 4, 23, 24, 110, 270,
359, 364
compulsion versus voluntarism 61
demand for earnings-related
pensions 113–16
difficulty of reform 109
double-payment problem 251, 253,
271, 276, 279, 281, 296,
355, 358
early leaver problem 118, 121,
189–91, 211, 352, 358
funding basis 17, 113, 129, 148, 159
inflation protection 147, 148–58
international comparisons 119, 313
low consumer knowledge 4, 23,
24, 364
market failure 333–4, 364
pensioner poverty 313, 314, 360,
364, 365
redistribution 118, 127, 130, 147,
160, 174, 279, 350, 364
regulatory failure 334–6
treatment of women 122, 127, 239,
278, 311, 328
Pensions World 321, 323, 331, 334
Pepper, Gordon 82

'Personal Equity Plans' 193
personal pensions 188, 235, 269,
270, 278, 285, 308, 353,
358, 364
administration costs 279, 280
charges 4, 293, 330–1, 360
expert warnings about 204–10,
279, 364
inadequate contributions 279, 328
incentives 235, 285, 287, 290, 296,
327, 355, 358
legacy of reforms to 364–5
minimum contributions 213,
283, 335
misselling 23, 207, 326–30, 360
advisers' training 330
origins of 133, 189–98
poor performance of 328,
330–1, 360
poor persistence of 329
reformulation as optional
substitute 283
regulation of 275, 291–3, 327
regulatory failure 331–3
Phillips curve 86
Phillips & Drew 293
Phoenix Assurance 201
Pierson, Paul 17, 109, 116, 138, 231,
251, 270, 271, 272, 276, 294,
297, 355, 356
Pirie, Madsen 81
Plant, Arnold 14
policy change 349, 357
historical institutionalism 271
incrementalism 20, 174, 187, 362
overview of approaches to
16–20
path dependence 17, 18, 116, 117,
138, 271, 349, 355, 356,
362, 364
system layering 359, 362
system replacement 1, 187, 270,
275, 358
Policy Studies Institute 241
Portillo, Michael 327
Posner, Richard 14, 55
Powell, Enoch 38, 84
Prior, Jim 153, 154
Private Eye 319
privatisation 5, 35, 188, 270, 285

projections 175
  economic growth 12
  national income devoted to pensions 4, 160, 165, 168, 169, 237, 273
  number of pensioners 160, 162, 169, 237
  relative income of pensioners 163, 170, 237
proletarianisation 49, 50, 58, 353
Prowse, Michael 281
Prudential Assurance Company 209, 214, 280
Prussia 44
public choice theory 57, 95
Public Expenditure Survey 155
Public Sector Borrowing Requirement (PSBR) 87, 148, 150, 250, 252, 254, 354
Pym, Francis 290

ratchet, socialist 22, 78, 147, 148, 150, 153, 157, 158, 174, 350, 351
Reagan, Ronald 39
Redwood, John 79, 82, 199, 200, 202, 211, 212, 216, 233, 237, 238, 242, 243, 246, 247, 249, 254, 255, 270, 286, 295, 353, 357, 359, 365
Rees, Peter 250, 254
regulation
  financial advice 291–3
  regulatory failure 331–3, 334–6, 364
  re-regulation 319–21
Reserve Pension Board 121
Reserve Pension Fund 122
Rhodes, R. A. W. 17, 34
Rhys Williams, Brandon 290
Ricardo, David 48
Ridley, Adam 82, 203, 236, 238
Ridley, Nicholas 168, 236
risk
  distribution of 1, 4, 15, 24, 58, 61, 174, 192, 277, 308, 350, 352, 354, 361, 364
Robbins, Lionel 14
Röpke, Wilhelm 41, 49, 51, 52
  on pensions 59
Rothschilds 79, 199
Rougier, Louis 41

Royal and Sun Alliance 332
Russian Revolution, 1917 45
Rüstow, Alexander 51, 52

Sandler, Ron 335
Save & Prosper 204, 205, 206, 207, 212, 281
Scott, Bernard
  report on public sector pensions 162
Seammen, Dianna 164, 167, 211, 257
Second World War 8, 11, 35, 41, 45, 76, 83, 95, 109, 111, 113, 193, 312
section 226 self-employed pension schemes 192, 239
Securities and Investment Board 292, 329, 330, 334
Seldon, Arthur 80, 81, 159
  Pensions in a Free Society (1957) 159
self-invested personal pension (SIPP) 327, 353
Shephard, Gillian 327
Sherman, Alfred 80, 81, 159, 161, 166, 191, 194, 195, 196, 214
Short, Eric 213, 289
Shultz, Theodore 56
Simons, Henry 55, 56
Smith, Adam 43
Soames, Lord 153
social democracy 36, 45–6, 90, 93, 353
Social Democratic Party 188, 283
social market 53, 77, 197
Social Security Advisory Committee 282
'Social Security Consortium' 291
Society of Pension Consultants 128, 207, 208, 332
Spencer, Herbert 43, 44
State Earnings-Related Pension Scheme (SERPS) 13, 128, 130, 136, 138, 143, 148, 188, 200, 210, 214, 234, 235, 237, 243, 247, 254, 270, 271, 274, 279, 282, 283, 286, 290, 308, 353, 357, 360
  consequences of reform 309–14, 359, 360
  contracting out of 128, 162, 235, 274, 275, 285, 287, 317, 322, 327, 328

guaranteed minimum pension
(GMP) 13, 130, 171, 232, 234,
235, 239, 286, 317
contribution rates 162
costs of 161, 162, 168, 171, 232,
234, 235, 237, 273, 274, 277,
279, 283, 288, 327, 353
quinquennial review (QR)
164–5, 232
costs of abolition 252, 358
difficulty of reform 170, 172, 253,
278, 285, 288
failed abolition of 269–97, 355
inflation protection 149
legacy of reforms to 364–5
ministerial decision to abolish
242–3, 244
modifications to 23, 163, 170, 172,
232, 234, 238, 278, 280, 282,
283, 284, 286, 289, 358
origins and overview 124–30
phased abolition of 355,
358, 359
proposals to abolish 23, 168, 172,
231–56, 269, 273, 277, 285,
353, 358
Green Paper 1985 252–4
MISC 111 proposals to
abolish 244–7
'20 best years rule' 164, 234, 238,
241, 283, 285, 286, 289
state Graduated Pension 12, 115–17,
121, 123, 136, 138
state Reserve Pension 12, 13, 121–3,
125, 126, 129
State Second Pension 310, 311, 335
Stewart, Colin 165, 166
Stigler, George 14, 55, 57
Sun Life 206
Superannuation Funds Office 327
supplementary benefit 125, 126, 168,
246, 273, 313
Switzerland 41, 243

Tebbit, Norman 253, 284
Thatcher governments
Cabinet decisions 151, 154,
155, 162
Cabinet U-turn 1985 281–7, 355
development over time 351–9

electoral strategy 157, 158
ministerial decision to abolish SERPS
243, 244, 278
MISC 111 proposals on pensions
244–7, 287
tensions within 147, 153, 155,
188, 272
Thatcher, Margaret 10, 38, 39, 76, 80,
82, 150, 154, 155, 157, 191,
193, 196, 198, 251, 253,
281, 286
beliefs 15, 36–7, 91, 269
decisions 158, 173, 200, 202,
243, 357
influence of upbringing 37
promises 149, 150, 152, 153, 158,
167, 174, 256, 277
role in Thatcherism 362
speeches and writings 155, 156, 194,
235, 269, 282
views on pensions reform 157, 195,
200, 211, 233, 357
Thatcherism
challenge to consensus 94–5
changes attributed to 6, 35–6
coherency and contingency
application of 34
definitions of 8, 21, 33, 34
as hegemonic project 36
histories of 2, 8, 33–9
ideas and arguments of 16, 17,
34, 361
implementation 34, 39, 336–7, 361
morality and vigorous virtues 36, 37,
78, 350, 353, 362
nature of 2, 7, 23, 34, 39, 146–7,
361–3
public spending and borrowing 148,
150, 154, 156, 158, 231,
269, 354
as reassertion of capital 36
relationship to conservatism 2, 6,
38, 361
relationship to neoliberalism 2, 5,
13, 15, 33, 39, 65, 83, 146,
174–6, 349, 352, 361
role of interests in 79–80
as response to economic crises of
1970s 35, 83–90, 350, 362
taxation 36

Thatcherism (*continued*)
  'Thatcher project' 5, 8, 15, 21, 34,
    39, 62, 64, 65, 75, 175, 351,
    361, 362
think tanks 8, 41, 75, 76, 77, 80–1,
    349, 351, 352
Thomas, Ken 206, 208
Thorneycroft, Peter 39
Times 82, 198, 278
Titmuss, Richard 115
Townsend, Peter 115
Trades Union Congress (TUC) 125,
    194, 204, 207, 208, 240, 241,
    260, 271, 278, 279, 280
  Social and Industrial Welfare
    Committee 280
trades unions 9, 13, 35, 36, 37, 43,
    86, 89, 95, 96, 112, 116, 117,
    119, 125, 130, 137, 146, 194,
    214, 216, 277, 280, 291,
    294, 356
Trumpington, Lady 291
Turnbull, Andrew 250, 253
Turner, Adair 3
Turner, Muriel 240, 242
Tyrie, Andrew 82

United States 19, 43, 44, 55, 80, 119,
    132, 194, 204, 243
  individual retirement account (IRA)
    204, 208, 235, 353
  social security system 271
University of Buckingham 201
University of Chicago 55

Viner, Jacob 55
Vinson, Nigel 79, 81, 131, 166, 192,
    193, 195, 196, 197, 198, 202,
    203, 204, 205, 206, 209, 213,
    214, 270, 295, 324

Virginia school 57
Volker Foundation 55

Wakeham, John 254
Walters, Alan 82
Ward, Sue 320, 321
'Washington consensus' 4
Wass, Douglas 82
Webb, Beatrice 112
Weinberg, Mark 201, 212, 292
welfare state
  changing nature of 353, 364
  early developments 12, 110–12
  international comparisons 17
Which? 206
White Papers
  *Better Pensions – Fully Protected
    against Inflation* 1974 12, 127,
    129, 160, 169, 232, 269,
    310, 311
  *Financial Services in the United
    Kingdom* 1985 275, 292
  *National Superannuation and Social
    Insurance* 1969 118, 124
  *Strategy for Pensions: The Future
    Development of State and
    Occupational Provision* 1971
    12, 121, 122, 124
Whitelaw, Willie 153, 254
Whitney, Ray 201
Wider Share Ownership Council 131
Willetts, David 216, 243, 246, 247,
    254, 270, 283, 285, 286, 288,
    289, 326, 353, 357, 359, 365
Williamson, Adrian 26
Wilson Committee 132, 187
Women's National Commission 241
World Bank 4, 312

Zurich Economic Society 194

Milton Keynes UK
Ingram Content Group UK Ltd.
UKHW020620101024
2102UKWH00009B/70